This is a remarkable book which will surely become the standard bearer for Amillennialism for years to come. Storms is particularly adept (and gracious) at critiquing premillennial positions, especially dispensationalism. His interaction with postmillennialism and preterism is equally intelligent and insightful. This is a book I will return to many times in my personal study and in pastoral ministry. Storms has given us a model for accessible, relevant, warm-hearted scholarship in service of the church.

KEVIN DEYOUNG,
Senior Pastor, University Reformed Church, East Lansing, Michigan

If Christians in the past were guilty of obsessing too much over the end times, evangelicals today may face the opposite problem of caring too little. The writings of Sam Storms are exactly what we need: faithful theology and careful exegesis served with a pastoral spirit and reverent worship. In these pages you will find Dr. Storms' mature reflections on the end times, honed over decades in the classroom and in the church. There is something in here to challenge and to encourage all of us, no matter our persuasion. I pray this book will help others in the same way it has helped me.

JUSTIN TAYLOR,
author and blogger, "Between Two Worlds"

Evangelicals continue to be divided over eschatology, and such divisions will likely continue until the eschaton. For some, premillennialism is virtually equivalent to orthodoxy. Sam Storms challenges such a premise with a vigorous defense of amillennialism. Storms marshals exegetical and theological arguments in defense of his view in this wide-ranging work. Even those who remain unconvinced will need to reckon with the powerful case made for an amillennial reading. The author calls us afresh to be Bereans who are summoned to search the scriptures to see if these things are so.

THOMAS R. SCHREINER,
James Buchanan Harrison Professor of New Testament Interpretation,
The Southern Baptist Theological Seminary, Louisville, Kentucky

Sam Storms' book, *Kingdom Come: The Amillennial Alternative*, is a substantial work on the viability of the Amillennial perspective on eschatology, including that of the Book of Revelation. While one may not agree with all that he says on this subject, the upshot of the book as a whole is a solid argument in favor of Amillennialism. His dialogue partners are Premillennial interpreters, whom he finds fall short in presenting a persuasive case for their view. Storms presents, in my own view, a very attractive way of understanding the millennial passage of Revelation 20:1-10, but his discussion of many other passages throughout the Bible also are adduced in an insightful way to support his view. He posits the surely correct hermeneutical approach that the rest of the Bible (e.g., Paul's epistles) should be understood as the main interpretive lens for eschatology and not any particular interpretation of Revelation 20, which too many have let control their understanding of eschatology elsewhere throughout the Bible. Among the discussions that I found particularly helpful was his study of the seventy weeks of Daniel 9. Even those who may disagree with Storms' Amillennial approach will definitely benefit from his book.

G. K. BEALE,
Professor of New Testament and Biblical Theology,
Westminster Theological Seminary, Philadelphia, Pennsylvania

Sam Storms' *Kingdom Come* is a remarkably comprehensive and informative study of eschatology from a Reformed perspective. Not only does he persuasively argue the amillennial position but he provides a clear and charitable understanding of the alternatives. On topic after topic, I marveled at Storms' sound handling and lucid teaching of difficult material. *Kingdom Come* is extraordinarily helpful to the student of eschatology and no Reformed library will be complete without this book.

RICHARD D. PHILLIPS,
Senior Minister, Second Presbyterian Church, Greenville, South Carolina

Sam Storms' *Kingdom Come: The Amillennial Alternative* is the most helpful book on the various millennial views I have seen since W. J. Grier's *The Momentous Event*. His work is marked by careful exegesis of pertinent texts, and ranges widely and deeply in all of the relevant Scriptural passages dealing with the end of the age. While no one book is universal in its range, this one comes close to it! Storms' work is lucid and fair; he certainly works with a point of view (amillennialism), but is scrupulous in not misrepresenting the views he critiques, and is charitable in spirit throughout his substantial volume. While he surveys in detail the three major views of the millennium (in a balanced way, in my opinion), probably the majority of his attention is directed to premillennial dispensationalism (so dominant in American Evangelicalism). He marshals many a passage to show why it is really not possible to hold this view, if one takes seriously the majority of the Scriptural texts involved (as for instance, the belief in the premillennial rapture). I do think he is humble before the teaching of the Scriptures, and wishes for the clear teaching written Word to be taken as it stands. His interpretation of the seventy weeks of Daniel chapter 9 is a model of clear, exegetical theology, as is his understanding of what is now called 'replacement theology. His discussion of the modern state of Israel is, I think, judicious and helpful. One does not have to agree with everything he says on the end of time to be able heartily to recommend this excellent book. I plan to use it in my teaching, and will be glad to have it available for the next time I teach Eschatology.

DOUGLAS F. KELLY,
Richard Jordan Professor of Systematic Theology,
Reformed Theological Seminary, Charlotte, North Carolina

Kingdom Come

The Amillennial Alternative

Sam Storms

ᴍENTOR

Sam is the Lead Pastor for Preaching and Vision at Bridgeway Church in Oklahoma City, Oklahoma, and the President of Enjoying God Ministries (www.samstorms.com). He has authored or edited 22 books and has published numerous journal articles and book reviews. He is a graduate of The University of Oklahoma (B.A.), Dallas Theological Seminary (Th.M.), and The University of Texas at Dallas (Ph.D.). He and his wife Ann have been married for 41 years and are the parents of two grown daughters and have four grandchildren.

Unless otherwise indicated Scripture quotations are from The Holy Bible, English Standard Version, copyright © 2001 by Crossway Bibles, a division of Good News Publishers. Used by permission. All rights reserved. ESV Text Edition: 2007.

Scripture quotations marked NASB are taken from the New American Standard Bible˚, Copyright © 1960, 1962, 1963, 1968, 1971, 1972, 1973, 1975, 1977, 1995 by The Lockman Foundation Used by Permission. (www.lockman.org)

hardback ISBN 978-1-78191-132-7
epub ISBN 978-1-78191-195-2
mobi ISBN 978-1-78191-196-9

Copyright © Sam Storms 2013

First published in 2013
in the
Mentor Imprint
of
Christian Focus Publications Ltd.,
Geanies House, Fearn,
Ross-shire, IV20 1TW, Scotland, UK

www.christianfocus.com

Cover design by Jesse Owens
Printed in the USA

MIX
Paper from
responsible sources
FSC® C014174

Contents

Contents cont.

Contents cont.

Introduction

Ihonestly can't remember giving a second thought to the second coming of Christ until my senior year in high school. My church believed in it, of course. I was raised Southern Baptist and undoubtedly must have heard a sermon here and there or sat through a Sunday school class when it was addressed. But I don't recall thinking deeply about the issue until First Baptist Church of Duncan, Oklahoma, held revival services either in late 1968 or early 1969. The only reason I know it was during that time span is that I was sitting with a particular young lady when the message was delivered and I most certainly do recall the time frame when we dated! Oh, the things we remember and forget!

The guest evangelist spoke forcefully on the events that had transpired in Israel which he believed were a harbinger of the return of Christ. I recall being quite frightened by stories of the Antichrist and false prophet and the impending forceful imposition of 666 on the foreheads of his followers.

In the summer of 1970, following my freshman year at the University of Oklahoma (OU), I lived in Lake Tahoe, Nevada, working on an evangelistic project with Campus Crusade for Christ. Aside from this being the season of violent anti-Vietnam War protests on many college campuses, as well as the time when the Jesus movement first emerged, it was the summer when Hal Lindsey's book, *The Late Great Planet Earth*, was released. All of us on the project quickly ingested every word and prayed that we would be ready should the rapture occur at any moment, which, of course, all of us believed it would (or at least could).

Upon returning to college in the fall I purchased a Scofield Reference Bible and began to devour its notes more passionately than I did the biblical text on which they commented. No one, as I recall, ever suggested there was another view, much less a wide range of options, when it came to the end times or to biblical prophecy. We cut our theological teeth on the dispensational, pretribulational, premillennialism of the Scofield Bible. Anyone who dared call it into question was suspected of not believing in biblical inerrancy.

While in school at OU I attended Metropolitan Baptist Church in Oklahoma City, then pastored by three graduates of Dallas Theological Seminary. Wednesday evenings at the church were often devoted to lectures by prominent theologians from around the country. I became quite accustomed to hearing a Dallas Seminary professor speak on the subject of eschatology. I was becoming ever more deeply ingrained in the dispensational school of thought and, again, never considered the possibility that other views might fall within the boundaries of orthodoxy. Anyone who dared question the pre-trib. rapture or the accuracy of Scofield was automatically viewed as either liberal or fast sliding down the slope thereto.

Upon graduating from OU in 1973, I began my studies at Dallas Theological Seminary (DTS) in pursuit of the Th.M., or Master of Theology, degree. My professors were a Who's Who of dispensational premillennialism: John Walvoord (then President of DTS), Charles Ryrie (author of *Dispensationalism Today* and *The Ryrie Study Bible*), and J. Dwight Pentecost (author of perhaps the most influential text on the subject at that time, *Things to Come*), just to mention the more well-known. Anything other than the dispensational premillennial perspective as found in Lewis Sperry Chafer's *Systematic Theology* and taught in the many DTS classrooms was considered less than evangelical. The only thing I recall hearing about amillennialism, for example, was how dangerous it was given the fact that it was popular among theological liberals who didn't take the Bible very seriously.

One incident in class is illustrative of the atmosphere in the 1970s at Dallas. We had just been exhorted by one of the professors (who will remain anonymous) to dig deeply into Scripture and particularly the eschatological passages and to read widely in the literature. The student sitting next to me (who likewise will remain anonymous) raised his hand and asked: "If we do what you say and end up embracing something other than dispensational, pretribulational premillennialism, can you promise us that we will still graduate on time?" The professor paused for a moment and then said, "No, I can't make that promise." Sure enough, during my senior year a classmate of mine expressed his belief in covenant theology and was told that his diploma would be withheld until such time as the faculty was confident that he properly understood the doctrine of eschatology. As I recall, he dropped out of Dallas and eventually obtained his degree at Reformed Theological Seminary.

Robert Gundry's book, *The Church and the Tribulation*, was released in 1973, the same year I began my studies at Dallas, and fell like a theological atom bomb on the campus. Everyone was reading it, and more than a few were being drawn to its post-tribulational perspective on the timing of the Rapture. Debates in the classroom, cafeteria, and elsewhere were many and quite heated. Someone obtained a copy of Daniel Fuller's Ph.D. dissertation in which he critiqued the hermeneutics of dispensationalism and more gasoline was thrown on the fire.

Upon my graduation from Dallas Seminary in 1977 I immediately immersed myself in a study of all aspects and schools of eschatological thought. However, without question the most influential and persuasive volume I read was *The Presence of the Future: The Eschatology of Biblical Realism* by George Eldon Ladd, then Professor of New Testament Exegesis and Theology at Fuller Theological Seminary in Pasadena, California. I'll have considerably more to say later about Ladd's writings and the influence he exerted on my thinking, but it is worth noting here that the distinction between Israel and the Church, on which dispensationalism is largely based, could not withstand Ladd's relentless assault.

It wasn't long before Ladd (and Gundry, together with a few others) had persuaded me that there was no basis in Scripture for a pretribulational rapture of the Church.[1] That was, in the eyes of many, bad enough. Indeed, I distinctly recall the horror (trust me, "horror" is by no means an exaggerated term to describe the reaction I received) in my church when I made it known that I could no longer embrace a pretribulation rapture. More than a few were convinced that I was well on my way into theological liberalism! But when in the early 1980s I abandoned premillennialism in all its forms, public reaction was such that you would have sworn I had committed the unpardonable sin. I'm not suggesting that all or even the majority of dispensational premillennialists feel this way today (I hope and pray that few do), but the atmosphere in the 1970s and 1980s was something less than amicable for those who departed from the accepted eschatological faith.

Over the next few years I continued my study of the subject and eventually, sometime in 1985, wrote the first draft of what is now the book you have in your hands. It was largely restricted to a critique of premillennialism and was graced by a Foreword from Anthony Hoekema whose book, *The Bible and the Future* (Eerdmans, 1979), had greatly shaped my thinking on the subject. I can only attribute it to the providential mercy of God that I never submitted the manuscript for publication, but waited until now when a more comprehensive work could be made available. As you might expect, the last quarter of a century has been one in which my understanding of this issue has, I hope, grown and improved, and I pray that the final product will be one that proves beneficial and edifying to the body of Christ. You, the reader, will alone be the judge on that point.

This book is not an exhaustive treatment of every issue or biblical text relating to end-time prophecy. No such book has ever been written and I doubt if it will. Therefore, I am quite prepared to be criticized for not addressing a number of passages and topics that

---

1. Another influential work that contributed to my doubts about pretribulationism was the Ph.D. dissertation of a DTS graduate, William E. Bell, Jr. The title of his work, written in 1967 and submitted to the School of Education of New York University, was: "A Critical Evaluation of the Pretribulation Rapture Doctrine in Christian Eschatology." As far as I know it was never formally published.

I suspect many of my readers were hoping I might explain. My primary aim will be to provide a biblical rationale for what is commonly known as amillennialism. In doing so I will of necessity be forced to account for what I also believe are the shortcomings of all varieties of premillennialism, and in particular the dispensational, pretribulational eschatology of the quite famous *Left Behind* series of books authored by Tim LaHaye and Jerry Jenkins. Along the way we will closely examine what Scripture says concerning the kingdom of God, the relationship between Israel and the Church and whether or not there is a distinct future for national Israel in God's redemptive purposes. I will also examine the third among the millennial options known as postmillennialism, as well as the biblical perspective on the beast of Revelation. As will become evident, the book is built around an in-depth analysis of the major biblical texts that inform our understanding of eschatology. In the final analysis, as I hope all of us will agree, the only thing that matters isn't the theology of a TV personality, the op-ed page of the *New York Times*, or the denominational tradition in which any of us were raised, but the word of God and only the word of God.

Chapter One

The Hermeneutics of Eschatology
Five Foundational Principles for the Interpretation of Prophecy [1]

Many who study biblical prophecy often fall into one of two camps, reflecting one of two perspectives. On the one hand, there are those who see prophetic texts as providing us with something of a crystal ball through which we can ascertain specific details about what the future holds. The biblical text, on this view, functions much like the blueprints for a new home, providing "specs" and dimensions concerning the future down to the smallest of details. On the other hand, there are those who read prophecy as if it were a stained-glass window, designed to paint in broad brush strokes the general principles that will govern how God brings this world to its consummation in Christ. Although there is a measure of legitimacy in both approaches, neither perspective is entirely adequate. Whereas one tends to demand an almost objective photographic precision from passages that are largely symbolic, the other can easily drift into a slippery subjectivism that treats the Bible like an impressionist work of art.

I certainly don't intend to provide a comprehensive remedy, as if in one short chapter I could even begin to articulate all the

---

1. For those unfamiliar with the term, *hermeneutics* simply refers to the science or study of interpretation. That is to say, it is concerned with the principles and patterns of analysis that enable us to make sense of the biblical text.

principles that help us interpret God's Word. What I would like to do, however, is set forth five basic hermeneutical assumptions that undergird and largely account for what you will encounter in the subsequent chapters. I make little effort to defend these principles (that in itself would require an entire book), but rather strive simply to explain them in a way that is intelligible (even if not persuasive!) to all my readers. So let me begin.

✤ ✤ ✤ ✤ ✤ ✤ ✤

1. The central and controlling thesis that I believe is warranted by the biblical text is that the fulfillment of Israel's prophetic hope as portrayed in the Old Testament documents is found in the person and work of Jesus Christ and the believing remnant, the Church, which he established at his first coming. The point is that Jesus Christ and his Church are the focal and terminating point of all prophecy.

This may sound somewhat trite at first hearing. After all, most Christians are quick to agree that Jesus is the center or focal point of all biblical revelation, that the Old Testament was a foreshadowing of his person and work, and that it is the Father's purpose to "unite all things in him, things in heaven and things on earth" (Eph. 1:10b). But I have in mind something far more specific, something far more comprehensive in terms of how the Old Testament finds its consummate fulfillment in the person of Christ and his body, the Church.

Jesus is the Temple

For example (from among several that I might cite), many affirm that Jesus was the true temple of God, the one in whom the Old Testament physical structure finds its perfect expression. But these same people also insist that God will approve and oversee the construction of yet another (third) physical temple in conjunction with events at the end of the age. Let's take a moment, therefore, and tease out this theme to see how it illustrates the hermeneutical principle in view.[2]

---

2. Much of the following discussion is adapted from my book, *A Sincere and Pure Devotion to Christ: 100 Daily Meditations on 2 Corinthians* (Wheaton: Crossway, 2010).

The starting point for understanding this crucial concept is the Old Testament narrative in which we find the visible manifestation of the splendor of God among his people, the *shekinah* of God, his majestic and radiant glory without which the Israelites would have been left in the darkness that characterized the Gentile world. Before Solomon's temple was built, God revealed his glory in the tent or tabernacle which Moses constructed. It was there that God would come, dwell, and meet with his people. "Let them make me a sanctuary," the Lord spoke to Moses, "that I may dwell in their midst" (Exod. 25:8). It was there that "the pillar of cloud would descend and stand at the entrance of the tent, and [there that] the LORD would speak with Moses" (Exod. 33:9). It was there that "the cloud covered the tent of meeting, and the glory of the LORD filled the tabernacle" (Exod. 40:34). The tabernacle was where the people of Israel would draw near to hear from God, to worship him, and to stand in his presence (cf. Lev. 9:23; Num. 14:10).

What was true of the tabernacle during the days of Israel's sojourn was even more the case in the temple of Solomon. When the Ark of the Covenant was brought "to its place, in the inner sanctuary of the house, in the Most Holy Place, underneath the wings of the cherubim" (2 Chron. 5:7), "the priests could not stand to minister because of the cloud, for the glory of the LORD filled the house of God" (2 Chron. 5:14).

It is against this preparatory backdrop that we read the stunning declaration of the Apostle John that "the Word became flesh and dwelt among us, and we have seen his glory, glory as of the only Son from the Father, full of grace and truth" (John 1:14). The word translated "dwelt" (*skenoo*) literally means "to pitch a tent" or "to live in a tabernacle" and unmistakably points back to the Old Testament when God's glory took up residence in the tent of Moses, the portable tabernacle, and eventually in Solomon's temple.

John's point is that God has now chosen to dwell with his people in a yet more personal way, in the Word who became flesh: in Jesus! The Word, Jesus of Nazareth, is the true and ultimate *shekinah* glory of God, the complete and perfect manifestation of the presence of God among his people. The place of God's glorious dwelling is the flesh of his Son! The glory which once shined in the tent/tabernacle/temple of old, veiled in the mysterious cloud, was simply *a fore-glow, a mere anticipatory flicker*, if you will, of that exceedingly excelling glory now embodied in the incarnate Word, Jesus Christ (cf. Col. 1:19).

God no longer lives in a tent or tabernacle built by human hands, *nor will he ever*. God's glorious manifest presence is not to be found in an ornate temple of marble, gold, and precious stones, but rather in Jesus. Jesus is the glory of God in human flesh, the one in whom God has finally and fully pitched his tent.

The point is that the temple of the Old Covenant was a type or foreshadowing of the glory of Christ (more on Typology below). It was the place where the Law of Moses was preserved, of which Jesus is now the fulfillment. It was the place of revelation and relationship, where God met with and spoke to his people. Now we hear God and see God and meet God in Jesus. It was the place of sacrifice, where forgiveness of sins was obtained. For that, we now go to Jesus (see Mark 2:1-12). Israel worshiped and celebrated in the temple in Jerusalem. We now worship in spirit and truth, regardless of geographical locale (cf. John 4:20-26).

In order to meet with God, to talk with him, and to worship him, we no longer come to a building or a tent or a structure made with human hands. We come to Jesus! Jesus is the Temple of God! Gary Burge is right: "Divine space is now no longer located in a place but in a person." [3]

But the story doesn't end there. *We, the Church, are the body of Christ* and therefore constitute the *temple* in which God is pleased to dwell. The *shekinah* of Yahweh now abides permanently and powerfully in us through the Holy Spirit. When Paul describes this in his letter to the Ephesians, he refers to Jesus Christ as the cornerstone, "in whom the whole structure, being joined together, grows into a holy temple in the Lord. In him you also are being built together into a dwelling place for God by the Spirit" (Eph. 2:21-22).

---

3. Gary M. Burge, *Jesus and the Land: The New Testament Challenge to "Holy Land" Theology* (Grand Rapids: Baker Academic, 2010), 52 (emphasis his).

Simply put, God's residence is "neither a literal temple in Jerusalem nor simply heaven, but the Church, of which the Gentile Christian readers in Asia Minor were a part." [4]

This formation of the temple is an on-going divine project, a continuous process (see also Ephesians 4:15-16). Although it may seem strange to speak of a "building" experiencing continuous "growth", Paul surely wants us to conceive of the Church as an *organic* entity. Recall that Peter also refers to believers somewhat paradoxically as "living stones" (1 Pet. 2:5)!

Again, Paul grounds his appeal to the Corinthians in this truth: "Do you not know that you are God's temple and that God's Spirit dwells in you? If anyone destroys God's temple, God will destroy him. For God's temple is holy, and you are that temple" (1 Cor. 3:16-17). In his plea for sexual purity, Paul again asks: "Or do you not know that your body is a temple of the Holy Spirit within you, whom you have from God? You are not your own, for you were bought with a price. So glorify God in your body" (1 Cor. 6:19-20; see also the graphic portrayal of this truth in 1 Pet. 2:4-10).

All this brings us to Paul's consummate declaration in 2 Corinthians 6:16b: "For we are the temple of the living God"! To reinforce this point he conflates several Old Testament texts (Lev. 26:11-12; Isa. 52:11; Ezek. 11:17; 20:34, 41; 2 Sam. 7:14) which prophesied of a coming temple, one of which is Ezekiel 37:26-27 where God declares: "I will make a covenant of peace with them. It shall be an everlasting covenant with them. And I will set them in their land and multiply them, and will set my sanctuary in their midst forevermore. My dwelling place shall be with them, and I will be their God, and they shall be my people."

Let me come straight to the point. Beginning with the incarnation and consummating in the resurrection of Jesus Christ, together with the progressive building of his spiritual body, the Church, God is fulfilling his promise of an eschatological temple in which he will forever dwell.

---

4. Andrew T. Lincoln, *Ephesians,* Word Biblical Commentary (Dallas: Word Books, 1990), 158.

But what about the literal, physical temple in Jerusalem? Has it lost its spiritual significance in God's redemptive purposes? To answer this we must look to Jesus' words in Matthew 23–24 (about which I'll have much to say in two subsequent chapters).

In his judgment against the Jewish people, the temple complex was abandoned by our Lord, both physically and spiritually, as he departed and made his way to the Mount of Olives. "Your house," said Jesus, "is left to you desolate" (Matt. 23:38). It has thus ceased to be "God's" house. When Jesus died and "the curtain of the temple was torn in two, from top to bottom" (Matt. 27:51), God forever ceased to bless it with his presence or to acknowledge it as anything other than *ichabod* (the glory has departed).

Just as dramatically as Jesus had entered Jerusalem (Matt. 21:1-17, the so-called "Triumphal Entry") and its temple, he now departs. This once grand and glorious house of God is now consigned exclusively to them ("See, *your* house is left to *you* desolate," Matt. 23:38; emphasis mine). The echoes of God's withdrawal from the temple in Ezekiel's vision reverberate in the words of our Lord (see Ezek. 10:18-19; 11:22-23). The ultimate physical destruction of the temple by the Romans in A.D. 70 is but the outward consummation of God's spiritual repudiation of it. Jesus has now left, never to return. Indeed, the action of Jesus in departing the temple and taking his seat on the Mount of Olives (Matt. 24:3) recalls Ezekiel 11:23 where we read that "the glory of the LORD went up from the midst of the city and stood on the mountain that is on the east side of the city."

This applies equally to any supposed future temple that many believe will be built in Jerusalem in the general vicinity where the Dome of the Rock now stands. It's entirely possible, of course, that people in Israel may one day build a temple structure and resume their religious activities within it. The political and military implications of such, not to mention the religious furor it would provoke, are obvious. Whether or not this will ever occur is hard to say, but if it does *it will have no eschatological or theological significance whatsoever*, other than to rise up as a stench in the nostrils of God. The only temple in which God is now and forever will be pleased to dwell is Jesus Christ and the Church, his spiritual body.

It would be an egregious expression of the worst imaginable *redemptive regression* to suggest that God would ever sanction the rebuilding of the temple. It would be tantamount to a denial that the Word became flesh and dwelt among us. It would constitute a repudiation of the Church as the temple of God and thus an affront to the explicit affirmation of Paul here in 2 Corinthians 6 and elsewhere.[5]

Finally, let's not lose sight of the practical point Paul is making in this passage in 2 Corinthians 6. It is because we as the Church are the place of God's presence in the world today that we must guard ourselves against any and every expression of idolatry. We are not simply another cultural institution or "social service meeting the felt needs" of our neighbors. "Instead, as the new covenant people of God, the church is the 'family of God' united by a common identity in Christ and gathered around her common worship and fear of 'the Lord Almighty.'"[6] May our lives always reflect that glorious and gracious identity.

Jesus fulfills the Feasts

Yet another example of this hermeneutical principle at work is seen in the way Jesus fulfills in his person and work all the feasts of Israel. One particular instance of this is made explicitly clear in John 7:37-44. The feast of Tabernacles was, if not the most popular celebration in Israel during the time of the old covenant, certainly the most joyful. It was celebrated in early fall, following harvest, after the crop was in the barn. Unlike the somber and serious mood of Passover, Tabernacles was a time of great festivity and rejoicing. For seven days in Jerusalem the people lived in booths or tabernacles made of leaves and branches. It was truly a time of joy, dancing, singing, and shouting (see Lev. 23:40).

On the seventh and final day of the feast, a typical celebrant would carry in his right hand a *lulabha*, the branch of a myrtle tree, one from

---

5. For an excellent explanation of how Ezekiel's vision (Ezekiel 40–48) of a restored temple fits in with the perspective developed here, see G.K. Beale, *The Temple and the Church's Mission: A Biblical Theology of the Dwelling Place of God* (Downers Grove: Inter Varsity Press, 2004), 335-64.
6. Scott Hafemann, *2 Corinthians,* NIV Application Commentary (Grand Rapids: Zondervan, 2000), 292.

a willow, and another from a palm tree, all tied together. In the left hand one carried an *ethrog*, or citrus branches bound as one. One of the priests would take in hand a golden pitcher and lead the crowd in festive procession, to the accompaniment of flutes and trumpets, to the pool of Siloam. He would fill the pitcher with water from the pool and then lead the worshiping parade back to the temple. He immediately proceeded to the altar where the sacrifice had been offered and there poured the water into a funnel which led to the base of the altar. Then, to the accompaniment of the flute, shaking the lulabha in the right hand and the ethrog in the left, all the people would chant, antiphonally, Psalms 113–118, climaxed by the public recitation of Psalm 118:24-29. The symbolic purpose of the water ritual, considered the high point of the festival, was to remind the people of the provision of water from God during the time of wilderness wandering (see Num. 20:7-11; Neh. 9:15, 19-20) as well as his showering the earth to make possible the growth of their crops.

It was then, with the ritual of water still fresh in the minds of the people, that a man from Nazareth stood up from a visible and prominent place and cried aloud: "If anyone thirsts, let him come to me and drink. Whoever believes in me, as the Scripture has said, 'Out of his heart will flow rivers of living water'"(John 7:37-38). Simply, yet profoundly, put, Jesus was saying: "This feast is all about **me**! The water that flowed from the rock in the wilderness symbolized **me**! The sacrifice on the altar is about **me**! The water in the golden pitcher points to **me**! The promise of refreshing waters of salvation refers to **me**! The water that I offer is better than that which flowed from the rock, better than that which falls from heaven to nourish your crops, better than that just taken from the pool of Siloam. I am the water that gives eternal life, eternal refreshment, and eternal joy! No longer do you need to go to the temple. No longer do you need to celebrate the feast. Celebrate **me**! Come and drink of **me**!"

Jesus is our Sabbath Rest

We also see this principle expressed in how Jesus responded to the accusation of the Pharisees that he and his disciples had profaned the Sabbath when they plucked heads of grain to satisfy their hunger (Mark 2:23-28). Matthew's version of the story includes this remarkable declaration by our Lord: "Or have you not read in the Law how on the Sabbath the priests in the temple profane the Sabbath and are guiltless? I tell you, something greater than the temple is here" (Matt. 12:5-6). Jesus is saying in response to their accusations: "I am greater than David! I am greater than the temple!" But he doesn't stop there: "And he said to them, 'The Sabbath was made for man [i.e., for his benefit and spiritual and physical welfare] not man for the Sabbath [the Sabbath has no needs that a human can fulfill]. So the Son of Man is lord even of the Sabbath'" (Mark 2:27-28).

Do you see what Jesus is saying? This isn't primarily a story about finding a loophole in the Sabbath regulations. This isn't primarily about finding precedent in the Old Testament for reaping and eating on the Sabbath. It isn't even primarily about whether or not you can do good by healing a man on the Sabbath. *This is a story about who Jesus is!* It is all about Jesus saying to them and to us: *I am greater than David. I am the fulfillment of all that David typified. I am greater than the temple. I am the fulfillment of all that the temple typified and symbolized. I am greater than the Sabbath. I bring to you a rest and satisfaction that not even the Old Testament Sabbath could provide.* In the words of N.T. Wright, "If Jesus is a walking, living, breathing Temple, he is also the walking, celebrating, victorious sabbath."[7]

Remember that the Sabbath was instituted by God as a sign of the old covenant with Israel (see Exod. 31:12-13, 16-17). However, as Paul makes clear in Colossians 2:16-17, Jesus is the fulfillment of all that the Old Testament prophesied, prefigured, and foreshadowed: "Therefore let no one pass judgment on you in questions of food and drink, or with regard to a festival or a new moon or a Sabbath. These are a shadow of the things to come, but the substance belongs to Christ."

The immediate purpose of the Sabbath in the Old Testament was to provide men and women with physical rest from their physical

---

7. N.T. Wright, *Simply Jesus: A New Vision of Who He Was, What He Did, and Why He Matters* (New York: HarperOne, 2011), 138.

labors. When Paul says that this Sabbath was a shadow, of which Christ is the substance, he means that the physical rest provided by the Old Testament Sabbath finds its fulfillment in the spiritual rest provided by Jesus. We cease from our labors, not by resting physically one day in seven, but by resting spiritually every day and forever in Christ by faith alone. We experience God's true Sabbath rest, not by taking off from work one day in seven, but by placing our faith in the saving work of Jesus. To experience God's Sabbath rest, therefore, is to cease from those works of righteousness by which we were seeking to be justified. The New Testament fulfillment of the Old Testament Sabbath is not one day in seven of physical rest, but an eternity of spiritual rest through faith in the work of Christ.

Physical rest, of course, is still essential. God does not intend for us to work seven days a week. Our body and spirit need to experience renewal and refreshment by resting. But resting on Sunday is not the same thing as the OT observance of the Sabbath day. Some Christians have chosen to treat Sunday as if it were a Sabbath, as if it were special, and that's entirely permissible. Don't let anyone tell you it is wrong. But neither should you tell anyone that it is wrong if they treat Sunday like every other day of the week. "One person esteems one day as better than another, while another esteems all days alike. Each one should be fully convinced in his own mind" (Rom. 14:5). If you want to observe Sunday as a day of rest to the exclusion of all other worldly pursuits or activities, that's fine. But you have no biblical right to expect others to do the same and therefore no biblical right to pass judgment on them if they don't.

My point is simply that for the Christian, for the person who is trusting in the work of Jesus Christ rather than in his own efforts, for those resting by faith in Jesus, *every day is the Sabbath!* Every day is a celebration of the fact that we don't have to do any spiritual or physical works to gain acceptance with God. We are accepted by him through faith in the works of Jesus Christ. If you are a child of God, born again, trusting and believing in Jesus for your acceptance with God rather than in your own works and efforts, you are experiencing the true meaning of Sabbath twenty-four hours a day, seven days a week. I observe the Sabbath every moment of every day to the degree that I rest in the work of Christ for me. Thus, for the Christian, Jesus is our Sabbath rest![8]

The same scenario, the identical claim on the part of Jesus, can also be made with regard to every Old Testament feast, holiday, type, celebration, or institution. Jesus is not only the fulfillment of the Old Testament Sabbath (Col. 2:16-17) but also of the Old Testament Passover (1 Cor. 5:7-8), the Old Testament temple (Matt. 12:6), as well as the entire Old Testament sacrificial system (Heb. 10:1-18). Everything and all that these events and institutions were designed to be and do, Jesus was and did. To suggest that any such Old Testament shadow might yet re-emerge in God's divine economy is worse than redemptive retrograde. It is tantamount to a denial of the coming of Christ Jesus and the sufficiency of all that he accomplished in his life, death, and resurrection. Thus any attempt to interpret Old Testament prophetic texts that, as it were, leapfrogs the incarnate Christ will ultimately mislead us into expecting at some future time what God never intended and never will bring to pass.

Jesus is the True Vine

One more example of this principle in operation is found in our Lord's claim to be "the true vine" in John 15:1-5. One of the primary metaphors in the Old Testament of Israel's rootedness in the land is that of the vineyard. We see this in numerous texts, such as Hosea 10:1 ("Israel is a luxuriant vine that yields its fruit"); as well as Jeremiah 2:21; 5:10; 12:11f.; Ezekiel 15:1-8; 17:1-10; 19:10-14; and Isaiah 5:7 ("For the vineyard of the Lord of hosts is the house of Israel"); 27:2-6. The most explicit statement is found in Psalm 80:7-11,

[7]Restore us, O God of hosts; let your face shine, that we may be saved!
[8]You brought a vine out of Egypt; you drove out the nations and

---

8. For more on this subject, see *Perspectives on the Sabbath: Four Views,* Charles P. Arand, Craig L. Blomberg, Skip MacCarty, Joseph A. Pipa, edited by Christopher John Donato (Nashville: B & H Academic, 2011). I especially recommend the chapter by Blomberg, 305-58.

planted it. [9]You cleared the ground for it; it took deep root and filled the land. [10]The mountains were covered with its shade, the mighty cedars with its branches. [11]It set out its branches to the sea and its shoots to the River.

But as Burge points out, "the crux for John 15 is that Jesus is changing the place of rootedness for Israel. The commonplace prophetic metaphor (the land as vineyard, the people of Israel as vines) now undergoes a dramatic shift. God's vineyard, the land of Israel, now has only one vine: Jesus. The people of Israel cannot claim to be planted as vines in the land; they cannot be *rooted* in the vineyard unless first they are *grafted* into Jesus."[9] God the vinedresser "now has one vine growing in his vineyard. And the only means of attachment to the land is through this one vine, Jesus Christ."[10]

Thus, just as we saw with the temple, here in the fourth gospel John "is transferring spatial, earthbound gifts from God and connecting them to a living person, Jesus Christ."[11] Whatever sense of identity or spiritual benefits and blessings God's people derived from the land in the Old Testament, they now can find only through a relationship of faith in Jesus. Burge here anticipates what we'll look at later with regard to the role of the "land" in God's prophetic purpose when he says that "those who pursue territory, religious turf, motivated by the expectation that it is theirs by privilege hoping that God will bless their endeavor, are sorely mistaken.... 'The way' [to God] is not territorial. It is spiritual."[12] In sum, here in John 15 "Jesus exploits the vineyard metaphor in order to take from it what Judaism had sought from the land. Now Jesus is the sole source of life and hope and future. The land as holy territory therefore should now recede from the concern of God's people. The vineyard is no longer an object of religious desire as it once had been."[13] Only Jesus is!

9. Gary Burge, *Jesus and the Land,* 54-55.
10. Ibid., 55.
11. Ibid.
12. Ibid.
13. Ibid., 56.

The Meaning of "Forever"

What, then, should we do with those texts where specific Old Testament institutions or practices are said to have been established by God "forever" or are declared to be "everlasting" (one example being the Sabbath; see again Exodus 31:12-13, 16-17). Whereas the immediate response of many is to assume that "When the Bible says 'forever' it means 'forever,'" a closer look reveals this to be a facile and erroneous conclusion. In fact, the Hebrew word for "forever" or "everlasting" is not nearly as chronologically or temporally "infinite" as it may sound in English. The Aaronic Levites as priests (1 Chron. 23:13) and the descendants of David as kings (2 Sam. 7:12-16) are said to have been instituted "forever", yet both have come to their end and are unmistakably seen as fulfilled in Christ in the new covenant. Thus, as Christopher Wright has noted, "when the land, the kings and the priests were declared to be 'forever', it meant that these dimensions were permanent and guaranteed while Israel as a nation was the limit of God's redemptive work and covenant relationship. Once this national and territorial basis was transcended through the coming of the Messiah and the extension of the gospel of redemption to Gentiles and Jews through him, then the 'forever-ness' of these things resides in Christ himself, the embodiment of Israel."[14] Thus these features do, in a sense, exist forever, but not simply in the concrete terms in which they were first expressed but in their consummate and transcendent expression when fulfilled and perpetuated eternally in Christ.

Thus, on occasion, "forever" can "designate something that is true presently and lasts indefinitely into the future, without interruption and without end"[15] (as, for example, when the psalmist declares: "Your testimonies are righteous forever," Ps. 119:144). But in countless other texts, notes Brent Sandy, "forever" "may or

---

14. Christopher Wright, "A Christian Approach to Old Testament Prophecy Concerning Israel," in *Jerusalem Past and Present in the Purposes of God*, edited by P.W.L. Walker (Cambridge: Cambridge University Press, 1992), 6.

15. D. Brent Sandy, *Plowshares & Pruning Hooks: Rethinking the Language of Biblical Prophecy and Apocalyptic* (Downers Grove: IVP, 2002), 98.

may not begin immediately, may be interrupted for long periods of time, and may achieve its perpetuity only in the distant future, when time essentially will no longer matter anyway." [16] In other places "forever" may "designate perpetuity in the present world, with no notion of its being without end. It is simply the notion of continuing." [17] "Forever" may also be used in hyperbole, especially in Old Testament poetic literature (see Isa. 34:10; Jer. 15:14; 17:27; 18:16; Jonah 2:6). In a number of texts "forever" is used "to add a sense of pregnancy to language, or a sense of power and emotion and mystery," rather than to indicate simply perpetuity. [18]

❖ ❖ ❖ ❖ ❖ ❖ ❖

2. The previous principle should not lead us to neglect the equally legitimate truth that whereas the Old Testament saw the consummation of God's redemptive purposes in one act, the New Testament authors portray it as coming in two phases. This is often seen in the New Testament in terms of the "overlapping" of the ages. The consummation of God's redemptive purpose has begun in Christ but we still abide in the present evil age. Some refer to this as the "inauguration of the end". God has acted in Christ to "fulfill" his prophetic promise but the "consummation" will come only when Christ does for a second time.

Thus the unfolding fulfillment of God's promises may be seen in terms of what Geerhardus Vos called a "binary configuration." [19] That is to say, human history reflects a tension between what was accomplished at the first advent of Christ and what awaits consummation at the second. Thus we live in "this present evil age" but partake, in part, of the glories of "the age to come." Hence there is a tension between what has "Already" been fulfilled (or at least

---

16. Ibid.
17. Ibid., 99. See 1 Kings 1:31; Neh. 2:3; Dan. 2:4; 3:9; 6:21; Josh. 4:7.
18. Ibid., 100. On p. 222 of his book, Sandy lists more than thirty texts in which "forever" does not mean literally "in perpetuity".
19. Geerhardus Vos, "The Eschatological Aspect of the Pauline Conception of the Spirit," in *Redemptive History and Biblical Interpretation: The Shorter Writings of Geerhardus Vos,* edited by Richard B Gaffin (Phillipsburg: Presbyterian & Reformed, 1980), 93-94.

partially inaugurated) and what has "Not Yet" been consummated. Examples of this abound, but here are only a few:

- Salvation is now, but also future (Eph. 2:8 / Rom. 5:10)
- Justification is now, but also future (Rom. 5:1 / Rom. 2:13)
- We have been adopted into God's family as his children, but our adoption is also yet to come (1 John 3:1; Rom. 8:23)
- We have been raised with Christ, but the resurrection is also yet future (Eph. 2; Rom. 6 / Phil. 3; 1 Cor. 15)
- We have been glorified, but will be glorified (Rom. 8:30 / Phil. 3; 1 John 3)
- We have been redeemed, but redemption is yet future (Eph. 1:4ff. / Rom. 8:23; 13:11).
- Regenerate believers are a "new creation" (2 Cor. 5:17), while we yet await the new heavens and new earth at the return of Jesus.

Thus, when reading the Old Testament one must reckon with the placement of events in close proximity, as if they happen simultaneously or in quick succession. The fact is, as both the New Testament and history have proven, events are often separated by significant intervals of time. This has often been called *prophetic foreshortening*. Donald Garlington provides this example:

The classic illustration is that of the advent of Messiah. The Prophets saw only one coming, with no distinction made between two phases of that coming. Thus, what is represented by the Prophets as transpiring once-for-all in "the latter days" is realized over an expanse of time which is already virtually two millennia in length. Therefore, it is in light of the New Testament we discern that Messiah's coming is in *two* stages, corresponding to the *inauguration and consummation* of God's eschatological purposes.[20]

---

20. Donald Garlington, "Reigning with Christ: Revelation 20:1-6 and the Question of the Millennium," in *Reformation and Revival Journal*, vol. 6, no. 2, 1997, 60-61.

3. Essential to this interpretive perspective is that "the New Testament serves, as it were, as the 'lexicon' of the Old Testament's eschatological expectation. In a nutshell, the Old Testament anticipates realities which are unpacked and explicated by the apostolic writings from the vantage point of salvation-historical realization in Christ." [21] In sum, Jesus is himself the inspired interpreter of the Old Testament. His identity, life, and mission provide the framework within which we are to read and approach the Old Testament (see especially Luke 24:25-27 and 1 Peter 1:10-12).

Let's look at this more closely with help from G.K. Beale. Certain Old Testament texts, he tells us, have "thick" content, the full meaning of which may have been unknown to its original author and is discernible only in the aftermath of Christ's coming and our access to the Scriptures in their final canonical form. In other words, biblical texts can "grow in meaning." [22] This can happen when an original author either consciously or, more likely, unconsciously writes in such a way that his text is "open-ended or indeterminate." [23] In other words, "authors may wish to include a potential in what they say to extend meaning into the indefinite future by espousing principles intended for an indefinite number of applications. Or, alternatively, authors may be aware that their original meaning has the potential to be recontextualized by subsequent interpreters who ascertain creative applications of the meaning to new contexts. In such cases a provision is made for subsequent readers to interpret in a way that 'extends meaning'. Thus an original meaning is so designed to tolerate some revision in cognitive content and yet not be essentially altered." [24]

Beale argues that this may be what is happening when New Testament authors cite or allude to Old Testament prophetic passages. The

---

21. Ibid., 56.
22. G.K. Beale, *The Temple and the Church's Mission: A Biblical Theology of the Dwelling Place of God* (Downers Grove: InterVarsity Press, 2004), 377.
23. Ibid.
24. Ibid.

original intent of a particular Old Testament author may not be "as comprehensive as the simultaneous divine intentions, which become progressively unpacked as the history of revelation progresses until they reach climax in Christ."[25] Old Testament authors thus prophesied of events that would occur in a distant time and in a new world inaugurated by Jesus. From their original context they might not fully grasp how their words would find fulfillment in a history radically transformed by the coming of Christ. Thus "the literal picture of Old Testament prophecy is magnified by the lens of New Testament progressive revelation, which enlarges the details of fulfillment in the beginning new world that will be completed at Christ's last advent."[26]

In sum, "the progress of revelation reveals enlarged meanings of earlier biblical texts, and later biblical writers further interpret prior canonical writings in ways that amplify earlier texts. These later interpretations may formulate meanings of which earlier authors may not have been conscious, but which do not contravene their original organic intention but may 'supervene' on it. This is to say that original meanings have 'thick' content and that original authors likely were not exhaustively aware (in the way God was) of the full extent of that content. In this regard, fulfillment often 'fleshes out' prophecy with details of which even the prophet may not have been fully cognizant."[27]

✠ ✠ ✠ ✠ ✠ ✠ ✠

4. We now come to a principle of interpretation apart from which the proper reading of prophetic texts may prove impossible. Brent Sandy points out, rightly so, in my opinion, that "our ideas about things we have never experienced are largely controlled by things we have experienced."[28] In other words, whenever the biblical authors sought to describe the future, which they had not experienced, they often employed language and imagery from the present, which they

25. Ibid., 379.
26. Ibid.
27. Ibid., 381.
28. Sandy, *Plowshares & Pruning Hooks*, 25.

had experienced. Or, as Richard Bauckham put it, "Prophecy can only depict the future in terms which make sense to its present. It clothes the purpose of God in the hopes and fears of its contemporaries."[29] It's the age-old problem of how to describe eschatological and heavenly concepts in human language. Sandy's argument is that "under divine empowerment, the prophets created metaphors and similes from their world to let us experience what the world of God and heaven is like – as best they could."[30]

This principle is especially helpful in enabling us to grasp the distinction often drawn between what is *literal* and what is *figurative*. Take, for example, the passage from which the title of Sandy's book was derived: "and they shall beat their swords into plowshares, and their spears into pruning hooks; nation shall not lift up sword against nation, neither shall they learn war anymore" (Isa. 2:4; Micah 4:3; cf. Joel 3:10). How *literal* is this prophetic utterance? Do the prophets mean to suggest that people in the end times will literally or physically reshape an actual sword into an actual plow or pruning hook? Or do they mean that those who have any instruments of warfare will transform them, by whatever means possible, into instruments of agriculture? Or it may be that the point of the imagery is simply that God will restore order to the earth in the sense that political peace among all nations and the complete absence of military conflict will come to pass. I'm inclined to think the last is true. As Sandy points out, "only when we reach the point of denying that anything will happen as a result of these words have we moved completely away from literal meaning. At that point to be nonliteral would mean to be nonhistorical (nonactual)."[31] His point, and this is critically important, is that one can interpret the prophets as speaking "literally" if, by that, we mean that what they *intended* to communicate will actually and historically come to pass. Whether or not there is a one-to-one "physical" equivalence between the words of predic-

---

29. Richard Bauckham, *The Climax of Prophecy: Studies on the Book of Revelation* (Edinburgh: T & T Clark, 1993), 450.

30. Sandy, *Plowshares & Pruning Hooks,* 28.

31. Ibid., 39.

tion and the event of fulfillment is of secondary importance. The key then becomes ascertaining authorial intent.

The point is that "if we fail to hear the communication as the authors intended and the hearers understood, it is because we are outside in the dark. When God chose to use the forms of communication and culture available in the biblical world, he simply left us with the challenge to enter into that world to understand his revelation."[32] In other words, it is a fatal mistake to think we can interpret the prophetic word apart from an understanding of the social, linguistic, historical, economic, cultural, theological and aesthetic conventions of the author, as well as the range of what the original audience could reasonably be expected to grasp from his words.

The Meaning of "Metaphor"

All this demands that we engage in a brief analysis of the nature of metaphor. Metaphors, Sandy notes, "begin with something non-figurative and make it figurative by using it to describe something beyond the scope of its normal meaning."[33] It's important to remember, then, that "metaphors speak truths, but the surface meaning of the words in metaphors speak untruths."[34] The surface meaning of, "We locked horns on that topic," is meaningless. Neither of the disputants had horns! But the statement communicates a real, actual, historical truth, namely, that I and another person disagreed and argued about a particular issue. Thus, figurative language, such as metaphor, hyperbole, simile, etc. may actually enhance the truth and power and force of utterances in a way that surface, flat-footed literalism never could. Or to illustrate yet again, "when people are nearly blind, we increase the font size. When people are nearly deaf, we turn up the volume. When people are mentally handicapped, we use visuals. The audience of prophetic language was sometimes blind, sometimes deaf and often mentally handicapped."[35] There-

---

32. Ibid., 57.
33. Ibid., 62.
34. Ibid., 63-64.
35. Ibid., 73.

fore, figurative language was employed to communicate more effectively the truth about God's eschatological purposes.

We simply cannot escape the fact that metaphor is dominant in Scripture, especially in prophetic texts. This recognition does not undermine the authority or infallibility of the word. Evangelicals must stop their knee-jerk reaction to the word as if it is nothing more than the liberal scholar's way of dismissing the historicity of the Bible. The concepts and principles communicated via figurative language are as true and real as those communicated via more "literal" language. To say that a text or phrase is metaphorical does not mean it isn't true or that it is emptied of concrete reality. It simply means that ordinary, flat-footed literalism would fail to fully and properly communicate what God intended.

The New Heavens and New Earth

This foundational principle in the interpretation of prophetic literature comes to light in the way one handles the Old Testament portrayal of the new heavens and new earth in Isaiah 65:17-25 (see also 66:22). The problem this text poses for all Christians, regardless of their millennial beliefs, is found in verses 20 and 23. There we read that in the new heavens and new earth there shall not be "an infant who lives but a few days or an old man who does not fill out his days, for the young shall die a hundred years old, and the sinner a hundred years old shall be accursed" (v. 20). And in verse 23 it appears to suggest that women during that time will bear children.

The principle we have been discussing is clearly articulated by Garlington:

> Prophecy is characteristically cast in terms of the limited understanding of the person to whom it was given. That is to say, the language of prophecy is conditioned by the historical and cultural setting in which the prophet and the people found themselves.... [Thus] the future kingdom is beheld as an extension and glorification of the theocracy, the most common representation of which is its condition in the reigns of David and Solomon. The prospect for the future, accord-

ingly, is portrayed in terms of *the ideal past,* in terms both familiar and pleasing to the contemporaries of the prophet. This phenomenon has been termed "recapitulation eschatology," i.e., the future is depicted as a recapitulation or repetition of the past glory of the kingdom.[36]

As noted earlier, the point is that the Old Testament author frequently spoke of the future in terms, images, and concepts borrowed from the social and cultural world with which he and his contemporaries were familiar. Since he likely could not fully grasp how his words would find fulfillment in a distant time and altogether new world transformed by the coming of Christ, he clothed the eschatological purposes of God, including the glory of the new heaven and new earth, in the beliefs, fears, and hopes of those to whom they were originally delivered. Thus, when prophets spoke about the future, says Christopher Wright, "they could only do so meaningfully by using terms and realities that existed in their past or present experience."[37] These realities included such things as the land, the law, the city of Jerusalem, the temple, the sacrificial system, and the priesthood. Therefore, "to speak of restoration without recourse to such concrete features of being Israel would have been meaningless, even if it had been possible."[38]

It should also be noted that the fulfillment of such prophecies, cast in terms of those contemporary realities with which the original audience was conversant, would often go beyond and transcend them. There is almost always an element of *escalation* or *intensification* in the fulfillment of any particular promise. The best and most intelligible way that the original author of this prophecy could communicate the *realistic future* glory of the new heaven and new earth, to people who were necessarily limited by the progress of revelation to that point in time, was to portray it in the hyperbolic or exaggerated terms of an *ideal present.* What greater glory was imaginable to

---

36. Donald Garlington, "Reigning with Christ," 61.
37. Christopher Wright, "A Christian Approach to Old Testament Prophecy Concerning Israel," 3.
38. Ibid. This principle may well provide us with the best possible explanation of the enigmatic prophecy of Zechariah 14:1-21.

the original audience to whom Isaiah wrote than to speak of an age in which a person dying at 100 would be thought of as an infant, an age in which the all too familiar anguish of childbirth was a thing of the past? His point isn't to assert that people will actually die or that women will continue to give birth. Rather, he has taken two very concrete and painful experiences from the common life of people in his own day to illustrate what to them, then, was an almost unimaginable and inexpressible glory yet to come. The explanation of this principle by Alec Motyer should suffice:

> Things we have no real capacity to understand can be expressed only through things we know and experience. So it is that in this present order of things death cuts life off before it has well begun or before it has fully matured. But it will not be so then. No infant will fail to enjoy life nor an elderly person come short of total fulfilment. Indeed, one would be but a youth were one to die aged a hundred! This does not imply that death will still be present (contradicting 25:7-8) but rather affirms that over the whole of life, as we should now say from infancy to old age, the power of death will be destroyed.[39]

✤ ✤ ✤ ✤ ✤ ✤ ✤

5. Our final principle concerns what is known as typology. In typology the student of Scripture finds a divinely orchestrated correspondence or parallel in one or more respects between a person, event, series of circumstances, or institution in the Old Testament (called the *type*) and a person, event, or thing in the New Testament (called the *antitype*). In most cases the Old Testament type finds a deeper realization or expression in some aspect of the life of Jesus, his redemptive work, his judgments, or in his future return and reign. The correspondence is based on the premise that God controls history. There is, therefore, a *providential pattern* in the type that is repeated in the antitype. The characteristic features of an earlier (Old Testament) individual, experience, or relationship

---

39. J. Alec Motyer, *The Prophecy of Isaiah: An Introduction and Commentary* (Downers Grove: IVP, 1993), 530.

between God and humanity reappear later (New Testament) with a finality and sense of fulfillment not initially apparent. God is the one who molds and shapes the specific details of history so that they occur originally as types and are later recognized by New Testament authors as such. Typology clearly assumes the organic unity of the two testaments in the sense that the Old is a preparatory foreshadowing of which the New is its continuation and consummation.

Most scholars recognize several important features in typology. For example, the Old Testament person, event, or institution which serves as the type must be historical and not something read back into the Old Testament text. R.T. France also points out that there is always some notable point of resemblance or analogy or correspondence between the "type" (Old Testament) and its "antitype" (New Testament):

> This correspondence must be both historical (i.e., a correspondence of situation and event) and theological (i.e., an embodiment of the same principle of God's working). The lack of a real historical correspondence reduces typology to allegory, as when the scarlet thread hung in the window by Rahab is taken as a prefiguration of the blood of Christ; both may be concerned with deliverance, but the situations and events are utterly dissimilar. On the other hand, the lack of a real theological correspondence destroys what we have seen as the very basis of typology, the perception of a constant principle in the working of God. This is not, of course, to demand a correspondence in every detail of the two persons or events, but simply that the same theological principle should be seen operating in two persons or events which present a recognizable analogy to each other in terms of the actual historical situation. Only where there is both a historical and theological correspondence is a typological use of the Old Testament justified.[40]

Of great significance is the fact that there is in the "antitype" an *intensification* or *escalation* of the "type." The relation between the

---

40. R.T. France, *Jesus and the Old Testament: His Application of Old Testament Passages to Himself and His Mission* (London: The Tyndale Press, 1971), 41.

two is not simply one of mere repetition, nor even of comparative increase. Rather, *in the "antitype" there is eschatological completion and consummation*. The nature of this intensification or escalation or consummation which we see in the "antitype" is often such that involves a movement from the external and earthly to the internal and spiritual. For example, France points to John 3:14-15 and the incident of the brazen serpent. The points of correspondence are "lifting up" and "life". Both the serpent and Christ were "lifted up," but the latter in a way far more significant and spiritual than the former. Similarly, those who "looked" at the serpent received "life" in the physical sense, i.e., they did not die of the snake bite; on the other hand, those who "look" to Christ (i.e., believe in him) receive "life" in the spiritual sense, eternal life.

It's also important that we differentiate typology from allegory, and in some sense also from prophecy. Bernard Ramm is helpful in the former case. Allegorical interpretation, he contends, "is the interpretation of a document whereby something *foreign, peculiar*, or *hidden* is introduced into the meaning of the text giving it a proposed deeper or real meaning…. *Typological interpretation* is specifically the interpretation of the Old Testament based on the fundamental theological unity of the two Testaments whereby something in the Old shadows, prefigures, adumbrates something in the New. Hence, what is interpreted in the Old is not foreign or peculiar or hidden, but rises naturally out of the text due to the relationship of the two Testaments." [41] A good example of allegory is the way in which one of the church fathers interpreted the story of Herod's slaughter of the infants of Bethlehem (Matthew 2). The fact that only the children of two years old and under were murdered while those of three presumably escaped is meant to teach us that those who hold the Trinitarian faith will be saved whereas Binitarians (those who recognize only two divine persons in the Godhead) and Unitarians (one divine person) will undoubtedly perish!

---

41. Bernard Ramm, *Protestant Biblical Interpretation: A Textbook of Hermeneutics* (Grand Rapids: Baker Book House, 1981), 223.

France also seeks to differentiate between typology and prophecy, although this is admittedly more difficult. A type, says France, is not a prediction. "In itself it is simply a person, event, etc. recorded as historical fact, with no intrinsic reference to the future. Nor is an antitype the fulfillment of a prediction; it is rather the re-embodiment of a principle which has been previously exemplified in the type. A prediction looks forward to, and demands, an event which is to be its fulfillment; typology, however, consists essentially in looking back and discerning previous examples of a pattern now reaching its culmination."[42]

There are number of different sorts of types in the Old Testament. One can find persons (Adam, Solomon, David, Jonah), events (the Passover, the experience of Israel in the wilderness), articles of religious life (the temple and its furnishings), institutions (the Levitical sacrificial system), offices (Aaron as priest and Moses as prophet), and certain actions (the lifting up of the brazen serpent, as noted earlier, is a case in point) that function in typological fashion.

One of the most common expressions of typology is in the way certain individuals in the Old Testament embody characteristics that later reappear in the life and ministry of Jesus. We see this with Jonah (Matt. 12:38-41; Luke 11:29-30,32), Solomon (Matt. 12:42; Luke 11:31), David (Mark 2:25-26; Matt. 12:3-4; Luke 6:3-4), Elijah and Elisha (Mark 6:35ff.; Matt. 14:15ff.; Luke 4:23-30; Luke 9:12ff.), and Isaiah (Mark 4:12; Matt. 13:13; Luke 8:10; see Isa. 6:9-10). A similar pattern exists between the temple and Jesus (Matt. 12:5-6), as well as Israel and Jesus (the temptation – Matt. 4:1-11; Luke 4:1-13; the Exodus and cross – Luke 9:31).

No one has proven more helpful than R.T. France in bringing to our awareness the implications of typology for eschatology, and in particular how typology accounts for how Jesus himself relates to the Old Testament.[43]

First, says France, typology reveals that *Jesus is in line with the Old Testament*. In response to accusations of being a revolutionary

---

42. France, *Jesus and the Old Testament*, 39-40.

43. I've summarized the argument as provided by France in *Jesus and the Old Testament*, 78-80.

and of setting himself against the Old Testament, Jesus claimed a continuity between God's working in the Old Testament and his own ministry. He was simply working out patterns already seen in the Old Testament. If in the Old Testament God worked through prophets, priests, and kings, then Jesus could point to all three as types of himself. If in the Old Testament God selected a people to whom he made promises of blessing, then Jesus could claim that in himself and his disciples that people was embodied, and those promises would find their fulfillment. Jesus understood the Old Testament Christologically: in its essential principles, and even in its details, it foreshadows the Messiah whom it promises. *The entire theological system of the Old Testament points forward to his work, and in his coming the whole Old Testament economy finds its perfection and fulfillment.*

Second, typology discloses how *Jesus is not only in line with the Old Testament but is superior to it.* God's working is not only repeated, but *repeated on a higher plane*, and with a greater glory and significance. Three times Jesus states this superiority of the antitype to the type in so many words: "I tell you, something greater than the temple is here" (Matt. 12:6); "something greater than Jonah is here" (Matt. 12:41); "something greater than Solomon is here" (Matt. 12:42). In Mark 2:25-26, a parallel argument to Matthew 12:6, although the superiority is not explicit, the argument depends on it. In Mark 6:35ff. Jesus repeats Elisha's miracle, but on a vastly greater scale. *Twice he succeeds where Old Testament Israel, the type, had failed (the temptation, and the resurrection, where Israel's vain hope comes to fruition in him).* And since Jesus is superior to the Old Testament types, the Jewish refusal to accept him as God's messenger must carry a greater condemnation. Their punishment, in the destruction of Jerusalem and the final rejection of the nation from their privileged status as the people of God, will be on a scale higher even than the most terrible disasters known to the Old Testament: "For in those days there will be such tribulation as has not been from the beginning of the creation that God created until now, and never will be" (Mark 13:19). The rejection of the Old Testament prophets brought severe condemnation, but, as the parable of the tenants shows, something greater than the prophets is here.

Finally, *Jesus is the fulfillment of the Old Testament.* In Jesus the age of fulfillment has come. *The patterns discerned in the Old Testament are not only repeated on a higher plane, but they are now finding their final and perfect embodiment.* All God's working in the Old Testament is now reaching its culmination, and the Old Testament economy is at an end. The new, messianic age has dawned.

This is seen, paradoxically, in the fact that Jewish unbelief has now reached its highest point, so that its punishment must this time be final and complete. *The true Israel of this eschatological age is no longer the nation of the old covenant, but the Christian community, inaugurated by a new covenant through a mediator greater than the Israelite priesthood; for Jesus not only repeats the work of prophet, priest and king, but in him it is perfected. In this new community the hopes of the Old Testament Israel are fulfilled.* The glorious fulfillment to which the Old Testament looked forward has come; these are the *"last days."* The words of Paul in 1 Corinthians 10:11 sum up the conviction of Jesus: "Now these things happened to them as an example, but they were written down for our instruction, on whom the end of the ages has come."

France's point is that Jesus saw his mission as the fulfillment of the Old Testament Scriptures, not just of those which predicted a coming redeemer, but the whole sweep of Old Testament ideas. The patterns of God's working which the discerning eye could trace in the history and institutions of Israel were all preparing for the great climax when all would be taken up into the final and perfect act of God which the prophets foretold. And in the coming of Jesus all this was fulfilled. That was why he could find "in *all* the scriptures the things concerning himself" (Luke 24:27b).

Conclusion

What these principles lead us to conclude, when applied to the many texts that we will shortly examine, is that Jesus Christ is not simply analogous to the Old Testament nation of Israel nor simply parallel to her in terms of his experience, and far less is he merely one more Israelite in a long line of individual descendants of Abraham, Isaac, and Jacob. Jesus **is** Israel in the sense that God's purposes, promises, and predictions for the nation are fulfilled in his life, death, resurrection, exaltation, session, and second coming. This principle of the consummate fulfillment of the nation's destiny in the person of Christ is necessarily extended to his spiritual body, the Church. Since the Church is the body of Christ, of which he himself is the Head, what God intended for him, God also intended for her. What is true of him is true of her. *Both Jesus and his body, the Church, constitute the true Israel in and for whom all the promises of the Old Testament find their fulfillment.* "The whole of the Old Testament is gathered up in him," notes France. "He himself embodies in his own person the status and destiny of Israel, and in the community of those who belong to him that status and destiny are to be fulfilled, no longer in the nation as such."[44]

For some, I've probably raised more questions in this chapter than I've provided answers. Even should that be the case, I hope that the exegetical conclusions in subsequent chapters will confirm the validity of these principles.

---

44. France, *Jesus and the Old Testament*, 76. See also his discussion of this theme in "Matthew and Israel," in *Matthew: Evangelist and Teacher* (London: The Paternoster Press, 1989), 206-41. For those who wish to delve more deeply into this theme, I can do no better than to recommend the comprehensive, and I believe persuasive, treatment as found in G.K. Beale's *A New Testament Biblical Theology: The Unfolding of the Old Testament in the New* (Grand Rapids: Baker Academic, 2011).

Chapter Two

Defining Dispensationalism

O ne can learn much from a brief visit to a typical American Christian bookstore. I certainly did. It only took me a few minutes to count the number of titles in the section labeled, "Prophecy / End Times." It took another fifteen minutes or so to divide them into meaningful theological categories. I shouldn't have been surprised, but I was more than a little disappointed. Of the 117 titles on the shelves, 102 were devoted to articulating and defending some version of the dispensational, pretribulational, premillennial perspective on biblical eschatology. I was struck by the fact that, in all likelihood, that is probably representative of what most evangelical believers themselves embrace. That is to say, if I had taken the time to poll 117 Christians in that store who, like me, were browsing, I suspect at least (and probably more than) 102 of them would have endorsed the "Left Behind", dispensational, point of view found in the best-selling novels of Tim Lahaye and Jerry Jenkins.[1]

---

1. In a recent poll conducted by the National Association of Evangelicals, 65% of evangelical leaders who participated affirmed their belief in premillennialism. Approximately 13% identified themselves as amillennialists, and only 4% indicated they were postmillennial in their eschatology. However, we need to remember that these were evangelical "leaders," pastors, and professors. My strong hunch is that if a similar poll had been taken among the rank and file of evangelical believers, the percentage that would identify with some version of premillennialism (whether dispensational or historic) would be significantly higher. See the article by *Christian Post* reporter, Audrey Barrick, "Poll: What Evangelical Leaders Believe about the End Times," Wed, Mar. 09, 2011, www.Christianpost.com.

As I said, I wasn't surprised by this discovery. After all, dispensationalism has been the dominant eschatological perspective in American evangelicalism for the last 100 years.[2] It first emerged as a distinct *system* of biblical interpretation with the Plymouth Brethren movement in early nineteenth century England. Key figures who advocated a sharp division between God's purposes for Israel and the Church included John Nelson Darby, William Kelly, William Trotter, and Charles Henry Mackintosh. Although few reading this book will recognize those names, several more well known individuals in America were highly influenced by the Brethren movement, at least in terms of its eschatology. These include Dwight L. Moody, James Inglis, James Hall Brookes, A.J. Gordon, and most important of all, C.I. Scofield (1843–1921). In 1909 the first edition of what came to be known as *The Scofield Reference Bible* (second edition in 1917) was published by Oxford Press.

Dispensational premillennialism quickly spread in popularity and remains the dominant view among conservative evangelical as well as charismatic believers today. There are a number of reasons for this, a few of which I will mention here.

First of all, dispensationalism claimed that it alone, among all attempts to understand the Bible, employed a consistent *literalism* in interpreting biblical texts. In their book, *The Truth Behind Left Behind: A Biblical View of the End Times,* co-authors Mark Hitchcock and Thomas Ice, both well-known dispensationalists, identify three essential elements in their approach to biblical eschatology, the first of which is literal interpretation.[3] Thus the image of taking the Bible seriously, "just for what it says," as over against the liberal

---

2. For an excellent overview of developments in dispensational thought over the past 150 years, I highly recommend Craig Blaising's chapter, "Dispensationalism: The Search for Definition," in *Dispensationalism, Israel and the Church: The Search for Definition*, edited by Craig A. Blaising and Darrell L. Bock (Grand Rapids: Zondervan, 1992), 13-34.

3. Mark Hitchcock and Thomas Ice, *The Truth Behind Left Behind: A Biblical View of the End Times* (Sisters, OR: Multnomah, 2004), pp. 185-88. The other two distinguishing features of dispensationalism, so they contend, are a distinction between Israel and the Church and the purpose of history being the glory of God.

attempt to "explain away" the Bible, appealed to the common Christian man/woman. As a result, dispensationalism seemed to provide the Christian public with understandable answers to gnawing questions about difficult Bible texts (such as the book of Revelation).

Dispensationalism is uniquely suited to draw correspondence between biblical prophecies and current events. People are understandably drawn to a system of theology that they believe can be empirically verified by simply reading the newspaper. It also helps when people feel as if their own lives and what they are experiencing on a daily basis are part of God's final act in human history. It's exhilarating to watch the news or read an internet report and see one's own world caught up in what is believed to be the literal fulfillment of ancient prophecies.

Dispensationalism's unwavering commitment to Israel also makes for a strong appeal to people in the West. This is especially the case following the horrors of the Holocaust and the collective guilt that non-Jews around the world have felt for what happened in Nazi Germany during World War II. A very understandable compassion for the Jewish people goes hand in glove with dispensationalism's belief that God is in the process of restoring their land to them and returning them, eventually, to their former glory.[4]

Many dispensationalists became visible and highly influential leaders in the emergence of the Christian right-wing political surge. Not only was it the case that to be a fundamentalist is to be a dispensationalist, but for many to be a Reagan Republican entailed dispensational convictions as well.

Dispensational end-time scenarios make for sensational news and readily captivate the interest and imagination of many people. It comes as no surprise, then, that the people writing best-selling fic-

---

4. For the relationship between evangelicalism in general (whether dispensational or not) and the nation of Israel, see Timothy P. Weber, *On the Road to Armageddon: How Evangelicals became Israel's Best Friend* (Grand Rapids: Baker Academic, 2004); Stephen Sizer, *Christian Zionism: Road-Map to Armageddon?* (Leicester: Inter-Varsity Press, 2004), and *Zion's Christian Soldiers: The Bible, Israel and the Church* (Downers Grove: Inter-Varsity Press, 2008); and Victoria Clark, *Allies for Armageddon: The Rise of Christian Zionism* (New Haven: Yale University Press, 2007).

tional novels about the end of history are dispensationalists. The same may be said for the many "rapture" films that portray the stunning and sudden departure of tens of millions of Christians, followed by the social and political chaos that such an event would bring in its wake. Add to this the fascination people have with prophecy charts and meticulous chronological scenarios for how history is to come to its close and one can see why dispensationalism is so popular. It is difficult to think of a non-dispensational writer whose books are geared for a popular audience. They more often than not tend to be more academic and scholarly. And whereas dispensationalism certainly has its fair share of biblical scholars, its most successful works bear a populist appeal and are written for a decidedly lay audience. "It is very significant," notes Timothy Weber, "that the best-selling dispensationalist books of all time are *fictionalized* accounts of the end-times scenario: no careful exegesis there, no laborious comparisons with other alternatives, just a ripping good story told well. This is exactly what one would expect in a populist millennialist movement." [5]

Perhaps, in the end, notes Weber, what makes dispensationalism so appealing is that its proponents "simply have a better story to tell. Laying all matters of truth aside, in a popularity contest the pretribulation rapture is always going to easily beat the posttribulational rapture." After all, "going through the tribulation is not nearly as appealing as escaping from it." [6]

It was only a matter of time before dispensationalism came to be identified with conservative Christianity. Virtually all other eschatological systems were dismissed as the fruit of liberal theology that didn't embrace the complete inspiration and inerrancy of the Bible. Since dispensationalism at this time was virtually indistinguishable from premillennialism, it benefited from the dubious association of both amillennialism and postmillennialism with liberal thinking.

---

5. Timothy P. Weber, "Dispensational and Historic Premillennialism as Popular Millennialist Movements," in *A Case for Historic Premillennialism: An Alternative to "Left Behind" Eschatology*, edited by Craig L. Blomberg and Sung Wook Chung (Grand Rapids: Baker Academic, 2009), p. 21.

6. Ibid.

When the "Fundamentalist–Modernist" controversy broke out in the first few decades of the twentieth century, dispensational premillennialists were extremely visible and vocal in their defense of the fundamental doctrines of the faith. Thus, to be a dispensationalist was to be a Bible-believing conservative Christian.

One cannot overestimate the influence of the Scofield Bible on the rank and file of average Christians throughout the country. With the aid of the famous "Scofield Notes," the Bible suddenly became accessible to the average, moderately educated, Christian citizen. Although Scofield certainly didn't intend for this to happen, it became difficult for many to differentiate between the inspired text of Scripture and the interpretive notes at the bottom of the page. Other study Bibles published in more recent times, such as those bearing the names of prominent evangelicals W.A. Criswell, Charles C. Ryrie, and John MacArthur, served only to reinforce the belief that this approach to biblical prophecy is the standard evangelical view.

In more recent years, the disintegration of society and the political, economic, and especially military unrest of the twentieth and now twenty-first centuries seemed to confirm the pessimistic perspective required by dispensationalism. In other words, events in the world at large seemed to bear witness to the dispensational interpretation of biblical prophecy concerning the end times.

The fact that virtually all well-known TV preachers (at least those who appear on TBN and most on the 700 Club) and radio teachers espouse the dispensational view of biblical prophecy lends an aura of evangelical credibility to the movement. Prominent dispensationalists who utilized the media to communicate their views include the late W.A. Criswell (former Senior Pastor of the mammoth and highly influential First Baptist Church of Dallas, Texas), M.R. and Richard DeHaan (the Radio Bible Class), Warren Wiersbe, Charles Stanley, Adrian Rogers (former Pastor of Bellevue Baptist Church, Nashville, TN), Jack Van Impe, Chuck Swindoll, Billy Graham, Luis Palau, Bill Bright (Campus Crusade for Christ), James Dobson (Focus on the Family), Jerry Falwell (Liberty University), David Jeremiah, John Ankerberg, and pastor John Hagee of San Antonio, Texas.

I struggle to think of a single TV evangelist or minister of a mega-church that regularly broadcasts in America who isn't a dispensationalist (the late D. James Kennedy, however, does come to mind). Many Christians are unaware that there are other interpretive options that remain true to Scripture. Thus for many believers the dispensational view of the end times is as much a foundational and fundamental doctrine of the Christian religion as is the deity of Christ or salvation by grace alone. To question dispensationalism, therefore, is often perceived as an indication that one is "going soft" on the authority of Scripture.

A great many of the evangelical Bible colleges and theological seminaries in America were birthed out of the Fundamentalist–Modernist controversy or were founded by men and/or denominations highly influenced by dispensationalism. Among those schools which include dispensationalism in their doctrinal statement or espouse its basic ideas are: The Master's Seminary in Los Angeles, Grace College and Grace Theological Seminary in Winona Lake, Indiana; Dallas Theological Seminary; Philadelphia Biblical University (formerly known as Philadelphia College of the Bible); Moody Bible Institute; Grand Rapids Theological Seminary and its sister institution, Cornerstone University; Western Seminary (formerly called Western Conservative Baptist Seminary); Criswell College; Biola University and the related Talbot School of Theology; Multnomah Biblical Seminary; Southeastern Bible College in Birmingham, Alabama; Washington Bible College / Capital Biblical Seminary; Liberty University; together with every college or seminary affiliated with the Assemblies of God denomination. And these are only a representative handful of the numerous schools and seminaries that espouse dispensationalism in one form or another.

Most of the more well-known para-church organizations were either established by dispensationalists or are highly influenced by their teachings. This includes Youth for Christ, Young Life, Inter-Varsity Fellowship (less so than the others, however), Campus Crusade for Christ (recently renamed Cru), and the Navigators. One can hardly underestimate the influence of such widely known and closely followed dispensational bible teachers, Kay Arthur

(Precepts) and Beth Moore. And yet perhaps the single greatest catalyst for the popularizing of dispensationalism in the last forty plus years is the influence of Hal Lindsey and his book *The Late Great Planet Earth* (1970), followed by the even more popular *Left Behind* series of Tim LaHaye and Jerry Jenkins.[7]

Finally, one must not overlook the significance of the fact that the most well-known and influential of the classical Pentecostal denominations, the Assemblies of God, made the key tenets of dispensational eschatology an article of faith required of all who are ordained in that denomination. Likewise, although it comes as a surprise to some, the vast majority of charismatic Christians today are thoroughly dispensational in their theology. I've often heard people argue that one cannot be a charismatic and a dispensationalist, but the reasons given for this are worse than weak. The notion that these two perspectives are incompatible has little if any biblical or theological basis, but is grounded more in the history of American conservative Christianity. Given the fact that virtually all fundamentalists were cessationists (i.e., believed that so-called miraculous gifts of the Spirit *ceased* sometime in the late first century A.D., or with the death of the last apostle), it was simply assumed that to embrace dispensational eschatology required a bias against the perpetuity and contemporary validity of all such gifts. But there is simply no escaping the fact that although most charismatics today shy away from the label, virtually all of them are dispensational.[8]

Dispensationalism at Dallas Seminary

My exposure to dispensational premillennialism came during my four years at Dallas Theological Seminary. There I studied under

---

7. The best book-length treatment of the rise and influence of Dispensational Premillennialism in American religious life is Paul Boyer's *When Time Shall Be No More: Prophecy Belief in Modern American Culture* (Cambridge: Harvard University Press, 1992).

8. "Although historical generalizations are often foolhardy," notes Timothy Weber, "this one is not: by the end of World War I, dispensationalism was nearly synonymous with fundamentalism and Pentecostalism" ("Dispensational and Historic Premillennialism," p. 16).

three of the most famous of all dispensational theologians of the twentieth-century: John Walvoord, Charles Ryrie, and J. Dwight Pentecost. Make no mistake: these men are among the most godly and gifted evangelicals that I have known. Their devotion to Christ and their commitment to the infallibility and authority of Scripture are remarkable. My disagreement with their theological convictions should in no way be interpreted as an assault on their Christian character. So what do dispensational premillennialists believe?

Those who embrace dispensational premillennialism contend that the Bible cannot be properly understood apart from recognizing distinct periods or eras or *dispensations* in which the unfolding purpose of God and his relationship with mankind are revealed. All dispensationalists recognize at least three such *dispensations* in biblical history: (1) the period before Pentecost (the age of the Mosaic covenant); (2) the period between Pentecost and the return of Christ (the church age); and (3) the period between the return of Christ and the eternal state (the millennium). Classical dispensationalists, following the lead of dispensationalism's founding father, John Nelson Darby (1800–1882), point to four additional periods. Thus:

1) **from creation to the fall** (the dispensation of *innocence*)
2) **from the fall to Noah** (the dispensation of *conscience*)
3) **from Noah to Babel** (the dispensation of *human government*)
4) **from Abraham to Moses** (the dispensation of *promise*)
5) **from Moses to Jesus** (the dispensation of *law*)
6) **from Pentecost to the rapture** (the dispensation of *grace*)
7) **the Millennium** (the dispensation of the *kingdom*)

It must be noted, however, that the recognition of distinct epochs or periods in biblical history is *not* the primary characteristic of dispensationalism. *All* Christians recognize the presence in Scripture of developments within God's redemptive purpose. What is unique about dispensationalism is the way these distinct periods in biblical history are used to justify or undergird a separation between Israel and the Church. Dispensationalism's principal feature is what might be called *redemptive dualism*, that is, the insistence that God has two distinct peoples, with distinct purposes for each. Variations within dispensationalism usually revolve around the question of whether and to what degree Israel and the Church share in the blessings and promises of God. Therefore, it is the *distinction between Israel and the Church and the purposes God has for each* that sets dispensationalism apart from other eschatological systems. Our task will be to see why dispensationalism draws this distinction between two peoples and purposes of God and how this affects their understanding of the kingdom.[9]

Dispensational Distinctives

The point of departure in Old Testament redemptive history, according to the dispensationalist, is Genesis 12 in which we see God entering into a covenant with Abraham and his seed. The promises made to this peculiar people, Israel, include an innumerable seed (Gen. 13:16; 15:5), and a land for an everlasting possession (13:14-18; 17:8). In God's covenant with David (2 Sam. 7:12-16) the promises initially given to Abraham are expanded. John Walvoord explains:

> What do the major terms of the covenant mean? By David's "house" it can hardly be doubted that reference is made to David's posterity, his physical descendants. It is assured that they will never be slain *in toto*, nor displaced by another family entirely. The line of David will always be the royal line. By the term "throne" it is clear that no reference is made to a material throne, but rather to the dignity and power which was sovereign and supreme in David as king. The right to rule always belonged to David's seed. By the term "kingdom" there is reference to David's political kingdom over Israel. By the expression "for ever" it is signified that the Davidic authority and Davidic kingdom or rule over Israel shall never be taken from David's posterity. The right to rule will never be transferred to another family, and its arrangement

---

9. Hitchcock and Ice (*The Truth Behind Left Behind*) speak for most classical dispensationalists when they refer to God as having "a distinct plan for Israel and a distinct plan for the Church" (186), although they also contend that the Church "currently shares in some of Israel's spiritual blessings (see Romans 15:27)" (187).

is designed for eternal perpetuity. Whatever its changing form, temporary interruptions, or chastisements, the line of David will always have the right to rule over Israel and will, in fact, exercise this privilege. This then, in brief, is the covenant of God with David.[10]

All these promises of an earthly/geographical, socio/political kingdom were both *unconditional* and *eternal*, which is to say that they do not depend for their ultimate fulfillment upon the obedience of the people of Israel, but solely upon God and his faithful promise, and they are to last forever as an everlasting possession. Thus Israel alone was to be the steward of God's blessings to the world (Gen. 12:2-3). To ethnic Israel and only to ethnic Israel did God give his Law (Mosaic code), a temple and a priesthood to minister in it, a sacrificial system to deal with sin, and the promise of agricultural, political, and economic prosperity in the land.

In the New Testament the dispensationalist recognizes that God again has a chosen people, only now they are called the *Church*. Like Israel, the people of God in the Old Testament, the Christian Church also has promises from God, which include, among other things, a heavenly position in Christ, a heavenly city, permanent forgiveness of sin, and a universal priesthood of believers. God, then, has *two separate peoples: Israel in the Old Testament with her distinctive set of earthly promises and destiny, and the Church in the New Testament with her distinctive set of heavenly promises and destiny.* But how came we to have two separate peoples? The answer to this question is the key to dispensational premillennialism. Let me unpack it for you in several interrelated stages.

Two Peoples of God

To begin, the promises given to Israel in the Old Testament were *never* literally and perpetually fulfilled. In spite of periods of prosperity, Israel never received the total fulfillment of the blessings contained in the Abrahamic covenant (notwithstanding what we read

---

10. John F. Walvoord, *The Millennial Kingdom* (Grand Rapids: Zondervan, 1975), 196.

in Josh. 21:43-45). Thus, it is only natural to assume that complete and literal fulfillment is yet future. This is largely the basis for the vastly popular belief among those known as Christian Zionists that the nation of Israel today has not merely a historical or political claim to the holy land, but a biblical one that is grounded in the covenant God made with Abraham. Dispensationalists will often point to the fact that even *after* the days of David and Solomon, days during which Israel enjoyed its most extensive geographical expansion, the prophets still speak of the possession of the land in its fullness to be *future*.[11]

The fulfillment of this covenant promise and prophetic hope was the purpose of Christ's first coming. The Father sent his Son to offer Israel the kingdom, that is, the fulfillment of all the promises he had given to her in the Old Testament (e.g., the land, political supremacy, a king [Christ himself] to sit on the Davidic throne).

But Israel as a whole rejected Christ and his offer of the kingdom. Consequently, God has ceased dealing with his people Israel, has *postponed* the fulfillment of the Old Testament promises, and has turned to deal with his second (and *new*) people, the Christian Church. After God has completed his purpose for the Church in this present dispensation/age, i.e., when the "fullness of the Gentiles" has come in (Rom. 11:25-27), God will remove the Church from earth to heaven (the pretribulation rapture) and again turn to deal with his people Israel in order to prepare her (by means of the great tribulation) for the fulfillment of the promises given in the Old Testament. We see, then, that *according to the dispensational premillennialist, this present Church age is a parenthesis in God's primary redemptive purpose.*[12]

Lewis Sperry Chafer, founder and first president of Dallas Theological Seminary and the man most responsible for giving systematic expression to Scofield's beliefs, did not think the word

---

11. See Isa. 11:1-11; Jer. 16:14-16; 30:10-11; Ezek. 34:11-16; Joel 3:17-21; Amos 9:11-15; Micah 4:4-7; Zeph. 3:14-20; Zech. 8:4-8

12. Again, Hitchcock and Ice concede that God's plan includes a purpose for the Church. However, "this is a temporary phase that will end with the Rapture. After the Rapture, God will complete His plan for Israel and the Gentiles" (180).

"parenthesis" was strong enough to express the radical distinction between God's Old Testament purpose for Israel and his New Testament purpose for the Church. Therefore, he chose to use the term "intercalation". Here is his explanation:

> In fact, the new, hitherto unrevealed purpose of God in the out calling of a heavenly people from Jews and Gentiles is so divergent with respect to the divine purpose toward Israel, which purpose preceded it and will yet follow it, that the term parenthetical, commonly employed to describe the new age purpose, is inaccurate. A parenthetical portion sustains some direct or indirect relation to that which goes before or that which follows, but the present age purpose is not thus related and therefore is more properly termed an *intercalation*. The appropriateness of this word will be seen in the fact that, as an interpolation is formed by inserting a word or phrase into a context, so an intercalation is formed by introducing a day or a period of time into the calendar. The present age of the Church is an intercalation into the revealed calendar or program of God as that program was foreseen by the prophets of old. Such, indeed, is the precise character of the present age." [13]

This fulfillment of the earthly promises to his earthly people (Israel) will take place in what is called the *millennium*, a period of 1,000 years *following* the great tribulation and second coming of Christ and *preceding* the final judgment and eternal state. The present age, therefore, is understood to be a parenthesis intervening between God's covenant *promise* to Israel in the Old Testament and God's *fulfillment* of that promise in the millennium.

Thus *the most fundamental aspect of dispensational premillennialism is the distinction between Israel and the Church.* According to the dispensationalist, God has *two* different peoples or groups for whom there are distinct promises, purposes, and destinies. Irrespective of whatever else in the dispensational system one may

---

13. Lewis Sperry Chafer, *Systematic Theology* (Dallas: Dallas Seminary Press, 1947-48), 4:40.

agree with, if he rejects the Israel/Church distinction, he is *not* a dispensationalist. Chafer writes:

> The dispensationalist believes that throughout the ages God is pursuing two distinct purposes: one related to the earth with earthly people and earthly objectives involved which is Judaism; while the other is related to heaven with heavenly people and heavenly objectives involved, which is Christianity.[14]

"This [Chafer's distinction]," writes Ryrie, "is probably the most basic theological test of whether or not a man is a dispensationalist, and it is undoubtedly the most practical and conclusive." [15] "The essence of dispensationalism, then," Ryrie concludes, "is the distinction between Israel and the Church." [16] This is why the *progressive dispensationalism* of more recent scholars is perceived as such a threat to the purity of *classical dispensationalism*. Progressive dispensationalism's proposal that there is a measure of continuity between Israel and the Church and that the latter shares, in part, in the Old Testament promises given to the former, is viewed as a departure from that one feature that sets dispensationalism apart from all other eschatological systems. See the Addendum for a brief explanation of this new expression of dispensationalism.

The Pretribulation Rapture

Beyond what one finds in the next few pages, very little will be said in this book about the so-called "Rapture Debate." I realize this may come as a disappointment to many, given the widespread popularity of the issue and the deeply emotional attachment that so many Christians have to the idea of a translation of all believers before the onset of the so-called "Great Tribulation." I suppose, then, that I should justify my relative neglect of the debate.

---

14. Chafer, *Dispensationalism* (Dallas: Dallas Seminary Press, 1936), 107.
15. Charles C. Ryrie, *Dispensationalism Today* (Chicago: Moody Press, 1965), 45.
16. Ibid., 47.

There are several reasons why I've chosen not to dig deeply into this controversial topic each of which will become evident only as one proceeds through the subsequent chapters. First, the very notion of a seven-year period immediately preceding the second coming of Christ, widely referred to as the "Great Tribulation," is largely dependent on the dispensational interpretation of Daniel 9. In the next chapter (Three) I argue that such a reading of Daniel's so-called "Seventy-Weeks Prophecy" is entirely unwarranted. Thus, to delve into a debate about the timing of the "rapture" as it relates to a period in history, the very existence of which I believe the Bible nowhere teaches, does not strike me as worthwhile.

Will there even be a "rapture," a moment in time when all living saints are resurrected and "caught up" both physically and spatially to meet Christ in the air? Yes, but this event is simultaneous with and inseparable from the parousia or the second coming of Christ itself. In the absence of a yet future seven-year season of great tribulation, to argue whether or not the "rapture" occurs before, during, or after "it," seems a needless waste of time, to state the obvious.

Second, the concept of a rapture of living saints before (hence, *pre*-tribulational) this purported seven-year time span is also, to a large extent, dependent on a distinction between Israel and the Church and God's separate purposes for each. But as you will discover upon reading Chapter Six, I do not believe the Scriptures justify such a distinction. Thus, again, to engage in a debate that makes little sense apart from the notion that God has two separate peoples, operating under the authority of two separate covenants to accomplish two separate purposes, is unwise, indeed highly misleading.

Third, as Chapters Seven and Eight will make clear, the so-called "Great Tribulation" to which Jesus refers in Matthew 24 is not a future expectation for the people of God but is an established fact of past history. The great tribulation is our Lord's way of describing the siege on Jerusalem in A.D. 66–70, by the armies of Rome, that resulted in the utter destruction of both the city and its temple.

Fourth, much of the rationale for a future seven-year period of great tribulation and the debate as to when the rapture occurs in relation thereto is tied up inextricably with the belief that God intends to save the great majority of ethnic Jews prior to the end of history and the coming of Christ (or perhaps in some way in conjunction with his coming). But as I argue in Chapter Ten in my treatment of Romans 11, the salvation of the elect who are ethnic Jews has been, is, and will continue to unfold and come to fruition in the same way God is saving the elect who are ethnic Gentiles, namely, throughout the course of the present church age. It is in this way that both the "fullness" of the Gentiles" and the "fullness" of Israel will ultimately have come in.

Fifth, the doctrine of the pretribulational rapture of the Church is to a large degree dependent on a strictly futuristic reading of the book of Revelation. In other words, it only makes sense on the assumption that what John describes in Revelation 6–18 is largely, if not entirely, in the future. The seal, trumpet, and bowl judgments that he describes are thought by pretribulationists to refer to what occurs wholly within that alleged seven-year tribulational period. In Chapter Thirteen I provide what I believe is a more persuasive way to understand the nature and sequence of these judgments and the chronological framework within which they occur.

Sixth, yet another alleged basis for the notion of a pretribulation rapture is the idea that the "restrainer" in 2 Thessalonians 2 refers to the Holy Spirit. The argument by dispensational pretribulationists is that if the Holy Spirit is removed or taken out of the way before the appearance of Antichrist and the inauguration of the seven-year period during which he holds sway, the Church itself must of necessity be removed or taken out from its present location on earth, all this by means of the rapture. Here I will only refer you to Chapters Sixteen and Seventeen where I not only offer a more cogent understanding of what Paul has in view in 2 Thessalonians 2 but also call into serious question whether or not John (in his epistles and the book of Revelation) has in mind a single individual when he speaks of the so-called "Antichrist" or beast of Revelation.

All that being said, I will take a brief moment to interact with what is typically believed to be the most important New Testament passage on the subject of the timing of the rapture. In defense of their doctrine, pretribulationists often point to the words Jesus spoke to the local church in the city of ancient Philadelphia: "Because you have kept my word about patient endurance, I will keep you from the hour of trial that is coming on the whole world, to try those who dwell on the earth. I am coming soon. Hold fast what you have, so that no one may seize your crown" (Rev. 3:10-11).

The pretribulational interpretation is that "the hour of trial" refers to a future seven-year period of intense persecution, during which the judgments of God are poured out on the earth. The promise to the Church is that God will "keep from" this hour all who believe in Jesus. The only way he can do this, so they say, is by physically removing the Church from the earth prior to the onset of this time of tribulation. A few observations should indicate why I don't believe that Jesus (or John) had any concept of a yet future pretribulation rapture of the Church in mind when these words were spoken/written.

First, the notion that any Christian is assured of special protection from trials, tribulations, and persecution is unbiblical. One can see repeatedly in the seven letters of Revelation 2–3 alone that suffering for the sake of Christ and the gospel is something all believers must embrace (see Rev. 2:2-3; 2:9-10; 2:13; 3:8-10). According to Paul, it is "through many tribulations (*thlipsis*; the same word used in Rev. 1:9; 7:14) we must enter the kingdom of God" (Acts 14:22). Jesus declared that "in the world you will have tribulation (*thlipsis*)" (John 16:33). Again, we are to "rejoice in our sufferings (*thlipsis*)" (Rom. 5:3; see also John 15:19-20; Acts 5:40-41; 1 Cor. 4:11-13; 2 Cor. 4:7-12; 11:24-25; 2 Tim. 3:12).

Second, the trial or tribulation that is coming is designed for the judgment of *unbelievers*, not Christians. "Those who dwell on the earth" (v. 10) or "earth-dwellers" is a stock phrase in Revelation that *always* refers to pagan persecutors of the church (6:10; 8:13; 11:10; 12:12; 13:8, 12, 14; 14:6; 17:2, 8). They are the ones who suffer the seal, trumpet, and bowl judgments of Revelation which *characterize the entire church age*, from the first coming of Christ to his second.

Third, the promise, then, is for *spiritual* protection in the midst of physical tribulation. Jesus is assuring his people that he will provide sufficient sustenance to preserve them in their faith, no matter what they face. The promise here is similar to what we find in Revelation 7:1-3,13-14 where the people of God are "sealed" lest they suffer spiritual harm from "the great tribulation (*thlipsis*)" (v. 14; cf. also Rev. 11:1-2; 12:6, 14-17). Clearly, believers endure and emerge from tribulation spiritually secure. As Beale notes, "they are not preserved from trial by removal from it, but their faith is preserved through trial because they have been sealed by God." [17]

Fourth, pretribulationists have typically insisted that the only way God's people can be spiritually protected from the outpouring of divine wrath is by being physically removed from the earth. But this is clearly not the case, as John 17:15 makes clear (as also does the presence of the Israelites in Egypt during the time of the ten plagues). In this Johannine text we find the only other place in the New Testament where the precise phrase "kept from" (*tereo ek*) is used. There Jesus prays to the Father: "I do not ask that you take them out of the world, but that you *keep them from* the evil one."

It's important to note in this text that "keep from" is actually *contrasted* with the notion of physical removal. Jesus prays not that the Father "take them out of the world" (i.e., physically remove them), *but* that the Father "keep them from" Satan's effort to destroy their spiritual life. Thus, when we turn to Revelation 3:10 we see that it is from the wrath of God poured out on "earth-dwellers" (unbelievers) that he promises to "keep" them. In the face of certain opposition and oppression from Satan, the beast, and unbelievers, this is a glorious promise indeed.

A related argument is that since this alleged "Great Tribulation" is to be a time when the *wrath* of God is poured out on an unbelieving world, Christians cannot be present. After all, believers will never suffer God's wrath, insofar as Christ has already suffered in their stead on the cross. But this falls short of a convincing reason to posit a pretribulation rapture. In the first place, even pretribula-

17. G.K. Beale, *The Book of Revelation* (Grand Rapids: Eerdmans, 1999), 292.

tionists concede that believers will be present on the earth during this "Great Tribulation" (having come to faith at some time subsequent to the rapture). But if they do not suffer God's wrath (and it is certain that they wouldn't), why should it be any different for those who were purportedly removed from the earth by the rapture? The simple fact is that no believer at any time in redemptive history will ever suffer divine wrath. Thus, if the pretribulationist admits that blood-bought believers will be in the "Tribulation", a time of God's wrath, on what basis does he say that blood-bought believers of the Church cannot be present? We mustn't forget that in Revelation the "wrath" of God never falls on the believer, but only on the wicked (this is true whether the term for "wrath" is *thumos,* as in Rev. 14:8, 10, 19; 15:1, 7; 16:1, 19; 18:3; 19:15; or *orge,* as in Rev. 6:16, 17, 14:10; 16:19; 19:15).

Fifth, we must never forget that it is precisely in remaining faithful unto death that our greatest victory is achieved (not in being "raptured" to safety; cf. Rev. 2:10). Believers conquer Satan and the beast "by the blood of the Lamb and by the word of their testimony, *for they loved not their lives even unto death*" (Rev. 12:11; emphasis mine).

But *what,* precisely, is "the hour of trial that is coming on the whole world," and *when* will it occur?

Of one thing I'm certain: the promise of protection must be of practical benefit and reassurance for the people of the church in Philadelphia *in the first century.* Thus, contrary to what is argued by dispensationalists, this "hour of trial" can't be restricted to (although it may be inclusive of) a time of tribulation at the end of the present age.

If you are inclined to insist on a strictly futurist interpretation of the "hour of trial", ask yourself whether it seems odd (dare I say, impossible) that Jesus would promise one church in Asia Minor in the first century that they were to be protected from an event that not one single individual in that church would ever see, indeed, an event that allegedly would not transpire for at least another 1,900 years! How could this "hour of trial" be an event centuries after the Philadelphian Christians lived, especially since their protection from it is the very specific reward *to them* of their very specific, and historically identifiable, resistance to persecution and steadfast faithfulness in proclaiming the word of God? *They* are promised protection because *they* "kept the word" of Christ's perseverance.

I'm persuaded that Jesus is referring to that "tribulation" (*thlipsis*) which has already begun for Christians (including the Philadelphians) and will continue throughout the present age. In writing to the churches, John identifies himself as their "brother and partner in the tribulation [*thlipsis*] and the kingdom and the patient endurance that are in Jesus" (Rev. 1:9). In other words, "the hour of trial" is likely a reference to *the entire, inter-advent church age*, during which there will always be suffering and tribulation for those who stand firm in their witness for Christ.

This isn't to deny that there will emerge an especially intensified and horrific period of tribulation in connection with the return of Christ at the end of history (regardless of how long you conceive it to be). But Jesus must have in mind an experience that was impending or already present for the Philadelphian believers in the first century and for all believers in subsequent centuries of the Church's existence.

Sixth, pretribulationists often argue that Revelation 3:10 must describe the removal of the Church from the earth insofar as the Greek word *ekklesia* ("Church") is wholly absent from Revelation 4–18, chapters that purportedly describe the "Great Tribulation." The *ekklesia* or "Church," so they say, must be present in heaven. But this argument cuts both ways, insofar as the word *ekklesia* is not found in any text in Revelation 4–18 that describes a *heavenly* scene. Should we conclude from this that the Church must be on the earth? Such arguments from silence are extremely dubious. After all, the word "Church" is not found in Mark, Luke, John, 2 Timothy, Titus, 1 Peter, 2 Peter, 1 John, 2 John, Jude, and not until the sixteenth chapter of Romans! Unless one is prepared to dismiss large portions of the New Testament as irrelevant to the Church, the absence or presence of the word itself cannot be made a criterion for determining the applicability of a passage to the saints of the present age.

We should also remember that the word "Church" as a denotation of the universal body of Christ considered in its totality does not occur at all in the book of Revelation. All nineteen occurrences of the word in chapters one through three refer to particular "local" congregations of Christians. Add to this the fact that terms commonly used to describe members of the Church, such as "servant" (Rev. 2:20; 7:3; 19:2), and "saints" (5:8; 8:3-4; 13:7, 10; 14:12; 16:6; 17:6; 18:24) are used throughout Revelation.

Finally, Jesus concludes with both a word of assurance and an exhortation: "I am coming soon. Hold fast what you have, so that no one may seize your crown" (Rev. 3:11). Is this "coming" the second advent at the close of history or a first-century disciplinary visitation? Possibly the former, but assuredly not the latter. After all, given the obedience of the Philadelphian church, there was no need for a "coming" of Jesus to judge or chastise (as was the case with Ephesus in 2:5, Pergamum in 2:16, and Sardis in 3:3).

However, there may be another option. Beale suggests that "the 'coming' referred to in this verse is the increased presence of Christ that will protect these believers when they pass through tribulation, as has just been mentioned in v. 10."[18] In other words, this may be a spiritual coming to provide comfort and the power to persevere, a drawing near to their hearts to energize them in their commitment. His "coming" or approach to them is not spatial, but spiritual and sanctifying, in which he intensifies his sustaining influence in their souls. If he can "come" to the churches at Ephesus, Pergamum, and Sardis to discipline, he can certainly "come" to the church at Philadelphia to strengthen and bless.[19]

The Dispensational Chronology

The key to understanding dispensational premillennialism is its view of the kingdom of God: its nature, offer, rejection, postponement, and ultimate fulfillment in the millennium. The best way to describe the dispensationalist's view of the millennial kingdom is

18. Ibid., 293.
19. For additional study of this topic, I highly recommend, *Three Views on the Rapture: Pretribulational, Prewrath, or Posttribulation*, edited by Stanley N. Gundry (with contributions from Alan Hultberg, Craig A. Blaising, Douglas J. Moo) (Grand Rapids: Zondervan, 2010).

chronologically, i.e., by means of the temporal order in which the events actually occur, beginning with the rapture. Although there are variations among those who call themselves dispensationalists, I will focus here only on the majority view known as dispensational, pretribulational, premillennialism.

First, according to this scheme of end-time events, Jesus will appear suddenly and unannounced in the heavens at which time he will *rapture* or translate or "catch up" to himself all Christians currently alive on the earth. All believers who had previously died will also be resurrected at this time. This event is *imminent,* which is to say that no other prophesied event must first occur. Dispensationalists often declare that the rapture could occur "at any moment" and without warning. All believers at that time are transformed or glorified and receive their resurrection bodies in conformity with that of the risen Lord himself. There is a small minority in the dispensational camp who embrace a "partial" rapture of the Church, insisting that only those who are living in expectation of Christ's return and the godliness that this necessarily entails will be caught up to their Lord in the heavens. All others will be "left behind" to endure the horror of the great tribulation, together with the unbelieving populace of the earth.

Second, subsequent to the rapture, there will ensue a period of seven years during which the judgments and wrath of God (as expressed in the seal, trumpet, and bowl judgments of the book of Revelation) will be poured out on the non-Christian peoples of the earth. This seven-year period is the seventieth and final week of Daniel's prophecy (Dan. 9:24-27), a passage we will carefully examine in a subsequent chapter. A world leader, popularly known as the Antichrist, will emerge. He will initially establish a covenant of peace with Israel, only to betray the agreement at the midpoint of the tribulation (3½ years), at which time he will orchestrate a global persecution of the Jewish people and any who may have come to saving faith in Christ subsequent to the rapture. Another minority view within dispensationalism contends that the judgments of God, in conjunction with the persecution sponsored by the Antichrist, will not begin until the midpoint of the great tribulation (3½ years into its span of time), and that the rapture will occur immediately before these judgments are poured out.

Third, at the Lord's second coming after the tribulation, in conjunction with the Battle of Armageddon where the Antichrist and the enemies of the gospel are finally and fully defeated, the vast majority of Israelites who survive that period of time will be converted to faith in Christ (Rom. 11:25-27). Those who remain in unbelief will be put to death and not permitted to enter the millennium (Ezek. 20:33-38). It's important to observe that according to this more popular version of dispensationalism, Christ's return is in *two stages*: a coming in the heavens (but not to earth) *before* the tribulation to rapture the Church, and a coming to earth at the *close* of the tribulation to defeat and judge his enemies at Armageddon.

Fourth, all Gentiles who also survived the tribulation will be judged (Matt. 25:31-46): the sheep (who are saved) being left on the earth to enter the millennium and the goats (the lost) being cast into everlasting fire and condemnation.

Fifth, these saved Israelites and saved Gentiles will therefore enter the millennium in their natural, physical, unglorified bodies (that is to say, in the same condition in which you who are reading this book now find yourselves).

Sixth, when Christ returns at the close of the tribulation there will also occur the bodily resurrection both of Old Testament saints and those believers who died during the tribulation period.

Seventh, Satan will at that time be bound and sealed for 1,000 years (he and the Antichrist having been defeated at the battle of Armageddon), wholly prevented from perpetrating evil during the millennial kingdom.

Eighth, Christ now begins his millennial reign. He ascends a throne in Jerusalem and rules over a predominantly Jewish kingdom, although Gentiles share in its blessings. The subjects of Christ's rule are primarily those Israelites and Gentiles who entered the kingdom in their natural bodies. Thus, at the *beginning* of the millennium there are no unregenerate/unbelieving people alive on the earth. This reign of Christ also fulfills the promises made to Israel in the Old Testament. According to Ryrie, "the earthly purpose of Israel of which dispensationalists speak concerns the national promise which will be fulfilled by Jews during the millennium as they live on the earth in *un*resurrected bodies. The earthly future for Israel does not concern Israelites who die before the millennium is set up."[20]

Ninth, those who have entered the millennium in their natural bodies will marry and reproduce, and though they will live much longer than they would have prior to Christ's coming, most of them will eventually die. This period is a time of unparalleled economic prosperity, political peace, and spiritual renewal. Worship in the millennium will center around a rebuilt temple in Jerusalem in which animal sacrifices will be offered: these sacrifices, however, will not be propitiatory, argues the dispensational premillennialist, but *memorial* offerings in remembrance of Christ's death.

Tenth, although dissimilarities exist, the millennial kingdom will see a virtual revival of much of the Mosaic and Levitical systems described in the Old Testament. J.D. Pentecost explains:

> In the millennial system we find the worship centers in an altar (Ezekiel 43:13-17) on which blood is sprinkled (43:18) and on which are offered burnt offerings, sin offerings, and trespass offerings (40:39). There is the re-institution of a Levitical order in that the sons of Zadok are set aside for a priestly ministry (43:19). The meal offering is incorporated in the ritual (42:13). There are prescribed rituals of cleansing for the altar (43:20-27), for the Levites who minister (44:25-27), and for the sanctuary (45:18). There will be the observance of new moon and sabbath days (46:1). Morning sacrifices will be offered daily (46:13). Perpetual inheritances will be recognized (46:16-18). The Passover feast will be observed again (45:21-25) and the feast of Tabernacles becomes an annual event (45:25). The year of jubilee is observed (46:17). There is a similarity in the regulations given to govern the manner of life, the dress, and the sustenance of the priestly order (44:15-31). This temple, in which this ministry

---

20. Ryrie, *Dispensationalism Today*, 146.

is executed, becomes again the place from which is manifested the glory of Jehovah (43:4-5). It can thus be seen that the form of worship in the millennium will bear a strong similarity to the old Aaronic order.[21]

Eleventh, all resurrected saints (i.e., Old Testament saints, Christians raptured before the great tribulation, and believers who came to faith during the tribulation but were put to death by the Antichrist) will live in the New Jerusalem (Rev. 21:1–22:5). This New Jerusalem will be above the earth, in the air, shedding its light and glory thereon. Resurrected saints will play some role in Christ's rule on the earth; their primary activity, however, will be in the New and Heavenly Jerusalem.[22]

Twelfth, children will be born to those believers (both Jew and Gentile) who entered the millennial kingdom in their natural bodies (and it is reasonable to assume that these children will themselves in turn live long lives, get married, and in turn bear yet more children). Many will come to faith in Christ and be saved. Those who persist in unbelief will be restrained by the righteous rule and government of Christ. At the end of the millennial kingdom Satan is released and will gather all unbelievers in one final conflict against Christ (Rev. 20:7-10). The rebellion will be crushed and Satan will be cast into the lake of fire, where the Antichrist and false prophet already languish (having been judged and cast there at the close of the tribulation).

Thirteenth, two more bodily resurrections now occur: that of all unbelievers of every age and that of believers who died during the millennial kingdom.

Fourteenth, the consummation will then come with the Great White Throne Judgment (Rev. 20:11-15), at which all unbelievers of every ethnicity and every era of human history will appear. They will be judged in accordance with "what they had done" (i.e., according to their works; Rev. 20:13-14).

21. J. Dwight Pentecost, *Things To Come* (Grand Rapids: Zondervan, 1971), 519.
22. For this view, see especially Ibid., 563-80.

Fifteenth, and finally, the new heavens and new earth are created as the everlasting dwelling place of God and his people, and thus begins the eternal state (Rev. 21:1-22:5).

This, then, is the perspective on redemptive history and the consummation of God's eternal purpose known as dispensational, pretribulational, premillennialism. Needless to say, I have offered little critique or response to these claims. My aim in this chapter was solely to explain what dispensationalism believes and to account for its meteoric rise in popularity, especially in the church in America. What I believe are the biblical and theological shortcomings of dispensationalism, and its concomitant premillennialism, will be taken up in subsequent chapters.

Addendum: Progressive Dispensationalism

The principal advocates of *Progressive Dispensationalism* are Craig Blaising and Darrell Bock, in their books, *Progressive Dispensationalism* (Wheaton: Victor Books, 1993), and *Dispensationalism, Israel and the Church: The Search for Definition* (Grand Rapids: Zondervan, 1992), together with Robert Saucy, *The Case for Progressive Dispensationalism* (Grand Rapids: Zondervan, 1993). At the heart of this development within dispensational theology is a growing recognition of greater *continuity*, not only among the many biblical covenants in the unfolding of redemptive history, but more importantly in the relation between Israel and the Church, both now and in the eternal state. According to Saucy, "this view seeks to retain a natural understanding of the prophetic Scriptures that appear to assign a significant role to the nation Israel in the future, in accordance with a dispensational system. But it also sees the program of God as unified *within* history, in agreement with non-dispensationalists, and it denies a radical discontinuity between the present church age and the messianic kingdom promises."[23] Thus progressive dispensationalists deny that the church age is a parenthesis

---

23. Robert L. Saucy, *The Case for Progressive Dispensationalism: The Interface Between Dispensational & Non-Dispensational Theology* (Grand Rapids: Zondervan, 1993), 27.

unrelated to that redemptive history which has preceded and the millennial age that follows.

Progressive dispensationalists also want us to believe that they affirm a fundamental unity between God's old covenant people Israel and the new covenant Church of Jesus Christ. Blaising contends that "progressive dispensationalists believe that the church is a vital part of *this very same [eternal] plan of redemption*. The appearance of the church does not signal a secondary redemption plan, either to be fulfilled in heaven apart from the new earth or in an elite class of Jews and Gentiles who are forever distinguished from the rest of humanity. Instead the church today is a revelation of spiritual blessings which *all the redeemed* will share in spite of their ethnic and national differences. Consequently, progressive dispensationalism advocates a *holistic and unified* view of eternal salvation."[24]

Before one jumps to the conclusion that this signals a significant deviation from older, more classical forms of dispensationalism, Blaising defines what he means. God will bless humankind "with the same salvation given to all without distinction; the same, not only in justification and regeneration, but also in sanctification by the indwelling Holy Spirit. These blessings will come to all without distinction through Jesus Christ."[25] Note well that the "blessings" that all share are "spiritual" and pertain to such things as regeneration by the Spirit and justification by faith alone, as well as sanctification. But when it comes to the so-called "national" or "geo-political" blessings, inclusive of the land promise, only believing ethnic Israelites are regarded as heirs.

Bruce Ware makes the same distinction. He refers to Israel and the church as a "*united people* of God," at the same time he insists they remain separate in their identity and specifically so when it comes to the "territorial and political aspects" of the new covenant

---

24. Craig A. Blaising, "The Extent and Varieties of Dispensationalism," in *Progressive Dispensationalism,* edited by Craig A. Blaising & Darrell L. Bock (Wheaton: Victor Books, 1993), 47.

25. Ibid., 47-48.

that do not apply to the Church.[26] Again, Ware affirms that "Israel and the church are in fact one people of God, who together share in the forgiveness of sins through Christ and partake of his indwelling Spirit with its power for covenant faithfulness, while they are nonetheless distinguishable covenant participants comprising what is one unified people."[27] The primary factor that distinguishes them is the promise, unique and exclusive to Israel alone, says Ware, of eventual restoration as a nation to its land. Needless to say, this is precisely the sort of distinction and exclusive promise that I believe is denied in Ephesians 2, Galatians 3, and elsewhere. See Chapter Six for my comments on these passages and their implications for the relationship between Israel and the Church.

Thus, notwithstanding what strike me as at best minimal changes, Darrell Bock points out that "Progressive dispensationalism still believes in the future of Israel in a land involving an earthly millennium and making a distinction between Israel and the church.... A pretribulational rapture... is still held to by the vast majority [of progressive dispensationalists]."[28]

My conclusion is that what at first appears to be a generous inclusion of the Church in Israel's covenant promises falters on a decisive exclusion from the latter's inheritance in the land. As much as progressive dispensationalists might want us to think they have moved beyond the distinctives of their classical ancestors, they yet retain a significant dichotomy between Israel and the Church. They want to speak of "one people of God" but can do so only in terms of a common inheritance of "spiritual" blessings. When it comes to the inheritance of the land and those promises associated with it, only ethnic Israelites are recipients.

---

26. Bruce A. Ware, "The New Covenant and the People(s) of God," in *Dispensationalism, Israel and the Church: The Search for Definition*, edited by Craig A. Blaising and Darrell L. Bock (Grand Rapids: Zondervan, 1992), 96-97.

27. Ibid., 97.

28. Darrell L. Bock, "Charting Dispensationalism," *Christianity Today* (September 12, 1994): 29.

Chapter Three

The Seventy Weeks of Daniel 9 and the Old Testament Roots of Dispensationalism

O ne might well argue that Daniel 9:24-27 is both the most complex and the most crucial text in either testament bearing on the subject of biblical prophecy. Its complexity is questioned only by those who have not studied it, or perhaps by those whose conclusions concerning its meaning were predetermined by unspoken theological commitments. That Daniel 9 is as crucial as I have suggested can hardly be denied. For example, dispensationalists have largely derived from Daniel 9 several of their more distinctive doctrinal and prophetic themes, among which are,

1) separate divine programs for *Israel* and the *Church* based on the idea of a prophetic and historical *gap*, during which time God's purpose for the former is suspended and his purpose for the latter engaged (that "gap," of course, being identified with this present "church" age);

2) the reality of a future period of intense tribulation, precisely seven years in length, during which the divine program for Israel is resumed;

3) the rebuilding of a temple in Jerusalem at the inception of this seven-year period and its subsequent destruction; and,

4) the emergence of a personal Antichrist who will establish a seven-year covenant with Israel, reinstitute the Levitical

71

sacrificial system, only to break the covenant after three and one half years.

One could conceivably make an argument that apart from the dispensational interpretation of Daniel 9, these and related prophetic doctrines would lack substantial biblical sanction.

There's simply no way to overemphasize how crucial this paragraph in Daniel 9 is for dispensationalism, as well as the role it plays in the debate over the timing of the rapture. Rarely if ever do I read in dispensational literature about the end times or the Antichrist or the rapture where reference isn't made to "Daniel's Seventieth Week" or the seven-year period of great tribulation. Most dispensational Christians simply take it for granted that the Bible teaches there will be a literal seven-year period of intense tribulation, either before, in the middle of, or immediately after which the rapture of the Church will occur, a seven-year period during which the Antichrist will exert his nefarious influence over the earth and oppress the nation of Israel. Were it to be discovered that Daniel 9 does not, in fact, teach any such thing, that would strike a severe, if not mortal, blow to the entire dispensational scenario.

My purpose, however, is not to offer an extensive critique of dispensationalism. It will, of course, be necessary to review briefly what dispensationalists have said about Daniel 9. But my goal is to be more constructive than destructive, and to that end I have devoted the bulk of this chapter to what I believe is the correct meaning of the text and its contribution to our understanding of God's purpose in redemptive history. The passage reads as follows:

[24]Seventy weeks are decreed about your people and your holy city, to finish the transgression, to put an end to sin, and to atone for iniquity, to bring in everlasting righteousness, to seal both vision and prophet, and to anoint a most holy place.

[25]Know therefore and understand that from the going out of the word to restore and build Jerusalem to the coming of an anointed one, a prince, there shall be seven weeks. Then for sixty-two weeks it shall be built again with squares and moat, but in a troubled time.

²⁶And after the sixty-two weeks, an anointed one shall be cut off and shall have nothing.[1] And the people of the prince who is to come shall destroy the city and the sanctuary. Its end shall come with a flood, and to the end there shall be war. Desolations are decreed.

²⁷And he shall make a strong covenant with many for one week, and for half of the week he shall put an end to sacrifice and offering. And on the wing of abominations shall come one who makes desolate, until the decreed end is poured out on the desolator.

The Dispensational Interpretation of Daniel 9:24-27

I've decided to approach this chapter in a manner somewhat different from how the other chapters are constructed. I believe the best and most instructive way to address this subject and to unpack what is admittedly a complex paragraph is by asking and then answering a series of related questions. So let me begin by asking several questions and answering them as I believe a dispensationalist typically would.

1. What are the seventy weeks of Daniel 9?

According to Daniel 9:24, "seventy sevens" have been decreed. The latter of these two terms, here translated "sevens," literally means *a unit of seven things* (hence, a "week"). The question, however, is: a unit of seven *what?* Seven Days? Seven Weeks? Hours? Months? Years? Most commentators of the dispensational school conclude that Gabriel had in mind units of *years.* Consequently, "seventy" of these "units of seven years" would equal 490 years. Although commentators refer to this period as Daniel's seventy "weeks," the period of time in view is one of 490 years.

2. When do the seventy weeks of Daniel begin?

According to verse 25 the seventy weeks (i.e., the 490-year period) begin with the issuing of a decree or "word" to restore and rebuild

---

1. Peter J. Gentry argues that the traditional rendering, "and shall have nothing," is inaccurate. The Hebrew can more accurately be rendered, "but not for himself", and likely points to the notion that "the coming king dies vicariously for his people" ("Daniel's Seventy Weeks and the New Exodus," in *The Southern Baptist Journal of Theology,* Volume 14, Number 1 [Spring 2010], 37).

Jerusalem. Dispensationalists have opted for either one of two dates for this decree. Some point to the seventh year of Artaxerxes in 458–457 B.C. (Ezra. 7:11-26), while others identify it with the twentieth year of Artaxerxes in 445–444 B.C. (Neh. 2:1-8). The latter of these two dates is preferred by most dispensationalists, and for *two reasons. First,* this decree pertains to the rebuilding of the "city," in accordance with Daniel 9:25. *Second,* verse 25 also indicates that between the decree and the coming of Messiah sixty-nine of the seventy weeks transpire. In other words, 483 years (or, 173,880 days, on the questionable assumption that a year = 360 days) from the decree brings us to Jesus Christ. If one begins with the first of Nisan (March 14), 445 B.C., and counts off 173,880 days (taking into account years that have an extra day due to leap year), one arrives at April 6, A.D. 32, allegedly the occasion of Christ's triumphal entry into Jerusalem. If one chooses to begin the count in 444 B.C., instead of 445, the sixty-ninth week terminates on March 30, A.D. 33. Many people are obviously quite impressed with this sort of chronological precision and have embraced the dispensational view because of it.

The dispensational view, therefore, appears to depend upon two crucial facts: (1) 445–444 B.C. is the only year in which a decree relative to the rebuilding of Jerusalem was issued; and (2) the 490 years or seventy weeks is a chronologically precise period of time, and must therefore span the period from the decree to the Messiah *to the very day.* If either or both of these assertions are false, the dispensational interpretation is seriously undermined. That is to say, *if* it can be shown that the decree of Cyrus in 538 B.C. meets all the qualifications for the decree which inaugurates the seventy weeks (Dan. 9:25), and *if* it can be shown that the 490 years or seventy weeks need not be taken with chronological and arithmetic precision, the dispensational view is considerably weakened.

3. What is the goal or purpose of the seventy weeks?

The goal of Daniel's 70 weeks is stated in the six-fold declaration of verse 24 – "to finish the transgression, to put an end to sin, and to atone for iniquity, to bring in everlasting righteousness, to seal both vision and prophet, and to anoint a most holy place." Without going into detail at this time, suffice it to say that most dispensationalists insist that some, if not all, of these goals will only be achieved at the second advent of Jesus at the end of the age, perhaps not even until the end of the "millennium." For this reason they insist that the seventieth week is yet future.

4. When exactly will the seventieth week begin?

The dispensationalist says that, according to verse 26, two events will occur *after* the sixty-ninth week but *before* the seventieth. In other words, these two events will occur in the alleged "gap" between the sixty-ninth and seventieth weeks. These two events are, first, the cutting off of Messiah (the crucifixion), and second, the destruction of Jerusalem and its temple in A.D. 70. When, then, is the seventieth week to occur? Only at the end of the present age when Christ returns to consummate the six-fold purpose outlined in verse 24. This seventieth week, the so-called "Great Tribulation," says the dispensationalist, is described in verse 27.

5. Who is the coming "prince" of verse 26 and the one who makes the covenant in verse 27?

Both the "prince" who is to come in verse 26 and "he" who, in verse 27, makes a covenant with the many for one week, refer, says the dispensationalist, to the final, personal Antichrist. This "one week" or seven-year covenant will entail the rebuilding of the temple in Jerusalem and the reinstitution and observance of sacrificial offerings. After 3½ years, i.e., in the middle of the week, Antichrist will break the covenant, persecute the people of God (Israel), only to be destroyed by the return of Christ Jesus at the close of the seven-year tribulation period (i.e., at the close of the seventieth week, during the battle of Armageddon).

6. On what basis does the Dispensationalist posit a "gap" between the sixty-ninth and seventieth weeks of Daniel 9?

Absolutely fundamental to the dispensational interpretation is that there is *a gap or interval or historical parenthesis* between the sixty-ninth and seventieth weeks. Thus far in history this alleged gap has spanned over 1,980 years. On what basis do dispensationalists justify this remarkable length of time?

Typically they appeal to the following points. First, if one believes the text is providing a strict historical or chronological sequence, a gap is implied. According to verse 25, a period of sixty-nine weeks is terminated by the appearance of Messiah. Two events then occur: the death of Messiah and the destruction of Jerusalem. Then, in verse 27, after the events of verse 26, the seventieth week occurs. Dispensationalists contend that since two of the prophesied events occur *after* the sixty-ninth week but *before* the seventieth week, a gap between the two is implied.

Dispensationalists also insist that the events outlined in verse 24 were not fulfilled at Christ's first coming nor have they been fulfilled at any time in history since his appearance. Therefore, the seventieth week, in which they will be finally fulfilled, must be future. Furthermore, since an unseen gap in prophetic time is not unusual in the Old Testament (see, for example, Isa. 61:1-2 and Luke 4:16-21), we shouldn't be surprised to find one here in Daniel 9. Finally, based on how most dispensationalists interpret the Olivet Discourse in Matthew 24 (esp. vv. 15ff.), Jesus himself declared that Daniel's seventieth week is still future. Although other arguments may be cited to support the gap theory, these are certainly the more important ones.

God's Final Jubilee

Instead of responding critically to the dispensational interpretation (although this will occur in subsequent chapters), I prefer to present what I believe is a far superior understanding of the text. By means of asking and then answering a series of ten questions, I hope that the sense of Daniel's seventy weeks will become clear to us.

1. What is the Historical and Literary context of Daniel 9?

The opening verses of Daniel 9 indicate that Daniel prayed to God in the light of the prophecy uttered by Jeremiah relative to the seventy-years' captivity of Israel (Jer. 25:1-11) and the punishment of Babylon when the seventy years were complete (Jer. 25:12). Daniel prays "in the first year of Darius, son of Xerxes" (9:1-2), that is to say, in the first year of Cyrus's reign (539–538 B.C.). If the beginning of the seventy years captivity is to be reckoned from 605 B.C. (Jer. 25:1, 9) when Daniel and his friends were deported to Babylon, it is obvious that the prophesied period was nearing completion. In fact, *sixty-six of the seventy years had passed.* This motivated Daniel to pray for the restoration of Israel and Jerusalem (9:16, 18, 20). Certainly, then, *Gabriel's response in Daniel 9:20-27 is to be understood as an answer to Daniel's prayer (see esp. 9:20-23).* Thus, Vern Poythress concludes:

> The logical conclusion from this language is that the beginning point of the 70 weeks basically coincides with the end of Jeremiah's 70 years. That is, it occurs in 538 B.C. or shortly thereafter. On the other hand, a beginning point in 444 B.C. would not really answer Daniel's prayer. It would not be quick enough to satisfy Daniel's urgency. And it would not be related to the basis of Daniel's prayer in Jeremiah's prophecy of 70 years.[2]

This relationship between the conclusion of Jeremiah's seventy-years prophecy and the beginning of Daniel's seventy-weeks prophecy is substantiated when we consider the nature and purpose of Cyrus' decree, to which we now turn our attention.

2. What is the "word" or "decree" of Daniel 9:25, or when do the seventy weeks begin?

In his first year, after the fall of Babylon in fulfillment of prophecy, the Persian king, Cyrus, issued a decree relative to the rebuilding of the temple in Jerusalem:

> Thus says Cyrus king of Persia, The LORD, the God of heaven, has given me all the kingdoms of the earth, and he has charged me to build him a house at Jerusalem, which is in Judah. Whoever is among you of all his people, may the LORD his God be with him. Let him go up (2 Chron. 36:23).

We are told explicitly in 2 Chronicles 36:21-22 that the decree of Cyrus signaled the end of Jeremiah's prophecy and the beginning

---

2. Vern Sheridan Poythress, "Hermeneutical Factors in Determining the Beginning of the Seventy Weeks (Daniel 9:25)," in *Trinity Journal* 6:2 (Fall 1985), 134.

of the restoration of Israel. This corresponds directly with Daniel's concern for the completion of Jeremiah's prophecy, on the basis of which he utters his prayer (9:2).

In Daniel 9:25 the decree that inaugurates the seventy weeks is "to restore and build Jerusalem," and that is precisely what *Isaiah* prophesied that Cyrus would do:

> [It is I] who says of Cyrus, "He is my shepherd, and he shall fulfill all my purpose"; saying of Jerusalem, "She shall be built," and of the temple, "Your foundation shall be laid." (Isa. 44:28)

> "I have stirred him up in righteousness, and I will make all his ways level; he shall build my city and set my exiles free, not for price or reward," says the LORD of hosts. (Isa. 45:13)

Let me now summarize. In 605 B.C. Jeremiah prophesied that Israel would be taken captive in Babylon for seventy years and that Jerusalem and its temple would be destroyed. He also prophesied that at the end of this period Babylon would fall. In 539 B.C. Babylon fell to Cyrus of Persia. Consequently, in that very year, sensing the completion of Jeremiah's prophecy, Daniel prays for the restoration of Jerusalem. Gabriel (as God's messenger) responds to Daniel's prayer with the prophecy of the seventy weeks, the beginning of which would be a decree to rebuild and restore the city. In 538 B.C Cyrus issued just such a decree! The point, then, is this. *The decree of Cyrus in 539–538 B.C. is both the conclusion of Jeremiah's prophecy of captivity (2 Chron. 36:21-23) and the beginning of Daniel's seventy-weeks prophecy of restoration (Dan. 9:25).*

3. Did Cyrus's decree pertain to the rebuilding of the city as well as the temple?

Dispensationalists insist that the decree of Cyrus in 538 B.C. cannot be the beginning of the seventy weeks because his decree did not include reference to the rebuilding of the *city*, but only the temple. Several things may be said in response to this charge.

First, as Vern Poythress points out, we must bear in mind that the Israelites

lived in an atmosphere where the restoration of the temple, the restoration of the city of Jerusalem, and the restoration of the land itself were closely bound up together. The city represented the heart-beat and security of the land around; the temple represented the heart-beat and security of the city (Jer. 7:4). Jeremiah prophesied desolation for the land, for the city of Jerusalem, and for the temple. In particular, Jeremiah's prophecy concerning 70 years of desolation speaks explicitly of restoration of the people to the land (Jer. 29:10,14), but is naturally interpreted to imply restoration of the city (Dan. 9:2,16,18) and of the temple (Dan. 9:17).[3]

Second, the focus of the decree in Ezra 1:2-4 and 2 Chronicles 36:23 is indeed the temple, but these passages may not give us the complete text of the decree. Ezra 6:3-5, an alternative report of the decree, contains details not mentioned in Ezra 1:2-4. When Josephus wrote of the decree he included direct reference to the city. But let us grant, for the sake of argument, that Josephus was wrong and that the decree of Cyrus contained no *explicit* reference to the rebuilding of the city. The restoration of the city, observes Poythress, "would nevertheless be presupposed as an accompaniment to the restoration of the temple. For one thing, there would have to be workers there in the city to engage in the restoration work on the temple. And the temple would make little sense without a body of priests to serve in it. Some priests would have to be settled in Jerusalem."[4]

Third, according to Daniel 9:2, Daniel himself believed that the desolation of the city of Jerusalem would last for seventy years. It is only natural, therefore, that the restoration of the city, as well as the temple, would begin when the seventy years were completed. "To say that the restoration of the city had to wait until Nehemiah's time [as the dispensationalist insists] is a denial of the validity of Jeremiah's prophecy."[5]

---

3. Ibid., 136.
4. Ibid.
5. Ibid., 137.

Fourth, we have already seen that Isaiah 44:28 and 45:13 include reference to the rebuilding of the *city*.

Fifth, numerous texts indicate that Jerusalem was at least partially inhabited *before* Nehemiah's time (cf. Hag. 1:4,9; Neh. 3:20, 21, 23, 24, 25, 28, 29; 7:3; Ezra 4:6; 5:1; 6:9). That the restoration was not at that time complete is no proof that it had not begun.

Sixth, and finally, what about Daniel 9:25b and the reference to "squares and moat"? This poses no problem, for one must distinguish between the *decree* itself and the historical *results*. It is the verbal (or literary) act that marks the beginning of the seventy weeks. Daniel 9:25b simply describes the non-verbal historical results.

Given the available evidence, I see no reason why we should look for any decree other than that of Cyrus in 539–538 B.C. as the fulfillment of Daniel 9:25 and thus the beginning (the *terminus a quo*) of the seventy weeks. Consequently, one of the principal foundations for the dispensational interpretation has crumbled.

4. What is the goal or purpose of the seventy weeks?

Daniel 9:24 makes it clear that the goal of the seventy-weeks prophecy is six-fold in nature: (1) "to finish (or, 'restrain') the transgression"; (2) "to put an end to sin" (or, 'to seal up sin'); (3) "to atone for iniquity"; (4) "to bring in everlasting righteousness"; (5) "to seal both vision and prophet"; and (6) "to anoint a most holy 'place.'"

Most are agreed that (3) pertains to the propitiatory sufferings of Jesus. The dispute concerning (1) and (2) focuses more on the time of their fulfillment. Are these statements descriptive of what our Lord already accomplished at his first advent, or do they pertain to what he will achieve at his second advent (particularly, for Israel)? My opinion is that this is a false disjunction. What Jesus *fulfilled* at his first advent, he will *consummate* at the second. More on this later.

The fifth purpose, "to seal both vision and prophet" (or "prophecy"), means that the season of preparation, foreshadowing, and type, what we know to be the time of the old covenant, will be "sealed" up, because its purpose has been completed. It will no longer be needed, since the age of messianic fulfillment has come.

Again, should one insist that the ultimate consummation of all prophetic utterance in the second coming of Christ is intended, no objection is forthcoming. One need not conclude, however, that the seventieth week is therefore altogether future. If the seventieth week of Daniel 9 is the present age, as I intend to argue, one may find the consummation of each goal in the second advent of Christ without conceding the validity of the dispensational scheme.

The sixth purpose, literally, "to anoint a most holy place" (literally, "to anoint a most holy"), is a reference to the baptism (anointing) of Jesus (cf. Acts 10:38; Luke 4:34, 41). There is absolutely no evidence in the Old Testament that the temple was ever anointed (aside from the single reference to Moses' anointing of the wilderness tabernacle in Lev. 8:10-11).

5. Who is the coming "prince" of Daniel 9:26?

Dispensationalists believe that this "prince" is the final Antichrist who will appear at the end of the age. However, we are told in verse 26 that the city and sanctuary are to be destroyed by the people of the prince who is to come. The dispensationalist rightly insists that "the people" refers to the Roman armies of A.D. 70. But the "prince", says the dispensationalist, to whom these armies or people belong, was not Titus, the Roman general, but a prince who is to arise from a revived Roman Empire conceivably 2,000 years *after* the people had died! E.J. Young has pointed out the shortcomings of this interpretation:

> Now it is impossible thus to speak of the Roman armies who attacked Jerusalem in A.D. 70. These armies cannot be said to belong to a prince who has not even now appeared, although nearly two thousand years have passed. The genitival relationship [people *of* a prince] shows clearly that the people and prince are contemporaries. The people belong to the prince, they are his people. Now, how can the Romans of A.D. 70 be said to belong to a prince who has not appeared yet? They are not his people; they belong to a prince who is their contemporary. Suppose that this prince should appear upon the scene of history; he cannot look back to the armies of Titus and call them his armies. To take a modern example, Mussolini could not have spoken of the

armies of Titus as being his own armies. The very language itself rules out this interpretation.[6]

Simply put: the "prince" who is to come (i.e., who is future to Daniel), is Titus, the Roman general, whose armies destroyed the city of Jerusalem and its temple in A.D. 70.[7]

6. Are verses 26 and 27 sequentially related, or are they parallel descriptions of the same series of events?

The key to the dispensational interpretation is that since verse 25 concludes with the sixty-ninth week and verse 27 opens with the seventieth, verse 26 must describe events that occur in a gap between the two. That gap has now stretched to more than 1,980 years. By way of response, two observations are in order.

First, according to Hans LaRondelle, "when Daniel announced that seventy weeks are determined for national Israel and that the Messiah will be 'cut off' after the first sixty-nine weeks, the natural presumption can only be that the death of the Messiah will take place sometime *during the last week*. J. Barton Payne [thus] concludes, 'What could be more naturally assumed than that it [the death of Messiah] concerns the 70th week?'"[8]

The dispensational argument for a gap between the sixty-ninth and seventieth weeks is based on the belief that verses 26 and 27 are phrased in a modern style of prose that describes events in a strictly sequential and chronological order. But a close examination of these two verses reveals that they are structured in the poetic style of synonymous (or perhaps synthetic) parallelism in which *verse 27*

6. E.J. Young. Unable to locate source for this quote.
7. Gentry argues that the "prince who is to come" of verse 26b is not Titus but Jesus, the "anointed" one of verse 25 and verse 26a. This would require that "the people" ("of" Jesus the prince) who destroy the city and sanctuary in A.D. 70 are the Jews, not the Romans. Gentry insists that "although the Roman army actually put the torch to Jerusalem, the destruction of the city was blamed squarely on the Jewish people themselves" (39). I find this unlikely, but even if true it would not affect my overall understanding of the passage.
8. Hans K. LaRondelle, *The Israel of God in Prophecy: Principles of Prophetic Interpretation* (Berrien Springs: Andrews University Press, 1983), 174.

repeats and elaborates the content of verse 26. Thus, events that occur "after" the sixty-ninth week (v. 26) occur "in" the seventieth week (v. 27). The death of Messiah and the destruction of Jerusalem are the two principal events portrayed in verses 26-27. Note especially the verbal correspondences between verse 26b and verse 27b.

7. The dispensationalist insists there is a gap between verse 26 and verse 27. Why is this not true?

The principal reason has just been given: verses 26 and 27 are not relating events that are sequential (i.e., A B C D) but rather parallel (i.e., A B A B). Even should we concede that some or all of the goals stated in verse 24 await the second advent of Christ for their fulfillment, a gap between the sixty-ninth and seventieth week is unnecessary. If it can be demonstrated that the seventieth week (or, more accurately, the latter half of the seventieth week) *is* the present age, then clearly it followed immediately upon the sixty-ninth. As noted earlier, what Jesus fulfilled at his first coming he will consummate at his second.

The appeal to the alleged gap between Isaiah 61:1-2a and 61:2b is invalid. Although our Lord in Luke 4 did not cite the entire passage, it may easily be demonstrated that the day of God's wrath as well as the day of redemption were inaugurated by our Lord's ministry (see Matt. 3:10-12; 23:37ff.).

It is also argued that the seventieth week is wholly future, a time period at the close of human history, because Jesus declared as much in the Olivet Discourse (see Matt. 24 and Mark 13). However, a careful study of these texts (that I will provide later in the book) will reveal that "the abomination of desolation" to which he refers, as well as the "great tribulation," both pertain to the events of A.D. 70 when Jerusalem and its temple were utterly destroyed.

Jeremiah's seventy years, on the pattern of which Daniel's seventy weeks were constructed, admit of no gap. Furthermore, there is no gap between the seven weeks and the sixty-two weeks (v. 25), making it unlikely for there to be a gap between the sixty-nine weeks (the seven + the sixty-two) and the seventieth.

After examining other cases in which prophecy refers to a determinate specification of time (Gen. 15:13; 45:6; Num. 14:34), Philip

Mauro concludes: "We are bold, therefore, to lay it down as an absolute rule, admitting of no exceptions, that when a definite measure of time or space is specified by the number of units composing it, within which a certain event is to happen or a certain thing is to be found, the units of time or space which make up that measure are to be understood as running continuously and successively." [9] Thus we would understand "seventy years" to mean seventy *continuous* years, and "seventy weeks" to mean seventy *continuous* weeks, and "seventy miles" to mean seventy *continuous* miles, and so on.

Assuming for the sake of argument that the 490 units of time equal 490 literal years, consider this: "Is it credible that this prophecy, which speaks so definitely of 70 weeks and then subdivides the 70 into 7 and 62 and 1, should require for its correct interpretation that an interval be discovered between the last two of the weeks far longer than the entire period covered by the prophecy itself? If the 69 weeks are exactly 483 consecutive years, exact to the very day, and if the 1 week is to be exactly 7 consecutive years [these are assumptions, again, made only for the sake of argument], is it credible that an interval which is already more than 1900 years, nearly four times as long as the period covered by the prophecy, is to be introduced into it and allowed to interrupt its fulfillment?" [10]

I am also convinced that the theory of a gap is motivated as much by the antecedent determination to find additional justification for distinguishing between Israel and the Church, as it is by any factors actually present in the text itself. In other words, if one had not *already* decided in favor of two distinct peoples of God with distinct dispensations in which God deals with each, would Daniel 9 ever have been interpreted in such a way as to yield the concept of a gap between the sixty-ninth and seventieth weeks? Or, again, to put it even more bluntly, dispensationalists find a gap in

---

9. Philip Mauro, *The Seventy Weeks and the Great Tribulation: A Study of the Last Two Visions of Daniel, and of the Olivet Discourse of the Lord Jesus Christ*, rev. ed. (Swengel, PA: Bible Truth Depot, 1944), cited by Young, *The Prophecy of Daniel*, 216.

10. Oswald T. Allis, *Prophecy and the Church* (Nutley, NJ: The Presbyterian and Reformed Publishing Company, 1972), 118.

Daniel 9 because they are *predisposed* to find one in order to justify an already existent theological construct.

8. What is the meaning of 9:27?

As noted earlier, in view of the parallel construction of verses 26 and 27, the Messiah or "anointed one" of verse 26a is identical with the "he" of verse 27a, and the "prince" of verse 26b is identical with the "one who makes desolate" of verse 27b, i.e., the Roman general Titus in A.D. 70. In addition to this, I conclude that he who, literally, "causes a covenant to prevail" is Jesus, the Messiah. This he does through the shedding of his blood (cf. Matt. 26:27-29; Mark 14:24; Luke 22:20; 1 Cor. 11:25; Heb. 8–10).

Finally, to what does Daniel refer when he speaks about Messiah putting "an end to sacrifice and offering"? There are two possibilities, as I see it. This may be a reference to the sacrifice of Christ whereby he abrogated the Jewish sacrificial system (see Heb. 7:11-12, 27; 9:26-28; 10:9; Matt. 27:51; Mark 15:38). Or, more likely still, this is a reference to the cessation of Jewish sacrifices by the destruction of Jerusalem and its temple in A.D. 70 (see Matt. 23:37–24:2).

9. Are the seventy weeks to be interpreted "chronologically" or "theologically"?

We are immediately made aware that the seventy weeks are probably not to be taken with chronological precision by the fact that the seventy years of Jeremiah's prophecy were not precisely seventy years. The fall of Babylon by which the end or conclusion of Jeremiah's prophecy is reached occurred in 539 B.C. There are several suggested beginning points for the prophecy, *none of which*, however, *add up to precisely seventy years:*

fall of Nineveh in 612 B.C. = 73 years; [11]
the battle of Carchemish or Nebuchadnezzar's accession, both of which were in 605 B.C. = 66 years;

---

11. Gentry says that "apparently" the seventy-year period begins with the death of Josiah in 608 B.C. He gives no reasons for making this claim, other than his belief that "a literal period of seventy years" is in view ("Daniel's Seventy Weeks," 32).

the beginning of the captivity in 597 B.C. = 58 years;
the destruction of the temple and city in 586 B.C. = 47 years.

My point is that "seventy years" is an approximate designation of length, such as we find in Jeremiah 27:7 and Ezekiel 4:6-8. In Mesopotamian culture, seventy years refers primarily to a certain period of desolation followed by the visitation of God. As we see in Zechariah 1:12, seventy years is the fixed term of divine wrath and indignation. Psalm 90:10 and Isaiah 23:15 both use the number "seventy" to indicate the totality of divine judgment. Jeremiah was emphatic in saying that the seventy years captivity would end with the punishment of the Babylonians (Jer. 25:11-12; 29:10), an event that Daniel explicitly acknowledges in the opening verses of chapter nine. If Jeremiah's seventy years began in 605 B.C., sixty-six of the seventy years had come and gone. This is likely what prompted Daniel's passionate prayer for the promised restoration. Daniel is not concerned that sixty-six does not equal seventy, and neither should we be. My point is that if Jeremiah's "seventy years" turn out to be only "sixty-six" or even "fifty-eight," we should not be overly concerned that Daniel's "seventy sevens" end up being something other than precisely 490 years.

It has been suggested that ever since the seven days of creation the number "seven" has pointed symbolically to the work or activity of God. "Seventy" is seven multiplied by the round number ten, again pointing to perfection or completion. Thus perhaps "seventy sevens" is symbolic of the divine work brought to consummate perfection. Although there is some truth to this, I believe the significance of the seventy weeks is more profound.

If the seventy weeks or 490 years is not to be applied with chronological and calendrical precision, what is its significance? In other words, what is the *symbolic* and *theological* meaning of the 70×7 units, or 490 years? Why did Gabriel communicate the answer to Daniel's prayer in terms of seventy weeks / 490 years rather than, say, a 500-year period or a period of forty weeks? What is so theologically special and distinctive about *seventy* weeks and *490* years?

To answer this question we must begin by noting the obviously *covenantal* character of the entire ninth chapter of Daniel. Meredith Kline offers this helpful explanation:

> The common focus of the prayer and the prophetic response, the theme that pervades the entire chapter, is Yahweh's covenant with Israel, particularly the actualization of the covenant sanctions through the faithfulness of God [N.B. Chapter 9 is the *only* chapter in Daniel in which the peculiarly covenantal name of God, *Yahweh*, occurs]. This central theme emerges at once in the opening words of Daniel's prayer. Setting his face toward God, he describes Him as the Lord who "keeps the covenant" (vs. 4). That is both the ground of Daniel's confidence and the subject of his plea. His prayer is that God would bring to realization the mercies of His covenant, as He had its curses. And the message of Gabriel's prophecy, answering to Daniel's prayer, is that God would straightway prove himself anew the keeper of the covenant, fulfilling the ancient Mosaic promise of restoration after exile (Lev. 26:42ff.; Deut. 30:3ff.) according to the specific terms of that promise as it had been reissued by Jeremiah (Jer. 29:10). Then in its revelation of the future of the covenant, Gabriel's answer moves on beyond the horizon of the prayer, disclosing that the ultimate purpose of the seventy weeks program was that the divine covenant keeper should not merely restore but consummate the covenant order He had given to Israel through Moses.[12]

When Daniel's prayer is analyzed we see that it belongs to the "*Todah*" genre, in which the petitioner acknowledges God's glory and grace in his actions toward his people, confesses the sins of the people in having broken the covenant, and pleads for its renewal. It is only to be expected that Gabriel's answer to Daniel's prayer will itself assume a covenantal pattern (see Lev. 26:40-45). This is,

---

12. Meredith Kline, "The Covenant of the Seventieth Week," in *The Law and the Prophets*, ed. John H. Skilton (Nutley, NJ: Presbyterian and Reformed, 1974), as found at www.monergism.com, p. 2.

in fact, precisely what we see. For the chronological mold in which the prophecy is cast is *sabbatical.*

Let us remember that not only were the Israelites themselves to rest on the seventh *day,* the *land* also was to rest in the seventh *year.* When Gabriel spoke of the "sevens," seventy of which were decreed for Israel, he had in mind the seven-year period, the seventh year of which was a sabbatical year of rest for the land (Lev. 25:2-7). Kline proceeds to make the point that the sabbath itself, whether for the people or the land, functioned "as a prophetic symbol of the consummation of the covenant order. As elaborated in the Mosaic covenant ... the sabbath served as a sign of the messianic age of redemptive liberation, restitution, and rest [see esp. Heb. 4:1-11]".[13]

It would appear, then, that this precise chronological or numerical framework was chosen not because Gabriel desired to set calendrical boundaries of a beginning and end in which the six-fold goal of 9:24 would be accomplished. Rather, he chose this framework, first, because it is sabbatical, and second, because the sabbath (and the number seven) bore special symbolic import for the nation Israel.

This point is confirmed when we observe that Gabriel spoke of "seventy" of these units of seven, hence 490 years. Why did he not choose thirty or fifty or eighty "sevens" instead of "*seventy* sevens"? The reason is found in Leviticus 25:8-55 and the observance of the year of *JUBILEE.* Let us note particularly vv. 8-12.

> [8]You shall count seven weeks of years, seven times seven years, so that the time of the seven weeks of years shall give you forty-nine years. [9]Then you shall sound the loud trumpet on the tenth day of the seventh month. On the Day of Atonement you shall sound the trumpet throughout all your land. [10]And you shall consecrate the fiftieth year, and proclaim liberty throughout the land to all its inhabitants. It shall be a jubilee for you, when each of you shall return to his property and each of you shall return to his clan. [11]That fiftieth year shall be a jubilee for you; in it you shall neither sow nor reap what grows of itself nor

---

13. Ibid., 5.

gather the grapes from the undressed vines. [12]For it is a jubilee. It shall be holy to you. You may eat the produce of the field.

When we examine the year of jubilee in detail we discover that its provisions were as follows: (1) the return of all property, according to the original Mosaic distribution, to the original owner or to his family; (2) the release of all Jewish slaves; (3) the cancellation of debts; and (4) the land is to lie fallow, i.e., it is neither to be sown, pruned, reaped, nor gathered for an entire year.

The jubilee, therefore, was a year in which social justice and equity, freedom, pardon, release, and restoration were emphasized and experienced. The jubilee signaled a new beginning, the inauguration of moral, spiritual, and national renewal. Hence *it is no surprise that the jubilee became a symbol and prefigurement of the ultimate redemption, release, and restoration that God would accomplish spiritually on behalf of his people.* Indeed, the eschaton, the final day of salvation to be inaugurated by Messiah, was conceived and described in terms of the release ordinance of the Mosaic year of jubilee.

This all takes on special significance when we realize that there is decreed for Israel a total period of seventy sevens of years or 490 years, which is to say **10 JUBILEE ERAS,** "an intensification of the jubilee concept pointing to the ultimate, antitypical jubilee." [14] The jubilary year of God in which the consummation of redemption and restoration is to occur is described in Isaiah 61:1-2:

> [1]The Spirit of the Lord GOD is upon me, because the LORD has anointed me to bring good news to the poor; he has sent me to bind up the brokenhearted, [2]to proclaim liberty to the captives, and the opening of the prison to those who are bound; to proclaim the year of the LORD's favor, and the day of vengeance of our God; to comfort all who mourn.

This is the passage that our Lord quotes in Luke 4:16-21 and applies to his own person and work. In other words, *the fulfillment*

14. Ibid.

and anti-type of the prophetic and typical jubilary year has come in the person and work of Jesus Christ! Thus both Isaiah and Luke employ the Mosaic instruction concerning the jubilee to describe the dawning of God's kingdom in the person and work of Jesus.

The purpose of the seventy-weeks prophecy, outlined in Daniel 9:24, was to secure that ultimate salvation, that release, redemption, and restoration of which the jubilee year was a type or symbolic prefigurement. *When Jesus declares that in himself the jubilee of God has come he is saying, in effect, that the seventy weeks of Daniel have reached their climax. The new age of jubilee, of which all previous jubilees were prefigurements, has now dawned in the person and minis-try of Jesus. THE GOAL OF THE SEVENTY-WEEKS PROPHECY IS THE CONSUMMATE JUBILARY SALVATION OF GOD!*

That is why the chronological frame of reference in which it is said to transpire is jubilary in nature: 10 jubilees = 490 years! The meaning of the period, therefore, is THEOLOGICAL, not calendrical. The seventy weeks are not designed to establish pre-cise chronological parameters for redemptive history. Rather, they serve to evoke a *theological image*, namely, that in "Messiah Jesus" God will work to bring about the final jubilee of redemptive history. The ten jubilee framework (i.e., the 490 years or seventy weeks) is thus symbolic of the divine work of redemption, at the conclusion of which the eternal and perfected jubilee will appear: THE NEW HEAVENS AND NEW EARTH (Rev. 21–22).

10. How, then, may we understand the contribution of Daniel's prophecy to the structure and flow of redemptive history?

According to the conclusions reached above, *the first half of Dan-iel's seventieth week runs from the baptism of Jesus to A.D. 70. The destruction of Jerusalem and its temple in A.D. 70 is the middle of the week, and the present church age is its latter half.* Kline concurs and summarizes as follows:

> When we survey the fulfillment of Gabriel's prophecy from our van-tage point, it appears that the last half of the 70th week is the age of the community of the new covenant, disengaged from the old covenant

order with whose closing days its own beginnings overlapped for a generation. In the imagery of the NT Apocalypse, the last half week is the age of the church in the wilderness of the nations for a time, and times, and half a time (Rev. 12:14). Since the 70 weeks are 10 jubilee eras that issue in the last jubilee, the 70th week closes with the angelic trumpeting of the earth's redemption and the glorious liberty of the children of God. The acceptable year of the Lord which came with Christ will then have fully come.[15]

Here, then, is a visual portrayal of the view I've defended, beneath which is a portrayal of the standard dispensational perspective.

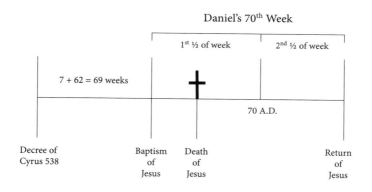

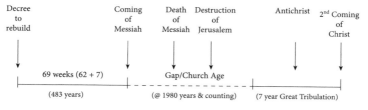

The Dispensational Interpretation of Daniel's 70 Weeks Prophecy

---

15. Ibid., 9.

Chapter Four

Daniel's Contribution to Biblical Eschatology

The significance of Daniel for biblical eschatology comes in three ways. First, as we have just noted in the previous chapter, Daniel 9 and the prophecy of the seventy weeks is one of the most important texts for the dispensational premillennial perspective, a passage, in fact, without which dispensationalism loses much of its credibility. Second, those from the dispensational school also largely derive from Daniel 2, 7, and 8 their belief in a revived Roman Empire at the end of history (they would, of course, also appeal to certain texts in the book of Revelation). Finally, Daniel is believed to provide extensive information concerning an end-time Antichrist. I earlier addressed the dispensational interpretation of Daniel 9 and will in this chapter focus more directly on the contribution, if any, that Daniel 2, 7, 8, and 11 make to our understanding of eschatology.

Nebuchadnezzar's Dream, Daniel's Interpretation, and the Four Kingdoms

Daniel 2:31-45 is of crucial importance, so I urge you to take the time to read through it slowly and carefully.

> [31]You saw, O king, and behold, a great image. This image, mighty and of exceeding brightness, stood before you, and its appearance was frightening. [32]The head of this image was of fine gold, its chest and

arms of silver, its middle and thighs of bronze, [33]its legs of iron, its feet partly of iron and partly of clay. [34]As you looked, a stone was cut out by no human hand, and it struck the image on its feet of iron and clay, and broke them in pieces. [35]Then the iron, the clay, the bronze, the silver, and the gold, all together were broken in pieces, and became like the chaff of the summer threshing floors; and the wind carried them away, so that not a trace of them could be found. But the stone that struck the image became a great mountain and filled the whole earth. [36]This was the dream. Now we will tell the king its interpretation. [37]You, O king, the king of kings, to whom the God of heaven has given the kingdom, the power, and the might, and the glory, [38]and into whose hand he has given, wherever they dwell, the children of man, the beasts of the field, and the birds of the heavens, making you rule over them all – you are the head of gold. [39]Another kingdom inferior to you shall arise after you, and yet a third kingdom of bronze, which shall rule over all the earth. [40]And there shall be a fourth kingdom, strong as iron, because iron breaks to pieces and shatters all things. And like iron that crushes, it shall break and crush all these. [41]And as you saw the feet and toes, partly of potter's clay and partly of iron, it shall be a divided kingdom, but some of the firmness of iron shall be in it, just as you saw iron mixed with the soft clay. [42]And as the toes of the feet were partly iron and partly clay, so the kingdom shall be partly strong and partly brittle. [43]As you saw the iron mixed with soft clay, so they will mix with one another in marriage, but they will not hold together, just as iron does not mix with clay. [44]And in the days of those kings the God of heaven will set up a kingdom that shall never be destroyed, nor shall the kingdom be left to another people. It shall break in pieces all these kingdoms and bring them to an end, and it shall stand forever, [45]just as you saw that a stone was cut from a mountain by no human hand, and that it broke in pieces the iron, the bronze, the clay, the silver, and the gold. A great God has made known to the king what shall be after this. The dream is certain, and its interpretation sure.

One of the central issues in the interpretation of Daniel is the identification of these four world empires or kingdoms described in chapter 2 and again in chapter 7. Traditionally, conservative scholars have argued that the four kingdoms are Babylon, Medo-Persia, Greece (or Macedonia), and Rome, and that they provide us with a prophetic scenario for how the remainder of human history will unfold. Most non-conservative scholars contend that they are Babylon, Media, Medo-Persia, and Greece. The latter view has been consistently rejected by evangelicals because most who embrace it are liberal critics who date the book of Daniel in the second century B.C. and deny its predictive prophecies. But recently several conservative scholars such as Robert Gurney,[1] John Walton,[2] and Marvin Pate and Calvin Haines[3] have argued for *both* a sixth-century date for the book of Daniel and that *Greece*, not Rome, is the fourth kingdom of Daniel 2 and the fourth beast of Daniel 7. These scholars have a very strong case and I will provide a more detailed explanation of their view later in this chapter.[4]

Before we delve into this debate, several important observations are in order.

First, this prophecy does not purport to describe every world power then or now. It is not intended to be exhaustive, but to

1. Robert Gurney, "The Four Kingdoms of Daniel 2 and 7," *Themelios* 2 (1977), 39-45.
2. John Walton, "The Four Kingdoms of Daniel," *JETS* 29/1 (March 1986), 25-36.
3. Marvin Pate and Calvin Haines, *Doomsday Delusions* (Downers Grove: IVP, 1995).
4. Others suggest the four are Babylon, Medo-Persia, Greece under Alexander the Great, and Greece under his successors. John Goldingay proposes a view that no one else, as far as I can tell, has ever entertained. He argues that since Daniel declares Nebuchadnezzar himself to be the "head of gold" the subsequent elements in the statue likewise refer to individual "kings" and not "kingdoms" or "empires". The four are, says Goldingay, Nebuchadnezzar, Belshazzar, Darius the Mede, and Cyrus the Persian. However, "king" and "kingdom" are frequently interchangeable in Scripture since the king was viewed as the embodiment of the kingdom. See also verse 39 which explicitly refers to "kingdoms" that follow Babylon. Tremper Longman argues that "though the vision begins with the Babylonian empire, its multivalent imagery intends to prohibit definite historical identifications with the remaining three beasts. Rather, the fourfold pattern simply informs us that evil kingdoms will succeed one another (at least seemingly) until the end of time" (*Daniel,* The NIV Application Commentary [Grand Rapids: Zondervan, 1999], 184).

describe the course of history from the Babylonian captivity to the inauguration of the messianic kingdom of God as it relates to his covenant people.

Second, as you read this chapter I hope you observed the emphasis on *deterioration and decline*. The image deteriorates in value, weight, unity, and in brittleness. You should also have taken note of the increasing strength of the image. "The metals increase in their degree of hardness, thus suggesting a paradox when seen alongside the emphasis on deterioration already mentioned."[5] Ford also points out how "the symbols quite clearly teach truths about the transitory nature of earthly kingdoms, compared with the reign of God, and the certainty of destructive judgments for all powers that oppose the divine will."[6]

There is also a marked contrast between the metals of the image and the unworked stone, cut without hands. It would seem to point to a transition from the efforts of mere humans to the creative work of God. One should likewise take note of the unity of the statue amidst the diversity. "Essentially, world powers are one, since they are human in nature; hence, the world powers are united in the *one* statue."[7] It is a "single statue" (2:31) which is destroyed *as a unity*. In other words, although the Babylonian empire, for example, had long since passed from the scene of history when Greece and Rome emerged, in some sense the four world powers are but successive forms of one unified entity. According to Daniel 2:35, the entire image was destroyed by the stone, and in 2:44 the four empires are envisioned as together existent when crushed by God.[8]

---

5. Desmond Ford, *Daniel* (Nashville: Southern Publishing Association, 1978), 96.
6. Ibid.
7. Edward J. Young, *The Prophecy of Daniel: A Commentary* (Grand Rapids: Eerdmans, 1980 [1949]), 71.
8. Patrick Fairbairn explains: "The language is purposely indefinite. It does not indicate at what particular time, or even under what precise dynasty, the kingdom represented by the stone should begin to develop itself on the theater of the world – though, from being mentioned the last in order, and from the fourth worldly kingdom being the one, with which alone it appears coming into collision, the natural inference obviously is, that the commencement of the

Finally, whereas the visions in chapters 2 and 7 are of the same world empires, they are presented under vastly diverse images. Nebuchadnezzar's conception, being that of an unregenerate man, is of a colossal and brilliant statue. In chapter 7, however, the divine perspective on these kingdoms is given to Daniel, which accounts for the imagery of ravenous, destructive beasts. That is to say, in chapter 7 prominence is given to the internal reality of each kingdom. "Viewed as a whole, the worldly kingdoms have their representation in so many wild beasts, because in them the beastly principle was predominant – that is, the earthly, sensual, groveling tendency, with all its selfishness of working and its debasing results."[9]

As noted above, most evangelical scholars have identified the four kingdoms as Babylon, Medo-Persia, Greece, and Rome. I will also make a case for the alternative reading, but for now we turn to a brief explanation of each kingdom according to this traditional understanding.

1. According to this interpretive scheme, *Babylon* is the head of gold (2:32a,36-38). Note the emphasis on the derivative character of Nebuchadnezzar's power: it has been *given* to him by God. The Babylonian empire ruled from 605 to 539.

2. The second kingdom, only briefly mentioned here in chapter 2 and represented by the breast and arms of silver (2:32:b, 39a),

---

heavenly kingdom is to be assigned to the fourth or last form of the earthly one. The whole of these successive monarchies of the world are taken together, as but different phases of the same worldly principle; in a somewhat different form the old always lived again in the new; so that the image which represents the entire series, appears still standing in its completeness – the several successive kingdoms, which it symbolized were to the last ideally present; but, from the nature of the case, they could only be so as seen in that which was more immediately represented by the legs and feet of the image" (*Prophecy: viewed in respect to its distinctive nature, its special function, and proper interpretation* [Grand Rapids: Baker Book House, 1976 (1865)], 292).

9. Ibid., 295. "The beasts," notes Longman, "(with the exception of the second) are like none to be found in God's creation. That is the point – they are symbols of forces ranged against God and his creation order. These beasts are bizarre; they are mutants, perversions of what God intended by his creation. As such, they evoke not only horror in the original reader, but also revulsion" (*Daniel*, 183).

is typically identified with *Medo-Persia*. On this scheme, Daniel considered the Medes and Persians as components of one and the same empire (see 6:8, 15; 8:20). The two arms have no more symbolic significance than do the two legs of the next empire. After all, what should one expect from a statue of a man but that it have two arms and two legs? Some, however, have argued that the two arms represent the two-fold nature of this empire: Media and Persia. The Medo-Persia kingdom ruled from 539 to 331.[10]

3. The third kingdom is often taken as *Greece*, with its belly and thighs of bronze (2:32c, 39b). Alexander the Great did indeed rule over "all the earth" as then conceived, from Egypt and Europe eastward to India. In 332, Alexander defeated the Medo-Persian empire in a series of decisive battles. His empire lasted from 331 to 146.

4. Finally, *Rome* is regarded by most evangelicals as the fourth kingdom, with its legs of iron, feet of iron and clay (2:33, 40-43). Rome dominated the world from the defeat of Carthage in 146 B.C. to approximately A.D. 400. Two important points are made in the description of the fourth kingdom. First, its strength and destructive power are symbolized by iron. Second, its inner divisions and eventual dissolution are symbolized by the curious mixture of iron and clay. Baldwin believes that "it has therefore an intrinsic weakness, for potter's clay and iron do not bond together. Unity is impossible and the kingdom is vulnerable because it is seeking to unite elements which will not coalesce."[11]

---

10. In what sense was Medo-Persia "inferior" (lit., "beneath you", v. 39) to Babylon when it actually controlled more territory? Most commentators believe the reference is to a progressive *moral deterioration*.

11. Joyce G. Baldwin, *Daniel: An Introduction & Commentary*, The Tyndale Old Testament Commentaries (Downers Grove: IVP, 1978), 93. According to Leon Wood, "The weakness of Rome, which led to its fall and which did come to existence especially in its later period, was a deterioration of moral fiber among the people. Idleness, luxurious living, and dissipation of character found their way into, and intermixed with, the still firmly structured aspects of government" (*A Commentary on Daniel* [Grand Rapids: Zondervan, 1973], 70).

The *messianic kingdom* is represented by the stone not cut by human hands but prepared solely by God (2:34-35, 44-45). Two crucial questions must be answered. First, when and in what manner does the "stone" shatter the pagan empires and establish its universal sovereignty? Second, when and in what manner does the messianic kingdom emerge, assert its dominion, and crush the "little horn" of Daniel 7? These questions will be addressed fully in our study of chapter 7.

The Four Beasts of Daniel 7

We should begin by once again carefully reading the passage. It is long and complicated but is deserving of close study.

> [2]Daniel declared, "I saw in my vision by night, and behold, the four winds of heaven were stirring up the great sea. [3]And four great beasts came up out of the sea,[12] different from one another. [4]The first was like a lion and had eagles' wings. Then as I looked its wings were plucked off, and it was lifted up from the ground and made to stand on two feet like a man, and the mind of a man was given to it. [5]And behold, another beast, a second one, like a bear. It was raised up on one side. It had three ribs in its mouth between its teeth; and it was told, 'Arise, devour much flesh.' [6]After this I looked, and behold, another, like a leopard, with four wings of a bird on its back. And the beast had four heads, and dominion was given to it. [7]After this I saw in the night visions, and behold, a fourth beast, terrifying and dreadful and exceedingly strong. It had great iron teeth; it devoured and broke in pieces and stamped what was left with its feet. It was different from all the beasts that were before it, and it had ten horns. [8]I considered the horns, and behold, there came up among them another horn, a little one, before which three of the first horns were plucked up by the roots. And behold, in this horn were eyes like the eyes of a man, and a mouth speaking great things.

---

12. On the significance of the "sea" as symbolic of evil, chaos, and anti-kingdom powers with whom Yahweh must contend, see Isa. 17:12, 13; 51:9-10; 27:1; 57:20; Rev. 17:8; 21:1; Jer. 46:7ff.; Job 26:7-13.

"9As I looked, thrones were placed, and the Ancient of Days took his seat; his clothing was white as snow, and the hair of his head like pure wool; his throne was fiery flames; its wheels were burning fire. 10A stream of fire issued and came out from before him; a thousand thousands served him, and ten thousand times ten thousand stood before him; the court sat in judgment, and the books were opened.

11"I looked then because of the sound of the great words that the horn was speaking. And as I looked, the beast was killed, and its body destroyed and given over to be burned with fire. 12As for the rest of the beasts, their dominion was taken away, but their lives were prolonged for a season and a time.

13"I saw in the night visions, and behold, with the clouds of heaven there came one like a son of man, and he came to the Ancient of Days and was presented before him. 14And to him was given dominion and glory and a kingdom, that all peoples, nations, and languages should serve him; his dominion is an everlasting dominion, which shall not pass away, and his kingdom one that shall not be destroyed.

15"As for me, Daniel, my spirit within me was anxious, and the visions of my head alarmed me. 16I approached one of those who stood there and asked him the truth concerning all this. So he told me and made known to me the interpretation of the things. 17'These four great beasts are four kings who shall arise out of the earth. 18But the saints of the Most High shall receive the kingdom and possess the kingdom forever, forever and ever.'

19"Then I desired to know the truth about the fourth beast, which was different from all the rest, exceedingly terrifying, with its teeth of iron and claws of bronze, and which devoured and broke in pieces and stamped what was left with its feet, 20and about the ten horns that were on its head, and the other horn that came up and before which three of them fell, the horn that had eyes and a mouth that spoke great things, and that seemed greater than its companions. 21As I looked, this horn made war with the saints and prevailed over them, 22until the Ancient of Days came, and judgment was given for the saints of the Most High, and the time came when the saints possessed the kingdom.

23"Thus he said: 'As for the fourth beast, there shall be a fourth kingdom on earth, which shall be different from all the kingdoms, and it shall devour the whole earth, and trample it down, and break it to pieces. [24]As for the ten horns, out of this kingdom ten kings shall arise, and another shall arise after them; he shall be different from the former ones, and shall put down three kings. [25]He shall speak words against the Most High, and shall wear out the saints of the Most High, and shall think to change the times and the law; and they shall be given into his hand for a time, times, and half a time. [26]But the court shall sit in judgment, and his dominion shall be taken away, to be consumed and destroyed to the end. [27]And the kingdom and the dominion and the greatness of the kingdoms under the whole heaven shall be given to the people of the saints of the Most High; his kingdom shall be an everlasting kingdom, and all dominions shall serve and obey him.' "

Let's look closely now at the "kingdoms" these "beasts" are designed to represent (7:17; cf. Ezek. 29:3ff; Isa. 27:1; 51:9).

The first beast is undoubtedly Babylon, here portrayed as a lion (7:4). The winged lion is familiar in Babylonian art and statues of this beast have actually been recovered from the ruins of Babylon. The lion is king of beasts and the eagle king of birds, an appropriate image for the power and might of ancient Babylon. On several occasions in the Old Testament Nebuchadnezzar and the Babylonians are described as being like both a lion (Isa. 5:25-30; Jer. 4:6, 7; cf. 25:9, 38; 49:19, 22; 50:17, 44) and an eagle (Deut. 28:49-53; 2 Kings 25:1-11; Jer. 49:19-22; Lam. 4:19; Ezek. 17:1-5, 11-14; Hab. 1:6-8). The plucking off of the lion's wings symbolizes the subduing of his pride and the reduction of his power during the time Nebuchadnezzar was reduced to living like a beast of the field (see Daniel 4). The description of a "mind of a man" being "given to it" also may allude to the restoration of Nebuchadnezzar's sanity after his seven-year dementia.

The second beast, a bear (7:5), has traditionally been identified with Medo-Persia (see Isa. 13:17, 18; cf. Hosea 13:8; Amos 5:19). Two things are said of the bear. First, it is raised up on one side. This may be symbolic of the double-sided nature of the kingdom – Media and Persia (see 8:20), while others suggest that the bear is raised up simply as an indication of its readiness to pounce on more prey. Wood believes that the one side raised "points to the greater importance assumed by the Persian division over the Median, in the Medo-Persian empire – a symbolism formed also by the two horns of the ram in Daniel's second vision (8:3), the second being made to grow higher than the first." [13] Perhaps all three suggestions are correct.

The second thing to note is that the bear has three ribs in its mouth, which may represent three nations conquered by the bear. The most likely candidates are Lydia (in Asia Minor), which fell to Cyrus in 546 B.C.; Babylon, annexed by Cyrus in 539; and Egypt, which Cyrus' son Cambyses acquired in 525.[14] Baldwin argues that the three ribs simply represent the "victim of a previous hunt which has not satisfied its [the bear's] appetite." [15] In other words, the three ribs portray the insatiable nature of the beast; not being content with one body it devoured many.[16]

Our third beast is like a leopard (7:6), pointing to Greece. Known for its sudden, swift, unexpected attacks, the leopard (with wings on its back) is an appropriate symbol for the military ventures of Alexander the Great. The significance of the four heads is not certain. Perhaps they represent the four generals among whom Alexander's kingdom was divided following his death: Cassander, already governor of Macedonia, was acknowledged as sovereign over all Greece; Seleucus received Syria and much of the Middle East; Lysimachus received Thrace and a large part of Asia Minor; and Ptolemy became ruler over Egypt. Or do they represent the four corners of the earth, thus pointing to the ecumenical and universal dominion of Alexander's rule? Joyce Baldwin believes the four heads simply refer to the fact that the leopard is looking in all directions for prey.

---

13. Leon Wood, *A Commentary on Daniel* (Grand Rapids: Zondervan, 1973), 183.
14. Gurney, who believes the bear is only Media, identifies the three as Ararat, Minni, and Ashkenaz, based on Jeremiah 51:27-29.
15. Baldwin, *Daniel,* 139.
16. Then again, the reference to "ribs" may simply mean "tusks" or "fangs" with no special symbolic significance at all.

The fourth beast may be Rome (7:7-8, 19-28). The point of this portrait is to emphasize its ferocity and strength, characteristics well suited to what we know of Rome. Two important components of the beast are its ten horns and the "little horn" which comes up among them, uprooting three of the ten in process. The identity of the "little horn" (7:17-18) will be examined below. Here we are concerned with the ten horns. What do they mean? These are the most popular interpretations.

Dispensationalists take the ten horns as referring to ten literal kingdoms. Since nothing of this nature occurred in the history of the Roman Empire (so they argue), they posit a revived Roman Empire at the end of the age. Wood explains: "The correct view can only be that there will be a time still future when the Roman empire will be restored, so that these representations can be true in the manner depicted: a time when ten contemporary kings will rule, among whom another will arise, uprooting three in the process, and then move on to become head of all." [17] Dispensationalists typically identify these ten horns in Daniel 7 with the "ten-nation confederacy" referred to in Revelation 17:12-18.

Others insist that the number ten is not necessarily to be taken as only ten kingdoms. According to Ford, "the number ten should no more be pressed in this context than in [Daniel] 1:20. It is a round number frequently used in Scripture. The reality must, however, be more than five or six, or the round number four would have been used. What is represented may indeed rise to a dozen or fifteen and not transcend the symbolism. This precisely fits the situation after the fall of the Roman Empire. The resulting fragments were sometimes more, sometimes less, and rarely stable for long. Thus the lists usually used to illustrate the prophecy differ slightly one from another." [18]

Here are several different theories and the persons who proposed them.

---

17. Leon Wood, *A Commentary on Daniel*, 187.
18. Desmond Ford, *Daniel*, 148-49.

(JOSEPH MEDE 1586–1638)	(ISAAC NEWTON 1642–1727)
Alemanes	Huns
Ostrogoths and Lombards	Ravena
Visigoths	Visigoths
Franks	Franks
Vandals	Vandals and Alans
Sueves and Alans	Suevians
Burgundians	Burgundians
Britons	Alans
Saxons	Britons
Greeks	Lombards

(BISHOP NEWTON 1704–82)	(URIAH SMITH 1832–1903)
Huns	Huns
Greeks in Ravena	Ostrogoths
Goths	Visigoths
Franks	Franks
Allemanes	Vandals
Senate of Rome	Suevi
Burgundians	Burgundians
Britons	Heruli
Saxons	Anglo-Saxons
Lombards	Lombards

In other words, on this view the ten horns are any and conceivably all of the pagan empires that emerged subsequent to the fall of Rome.

E.J. Young suggests that "like the number four in vs. 6, the number ten here is to be taken in a symbolic sense as indicating 'a multiplicity of rulers, or an indefinitely large number of kings,' 'comprehensive and definite totality.' " [19] Young thus sees the history of the fourth beast or Rome in three phases or stages. First, the beast itself is presented in the vision, a prophetic portrait of the

---

19. Young, *The Prophecy of Daniel*, 147.

emergence and power of Rome following the demise of Greece (and extending at least beyond the close of the apostolic age). Second, is the period of the ten horns themselves: "Although, in order to indicate the essential unity of the fourth kingdom, the horns appear upon the head of the beast, it is obvious that these horns represent a later phase of the beast's existence."[20] The ten horns come out of this kingdom. "By arising out of it must be meant, that they were to be historically connected with it, and to be in a sense its continuation; as there can be no doubt that the various kingdoms, which sprung up after the irruptions of the barbarians into the Roman empire, had much in common with Rome, while in policy and character they were diverse from it; they still had her laws, her language and literature, her institutions and customs, for the basis of theirs."[21] Third, is the period of the little horn, which most believe to be the Antichrist. Young concludes:

> As I have previously tried to indicate, we are not to look for ten kingdoms which shall exist side by side when the little horn appears. If the number ten is to be pressed, all we need insist upon is that, from the time when the fourth empire lost its beast form (i.e., the destruction of the Roman Empire) to the appearance of the little horn, there have been ten kingdoms which truly partake of the character of the beast. If, however, the number ten be regarded merely as the symbol of completeness, as I am inclined to regard it, the vs. means that from the time of the destruction of the Roman Empire to the appearance of the little horn there will be a number of kingdoms, which may truly be said to originate from the ancient Roman Empire. To seek to identify these kingdoms, when Scripture furnishes no clue as to their identity, is very precarious and probably unwarranted.[22]

---

20. Ibid., 148.
21. Fairbairn, *Prophecy*, 298.
22. Young, *The Prophecy of Daniel*, 149-50. In support of this view, Fairbairn observes that the number ten is often used as a symbol of "completeness, on which account the ancients called it the perfect number, which comprehends all others in itself.... When, therefore, the divided state into which the modern Roman world fell, is represented under ten horns or kingdoms, it

Daniel 7, Continued ...

Before proceeding, a brief review is in order. According to Daniel 7:7b-8, the fourth beast, supposedly representative of Rome, had ten horns, among which there emerged an eleventh called "a little horn." In our brief discussion of the significance of the ten horns we took note of the three most frequently suggested interpretations. To these I now want to add a fourth. Here again are the options before us:

(1) The ten horns are symbolic of precisely ten actual kings or kingdoms that will appear at the end of history (usually identified with the "ten-nation confederacy" of Revelation 17:12-18). This is the dispensational interpretation.

(2) Another view is that the number ten is not to be pressed, as if neither nine nor eleven kings/kingdoms could fulfill the prophecy. The ten horns simply portray the emergence from the Roman Empire of a multiplicity of kings or kingdoms, i.e., any and all of the pagan empires that arose subsequent to the fall of Rome. This is the view presented by Desmond Ford in his commentary on Daniel.

(3) E.J. Young suggests that the number ten simply indicates a multiplicity of rulers, an indefinitely large number of kings, what he calls a *comprehensive and definite totality*. The emergence of ten horns from the beast indicates the diversification and extension of the power of the beast into all the world. The beast is ever present in its horns precisely because the horns *are* the beast in multiple and widespread manifestation (this latter point differs somewhat from Young's view). They symbolize the diffusion, diversification, and universal dominion of the beast's reign. Thus any and all actual historical empires that have and do embody the evil and Satanic characteristics of the beast constitute the ten horns.

---

may well be doubted whether this should be pressed farther than as indicating, by a round number, the totality of the new states – the diversity in the unity – whether or not it might admit of being exactly and definitely applied to so many historical kingdoms" (*Prophecy*, 431). Baldwin suggests that "the horns of an animal represent its strength in self-defence or attacks. Ten horns, 5 times the natural 2, represent pictorially the extraordinary power of this beast" (*Daniel*, 140). In other words, she suggests that these ten horns have nothing at all to do with subsequent kingdoms or empires.

(4) Another view, advocated by Alan Johnson in his commentary on Revelation and based upon his explanation of the imagery found in Revelation 12:3; 13:1; 17:3,7-13, is similar to that of the previous two interpretations in that the number ten need not be taken with arithmetical precision. "Ten," says Johnson, "symbolizes a repeated number of times or an indefinite number. It is perhaps another number like seven, indicating fullness (Neh. 4:12; Dan. 1:12; Rev. 2:10). Thus the number should not be understood as referring specifically to ten kings (kingdoms) but as indicating the multiplicity of sovereignties in confederacy that enhance the power of the beast." [23] Johnson then goes on to identify the ten with "the principalities and powers, the rulers of the darkness of this world, the spiritual forces of evil in the heavenly realms that Paul describes as the true enemies of Jesus' followers (Eph. 6:12). To be sure, they use earthly instruments, but their reality is far greater than any specific historical equivalents. These 'kings' embody the fullness of Satan's attack against the Lamb in the great eschatological showdown. They are the 'kings from the east' (16:12-14, 16), and they are also the 'kings of the earth' who ally themselves with the beast in the final confrontation with the Lamb (19:19-21)." [24]

One can only conclude that any tendency to dogmatize on the interpretation of the ten horns must be resisted. We simply do not know to what or to whom they refer. Perhaps Daniel and John intended it that way. The same may be said for the three horns which are uprooted in consequence of the emergence of the little horn (Dan. 7:8, 20, 24). Those who identify the "little horn" with Antiochus Epiphanes, the Syrian ruler who persecuted the Jews in the second century B.C., are quick to identify the three horns (or kings/ kingdoms) as "Demetrius, whom Antiochus IV replaced because of his absence in Rome..., another Antiochus, son of Antiochus III, and Heliodorus who, though not of the royal line, was a schem-

23. Alan Johnson, *Revelation*, The Expositor's Bible Commentary (Grand Rapids: Zondervan, 1981), 561.
24. Ibid., 562.

ing aspirant to the throne."[25] The problem with identifying the little horn as Antiochus Epiphanes is that it would demand identifying the fourth beast as Greece and not Rome. In other words, the four beasts would then be Babylon, Media, Medo-Persia, and Greece, out of the last of which the "little horn" or Antiochus emerges. This view of the four kingdoms, however, has not been popular among evangelical scholars, although we will look more closely at it below.

Those who argue for a revived, end-of-the-age, Roman Empire in which precisely ten literal kings will rule, similarly insist that the uprooting here noted is an actual historical event involving precisely three literal kings whom the Antichrist ("little horn") will depose. Others prefer not to speculate on the issue while some see in this imagery a symbolic description of dissension, that is, a reference to disunity and internecine conflict throughout the entire reign of the beast.

We may now turn to the three primary issues before us. First, what is the relation of the messianic kingdom to that of the fourth beast and the little horn? In Daniel 2 we are told of the advent of the kingdom of God, symbolized by a stone cut out without hands, that crushes and eventually replaces the anti-God pagan empires of this world (2:34-35). In 2:44 reference is again made to the messianic kingdom of God being set up, never to be destroyed. When did this occur, or when shall it occur, and what form did it or will it assume? The emergence of this kingdom is again described in 7:13-14 (especially v. 14). We are told in the interpretation of the vision which follows (7:15-28) that, although the fourth pagan beast (empire, king/kingdom) will oppress and persecute the messianic people (7:21), the ultimate vindication of the saints and their dominion in the messianic kingdom is assured (7:22). Again we read that notwithstanding the persecuting power of the beast, which shall continue for "a time, times, and half a time," the kingdom of God will overpower and destroy it and eternal and universal dominion will be given to the saints of the Most High (7:26-27).

---

25. Robert A. Anderson, *Signs and Wonders: A Commentary on the Book of Daniel* (Grand Rapids: Eerdmans, 1984), 81.

The fundamental question then becomes: When and in what form does the messianic kingdom come and destroy the kingdom of the beast? When and in what form do the people of God receive dominion? The answer is found in the present fulfillment of the kingdom of God in the first coming of Jesus and the future consummation of the kingdom of God in the second coming of Jesus. I will devote an entire chapter to this theme and refer you to it. Here I would only say that the point is that the establishment of the messianic kingdom and the destruction of the pagan empires is not an instantaneous event. In his vision Daniel is alone concerned with the *fact* that God and his Christ will ultimately emerge victorious over the beast. The time and manner in which this occurs are not addressed by Daniel. In other words, Daniel is concerned with the goal or end and not the means and manner whereby it is achieved. Consequently, like so many of the Old Testament prophets, Daniel did not differentiate between the first and second comings of King Jesus, nor did he perceive the manner or phases in which the messianic kingdom would emerge corresponding to the nature of the two comings of Christ.

In sum, the answer to our first question as it is raised by Daniel 2 and 7 is this: the messianic kingdom *has been* established and the saints of God *now* rule, and, the messianic kingdom *will be* established and the saints of God *will* rule. It is the relationship between fulfillment in the present and consummation in the future.

Second, who or what is the "little horn" mentioned in Daniel 7:8, 11, 20, 21, 24, and 25? Is it/he identical with or different from the "little horn" of Daniel 8? It would appear that the "little horn" of Daniel 8 is assuredly Antiochus Epiphanes (175–164 B.C.). On the other hand, the "little horn" of Daniel 7, say many, is the end-time antichrist. More on this below.

Third, I provide an explanation of the meaning of the phrase, "a time, times, and half a time" (7:25) in Chapter Sixteen, and I refer the reader to the relevant portions of that discussion.

Reconsidering the Four Kingdoms

Although not popular with most evangelicals, we should give more serious consideration to the suggestion that the four kingdoms in

Daniel 2 and 7 are not Babylon, Medo-Persia, Greece, and Rome, but Babylon, Media, Medo-Persia, and Greece. Let's take a closer look at the evidence in favor of this view.

The existence of the Median Empire under the leadership of Astyages (585–550 B.C.) and Cyaxares II is not well-known, but it is clearly documented. Its territory was roughly equivalent to that of Babylon. One of Astyages' daughters married Nebuchadnezzar, while yet another married Cambyses I of Persia. The latter couple gave birth to Cyrus whose Medo-Persian Empire conquered Babylon in 539 B.C. A case can be made that whereas the Median Empire was contemporaneous with that of Babylon, the former succeeded the latter in power following the death of Nebuchadnezzar.

If Media is the second empire in Daniel 2, it is the second beast in Daniel 7. The second beast is said to have "three ribs in its mouth" (7:5). Gurney points us to Jeremiah 51:27-29 where three nations are mentioned as linked with the Medes and coming against Babylon. These three are Ararat, Minni, and Ashkenaz: Ararat = Urartu which was subdued by the Medes in 605 B.C.; Minni = Mannaea (an ally of Assyria), which fell to the Medes shortly after the collapse of Assyria; and Ashkenaz = the Scythians who were defeated by the Medes in the reign of Cyaxares II. The "three ribs" might refer to the Babylonian kings known to Jewish tradition: Nebuchadnezzar, Evil-Merodach, and Belshazzar. But these Babylonian kings were not conquered by Media, if in fact being in the "mouth" of the bear symbolizes military conquest.

On this view, the third kingdom and beast (the leopard with four wings and four heads; Dan. 7:6) is Medo-Persia. The "four wings of a bird" are believed to suggest the celerity with which Cyrus, king of Persia, extended his domain,[26] while the "four heads" are taken as referring either, a) to the four corners of the earth, thus indicating Persia's claim to universal dominion, or b) to the four Persian kings of Daniel 11:2 (Cyrus, Artaxerxes, Xerxes, Darius III [who was defeated by Alexander the Great]; others identify them as Cyrus, Cambyses, Darius, and Xerxes). Gurney also points out that

---

26. Anderson, *Signs and Wonders,* 79; cf. Isa. 41:3.

the superiority of the third kingdom over the second (Dan. 2:39; 7:6) better fits Persian supremacy over the inferior Median empire than Greece's relationship to Persia (since both the latter were world powers). Another argument against identifying Greece as the third kingdom is that "the four successors to Alexander [who are alleged to be the four heads on the leopard], both in history and in Daniel 8, represent diluted strength, whereas in Daniel 7 the four heads seem to represent the strength itself."[27]

On this view, the fourth kingdom of Daniel 2 (strength of iron, feet/toes of clay and iron) and the fourth beast of Daniel 7 both refer to Greece. Several arguments have been cited to support this reading. (1) Alexander the Great's army was invincible (Dan. 2:40; 7:7, 19), whereas Rome was stopped by Parthia in its attempted expansion. (2) The "western" civilization and culture of Greece was quite different from the three previous oriental empires (Dan. 7:7b, 19a), whereas Rome was in many ways similar to Greece. (3) The fourth empire is said to crush the other three (7:7, 19). Greece did in fact conquer the territory of Babylon, Media, and Persia, whereas the latter three were outside the area of the Roman Empire. (4) Daniel 2:40-43 says that this fourth kingdom will be divided (iron and clay) and weakened, a likely reference to the Seleucid kingdom (Syria, the stronger part, iron) and the Ptolemaic (Egypt, the weaker part, clay, which was eventually overrun by the Seleucids). "The reference to the two substances not mixing together distinctly reminds one of the rupture between the two kingdoms, which occurred despite the intermarriage between them."[28] (5) In Daniel 7:8, 20-22, 24-25, we read of a "little horn" emerging from the "ten horns" and before whom three of the latter fall. This "little horn" is portrayed as severely persecuting the people of God. On this view, the three uprooted horns (kings) were Cappadocia, Armenia, and Parthia. These three were actually defeated by Antiochus the Great, father of the infamous Antiochus Epiphanes. The defeat of the three by Antiochus the Great would then be seen as the beginning of the kingdom of the "little horn"

---

27. Walton, "The Four Kingdoms of Daniel," 31.
28. Pate & Haines, *Doomsday Delusions,* 68.

which was continued and brought to culmination under Antiochus Epiphanes.[29]

If Greece is the fourth kingdom/beast, one must account for its "ten horns" in Daniel 7 and its "four horns" in Daniel 8 (vv. 8, 22). Clearly, these cannot be referring to the same phenomenon. The four horns are assuredly the four generals who succeeded Alexander the Great (Cassander, Lysimachus, Seleucus, Ptolemy). The ten horns may well be the ten independent states that emerged by the latter part of the third century B.C.: Ptolemaic Egypt, Seleucia, Macedon, Pergamum, Pontus, Bithynia, Cappadocia, Armenia, Parthia, and Bactria. So, at one stage of its existence the "beast" of the Greek empire had "four horns," and at a later stage of its existence had "ten horns," from which emerged an eleventh or "little horn".

The "little horn" of both Daniel 7 and 8 who oppresses the people of God will do so for "a time, times, and half a time" (7:25). Antiochus IV Epiphanes (ruled 175–164 B.C.), besides persecuting the Jews, suppressed the observance of their religious festivals and sacred days (especially the Sabbath; see 2 Macc. 6:6) and prohibited reading of the Torah (1 Macc. 1:41-64). According to Lacocque, "this first religious persecution in the history of Israel lasted for just over three years between 168 and 165. The expression 'one period [a time], two periods [times], and a half period [half a time]' should be understood from this perspective as 'one year, two years, and a half year.'"[30]

Finally, "in Daniel 8 the two beasts are said to concern the 'final indignation' and the 'time of the end' (8:19), which would suggest that it is dealing with the third and fourth empires rather than the second and third as must be assumed in the Roman view. Daniel 11 also focuses its attention on the Greek empire, while reference to

29. Others have suggested that the "three horns" uprooted refer to Antiochus's capture of Ptolemy VI Philometor in Egypt, and his victories in the east against Parthia and Bactria.

30. Andre Lacocque, *The Book of Daniel* (Atlanta: John Knox Press, 1979), 153-54.

Rome is nothing more than incidental. There also the time of the end is the focus."[31]

If one adopts the view in which Greece is the fourth beast, then Antiochus Epiphanes is the "little horn" of both Daniel 7 and 8. This would lead to the conclusion that all that Daniel has written about the four kingdoms of Daniel 2 and the four beasts and ten horns of Daniel 7, has already been fulfilled in history. We should not, therefore, be looking to any future, end-of-the-age fulfillment of these prophecies.

Daniel 8:1-27

The purpose of Daniel 8 is to fill in the details omitted in chapters 2 and 7 relative to the second and third kingdoms (or third and fourth kingdoms if you adopt the view in which the fourth kingdom is Greece). According to the view that the fourth kingdom is Rome, the only thing we read in Daniel 2 concerning these is: "And after you (Nebuchadnezzar) there will arise another kingdom inferior to you, then another third kingdom of bronze, which will rule over all the earth" (2:39). In Daniel 7 the explanation of these two kingdoms is only slightly more detailed (7:5-6; or, again, 7:6-8 if you adopt the Greek view). Here in chapter 8, therefore, Daniel provides us with a much more in-depth study of the kingdoms of Medo-Persia and Greece (you will observe that whereas he still employs animals in his imagery, he now uses a ram and goat).

We must note well that one's interpretation of the fourth kingdom, whether it be Rome or Greece, has no bearing on the interpretation of Daniel 8. Everyone acknowledges that this chapter concerns Medo-Persia (the ram) and Greece (the he-goat). Virtually everyone also acknowledges that the "little horn" of Daniel 8 is Antiochus Epiphanes, Syrian ruler of the second century B.C. who persecuted the Jews.[32]

---

31. Walton, "The Four Kingdoms of Daniel," 36.
32. We should remember that the vision of chapter 7 (553 B.C., the first year of Belshazzar) and of chapter 8 (551 B.C., the third year of Belshazzar) were experienced by Daniel (sixty-nine years old in chapter 8) before the events recorded

The vision of the ram (8:3-4), the goat (8:5-8) and the little horn (8:9-14) occupies the first fourteen verses of this chapter. The description of the ram (see Ezek. 34:17; 39:18; cf. Jer. 51:40; Zech. 10:3) fits what we know of the relationship between Media and Persia: the former emerged first but was subordinate in its subsequent merger with Persia. Its conquests include: west (Babylonia, Syria, Asia Minor), north (Armenia, region of Caspian Sea), and south (Egypt and Ethiopia). It is also interesting that in the Zodiac, Persia was under Aries, the ram. Evidence also exists that when Persian kings were on a military march they carried a gold ram's head with them.

The goat (8:5-8) is best taken as representative either of the Macedonian kingdom in the abstract or of the country over which a series of kings would rule. Coming "from the west" points to the position of Greece: to the west of Medo-Persia and Palestine. The "conspicuous" ("prominent" – NIV) horn is obviously a reference to Alexander the Great (356–323 B.C.). His conquest of the Medo-Persian Empire and all other surrounding enemies is well chronicled. The phrase "without touching the ground" is a reference to the rapidity with which the Greek Empire conquered its foes. Indeed, Goldingay notes that "over a period of four years between 334 and 331 B.C. Alexander quite demolished the Persian empire and established an empire of his own extending from Europe to India."[33] He crossed the Hellespont and engaged the Persians in battle at the Granicus River where he soundly defeated them in 334 B.C. He defeated Darius III at Issus in the Taurus mountains. He laid siege to Tyre and eventually occupied all of Egypt. He proceeded east to the Tigris and defeated the Persians in 331 at the battle of Gaugemela. He captured and sacked Shushan, Ecbatana, and Persepolis. His subjugation of Persia was complete.

The "four conspicuous (prominent) horns" (8:8) that arose subsequent to the death of Alexander the Great (June 13, 323 B.C.)

---

in chapter 5 (539 B.C., the fourteenth and final year of Belshazzar). Most likely Daniel "saw" or "envisioned" himself to be in Susa, but was not actually there. Susa was 230 miles east of Babylon, about 120 miles north of the Persian Gulf.
33. John Goldingay, *Daniel*, 209.

point to the four-fold division of the kingdom among his generals: Cassander (Macedonia and Greece), Lysimachus (Thrace and much of Asia Minor), Seleucus (Syria and other regions to the east), and Ptolemy (Egypt).

The "little horn" in Daniel 8:9-14 is clearly a reference to Antiochus Epiphanes, eighth ruler in the Seleucid line, 175–164 B.C. (he died in 163). This raises the question of the relationship between the "little horn" of Daniel 7:8, 11, 19-26 and the "little horn" described here in Daniel 8. According to the view which believes Rome is the fourth kingdom/beast, the "little horn" of Daniel 7 and that of Daniel 8 are different (the latter being Antiochus Epiphanes, the former being the end-of-the-age Antichrist). But according to the view which believes Greece is the fourth kingdom/beast, the two chapters are describing the career and demise of the same person: Antiochus Epiphanes IV.

The nature of Antiochus' oppressive rule is described in 8:9-12.[34] He had conquests in "the south" (Egypt), "the east" (Persia, Parthia, Armenia), and "the Beautiful Land" (Palestine). In view of verse 24, the reference to the "stars" in verse 10 is most likely a symbolic allusion to the people of God as shining lights or glorious ones. Some contend that only the priesthood is in view. In any case, "an attack on the Jerusalem temple, the people of Israel, and the priesthood is presupposed to be implicitly an attack on the God worshiped there and on his supernatural associates who identify with Israel [in particular, Michael and his angelic hosts]."[35] Antiochus' persecution of the Jews began in 171 B.C. with the assassination of the high priest Onias III and ended in 163 B.C. with the death of Antiochus himself. The "prince" of verse 11 ("commander" in NASB) has been taken as a reference either to Onias or, more likely, to God. In 167 B.C. Antiochus ordered that all ceremonial observances to Yahweh were forbidden. The "place of his

---

34. The best description of the rule of Antiochus Epiphanes and his oppression and persecution of the Jews is provided in the apocryphal work of *1 and 2 Maccabees* (especially the former).

35. John Goldingay, *Daniel*, 210.

sanctuary" may refer to Jerusalem, but more likely is the temple itself. The phrase "because of transgression" (or, "because of rebellion") in verse 12 has been taken in one of two ways. Some say it refers to the sins of the Jewish people themselves who abandoned God for the ways of their Greek captors and thus incurred divine judgment (cf. 1 Macc. 1:11-15, 43). Others insist it refers to the sins committed by Antiochus against the Jews.

The duration of his rule (8:13-14) has been the cause of considerable debate. The "transgression that makes desolate" is probably an allusion to Antiochus' blasphemous act of setting up a statue of Zeus in the temple. This is referred to in 11:31 as "the abomination that makes desolate" or more commonly known as "the abomination of desolation." Before we examine the various theories of the "2300 evenings and mornings" (8:14). let's review the chronology of this period.

- **175–164 B.C.** – the rule of Antiochus Epiphanes (he died in 163)
- **175** – Onias III, Jewish high priest, is deposed
- **171** – Onias is murdered by Menelaus (who had bribed Antiochus in exchange for being made high priest)
- **169** – Antiochus attacks Jerusalem, butchers many of its inhabitants, and loots the temple
- **167 December (25 Kislev)** – Antiochus orders the cessation of all ceremonial observances. The sacrifice of a pig was performed on the altar to Zeus which had been erected on the altar of burnt offering in the temple (this is the "Abomination of Desolation" referred to in Daniel 11:31 and 12:11 and the "transgression that causes horror" in 8:13)
- **164 December (25 Kislev)** – three years to the day after it had been profaned, Judas Maccabeus, having led a successful revolt against Antiochus, rededicated the temple and a new altar of burnt offering.

There are basically four views as to the meaning of the 2,300 days. (1) Some believe that Daniel is referring to the evening and morning sacrifices which Antiochus will cut off. Hence, the duration is in fact only 1,150 days in each of which two sacrifices were made (one in the morning and one in the evening). The beginning of this 1,150-day period is reckoned as December 167 B.C. when Antiochus set up an altar (and possibly a statue) to Zeus in the temple (1 Macc. 1:54). The termination of this period would be December 14, 164 B.C. (1 Macc. 4:52), when Judas Maccabeus rededicated the temple. However, this doesn't equate to exactly 1,150 days, but is closer to 1,100. Advocates of this view suggest that perhaps the date is to be taken as a close approximation or the daily sacrifice may have been abolished even before the altar was erected (i.e., the beginning point would then be sometime in mid-October 167).

(2) Others contend that 2,300 days are meant to point out that when the Hebrews wished to express separately day and night, the component parts of a day of a week, then the number of both is expressed. They say, e.g., forty days and forty nights (Gen. 7:4,12; Exod. 24:18; 1 Kings 19:8), and three days and three nights (Jonah 1:17; Matt. 12:40), but not eighty or six days-and-nights, when they wish to speak of forty or three full days. "A Hebrew reader," says Keil, "could not possibly understand the period of time 2300 evening-mornings of 2300 half days or 1150 whole days, because evening and morning at the creation constituted not the half but the whole day." [36] Those who embrace this view still face the problem in figuring out how these days fit into the period of history during which Antiochus reigned. Leon Wood argues that the end or last of the 2,300 days must be the restoration of the temple on December 25, 165 B.C. (8:14b; note that Wood adopts the 165 B.C. rather than standard 164 B.C. dating). Reckoning back 2,300 days would bring us to September 6, 171 B.C., but we have no concrete evidence of anything significant happening on that day (although it was in 171 that Onias III was murdered). Wood nevertheless contends that in the year 171 B.C. the hostility of Antiochus against the Jews began to intensify (see 2 Macc. 4:7-50).

---

36. C.F. Keil, *Daniel*. Commentary on the Old Testament, Vol. 9 (Grand Rapids: Eerdmans, 1975), 304.

Dispensationalist John Walvoord contends that "the best conclusion is that the twenty-three hundred days of Daniel are fulfilled in the period from 171 B.C. and culminated [in contrast to Wood's view] in the death of Antiochus Epiphanes in 164 B.C. (except that AE died in 163). The period when the sacrifices ceased was the latter part of this longer period. Although the evidence available today does not offer fulfillment to the precise day, the twenty-three hundred days, obviously a round number, is relatively accurate in defining the period when the Jewish religion began to erode under the persecution of Antiochus, and the period as a whole concluded with his death." [37]

(3) Desmond Ford, along with a host of Seventh-Day Adventist commentators, adopts the *year–day* principle: thus the 2,300 days = 2,300 years. Ford begins his reckoning with 457 B.C. (when the Jews returned to rebuild Jerusalem) and brings us to A.D. 1844. "In 1844 began the cleansing of the sanctuary, the restoration in fullness of the everlasting gospel that the daily services prefigured, the vindicating work of God in heaven above and in the earth beneath." [38]

---

37. John F. Walvoord, *Daniel: The Key to Prophetic Revelation* (Chicago: Moody Press, 1971), 190. Stephen Miller offers a similar conclusion: "December 164 (the reconsecration of the sanctuary) is the termination date given in the text, thus the 2,300 days began in the fall of 170 B.C. Something significant must have occurred at that time that marked the beginning of the persecution, and such an event did take place. In 170 B.C. Onias III (a former high priest) was murdered at the urging of the wicked high priest Menelaus, whom Antiochus had appointed to that position for a bribe. [But most date the murder of Onias in 171, not 170.]... The altar to Zeus was not set up until 167 B.C., but the persecution had been going on long before that event. According to the 2,300-day view, therefore, the whole persecution period (the time that the saints 'will be trampled underfoot') was involved, not just the span from the cessation of the sacrifice and the desecration of the sanctuary until the rededication of the temple. Verse 14 concludes by stating that after this period of persecution, the temple would be 'reconsecrated.' Just over three years after the altar to Zeus was set up, Judas Maccabeus cleansed and rededicated the temple on December 14, 164 B.C. (cf. 1 Macc. 4:52). Today the Jews celebrate the Feast of Hanukkah ('dedication') to commemorate this momentous event (cf. John 8:12)" (*Daniel. The New American Commentary*, Vol. 18 [Nashville: Broadman & Holman Publishers, 1994], 229-30).

38. Ford, *Daniel*, 189.

118

William Miller (1782–1849) used a similar method of reckoning to conclude that Christ would return between March 21, 1843, and March 21, 1844. When the year came and went and Christ did not return, many were discouraged. Samuel S. Snow, one of Miller's followers, concluded that the 2,300 days/years would end, not in the spring of 1844, but in the fall. He insisted that Christ would return on October 22, 1844, the calendar equivalent of the Jewish Day of Atonement (the tenth day of the seventh month, Tishri). What resulted has come to be called "The Great Disappointment" when Christ did not return. Later another follower, Hiram Edson, concluded that instead of Jesus coming out of the holy of holies of the heavenly sanctuary to earth at the end of the 2,300 days/years, he had simply for the first time passed from the holy place of the heavenly sanctuary into the heavenly holy of holies.

(4) Both Keil and Young believe it doubtful whether the number revealed by the angel is of a literal period of time that can be marked chronologically on a calendar. In keeping with the way numbers are used elsewhere in Daniel, they argue that this one is similarly symbolic. The number 2,300 itself, of course, is not symbolic in the way that 3, 7, 12, 40, or 70 typically are. However, 2,300, says Keil, "can stand in such a relation to the number seven as to receive a symbolical meaning. The longer periods of time are usually reckoned not by days, but by weeks, months, or years; if, therefore, as to the question of the duration of the 2,300 days, we reduce the days to weeks, months, and years, we shall find six years, three or four months, and some days, and discover that the oppression of the people by the little horn was to continue not fully a period of seven years. But the times of God's visitations, trials, and judgments are so often measured by the number seven, that this number came to bear stamped on it this signification [cf. Dan. 4:23; 7:25; Gen. 29:18, 27; 41:26ff.; Judg. 6:1; 2 Sam. 24:13; 2 Kings 8:1].… Thus the answer of the angel has this meaning: The time of the predicted oppression of Israel, and of the desolation of the sanctuary by Antiochus… shall not reach the full duration of a period of divine judgment."[39]

---

39. Keil, *Daniel*, 306-07.

The interpretation of the vision is provided in Daniel 8:15-26. The appearance of one who "had the appearance of a man" (v. 15) and spoke to Gabriel is probably a reference to God himself. He is said to have spoken from "between the banks of the Ulai" river, thus perhaps depicting a hovering, as it were, in the air above the middle of the river. The reference in verse 17 to "the time of the end" and in verse 19 to "the latter end of the indignation" and "the appointed time of the end" remind us that we should not too quickly assume that such terminology refers to the end of the age (the second coming of Christ). Here it clearly points to the end of events prophesied in this chapter (i.e., the persecution of the Jews by Antiochus Epiphanes).

The "transgressors" or "rebels" in verse 23 again probably refers to those Jews who had rebelled against God (cf. v. 12). The statement in verse 24 that Antiochus will rise to prominence "not by his own power" is an allusion either to God's providential role in putting him in place or a reference to Satan's energizing presence in his oppressive rule. Antiochus certainly did "in his own mind" "become great" (v. 25), as seen in his decree that the coins of the day bear the inscription *theos epiphanes*, i.e., "God manifest." Although Antiochus did not actually claim to be God, he did understand himself as the earthly representative of deity. He will be broken "but by no human hand" (v. 25), probably a reference to his death, not by assassination or in battle, but from grief and remorse after numerous military setbacks. Others say he died of consumption (tuberculosis). Numerous other accounts of his death emerged: he fell from his chariot and later died from internal wounds; he was eaten by worms; etc.

To sum up, I am now persuaded that Babylon is represented by the head of gold in Daniel 2 and the first beast of Daniel 7. Media is represented by the breast and arms of silver in Daniel 2 and the second beast in Daniel 7. Medo-Persia is symbolized by the belly and thighs of bronze in Daniel 2 and the third beast of Daniel 7. Greece is represented by the feet of iron and clay in Daniel 2 and the fourth beast of Daniel 7. Based on this identification of the four empires, I conclude that the "little horn" of Daniel 7 is not any supposed end-of-the-age Antichrist but, together with the "little horn" of Daniel 8, is in fact Antiochus Epiphanes, the Greek king who defiled the sacrifice of Israel in 168 B.C.

Daniel 11:2–12:13

Daniel 11–12 contains a vision communicated to Daniel by the angel Gabriel (11:2–12:3) as well as the latter's final instructions to him (12:4-13). The best way to proceed through the difficult eleventh chapter is by reading the text with appropriate identifications of the principal figures involved. All are agreed that chapter 11 begins with a reference to the Persian kings who followed Cyrus, extends through Alexander the Great and his successors, and then provides a detailed summary of the on-going conflict between the Seleucid and Ptolemaic dynasties (the primary powers of the Greek empire), with special emphasis on Antiochus IV Epiphanes. As we will note in just a moment, many (but not I) also believe that the latter half of this chapter (vv. 36-45) leaps forward to the end of the age and describes the end-time Antichrist.

Perhaps the best way to navigate through this difficult and complex chapter is to simply insert the relevant interpretive explanations and identification of important figures along the way. So let's begin with the vision of Greek domination in 11:2–12:3.[40]

And now I will tell you the truth. Behold, three more kings [**after Cyrus: Cambyses (530–522), Smerdis (pseudo-Smerdis or Gaumata; 522) and Darius I Hystaspes (522–486)**] are going to arise in Persia. Then a fourth [**Xerxes I (486–465)**] will gain far more riches than all *of them*; as soon as he becomes strong through his riches, he will arouse the whole *empire* against the realm of Greece [**In this one verse (v. 2) the period from 538 to 331 is covered**]. And a mighty king [**Alexander the Great (336–323)**] will arise, and he will rule with great authority and do as he pleases. But as soon as he has arisen, his kingdom will be broken up and parceled out toward the four points of the compass [**perhaps a reference to the four generals among whom the**

---

40. In our study of Daniel 11, I've employed the NASB rather than the ESV.

Greek empire, subsequent to Alexander, was divided, or perhaps the "four major units (that) eventually emerged from Alexander's fragmented empire, centered on Macedon and Greece, Thrace, Syria and the east, and Egypt], though not to his *own* descendants [Alexander's two sons, Alexander IV and Herakles, were both murdered], nor according to his authority which he wielded; for his sovereignty will be uprooted and *given* to others besides them.

[Verses 5-20 contain a history of the on-going conflict between two divisions of the Greek empire: the Ptolemaic (Egyptian; the "southern king") and the Seleucid (Syrian; the "northern king"), from the death of Alexander (323 B.C.) to the reign of Antiochus Epiphanes (175–163)] Then the king of the South [Ptolemy I Soter (323–285), ruler of Egypt, who had been one of Alexander's four generals] will grow strong, along with *one* of his princes [Seleucus I Nicator (312/11–280; another of Alexander's four generals)] who will gain ascendancy over him and obtain dominion; his domain *will be* a great dominion *indeed*. And after some years they will form an alliance [Ptolemy II (285–246) made a treaty of peace in 250 with the Seleucid ruler, Antiochus II Theos (grandson of Seleucus; 261–246)], and the daughter of the king of the South [Berenice, Ptolemy's daughter] will come to the king of the North to carry out a peaceful arrangement. But she will not retain her position of power [Berenice was murdered, along with Antiochus, by the latter's powerful ex-wife, Laodice], nor will he remain with his power, but she will be given up, along with those who brought her in, and the one who sired her, as well as he who supported her in *those* times. But one of the descendants of her line [Ptolemy III Euergetes (246–221), Berenice's brother] will arise in his place, and he will come against *their* army and enter the fortress of the king of the North [in retaliation for the murder of his sister], and he will deal with them and display *great* strength. And also their gods with their metal images *and* their precious vessels of silver and gold he will take into captivity to Egypt, and he on his part will refrain from *attacking* the king of the North for *some* years [for two years, to be exact]. Then the latter [i.e., the King of the North] will enter the realm of the king of the South, but will return to his *own* land. And his sons [Seleucus III Ceraunus (226–223) and Antiochus III (the "Great", 223–187)] will mobilize and assemble a multitude of great forces; and one of them will keep on coming and overflow and pass through, that he may again wage war up to his [i.e., the King of the South's] *very* fortress. And the king of the South [Ptolemy IV Philopator (221–204)] will be enraged and go forth and fight with the king of the North. Then the latter will raise a great multitude, but *that* multitude will be given into the hand of the *former* [Ptolemy's victory occurred in 217 at Raphia, near Palestine]. When the multitude is carried away, his heart will be lifted up, and he will cause tens of thousands to fall; yet he will not prevail.

[Ptolemaic supremacy, however, did not long continue. Verses 13-35 describe the ensuing period of Seleucid supremacy.] For the king of the North [Antiochus III] will again raise a greater multitude than the former, and after an interval of some years [in 202] he will press on with a great army and much equipment. Now in those times many [Antiochus III, Philip V of Macedon and other insurrectionists in Egypt] will rise up against the king of the South; the violent ones among your people [i.e., Jews who sided with and aided Antiochus] will also lift themselves up in order to fulfill the vision, but they will fall down. Then the king of the North [Antiochus] will come, cast up a siege mound, and capture a well-fortified city [Sidon, an Egyptian fortified city]; and the forces of the South will not stand *their ground*, not even their choicest troops, for there will be no strength to make a stand. But he [Antiochus] who comes against him will do as he pleases, and no one will *be able to* withstand him; he will also stay *for a time* in the Beautiful Land [Palestine], with destruction in his hand. And he will set his face to come with the power of his whole kingdom, bringing with him a proposal of peace which he will put into effect; he will also give him [Ptolemy V] the daughter of women [Cleopatra; not the one who lived in the time of Julius Caesar and Mark Antony (69–30)] to ruin it. But she will not take a stand *for him* [i.e., for her father, Antiochus; rather she proved loyal to her husband, Ptolemy], or be on his side. [verses 18-19 prophesy Antiochus' defeat and ignominious end.] Then he will turn his face to the coastlands [the islands or countries around the Mediterranean Sea] and capture many. But a commander [Lucius Cornelius Scipio, a Roman general, in cooperation with their Greek allies] will put a stop to his scorn against him; moreover, he will repay him for his scorn. So he will turn his face toward the fortresses of his own land, but he will stumble and fall and be found no more [**having suffered a humiliating defeat, Antiochus returned to his country where he was murdered by an angry mob in 187. His son, Antiochus IV Epiphanes was taken to Rome as a hostage**]. Then in his place one will arise [**i.e., Seleucus IV Philopator (187–175)**)] who will send an oppressor [**Heliodorus, a "tax collector" of sorts**] through the Jewel of *his* kingdom; yet within a few days he will be shattered, though neither in anger nor in battle [**Heliodorus attempted to pillage the treasury of the Jerusalem temple to help Seleucus make payments to Rome in fulfillment of a debt incurred by the latter's father, Antiochus III**].

[Verses 21-35 are acknowledged by virtually all to be a description of the reign of terror by Antiochus Epiphanes IV. The debate is whether Antiochus is also being described in verses 36-45 or is the end-time Antichrist in view? Before proceeding further, here is a list of the two dynasties whose conflicts we have just noted:]

The South (Ptolemies – Egypt)	The North (Seleucids – Syria)
Ptolemy I (Soter) 323–285	*Seleucus I (Nicator) 312–280*
Ptolemy II (Philadelphus) 285–246	*Antiochus I (Soter) 280–261*
	Antiochus II (Theos) 261–246
Ptolemy III (Euergetes) 246–221	*Seleucus II (Callinicus) 246–226*
	Seleucus III (Ceraunus) 226–223
Ptolemy IV (Philopator) 221–204	*Antiochus III (the Great) 223–187*
Ptolemy V (Epiphanes) 204–181	*Seleucus IV (Philopator) 187–175*
Ptolemy VI (Philometor)181–145	*Antiochus IV (Epiphanes) 175–163*

And in his place a despicable person will arise, on whom the honor of kingship has not been conferred, but he will come in a time of tranquility and seize the kingdom by intrigue [**Demetrius I, young son of Seleucus IV, was next in line to receive the crown. Through skillful maneuvering, Antiochus IV captured the throne**]. And the overflowing forces will be flooded away before him and shattered, and also the prince of the covenant [**a reference to Ptolemy VI Philometor of Egypt; on the other hand, some believe this is Onias III, the**

Jewish high priest whom Antiochus deposed]. And after an alliance is made with him he will practice deception, and he will go up and gain power with a small *force of* people. In a time of tranquility he will enter the richest *parts* of the realm, and he will accomplish what his fathers never did, nor his ancestors; he will distribute plunder, booty, and possessions among them, and he will devise his schemes against strongholds, but *only* for a time. [**There begins here a more detailed account of Antiochus's involvement with Egypt**] And he will stir up his strength and courage against the king of the South with a large army; so the king of the South will mobilize an extremely large and mighty army for war; but he will not stand, for schemes will be devised against him. And those who eat his choice food will destroy him, and his army will overflow, but many will fall down slain. As for both kings, their hearts will be *intent* on evil, and they will speak lies *to each other* at the same table; but it will not succeed, for the end is still *to come* at the appointed time. Then he will return to his land with much plunder; but his heart will be *set* against the holy covenant, and he will take action and *then* return to his *own* land [**V. 28 sums up briefly the measures taken by Antiochus in suppressing the religious liberties of Judah from 172 to 168**]. At the appointed time he will return and come into the South [**Egypt**], but this last time it will not turn out the way it did before. For ships of Kittim [**i.e., Cyprus**] will come against him; therefore he will be disheartened, and will return and become enraged at the holy covenant and take action; so he will come back and show regard for those who forsake the holy covenant. And forces from him will arise, desecrate the sanctuary fortress, and do away with the regular sacrifice. And they will set up the abomination of desolation [**Here we have a brief description of what occurred in December 168 B.C. when Antiochus placed a statue of Zeus on the altar of the temple in Jerusalem**]. And by smooth *words* he will turn to godlessness those who act wickedly toward the covenant, but the people who know their God will display strength and take action [**although applicable in principle to all believers, this refers specifically to the sons of the Jewish priest Mattathias: Judas, Jonathan, and Simon, known as the Maccabees, and the other heroic patriots who resisted Antiochus and eventually rededicated**

the temple to God in December of 165]. And those who have insight among the people will give understanding to the many; yet they will fall by sword and by flame, by captivity and by plunder, for *many* days. Now when they fall they will be granted a little help, and many will join with them in hypocrisy. And some of those who have insight will fall, in order to refine, purge, and make them pure, until the end time; because *it is* still *to come* at the appointed time.

[As noted earlier, a major point of dispute is the identity of the person described in verses 36-45. Some believe these verses refer not to an individual but to Rome, the fourth empire (assuming one takes Rome, not Greece, to be the fourth empire). Others believe Herod the Great is in view, while some have pointed to Constantine of the early fourth century A.D. Many evangelical interpreters believe that with verse 36 the angel leaps forward several thousand years to the end of the age and begins describing the Antichrist, of whom Antiochus is the prototype, who will appear just preceding the coming of Jesus.

Walter Kaiser is typical in this regard and cites three reasons why he believes Antiochus is not in view in verses 36-39. First, "Antiochus is never referred to with the article as 'the king,' even though he (and his predecessors) was labeled as the 'king of the North' (11:6). Moreover, this one called 'the king' is set over against another called 'the king of the South,' whom 'the king' will oppose in Daniel 11:40." [41] But why does the presence or absence of the definite article matter? By what grammatical rule or theological principle does Kaiser justify concluding this can't be Antiochus because the word "the" is not used? And if Antiochus and his predecessors are referred to as "the" king of the North in 11:6, why would Kaiser make a point of what is now a false premise, namely that he "is never referred to with the article as 'the king'?" And why does the fact that "the king" is set over against another called "the king of the South", whom "the king" will oppose, prove that "the king" can't be Antiochus? Kaiser is simply making observa-

41. Kaiser, *Preaching and Teaching the Last Things*, 126.

tions on the text that yield no conclusions and bear no evidential weight.

Second, Kaiser thinks it "strange" that Daniel would describe "the character and policies" of Antiochus in verses 36-39 since "we have had him and his work already presented in this context." [42] This makes even less sense than his first point. It's as if Kaiser is saying, "Because Daniel said things about Antiochus earlier in this chapter he cannot possibly be saying anything else about Antiochus later in this chapter." There's nothing inconsistent or strange about Daniel providing additional information concerning Antiochus and his character and policies, unless of course, this new information is either contradictory to what he had earlier said (which it isn't) or entirely redundant and unnecessary (which it isn't).

Third, Kaiser appeals to the oft-heard argument that "numerous details are set forth in verses 40-45 that do not match the era or events in the life of Antiochus." [43] Note well, Kaiser is not claiming that the details in these verses contradict or are inconsistent with other details we know about Antiochus from the biblical record. He's simply saying that Daniel would be understood as providing us with details about Antiochus that we don't read about in any extra-biblical literature about his career and character. [44] But this sort of argument from historical silence is tenuous at best. No one has yet produced evidence that verses 40-45 can't be descriptive of Antiochus. There's nothing in these verses that contradicts what Daniel says about him elsewhere. Neither Kaiser nor anyone else has exhaustive records of Antiochus's life and activity such that it may be compared with what Daniel writes and thereby be determined to be incorrect.

Finally, Kaiser's fourth argument is truly strange. He admits that Antiochus is referred to by Daniel as a "king" in 11:27. He then

---

42. Ibid.

43. Ibid.

44. In particular, as Longman points out, "Antiochus did not 'extend his power over many countries; Egypt will not escape' (v. 42). Nor did he die when he 'pitch[ed] his royal tents between the seas at the beautiful holy mountain' (v. 45)" (*Daniel*, 281).

argues that he therefore can't be referred to as a "king" in verses 40-45. This one escapes me. Are we really being asked to believe that because Antiochus is only referred to as "king" one other time in Daniel that he therefore cannot be referred to as "king" in another text in the same chapter?

Although we should avoid dogmatism on this point, my belief is that the weight of evidence leans to the conclusion that these verses are simply a continuation of the description of Antiochus Epiphanes in the second century B.C. Observe closely that there is no indication of a break or a change of subject. Verses 36-45 flow in unbroken continuity with the preceding paragraph. There is reference to the "king" and to the "king of the South" and "king of the North" without the slightest indication that the three are any different from those in the fourth–second centuries B.C. who are described by the same names in the preceding verses.[45]]

> (11:36) Then the king will do as he pleases [see **11:3,16**], and he will exalt and magnify himself above every god [**this may be an allusion to Antiochus' title, "Epiphanes," (God) manifest, or perhaps to his use on coins of the title *Theos* = "God" and to his plundering of temples and suppression of other religions**], and will speak monstrous things against the God of gods; and he will prosper until the indignation is finished, for that which is decreed will be done. And he will show no regard for the gods of his fathers [**some say he replaced Apollo by Zeus as *the* god of the Seleucid dynasty; others find little evidence for this and contend that this is probably deliberate polemical distortion, to portray the godlessness of Antiochus in the most extreme terms possible**] or for the desire of women, nor will he show regard for any *other* god; for he will magnify himself

---

45. Longman agrees. The difficulty with seeing an end-time Antichrist in this paragraph "is that there is no clear transitional statement between verses 35 and 36 or later between verses 39 and 40. In the earlier part of the chapter, there are clear signals that the narrator moves from one king to the next (cf. vv. 2, 7, 20-21), but not in the present section. Here we have the primary textual reason why we cannot simply rule out of court the argument that verses 36-45 continue the 'prophecy' of Antiochus Epiphanes" (*Daniel*, 281).

above *them* all ["**the desire of women" may well be Adonis or Diony-
sus, deities favored in Egypt whom Antiochus slighted during his
various encroachments into that region; some point to Tammuz
in Ezekiel 8:14, a deity worshiped by women**]. But instead he will
honor a god of fortresses, a god whom his fathers did not know; he
will honor *him* with gold, silver, costly stones, and treasures. And he
will take action against the strongest of fortresses with *the help of* a
foreign god; he will give great honor to those who acknowledge *him,*
and he will cause them to rule over the many, and will parcel out land
for a price.

And at the end time the king of the South will collide with him,
and the king of the North will storm against him with chariots, with
horsemen, and with many ships; and he will enter countries, overflow
them, and pass through. He will also enter the Beautiful Land, and
many *countries* will fall; but these will be rescued out of his hand:
Edom, Moab and the foremost of the sons of Ammon. Then he will
stretch out his hand against *other* countries, and the land of Egypt will
not escape. But he will gain control over the hidden treasures of gold
and silver, and over all the precious things of Egypt; and Libyans and
Ethiopians *will follow* at his heels. But rumors from the East and from
the North will disturb him, and he will go forth with great wrath to
destroy and annihilate many. And he will pitch the tents of his royal
pavilion between the seas and the beautiful Holy Mountain; yet he
will come to his end, and no one will help him.

(12:1) Now at that time Michael, the great prince who stands
guard over the sons of your people, will arise. And there will be a time
of distress such as never occurred since there was a nation until that
time [**depending on how one interprets 11:36-45, this would refer
either to the events of 168–165 when Antiochus oppressed the Jews
(i.e., the events just described in 11:40-45), or to some later time
of tribulation (perhaps A.D. 66–70 and the destruction of Jerusalem by the armies of Titus; some see here the end-time tribulation
under the final Antichrist)**]; and at that time your people, everyone
who is found written in the book, will be rescued. And many of those
who sleep in the dust of the ground will awake, these to everlasting
life, but the others to disgrace and everlasting contempt [**some con-**

tend that this is not a description of bodily resurrection but a figurative portrayal, using Old Testament terms and imagery (see, e.g., Pss. 6, 69, 79), of the spiritual vindication and triumph of God's people over their enemies; others see it as a prophecy of the final resurrection (cf. Isa. 26:19). If the latter be the case, one must then decide whether it is simply a general declaration that just such a resurrection will occur for believers or whether it is saying that this resurrection will occur *immediately following* the persecution described in verse 2]. And those who have insight will shine brightly like the brightness of the expanse of heaven, and those who lead the many to righteousness, like the stars forever and ever.

Gabriel's final instructions are found in Daniel 12:4-13. The point of the command to "shut up the words and seal the book, until the time of the end" (v. 4), is both that the prophecies of Daniel be kept hidden or secret and that they be kept safe (cf. Jer. 32:9-12), with emphasis on the latter. When the time of fulfillment is at hand their truths will be relevant and encouraging to those who are suffering. Archer explains that "in the ancient Near East, important documents such as contracts, promissory notes, and deeds of conveyance were written out in duplicate. The original document was kept in a secure repository, safe ('closed up') from later tampering, in order to conserve the interests and rights of all parties to the transaction. Though copies might be made from it, the original was to remain secure so that it might be consulted if any future challenge of its terms were made."[46]

The "sealing" of the document also points to its preservation, unaltered, down to the day when its predictions would be fulfilled. It is because the truths of Daniel's prophecies are not immediately accessible that many people "will run to and fro, and knowledge shall increase." When one looks at this oft-quoted verse in context it becomes clear that it has nothing to do with a supposed increase in travel and the amount of human knowledge at the end of the

46. Gleason L. Archer, Jr. *Daniel*. The Expositor's Bible Commentary, Vol. 7 (Grand Rapids: Zondervan, 1985), 153.

age![47] The point is that people will be unable to find a word from God concerning his purposes because the book of Daniel will have been sealed. This verse echoes what we read in Amos 8:11-12, "'Behold, the days are coming,' declares the Lord God, 'when I will send a famine on the land – not a famine of bread, nor a thirst for water, but of *hearing the words of the Lord. They shall wander from sea to sea, and from north to east; they shall run to and fro, to seek the word of the Lord, but they shall not find it*'" (emphasis mine).

Daniel suddenly sees two additional angelic figures standing on either side of the river (12:5-7). One speaks to the man dressed in linen, i.e., the being (Gabriel? pre-incarnate Christ? another angel?) already graphically described in 10:5-6. In response to a question from one angel concerning the duration of the prophesied distress, the man in linen raises both hands toward heaven and swears "by him who lives forever" (v. 7a). Raising the hand when giving an oath was customary (cf. Gen. 14:22; Deut. 32:40), "but raising both hands and swearing to keep the oath in the name of the eternal God (cf. Rev. 10:5-6) gives the greatest possible assurance that the words spoken are true."[48]

The reference to "time, times, and half a time" links this verse with 7:25 and is descriptive of the brutal reign either of Antiochus in the second century B.C. or the end-time Antichrist, or perhaps both. I take it to be the former. Thus the "shattering of the power of the holy people" is "presumably the events of 11:21-45, or perhaps the whole period from the exile."[49]

In verses 11-12 we finally get an answer to the question posed in verse 6. 1,260 days is familiar enough (= 3 ½ years). But what is the purpose of the extra thirty days? And why is there then

---

47. Two renderings of the phrase are possible: (1) "Many will run to and fro, *and* knowledge shall increase," i.e., people will gain knowledge, to be sure, but not the knowledge of God's purposes as revealed in the book of Daniel. Or, (2) "many will run to and fro, *that* knowledge will increase," i.e., their going back and forth is for the purpose of gaining knowledge, unsuccessful though it be. The former is more likely.

48. Miller, *Daniel*, 323.

49. Goldingay, *Daniel*, 309.

appended to the 1,290 days an additional forty-five? No one knows! "The beginning of v. 11," notes Goldingay, "could be the time of one of Antiochus's edicts, the actual desecration of the temple, or the enforcement of the ban on the regular sacrificial order (11:31-33).... Vv. 11-12 could terminate with Judas's [the Maccabees] victories, the temple rededication, Antiochus's death, the arrival of news of his death, or the further events envisaged by 11:45-12:3."[50] In any case, Baldwin points out that "a particular blessing awaits the one who goes on expectantly even after the time for the fulfillment of the prophecy is apparently passed, as in the parable of Jesus there is a special blessing for the servant who continues to be faithful even when his master does not come home at the stated time (Matt. 24:45-51)."[51]

Conclusion

To be brief, if the fourth kingdom in Daniel 2 and 7 is Greece and not Rome, as I have tentatively suggested, and if the "king" in Daniel 11:36-45 is indeed Antiochus Epiphanes IV, we should not look to this Old Testament book for extensive detail concerning an alleged "Antichrist" or the second coming of Christ and the end of human history. Rather we should understand its principal focus to be on the emergence of Antiochus, referred to by Daniel as the "little horn," and his oppression of the Jewish people and profanation of the Temple (the "Abomination of Desolation"), all of which took place in the second century B.C.[52] Similarly, Daniel provides no support for the expectation that the end of history will witness a seven-year period of "Great Tribulation" or the emergence of a revived or renewed Roman Empire. What Daniel does say unequivocally, which is of paramount importance, is that with the coming of the Son of Man his kingdom has been inaugurated,

---

50. Ibid., 310.
51. Joyce Baldwin, *Daniel*, 210.
52. It's entirely possible, of course, that we are to understand Antiochus and his actions as prototypical of an end-time Antichrist. On this, see Chapter Sixteen.

will continue to expand its influence throughout the earth, and that his dominion, together with his saints, will never pass away (Dan. 2:44-45; 7:13-14, 18, 27).

Chapter Five

Problems with Premillennialism

Premillennialism is by far and away the most widely held perspective on the end of human history. Whether one is a dispensational premillennialist or a historical premillennialist, *all* premillennialists affirm that following the second coming of Christ there will be a chronologically literal 1,000-year period during which Jesus will live upon this present, unredeemed, earth and rule in righteousness with his people and over his enemies. This 1,000-year earthly kingdom intervenes between the second coming and the inauguration of the new heavens and new earth in the eternal state. It is called *pre*-millennialism because the second coming of Christ is believed to occur before (hence, *pre*) the millennial kingdom.

My departure from premillennialism was gradual and came as a result of two discoveries as I studied Scripture. First, I devoted myself to a thorough examination of what the New Testament said would occur at the time of Christ's second coming (or parousia). What I found was a consistent witness concerning what would either *end* or *begin* as a result of our Lord's return to the earth. Sin in the lives of God's people, corruption of the natural creation, and the experience of physical death would terminate upon the appearance of Jesus Christ. Furthermore, the resurrection of the body, the final judgment, and the inauguration of the new heavens and new earth would ensue. But why is this a problem for premillennialism? Good question.

If you are a premillennialist, whether dispensational or not, there are several things with which you must reckon:

135

You must necessarily believe that physical death will continue to exist beyond the time of Christ's second coming. The reason for this is that all premillennialists must account for the rebellious and unbelieving nations in Revelation 20:7-10 who launch an assault against Christ and his people at the end of what they believe is the millennial age. Where did these people come from? They must be the unbelieving progeny born to those believers who entered the millennial age in physical, unglorified bodies. Not only they, but also the *believing* progeny born to those believers will be subject to physical death (notwithstanding the alleged prolonged life-spans experienced by those who live during the millennial reign of Christ).

You must necessarily believe that the natural creation will continue, beyond the time of Christ's second coming, to be subjected to the curse imposed by the fall of man. The reason for this is that all premillennialists must concede that unbelievers will continue to populate and infect the earth during the millennial reign of Christ. Notwithstanding the presence of Christ himself, as premillennialists argue, the earth will continue to be ravaged by war and sin and death, even if only at the millennium's end (Rev. 20:7-10). As a premillennialist, you must necessarily believe that the redemption of the natural creation and its being set free from bondage to corruption does not occur, at least in its consummate expression, until 1,000 years subsequent to Christ's return.

You must necessarily believe that the new heavens and new earth will not be introduced until 1,000 years subsequent to the return of Christ. This is not in itself problematic, except for the fact that the New Testament appears to teach that the new heavens and new earth are inaugurated at the time of Christ's second coming, not 1,000 years thereafter. More on this later when we look at 2 Peter 3.

You must necessarily believe that unbelieving men and women will still have the opportunity to come to saving faith in Christ for at least 1,000 years subsequent to his return. The reason for this is that, according to premillennialism, countless millions of people will be born during the course of the millennial reign of Christ. Are premillennialists asking us to believe that upon their attaining to an age when they are capable of understanding and responding to the revelation of God and the personal, physical presence of the risen and glorified Christ Jesus himself, that *none* of them will be given the opportunity to respond in faith to the claims of the gospel?

You must necessarily believe that unbelievers will not be finally resurrected until at least 1,000 years subsequent to the return of Christ. All premillennialists affirm that the final resurrection of the unsaved occurs at the close of the millennial kingdom.

You must necessarily believe that unbelievers will not be finally judged and cast into eternal punishment until at least 1,000 years subsequent to the return of Christ.

So what's wrong with believing these things, asks the premillennialist? What's wrong is that these many things that premillennialists *must* believe (because of the way they interpret Scripture), *the New Testament explicitly denies.* In other words, in my study of the second coming of Christ I discovered that, contrary to what premillennialism requires us to believe (see above), death is defeated and swallowed up in victory at the parousia, the natural creation is set free from its bondage to corruption at the parousia, the new heavens and the new earth are introduced immediately following the parousia, all opportunity to receive Christ as Savior terminates at the parousia, and both the final resurrection and eternal judgment of unbelievers will occur at the time of the parousia. Simply put, the New Testament portrayals of the second coming of Christ forced me to conclude that a millennial age, subsequent to Christ's return, of the sort proposed by premillennialism was impossible.

The second factor that turned me from premillennialism to amillennialism was a study of Revelation 20, the text cited by all premillennialists in support of their theory. Contrary to what I had been taught and long believed, I came to see Revelation 20 as a strong and immovable support for the amillennial perspective.

I will examine Revelation 20 in detail in subsequent chapters. But in this chapter I want to look closely at those texts in the New Testament that, in my opinion, render impossible a post-parousia millennial kingdom on earth.

A Crucial Interpretive Principle

Before we examine the relevant texts, a brief word is in order concerning a principle of interpretation that underlies all that will follow. Some have referred to this principle as *The Analogy of Faith* (*analogia fidei*).[1] What is meant by it, quite simply, is that no part of Scripture should be interpreted in such a way as to render it in conflict (i.e., yielding logically contradictory propositions) with what is *clearly* taught elsewhere in Scripture. No *single* statement of Scripture in an admittedly obscure context should be permitted to set aside a doctrine that is established by several passages in admittedly clearer contexts. Again, *Scriptura Scripturae interpres*, by which is meant (with some paraphrase and expansion) that the whole of Scripture is to be the interpreter of the part. The singular text must yield to a plurality.[2]

This principle does not mean, however, that a statement of Scripture cannot be accepted as authoritative and binding unless substantiated by other passages. We cannot reject a biblical proposition or practice simply because it occurs but once in Scripture. "Nor can we set aside," writes Milton Terry, "any legitimate inference from a statement of Scripture on the ground that such inference is unsupported by other parallel statements."[3] Terry rightly concludes that "unless it be clearly contradicted or excluded by the analogy of faith, or by some other equally explicit statement, one

---

1. This principle has been the focus of criticism by some. See Daniel P. Fuller, "Biblical Theology and the Analogy of Faith," in *Unity and Diversity in New Testament Theology: Essays in Honor of George E. Ladd* (Grand Rapids: Eerdmans, 1978), pp. 195-213; Walter C. Kaiser, *Toward an Exegetical Theology* (Grand Rapids: Baker, 1981), pp. 134-40; and Robert Thomas, "A Hermeneutical Ambiguity of Eschatology: The Analogy of Faith," *JETS* 23 (1980): 45-53. A more constructive treatment is provided by Robert D. Preus, "A Response to the Unity of the Bible," in *Hermeneutics, Inerrancy and the Bible*, edited by Earl D. Radmacher and Robert D. Preus (Grand Rapids: Zondervan, 1984), pp. 671-90.

2. This principle obviously assumes biblical inerrancy. See R.C. Sproul, "Biblical Interpretation and the Analogy of Faith," in *Inerrancy and Common Sense*, eds. Roger Nicole and J. Ramsey Michaels (Grand Rapids: Baker, 1980), pp. 119-35.

3. Milton Terry, *Biblical Hermeneutics: A Treatise on the Interpretation of the Old and New Testaments* (Grand Rapids: Zondervan, 1976), p. 581.

positive declaration of God's word is sufficient to establish either a fact or a doctrine."[4]

This truth is what differentiates my use of the analogy of faith from that of, say, Paul K. Jewett in his book, *Man as Male and Female*. D.A. Carson explains:

> As Jewett develops his appeal to *analogia fidei*, it becomes clear he is in fact operating with a 'canon within the canon.' He isolates (at least to his own satisfaction) the central teachings of the Scriptures on his chosen subject and on that basis excludes Paul's argument in 1 Timothy 2:11-15 on the ground that it does not cohere with the *analogia fidei* he has constructed *on the basis of his now-limited canon....* If Jewett wishes to follow that line of argument, that is his business; but it is illicit to christen it with the *analogia fidei* argument, which traditionally assumes that the canon is the given.[5]

My treatment of Revelation 20:1-6, in relation to eschatology, is *not* parallel to the way in which Jewett, in relation to male/female roles, dismisses the authoritative truth claims of 1 Timothy 2:11-15. Jewett evidently believes that 1 Timothy 2 is irrevocably at odds with other Pauline utterances (such as Gal. 3:28) on the role of women in the Church and thus feels no need to attempt any form of harmonization. Conversely, my use of the analogy of faith is not intended to deprive Revelation 20 of its canonical and authoritative status, nor am I willing to concede that John was inconsistent with his own writings elsewhere or with other New Testament statements bearing on prophetic themes.

Therefore, in the interests of Scripture and a proper application of the analogy of faith, it is essential that I offer a viable amillennial alternative to the premillennial interpretation of Revelation 20.

---

4. Ibid.
5. Donald A. Carson, "Unity and Diversity in the New Testament: The Possibility of Systematic Theology," in *Scripture and Truth*, eds D.A. Carson and John D. Woodbridge (Grand Rapids: Zondervan, 1983), pp. 92-93. The full title of Jewett's work is *Man as Male and Female: A Study in Sexual Relationships from a Theological Point of View* (Grand Rapids: Eerdmans, 1975).

I seek to do this in subsequent chapters. But the analogy of faith permits, indeed demands, that, on the basis of what I believe are a multiplicity of explicit assertions supportive of the amillennial scheme, I embrace the latter view even should my current interpretation of Revelation 20 prove less than convincing (which is not to suggest, however, that I am unconvinced by it, far less that the premillennial exegesis is more satisfying). It would prove theologically disastrous should one feel compelled to withhold commitment to a doctrinal proposition until each and every problem passage is perfectly explained.

Returning now to the issue at hand, the question reduces to this: Does a premillennial interpretation of Revelation 20 *contradict* the eschatological assertions in other New Testament books? Or, to reverse the matter, do the statements in other New Testament books concerning end-time chronology *necessarily and logically preclude* the notion of a post-parousia millennial age in Revelation 20? I am convinced that both questions must be answered affirmatively.

In his masterful treatment of Pauline eschatology, Geerhardus Vos was evidently thinking of the analogy of faith when he wrote the following:

> Were it confined to the elucidation of the Pauline eschatology alone, the settlement [of the millennial dispute] should not appear overdifficult. Unfortunately, where one undertakes to do this, he must expect to have the scheme outlined in Rev. xx. 4ff. brought to his attention with the insistent demand, that a laborious effort at harmonizing shall be forthwith undertaken in which the large mould of the Pauline eschatological teaching shall be reduced to the narrower, pictorial measures of the Apocalyptic vision. With all due respect to the authoritativeness of biblical prophecy, it is difficult to escape the feeling that this is an unmethodical procedure. The minor deliverances ought in the harmonizing process be made to give way to the far-sweeping, age-dominating program of the theology of Paul. After the latter has been interpreted to a satisfactory degree of clearness and certainty, then, and not until then, will come the time to look the Apocalypse in the

face, and to endeavor to bring it into consonance with the Pauline deliverances. The law of proportion cannot be entirely waived in so far-reaching a matter as this.[6]

When I first let it be known to several of my premillennial friends that I had embraced amillennialism, I was, as Vos predicted, confronted with the "insistent demand" to subject my conclusions drawn from the Pauline literature to the singular declaration of Revelation 20. It seemed to me at the time, and still does, to be more than merely hermeneutically "unmethodical" (to use Vos' odd term). It seemed flatly illogical. Let me explain why.

I am *not* saying that the passages to be discussed in the subsequent pages simply *omit* reference to a post-parousia millennial age. If that were the case it is conceivable that we might harmonize Revelation 20 with them, making room, as it were, for the former in the latter. But the texts to be considered are not such as may be conflated with the notion of a future millennial kingdom. As I studied them, they appeared logically to *preclude* the existence of such a kingdom. Therefore, it is not a matter of simply conceding the eschatological advance in Revelation and then re-reading the gospel and epistolary literature in its light. This is apparently what George Ladd wishes us to do:

> Divine revelation within the Scriptures is not static but progressive. The implications of progressive revelation are always applied in the study of the relationship between the New Testament and the Old and

---

6. Geerhardus Vos, *The Pauline Eschatology* (Grand Rapids: Baker, 1979 [1930]), p. 226. Similarly, Benjamin B. Warfield suggests that "there is a sense in which it is proper to permit our understanding of so obscure a portion of Scripture [Rev. 20:1-10] to be affected by the clearer teaching of its more didactic parts. We must guard, no doubt, against carrying this too far and doing violence to the text before us in the interests of Bible harmony. But within due limits, surely, the order of investigation should be from the clearer to the more obscure" ("The Millennium and the Apocalypse," *PTR* 2 [Oct 1904], 599). More recently Moises Silva has voiced a similar perspective in *Biblical Words and their Meaning: An Introduction to Lexical Semantics* (Grand Rapids: Zondervan, 1983), pp. 157-59.

within the movement from Moses to the post-exilic prophets in the Old Testament writings. There is no reason why there might not be a further application of progress in revelation in the New Testament books. It might well be that in the Apocalypse, elements of a new revelation were imparted to John by the Lord, to the effect that there should be a millennial interregnum.[7]

Ladd is certainly correct, to a point. Divine revelation is undoubtedly organic and progressive, in which temporally subsequent revelation often develops, unfolds, and illuminates, but never contradicts, antecedent truth. It is with Ladd's concluding sentence, however, that I wish to take exception. For my argument will be that a premillennial interpretation of Revelation 20 actually *contradicts* the clear and unequivocal assertions in such texts as 1 Corinthians 15, Romans 8, and others. No one questions that the Revelation sheds much additional light upon the eschatological constructs of Paul and Peter. It undoubtedly fills in much of the detail not addressed by the other New Testament authors. But I am convinced that the premillennial interpretation of Revelation 20 neither sheds light upon nor fills in but rather contradicts the assertions of other, decidedly more lucid, prophetic passages.

Most premillennialists read these texts through the grid of Revelation 20. As Vos indicated, one is rarely permitted to discuss other relevant passages prior to the interpretation of Revelation, but only the former in the allegedly clear and antecedent light of the latter. Often the premillennial interpretation of Revelation 20 has become so deeply embedded in the minds of its advocates that it borders on unconscious assumption. This makes it difficult for them to read other portions of God's word through anything other than premillennial spectacles. This, I suggest, is contrary to good hermeneutical sense. It is contrary to the analogy of faith. It would not be, were it the case that a premillennial interpretation of Revelation 20 could be harmonized with the rest of Scripture. I will contend, however, that it cannot.

---

7. George E. Ladd, *Crucial Questions About the Kingdom of God* (Grand Rapids: Eerdmans, 1968 [1952]), pp. 181-82.

My point, then, is that sound hermeneutical procedure would appear to demand that we interpret the singular and obscure in the light of the plural and explicit. To make the rest of the New Testament (not to mention the Old Testament) bend to the standard of one text in the most controversial, symbolic, and by scholarly consensus most difficult book in the Bible, is hardly commendable hermeneutical method. The first reason, therefore, for my theological shift to amillennialism is that I can in good conscience no longer allow the apocalyptic tail to wag the epistolary dog. I must not force the whole of Scripture to dance to the tune of Revelation 20.

1 Corinthians 15:22-28 [8]

[22]For as in Adam all die, so also in Christ shall all be made alive . [23]But each in his own order: Christ the firstfruits, then at his coming those who belong to Christ. [24]Then comes the end, when he delivers the kingdom to God the Father after destroying every rule and every authority

---

8. A brief but helpful treatment of the grammatical and structural aspects of this text is provided by Ralph Martin, "The Hope of the Resurrection," in *New Testament Foundations,* Vol. 2 (Grand Rapids: Eerdmans, 1978), pp. 408-17. See also his book, *The Spirit and the Congregation: Studies in 1 Corinthians 12–15* (Grand Rapids: Eerdmans, 1984), pp. 110-18. For a defense of the premillennial view, see Wilbur Wallis, "The Use of Psalms 8 and 110 in 1 Corinthians 15:25-27 and Hebrews 1 and 2," *JETS* 15 (1972): 25-29, and "The Problem of an Intermediate Kingdom in 1 Corinthians 15:20-28," *JETS* 18 (1975): 229-42. Two of the better amillennial treatments are Geerhardus Vos, *The Pauline Eschatology,* pp. 226-60, and W.D. Davies, *Paul and Rabbinic Judaism* (Philadelphia: Fortress Press, 1980 [1948]), pp. 291-98. It is difficult to know which view Murray J. Harris is espousing in his *Raised Immortal: Resurrection and Immortality in the New Testament* (Grand Rapids: Eerdmans, 1983). Whereas he argues that 1 Corinthians 15:22-28 does not envision a post-parousia millennial age, he goes on to say: "That Paul nowhere explicitly refers to the millennium does not prove that he was unaware of this element of Johannine theology [a reference to Revelation 20:1-6] but simply indicates that he did not regard this as a crucial part of Christian eschatology" (180). My understanding of 1 Corinthians 15, however, is not simply that Paul was "unaware" of a millennial age but that his words explicitly and logically preclude the possibility of such an interregnum. That is to say, if "death dies" at the second advent of Christ, as Paul clearly says it does, then there *cannot* be a millennium subsequent to his coming during which death still reigns. If Revelation 20 teaches a post-parousia millennium, as the premillennialist contends, Paul *could not* say that death is swallowed up in victory at the time of Christ's return.

and power. ²⁵For he must reign until he has put all his enemies under his feet . ²⁶The last enemy to be destroyed is death. ²⁷For "God has put all things in subjection under his feet." But when it says, "all things are put in subjection," it is plain that he is excepted who put all things in subjection under him. ²⁸When all things are subjected to him, then the Son himself will also be subjected to him who put all things in subjection under him, that God may be all in all.

The premillennialist argues from this passage that since there is a lengthy gap between the resurrection of Christ and the resurrection of his people (v. 23; it is now almost at 2,000 years), so also there is a gap between the resurrection of his people (at the time of the second coming) and "the end" (*to telos*, v. 24). In other words, when Paul says in verse 24, "then comes the end," he does not mean "thereupon" or immediately after the resurrection of believers described in verse 23, but only after the millennium or 1,000 years later. At the close of the millennium, i.e., when "the end" comes, Christ will deliver up the kingdom to God the Father (v. 24a) after having abolished all rule and authority and power.

This reign of Christ, says the premillennialist, which entails his abolishing of all rule, authority, and power, occurs during the earthly millennium, a reign Paul further describes in verse 25 as the putting of all his enemies under his feet. The last of these enemies is death (v. 26). Clearly, then, for the premillennialist, death will not be destroyed or defeated or abolished until the close of the millennial age.

Before proceeding, note well that the matter under dispute is not whether the terms Paul used (*epeita* and *eita*; both of which are translated "then" by the ESV) will admit of a time gap. Obviously they may. The question is whether or not in this context they do. I will argue below that other factors in the text prohibit our interpreting Paul as saying that there is a gap of 1,000 years (the millennium) between the resurrection of Christ's people at his second coming (v. 23b) and "the end" (v. 24a).⁹ This is not to deny the

---

9. Geehardus Vos has pointed out that "of course, a brief interval in logical conception at least, must be assumed: *to telos* [the end] comes, speaking

obvious gap between the resurrection of Christ (v. 23a) and that of Christians (v. 23b). But no such gap, I will argue, is possible in the case of our resurrection and "the end."

Look again at verse 24 where Paul declares that "the end" occurs "when" (*hotan*) Christ delivers the kingdom to God the Father, "when" (*hotan*) he has abolished all rule and authority and power.[10] This second "when" clause is retrospective and describes the condition that must be fulfilled before the kingdom is handed over to the Father. Paul's thesis, then, is that the subjugation of Christ's enemies precedes and is consummated by his delivering of the kingdom to God the Father. This reign of Christ consists in the putting of all his enemies under his feet (v. 25), the last of which is death (v. 26).

In summary, "the end" (*to telos*) marks the close of Christ's reign, or at least that phase of it with which Paul is concerned. It is brought to its climax by the complete and final overthrow of death. The point of dispute is the time of the "end." The premillennialist argues that the "end" is the end or close of the millennial age, 1,000 years after Christ has returned to earth. The amillennialist argues that the "end" is the end or close of the *present* church age, signaled and brought to fruition by Christ's second coming.

It seems clear that all one need do is demonstrate which of these two options is correct and the millennial debate would come to a close. This isn't as difficult as one might think. *Since both eschatological schools agree that Christ's reign consummates with the destruction of death, and since the destruction of death signals the end, we need only ascertain the time of "death's death"!*

So, does Paul tell us when death dies? Yes, I believe he does. As I read 1 Corinthians 15:50-58, *the defeat of death occurs at the second coming of Christ* (see more on this text below). Therefore, we must understand the reign of Christ, consisting of his progressive abol-

---

in terms of strict chronology, after the rising of *hoi tou christou* [those who are Christ's]. But that by no means opens the door to the intercalation of a rounded-off chiliad of years" (*The Pauline Eschatology* [Grand Rapids: Eerdmans, 1961], 243).

10. Observe that the ESV translates the first *hotan* as "when" and the second instance as "after".

ishing of all rule, authority, and power, as presently occurring. The last of these enemies is death, which is abolished or swallowed up at our Lord's second coming when he delivers the kingdom to God the Father. That is "the end". C.K. Barrett explains:

> In some way (never specified by Paul) ... authority has come into the hands of evil powers, whom God has to dispossess in order to reassert his own sovereignty. In the passage before us Christ appears to reign during the period in which this dispossessing takes place, one enemy after another (cf. v. 26) being overpowered. When the kingdom has been fully re-established, the Son hands it over to the Father, and the kingdom of Christ gives place to the kingdom of God. There is ... nothing to suggest that this developing reign of Christ falls between the *parusia* [sic] and the End; it **culminates** in the *parusia* [sic; emphasis mine]. This is supported in the following verses, in which it is said that Christ reigns until all his enemies are defeated, and that the last enemy to be overcome is death; the defeat of death however is naturally taken as belonging to the time of the resurrection of Christ's people (v. 23) [at his second coming].[11]

If the premillennialist should question whether in fact Christ is *presently* ruling or reigning over every rule and authority and power, one need only read Ephesians 1:20-23 where precisely the same terms are used (*arche, exousia, dunamis*) in Paul's description of what has been put in subjection under Christ's feet (cf. also Colossians 1:13; 2:10,15).

The premillennialist does not believe that Christ will abolish death at his second coming. He believes that death will continue on into the 1,000-year earthly reign of Christ and will in fact assume massive proportions at its close (see Rev. 20:9-10).[12] But how can

---

11. C.K. Barrett, *A Commentary on the First Epistle to the Corinthians* (New York: Harper & Row, 1968), 357.
12. According to premillennialism, one's lifespan in the millennial age will be noticeably extended. They often appeal to Isaiah 65:20 for proof. However, this passage clearly describes in figurative language a condition that will obtain in the New Heavens and New Earth (see Isa. 65:17). For an excellent

this be when Paul places the destruction of death at Christ's second coming? The end of death *at that time* precludes the millennium of the premillennialist, for according to the latter death still prevails.

Although not an amillennialist (he's a postmillennialist), John J. Davis finds additional evidence in 1 Corinthians 1:7 for identifying "the end" with the parousia. "More specifically," says Davis, "in this very epistle [1 Corinthians] Paul clearly understands the 'end' to be coterminous with the second coming: 'as you wait for the revealing of our Lord Jesus Christ; who will sustain you to the end (*telos*), guiltless in the day of our Lord Jesus Christ' (1 Cor. 1:7-8). The 'day of the Lord' is clearly the day of the second coming, as may be seen from 1 Thessalonians 5:2…. The point is that the 'end' does not come, say, a thousand years after the second coming; for Paul, the second coming *is* the end."[13]

It was precisely this sort of thing that I encountered as I studied what the New Testament said would occur at the time of Christ's second coming at the close of the present age. When he comes, death dies. That is why there cannot be a millennium of history beyond the time of the second coming during which death continues to live (if I may so speak). Herman Ridderbos provides an excellent summation of the point I've labored to make:

> It is difficult to conclude otherwise from 1 Corinthians 15:50ff. than that the parousia itself and the resurrection taking place with it signify the end of the power of death. And inasmuch as death is the last enemy, the destruction of the remaining powers ("when he shall have destroyed all rule and authority and power") will have to be understood not as a final struggle beginning after the parousia, but as the definite victory of Christ that has already begun in his cross and resurrection and exaltation (cf., e.g., Col. 2:15), and is now finally settled at, and in virtue of, his parousia (cf. 2 Thess. 2:8). This view seems

---

discussion of this passage, see Anthony Hoekema, *The Bible and the Future* (Grand Rapids: Eerdmans, 1979), 201-03.

13. John J. Davis, *Christ's Victorious Kingdom: Postmillennialism Reconsidered* (Grand Rapids: Baker, 1987), p. 57.

to us, at least on the ground of the Pauline pronouncements, much more acceptable than that one still has to conceive of a battle for the destruction of the powers and of death, which would in the parousia have only its beginning and point of departure. Such a final phase or intermediate kingdom must in any case be introduced into the text as a presupposition, and has no basis in all Paul's preaching of the last things, so far as that is known to us.[14]

The Premillennial View

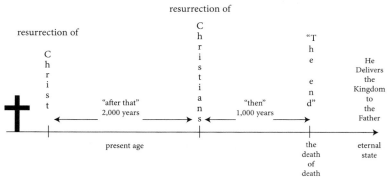

The Amillennial View

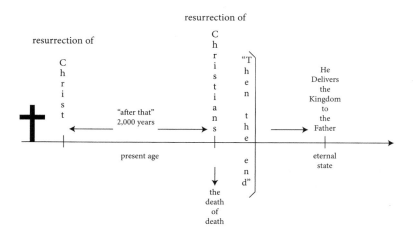

14. Herman Ridderbos, *Paul: An Outline of His Theology*, translated by John R. De Witt (Grand Rapids: Eerdmans, 1975 [1966]), 559.

1 Corinthians 15:50-57

[50]I tell you this, brothers: flesh and blood cannot inherit the kingdom of God, nor does the perishable inherit the imperishable. [51]Behold! I tell you a mystery. We shall not all sleep, but we shall all be changed, [52]in a moment, in the twinkling of an eye, at the last trumpet. For the trumpet will sound, and the dead will be raised imperishable, and we shall be changed. [53]For this perishable body must put on the imperishable, and this mortal body must put on immortality. [54]When the perishable puts on the imperishable, and the mortal puts on immortality, then shall come to pass the saying that is written: "Death is swallowed up in victory". [55]"O death, where is your victory? O death, where is your sting?" [56]The sting of death is sin, and the power of sin is the law. [57]But thanks be to God, who gives us the victory through our Lord Jesus Christ.

Take note first of Paul's declaration that "flesh and blood cannot inherit the kingdom of God" (v. 50). Simply put, a corruptible and perishable nature can neither possess nor participate in an incorruptible and imperishable kingdom. Neither the living ("flesh and blood") nor the dead ("the perishable") can inherit the kingdom in their present state.[15] Several factors contribute to make this a strong argument for amillennialism and against premillennialism.

Here Paul insists not merely on the necessity of regeneration but of resurrection, which is to say the ultimate glorification of the believer that will occur at the second coming of Christ (cf. 1 Thess. 4:13-18). In a word, only those who have been consummately transformed in body and spirit by that resurrection / glorification brought to pass at the return of Christ shall inherit the kingdom of God.

---

15. According to Joachim Jeremias, "the two lines of v. 50 are contrasting men of flesh and blood on the one hand, and corpses in decomposition on the other. In other words, the first line refers to those who are alive at the parousia, the second line to those who died before the parousia. The parallelism is thus not synonymous, but synthetic and the meaning of v. 50 is: neither the living nor the dead can take part in the Kingdom of God – as they are" ("Flesh and Blood Cannot Inherit the Kingdom of God," in *NTS* 2 [1955-56], 152).

The "kingdom" in view, according to the premillennialist, is the millennial kingdom, that very "reign" of Christ we noted above in 1 Corinthians 15:24.[16] But how can that be? The premillennialist argues that many believers will enter and inherit and enjoy the blessings of the millennial kingdom in their natural, unglorified, untransformed, "flesh and blood" bodies. But that is precisely what Paul denies could ever happen. Most premillennialists also contend that these believers will bear children, many of whom likewise may come to faith and "claim" their inheritance while yet in "flesh and blood" bodies. The problem for premillennialism is acute: either deny these believers that inheritance of the kingdom which Christ has promised, and into the experience of which he gives them entrance (Matt. 25), or recognize that 1 Corinthians 15:50 precludes the millennial age traditionally defined and defended by the premillennialist.

I'm compelled to conclude that Paul's declaration that unglorified, "flesh and blood" bodies cannot inherit the kingdom of God precludes a millennium following the second coming of Christ. The kingdom of God into which all believers are granted entrance at the time of their glorification (i.e., at the second coming of Christ), is the *eternal* phase of God's kingdom rule. This eternal phase, at the beginning of which Jesus "delivers the kingdom to God the Father" (v. 24) follows immediately upon the second coming of the Lord Jesus. It is then that "we shall all be changed, in a moment, in the twinkling of an eye, at the last trumpet" (vv. 51-52).

More important still, according to verses 54-55, the end of death at the second coming of Christ is the fulfillment of Isaiah 25:8. There we read that God "will swallow up death forever; and the Lord GOD will wipe away tears from all faces, and the reproach

---

16. J. Dwight Pentecost (*Things to Come* [Grand Rapids: Zondervan, 1971 (1958)], 175) explicitly equates the "kingdom" of verse 50 with the 1,000 year post-Parousia rule of Christ, as also does Alva McClain (*The Greatness of the Kingdom* [Chicago: Moody Press, 1968 (1959)], 433. McClain proceeds to say that verse 50 is parallel to Christ's words in Matthew 25:34, another alleged reference to the millennial age.

of his people he will take away from all the earth." In light of this, I have two questions for my premillennial readers.

First, how can God "swallow up death forever" at the time of the return of Christ and the resurrection of our bodies if, according to premillennialism, death continues to prevail for 1,000 years after the parousia? Look again closely at the development of Paul's argument in this paragraph. The final generation of Christians who are physically alive when Christ returns will "all be changed" (v. 51b). It will happen "in a moment, in the twinkling of an eye" (v. 52a). When will this occur? It will happen "at the last trumpet" (v. 52b). I don't know of anyone who denies that this is Paul's description of the second coming of Christ. When this occurs, "the dead will be raised imperishable, and we shall be changed" (v. 52b). He's clearly talking about the resurrection. This resurrection (which I believe is synonymous with the rapture) means that "this perishable body" will put on "the imperishable," and "this mortal body" will put on "immortality" (v. 53). Are you following me, or better yet, are you following Paul? When all this happens, or as Paul says, "when the perishable puts on the imperishable, and the mortal puts on immortality" (v. 54), which all agree happens at the time of the second coming of Christ, "**THEN** shall come to pass" the fulfillment of Isaiah 25:8 where it was prophesied that "death is swallowed up in victory."

Let's now put two and two together and see if it actually comes up four. The "end" (1 Cor. 15:24) is marked by the destruction of the "last enemy," namely, "death" (1 Cor. 15:26). All millennial views agree on this. And when is "death" destroyed? When does "death" cease to prevail? When is "death" going to be "swallowed up in victory"? Paul's answer couldn't have been clearer or more explicit: *Death is defeated, death dies, death is swallowed up in victory and is utterly and absolutely no more, as Isaiah 25:7-9 has prophesied, at the very moment that the last trumpet is sounded, at the very moment we are all changed, at the very moment when the perishable puts on the imperishable and the mortal puts on immortality!* And when, might I ask, is that? It is at the time of the second coming of Christ (and not some 1,000 years later as death continues to exert its horrid influence on the human race).

151

And now for the second question. In conjunction with the death of death, or its being swallowed up in victory, something else will happen. According to Isaiah 25:8, not only will God "swallow up death forever," he will also at that time "wipe away tears from all faces." Both these events will occur, as we've seen, at the time of the second coming. But according to Revelation 21:1-4, it is at the time of the creation of the new heavens and new earth that God "will wipe away every tear from their eyes, and death shall be no more" (21:4). My question is this: How can these two prophesied events (Isa. 25:7-9) find their fulfillment at the close of a 1,000-year post-parousia millennial kingdom when Paul has so clearly stated that they find their fulfillment at the time of the second coming of Christ? Is it not obvious that at the second coming of Christ the new heavens and new earth are created and the eternal state begins? Is it not equally obvious, therefore, that there is no room or place or role in either Paul's or John's theology for an intervening millennial kingdom? Is it not obvious that death's death at the second coming and the wiping away of all tears at the second coming, both of which mark the inauguration of the new heavens and new earth, preclude the existence of any such millennial kingdom?

Romans 8:18-23

[18]For I consider that the sufferings of this present time are not worth comparing with the glory that is to be revealed to us. [19]For the creation waits with eager longing for the revealing of the sons of God. [20]For the creation was subjected to futility, not willingly, but because of him who subjected it, in hope [21]that the creation itself will be set free from its bondage to corruption and obtain the freedom of the glory of the children of God. [22]For we know that the whole creation has been groaning together in the pains of childbirth until now. [23]And not only the creation, but we ourselves, who have the firstfruits of the Spirit, groan inwardly as we wait eagerly for adoption as sons, the redemption of our bodies.

Paul describes the deliverance or redemption of the natural creation as inseparably connected with that of the children of God. It is when the sons of God are revealed (v. 19) that the creation itself will experience its redemption. That is why the creation is personified as "waiting eagerly for the revealing of the sons of God" (NASB). The creation anxiously awaits the return of Christ and our glorification, for it is *then* that it too shall be set free from "its bondage to corruption" into that very "freedom of the glory of the children of God" (v. 21).

The creation waits *for* the revealing of the sons of God (v. 19) because it is *into* that very freedom that the creation too will be delivered (v. 21). In other words, *the natural creation and the children of God are intimately intertwined both in present suffering and in future glory. As there was a solidarity in the fall, so also there will be a solidarity in the restoration.*

The redemption we will experience at Christ's return is the complete and final eradication of all sin, of every trace of the corruption in spirit and flesh that was ours prior to that moment. Paul's point is that the natural creation awaits that day because then, it will in like fashion be fully redeemed and delivered.

If the creation should somehow fall short of complete deliverance from its present corruption, the finality and fullness of *our* redemption are seriously undermined. Inasmuch as the natural realm will enter into "the freedom of the glory of the children of God," any deficiency that it might experience must obtain in the case of Christians as well. To the extent that the created order is not wholly and perfectly redeemed, *we* are not wholly and perfectly redeemed. *The redemption and glory of creation are coextensive and contemporaneous with ours.*

The problem this poses for premillennialism is clear: the consummate redemption of creation that occurs when Christ returns to redeem and glorify his people would appear to preclude any suffering or corruption of creation *subsequent* to that return. And yet the millennial age for which the premillennialist argues is one that includes the corrupting presence of both sin and death.[17] The

---

17. This objection to premillennialism is developed in detail by Arthur H. Lewis in his book, *The Dark Side of the Millennium: The Problem of Evil in Revelation 20:1-10* (Grand Rapids: Baker, 1980).

question, then, is this: What kind of deliverance from corruption is it when corruption persists? How can the creation be delivered from the crippling effects of sin and death *when we are*, namely, at Christ's second coming, if during the millennium it must yet suffer the presence and perversity of its enemies?

To insist, as the premillennialist must, that the natural realm will undergo a *dual renewal*, a preliminary and incomplete one prior to the millennial age and a final and perfect one after it, demands that we anticipate a similar *dual renewal* in the case of all Christians. It seems more reasonable to me that Paul's description of the day of redemption for both Christians and the created order (i.e., the second coming of Jesus) is identical with the advent of the new heavens and new earth portrayed in such texts as 2 Peter 3:10-13; Revelation 21:1ff.; and Matthew 19:28. If so, there is no place for a "millennium" subsequent to the return of Christ.

Where do the Dead go?

More needs to be said about the difficulties presented by the premillennial belief that physical death will continue beyond the time of the second coming of Christ. Let's be sure, once again, that we understand what is *necessarily entailed* by all forms of premillennialism, whether dispensational, historical, or other. As stated earlier, premillennialists believe that during the 1,000-year earthly reign of Christ following his second coming, there will be countless men, women, and children living on the earth in their natural physical bodies. These people are typically seen as coming from one of two groups, or perhaps both. On the one hand, perhaps not all unbelievers are killed when Christ returns in triumph at the battle of Armageddon. Those who survive this war will thus enter the millennium in their natural, physical, unglorified bodies. Aside from the fact that Revelation 19:11-21 appears to say that all enemies of Christ are destroyed at the time of the second coming, how could they be permitted to enter into an alleged phase of the kingdom of God that is designed for the blessing of God's people and the promotion of righteousness? On the other hand, some premillennialists argue that many will be converted at the time of Christ's second coming but will not be resurrected or glorified at that time. They will remain in their natural bodies and enter the millennial kingdom susceptible to the presence of disease and death. It really matters little, for our present purpose, how they make their way into the millennium. The only relevant issue is that premillennialism requires that there be people living on the millennial earth in their natural, unglorified bodies.

You will recall that the reason for insisting that unglorified, mortal people will enter the millennial kingdom is that the premillennialist believes that a massive, global rebellion by unregenerate men and women will occur at the close of the millennium (Rev. 20:7-10). Thus there must have been present during this 1,000-year period a significant number of people (whether regenerate or unregenerate) who marry, reproduce, and whose descendants remain in unbelief and are present at the close of the millennium, susceptible to Satan's deception and thus participants in his final rebellion.

This, however, is not my primary concern (as problematic as it is). What concerns me is the presence on earth during this alleged millennial reign of men, women, and children who are born anew and come to saving faith in Christ. After all, Jesus is himself personally and physically present on the earth during this time. No premillennialist of whom I am aware has ever denied that men and women will be saved during the millennial reign of Christ. Of course, I have also argued that this, too, is problematic, in that the New Testament consistently portrays this present church age as the time of salvation, a time and opportunity for repentance and faith that ends when Christ appears. But I digress.

Our Lord, so they say, will be personally present in his resurrected and glorified body. Gone are the days of his humiliation and weakness. Gone are the days when people wondered at his identity or mocked his teachings. Gone are the days when an argument could be made that there was insufficient evidence to support his claims. Jesus will be bodily and visibly present to all, his omnipotent power and divine nature fully and unmistakably revealed (so says the premillennialist). All people will have immediate access to the undeniable proof that he is who he claimed to be. There will be no doubt or ambiguity as to the meaning of Scripture that bears witness to him. There will be no question as to the way in which he fulfills the Old Testament prophecies regarding a coming Messiah. I say all this simply to remind us that if the premillennialist is correct (and I only concede that he is for the sake of argument), it is difficult to understand how anyone would *not* come to saving faith while standing for a lifetime in Christ's glorified presence. In any case, all premillennialists admit that many, if not all, will come to faith.

My question is this: *What becomes of these born again believers who die physically during the millennial age?* The premillennialist insists that conditions will prevail during the millennium such that physical life will be unusually prolonged, much as it was in the days preceding the flood of Noah. Be that as it may, physical death will still occur. So what becomes of those who die in faith? *Where do they go? What do they experience?*

The Apostle Paul makes it clear in both Philippians 1 and 2 Corinthians 5 that when a believer dies he/she immediately enters the presence of Christ. To be absent from the body is to be present with the Lord. We rejoice in knowing that our friends and family who know Christ and have died are now with him in what theologians refer to as the intermediate state. They are even now in the presence of their Savior, gathered around the throne of the Lamb in festive worship and celebration (Heb. 12; Rev. 4–5).

But during the so-called millennial age, Jesus is not in heaven. He's on earth. So where are those who have died during this time period? Are we to envision them continuing to exist in a disembodied state, floating around, as it were, somewhere in the vicinity of the earth where Christ is physically present? Will their presence be known and seen by those who are still in their physical, unglorified bodies? What relationship will they sustain to believers who are on the earth in their resurrected, glorified bodies? Or will these who have died in faith during the millennium be escorted into some heavenly realm, away from Christ, there to await the final resurrection of the body?

Some premillennialists may respond by insisting that each time a born again man or woman dies during the millennial age he/she immediately receives a resurrection body. In other words, they do not wait for the final resurrection of the dead as described in Revelation 20:11-15 but are, upon their physical deaths, instantly resurrected and glorified and thus live with Christ on the millennial earth together with others who have already received their glorified bodies. But if that is what will happen, we must then conclude that countless thousands, perhaps even millions, of bodily resurrections are occurring all through the 1,000 years of the millennial kingdom! I have argued elsewhere that the New Testament appears to argue for a single, unified, consummate resurrection for all mankind, both believers and unbelievers. Premillennialists, on the other hand, must embrace the existence of multiple resurrections. Pretribulational premillennialists believe that some are resurrected at the time of the rapture, another resurrection occurs at the second coming, seven years later, and yet another resurrection at the close of the millennial age. Historic premillennialists must affirm at least two resurrections: one at the second coming of Christ, before the millennium, and another at the close of the millennium, prior to the final judgment. But we now see that if premillennialism is true, there may well be thousands, if not millions, of bodily resurrections happening all the time, throughout the course of this millennial age, each and every time a Christian passes away.

Is it not becoming increasingly evident that premillennialism necessarily entails a scenario that is simply bizarre, not to mention without biblical warrant? Is it really the case that the Bible teaches an earthly reign of Christ in which millions of physically dead believers hover in his presence, strangely mingling with physically alive unregenerate people, as well as physically alive but unglorified regenerate people, as well as resurrected and glorified people? For the premillennialist, the alternative to this bizarre and unbiblical scenario, as noted, is to assert, without the slightest hint in the Scriptures, that untold multitudes of individual bodily resurrections occur every time a believer dies physically during the millennial age.

If you are finding it difficult to make sense of this, that is precisely what happens when you embrace premillennialism! This eschatological system necessarily entails such bizarre and unbiblical ad hoc developments and explanations that it stretches credulity beyond the breaking point.

2 Peter 3:8-13 [18]

Following his reference to "mockers" who question whether Christ will ever return (vv. 3-7), Peter writes this:

> [8]But do not overlook this one fact, beloved, that with the Lord one day is as a thousand years, and a thousand years as one day. [9]The Lord is not slow to fulfill his promise as some count slowness, but is patient toward you, not wishing that any should perish, but that all should reach repentance. [10]But the day of the Lord will come like a thief, and then the heavens will pass away with a roar, and the heavenly bodies will be burned up and dissolved, and the earth and the works that are done on it will be exposed. [11]Since all these things are thus to be dissolved, what sort of people ought you to be in lives of holiness and godliness, [12]waiting for and hastening the coming of the day of God, because of which the heavens will be set on fire and dissolved, and the heavenly bodies will melt as they burn! [13]But according to his promise we are waiting for new heavens and a new earth in which righteousness dwells.

Here Peter echoes the words of Paul in 1 Thessalonians 5:2-3, both of whom refer to "the day of the Lord", i.e., the second coming/advent of Christ (1 Thess. 4:13-18; 2 Pet. 3:4, 8-9). Peter tells us that it is on account of the coming of this "day of the Lord/God" (vv. 10, 12), i.e., the second coming/advent of Christ, that the heavens

---

18. I mention only in passing that many preterists find the fulfillment of this passage not at the end of history, at the second coming of Christ, but in the events of A.D. 70. See the especially challenging defense of this view by David Chilton in "Looking for New Heavens and a New Earth: A Study of 2 Peter 3," in Gary DeMar, *Why the End of the World is Not in Your Future: Identifying the Gog-Magog Alliance* (Powder Springs, GA: American Vision Press, 2008), pp. 175-87.

will be dissolved. The purification of this present heavens and earth is the effect of the coming of Christ. According to verse 10, the coming of Christ entails the consummate judgment (and eventual renewal) of the heavens and earth. Note well: "the day of the Lord" is the time, literally, "in which" or "when" (ESV) "the heavens will pass away." Peter's point is that the return of Christ and the judgment of the heavens and earth are causally related in that complex of events which will herald the end of the present age. The "present heavens and earth," literally, the "*now* heavens and earth" (v. 7), are being reserved for this "day" of judgment.

Note also that the "present (now) heavens and earth" are contrasted with the former heavens and earth, literally, "the *then* world" (v. 6). Thus Peter looks at biblical history as consisting of three great periods: (1) the heavens and earth before Noah, which were destroyed by God's judgment, out of which he formed anew (2) the heavens and earth that now are, which are being reserved for judgment, and out of which he will create anew (3) the heavens and earth that shall be, which are the object of our hope. "Since you look for these things," says Peter, that is, for the new heavens and new earth in which righteousness dwells (v. 13), be diligent to be righteous.

Where is there room in Peter's scenario for an earthly millennium intervening between Christ's second coming and the new heavens and new earth? On the contrary, the present heavens and earth will be judged at Christ's return, at which time the *new heavens and new earth* (not a millennium) shall emerge as an eternal dwelling for God's people.

Note Peter's use of the word translated "look for" in verses 12, 13, 14 (NASB; "wait for" in the ESV). We are to "look for" the day of God (the Lord), i.e., the return of Christ (v. 12). In verse 13 we are to "look for" the new heavens and new earth. In verse 14 we "look for" these things, i.e., the coming of Christ which brings judgment against the present world and righteousness for his people. It seems clear that the object of our expectation, that for which we are to "look" and "wait" is the *return of Christ when the present heavens and earth give way to the new heavens and earth.* If the new heavens and new earth come at the time of Christ's second advent, there can be no earthly millennial reign intervening between the two. Remember that the premillennialist places the creation of the new heavens and new earth *after* the millennium (Rev. 21–22). However, if the new heavens and new earth come with Christ (as Peter indicates they will), the millennium must in some sense be identified with this present age and not some future period subsequent to Christ's return.

Finally, the premillennialist argues that during the millennial age it will be possible for people to come to saving faith in Christ. But Peter's argument is that the very reason why Christ has not yet returned is in order that he might patiently extend the opportunity for men to repent. This is meaningful only if it is *impossible* to repent *subsequent* to Christ's return. If souls may be saved after Christ returns, the patience he now displays is unnecessary. The urgency of the moment can be explained only on the supposition that "now is the acceptable time, behold now is the day of salvation" (2 Cor. 6:2).

Matthew 25:31-46

[31]When the Son of Man comes in his glory, and all the angels with him, then he will sit on his glorious throne. [32]Before him will be gathered all the nations, and he will separate people one from another as a shepherd separates the sheep from the goats. [33]And he will place the sheep on his right, but the goats on the left. [34]Then the King will say to those on his right, "Come, you who are blessed by my Father, inherit the kingdom prepared for you from the foundation of the world. [35]For I was hungry and you gave me food, I was thirsty and you gave me drink, I was a stranger and you welcomed me. [36]I was naked and you clothed me, I was sick and you visited me, I was in prison and you came to me". [37]Then the righteous will answer him, saying, "Lord, when did we see you hungry and feed you, or thirsty and give you drink? [38]And when did we see you a stranger and welcome you, or naked and clothe you? [39]And when did we see you sick or in prison and visit you?" [40]And the King will answer them, "Truly, I say to you, as you did it to one of the least of these my brothers, you did it to me". [41]Then he will say to those on his left, "Depart from me, you cursed,

into the eternal fire prepared for the devil and his angels. [42]For I was hungry and you gave me no food, I was thirsty and you gave me no drink. [43]I was a stranger and you did not welcome me, naked and you did not clothe me, sick and in prison and you did not visit me". [44]Then they also will answer, saying, "Lord, when did we see you hungry or thirsty or a stranger or naked or sick or in prison, and did not minister to you?" [45]Then he will answer them, saying, "Truly, I say to you, as you did not do it to one of the least of these, you did not do it to me". [46]And these will go away into eternal punishment, but the righteous into eternal life.

The premillennialist believes that this event, known as the "Sheep/ Goat Judgment," will occur at the close of the tribulation and just *before* the inauguration of the millennial age. Indeed, most premillennialists believe that the purpose of the judgment is to determine (or at least reveal) who is worthy of entrance into that millennial kingdom. He will gather all the nations of the earth (cf. Matt. 13:30, 39-41, 49-50), separate them (cf. Matt. 13:49), and pass judgment.

This judgment is said to issue in *eternal* fire (v. 41) and *eternal* punishment (v. 46) for the "goats" (the unsaved) and *eternal* life (v. 46) for the "sheep" (the saved). The problem this poses for premillennialism is obvious. As noted above, premillennialism believes this judgment occurs *before* the millennial age and is distinct from the Great White Throne judgment of Revelation 20:11-15 which occurs *after* the millennial age. But also as noted above, and is obvious from a reading of the text, the goats (the unsaved) go into the *eternal* (lake of) fire: "Depart from me, you cursed, into the eternal fire prepared for the devil and his angels" (v. 41), which in verse 46 is defined further as *eternal punishment*.

How can this be, when the premillennialist insists that the judgment which results in the lake of fire occurs *after* the millennial kingdom, 1,000 years following Christ's return in glory (Rev. 20:15)? There are two ways the premillennialist can respond to this difficulty.

First, he can argue that Matthew does not intend to suggest that Christ casts the goats into eternal fire *when* he returns in glory.

161

But how, then, should we account for the text which declares that "when" (*hotan*) the Son of Man comes in glory, "then" (*tote*) he will gather the nations, separate them, and pass judgment?

One way of dealing with this problem is to argue that there are, in fact, *two* different introductions into God's kingdom (in the case of the saved) and into eternal fire (in the case of the unsaved). That is to say, a premillennialist might suggest that the goats are judged before the millennium and at that time cast into eternal fire. Then, after the millennium, they are pulled out of eternal fire, judged yet again, and then cast back in. Likewise, he would have to argue that the sheep are granted entrance into *eternal life* before the millennium, and then again at its close. Dare I say that this sort of "exegesis" speaks for itself? It is indicative of the baseless duplication of eschatological events required to sustain belief in a post-parousia millennial kingdom.

The passage makes perfectly good (dare I say, literal) sense if interpreted to say that at the second coming of Christ the lost are judged and cast into eternal fire, to be punished eternally (v. 46), whereas the saved are granted entrance into eternal life, God's eternal kingdom, which has been prepared for them from the foundation of the world. The "Sheep/Goat Judgment" of Matthew 25 and the "Great White Throne Judgment" of Revelation 20, therefore, are one and the same, each described in different but complementary terms, occurring at the time of the second coming of Christ.

There is one other alternative for the premillennialist, as articulated by Robert Gundry. Gundry concedes that this judgment is the final one, identical with that judgment we see in Revelation 20:11-15 which will occur at the close of the millennial age, and that it is eternity, either of life or death, of blessedness or punishment, into which the sheep and goats enter respectively. He then suggests this solution to escape from the problem posed by verse 31 which appears to link this judgment with Christ's second coming *before* the millennial age:

A gap may intervene between the second coming and this judgment: "But when the Son of Man comes in His glory, and all the angels with Him, [millennium] then He will sit on His glorious throne." Or, "He will sit on His glorious throne. [Millennium] And all the nations will be gathered before Him." ... But better yet, the statement, "He will sit on His glorious throne," itself summarizes the millennial reign of Christ.[19]

Although Gundry's suggestion is slightly more plausible than the other noted above, it does not sufficiently bear the weight of Christ's words. Note well that "when" the Son of Man comes, "then" he will engage in a series of interrelated activities. These activities are logically and temporally successive. They sequentially build upon one another. When he comes, then he will sit ... and the nations will be gathered ... and he will separate ... and he will put ... then he will say, etc. It seems unduly strained to suggest that the gathering of the nations and all that subsequently follows is not to occur *when* our Lord returns but only 1,000 years *after* he initially sits on his glorious throne.

2 Thessalonians 1:5-10

[5]This is evidence of the righteous judgment of God, that you may be considered worthy of the kingdom of God, for which you are also suffering – [6]since indeed God considers it just to repay with affliction those who afflict you, [7]and to grant relief to you who are afflicted as well as to us, when the Lord Jesus is revealed from heaven with his mighty angels [8]in flaming fire, inflicting vengeance on those who do not know God and on those who do not obey the gospel of our Lord Jesus. [9]They will suffer the punishment of eternal destruction, away from the presence of the Lord and from the glory of his might, [10]when he comes on that day to be glorified in his saints, and to be marveled at among all who have believed, because our testimony to you was believed.

The conclusions drawn from Matthew 25 are reaffirmed in 2 Thessalonians 1. This passage also indicates that *it is at the time of Christ's second coming/advent, not 1,000 years later, that the eternal punishment of the lost occurs.*

---

19. Robert Gundry, *The Church and the Tribulation* (Grand Rapids: Eerdmans, 1973), 168.

When does the eternal destruction of the unsaved occur? When shall they pay the penalty of eternal destruction away from the presence of the Lord? Paul's answer is: "*when* he comes *on that day* to be glorified in his saints" (v. 10; emphasis mine). The climactic and final punishment of the lost is not reserved for a judgment 1,000 years after Christ's return, but is *simultaneous* with it. And since this judgment is elsewhere said to follow the millennium (Rev. 20:11-15), the millennium itself must be coterminous with the present age.[20]

John 5:28-29

[28]Do not marvel at this, for an hour is coming when all who are in the tombs will hear his voice [29]and come out, those who have done good to the resurrection of life, and those who have done evil to the resurrection of judgment.

An hour is coming *when* (lit., "in which") *all* who are in the tombs, i.e., the physically dead, whether believer or unbeliever, shall hear his voice and come forth in the resurrection.

The premillennialist, however, is unable to accept this straightforward declaration. He insists that a 1,000-year earthly reign of Christ must intervene between the resurrection of believers and the resurrection of unbelievers. He points to John 5:25 where the word "hour" encompasses the whole of this present age. Why, then, can't the "hour" in verse 28 also span the 1,000 years of a millennial age? Anthony Hoekema answers this question:

First, in order to be parallel to what is said in verse 25, the resurrection of believers and unbelievers should then be taking place throughout this thousand-year period, as is the case with the regeneration of people during the "hour" mentioned in verse 25. But, according to the theory under discussion (Premillennialism), this is not the case; rather this theory teaches that there will be one resurrection at the beginning of

---

20. An excellent and extended treatment of this text as it bears on all eschatological views is provided by Vern S. Poythress, "2 Thessalonians 1 Supports Amillennialism," in *JETS* 37/4 (1995):529-38.

the thousand years and another at the end. Of this, however, there is not a hint in this passage. Further, note the words "all who are in the tombs will hear his voice." The reference would seem to be to a general resurrection of all who are in their graves; it is straining the meaning of these words to make them describe two groups (or four groups) of people who will be raised at separate times. Moreover, this passage states specifically that all these dead will hear the voice of the Son of Man. The clear implication seems to be that this voice will be sounded once, not two times or four times. If the word "hour" is interpreted as standing for a period of a thousand years plus, this would imply that the voice of Jesus keeps sounding for a thousand years. Does this seem likely?[21]

No, it doesn't.

My conclusion is that when we examine what the New Testament says will occur at the time of the second coming/advent of Jesus Christ, there is no place for a 1,000 year earthly reign to follow. At the time of the second coming there will occur the final resurrection, the final judgment, the end of sin, the end of death, and the creation of the new heavens and new earth. As Peter has said, "Therefore, beloved, since you are waiting for these [things], be diligent to be found by him without spot or blemish, and at peace" (2 Pet. 3:14).

An Amillennial Response to Miscellaneous Premillennial Arguments

In a recent volume on the second coming of Christ, noted author and theologian Craig Blaising articulated additional arguments in favor of premillennialism that warrant consideration.[22] Blaising's first argument for premillennialism is an appeal to several Old Testament passages that he believes portray a phase of the kingdom

---

21. Hoekema, *The Bible and the Future*, 241.
22. Blaising's chapter, "The Kingdom that comes with Jesus: Premillennialism and the Harmony of Scripture" (pp. 141-59), can be found in the book, *The Return of Christ: A Premillennial Perspective*, edited by David L. Allen and Steve W. Lemke (Nashville: B & H Academic, 2011). This chapter appeared in a somewhat shorter form in *The Southern Baptist Journal of Theology* 14 (Spring 2010):4-13.

on earth that is subsequent to the return of Christ but anteced-ent to the final judgment and the inauguration of the new heav-ens and new earth. Such texts envision a time where the sin and rebellion of humans is judged and physical death is still present. Blaising does not believe this is descriptive of the present church age and insists that the eternal state cannot be in view (after all, everyone agrees that in the eternal state all sin and death will be altogether absent).

One such text is Isaiah 65:17-20. In spite of the fact that Isaiah explicitly identifies this time period as the new heavens and new earth (a not insignificant point that Blaising altogether ignores), and in spite of the fact that, as Blaising himself acknowledges, "the language is similar to Revelation 21," [23] which all agree refers to the eternal state, he insists this is descriptive of an earthly phase of the kingdom following Christ's return and preceding eternity. He does this because he believes that otherwise Isaiah 65 would contradict Isaiah 25:7-9. Both texts, he argues, cannot refer to the eternal state. After all, in the latter text "death will be no more," [24] whereas in the former text death is still present. Blaising believes the only way to resolve this conflict is to argue that Isaiah 65 describes the millen-nial phase of God's kingdom preceding the eternal state (in spite of the fact that Isaiah calls it the eternal state, i.e., the new heav-ens and new earth), while Isaiah 25 describes the eternal phase of God's kingdom. But no such differentiation is needed.

First, note carefully that Blaising's appeal to Isaiah 25:7-9 as descriptive of conditions in the new heavens and new earth actually contradicts and precludes premillennialism altogether. As we saw earlier in this chapter, the Apostle Paul, in 1 Corinthians 15:50-57, describes for us what will happen at the second coming of Christ. No one denies this. Yet in doing so, he explicitly declares that when Christ returns and "when the perishable puts on immortality, *then* (emphasis mine) shall come to pass the saying that is written: 'Death is swallowed up in victory.' 'O death, where is your victory?

---

23. Blaising, 143.
24. Ibid. 144.

O death, where is your sting?'" (1 Cor. 15:54b-55). In other words, for Paul the death of death, the termination of all physical suffering and human mortality, occurs at the time of the return of Christ and the resurrection of the body. *At that time, says Paul, Isaiah 25:7-9 (he specifically quotes v. 8) will be fulfilled. "Death will be swallowed up in victory" at the time of the second coming. No physical death can occur after the second coming. If it could, Paul would be wrong in saying that death is swallowed up in victory, in fulfillment of Isaiah 25, at the moment of the second coming.*

Blaising is asking us to believe that Isaiah 25:7-9 describes events and conditions 1,000 years subsequent to the second coming, in the eternal state, which is to say in the new heavens and new earth. I agree with Blaising that it describes the eternal state, the new heavens and new earth, but Paul, contra Blaising, places this *at the time of the second coming.* The point, quite simply again, is that there is no place in Paul's scheme for a 1,000-year interregnum between the return of Christ (when death is "swallowed up in victory") and the new heavens and new earth.

So once again, in simpler terms (I hope!), here is what Paul is saying. When "the trumpet will sound, and the dead will be raised imperishable, and we shall be changed" (1 Cor. 15:52), all of which occurs at the second coming, Isaiah 25:7-9 will be fulfilled: Death will be swallowed up in victory! Blaising is correct in saying this Old Testament passage describes the end or termination of all death. But Blaising is clearly wrong in placing death's death 1,000 years *after* Christ's return, for the Apostle Paul places it *simultaneous with* Christ's return. Therefore, I'm left with the only obvious conclusion: there can be no millennial kingdom, in which physical death continues to exist, intervening between the coming of Christ and the coming of eternity. Why? Because Paul says so!

Let's return for a moment to this alleged inconsistency between Isaiah 25 and Isaiah 65. Yes, it is true that the prophet in chapter 25 envisioned the eternal state as one in which death was altogether absent. Yes, it is true that the prophet in chapter 65 portrayed the eternal state (he himself calls it the new heavens and new earth) as one in which death appears to be present. But note carefully that Isaiah does not merely assert that physical death will exist in the new heavens and new earth. Rather he portrays conditions in which "no more shall there be in it an infant who lives but a few days, or an old man who does not fill out his days, for the young man shall die a hundred years old, and the sinner a hundred years old shall be accursed" (v. 20). I earlier explained in Chapter One why Isaiah chose to speak in such terms, and I urge you to go back and read again my comments. Here I would simply say that it is not at all the case that Isaiah is incapable of envisioning a scenario in which physical death is altogether absent. Clearly chapter 25 indicates that he can. Rather, the prophet is seeking a way to communicate vividly and effectively to a people who were constantly burdened with the anguish of premature infant death and the sorrows that it invariably would bring. He is, in effect, saying: "People, can you imagine a time and place where if someone were to only live 100 years we would all lament the fact that he/she had died so young?" We need *not* insist that Isaiah is saying, "Yes, and in literal fact, people in that time *will* die prematurely at age 100." Isaiah is simply doing what not only other biblical authors but we today do as well: he is using the idealized language of the present to portray in terms intelligible to the people of his day the reality of future glory in the age to come. He may not be describing it in as exalted and exhaustive terms as he is capable, but why should we insist that he do so?

Walter Kaiser's attempt to account for the language of Isaiah 65 is even less persuasive. He is certainly correct in pointing out that "the point of Isaiah 65:20-24 is that in the future one may disregard any thoughts of an untimely death." [25] But rather than embrace the explanation proposed above, he argues that the "Jerusalem" of verses 20-24 is different from the "Jerusalem" of verses 17-19. Although nothing in the text even remotely suggests that the prophet had such a radical distinction in mind, Kaiser insists that in verses 17-19 "Jerusalem" refers to the renewed city of the eternal state, whereas in verses 20-24 "Jerusalem" refers to a millennial city. He says this, mind you, in

25. Walter C. Kaiser, Jr., *Preaching and Teaching the Last Things: Old Testament Eschatology for the Life of the Church* (Grand Rapids: Baker Academic, 2011), 160.

spite of the fact that the antecedent of "it" in verse 20 (the Jerusalem where Kaiser insists death will continue to reign) is the "Jerusalem" of the new heavens and new earth described in verses 17-19. "No more shall there be in *it* an infant who lives but a few days, or an old man who does not fill out his days," etc. The reference is to the "Jerusalem" of the "new heavens" and "new earth" (vv. 17-19). Why, then, does he make this proposal? It would appear that he comes to this prophecy in Isaiah already committed to premillennialism and imposes the latter upon the text, forcing it to conform to a preconceived eschatological scenario.

Blaising also refers to Isaiah 11:4 where God "strikes the earth with the rod of his mouth." He believes this "indicates the presence of rebellious activity not in keeping with the eternal kingdom order in which sin is absent."[26] But why does he conclude that it must therefore describe what will occur in the millennial kingdom? Because he *needs* it to! He actually concedes that whereas "it is possible that the reference to the rod in Isa 11:4 refers to the definitive final judgment, more likely it is to be understood as a general feature within the overall description of the messianic reign."[27] Why is this "more likely"? It is "more likely" not for any obvious exegetical or theological reasons but because otherwise Blaising loses another potentially premillennial Old Testament text! The fact is, Isaiah 11:4 falls within a larger context that describes the characteristics of the coming Messiah, a passage that Jesus himself cites and applies to his own person and work in the first century (see Luke 4:16ff.)! Thus the sort of judgment that is portrayed in verse 4 (in highly figurative language I might add: Isaiah speaks of the "rod" of Messiah's mouth and of his killing the wicked "with the breath of his lips," terms that no one would insist on taking in a physically literal sense) could easily be what the reigning Lord Jesus exercises throughout the course of the present church age as well as the judgment that he will inflict at the time of his second coming. The only reason anyone might argue that it must or even likely describes the sort of judgment that will

26. Blaising, 144.
27. Ibid.

occur in an intermediate messianic kingdom is because they need Old Testament texts that warrant belief in the existence of such. But nothing in the text itself justifies interpreting it in such a fashion.

Other alleged Purposes of an Earthly Millennial Kingdom

One of the arguments often found among premillennialists is that a 1,000-year earthly millennium following the second coming of Christ is necessary in order for God's kingdom to appear in *history* prior to the eternal state. To be sure, a millennium of this sort *would* disclose a phase of God's kingdom prior to its consummation in the new heavens and new earth. But that is altogether different from saying that God's kingdom would fail of its purpose or be in some sense deprived of the end for which God ordained it if there were no earthly millennium. The Bible distinguishes between "this age" and "the age to come," but there is no indication that it does so in order that God's kingdom might have an earthly fulfillment in the former, antecedent to the latter.

The historic premillennialist insists there are other reasons why a millennium is necessary. Alan Johnson, for example, in addition to the argument just noted, mentions three other factors which give meaning and purpose to a millennial age. He says that "the Millennium will reveal that man's rebellion against God lies deep in man's own heart, not in the devil's deception. Even when Satan is bound and righteousness prevails in the world, some people will still rebel against God. The final release of Satan will openly draw out this hidden evil."[28] Again, I readily concede that a millennium in which Satan is bound until its end *would* reveal the depths of human sin. But I see nothing in Scripture, not even in Revelation 20, which demands that this fact be revealed in precisely this way. In other words, if there should be no earthly millennium in which this might occur, is there anyone who for that reason might argue that man is *not* inherently sinful or that Satanic deception is the real cause of our rebellion? We know that "man's rebellion

---

28. Alan F. Johnson, *Revelation*, The Expositor's Bible Commentary (Grand Rapids: Zondervan, 1981), 581.

against God lies deep within man's heart, not in the devil's deception" from what both Scripture and experience already tell us. The certainty of that truth and our knowledge of it are not portrayed anywhere in Scripture as dependent on a millennial age in which it may be visibly demonstrated.

Johnson goes on to suggest that "the release of Satan after the Millennium shows the invulnerability of the city of God and the extent of the authority of Christ, since the devil is immediately defeated and cast into the lake of fire forever." [29] But again, where in Scripture does it say that a millennium is necessary if we are to be convinced of the invulnerability of the city of God? That God's city is invulnerable and that Christ's authority is extensive are certainly marvelous truths. But we know this from countless texts of Scripture wholly unrelated to any notion of a future earthly millennial age. In other words, what a millennium might accomplish *if* it were to exist is irrelevant, unless that goal cannot be accomplished or that truth cannot be establish apart from an earthly millennium.

Finally, Johnson says that "the Millennium will serve as a long period required to do the general 'housecleaning' needed after the preceding ages of sin, during which sin was prevalent." [30] I beg to differ. Why, and on the basis of what biblical texts concerning either the nature of God or the present age, is it "required" that there be a millennium if sin is to be removed from the cosmos? If God has determined to do so, he is certainly capable of "cleaning house" in a millisecond. To suggest that a millennium is required for God to rid the earth of sin is ludicrous. Are we to believe that an extended period is required for the general housecleaning of our bodies simply because we have lived in sin for many years? Obviously not, for Paul says that this transformation will occur "in a moment, in the twinkling of an eye" (1 Cor. 15:52). Assuming that he is willing, God is certainly able to destroy the present heavens and earth, along with its sin, and create the new heavens and earth in a moment, in the twinkling of an eye (cf. 2 Pet. 3:10).

---

29. Ibid.
30. Ibid.

Premillennialism and the Early Church

One final issue that is all too often brought up is that premillennialism was the dominant position embraced by the early church fathers. Walter C. Kaiser is typical in this regard when he says that "nearly everybody will agree that the major millennial view of the early church in its first three or so centuries was a premillennial position."[31] Or again, David Allen declares categorically: "Premillennialism was the dominant position among the ante-Nicene church fathers."[32] I've become accustomed to such sweeping statements, but am not persuaded by them.

Whenever the issue of church history is brought up, one particular resource is typically cited. Alan Patrick Boyd wrote his Th.M. thesis for Dallas Theological Seminary on the theme: "A Dispensational Premillennial Analysis of the Eschatology of the Post-Apostolic Fathers (until the Death of Justin Martyr)."[33] As it turns out, Boyd and I were classmates at DTS, both majored in historical theology, and graduated together in 1977. I have a copy of Boyd's thesis and have read it on numerous occasions.

Those who appeal to Boyd's thesis have often failed to grasp both its purpose and the conclusions to which he ultimately came. Boyd's intent was to determine whether or not Christian authors in the time frame he studied affirmed or were even aware of the dispensational premillennial perspective advocated by DTS professors Charles Ryrie and John Walvoord. More specifically, "the purpose of this thesis is to determine whether Dr Ryrie's 'premillennialism' is similar to, or dissimilar to, the premillennialism exhibited in some of the patristic writings under consideration."[34]

---

31. Walter Kaiser, *Preaching and Teaching the Last Things,* 143.

32. David Allen, "The Millennial Reign of Christ," in *The Return of Christ: A Premillennial Perspective,* edited by David L. Allen & Steve W. Lemke (Nashville: B & H Academic, 2011), 75.

33. Submitted to the faculty of the Department of Historical Theology in May of 1977.

34. Alan Patrick Boyd, "A Dispensational Premillennial Analysis of the Post-Apostolic Fathers (until the Death of Justin Martyr)," Th.M. thesis, Dallas Theological Seminary, 1977, 2.

After a close examination of authors prior to Papias (specifically, 1 Clement, 2 Clement, the Epistle of Barnabas, the Didache, Ignatius, and Hegesippus), Boyd discovered that the "differences" between them and the premillennial construct of Ryrie are "profound, and disqualify any claim that pretribulational, dispensational premillennialism existed *in any form* in the period."[35] Such authors did not employ a consistently literal interpretation of the biblical text and a distinction between Israel and the Church is missing. Dispensationalism, as articulated by contemporary authors, is absent. In sum, "it is quite evident that traces of modern pretribulational, dispensational premillennialism simply did not exist in the immediate post-apostolic period."[36]

Boyd then turns his attention to Papias (c. 70–155), whom he describes as "the first <u>orthodox</u> chiliast."[37] Although Papias was assuredly a premillennialist, he "did not perceive the Millennium to be the climax of God's dealings with Israel,… did not apply a consistently literal interpretation;… [and] did not have a concept of a secret rapture."[38] Boyd's conclusion is that the premillennialism of Papias "was of a markedly different character than the modern variety [of Ryrie and Walvoord] used as a construct for this thesis."[39]

The Shepherd of Hermas, Polycarp, and Aristides, the immediate predecessors of Justin Martyr, are then examined. The fragmentary remains of Aristides make it impossible to determine with certainty what he believed. As for the writings of Hermas and Polycarp, "1). there is no concept of the Rapture, 2). the resurrection of believers occurs at the inception of the Kingdom, 3). there is no imminency to the Second Advent, 4). there is an eschatological Tribulation through which the Church will pass, 5). the Kingdom is the completed Church, not the culmination of YHWH's work with Israel, 6). the Church and Israel are not consistently distinguished and 7). a consistently applied literal interpretation is not employed."[40] Boyd's

---

35. Ibid., 49.
36. Ibid., 50.
37. Ibid., 52.
38. Ibid., 62.
39. Ibid.
40. Ibid., 72.

conclusion is that "claims for chiliasm/premillennialism being existent in Hermas and Polycarp are historically unfounded."[41]

An entire chapter is then devoted to the eschatology of Justin Martyr (c. 100–165). Although Justin affirms the existence of an earthly millennium, he applies "aspects of the national promises [given to Israel] to Christians, and not the Jews. For example, he claims that the Jews will not inherit anything promised to Abraham. Instead, the land of Israel will be given to the Christians for an eternal inheritance, because Christians are the nation promised to Abraham. In line with this, he claims that the Church is the true Israelite race, thereby blurring the distinction between Israel and the Church."[42] It is apparent, Boyd concludes, "that the eschatology of Justin Martyr and of dispensational premillennialism are radically dissimilar."[43]

Boyd's careful analysis thus led him to the conclusion that Ryrie's claim that "Premillennialism is the historic faith of the Church"[44] is invalid. The reasons for this conclusion are that the writers in the period studied "did not generally adopt a consistently applied literal interpretation;... [and] did not generally distinguish between the Church and Israel." There is no evidence "that they generally held to a dispensational view of revealed history;... [and] although Papias and Justin Martyr did believe in a Millennial kingdom, the 1,000 years is the only basic similarity with the modern system (in fact, they and dispensational premillennialism radically differ on the basis for the Millennium);... they had no concept of imminency or of a pretribulational Rapture of the Church;... in general, their eschatological chronology is not synonymous with that of the modern system. Indeed, this thesis would conclude that the eschatological beliefs of the period studied would be generally inimical to those of the modern system (perhaps, seminal amillennialism,

---

41. Ibid.
42. Ibid., 85-86.
43. Ibid., 86.
44. Charles C. Ryrie, *The Basis of the Premillennial Faith* (Neptune, NJ: Loiseaux Brothers, 1953), 17.

and not nascent dispensational premillennialism ought to be seen in the eschatology of the period)."[45]

Charles E. Hill has also written a magisterial treatment of eschatology among the early church fathers, *Regnum Caelorum: Patterns of Millennial Thought in Early Christianity*, second edition (Grand Rapids: Eerdmans, 2001), which directly conflicts with and counters the claims of premillennialists like Kaiser.[46] Hill has identified several prominent figures among the Apostolic Fathers who were *not* premillennial (or "chiliastic," as Hill prefers). Among them are Clement of Rome, Ignatius of Antioch, Polycarp of Smyrna, Hermas, and the author of 2 Clement. Turning to three prominent second-century Apologists, the author of the Epistle to Diognetus, Melito of Sardis, and Athenagoras, Hill "looks in vain for any clear indication of a chiliastic [premillennial] expectation."[47] Likewise, none of the Christian pseudepigraphical writings of the second and early third centuries show "any sure sign of being chiliastic" in their "view of future history and the coming of Christ."[48] These would include the *Ascension of Isaiah,* the *Apocalypse of Peter, 5 Ezra,* the *Epistula Apostolorum,* as well as the Syrian Pseudipigrapha: *Odes of Solomon; Acts of Thomas;* and the Abgar Legend.

The literature that documented early Christian martyrdoms also betrays the absence of any form of premillennialism. These would include the Confession of Jude's Grandsons, the *Martyrdom of Polycarp,* the *Martyrdom of Justin,* the *Epistle of Vienne and Lyons,* and the *Acts of the Scillitan Martyrs.* Scholars have long held that the Montanists were proponents of premillennialism and that their excesses contributed greatly to the demise of chiliasm in the early church. Hill challenges this, but is modest in his conclusion,

---

45. Boyd, 89-91.
46. In addition to Hill's book and Boyd's thesis, an excellent treatment of the historical evidence is provided by Gary DeMar and Francis X. Gumerlock, "Premillennialism and the Early Church," in *The Early Church and the End of the World* (Powder Springs, GA: American Vision, 2006), 39-64.
47. Charles E. Hill, *Regnum Caelorum: Patterns of Millennial Thought in Early Christianity,* second edition (Grand Rapids: Eerdmans, 2001), 108.
48. Ibid., 109.

suggesting that "if the evidence that the early Montanists held a non-chiliastic [i.e., amillennial] eschatology is not fully conclusive, it is still stronger than the evidence for the alternative [i.e., premillennialism]."[49] Indeed, "in all probability, the original New Prophets were not chiliasts."[50] Hippolytus, Clement of Alexandria, Origen, and Cyprian were all committed amillennialists.

Does any of this prove either millennial position? No. Alan Boyd's exhortation in this regard is well-taken: "... one cannot *assume* the truthfulness of his eschatological position simply because there are adumbrations of it in the patristic writings. Conversely, a modern eschatological position *can not* [*sic*] be demonstrated to be in error simply because there are no adumbrations of it in the patristic writings."[51] In brief, we are ultimately subject to the final authority of Scripture and not to the individual or collective views of anyone in the course of church history.

---

49. Ibid., 153.
50. Ibid., 159.
51. Boyd, Preface.

Chapter Six

Who are the People of God? Israel, the Church, and "Replacement" Theology

A friend once wrote to me asking my opinion on whether or not the modern state of Israel has a biblical right to the Holy Land. That is to say, can Israel appeal to the covenant made with Abraham, Isaac, and Jacob as grounds for their presence in and possession of the land of Palestine? My friend wondered if the view I espouse is what many have called "Replacement" theology. Let me take this opportunity to address the point.

I want to make an appeal to all who engage in this debate that we do so with civility and generosity towards those with whom we disagree. I make this request because I have noticed that to disagree with what has come to be known as "Christian Zionism" exposes one either to the charge of anti-Semitism or a demonically induced blindness. I hope we can all agree that this is an issue that requires careful and patient examination of the Scriptures and a willingness to dialogue with an open mind.

All of us are by now familiar with the comments of the president of Iran, Mahmoud Ahmadinejad, who has repeatedly called for Israel to be "wiped off the map." He has also denounced attempts to recognize Israel or normalize relations with her. In one article I read the Iranian president declared that "anybody who recognizes Israel will burn in the fire of the Islamic nation's fury." After numerous heads of state denounced the Iranian president for these comments, mass demonstrations broke out in Iranian cities that expressed rage and contempt for the existence of the nation of Israel.

Let me be perfectly clear. As an American, I hope and pray that all American citizens and all other peoples, whether Christian or not, would stand firmly in their opposition to this sort of evil and irresponsible rhetoric. I believe that Israel has every right to exist and flourish as a nation, and I hope that the United States will maintain its vigilance in defense of Israel against all such Islamic threats and future attacks. Clearly, then, I believe Israel has a right to exist in the land and that we have a moral and political obligation to stand with her against all enemies. But this is not the same as saying that Israel has a *biblical* or *covenantal* right to the territory over which so much blood has been shed in recent years (indeed, in recent centuries). Nor does it address the question of what role, if any, the "promised land" will have in God's redemptive purposes for his people and this earth. To that particular issue, I now turn.

Searching the Scriptures

First, when God established his covenant in Genesis 12, he affirmed that the *seed* (some translations render it "offspring") of Abraham would inherit the land of Canaan (among other things) in fulfillment of the promise. But we must never read such promises, or anything in the Old Testament, as if Jesus had not come and the New Testament had not been written. Or to put it in more positive terms, the Old Testament must always be read in light of the New. I never read such Old Testament texts without immediately asking, "Does the New Testament shed additional light on how I am to understand the nature of such promises and their recipients?"

There are several texts that shed considerable light on how we are to understand the covenant made with Abraham and his progeny.

(1) Consider **Romans 9:6-7**. There the Apostle Paul writes: "But it is not as though the word of God has failed. For not all who are descended from Israel belong to Israel, and not all are children of Abraham because they are his offspring, but 'Through Isaac shall your offspring be named.'"

The context of this passage is Paul's response to the charge that God cannot be trusted because so many Israelites, his "kinsmen according to the flesh" (9:3), are in unbelief. If God cannot be trusted to fulfill his covenant promise to Old Testament Israel, how can he be trusted to fulfill any of his promises to the New Testament Church? Or again, we could put it this way: If Israel is God's covenant people, to whom so many glorious privileges have been given (Rom. 9:4-5), why are so few Israelites saved? Why are so many of them "accursed, separated from Christ"? Has God's word failed? Have God's covenant promise and eternal purpose come to nothing? Has the rejection of Jesus Christ by the majority of Israelites thwarted God's purpose? Have the trustworthiness and finality of God's word been undermined by the unbelief of so many Jews? His response to the question is a resounding *No!*

If God's word of promise and covenant is that *all ethnic* Israelites, i.e., all those who are physically descended from Israel, are to be saved, then clearly his purpose *has* failed and his word *is* void. But Paul denies that God *ever* intended to save all ethnic Israelites. His purpose has always been to save a remnant within, but not the entirety of, ethnic Israel. This is the force of his declaration that "not all who are descended from Israel belong to Israel" (9:6). Paul's point is that there is an *Israel* within Israel. There is a *spiritually elect remnant* within the *physically ethnic nation.* John Murray explains:

> The purpose of this distinction is to show that the covenantal promise of God did not have respect to Israel after the flesh but to this *true* Israel and that, therefore, the unbelief and rejection of ethnic Israel as a whole in no way interfered with the fulfillment of God's covenant purpose and promise. The word of God, therefore, has not been violated.[1]

Simply put: *Not every person who is a physically ethnic Israelite is a spiritually elect Israelite.* Douglas Moo summarizes this way:

> If the OT teaches that belonging to physical Israel in itself makes a person a member of God's true spiritual people, then Paul's gospel is

1. John Murray, *The Epistle to the Romans* (Grand Rapids: Eerdmans, 1965), II:10.

in jeopardy. For were this the case, the gospel, proclaiming that only those who believe in Jesus Christ can be saved (cf. 3:20-26), would contradict the OT and be cut off from its indispensable historical roots. Paul therefore argues in [Romans 9] vv. 6b-29 that belonging to God's true spiritual people has always been based on God's gracious and sovereign call and not on ethnic identity. Therefore, God is free to "narrow" the apparent boundaries of election by choosing only some Jews to be saved (vv. 6-13; 27-29). He is also free to "expand" the dimensions of his people by choosing Gentiles (vv. 24-26).[2]

Thus we see that the initial promise in Genesis 12 did not mean that all physical descendants of Abraham, Isaac, and Jacob would be saved or inherit the blessings, such as the land, entailed by that covenant. We must remember, says Paul (with added paraphrase), that "not all who are descended from Israel [i.e., the physical seed] belong to Israel [i.e., the spiritual seed], and not all are children of Abraham [which is to say, heirs of the promise] because they are his [physical or ethnic] offspring" (9:6b-7).

(2) Romans 9:6-7 isn't the only passage that provides clarification concerning the identity of "true" Israel, which is to say, the people for whom the covenant promises will be fulfilled. Perhaps the most explicit text is found in **Ephesians 2:11-22**.

In my second year at Dallas Seminary I took a course in the Greek exegesis of Ephesians. One of the requirements for the class was an exegetical paper on a particular paragraph of the book that was assigned at random. I was given Ephesians 2:11-22, where Paul writes:

> Therefore remember that at one time you Gentiles in the flesh, called "the uncircumcision" by what is called the circumcision, which is made in the flesh by hands – remember that you were at that time separated from Christ, alienated from the commonwealth of Israel and strangers to the covenants of promise, having no hope and without

<hr>

2. Douglas J. Moo, *The Epistle to the Romans* (Grand Rapids: Eerdmans, 1996), 568-69.

God in the world. But now in Christ Jesus you who once were far off have been brought near by the blood of Christ. For he himself is our peace, who has made us both one and has broken down in his flesh the dividing wall of hostility by abolishing the law of commandments and ordinances, that he might create in himself one new man in place of the two, so making peace, and might reconcile us both to God in one body through the cross, thereby killing the hostility. And he came and preached peace to you who were far off and peace to those who were near. For through him we both have access in one Spirit to the Father. So then you are no longer strangers and aliens, but you are fellow citizens with the saints and members of the household of God, built on the foundation of the apostles and prophets, Christ Jesus himself being the cornerstone, in whom the whole structure, being joined together, grows into a holy temple in the Lord. In him you also are being built together into a dwelling place for God by the Spirit.

As we saw in an earlier chapter, dispensationalism is built on the belief that Israel and the Church are two separate peoples of God, each with its own covenant promises. I never questioned this until I began to dig deeply into this text in Ephesians 2. The context of this paragraph and its relation to what precedes is important. In 2:1-10 Paul explained the meaning and spiritual dynamics of salvation in relation to the individual, whether Jew or Gentile. Death in sin is common to all, irrespective of ethnic origin (2:1-3). Likewise, none is saved but by the grace of God in Christ (2:4-10).

This salvation of the individual, however, also has social and corporate implications. The redemptive work of Christ has forever abolished the inequalities that once existed between Jew and Gentile. The latter, at one time both physically and spiritually far away from the blessings of God, have now been brought near. Christ has abolished the barrier that not only separated God from Gentile but also Jew from Gentile. Through the blood of Christ the believing Gentile has been incorporated as a fellow-citizen into the household of God, receiving equal status with the believing Jew, the two together forming one new man in Christ, the Church. In describing this great event, Paul first portrays the condition of the Gentiles before the cross (2:11-12). He then explains what Christ has done to reverse their lost condition (2:13-18), and finally he describes what we, as believing Gentiles, in conjunction with believing Jews, have become: the Church of Jesus Christ, a holy temple in the Lord (2:19-22).

Paul begins by describing the horrid and Christless condition of Gentiles during the period of the Old Testament. The so-called "uncircumcision" (v. 11) suffered a five-fold plight: they were (1) "separated from Christ," (2) "alienated from the commonwealth of Israel," (3) "strangers to the covenants of promise," (4) devoid of "hope", and (5) "without God in the world." Not a very pretty picture for non-Jews!

A closer look at Paul's language will help. The label "uncircumcised", used by Jews of Gentiles, was one of derision and scorn. Yet, referring to Jewish circumcision as "so-called" may be Paul's way of pointing to the worthlessness of the physical rite as a guarantee of acceptance with God (cf. Rom. 2:28-29; 1 Cor. 7:19; Phil. 3:3; Gal. 5:6 ["for in Christ Jesus neither circumcision nor uncircumcision means anything, but faith working through love"]).

The word translated "by human hands" (*cheiropoietos*) and its opposite are used in the New Testament to contrast what is made by humans with what is made by God. It also points to the contrast between the external material aspects of the old order of Judaism under the Mosaic covenant and the internal spiritual efficacy of the new order under the new covenant (Mark 14:58; Acts 7:48; 17:24; Heb. 9:11, 24). Thus, to speak of something "not made by human hands" (*acheiropoietos*) is to assert that God himself has created it (e.g., the temple that Jesus would build in three days in Mark 14:58; the heavenly house [i.e., body] which believers receive at death in 2 Cor. 5:1; and that true, spiritual circumcision of the heart which comes through the death of Christ in Col. 2:11). Paul's point is that the circumcision performed in the flesh with human hands is no longer the real or spiritually meaningful circumcision.

The word translated "separate" is used in only two other places (Eph. 4:18; Col. 1:21) and means alienation or estrangement from

God. But now those once so described are "in Christ"! The question is raised: How can it be that having been separate from Christ is parallel to having been separated from Israel? It would appear that Paul "can make this point because he conceives of Christ as the Messiah belonging to Israel [or, as Best says, 'the Messiah for whom Israel hoped'[3]]. His thought here, and later in this verse, appears to be dependent on Rom. 9:4,5, where Paul could say 'and of their race, according to the flesh, is the Christ.'"[4]

The word "commonwealth" conveys the idea not only of a state or government but even more so of the rights extending to its citizens, i.e., privileges, blessings, resources, duties, etc. During the time of the old covenant God had restricted his elective purposes to Israel, but now, with the coming and cross of Christ, believing Gentiles are "fellow-citizens" (v. 19).

Perhaps even more significant is Paul's reference to the "covenants of promise." The plural "covenants" points to a series of covenants: with Abraham (Gen. 15; 17), Isaac (Gen. 26:2-5), Jacob (Gen. 28:13-15), and David (2 Sam. 7). These covenants were all characterized by or based on "promise," namely, God's pledge to be faithful to his people and to fulfill his word to them. One might even translate the phrase, "the covenants which embodied the promise" of God. Though Gentiles had no part in this promise they are now co-heirs with Christ. As if all this weren't enough, Gentiles were also without hope or God in the world. In sum: they were "Christless, stateless, friendless, hopeless, and Godless."[5]

But verse 13 makes the startling assertion that "now," because of what Christ has accomplished, Gentile believers "have been brought near"! "Now" contrasts with "at that time" of v. 12. "In Christ" contrasts with "apart from Christ" of verse 12. "Near" and "far" have both a geographical or spatial as well as spiritual mean-

3. Ernest Best, *A Critical and Exegetical Commentary on Ephesians* (Edinburgh: T & T Clark, 1998), 241.
4. Andrew Lincoln, *Ephesians*, Word Biblical Commentary (Dallas: Word Books, 1990), 137.
5. William Hendriksen, *Ephesians* (Grand Rapids: Baker Book House, 1967), 129.

ing (see Deut. 4:7; Ps. 148:14; Dan. 9:7; Acts 2:39; 22:21). The *spatial* distance of the Gentiles was symbolic of their *spiritual* and *moral* separation as well (see Deut. 28:49; 29:22; 1 Kings 8:41; Isa. 5:26; Jer. 5:15).

To what have Gentiles been brought "near"? Certainly, near to Christ or to the salvation and forgiveness that his "blood" (v. 13) has obtained. But as I examined this passage more closely I began to realize that it wasn't simply salvation to which Gentiles had been brought near but *to the very things stated in verse 12 from which they had previously been separated.* In particular, Gentile believers have been incorporated into "the commonwealth of Israel" and made heirs of the "covenants of promise." More than that, by the work of Christ, God has made the two, that is, Jew and Gentile, into "one new man" (v. 15). Though surely separate and distinct before the coming of Jesus, Jewish believers and Gentile believers, since the coming of Jesus, have been made "one" (v. 14).

Initially, I thought that what Paul had in mind was the *spiritual unity* of Jew and Gentile in Christ. In other words, perhaps Paul was saying no more than that Gentiles are justified equally by grace through faith, no less so than Jews who believe in Jesus. They are "one" or equal only in the sense that salvation has now extended beyond the boundaries of Old Testament Israel to encompass people of any and every race who happen to trust Jesus for the forgiveness of sin. But Paul's language goes far beyond merely asserting the salvific equality of Jew and Gentile. I simply couldn't escape the fact that *Gentile believers are said to have been brought near not merely to Christ, hope, and God, but also to "the commonwealth of Israel" and "the covenants of promise"!* If that were not enough, Paul expands on this in verse 19 by saying that Gentile believers are "no longer strangers and aliens" (cf. the same language in v. 12) but are "fellow citizens and members of the household of God"! And if that weren't enough, in the verses that conclude the chapter Paul identifies all believers, both Jew and Gentile, as together constituting the true temple of God in whom the Holy Spirit is pleased to dwell.

All thoughts of Jewish superiority suddenly vanished. Any thought that being a Jew afforded one a greater privilege or share in the covenant established with Abraham, Isaac, and Jacob was shattered by the weight of Paul's momentous declaration. What formerly belonged exclusively to Jewish believers is now shared equally by Gentile believers. *So far as Paul is concerned, the ethnic categories of "Jew" and "Gentile" were no longer relevant to determining who would inherit what in the kingdom of God. The only thing that now matters is faith in Jesus Christ.* Anyone who believes, all who believe, together constitute "one new man," that is to say, the Church.

The reference to the "commonwealth of Israel" and the "covenants of promise" alerted me to the fact that whatever privileges and blessings they entailed were now equally shared by Gentile believers. Any thought of Jewish priority or some unique and separate inheritance couldn't explain Paul's language. The "one new man," i.e., the Church, in which both believing Jews and believing Gentiles were united by the blood of Christ, was heir to all the promises given to Abraham, Isaac, and Jacob. The dispensational idea that in the age to come Israel would hold privileged status and be the unique focus of God's eschatological activity and blessing was ruled out by this passage. *Whatever a believing Jew can point to in the Old Testament and say, "Mine," is no less the inheritance and future of a believing Gentile.*[6]

By "new man" Paul means the Christian community in its corporate identity, the Church. This new man is not simply an amal-

---

6. What I'm contending for is clearly contrary to the view of progressive dispensationalist Bruce Ware, for example, who insists that "Israel is given territorial and political aspects of the new-covenant promise not applicable to the church" ("The New Covenant and the People(s) of God," in *Dispensationalism, Israel and the Church*, edited by Craig A. Blaising and Darrell L. Bock [Grand Rapids: Zondervan, 1992], 96-97). Ware affirms that "Israel and the church are in fact one people of God, who together share in the forgiveness of sins through Christ and partake of his indwelling Spirit with its power for covenant faithfulness, while they are nonetheless distinguishable covenant participants comprising what is one unified people" (97). The primary factor that distinguishes them is the promise, unique and exclusive to Israel alone, of eventual restoration as a nation to its land. Needless to say, this is precisely the sort of distinction and exclusive promise that I believe Paul denies in Ephesians 2 and elsewhere.

gam of the old in which the best of Judaism and the best of the Gentile world are combined. This is a completely *new creation* in which distinctives of Jewishness and Gentileness are irrelevant. Thus, as Lincoln says, "they have not just been brought into a mutual relationship, but have been made one in a unity where both are no longer what they previously were (cf. vv. 15, 16, 18). In accomplishing this, Christ has transcended one of the fundamental divisions of the first-century world."[7] Therefore, it's not as though Gentiles are transformed into Jews or Jews into Gentiles. Rather "the resulting new humanity transcends the two old entities, even though unbelieving Israel and disobedient Gentiles continue to exist."[8] For Paul, there are but three groups of people in the world: unbelieving Jews, unbelieving Gentiles, and the Church (cf. 1 Cor. 10:32; see esp. Col. 3:11; Gal. 3:28; 6:15).

Consider also the implications of the word translated "access" (cf. Eph. 3:12; Rom. 5:1, 2). Whereas some have argued that the reference is to an oriental court scene in which a person is granted an audience with a king or emperor, Paul's imagery most likely derives from the Old Testament sacrificial system in which offerings were brought into the presence of God (Lev. 1:3; 3:3; 4:14). But notice the emphasis: "we *both* have *our* access..." As O'Brien points out, "it is not simply that individual Gentiles and Jews have unhindered entry into the presence of God, wonderful as this is. In addition, both of them as *one new humanity* can come into his presence. 'Jew and Gentile stand together as one people in God's presence with old distinctions no longer having significance.'"[9]

Believing Gentiles are thus "fellow-citizens" (v. 19a) with believing Jews. If there is a distinction between the terms "strangers" and "aliens" it would be that the former describes a person from another country while the latter points to the stranger who lives in the land as a resident alien. The good news, however, is that believing Gen-

---

7. Lincoln, *Ephesians,* 140-41.
8. Peter O'Brien, *The Letter to the Ephesians* (Grand Rapids: Eerdmans, 1999), 184.
9. Ibid., 209.

tiles are now neither homeless nor second-class citizens in someone else's kingdom or homeland: they are fellow-citizens with the saints.

In the second half of verse 19, the imagery shifts from the political realm of citizenry and its rights to the intimacy of a family and a home. It is not simply that Jews and Gentiles are fellow-citizens under God's rule: they are now children together, brothers and sisters, in God's family. Lincoln's comments are worthy of note:

> As the text stands, the Gentiles' former disadvantages have been reversed, not by their being incorporated into Israel, even into a renewed Israel of Jewish Christians, but by their being made members of a new community which transcends the categories of Jew and Gentile, an entity which is a new creation, not simply a merging of the former groupings.... Gentiles no longer lack a commonwealth. Yet this is not because they are now part of the commonwealth of Israel, but because they are fellow citizens with all the saints *in the Church* [emphasis mine].... [Thus] there is no escaping the conclusion that Eph. 2 depicts the Church in terms of a new third entity, one which transcends the old ethnic and religious entities of Jew and Gentile.[10]

The word translated "dwelling" (*katoiketerion*) is used in the Old Testament of God's dwelling in the temple at Jerusalem (1 Kings 8:13) and of his heavenly dwelling place (1 Kings 8:39, 43). "Now his dwelling place can be said to be neither a literal temple in Jerusalem nor simply heaven, but the Church, of which the Gentile Christian readers in Asia Minor were a part."[11] What theological and practical (indeed, *political*) significance is there in the fact that Paul says the individual Christian and the church corporately are the "temple" of God?[12] You may want to return to Chapter One and read again my comments on the significance of the temple and its fulfillment in Christ and the Church.

10. Lincoln, *Ephesians,* 163.
11. Ibid., 158.
12. On this, see especially 1 Cor. 3:16-17; 6:19-20; 2 Cor. 6:16-18; 1 Peter 2:4-10; see also John 1:14; 2:19-22; Acts 7:48-50.

The unmistakable language of the apostle here in Ephesians 2 forced me to conclude that all distinctions, all spiritual privileges, all grounds for separation and alienation based on one's ancestry, have been abolished by the blood of the cross. One's genetic history no longer has bearing or weight or significance in the sight of God. One's ethnic identity no longer has relevance when it comes to the experience of spiritual privilege. The focus of God's presence, the repository of his power, is no more and never again shall be an ethnically united people-group who share a common ancestry, but rather a spiritually united Church who share a common faith in Jesus Christ.

I tried to wriggle free from the implications of this passage. I did everything I could to avoid drawing the conclusion to which Paul's explicit language was inexorably drawing me. But I eventually conceded his point, and felt my dispensationalism slowly but surely slipping through my theological fingers. I should also point out that believing Gentiles do not "replace" anyone as recipients of God's covenant promise. No believing Jew in any age has been either displaced or replaced by a believing Gentile. Rather, believing Gentiles have been admitted into the commonwealth of Israel to share equally in the promised blessings, the two (believing Jew and believing Gentile) now comprising "one new man", the Church. The "Israel of God" (Gal. 6:16), therefore, in and for whom the promises will be fulfilled, consists of believing Jews and Gentiles, the natural and unnatural branches in the one olive tree of God. [13]

---

13. Christopher Wright concurs: "In all of this, then, it is not a case of abolishing and 'replacing' the realities of Israel and the Old Testament, but of taking them up into a greater reality in the Messiah. Christ does not *deprive* the believing Jew of anything that belonged to Israel as God's people; nor does he give to the believing Gentile anything *less* than the full covenantal blessing and promise that was Israel's. On the contrary, we share together in all of it and more – in him, and for ever" ("A Christian Approach to Old Testament Prophecy Concerning Israel," in *Jerusalem Past and Present in the Purposes of God*, edited by P.W.L. Walker [Cambridge: Cambridge University Press, 1992], 19). In addressing this point, Samuel E. Waldron contends that "as the butterfly surpasses the caterpillar from which it emerges, so the Church as the

For the next two years of my seminary education I continued to grow in my realization that the relationship between Old Testament Israel and the New Testament Church was one of continuity, not discontinuity. No one helped me see this quite like George Eldon Ladd, then professor of New Testament at Fuller Theological Seminary in Pasadena, California. Ladd's many books began to circulate everywhere on campus. *Crucial Questions about the Kingdom of God* and *The Blessed Hope* were among them. But it was his book, *The Presence of the Future* (1974), which had the greatest impact, at least on me. To this day I attribute my eschatological shift to this remarkable volume. But before I explain the significance of Ladd's book, we must continue to observe the teaching of the New Testament concerning the relationship of Israel and the Church.

(3) Additional light is shed on the answer to our question in **Galatians 3** where Paul makes an astounding statement. He provides us with an inspired commentary on, or interpretation of, those Old Testament passages dealing with the promises contained in the covenant with Abraham. In 3:16 he declares, "Now the promises were made to Abraham and to his offspring [or, seed]. It does not say, 'And to offsprings' [or 'seeds'], referring to many, but referring to one, 'And to your offspring [seed],' who is Christ." Amazing! Here Paul unequivocally says that the "seed" or "offspring" of Abraham with whom God established his covenant and to whom the land and all its blessings were promised was ultimately only ONE of Abraham's physical progeny, Jesus the Messiah! Jesus is "THE SEED" of Abraham whom God had in mind when he made his covenant promise.

New Israel surpasses the Old Israel. The butterfly does not exactly replace the caterpillar. *It is the caterpillar in a new phase of existence.* In the same way, to speak of the Church replacing Israel is to forget that the Church *is* Israel in a newly reformed and expanded phase of existence. In a word, terminology like replacement theology or supersessionism disguises the biblical fact that the Church is really the *continuation* of Israel" (*MacArthur's Millennial Manifesto: A Friendly Response* [Owensboro, KY: RBAP, 2008], 7).

Upon reading this one might think that the door has now been shut on everyone else, whether Jew or Gentile, and that only Jesus will inherit the promises. But just when you think that Paul has narrowed it down to one person and one person only, he throws wide open the gate into God's kingdom blessings by saying at the close of Galatians 3, "There is neither Jew nor Greek, there is neither slave nor free, there is neither male nor female, for you are all one in Christ Jesus. *And if you are Christ's, then you are Abraham's offspring* [i.e., seed], *heirs according to promise*" (vv. 28-29; emphasis mine).

Here is Paul's stunning point: Jesus the Messiah is the one seed or progeny or offspring of Abraham to whom the promises were given. But, if you are "in Christ" through faith and thus belong to him, then you too "are Abraham's offspring" or "seed" and thus you too are an heir of the covenant promises! This is why Paul can say "that it is those of faith who are the sons of Abraham" (Gal. 3:7) and that "those who are of faith are blessed along with Abraham, the man of faith" (Gal. 3:9; cf. 3:14).

Paul's conclusion is that in the final analysis one's ethnicity has nothing to do with who will or will not inherit the promises. Neither does gender ("neither male nor female") or socio-economic status ("there is neither slave nor free"). The only relevant criterion is whether or not you are related by faith to the one seed of Abraham for whom the covenant promises were intended. Are you "in Christ"? If so, you (regardless of ethnicity, gender, or social status), no less than he, are Abraham's seed and thus the ones for whom the covenant was intended and in whom the covenant blessings will be fulfilled.

Someone might say, "But wait a minute. That's not what the Old Testament texts say. They say that the promises were only given to and will be fulfilled in believing *Jews*." That's right. That's why Paul said as clearly as he could in Ephesians 3:4-6 that Gentile inclusion as co-heirs is the "mystery" of Christ "which was not made known to the sons of men in other generations" (i.e., in the time of the Old Testament) but has "now been revealed to his holy apostles and prophets by the Spirit" (3:5). *Believing Gentiles are as "Jewish", in the only way that matters to God, namely, spiritually (cf. Rom. 2:28-29),*

as are any of the physical descendants of Abraham, Isaac, and Jacob.
Once again, this reminds us of the danger of reading the Old Testament in isolation from the New. Simply reading and loudly asserting what the Old Testament says concerning who Israel is and what the promises to her are without then reading the New Testament to see if the inspired authors expand upon this theme is highly irresponsible.

So, yes, it is true that only believing "Jews" will inherit the promises given to Abraham, Isaac, and Jacob. But the "true Jews" who are heirs include all of any ethnic derivation who are "in Christ" by faith.

There are numerous other New Testament texts that affirm the same truth (see below). My point here is simply to clarify why I see the Church as the "one new man," the true Israel of God in and for whom all the promises will be fulfilled. The promises will not be fulfilled exclusively in and for a separate "nation" of ethnic Israelites but in and for all believing ethnic Israelites together with all believing ethnic Gentiles, that is to say, in the Church.

(4) At the close of his epistle to the Galatians, Paul pronounces a blessing that has been the source of seemingly endless controversy. The ESV renders the passage this way: "And as for all who walk by this rule, peace and mercy be upon them, and upon the Israel of God" (**Gal. 6:16**). The NIV renders it slightly differently: "Peace and mercy to all who follow this rule, even to the Israel of God."

Those who embrace the first (ESV) translation typically recognize two groups: (1) "all who walk by this rule," a reference either to Gentile believers or all who are in the Church, whether Jew or Gentile, and (2) all believing Jews or elect ethnic Israelites. According to the second (NIV) translation, Paul has in view only one group. The Greek conjunction *kai,* most often translated simply as "and," is taken as *explanatory* (or the more technical term, "epexegetical") and is rendered "even," or in some translations is simply omitted altogether. A somewhat expanded paraphrase would be, "Peace and mercy to all who follow this rule, which is to say, to the

Israel of God." Thus in the NIV Paul identifies those "who follow this rule" with "the Israel of God." They are one and the same.[14]

Some have suggested that by "the Israel of God" Paul has in view all ethnic Jews, the nation as a whole, whether they believe in Jesus or not. But this is highly unlikely, if not altogether impossible. It is simply inconceivable that Paul would have considered those who reject Christ as being "of God" on whom a spiritual blessing is pronounced. We must not forget that Paul earlier in Galatians pronounced a curse (or "anathema"; Gal. 1:8-9) on those who corrupt the gospel by insisting on circumcision or any other ritual or work as a condition for acceptance with God. There is simply no way that Paul would now reverse himself and pronounce on them both "peace and mercy." Thus, when it comes to "the Israel of God," the two options available to us are (1) Jewish believers, or (2) Jewish and Gentile believers alike, together who constitute the Church, the one true Israel of God.

The first task in bringing us to a responsible conclusion is to define what Paul means by "this rule." The "rule" by which Paul calls upon all to live may well be the entirety of what he has written in the letter. But more likely the reference is closer at hand. In verse 15 Paul has declared, as if in a summary of the message of the book, that neither circumcision nor uncircumcision counts for anything. That is to say, external marks of a particular ethnicity matter nothing to God, and therefore they should matter nothing to us. Our lives should be shaped and controlled by the "rule" of the "new creation," namely, that regardless of one's ancestry, blood, or ethnicity, faith in Jesus alone counts in the sight of God and alone should dictate how we see others and their ultimate destiny and how we relate to them in the body of Christ.

Throughout Galatians Paul has labored to make the critical point that one need not become a Jew and be circumcised in order to be a part of the people of God. The false teachers whom the apos-

---

14. Most commentators acknowledge that *kai* can be rendered in either way and that grammar alone cannot decide the interpretive outcome. Context must be the deciding factor.

tle opposes insisted that obedience to the law, and in particular the requirement of circumcision, were essential conditions for acceptance with God. But Paul has argued repeatedly that only faith in Jesus Christ is required. Indeed, he went so far as to describe Gentiles who believe in Jesus as the "offspring" or "seed" of Abraham (Gal. 3:16, 29) in and for whom the covenant promises are fulfilled. Thus, whether one is ethnically Jewish or ethnically Gentile is irrelevant to one's status with God. One need only be "in" Christ, who is himself the One true seed or "offspring" to whom the promises were originally made. As Tom Schreiner explains,

> it would be highly confusing to the Galatians, after arguing for the equality of Jew and Gentile in Christ (3:28) and after emphasizing that believers are Abraham's children, for Paul to argue in the conclusion that only Jews who believe in Jesus belong to the Israel of God. By doing so a wedge would be introduced between Jews and Gentiles at the end of the letter, suggesting that the latter were not part of the true Israel. Such a wedge would play into the hands of the opponents, who would argue that to be part of the true Israel one must be circumcised.[15]

Let's recall that Paul has described believers, whether Gentile or Jewish, as both the "sons" (Gal. 3:7) and "offspring", or "seed", of Abraham, a status attained by grace alone through faith alone in Christ alone (Gal. 3:16, 29; and in Philippians 3:3 all such believ-

---

15. Thomas R. Schreiner, *Galatians,* Zondervan Exegetical Commentary on the New Testament (Grand Rapids: Zondervan, 2010), 383. Again, if one takes "Israel of God" as referring to all elect Jews, i.e., ethnic Israelites who believe in Jesus, Paul would be violating the very rule that "he himself has just established by pronouncing his blessing over elect Jews who did use circumcision to identify themselves as the people of God. 'The Israel of God' would be a group of people other than all those who make it a practice never to regard a distinction between Jew and Gentile as a basis for identifying the people of God. But this would have Paul contradicting his own line of argument" (O. Palmer Robertson, *The Israel of God: Yesterday, Today, and Tomorrow* [Phillipsburg: P & R Publishing, 2000], 41).

ers are called the true "circumcision, who worship by the Spirit of God"). Gordon Fee concludes from this that "what Paul has done in fact is to make a final, deliberately 'in your face,' statement over against the agitators [false teachers or Judaizers]. They are trying to make Gentiles become a part of ancient Israel; Paul has spent the entire letter arguing vigorously against them. With this final coup [6:16] he designates those who are truly Israel, God's Israel, as those who abide by the canon ['rule'] that the circumcision that the agitators are urging on these Gentiles counts for nothing. Christ is all and in all; and those who follow him are now designated by Paul with this neologism: they are 'God's Israel,' the real thing." [16]

These, then, are the principal considerations that lead me to agree with Gary Burge when he says that "the apostle is redrawing the definitions for self-identity. No longer based on ethnic or historic claims to race or identity, Israel now is the title for the people of God who belong to Abraham no matter their ethnic make-up." [17]

(5) Much the same point is made in **Romans 11** (I encourage you to read the entire chapter, but especially verses 17-24) where Paul uses the imagery of the *olive tree* to instruct concerning the nature of the people of God (cf. Jer. 11:16; Hosea 14:6). I also deal more extensively with Romans 11 in Chapter Nine of this book.

The "branches" refers to individual Israelites. Because of unbelief (rejection of Messiah) most of the natural branches were broken off (v. 17). This does not mean, however, that God has cast off his people (vv. 1-2), nor that he has nullified the covenant promises given to Israel in the Old Testament. We must remember that those promises were never intended for the whole of the nation, but for the chosen/believing remnant within that nation. That the majority of Israelites ("natural branches") rejected Messiah and were consequently broken off does not counteract God's purposes nor

16. Gordon D. Fee, *Galatians*, Pentecostal Commentary Series (Dorset, UK: Deo Publishing, 2007), 253.
17. Gary M. Burge, *Jesus and the Land: The New Testament Challenge to "Holy Land." Theology* (Grand Rapids: Baker Academic, 2010), 84.

abrogate the promises. It simply proves Paul's point that "they are not all Israel, who are of Israel" (my translation). That is, not all physical descendants of Abraham, Isaac, and Jacob are the chosen recipients of the covenant blessings. Of course, the nucleus of the early Church was *Jewish*. They were members of the Church, however, *not* because they were *Jewish*, but because they were *believers*!

When the majority of the natural branches were broken off, unnatural branches (Gentiles) were grafted in (vv. 17, 24). These are Gentiles who received Jesus Christ as Lord and Savior (both then and *now*); they are the "other nation" (Matt. 21:43) to whom the stewardship of the kingdom has been given. One cannot read Romans 11 and conclude that the Church is wholly separate from Israel. Although we can surely speak of believing *Israelites* (i.e., the physical descendants of Abraham who come to faith in Christ) and believing *Gentiles*, they are together, as natural and unnatural branches respectively, one people of God, one olive tree.

Replacement theology would assert that God has uprooted and eternally cast aside the olive tree which is Israel and has planted, in its place, an entirely new one, the Church. All the promises given to the former have been transferred to the latter. But this is not what Paul says. He clearly states that there is but one olive tree, rooted in the promises given to the patriarchs. In this one tree (i.e., in this one people of God) there are both believing Jews (natural branches) and believing Gentiles (unnatural branches). Together they constitute the one people of God, the one "new man," the true Israel in and for whom the promises will be fulfilled. This one people, of course, is the Church.

Neither believing Jew nor believing Gentile has any advantage over the other. When it comes to inheriting the promises, which is inclusive of the "land", they are co-heirs. Indeed, when it comes to inheriting the promises, *ethnicity is irrelevant*. The only relevant factor is one's relationship to Jesus Christ by faith.

The Restoration of "Israel"

There are numerous passages in the New Testament where Old Testament prophecies concerning Israel's regathering and restoration are applied to the Church, indicating that the latter is the "true Israel" comprised of both believing Jews and believing Gentiles in whom the promises will be fulfilled. Or, to put it in other terms, the Church does not replace Israel but takes up and perpetuates in itself the believing remnant within the nation as a whole. The "true Israel" of God, which in the Old Testament was comprised of all ethnic Jews who were circumcised in heart, finds its New Testament expression in the Church, now comprised of all believing ethnic Jews and all believing ethnic Gentiles. Or, to use Paul's imagery from Romans 11, the one Olive Tree = True Israel = the Church in which are both natural (Jewish) branches and unnatural (Gentile) branches, but in all cases "*believing* branches."

This is the only way I can explain or account for those many texts in which prophecies and promises and titles and privileges descriptive of Israel in the Old Testament are applied to and fulfilled by the Church in the New Testament. A few representative examples will have to suffice.

(1) A good place to begin is in Matthew's Gospel where we find numerous indications that the Old Testament promise of ethnic Israel's future regathering is being fulfilled now, in the present age, in that community of faith known as the Church, a people in whom we find all ethnicities united by a common faith in Jesus Christ.

Let's begin with a brief look at **Matthew 8:10-12**. In verse 10 Jesus comments on the remarkable faith of a *Gentile* centurion: "Truly, I tell you, with no one in Israel have I found such faith." He then turns immediately to speak of a time when "many will come from east and west and recline at table with Abraham, Isaac, and Jacob in the kingdom of heaven, while the sons of the kingdom will be thrown into the outer darkness. In that place there will be weeping and gnashing of teeth." The reference to those coming from "east and west" does not find an exact parallel in the Old Testament, but in both Psalm 107:3 and Isaiah 43:5-6 (cf. Isa. 49:12) similar wording is found which speaks of God's gathering of *Israel* from all quarters of the earth. When we combine this with the many texts which speak of the Gentiles worshiping God throughout the earth (Isa. 45:6; 59:19; Mal. 1:11), it appears that Jesus is telling us that the coming from east and west of believing Gentiles into the kingdom is itself the fulfillment of the Old Testament expectation that Israel would again be gathered. Thus as "Israel had been gathered from foreign lands in Old Testament times, so the true Israel [i.e., believing Gentiles, together with believing Jews, who constitute the Church of Jesus Christ] was now to be gathered from all the world."[18]

The language used here of reclining at table (v. 11) with Abraham, Isaac, and Jacob would have been understood immediately as a reference to participation in the messianic banquet by Jews in the eschaton. These "foreigners" do not merely share "the residue of Israel's eschatological blessings" but are portrayed as "reclining at the same table as the Hebrew patriarchs who, we are to assume, do not fear ritual defilement by eating with those who do not share Israel's purity."[19] Jesus remarkably declares that, in point of fact, "many" (v. 11a) Gentiles, from the "east and west" will be included while those who simply assumed that, by virtue of their Jewish ethnicity ("the sons of the kingdom," v. 12a), they would be present are excluded. Thus we see, as we have on multiple occasions already, that membership in and enjoyment of the blessings of the kingdom of heaven is *based not on blood but belief.* This is consistent with what we regularly see in the New Testament where familiar Old Testament categories are taken up, redirected, and applied in a new and surprising way.

(2) As I'll explain later and in more detail in our study of the Olivet Discourse (Matt. 24; Mark 13; Luke 21), our Lord's prediction that "he will send out his angels with a loud trumpet call, and they will gather his elect from the four winds, from one end of heaven to the other" (Matt. 24:31) is *not* a reference to what will occur only at the second advent at the close of history. This text is primarily a description of Christ's ingathering of his people into the Church

18. R.T. France, *Jesus and the Old Testament,* 63.
19. R.T. France, *The Gospel of Matthew* (Grand Rapids: Eerdmans, 2007), 319.

throughout the course of the present age following the judgment that befell national Israel in A.D. 70. The passage is a clear allusion to both Deuteronomy 30:4 and Zechariah 2:6. There we read: "If your outcasts are in the uttermost parts of heaven, from there the Lord your God will gather you, and from there he will take you" (Deut. 30:4); "Up! Up! Flee from the land of the north, declares the Lord. For I have spread you abroad as the four winds of the heavens, declares the Lord" (Zech. 2:6).

The text in Deuteronomy is a promise that God will restore his people to the land if they repent following their time in exile. In Zechariah, God is addressing the people who remained in Babylon after the time of captivity. I believe France is right that, in applying these texts to the gathering of the Gentile church in the age subsequent to the fall of Jerusalem, "Jesus is again taking up Old Testament predictions which had been, partially at least, fulfilled in Old Testament times, and regarding that partial Old Testament fulfillment as a type of the greater gathering in of the people of God which he had come to inaugurate."[20] This is confirmed by the reference to "a loud trumpet call" (Matt. 24:31), a likely allusion to Isaiah 27:12-13 which speaks of the conclusion of Israel's dispersion when she "will be weeded out within the ideal limits of the promised land (verse 12), and the great trumpet will summon those dispersed to Assyria and Egypt to return and worship Yahweh in Jerusalem."[21]

If someone should object, as no doubt they will, that these Old Testament passages when read in their original context pertain to God's prophesied purpose for Israel, the physical descendants of Abraham, Isaac, and Jacob, I happily concur. But again we cannot read, interpret, and apply such texts in isolation from the more complete revelation in the New Testament concerning the identity of God's covenant people. As we'll see on several occasions, *all believing Jews are included in these predictions.* No one is replaced by a believing Gentile. But all those who are by faith in Christ, the

---

20. France, *Jesus and the Old Testament*, 64.
21. Ibid.

true seed of Abraham, are now themselves "one new man" and thus co-heirs with believing Jews of the promises made to the fathers. The Church is, therefore, the true Israel in and on behalf of whom all the Old Testament prophecies are fulfilled. Thus, when we read about prophesied regatherings of Israel into their land, we are to see in them a type of the future gathering of believing men and women from all nations of the earth into the Christian community that we know as the Church.

(3) Perhaps the most explicit affirmation that the ingathering of believers in the present age from all ethnic groups is the fulfillment of the Old Testament's prophesied regathering of ethnic Israel is found in **Acts 15:14-18**. Because of its importance, I've devoted an entire chapter to unpacking this powerful text. Briefly, James interprets the prophecy of Amos 9 that describes the rebuilding of David's tabernacle as finding its fulfillment in the calling out of Gentiles and the progressive formation of the Christian Church. Again, for a complete exposition of this passage, see Chapter Nine in this book.

(4) In **Romans 9:25-26**, Paul cites two passages in Hosea (2:23 and 1:10) that were addressed to the ten apostate northern tribes of Israel before the Assyrian exile in 722–721 B.C. They describe both the rebellious condition of Israel ("not my people"/"not beloved") and her prophesied future restoration ("my people"/"beloved"/"sons of the living God"):

> As indeed he says in Hosea, "Those who were not my people I will call my people, and her who was not beloved I will call beloved." And in the very place where it was said to them, "You are not my people," there they will be called sons of the living God" (Rom. 9:25-26).

But observe carefully how Paul applies these two Old Testament texts. He uses them to describe what God is doing in calling out a people for himself "not from the Jews only but also from the Gentiles" (9:24). In other words, two passages that in the Old Testament unmistakably describe the restoration and future salvation of Israel, Paul applies directly to what God is doing in saving the Church! The Church, which consists of both believing Jews and believing Gentiles, is the true people of God to whom these Old Testament texts ultimately pertained. "It follows inescapably," notes George Ladd, "that the salvation of the Gentile church is the fulfillment of prophecies made to Israel. Such facts as this are what compel some Bible students, including the present writer [not only Ladd, but also Storms], to speak of the church as the New Israel, the true Israel, the spiritual Israel." [22]

In other words, the Old Testament prophetic promise of Israel's regathering in covenant faith to Yahweh is being progressively fulfilled in the salvation of believing Jews and Gentiles in this present age, that is to say, in the *Church. The calling out of Gentiles from among every tribe, tongue, people, and nation* **is** *the prophesied restoration of Israel, for the Church is the continuation and maturation of Israel's believing remnant.*

Before moving on, I should take note of how dispensationalists typically respond to these sorts of texts and the conclusions which Ladd, I, and others draw from them. What they often say in response is that *the way in which* God is saving Gentiles in the present age corresponds to or is *merely analogous with* the way God will eventually save, regather, and restore national Israel in the future. In other words, no matter how many texts I might cite in this chapter in which New Testament authors apply to the Church Old Testament texts that pertained to national Israel, they have a quick and seemingly insurmountable response: The *principle* according to which God saved and will restore Israel is much the same principle on the basis of which he is saving the Church today. For example, Michael Vlach insists this is precisely what Paul is doing in Romans 9:

> To show that God in His sovereignty can take a disobedient people and make them His people, Paul quotes the clearest passages *to high-*

---

22. George Eldon Ladd, *The Last Things: An Eschatology for Laymen* (Grand Rapids: Eerdmans, 1978), 23.

light this principle. In this sense, God's electing purposes for Gentiles is *parallel or analogous to* God's choosing Israel. The main point of analogy is God's election. In this sense, there is a *divine correspondence* between God's calling of Israel and His calling of Gentiles.[23]

The reason I describe this as a "seemingly insurmountable response" isn't to suggest that I find it convincing, but rather because it is, at least on the surface, theologically unfalsifiable. What I mean is that no matter how many texts from the Old Testament are applied to the Church, no matter how clear and explicit those texts may be, no matter how many Old Testament titles or names or descriptive phrases for Israel are applied to the Church in the New Testament, one need only fall back on the principle employed by Vlach and insist that it is a matter of *correspondence* or *analogy* or *parallel*, but by no means is it a pattern of fulfillment. Of course, Vlach and others who share his view may be right. But their use of this hermeneutical approach makes it virtually impossible to prove them wrong. In the final analysis each of you must decide whether or not the cumulative effect of the many texts cited in this chapter and elsewhere in the book which portray the Church as the true Israel of God, the ultimate fulfillment of God's redemptive purposes that began with the covenant established with Abraham, can so easily be set aside as nothing more than illustrations of a principle. Is that all the New Testament authors are saying to us about the nature and identity of the Church and her place in God's prophetic purposes? Perhaps we should now return and look at other such passages and see if they can so easily be set aside as little more than illustrative of some theological principle.

(5) In **Revelation 2:17**, John (quoting Jesus) promises to the overcomers (i.e., the Church) a "new name" that "no one knows except the one who receives it." This is a clear reference to the prophecy in Isaiah 62:2 ("The nations shall see your righteousness, and all

---

23. Michael J. Vlach, *Has the Church Replaced Israel? A Theological Evaluation* (Nashville: B & H Academic, 2010), 103 (emphasis mine).

the kings your glory and *you shall be called by a new name*, that the mouth of the Lord will give") and 65:15 ("but his servants he will call by *another name*") about Israel's future kingly status and restoration to Yahweh, both of which are now applied to individuals within the Church.

(6) **Revelation 3:9** is especially instructive. Here Jesus promises the church in Philadelphia that he "will make those of the synagogue of Satan who say that they are Jews and are not, but lie – behold, I will make them come and bow down before your feet and they will learn that I have loved you." There are two important points to make.

First, Jesus refers to people who "say they are Jews and are not, but lie" (for an almost identical statement, see Rev. 2:9). Clearly, in one sense, these people *are* Jews, the physical descendants of Abraham, Isaac, and Jacob, who met regularly in the synagogue to worship. Yet, in another sense, i.e., inwardly and spiritually, they are *not* Jews, having rejected Jesus and now persecuted and slandered his people. Indeed, their gatherings at synagogue are energized by Satan himself. But if they are *false Jews*, who, then, are the *true Jews*? If they are a *synagogue of Satan*, who, then, constitutes a *synagogue of God*? John does not provide an explicit answer, but the implication seems clear. Ladd explains:

> true Jews are the people of the Messiah. Paul says the same thing very clearly: "For he is not a real Jew who is one outwardly, nor is true circumcision something external and physical. He is a Jew who is one inwardly, and real circumcision is a matter of the heart, spiritual and not literal" (Rom. 2:28-29). That this "Judaism of the heart" is not to be limited to believing Jews but includes believing gentiles is clear from Paul's words to the Philippians: "For we are the true circumcision, who worship God in spirit, and glory in Christ Jesus" (Phil. 3:3). We must conclude, then, that John makes a real distinction between literal Israel – the Jews – and spiritual Israel – the church. [24]

---

24. George E. Ladd, *A Commentary on The Revelation of John* (Grand Rapids: Eerdmans, 1972), 43-44. "John is not condemning the Jews as a race of

The second important thing about this text is that in it we find an allusion to several Old Testament passages in which it is prophesied that *Gentiles* will come and bow down before Israel in the last days. For example:

> The sons of those who afflicted you shall come bending low to you, and all who despised you shall bow down at your feet; they shall call you the City of the LORD, the Zion of the Holy One of Israel. (Isa. 60:14)

> Thus says the LORD: "The wealth of Egypt and the merchandise of Cush, and the Sabeans, men of stature, shall come over to you and be yours; they shall follow you; they shall come over in chains and bow down to you. They will plead with you, saying: 'Surely God is in you, and there is no other, no god besides him.'" (Isa. 45:14)

> Kings shall be your foster fathers, and their queens your nursing mothers. With their faces to the ground they shall bow down to you, and lick the dust of your feet. Then you will know that I am the LORD; those who wait for me shall not be put to shame. (Isa. 49:23)

But as David Aune points out, "The ironical use of this motif is clear: in all these passages the Gentiles are expected to grovel before Israel, while in Rev. 3:9 it is the Jews who are expected to grovel before the feet of this (largely gentile) Christian community."[25]

What makes this even more intriguing is the fact that in Isaiah 60:14 "they" (the Gentiles) will call "you" (the Israelites) *the City of the Lord,*

---

people," notes Philip Mayo, "or even as a religion. John himself is a Jew. It would be anachronistic to suggest that he is being anti-Semitic or even anti-Jewish. He is condemning those Jews who are opposing God and his people, for a true Jew would not act in such a manner. John's definition of a 'Jew' has broadened as it had for the Apostle Paul (Rom. 2.28-29). God's people, the 'true Jews,' now constitute both Jews and Gentiles who have accepted Jesus as the Messiah" (*"Those Who Call Themselves Jews": The Church and Judaism in the Apocalypse of John* [Eugene, OR: Pickwick Publications, 2006], 72).

25. David E. Aune, *Revelation 1-5*, Word Biblical Commentary (Dallas: Word Books, 1997), 237-38.

the Zion of the Holy One of Israel". This is precisely what we see in Revelation 3:12, except that in the latter it is said of the *Church*! There we read that these very overcomers before whom these Jews prostrate themselves are given the name of … "*the city of my God, the new Jerusalem*"! And be it noted that the name by which Jesus identifies himself to the Philadelphian believers is "*the Holy One*" (thereby reinforcing the link between Revelation 3 and Isaiah 60).

Similarly, the words they will "know that I have loved you" may be an allusion to Isaiah 43:4 ("Because you [Israel] are precious in my eyes, and honored, and I love you …"), thereby reinforcing the notion that John saw in the Church the fulfillment of these Old Testament prophetic promises. In other words, the fulfillment of these Isaianic prophecies "will be the reverse of what the Philadelphian Jews expect: *they* will have to 'bow down before *your* feet', and acknowledge 'that I have loved *you*'. Let the Christians take heart, for it is on them that the Lord has set his favour." [26]

(7) **Revelation 7:15** is also relevant in this regard, and I will address it at length below.

(8) In **Revelation 21:14** the wall of the New Jerusalem has "twelve foundation stones" on which were written the names of the twelve apostles (v. 14). The number "twenty-four", the sum of the twelve tribes and twelve apostles, has already occurred in Revelation 4:4. Some point to David's organization of the temple servants into twenty-four orders of priests (1 Chron. 24:3-19), twenty-four Levitical gatekeepers (26:17-19), and twenty-four orders of Levites (25:6-31). I agree with Beale that "the integration of the apostles together with the tribes of Israel as part of the city-temple's structure prophesied in Ezekiel 40–48 confirms further… that the multiracial Christian church will be the redeemed group who, together with Christ, will fulfill Ezekiel's prophecy of the future

---

26. Michael Wilcock, *The Message of Revelation: I Saw Heaven Opened* (Downers Grove: Inter-Varsity Press, 1975), 54.

temple and city." [27] Thus here again we see an emphasis on the *one people of God*, comprised of believing Jews and believing Gentiles, who together equally inherit the promises.

I mentioned earlier the massive work of G.K. Beale in which he points to numerous texts where Jesus is identified as the true embodiment of Israel and his Church as what he calls "the Transformed and Restored Eschatological Israel." Beale's thesis, which is identical to the one for which I have also argued, is as follows:

> Christ is the true Israel, and as true Israel, he represents the church as the continuation of true Israel from the OT. Christ came to do what Israel should have done but failed to do. Those who identify by faith with Christ, whether Jew or gentile, become identified with him and his identity as true eschatological Israel. [28]

Beale makes a persuasive case that "it is not an allegorical or spiritualizing hermeneutic by which the predominantly gentile church is to be identified with Israel but it is what we might call a 'legal representative' or 'corporate' hermeneutic that underlies this identification of the church." [29] That is why both Jesus and the Church "do not merely resemble what restored Israel was to be [contrary to the claims of dispensationalism]; they are the actual beginning of eschatological restored Israel. In particular, the idea is that Jesus as the individual messianic king of Israel represented the true continuing remnant of Israel, and all those identifying with him become a part of the Israelite remnant that he represents." [30]

In addition to the many texts cited in this chapter, Beale points to other passages that highlight the fact that "the church is actually considered to be true end-time Israel, composed of believing ethnic Jews and gentiles." [31] Among these are:

---

27. Ibid., 1070.
28. Beale, *A New Testament Biblical Theology*, 652.
29. Ibid., 655.
30. Ibid., 656.
31. Ibid., 669.

God calls Israel "beloved" in Deuteronomy 32:15; 33:12; Isaiah 44:2; Jeremiah 11:15; 12:7; Psalms 60:5; 108:6. Likewise, the Church is called "beloved" in 1 Thessalonians 1:4 and Romans 9:25.

Israel was repeatedly referred to as God's "son(s)" in Exodus 4:22-23; Deuteronomy 14:1; Isaiah 1:2, 4; 63:8; Hosea 1:10; 11:1; as is the Church in Galatians 3:26 (and other texts).

As Israel was the wife of Yahweh in the Old Testament (Isa. 54:5-6; Ezek. 16:32; Hosea 1:2), so the Church is the bride of Christ in the New Testament (2 Cor. 11:2; Eph. 5:25-27).

Israel was on occasion portrayed as God's "vineyard" or "cultivated field" in the Old Testament (Isa. 5:1-7; Jer. 12:10). Likewise, we see the same imagery applied to Jesus and the Church in the New Testament (John 15:1-5; 1 Cor. 3:9).

Israel and certain of its leaders are depicted as an "olive tree" in the Old Testament (Isa. 17:6; Jer. 11:16; Hosea 14:6; Ps. 128:3; Judg. 9:8-9; Ps. 52:8; Zech. 4:3, 11-12). In Romans 11:17 and 24 Paul envisions believing Gentiles as wild branches that are grafted into the cultivated "olive tree" of Israel.

As Israel was described as God's "special people" (Exod. 19:5; 23:22; Deut. 7:6; 14:2; 26:18), so also the Church (Tit. 2:14; cf. also the latter text with Ps. 130:8).

Israel was a "kingdom of priests" unto God (Exod. 19:6) and so too is the Church (1 Pet. 2:9; Rev. 1:6; 5:10).

The Church in its collective witness to the nations is portrayed as "lampstands" and "olive trees" in Revelation 2:1, 5 and especially in 11:3-4, linking her with Israel in Zechariah 4:14 (cf. 4:2-3, 11-14).

One final example will have to suffice. Beale directs our attention to Matthew 12:46-50 where Jesus appears to redefine what a true Israelite is:

> While he was still speaking to the people, behold, his mother and his brothers stood outside, asking to speak to him. But he replied to the man who told him, "Who is my mother, and who are my brothers?" And stretching out his hand toward his disciples, he said, "Here are my mother and my brothers! For whoever does the will of my Father in heaven is my brother and sister and mother."

Beale's explanation follows:

> Here Jesus redefines a true Israelite as "whoever does the will of My
> Father" (the parallel in Luke 8:21 has "who hear the word of God and do
> it"). Jesus's true family consists of those who trust in him, not those who
> are related to him by blood. Because Jesus is restoring not only Israel
> but also all of creation, including gentiles (Matt. 15:21-28; 21:40-44),
> the true people of God no longer can be marked out by certain nation-
> alistic badges that distinguish one nation from another. Therefore, in
> order to become a true Israelite and part of Jesus's real family, one no
> longer needs to keep all the specific requirements of Israel's law that
> marked Israel out as Israel in contrast to the rest of the nations: laws of
> circumcision, diet, the temple, the Sabbath, and so on. Jesus is redefin-
> ing the true Israel, the true people of God, by saying that loyalty to him
> is the mark of a faithful Israelite. People no longer must possess the
> badges of old national Israel in order to be part of the true, new Israel....
> You do not have to be of the bloodline of Abraham to be his true child,
> nor do you have to move to Israel geographically to become an Israelite;
> you merely have to move to Jesus, true Israel, and embrace him.[32]

These are by no means all of the texts that affirm this truth. To
delve into the Synoptic Gospels alone would reveal numerous
other instances in which the Church is portrayed as the continuation and maturation of the believing remnant of Old Testament
Israel and thus heirs according to promise. Let me say it again
clearly. Not one single ethnic Jew who believes in Jesus Christ as
the Messiah has been "replaced" or lost his/her inheritance in the
blessings of the covenant. Rather, every single ethnic Gentile who
believes in Jesus Christ as the Messiah has been "included" in the
commonwealth of Israel and grafted into the one olive tree. Thus
the true Israel, the true "seed" of Abraham, which is to say, any and
all who are "in Christ" by faith, regardless of ethnicity, will together
inherit the blessings of the covenant.

---

32. Ibid., 424-25. Other texts that make much the same point include Matthew
3:9; 19:29; and Luke 11:27-28.

What about the "Land"?

I have argued that the New Testament provides us with an expanded definition of what constitutes an "Israelite" or a "Jew". Or perhaps we might say that the New Testament provides us with a *Christified* perspective on the people of God. Ethnicity is no longer the primary concern. Having Abraham's blood in one's veins is not the primary consideration, but rather having Abraham's faith in one's heart. Jesus is the true "seed" of Abraham to whom the promise was given. But if anyone is "in Christ" by faith, he or she is the "seed" of Abraham and thus an heir according to the promise. Where we left off is with the question of the ultimate disposition of the land that was included in the Abrahamic covenant. What becomes of that element in the promise? [33]

I believe that promise will be *literally* fulfilled, but not merely (or even primarily) in the land of Canaan. It's important we note that the initial covenant promises of the land of Canaan to Abraham (Gen. 12; 13; 15; 17) undergo considerable *expansion* in Scripture, an expansion of such a nature that the ultimate fulfillment could only be realized on the New Earth. I find Anthony Hoekema's description helpful. He refers to Genesis 17:8 and the land promise to Abraham, and says:

> Note that God promised to give the land of Canaan not just to Abraham's descendants but also Abraham himself. Yet Abraham never owned as much as a square foot of ground in the land of Canaan (cf. Acts 7:5) – except for the burial cave which he had to purchase from the Hittites (see Gen. 23). What, now, was Abraham's attitude with respect to this promise of the inheritance of the land of Canaan, which was never fulfilled during his own lifetime? We get an answer to this question from the book of Hebrews. In chapter 11, verses 9-10, we read, "By

---

33. Among the numerous books that treat the issue of the "land" in biblical eschatology, I strongly recommend Gary M. Burge, *Jesus and the Land: The New Testament Challenge to "Holy Land" Theology* (Grand Rapids: Baker Academic, 2010); Peter W.L. Walker, *Jesus and the Holy City: New Testament Perspectives on Jerusalem* (Grand Rapids: Eerdmans, 1996); and Philip Johnston & Peter Walker, editors, *The Land of Promise: Biblical, Theological and Contemporary Perspectives* (Downers Grove: IVP, 2000).

faith he [Abraham] sojourned in the land of promise, as in a foreign land, living in tents with Isaac and Jacob, heirs with him of the same promise. For he looked forward to the city which has foundations, whose builder and maker is God." By "the city which has foundations" we are to understand the holy city or the new Jerusalem which will be found on the new earth. Abraham, in other words, looked forward to the new earth as the real fulfillment of the inheritance which had been promised him – and so did the other patriarchs.[34]

And again:

When we properly understand biblical teachings about the new earth, many other Scripture passages begin to fall into a significant pattern. For example, in Psalm 37:11 we read, "But the meek shall possess the *land*." It is significant to observe how Jesus' paraphrase of this passage in his Sermon on the Mount reflects the New Testament expansion of the concept of the land: "Blessed are the meek, for they shall inherit the *earth*" (Matt. 5:5). From Genesis 17:8 we learned that God promised to give to Abraham and his seed all the land of Canaan for an everlasting possession, but in Romans 4:13 Paul speaks of the promise to Abraham and his descendants that they should inherit the world – note that the *land of Canaan* in Genesis has become the *world* in Romans.[35]

As Hoekema noted above, a significant passage that addresses this issue is found in Hebrews 11. Let me begin with a question: How do we explain that when Abraham finally arrived in the land of promise he only *sojourned* there, as a stranger and exile, "as in a foreign land"? (Heb. 11:9, 13). Philip Hughes rightly asks: "In what sense could he be said to have received this land as an inheritance when it was a territory in which he led no settled existence and to which he had no claim of ownership?"[36] We need not speculate an

---

34. Hoekema, *The Bible and the Future*, 278.
35. Ibid., 281-82.
36. Philip Edgcumbe Hughes, *A Commentary on the Epistle to the Hebrews* (Grand Rapids: Eerdmans, 1977), 467.

answer, for the text provides its own in verse 10, "for he was looking forward to the city that has foundations, whose designer and builder is God."

What is this *city*? It is that city which God has prepared for them (v. 16), mentioned again in Hebrews 12:22 as the "city of the living God, the heavenly Jerusalem." See also Hebrews 13:14, where we read that "here [that is, on this present earth] we have no lasting city, but we seek the city that is to come." This surely refers to the heavenly Jerusalem of Hebrews 12:22, the city which has foundations (v. 10). Note also Revelation 21:1-2, especially verse 2 where we read that John "saw the holy city, the new Jerusalem, coming down out of heaven from God" (cf. 21:9-11). The reason, then, why Abraham was a sojourner and exile in Canaan was because he viewed that earthly land to be a type of the heavenly and more substantial land/country.

The point is that the patriarchs did not seek in the physical land of Canaan their everlasting possession. The focal point of the Old Testament land promise was on *land*, to be sure, but on the *heavenly land* (or "country", Heb. 11:16) of the new earth with its central feature, the New Jerusalem. Abraham, the one to whom the land of Canaan was originally promised, is said to receive the fulfillment of that promise, not in geographic Canaan, but in heavenly Jerusalem. Abraham is heir, not merely of Canaan, but of the world! Indeed, according to Hebrews 11:9-10, it was Abraham's expectation of permanent and perfect blessing in the heavenly city that enabled him to submit patiently to the inconvenience and disappointments during his pilgrimage in Canaan.

We must also consider Hebrews 11:13-16. The patriarchs themselves "acknowledged that they were strangers and exiles on the earth" (v. 13). They died without receiving the promise, having only seen it from afar. Their hope was not focused on any this-earthly-inheritance, but, as verse 16 indicates, on "a better country, that is, a heavenly one." F.F. Bruce sums it up well by noting that, according to verse 16, "their true homeland was not on earth at all. The better country on which they had set their hearts was the heavenly country. The earthly Canaan and the earthly Jerusalem were but temporary object-lessons pointing to the saints' everlasting rest, the well-founded city of God."[37] The Abrahamic land promise, as well as prophecies such as Isaiah 65:17; 66:22; 32:15; 35:2, 7, 10; 11:9, which speak of a restoration of the cosmos, are to be fulfilled on the new earth in the new creation, not on a millennial earth in the old one.[38]

Typically at this point someone will ask: "But doesn't the fulfillment have to sustain a literal one-to-one correspondence with the promise?" In other words, the fulfillment must consist of what can only be called a "photographic reproduction" of the promise. Therefore (so goes the argument), God has failed to carry through on his covenantal commitment to the nation Israel if he does not bring her into possession and enjoyment of the precise geographical dimensions as outlined in Genesis 12, 13, 15, and 17.

Clearly, I believe this fundamentally misunderstands the nature of promise and fulfillment as well as the relationship between the two testaments. But consider this illustration, as provided by Greg Beale in his excellent book, *The Temple and the Church's Mission*. Imagine that a father, in 1900, promises his young son a horse and buggy when he grows up and gets married:

> During the early years of expectation, the son reflects on the particular size of the buggy, its contours and style, its beautiful leather seat and the size and breed of horse that would draw the buggy. Perhaps the father

---

37. F.F. Bruce, *The Epistle to the Hebrews* (Grand Rapids: Eerdmans, 1973), 305.
38. Walter C. Kaiser, Jr., tries to evade this point in Hebrews by arguing that the "city" referred to in 11:10 is the Jerusalem that will be "found in the millennial rule and reign of Messiah prior to the eternal state" (*Preaching and Teaching the Last Things,* 157). Needless to say (as noted above), this entirely ignores the fact that this "city" is part of a "better country, that is, a heavenly one" (Heb. 11:16). Again, if the "city" that Abraham desired was part of an alleged millennial earth, within history, as Kaiser contends, why did he (Abraham) and all the patriarchs acknowledge that "they were strangers and exiles on the earth" (v. 13), at the very time they were living upon it? And does not Kaiser's view also require us to ignore the obvious reference yet again to "the heavenly Jerusalem" (12:22) and "the city that is to come" (13:14b), which is explicitly contrasted with all transient-this-earthly cities (13:14a), which would certainly include any purported millennial Jerusalem?

had knowledge from early experimentation elsewhere that the invention of the automobile was on the horizon, but coined the promise to his son in terms that his son would understand. Years later, when the son marries, the father gives the couple an automobile, which has since been invented and mass-produced. Is the son disappointed in receiving a car instead of a horse and buggy? Is this not a "literal" fulfillment of the promise? In fact, the essence of the father's word has remained the same: a convenient mode of transportation. What has changed is the precise form of transportation promised. The progress of technology has escalated the fulfillment of the pledge in a way that could not have been conceived of when the son was young. Nevertheless, in the light of the later development of technology [corresponding to the redemptive impact of the coming of Christ], the promise is viewed as "literally" and faithfully carried out in a greater way than earlier apprehended. [39]

Revelation 7:1-8

One of the more important passages in the New Testament addressing the relationship between Israel and the Church is found in Revelation 7 and John's vision of the 144,000 and the so-called innumerable multitude. A close examination of this passage will reveal once again that the Church is the true Israel of God, the one people on whose behalf all of the covenant promises will be fulfilled.

[1]After this I saw four angels standing at the four corners of the earth, holding back the four winds of the earth, that no wind might blow on

---

39. G.K. Beale, *The Temple and the Church's Mission: A Biblical Theology of the Dwelling Place of God* (Downers Grove: Inter Varsity Press, 2004), 352-53. I first encountered this illustration in Christopher J.H. Wright, *Knowing Jesus Through the Old Testament* (Downers Grove: Inter-Varsity, 1992), 71. Wright is quick to remind us that "just because the gift turns out to be a motor car [i.e., automobile] doesn't mean we should try to argue that the promise of a horse was only meant figuratively. A horse was meant and a horse was expected. But the changed circumstances and the progress of history enabled the promises to be fulfilled in a different and superior way, without emptying the promise either of its purpose (to give a means of transport), or of its basis in a relationship of fatherly love" (76).

earth or sea or against any tree. [2]Then I saw another angel ascending from the rising of the sun, with the seal of the living God, and he called with a loud voice to the four angels who had been given power to harm earth and sea, [3]saying, "Do not harm the earth or the sea or the trees, until we have sealed the servants of our God on their foreheads." [4]And I heard the number of the sealed, 144,000, sealed from every tribe of the sons of Israel: [5]12,000 from the tribe of Judah were sealed, 12,000 from the tribe of Reuben, 12,000 from the tribe of Gad, [6]12,000 from the tribe of Asher, 12,000 from the tribe of Naphtali, 12,000 from the tribe of Manasseh, [7]12,000 from the tribe of Simeon, 12,000 from the tribe of Levi, 12,000 from the tribe of Issachar, [8]12,000 from the tribe of Zebulun, 12,000 from the tribe of Joseph, 12,000 from the tribe of Benjamin were sealed.

The list of tribes here in Revelation 7 corresponds to none of the nearly twenty different variations found in the Old Testament. Judah, listed first here, is found in that position in the Old Testament only when the tribes are arranged geographically, moving from south to north (Num. 34:19; Josh. 21:4; Judg. 1:2; 1 Chron. 12:24). The only exception to this is Numbers 2:3 (followed by 7:12; 10:14). Perhaps Judah's priority here "emphasizes the precedence of the messianic king from the tribe of Judah (cf. Gen. 49:10; 1 Chron. 5:1-2) and thus refers to a fulfillment of the prophecy in Gen. 49:8 that the eleven other tribes 'will bow down' to Judah." [40]

One can hardly fail to note that the tribes of Dan and Ephraim are omitted. One tradition believed that the Antichrist was to come from the tribe of Dan (based on a misinterpretation of Jeremiah 8:16 and first found in Irenaeus, c. A.D. 200); whereas yet another tradition alleged that the mother of the Messiah would be a Danite. Dan was also closely associated with idol worship (Judg. 18:16-19; 1 Kings 12:28-30; cf. Gen. 49:17; Judg. 18:30; Jer. 8:16), as was Ephraim (Hosea 4:17–14:8). In Revelation 7, Joseph and Manasseh substitute for Dan and Ephraim. In the final analysis, there is no clear reason for this and we may never know why (unless the proposal by Smith, noted below, is correct).

---

40. Beale, *Revelation*, 417.

Who are these *144,000* who receive the seal of the living God? Several things should be noted about them.

First, it would initially appear that those who are sealed are part of a larger group, for the Greek construction (*ek* plus the genitive) is partitive in nature: literally, "*out of* all the tribes of Israel ... *out of* the tribe of Judah ... *out of* the tribe of Reuben ... etc." Thus, whoever these people are, 12,000 from each tribe might mean a *portion* of those who make up the whole tribe. This is confirmed when we realize that this passage is an allusion to Ezekiel 9:4 where only *some* of the inhabitants of Jerusalem were marked in order to be preserved from the judgment that followed. The point is that the idea of the *remnant* may be in view (see Rom. 11:7). On second thoughts, too much should not be made of this. After all, no one denies that there were more than 12,000 in each tribe. But if there was a theological reason for limiting the vision to only 144,000 of the total (and I believe there was), how else could John have described it except in the way that he did? In other words, I will argue below that the 12,000 from each of the twelve tribes represent all in every tribe.

Second, there are several noticeable differences between the 144,000 in verses 4-8 and the great multitude in verses 9-17. The most obvious difference is that the first group is specifically numbered (144,000) whereas the second is innumerable. Furthermore, the members of the 144,000 are all taken from one nation, Israel, whereas those in the innumerable multitude are taken from "every nation and tribe and people and language" (7:9). Another difference is their location: the 144,000 appear to be on earth, whereas the multitude is in heaven, before the throne of God (7:9). Finally, the 144,000 are in imminent peril and thus require divine protection, whereas the multitude is in a condition of absolute peace and joy. Do these differences mean that the two groups are entirely different, or is it the same group viewed from different perspectives, at different stages of their existence and experience?

Third, these in 7:4-8 are surely identical with the *144,000* mentioned in Revelation 14:1-5. In both cases it is said that they received the seal of God on their "foreheads" (7:3 and 14:1). In 14:3 they are

described as those who had been "redeemed from the earth" and
again in 14:4 they were "redeemed from mankind". This echoes 5:9
where the Lamb is said to have "ransomed" for God people from
every tribe, tongue, people, and nation. This same phrase is used
again in 7:9 to describe the innumerable multitude. This would
seem to indicate that the 144,000 = the innumerable multitude =
the redeemed of all ages, and *not some special remnant of humanity*.

Fourth, there is one statement, however, in 14:4 that may support the idea that the 144,000 are less than the total number of
the redeemed. There they are described as "firstfruits" (*aparche*)
to God and to the Lamb. This word occurs nine times in the New
Testament, seven of which are in Paul. It may refer to new converts
who were the first of many more to come (Rom. 16:5; 1 Cor. 16:15;
2 Thess. 2:13). It also refers to the Holy Spirit as the first evidence
of a greater end-time inheritance (Rom. 8:23). It is also used of
Christ's resurrection as the beginning of the subsequent resurrection of all believers (1 Cor. 15:20, 23), and of believers as the
beginning of the new creation (James 1:18). In Romans 11:16 it is
used to speak of the Old Testament patriarchs as fathers of later,
faithful descendants. If that is the meaning in Revelation 14:4 the
idea would be that the 144,000 were an initial group, perhaps a
remnant, of believers whose salvation was a foreshadowing of a yet
greater ingathering or harvest of believers in the end time. Beale
counters by pointing out that in Jeremiah 2:2-3, for example, the
entire nation of Israel is called the "firstfruits" of God. This seems
unlikely to me. More probable is the suggestion that the 144,000
represent the totality of God's redeemed *at that time*, and thus
"firstfruits" of the remainder of *all the redeemed* who will be gathered in the final harvest at the close of history.

Fifth, these 144,000 are called the "servants" (*douloi*) of God.
Whenever the word "servants" is used in Revelation (2:20; 19:5;
22:3) it refers to the entire community of the redeemed. Also, if
Satan puts a seal or mark on all his followers (13:16-17; 14:9-11), it
seems reasonable that God would do likewise for his people.

Sixth, another interesting fact is that the numbering (144,000)
is probably used to evoke images of the Old Testament census,

which was designed to determine the military strength of the nation (see Num. 1:3,18,20; 26:2,4; 1 Chron. 27:23; 2 Sam. 24:1-9). The point is that these in Revelation 7 constitute a *messianic army* called upon, like Jesus himself, to conquer the enemy through sacrificial death. In the Old Testament those counted were males of military age (twenty years and over). This explains why the 144,000 in Revelation 14:1ff. are *adult males*, i.e., those eligible for military service. According to Numbers 31:4-6, 1,000 soldiers from each of the twelve tribes were sent into battle against Midian. Some have countered that the tribe of *Levi* is out place in a military census. However, as Bauckham points out, "although the priests and Levites do not fight with weapons, they play an essential part in the conduct of war, conducting prayers before, during and after battle, and blowing the trumpets which both direct the troops and call divine attention to the battle. Without them the war could not be a *holy war*."[41]

Seventh, this "military force" in 7:4-8, notes Beale, "conquers its enemy ironically in the same way in which the Lamb has ironically conquered at the cross: by maintaining their faith through suffering, the soldiers overcome the devil.... Consequently, they are those who 'follow the Lamb wherever he goes' (14:4). In particular, 7:4-8 portrays an army ready to fight, and 7:14 interprets the manner of their fighting: they conquer in no other way than that of the Lamb, by persevering in the midst of suffering."[42]

Eighth, whereas John uses holy war *language* in Revelation 7, he transfers its *meaning* to non-military means of triumph over evil. In other words, *the people of God are portrayed as engaging in holy war, but in a spiritual, non-violent way.* John's aim is to show that "the decisive battle in God's eschatological war against all evil, including the power of Rome, has already been won – by the faithful witness and sacrificial death of Jesus. Christians are called to participate in his war and his victory – but by the same means as he employed:

41. Richard Bauckham, *The Climax of Prophecy: Studies on the Book of Revelation* (Edinburgh: T & T Clark, 1993), 222.
42. Beale, *Revelation*, 423.

bearing the witness of Jesus to the point of martyrdom."[43] Thus, later on, when the beast puts the martyrs to death, who wins? From an earthly perspective, the beast does (cf. 11:7; 13:7). But from a heavenly perspective, the martyrs are the real victors. They conquer by dying in their faith, committed to the end to Jesus.[44]

So, who are they?

So, who are the 144,000? Are they different from or one and the same with the innumerable multitude?

Most dispensational, pretribulational, premillennialists, that is, most who read the book of Revelation in a futurist sense, understand the 144,000 to be a Jewish remnant saved immediately after the rapture of the Church. Many then argue that, in the absence of the Church, they serve as *evangelists* who preach the gospel during the Great Tribulation. In other words, these are literally 144,000 (arithmetically speaking, neither 143,999 nor 144,001) ethnic descendants of Abraham, Isaac, and Jacob. The innumerable multitude, some go on to argue, are Gentiles saved in the tribu-

43. Bauckham, *The Climax of Prophecy,* 234.
44. Christopher Smith ("The Portrayal of the Church as the New Israel in the Names and Order of the Tribes in Revelation 7.5-8," *JSNT* 39 [1990]: 111-18; and again, "The Tribes of Revelation 7 and the Literary Competence of John the Seer," *JETS* 38 [1995]: 213-18), believes that the order in which the tribes are listed in Revelation 7 symbolizes the inclusion of Gentiles among the sealed and protected people of God. When the list in Revelation 7 is compared with that in Genesis 35:23-26, the changes are revealing. Judah is moved from fourth to first (perhaps because this is the tribe of Jesus). The sons of the concubines, Bilhah and Zilpah, are moved, dare we say "promoted," from last in the list in Genesis to positions three through six in Revelation (above six of the sons of the wives, Leah and Rachel). Dennis Johnson, taking up Smith's theory, concludes that "the elevation of these descendants of women who were outsiders to the covenant family signifies the inclusion of the Gentiles among 'the bond-servants of our God' (Rev. 7:3).... Thus the order of the tribes in Revelation 7 symbolizes the reign of Jesus, from the tribe of Judah; the incorporation of outcasts; and the exclusion of idolaters [specifically Dan and Ephraim] from the covenant community that God shields from his terrible wrath" (*Triumph of the Lamb: A Commentary on Revelation* [Phillipsburg: P & R Publishing, 2001], 132).

lation through the evangelistic efforts of the 144,000. Be it noted, however, that there is nothing explicitly said in this passage about these people functioning as evangelists or being responsible for the salvation of the multitude.[45]

My problem with this perspective begins with the fact that it depends entirely on a futurist interpretation of the book. Furthermore, why would God protect *only Jewish* believers and leave Gentile believers to endure such horrific judgments? And why would God protect *only 144,000* Jewish believers? Why would he not protect all of them? In Revelation 9:4 we read that only those with the seal of God on their foreheads are exempt from the demonic torments that are so horrible and agonizing that men will long to die. Is it feasible or consistent with the character of God that he should protect only a select group from such wrath while afflicting the rest of his blood-bought children with it? The answer is a resounding No. Therefore, those who are sealed on their forehead in 7:4-8 (and 9:4) must be *all* the redeemed, not a select few.

Robert Gundry, who believes in a post-tribulational rapture, argues that the 144,000 "constitute a Jewish remnant – not members of the Church and therefore not to be raptured – physically preserved through the tribulation, converted immediately after the rapture as they see their Messiah descending onto the earth (Zech. 3:8, 9; 12:9–13:1; Mal. 3:1-5; Rom. 11:26-27), and entering the millennium in their natural bodies to form the nucleus of the re-established Davidic kingdom. They would be 'orthodox' (though unconverted) Jews who will resist the seductions of the Antichrist. The designation 'bond-servants' (7:3), then, anticipates their role in the reestablishment of the Davidic kingdom.... Thus, the 144,000 will include both men and women who will populate and replenish the millennial kingdom of Israel. If they will resist the Antichrist but remain unbelievers in Christ until the second

---

45. Some find a problem with the literal interpretation in that "ten of the tribes had lost their national identity in the Assyrian exile, and the same fate befell Benjamin and Judah in A.D. 70 when the temple and Jerusalem were destroyed" (Beale, 419). However, see Acts 26:6-7.

coming, the reason for their sealing at once becomes apparent: their unconverted state will require special protection from the wrath of God and the persecution of the Antichrist." [46] One could hold this view without insisting that *only* 144,000 are saved. In other words, this view is compatible with taking the number figuratively.

Others contend that the number 144,000 is symbolic (as is the case with virtually every number in Revelation). "twelve" is both squared (the twelve tribes multiplied by the twelve apostles? cf. 21:12, 14) and multiplied by 1,000, a two-fold way of emphasizing completeness. Hence, John has in view *all the redeemed, all believers, whether Jew or Gentile, i.e., the Church.* Thus the 144,000 in Revelation 7:3-8 and the innumerable multitude in 7:9-17 refer to the same group of people viewed from differing perspectives. The former is the redeemed standing on the brink of battle, while the latter is the redeemed enjoying their heavenly reward. As Beale points out, "if Gentile believers are clearly identified together with 'the twelve tribes of the sons of Israel' as part of the new Jerusalem (21:12, 14, 24; 22:2-5), then it is not odd that John should refer to them together with Jewish Christians in 7:4 as 'the twelve tribes of the sons of Israel.'" [47] Let us also not forget that the "seal" of 7:2-3 is equivalent to their receiving a *name.* And one of the names written on Gentile believers, in addition to the name of God and Jesus, is "the name of the new Jerusalem" (3:12)! Finally, as noted earlier, in Revelation 9:4 the demonic scorpions are told to harm only those "who do not have the seal of God on their foreheads," implying that all Christians (whether Jewish or Gentile) have such a seal.

Earlier in this chapter I pointed out how Christians, i.e., the Church, comprised of both believing Jews and believing Gentiles, are described in Revelation as the true people of God, the true Israel (as seen from the application of Exod. 19:6 to the Church in Revelation 1:6 and 5:10; see also Isa. 62:2 and 65:15 applied to

---

46. Robert H. Gundry, *The Church and the Tribulation* (Grand Rapids: Zondervan, 1973), 82-83.

47. Beale, *Revelation,* 417.

the Church in Rev. 2:17 and 3:12; and Isa. 43:4; 45:14; 49:23; and 60:14 applied to the Church in Rev. 3:9). This is in keeping with other texts in the New Testament where the new covenant community, the Church, is referred to with designations and titles previously used exclusively of Old Testament Israel (Rom. 2:29 [cf. 9:6]; 2 Cor. 1:20-21; Gal. 3:29; 6:16; Eph. 1:11, 14; Phil. 3:3-8; Titus. 2:14; James 1:1 [where the Church is addressed as "the twelve tribes in the Dispersion"]; 1 Pet. 1:1 [where the Church is addressed as "elect exiles of the dispersion"]; 2:9).

Revelation 7:9-17

[9]After this I looked, and behold, a great multitude that no one could number, from every nation, from all tribes and peoples and languages, standing before the throne and before the Lamb, clothed in white robes, with palm branches in their hands, [10]and crying out with a loud voice, "Salvation belongs to our God who sits on the throne, and to the Lamb!" [11]And all the angels were standing around the throne and around the elders and the four living creatures, and they fell on their faces before the throne and worshiped God, [12]saying, "Amen! Blessing and glory and wisdom and thanksgiving and honor and power and might be to our God forever and ever! Amen." [13]Then one of the elders addressed me, saying, "Who are these, clothed in white robes, and from where have they come?" [14]I said to him, "Sir, you know." And he said to me, [15]"These are the ones coming out of the great tribulation. They have washed their robes and made them white in the blood of the Lamb. "Therefore they are before the throne of God, and serve him day and night in his temple; and he who sits on the throne will shelter them with his presence. [16]They shall hunger no more, neither thirst anymore; the sun shall not strike them, nor any scorching heat. [17]For the Lamb in the midst of the throne will be their shepherd, and he will guide them to springs of living water, and God will wipe away every tear from their eyes."

In light of the evidence given above, I believe the innumerable multitude and the 144,000 constitute one group of people: the redeemed of the Church. In Revelation 7:4-8 they are numbered,

like unto the census of Old Testament Israel, because they constitute a messianic army called to carry on the battle of the Lion of
Judah. They are the true Israel of God, the remnant of believers
whose salvation and preservation have been secured by the seal
of God. Perhaps also they are numbered to highlight the fact that
"God has determined exactly who will receive his redemptive seal,
and only he knows the precise number of his true 'servants' (so 7:3;
2 Tim. 2:19)."[48] In Revelation 7:9-17 they are innumerable, at least
from a human point of view, because the redeemed are viewed in
terms of their actual number.

The "great multitude" that John sees are precisely those in Revelation 5:9 whom Jesus redeemed "from every tribe and language
and people and nation". The language John uses, "a great multitude, that no one could number," sounds remarkably similar to the
promise given to Abraham. That promise consisted primarily of
two elements. First, Abraham was promised that he would have
innumerable descendants, described as "the dust of the earth,"
"the stars of the sky," and "the sand of the sea" (Gen. 13:16; 15:5;
22:17-18). In Genesis 16:10 God said to Abraham: "I will surely
multiply your offspring so that they cannot be numbered for multitude." This promise was repeated to Isaac (Gen. 26:4) and to Jacob
(Gen. 28:14; 32:12), and is found in numerous other Old Testament texts (Exod. 32:13; Deut. 1:10; 10:22; 28:62; 2 Sam. 17:11;
1 Kings 3:8; 4:20; Neh. 9:23; Isa. 10:22; 48:19; 51:2; Hosea 1:10).
Second, God promised Abraham that he would be the father of
many nations (Gen. 17:4-6, 16), a promise also repeated to Isaac
and Jacob (Gen. 28:14; 32:12; 35:11; 48:19).

In these Old Testament texts it is the physical progeny of Israel
who are in view. But amazingly here in Revelation 7:9 it is the
Church in whom those promises appear to be fulfilled. Verse 9a
points to the fulfillment of the first promise above, while verse 9b
points to the fulfillment of the second. It may well be, then, that
John views the innumerable multitude of Revelation 7:9 as the
consummate fulfillment of the Abrahamic promise.

---

48. Beale, *Revelation*, 424.

In verse 10 the saints attribute their "salvation" to God and to the Lamb. In Paul's writings this noun normally refers to deliverance from sin and guilt. In this context, however, something else may be in view. John is describing the preservation and protection of the saints in the midst of suffering. Their "sealing" is designed to safeguard their souls, lest they deny Jesus under the pressures of persecution. The focus of Revelation 7:9-17 is the heavenly reward for those who do, in fact, persevere. Therefore, it may be that by "salvation" John refers not so much to the forgiveness of sins but to their preservation in faith in the midst of trials.

The words "great tribulation" occur only elsewhere in the New Testament in Matthew 24:21 where they point to the destruction of Jerusalem and its temple, an expression of the judgment of God against Israel for its calloused rejection of the Messiah. If my later argument is correct (see the chapters on Matthew 24 and the Olivet Discourse) – that the events of A.D. 33–70 are a microcosmic foreshadowing of what happens on a macrocosmic scale throughout the present age – the use of such terminology here is understandable.

On the other hand, "tribulation" is nothing new or unexpected for Christians in any age. John's presence on the island of Patmos is described as "tribulation" (1:9; see also 2:9-10, 22). Tribulation is the normative experience for all believers, as several texts indicate (John 16:33; Acts 14:22; Rom. 5:3; 8:35-36; 2 Tim. 3:12). In fact, twenty-one of Paul's twenty-three uses of this term (*thlipsis*) refer to an on-going, present day experience of the Christian. The tribulation we suffer is "great" because of the intensity of opposition from the world and its god, the devil.

Either of these views, or perhaps a combination of both, is probably in John's mind. In any case, nothing requires us to think of the "great tribulation" as a special period of time reserved exclusively for the end of the age through which only the last generation of believers might pass. All Christians in every age face the reality of what John describes.

Further, there is nothing to indicate that only martyrs are in view. If they are the focus of John's comments, they could also serve to represent all believers who must suffer, whether or not they actually lose their lives. That "they have washed their robes and made them white in the blood of the Lamb" (7:14) would mean that, notwithstanding the intensity of persecution and resistance, they have retained their faith and testimony concerning the death of Jesus on their behalf and the cleansing power of his shed blood. On the other hand, we noted above that the 144,000 (= innumerable multitude) may be a way of portraying the people of God as a messianic army ready to engage in holy war (spiritually speaking, of course). If so, the reference to the "washing" of their clothes may be an allusion to Numbers 31:19-20, 24 where such was required for ritual purification after the shedding of blood.

There may also be here an allusion to the Exodus event of the Old Testament. More than an allusion, it may be John's way of saying that the Church is the true Israel in whom the Old Testament exodus event finds its typological fulfillment. We simply can't ignore these unmistakable facts: a great multitude comes out of trial and tribulation (*thlipsis* is used in the LXX of Exodus 4:31 to describe Israel's experience); Israel is portrayed as washing their garments (Exod. 19:10, 14) and being sprinkled with blood (Exod. 24:8) to prepare them for God's tabernacling among them, as a result of which they receive food, water, protection, and comfort.

Revelation 7:15 speaks of the saints in God's heavenly "temple" and of God "spreading his tabernacle over them" (or "he ... will shelter them with his presence," ESV). This is a clear allusion to Ezekiel 37:26-28, a passage that in its Old Testament context is a prophecy of Israel's restoration. There God says, "I will make a covenant of peace with them. It shall be an everlasting covenant with them. And I will set them in their land and multiply them, and will set my sanctuary in their midst forevermore. My dwelling place shall be with them, and I will be their God, and they shall be my people. Then the nations will know that I am the Lord who sanctifies Israel, when my sanctuary is in their midst forevermore." Beale's conclusion deserves close consideration:

> The link with Ezekiel is confirmed from the parallel in Rev. 21:3, where Ezek. 37:27 is quoted more fully and is immediately followed

in 21:4,6b by the same OT allusions found in 7:16-17. Yet again, the innumerable multitudes of redeemed in the church are viewed as the fulfillment of a prophecy concerning Israel's latter-day restoration. The application of Ezek. 37:27 to the church is striking because Ezekiel emphasizes that when this prophecy takes place the immediate result will be that "the nations will recognize that I am the Lord who sanctifies Israel, when my sanctuary is in their midst" (37:28). Therefore, Ezekiel 37 was a prophecy uniquely applicable to ethnic or theocratic Israel in contrast to the nations, yet now John understands it as fulfilled in the church. [49]

The comforts and blessings of God's presence are portrayed in terms drawn from Isaiah 49:10, yet another text that refers to the results of Israel's restoration: "they shall not hunger or thirst, neither scorching wind nor sun shall strike them, for he who has pity on them will lead them [i.e., he will be their shepherd], and by springs of water will guide them." As if that were not enough, another prophetic promise tied to Israel's restoration is appended to this list of blessings now applied to the Church: "God will wipe away every tear from their eyes" (Isa. 25:8; Rev. 7:17).

There seems to be no escaping the fact that John sees the Old Testament hope of Israel's restoration and all its attendant blessings fulfilled in the salvation of the Christian multitudes who comprise the Church, both believing Jews and Gentiles.

Conclusion

We come finally to the current nation of Israel and its claim to possession of the land in which it dwells. I can do no better here than to quote the words of John Piper in a sermon he preached on Romans 11. His comments deserve a wide hearing:

> The promises made to Abraham, including the promise of the Land, will be inherited as an everlasting gift only by true, spiritual Israel, not disobedient, unbelieving Israel. In other words, the promises cannot be

---

49. Beale, *Revelation*, 440.

demanded by anyone just because he is Jewish. Jewish ethnicity has a place in God's plan, but it is not enough to secure anything. It does not in itself qualify a person to be an heir of the promise to Abraham and his offspring. Romans 9:8 says it clearly: "It is not the children of the flesh who are the children of God, but the children of the promise are counted as offspring." Being born Jewish does not make one an heir of the promise – neither the promise of the Land nor any other promise.

Be careful not to infer from this that Gentile nations (like Arabs) have the right to molest Israel. God's judgments on Israel do not sanction human sin against Israel. Israel still has *human* rights among nations even when she forfeits her present *divine* right to the Land. Remember that nations which gloated over her divine discipline were punished by God (Isaiah 10:5-13; Joel 3:2).

So the promise to Abraham that his descendants will inherit the Land does not mean that all Jews inherit that promise. It will come finally to the true Israel, the Israel that keeps covenant and obeys her God.

Therefore, the secular state of Israel today may not claim a present divine right to the Land, but they and we should seek a peaceful settlement not based on present divine rights, but on international principles of justice, mercy, and practical feasibility.

[Therefore] … we should not give blanket approval to Jewish or to Palestinian actions. We should approve or denounce according to Biblical standards of justice and mercy among peoples. We should encourage our representatives to seek a just settlement that takes the historical and social claims of both peoples into account. Neither should be allowed to sway the judgments of justice by a present divine claim to the land. . . .

Therefore Jewish believers in Jesus and Gentile believers will inherit the Land. And the easiest way to see this is to see that we will inherit the world which includes the Land. Jewish Christians and Gentile Christians will not quibble over the real estate of the Promised Land because the entire new heavens and the new earth will be ours. 1 Corinthians 3:21-23, "All things are yours, whether Paul or Apollos or Cephas or the *world* or life or death or the present or the future – all are yours, and you are Christ's, and Christ is God's." All followers of

Christ, and only followers of Christ, will inherit the earth, including the Land. [50]

In yet another sermon from Romans, Piper declares that

> a covenant-breaking people does not have a present claim on covenant promises. Therefore it is wrong for America or for Christians to be unquestioningly pro-Israel and anti-Palestinian in the political and geographical situation of the Middle East. It may be right to be pro-Israel or pro-Palestinian on any given issue, but while Israel is breaking the covenant with her God by rejecting his Messiah, the criterion for what is right in the Middle East should be equally applied standards of justice and mercy among nations, not divine rights or covenant privileges. Our relation to Jews and Palestinians should be to love them and treat them with mercy and justice, as we do all others. Anti-Semitism is sin. And unquestioning rejection of possible rights of Palestinians is sin. [51]

I'll conclude with two important observations.

(1) The view that I've defended in this chapter is consistent with either historic premillennialism or amillennialism. John Piper, among many others, is a premillennialist. I, on the other hand, am an amillennialist. But we both agree that there is only one people of God, the Church, comprised of believing Jews and believing Gentiles.

(2) In all of this discussion I have not addressed the question of whether the Bible teaches a widespread salvation of Jewish people at the close of this present age. Piper believes that in Romans 11 Paul affirms just such a massive salvific ingathering of ethnic Jews in some way associated with the second coming of Christ. I do not, as I explain in detail in Chapter Ten.

---

50. John Piper, a sermon on "Israel, Palestine and the Middle East," March 7, 2004; www.desiringgod.org.

51. Piper, "The Gentiles are Included," a sermon on Romans 9:24-29, April 27, 2003; www.desiringgod.org.

Whatever view one may take on that point (and the interpretation of Romans 11:25-27), more important still is that whoever among the Jewish people is saved, regardless of when that may occur, will enter the kingdom in the same manner and on the same terms as do Gentile believers. Whether that salvation is eschatological (at the end of the present age) or historical (progressively, throughout the course of the present age), I do not believe it is God's purpose to reconstitute or re-establish a theocratic nation separate from the Church. The Church is the only "holy nation" (1 Pet. 2:9) that will inherit the promises of the covenant.

Chapter Seven

The Eschatology of Jesus: Matthew 24 and The Olivet Discourse (1)

A side from the book of Revelation, there is hardly a more important section of Scripture on the subject of biblical eschatology than Matthew 24, the famous Olivet Discourse delivered by Jesus to his disciples shortly before his betrayal into the hands of his enemies.[1] Most Christians simply assume that Jesus is describing the end of human history and his second advent. In fact, this interpretation has become so firmly entrenched in the evangelical community that people are shocked to learn that anyone would dare question it. The language and imagery of this chapter have been quoted with such frequency and invariably associated with the "signs" of Christ's imminent return that it's difficult to gain a hearing for any alternative suggestions. Permit me but one illustration.

The advertisement is seemingly ubiquitous. It has appeared in virtually every daily newspaper of every major city in the U.S. I most recently saw it in the Sports section of *USA Today* (Wednesday, March 31, 2010). If you haven't seen it, you are surely among the minority. It is, if nothing else, bold and unequivocal in its prediction that ***Christ is Coming Very Soon!*** The article proceeds to identify "8 Compelling Reasons" why this is true.

---

1. Largely parallel versions of the discourse are found in Mark 13:1-37 and Luke 21:5-36.

What I find most interesting and instructive for our purposes in this book is that, in five of the eight "compelling reasons," Matthew 24 and the Olivet Discourse of Jesus figure prominently. I don't think it is a stretch to say that without the Olivet Discourse the article would never have been written, or, if it had, it would lack substantive punch. For example, the increase of "famines, violence and wars" is allegedly a sign that the return of Christ is near (citing Matt. 24:6-8). The increase in earthquakes is also cited as an indication that the end is near (citing Matt. 24:7). The explosion of cults and counterfeit spirituality (Matt. 24:24), as well as the deceptive activity of Antichrist (Matt. 24:15) are all cited as infallible signs of the impending second coming.

I've drawn our attention to this article simply to illustrate a commonplace among evangelical believers today, namely, the appeal to the words of Jesus in the Olivet Discourse as the clearest and most "compelling" evidence for his soon return. This makes what I'm going to ask of you indescribably difficult, especially for those who have almost unconsciously embraced the prophetic scenarios outlined by modern dispensationalism. My challenge to us all is that we read this narrative with keen sensitivity to the immediate historical context in which Jesus was speaking and against the background, not of the *Wall Street Journal*, TBN, or *USA Today*, but the Old Testament Scriptures in which both Jesus and his disciples were well-versed. In other words, we must permit Jesus himself to establish the focus of his discourse and the Old Testament to define the terms he uses. I therefore concur with Andrew Perriman that we should try "to read forwards from the first century rather than backwards from the twenty-first century. One of the reasons why the apocalyptic language of the New Testament can be so puzzling to the modern interpreter is that we cannot help but read it retrospectively and with the advantage, which more often than not turns out to be the disadvantage, of hindsight. It is rather like words written on a glass door. Once we have gone through the door, the text is reversed and becomes difficult to decipher. To make sense of it, we must at least *imagine* how it must have appeared from the other side of the door – as it would have been viewed by those for whom it was written."[2] When this is done it will become evident that Jesus was actually describing, in response to his disciples' question, the fall of Jerusalem and the destruction of the Temple in A.D. 70

An Overview of Matthew 24:1-31

Much of the confusion over what Jesus said comes from the artificial chapter divisions in our English Bibles. Instead of beginning with Matthew 24:1, we need to back up into chapter 23 and take note of his scathing denunciation of the religious leaders of his day. On them, said Jesus, will come the judgment for "all the righteous blood shed on earth" (23:35). And then to reinforce his point he declares, "Truly, I say to you, all these things will come upon this generation" (23:36), an unmistakable reference to his contemporaries. This isn't the first time Jesus has issued a warning of impending judgment on the people of Israel. One should also read Matthew 21:33-46, the most important statement of which is found in verse 43: "Therefore I tell you, the kingdom of God will be taken away from you and given to a people producing its fruits" (see also Matt. 22:1-14, especially v. 7). The most explicit and ominous statement comes at the close of Matthew 23, following his plaintive cry for repentance: "O Jerusalem, Jerusalem, the city that kills the prophets and stones those who are sent to it! How often would I have gathered your children together as a hen gathers her brood under wings, and you would not! See, your house is left to you desolate. For I tell you, you will not see me again, until you say, 'Blessed is he who comes in the name of the Lord'" (23:37-39).

Undoubtedly in great consternation by his words, the disciples point out to him "the buildings of the temple" (24:1b). Jesus' response is decisive and inescapable: "You see all these, do you not? Truly, I say to you, there will not be left here one stone upon another that will not be thrown down" (24:2).[3] He could hardly

---

2. Andrew Perriman, *The Coming of the Son of Man: New Testament Eschatology for an Emerging Church* (Waynesboro, GA: Paternoster, 2005), 3.

3. As for the reference to the "stones", as well as a general description of the physical features of the temple, see Josephus, *Wars* 5.184-226 (cf. *Antiquities*,

have been more explicit about the impending visible and gruesome destruction of both the city and temple that was to occur in A.D. 70. To put it bluntly, as Jesus did, the temple will be flattened!

Just as dramatically as Jesus had entered Jerusalem (Matt. 21:1-17, the so-called "Triumphal Entry") and its temple, he now departs. This once grand and glorious house of God is now consigned exclusively to them ("See, **your** house is left to **you** desolate," 23:38; emphasis mine). The echoes of God's withdrawal from the temple in Ezekiel's vision reverberate in the words of our Lord (see Ezek. 10:18-19; 11:22-23). The ultimate physical destruction of the temple is but the outward consummation of God's spiritual repudiation of it. Jesus has now left, never to return. Indeed, the action of Jesus in departing the temple and taking his seat on the Mount of Olives (Matt. 24:3) recalls Ezekiel 11:23 where we read that "the glory of the Lord went up from the midst of the city and stood on the mountain that is on the east side of the city." [4]

15.392-402, 410-20 for similar comments). All citations from Josephus are taken from *The Works of Josephus*, translated by William Whiston (Hendrickson Publishers, 1987).

4. We should note the connection between Matthew 23:38 and v. 39 ("for"). This suggests that the only condition on which the abandonment of the "house/temple" can be reversed or averted is now to be stated. "This act of judgment," notes R.T. France, "can be averted only if the people of Jerusalem are prepared to follow the lead given by the Galilean pilgrims in 21:9 (the acclamation from Ps 118:26 is here given in the same words) and welcome Jesus as their Messiah" (*The Gospel of Matthew* [Grand Rapids: Eerdmans, 2007], 884). Contrary to what many have thought, "there is no prediction here, only a condition. Or, rather, the only prediction is an emphatic negative, 'from now on you will certainly not see me,' to which the following 'until' clause provides the only possible exception. They will not see him again *until* they welcome him, but the indefinite phrasing of the second clause gives no assurance that such a welcome will ever be forthcoming" (ibid., 884-85). Therefore, this statement "spells out the condition on which Jerusalem may be restored to a relationship with its Messiah, but it gives no indication as to whether or not that condition will ever be met" (ibid., 885). "*Heos an* with the subjunctive," notes France, "makes this in effect what grammarians call an unreal condition: if you were to do this, you would see me, but whether you will do so remains unknown.... It is remarkable that so many interpreters can find a positive prediction in what

Thus the temple has been abandoned, not only geographically and physically but spiritually and symbolically. The glory of God's presence has departed. They cross over the Kidron Valley and climb up the western slope of the Mount of Olives. There, as they look back over the valley at the magnificence of that structure in full view, the disciples approach Jesus with a question: "Tell us, when will these things be, and what will be the sign of your coming and of the close of the age?" (24:3; see also Mark 13:1; Luke 21:5-6).

Jesus responds with two crucial answers. First, he tells them when the temple will be destroyed, *but*, second, he also tells them that, contrary to their expectations, his second coming and the end of the age are *not* to occur at that time (i.e., not at the same time as the destruction of the temple). In other words, the destruction of the temple *can* be dated by signs, but the second coming of Christ *cannot*.

Matthew 24:4-28 thus contains a description of events prior to and inclusive of the destruction of the temple. (1) Verses 4-14 refer to events that are to characterize the entire period from A.D. 33 to A.D. 70, none of which, in themselves, are signs that the end of the city and its temple are immediately at hand. (2) Verses 15-28 refer to the one sign that indicates the prophesied destruction is about to occur. Whereas the events of verses 4-14 are characteristic of the time, and signal only the beginning of birth pains, verse 15 provides a sign (the *"abomination of desolation"*) that unmistakably confirms the consummation of God's judgment against Israel has come.

The debate surfaces with the interpretation of verses 29-31. Three views contend for our allegiance. Some, indeed most, believe that verses 29-31 describe the second coming at the end of history. A few insist that verse 29 describes the present inter-advent age, while vv. 30-31 portray the second coming. The view that I will defend is that verses 29-31 have *nothing* directly[5] to say about

---

is in fact an emphatically negative prediction (*ou me* with subjunctive) with only an indefinite possibility (*heos an*) set against it" (ibid.).

5. Although not a "direct" reference to the second coming, it is possible that these verses "indirectly" allude to the return of Christ at the close of history. The argument is often made that what happened locally in conjunction with the judgment of Jerusalem and its temple in the first century is a pattern or template

the second coming of Christ. Rather, they are a symbolic description of the fall of Jerusalem in A.D. 70 and the inauguration of the church age in which the gospel is proclaimed and the elect of God are saved. This period of unprecedented tribulation (A.D. 66–70) inaugurates or introduces a time of undetermined length, during which tribulation will be prominent, but during which also we are alertly to look for the second coming of Christ. This is the present age in which we live, called by Luke "the times of the Gentiles" (Luke 21:24; cf. Rom. 11:25).[6]

Thus, *"the tribulation of those days"* (v. 29) refers to all that occurred from 33 to 70, with special reference to the events relating to the siege and sack of Jerusalem in 66–70 (called the *"great tribulation"* in v. 21). The generation to whom Jesus was speaking would live to see "all these things" occur, "these things" being a reference to the events leading up to and including the destruction of Jerusalem and the temple (Matt. 24:34-35). Although there will be signs and events indicating when the temple will fall, the second coming of Jesus at the end of the age (what he refers to in verse 36 as "that day and hour") will be unannounced: so be prepared (vv. 36-51).

Let me summarize. Although this entire present age intervening between the first and second comings of Christ is one of *tribulation*, trial, and distress, the so-called *great tribulation* mentioned in verse 21 (and described in verses 15-31) *has already come and gone*. It is to be identified with the siege on Jerusalem during the years 66–70, which culminated in the destruction of the city and its temple by the armies of Rome (the latter being the "abomination of desolation" referred to in verse 15). Thus **"The Great Tribula-**

---

for what will happen globally at the close of history. More on this later.

6. It should be noted that some argue that "the times of the Gentiles" (Luke 21:24) was the very short span of time between the beginning of the siege of Jerusalem and the city's final destruction. In other words, "the times of the Gentiles" does not refer to the present age but to that period 66–70 during which the Gentiles (in particular, the Romans) "trampled under foot" Jerusalem and destroyed her temple. If so, "the 'trampling' then refers to the physical acts involved in laying waste the city" (Peter W. L. Walker, *Jesus and the Holy City: New Testament Perspectives on Jerusalem* [Grand Rapids: Eerdmans, 1996], 101, n. 167).

tion" of Matthew 24:21 (called "days of vengeance" in Luke 21:22 and "days of affliction" in Mark 13:19) **is not a future event but an established fact of past history.**

A Brief Defense

There are several initial reasons why I understand the passage in this way. First, the context pertains to the predictions of God's wrath against the *current* (first-century) generation of Israel. We saw this clearly in Matthew 23:35, 36, 38. This leads to the expectation of fulfillment at that historical moment. Second, the *question* posed by the disciples pertained to the temple then standing in Jerusalem, out of which they had just departed, at which they were then looking, and about whose prophesied destruction they were wondering. Third, Jesus' *answer* pertains to the then-standing temple, not some future temple (cf. v. 2). Fourth, the circumstances described in verses 15-22 are geographically, historically, and culturally limited to conditions relevant in the first century.

Fifth, the entire section is couched in terms of what his actual (original) hearers are to see, hear, and experience. One cannot easily dismiss the repeated use of the second person in Jesus' warnings and instructions (e.g., "**you** will hear" [24:6], "see that **you** are not alarmed" [24:6], "they will deliver **you** up to tribulation, and put **you** to death, and **you** will be hated" [24:9], "so when **you** see the abomination of desolation" [24:15], "if anyone says to **you**" [24:23], "I have told **you** beforehand" [24:25], "so also, when **you** see all these things" [24:33]).

Sixth, and most important of all, Jesus says that this prophetic scenario applies to "***this generation***" (v. 34). Some try to evade this point by arguing that the word translated "generation" actually means "race" and that Jesus, therefore, was simply saying that the "Jewish race" would not die out until all these things took place. But this would require the Greek word *genos*, whereas the word here is *genea*. Furthermore, the word *genea* occurs twenty-seven times in the Gospels and *never once* means "race".[7] Additional study reveals

7. See Matt. 1:17; 11:16; 12:39, 41, 42, 45; 16:4; 17:17; 23:36; 24:34; Mark 8:12, 38; 9:19; 13:30; Luke 1:48, 50; 7:31; 9:41; 11:29, 30, 31, 32, 50, 51; 16:8; 17:25; 21:32.

that the word "generation" is used elsewhere in Matthew (and the other gospels) of *those living in Christ's day* (see Matt. 12:38-39; 16:4; 17:17). Every time the words "this generation" occur in the Gospels they mean *Jesus' contemporaries*, i.e., the sum total of those living at the same time he did (read Matt. 11:16; 12:41, 42, 45; and especially 23:36). Moreover, the adjective "this" points to the contemporary nature of the generation Jesus had in mind; if he had in mind a future generation he would more likely have chosen the adjective "that."

I agree, then, with Gentry: "Surely Jesus does not denounce the first-century temple in which He is standing (24:1) by declaring it 'desolate' (23:38), prophesying its total destruction (24:2), then answering the question 'when shall these things be?' (v. 3), and warning about the temple's 'abomination of desolation' (v. 15) only to speak about the destruction of a totally different temple some two thousand years (or more) later!"[8]

Their Question, His Answer

Upon reading Matthew 24:2, we need to remember that Micah (3:12) and Jeremiah (7:12-14) had dared to make similar predictions of Solomon's temple in the sixth century B.C., both of which were fulfilled in 587 B.C. By the time of Jesus, however, it was generally believed among the Jews that the temple was indestructible.

Let's look again at the question the disciples put to Jesus: "Tell us, when will these things be, and what will be the sign of your coming and of the close of the age" (24:3). "These things" can only be a reference to the prophesied destruction of Jerusalem and its temple (first, in 23:36-38; again, in 24:2). I believe Jesus answers this first question in 24:4-35.

The disciples appear to believe that when this destruction occurs, the second coming (or *parousia*) of Christ will likewise take place. They evidently believed, as did most in that day and time, that the

8. Thomas Ice and Kenneth L. Gentry Jr., *The Great Tribulation: Past or Future, Two Evangelicals Debate the Question* (Grand Rapids: Kregel Publications, 1999), 24.

temple was as permanent as the world itself. If the former was to be destroyed, it must mark the consummation of history as we know it. Jesus corrects this mistaken assumption. Thus, he says, in effect: "No, the two events are not simultaneous. 'These things' concerning the destruction of Jerusalem and the temple will indeed occur in the lifetime of 'this generation' (23:36; 24:34). There will be signs that point to it [which Jesus will outline in verses 4-28]. But my coming and the end of history will not occur at that time. There will follow a lengthy delay (described in 24:36–25:30). No signs will point to the precise moment of my return. Therefore, you must remain alert at all times [as is described in 24:36-51 and the many parables in 25:1-30]."

Thus, I agree with R.T. France that Matthew 24:4-35 "is concerned with the destruction of the temple, answering the question 'When?' with a clear time-scale summed up in v. 34, and that the second question about the *parousia* comes into the frame only with the new beginning in 24:36 ('but concerning…'), which, in contrast with what has gone before, speaks of a 'day and hour' which no one can predict, not even Jesus himself (who has just predicted quite specifically the time within which the temple will be destroyed)."[9]

It's actually quite straightforward, but I'll repeat myself for the sake of clarity. In response to the question, "When will these things be?" i.e., when will the temple be destroyed in fulfillment of our Lord's prediction, Jesus provides the answer in verses 4-35. He provides a clear time framework: it will happen within the lifespan of the current generation (v. 34). In response to the second question, "what will be the sign of your coming and of the close of the age?", Jesus again provides an answer beginning in verse 36. Whereas in the first case there are clear time indicators, there are none in the second. "Thus one event (the destruction of the temple) falls within defined and predictable history, and those who know what to look for can see it coming, while the other (the *parousia*) cannot

---

9. R.T. France, *The Gospel of Matthew* (Grand Rapids: Eerdmans, 2007), 890.

be tied down to a time frame, and even Jesus does not know when it will be and so will offer no 'sign.'"[10]

Signs of the Times

Our Lord's comments in verses 4-14 are designed to prevent premature excitement and speculation about when the events of verse 3 would occur. "Don't jump to any hasty conclusions," says Jesus. The main point is that these are *not* signs of the impending destruction of Jerusalem nor are they signs of Christ's second advent. These events are only the beginning of birth pains. They serve no

---

10. Ibid., 899. Some interpreters contend that the three questions asked in v. 3 have a single focus. The disciples were asking about the time when Jesus would "come" in judgment to destroy the temple and bring the Jewish "age" to an end. These interpreters, among whom N.T. Wright is the most articulate, point out that "within the mainline Jewish writings of this period, covering a wide range of styles, genres, political persuasions and theological perspectives, *there is virtually no evidence the Jews were expecting the end of the space-time universe....* What, then, did they believe was going to happen? They believed that *the present world order* would come to an end – the world order in which pagans held power, and Jews, the covenant people of the creator God, did not" (*The New Testament and the People of God* [Minneapolis: Fortress Press, 1992], 333). The disciples, then, says Wright, were "looking for the fulfillment of Israel's hopes, for the story told so often in Israel's scriptures to reach its appointed climax. And the 'close of the age' for which they longed was not the end of the space-time order, but the end of the present evil age..., and the introduction of the (still very much this-worldly) age to come... – in other words, the end of Israel's period of mourning and exile and the beginning of her freedom and vindication. Matthew 24.3, therefore, is most naturally read, in its first-century Jewish context, not as a question about (what scholars have come to call, in technical language) the 'parousia', but as a question about Jesus' 'coming' or 'arriving' [parousia] in the sense of his actual enthronement as king, consequent upon the dethronement of the present powers that were occupying the holy city....The question... seen from within the story the disciples have in their minds, must be read to mean: When will you come in your kingdom? When will the evil age, symbolized by the present Jerusalem regime, be over?" (Wright, *Jesus and the Victory of God* [Minneapolis: Fortress Press, 1996], 345-46). For a careful and convincing response, see Kenneth Gentry, *The Olivet Discourse Made Easy* (Draper, VA: Apologetics Group Media, 2010), 43-50.

purpose at all in telling us when or how soon Jesus is coming back. They are events which will characterize the period 33 to 70.

It's actually quite ironic "how often occurrences such as those mentioned in these verses are appealed to by those who are trying to work out a pattern for eschatological events, whereas in fact they are mentioned here precisely in order to *discourage* such speculation and to assert that the events described are *not* part of an eschatological scenario, but rather routine events within world history which must not be given more weight than they deserve."[11] In any case, let's take note of those events that Jesus insists will characterize the next forty or so years leading up to and culminating in the destruction of city and temple.

He begins by mentioning the appearance of *religious impostors and messianic pretenders* (v. 5), examples of which we find in the book of Acts (see 5:36-37; 8:9-10; 13:6; 21:38). Josephus reports that during the reign of Nero deceivers and false prophets were arrested on a daily basis.[12] In his *Ecclesiastical History*, Eusebius refers to the prevalence of false messiahs in this period.

As for *military conflict* (v. 6), the period A.D. 33-70 witnessed countless military disturbances. An uprising in Caesarea took 20,000 Jewish lives; at Scythopolis 13,000 Jews were killed; in Alexandria 50,000 were slain; 10,000 were killed in Damascus. When the Emperor Caligula ordered his statue to be erected in the temple at Jerusalem (A.D. 40), the Jews refused. As a result, they lived in a state of fearful anxiety over imminent war with Rome and were in such distress that they even neglected to till the land.

The *Annals* of Tacitus, which covers events from A.D. 14 to 68, describes the turmoil of this period with phrases such as "disturbances in Germany," "commotions in Africa," "commotions in Thrace," "insurrections in Gaul," "intrigues among the Parthians,"

---

11. France, *Matthew*, 901-02.
12. See Josephus, *Antiquities* 18.85-87 (a Samaritan), 20.97-99 (Theudas), 102 (the sons of Judas of Galilee), 169-72 ("the Egyptian"), 160-61, 167-68, 188 (various unnamed "impostors").

"the war in Britain," and "the war in Armenia."[13] The "end" (v. 6) that these events do *not* signal refers to the end or termination of Jewish national existence; the end of the city; as well as the end of the temple (primarily the latter).

Political upheaval and turmoil (v. 7a) were also very much characteristic of this period of time, as has been exhaustively documented by N.T. Wright.[14] As for *natural disasters* (v. 7b), the famine described in Acts 11:28 occurred in the year 44. It resulted in the disciples at Antioch mounting a huge relief effort to ease the burden of the Christians in Judea (Acts 11:29). Three other famines occurred during the reign of Claudius. The Roman historians Tacitus and Suetonius both mention the prevalence of famines in this period of history (in particular the widespread famine in Rome in 51). Earthquakes were also common (see Acts 16:26). There were recorded earthquakes in Crete, Smyrna, Miletus, Chios, Samos, Apamea, Campania, and Rome. The cities of Laodicea, Hierapolis, and Colossae were devastated by a quake in the year 60. In A.D. 58 Seneca wrote:

> How often have the cities of Asia and Achaea fallen with one fatal shock! How many cities have been swallowed up in Syria! How many in Macedonia! How often has Paphos become a ruin. News has often been brought to us of the demolition of whole cities at once.[15]

In Luke 21:11 we read about "terrors and great signs from heaven," which when taken in the immediate context of famines and earthquakes probably refer to natural phenomena. In particular, we know that a comet appeared around 60 during Nero's reign, leading to public speculation that some change in the political scene was imminent. Then *Halley's Comet* appeared in 66. Not long after this, Nero committed suicide. Josephus wrote in *The War of the*

---

13. Cited by Gary DeMar, *Last Days Madness: Obsession of the Modern Church* (Atlanta: American Vision, 1997), 53.
14. For an extensive treatment of these events, see N.T. Wright in chapter 6 of his book, *The New Testament and the People of God*.
15. Seneca, *Epistles*, 91. Cited in Gentry, *The Olivet Discourse Made Easy*, 75.

Jews that "there was a star resembling a sword, which stood over the city, and a comet, that continued a whole year." [16]

As verse 8 makes clear, none of these "birth pains" were meant at any time to mislead Christians into thinking that either Christ's second coming was imminent or that God's judgments against Jerusalem were about to begin. "Birth pains" in itself means "not yet," especially when combined with the word "beginning".

Persecution and martyrdom are mentioned in verses 9-10. This marks a turn from widespread phenomena to what will occur among Jesus' disciples and the community of faith. Mark's version reads as follows: "But be on your guard. For they will deliver you over to councils, and you will be beaten in synagogues, and you will stand before governors and kings for my sake, to bear witness before them" (13:9). The reference to "courts/councils/synagogues" indicates that Jesus has in mind a first-century fulfillment. After 70, when the Jewish religious and political systems ceased to exist, there were no councils or synagogues. We see fulfillment of this word in Acts 4:1-18; 5:17-40 (synagogues) and 12:1; 23:24; 24:27 (governors and kings; see also Acts 8:1). The reality of verse 10 is caused by the pressures and pains of verse 9 (cf. 1 John 2:19; 2 Tim. 1:15 ["all those in Asia have turned away from me"]; 4:10 ["Demas has forsaken me, having loved this present world"], 16 ["at my first defense no one stood with me, but all forsook me"]).

In speaking of *false prophets* (v. 11), one need only remember that much of what we read in Galatians, Colossians, 2 Corinthians, 2 Timothy, 2 Peter, 1 John, and Jude was written to counter the activity and influence of false prophets in the early Church. See especially Paul's warning in Acts 20:29-30; Romans 16:17-18; 2 Corinthians 11:13; Galatians 2:4; and Peter's in 2 Peter 2:1; and John's in 1 John 4:1.

Religious insurrection and indifference (v. 12) call for perseverance (v. 13), the proof of eternal life. Jesus assures his followers that "the one who endures to the end will be saved" (v. 13). The "end" may mean "right through, all the way, perhaps to the *end*

---

16. Josephus, *Wars*, 6.289.

of one's life," or "for as long as may be necessary." Thus whoever stands firm and perseveres throughout the series of events that will eventually lead to and culminate in the destruction of the temple will be saved.

Finally, Jesus predicts *widespread preaching of the gospel* (v. 14). This is perhaps the single most oft-cited passage in defense of the interpretation that Jesus is describing the end of human history. After all, how could this possibly have occurred in the period 33–70? It may at first seem strange, but "fundamental principles of interpretation lead us to bear in mind contextual clues: the time indicator ('this generation'), the audience (the disciples who ask about the temple), the specific concern (the destruction of the temple), and the harmony of the preceding signs with the first-century experience. All of these should dispose us to seek a first-century fulfillment of this verse."[17]

Before I try to make sense of this passage, I want to make it clear that I believe passionately in the responsibility of the Church to preach the gospel throughout the world and to every people group on the globe. Nothing that I say in the next few paragraphs should be taken as an excuse to diminish our zeal or commitment to make known the gospel to every creature on earth. The Great Commission in Matthew 28 leaves no loopholes. We simply *must* labor in the grace of God to proclaim the gospel of God and to make disciples of all nations. My point in what follows is simply that Matthew 24:14 is not concerned with that task. Make no mistake: that task is essential, and it is nothing short of rank disobedience for the Church to ignore this calling of God on all Christians. I trust that point is settled.

Now, note two important facts. First, the words "whole world" (ESV and NASB) are a translation of the term *oikoumene*, which typically means an inhabited area, a standard term at that time for the Greek world, then for the Roman Empire, and subsequently for the *then known world*. Again, I encourage you *not* to read a statement like this in view of our *global* perspective of the twenty-first

---

17. Gentry, *The Great Tribulation*, 44.

century, but in light of the much more limited point of view of the people living in the first century. When we do that we discover that in Jesus' day this word "meant primarily the area surrounding the Mediterranean and the lesser known areas to the east, around which stretched mysterious regions (comprising much of our 'old world') beyond the fringes of civilization." [18]

The same Greek word is used in Luke 2:1 – "In those days a decree went out from Caesar Augustus that all the world (*oikoumene*) should be registered." In Acts 11:28 we read that "one of them named Agabus stood up and foretold by the Spirit that there would be a great famine over all the *world* (this took place in the days of Claudius"). Again, in Acts 24:5, "For we have found this man [Paul] a plague, one who stirs up riots among all the Jews throughout the *world*, and is a ringleader of the sect of the Nazarenes." Often our immediate, knee-jerk interpretation is that the events described with these words describe global events. Yet we know that they were limited to the Roman Empire of the first century. The reference to the "nations" also indicates that the point is not that every geographical area on the globe must be covered but that all the *Gentiles* must be reached. Did this occur as Jesus prophesied? Let's allow the biblical text to answer that question.

Writing before the fall of Jerusalem in 70, Paul says to the Colossians: "Of this you have heard before in the word of the truth, the gospel, which has come to you, as indeed *in the whole world* it is bearing fruit and growing – as it also does among you, since the day you heard it and understood the grace of God in truth" (1:5b-6; emphasis mine; cf. Col. 1:23b). Similarly, in his letter to the Romans Paul writes: "I thank my God through Jesus Christ for all of you, because your faith is proclaimed in *all the world*" (Rom. 1:8; emphasis mine). Again, in Romans 10:18, Paul says in regard to gospel proclamation

---

18. France, *Matthew*, 909. Gary DeMar's excellent treatment of this matter came to my attention only after my book was already in production, thus making it possible only that I mention it in this footnote. See the chapter, "The Myth that the Gospel Has Yet to be Preached in the 'Whole World,'" in his book, *10 Popular Prophecy Myths Exposed and Answered: The Last Days Might Not Be As Near As You Think* (Powder Springs, GA: American Vision Press, 2010), pp. 119-50.

that "Their voice has gone out to all the earth, and their words to *the ends of the world* [*oikoumenes*; emphasis mine]." Furthermore, in both Colossians 1:6a and Romans 1:8, the word "world" is a translation of the Greek *kosmos*, a term that is broader and far more encompassing than merely the "inhabited earth" (*oikoumene*). Thus, if Paul can confidently say that in his day the gospel is bearing fruit and the faith of the Roman believers is proclaimed in all (or the whole) *kosmos* ("world"), we should not struggle in the least to embrace our Lord's prediction that the gospel of the kingdom, within the same general time frame, would be proclaimed to the Gentiles throughout the *oikoumene* ("inhabited earth"). The point here is simply that what appears to be "universal" or "global" language to our ears today had a much more restricted meaning in the first century.[19]

As far as Jesus' prophecy in Matthew 24:14 is concerned, his point is that following his resurrection the gospel will be preached outside the boundaries of Judea, such that the Gentile nations in the inhabited world known as the Roman Empire will hear the testimony of his redemptive work. Only thereafter, says Jesus, will the "end" of the city and temple occur.

The Great Tribulation

With Matthew 24:15 we come to a critical juncture in the discourse. To this point Jesus has referred to general signs that would characterize the period preceding Israel's collapse. Here in verse 15, though, he refers to one sign that unmistakably signals that the prophesied destruction is at hand. It would serve to alert the people of *that* generation to the proximity of Jerusalem's ruin. In response to the question, "When will these things be?" Jesus now answers "When you see ..." (v. 15).

Perhaps we should begin with a general overview of the events that transpired in the critical period of 66–70. The Jewish revolt

---

19. One should also take note of what Luke says occurred on the day of Pentecost when Peter preached the gospel: "Now there were dwelling in Jerusalem Jews, devout men *from every nation under heaven*" (Acts 2:5; emphasis mine). No one would argue that Luke intends for us to understand that there were present that day Jews from Australia and China and the United States!

began in 66 and by 67–68 Vespasian had conquered most of Palestine. The Roman civil war in 68–69 required a temporary suspension of the siege, but during that period "Jerusalem was torn apart by its own civil war, as different Jewish parties battled for control, with the temple (the inner courts controlled by the Zealots under Eleazar and the outer court by John of Gischala) at the center of the fighting. When eventually the Roman attack was resumed in 69, Jerusalem was already in a weakened and demoralized state." [20] Titus then put Jerusalem under siege for five months until the temple and city were destroyed in 70.

Abomination of Desolation is literally, the abomination that causes desolation. In the Old Testament, "abomination" referred to an object of disgust or hatred, something that causes revulsion; an idolatrous offense or affront to the true worship of God. The Abomination of Desolation is referred to four times in Daniel 8:13; 9:27; 11:31; 12:11. The first and immediate reference was to the Syrian king Antiochus who ruled over Palestine in 175–165 B.C. He called himself *Theos Epiphanes* ("manifest God") but his enemies called him *Epimanes* ("madman; the insane one").

In 168 B.C. Antiochus Epiphanes slaughtered 40,000 Jews and plundered the temple. He sacrificed a pig on the altar of burnt offering and sprinkled broth from the unclean flesh all over the holy grounds as an act of deliberate defilement. He then erected an image of Zeus above the altar. It was a sacrilege of indescribable proportions indelibly imprinted on the minds of the Jews in Jesus' day.

It would appear that Jesus envisioned something of a repeat performance in his day of what happened in 168 B.C. under Antiochus. When he says "let the reader understand" he means "let the reader of the Old Testament book of Daniel understand" the true meaning and fulfillment of the coming Abomination of Desolation. The Abomination of Desolation, therefore, refers first to Antiochus Epiphanes and his desecration of the temple in 168 B.C. and, second, to something that was to occur in relation to the entire city of Jerusalem and the temple within the lifetime of his

---

20. France, *Matthew*, 910.

contemporaries. So what, then, was the Abomination of Desolation to which Jesus referred? There are at least four possibilities.

(1) Some point to the *Zealots*, the so-called "patriotic freedom fighters" who rose up against Roman oppression in defense of Jewish traditions and religion. They first emerged in A.D. 6 following the death of Herod the Great. At the outbreak of the Jewish War the Zealots stormed the city and occupied the temple area. They committed numerous sacrileges, including murder, within the Holy of Holies. In the winter of 67–68 they installed Phanni as high priest. Eventually the Zealots retreated to the mountain fortress *Masada*. The surviving 960 rebels committed mass suicide in May of 73 to prevent capture by the Romans.

(2) The *Idumeans* have also been considered as potential candidates. They occupied the territory once held by the ancient kingdom of Edom and came to Jerusalem at the request of Zealot leaders to participate in their revolution. After gaining entrance to the city, they killed more than 8,000 Jews in the outer court of the temple, including the chief priest Ananus. The Idumeans later withdrew from the city.

(3) Some argue that the *Jewish* religious leaders are in view, insofar as their rejection of Jesus as Messiah reduced the Jewish temple sacrifices to an abomination. One is reminded of Ezekiel 5:11 – "Therefore, as I live, declares the Lord GOD, surely, because you have defiled my sanctuary with all your detestable things and with all your abominations, therefore I will withdraw. My eye will not spare, and I will have no pity" (cf. John 2:16; Matt. 21:13).

(4) The most likely identification is *Titus and the armies of Rome*. While the city of Jerusalem was still burning, the soldiers brought their legionary standards into the temple precincts and offered sacrifices there, declaring Titus to be victor. The idolatrous representations of Caesar and the Roman eagle on the standards would have constituted the worst imaginable blasphemy to the Jewish people.[21]

---

21. France points out that the participle "standing" is neuter (in agreement with *bdelugma*), "which indicates an (idolatrous) object 'set up' rather than a person 'standing'" (897).

Identifying Titus and his armies with the Abomination of Desolation is most popular because it seems to parallel the action of Antiochus Epiphanes in the second century B.C. It is important to note that in Luke 21:20 the surrounding of Jerusalem by armies was the signal that her desolation (Gk, *eremosis*, the same word used in Matthew 24:15) had drawn near. We read in Josephus: "the Romans, upon the flight of the seditious into the city, and upon the burning of the holy house itself, and of all the buildings round about it, brought their ensigns to the temple, and set them over against its eastern gate; and there did they offer sacrifices to them, and there did they make Titus imperator, with the greatest acclamations of joy." [22] Thus, although the Abomination of Desolation "involves the destruction of Jerusalem (beginning with its several encirclings by Cestius, Vespasian, Simon, and Titus), it culminates in this final abominable act within the temple itself." [23] I find this view the most likely one.

Why did Matthew use the terms *Abomination of Desolation* whereas Luke identifies it explicitly as the activity of the invading Roman armies? The most likely explanation is that Matthew was writing to a *Jewish* audience and wanted to link up the A.D. 70 prophecy with the prophecy in Daniel. Luke, on the other hand, was writing to *Gentiles* outside the borders of Judea. Thus, the terminology "Abomination of Desolation" would have been confusing and enigmatic to them, prompting Luke to graphically identify precisely what Jesus had in mind: the Abomination that brings desolation to Jerusalem and its temple is the invading army under the leadership of Titus. We must remember that Jesus is answering the question of the disciples concerning "these things", "this temple", "these stones that you see", all of which would occur in the lifetime of "this generation" (v. 34). [24]

---

22. Josephus, *Wars*, 6.316.
23. Gentry, *The Great Tribulation*, 50.
24. None of these three [four or five?] events quite fits what this verse says. As France points out, "the Roman presence in the sanctuary [was] too late to provide a signal for escape before the end came" and "the Zealot occupation, which took place at the right time, was perhaps not quite the type of pagan defilement envisaged by Daniel. It seems wiser not to claim a specific tie-up with recorded

In verses 16-20 Jesus gives them a plan of escape. The appearance of the Abomination of Desolation was the sign for immediate flight from Judea. Luke even includes the warning not to enter the city at this time (21:21). As Wright observes, "the disciples are not to stay and fight for the physical survival of Jerusalem. They are not to be implicated in the coming war. Jesus will die at the hands of the Romans on the charge of being a Jewish rebel, but they are not to do so. No mistaken sense of loyalty must sway them into trying to bring the kingdom after all by means of the sword. Rather, they are to waste no time: they must run away." [25]

Those in the countryside of Judea (v. 16) must take to the hills as the Romans come to ravage farmlands and villages (this is, in fact, precisely what occurred; pillaging and killing were widespread). "The reference to 'Judea' suggests that the period envisaged is before the final siege of Jerusalem, when the wider province was being brought under Roman control, but when escape was still possible (as it would not be for those in Jerusalem itself after the siege began)." [26] Jewish houses within walled cities were flat-roofed structures that often formed a continuous terrace extending to the outer walls of the city, making it possible to quicken one's departure by following this "elevated highway" to the gates of the city (v. 17).

Working men will have to get by with the clothes they have on. There will be no time to go home and pack (v. 18). Nursing mothers and pregnant women are obviously ill-prepared for hasty escape (v. 19). In Palestine during the winter, roads were practically impassable because of mud; harsh weather and cold temperatures would slow down one's journey and make mountain hideaways unbearable (v. 20a). On the Sabbath, gates would be closed; it would be difficult to obtain provisions (Jews prohibited anything more than a one-day's journey on the Sabbath); buying and selling were not permitted; one traveling on a Sabbath would receive no assistance from the Jewish populace (v. 20b).

history, but to recognize that desecration of the temple was an ever-present threat once the Roman invasion had been provoked" (*Matthew*, 913).

25. Wright, *Jesus and the Victory of God*, 359.
26. France, *Matthew*, 914.

These instructions were in fact followed by Christians in Judea and Jerusalem. Some point to the fact that, in late 66, the Christian community, under the leadership of Symeon (a cousin of Jesus), withdrew to the village of Pella in Perea, a mountainous region east of the Sea of Galilee. History records that the commander Cestius inexplicably and without warning ordered his troops to withdraw. This gave the Jewish believers an opportunity to flee the city in accordance with Jesus' advice (Luke 21:21). According to Josephus, after Cestius' siege and retreat the Jews left Jerusalem like swimmers from a sinking ship.[27] By all accounts, no Christian died in the holocaust that engulfed Jerusalem shortly thereafter. William Whiston (1737), Josephus' best-known English translator, writes:

> There may be another very important, and very providential, reason be here assigned for this strange and foolish retreat of Cestius; which, if Josephus had been now a Christian, he might probably have taken notice of also; and that is, the affording the Jewish Christians in the city an opportunity of calling to mind the prediction and caution given them by Christ about thirty-three years and a half before, that "when they should see the abomination of desolation" [the idolatrous Roman armies, with the images of their idols in their ensigns, ready to lay Jerusalem desolate], "stand where it ought not;" or, "in the holy place;" or, "when they should see Jerusalem encompassed with armies," they should then "flee to the mountains." By complying with which those Jewish Christians fled to the mountains of Perea, and escaped of Cestius, this destruction.[28]

The Horror of A.D. 70

Matthew 24:21-22 explains the reason for the extreme urgency of escape. The reference is to the events of April–September in 70. Flavius Josephus (c. 37–100) was a Jewish author and historian who wrote a comprehensive (200 pages) eye-witness account ("The Wars of the Jews") of the Jewish revolt (66–70) and the fall of Jerusalem.

---

27. Josephus, *Wars*, 2.556.
28. Whiston, Josephus, *Wars*, 2.539, note b.

His book was first published in 75 when the facts of this holocaust were still vividly in the minds of many.[29]

The war that broke out in 66 between Rome and the Jewish people was simply an intensified continuation of hostilities that had been brewing for years. Jerusalem, the last Jewish stronghold, was the focus of Rome's most brutal rage. Multitudes of thieves, Zealots, and murderers had flocked to the city seeking refuge. The city was without law and order. Chaos and anarchy reigned. The city divided into warring factions who took turns attacking each other. In one incident, more than 12,000 of the city's nobles and leading citizens were tortured and killed by the Zealots. Those who tried to escape had their throats slit and their bodies were left to rot in the streets. Burial became impossible. Huge piles of cadavers filled the streets or were thrown from the city's walls. Josephus describes it:

> The noise also of those that were fighting was incessant, both by day and by night; but the lamentation of those that mourned exceeded the other [i.e., the noise of the fighting].... They, moreover, were still inventing somewhat or other that was pernicious against themselves; and when they had resolved upon anything, they executed it without mercy, and omitted no method of torment or of barbarity.[30]

It was the Passover season, and a momentary lull in hostilities led to the city's gates being thrown open for all those who desired to observe the feast. The population of the city swelled and contributed to the tremendous slaughter that was to take place. The Roman general Vespasian was recalled because of Nero's death and was himself soon declared emperor. His son Titus assumed responsibility for the battle. He repeatedly offered clemency to the Jews and often sent Josephus to the walls of the city to appeal for their surrender. Famine soon set in. The city's granaries and store-

---

29. See William Kimball's book, *The Great Tribulation* (Grand Rapids: Baker Book House, 1983), pp. 94-109, for a helpful summary of these events.
30. Josephus, *Wars*, 5.31,35.

houses were deliberately burned and the water reservoirs were polluted. Again, Josephus:

> The madness of the seditious did also increase together with their famine, and both those miseries were everyday inflamed more and more; for there was no corn which anywhere appeared publicly,... It was now a miserable case, and a sight that would justly bring tears into our eyes,... insomuch that children pulled the very morsels that their fathers were eating out of their very mouths... so did the mothers do as to their infants.[31]

People not only sold their homes but their children as well to obtain food. People regularly ate from the public sewers, cattle and pigeon dung, leather shields, hay, clothing, and things that scavenger dogs would dare not to touch! Unbelievable forms of torture were inflicted on those suspected of hiding food:

> It is therefore impossible to go distinctly over every instance of these men's iniquity. I shall therefore speak my mind here at once briefly: – That neither did any other city suffer such miseries, nor did any age ever breed a generation more fruitful in wickedness that [than] this was, from the beginning of the world.[32]

In desperation, some left the city at night to hunt for food but were captured by the Romans. Thousands were crucified in plain sight of the city walls, often at a rate of 500 per day. So many were killed in this manner that "room was wanting for the crosses, and crosses wanting for the bodies."[33]

After several unsuccessful assaults on the city, Titus ordered his troops to surround the city with a wall to cut off any remaining avenues of escape, seemingly in fulfillment of Jesus' word: "your enemies will set up a barricade around you and hem you in on

---

31. Ibid., 5.424-425, 429-430.
32. Ibid., 5.442.
33. Ibid., 5.451.

every side" (Luke 19:43). This served to intensify the famine. Josephus explains:

> Then did the famine widen its progress, and devoured the people by whole houses and families; the upper rooms were filled with women and children dying by famine; and the lanes of the city were full of the dead bodies of the aged; the children also and the young men wandered about the market places like shadows, all swelled with the famine, and fell down dead wheresoever their misery seized them.... Thus did the miseries of Jerusalem grow worse and worse every day.... And indeed the multitude of carcasses that lay in heaps one upon another, was a horrible sight, and produced a pestilential stench, which was a hindrance to those that would make sallies out of the city and fight the enemy. [34]

Josephus tells of one woman who killed her son, roasted his body, ate half of him and hid the remaining half. When the smell drew others desperate for food, she offered to share his body, inciting horror among the multitudes. The wall of the city was finally breached. The temple was set aflame.

> While the holy house was on fire, everything was plundered that came to hand, and ten thousand of those that were caught were slain; nor was there a commiseration of any age, or any reverence of gravity; but children and old men, and profane persons, and priests, were all slain in the same manner;... many of those that were worn away by the famine, and their mouths almost closed, when they saw the fire of the holy house, they exerted their utmost strength, and broke out into groans and outcries again. Perea did also return the echo, as well as the mountains round about [the city], and augmented the force of the entire noise. Yet was the misery itself more terrible than this disorder; for one would have thought that the hill itself, on which the temple stood, was seething hot, as full of fire on every part of it, that the blood was larger in quantity than the fire, and those that were slain more

---

34. Ibid., 5.512-513; 6.1-2.

in number than those who slew them; for the ground did nowhere appear visible because of the dead bodies that lay on it.[35]

Josephus reports the activity of numerous false prophets who misled the people and contributed to their demise, again in fulfillment of the words of Jesus in Matthew 24:23-26. When the Romans finally penetrated the heart of the city the slaughter continued until the soldiers "grew weary of killing." Josephus stated that the soldiers,

> when they went in numbers into the lanes of the city, with their swords drawn, they slew those whom they overtook, without mercy, and set fire to the houses whither the Jews had fled, and burnt every soul in them, and laid waste a great many of the rest; and when they were come to the houses to plunder them, they found in them entire families of dead men, and the upper rooms full of dead corpses, that is of such as died by the famine; they then stood in a horror at this sight, and went out without touching anything. But although they had this commiseration for such as were destroyed in that manner, yet had they not the same for those that were still alive, but they ran everyone through whom they met with, and obstructed the very lanes with their dead bodies, and made the whole city run down with blood, to such a degree indeed that the fire of many of the houses was quenched with these men's blood.[36]

Almost 100,000 Jewish survivors were sold into slavery. Others were consigned to die in the gladiatorial exhibitions or were selected to be paraded in Titus' triumphal procession through the streets of Rome. According to Josephus, more than 1,100,000 died during the siege of the city! He also describes how "Caesar gave orders that they should now demolish the entire city and temple,… [and] it was so thoroughly laid even with the ground by those that dug it up to the foundation, that there was left nothing to make

---

35. Ibid., 6.271-276.
36. Ibid., 6.404-406.

those that came thither believe it had ever been inhabited." [37] Here is his final verdict:

> The war which the Jews made with the Romans hath been the greatest of all those, not only that have been in our times, but, in a manner, of those that ever were heard of; both of those wherein cities have fought against cities, or nations against nations;... Accordingly it appears to me, that the misfortunes of all men, from the beginning of the world, if they be compared to these of the Jews, are not so considerable as they were. [38]

The Great Tribulation

In Matthew 24:21 Jesus describes this event to be "such as has not been from the beginning of the world until now, no, and never will be." Many insist that this "great tribulation" (v. 21a) cannot refer to the events of 70 because worse and more severe tribulations have since followed (World War II and the Holocaust, Stalin, Pol Pot's genocidal campaign in Cambodia, etc.). Let me say several things in response to this objection.

Assuming Jesus is speaking in strictly literal terms, it is unlikely that he is referring to a time of tribulation at the end of the age, because of the phrase "no, and never will be." In other words, this phrase envisions a time following this tribulation in which other, albeit less severe tribulations, might occur. But if the supposed future tribulation is followed immediately by the millennium or the eternal state, it would be pointless to say that a tribulation of such magnitude will never take place again, for there would be no remaining time to prove the assertion.

Once one grasps the dimensions of what occurred in 70, one realizes that the savagery, cruelty, and the monstrosities that occurred were beyond comparison. Also, never so high a percentage of one city's population was destroyed. *Everyone was either killed or sold into slavery.* As noted earlier, approximations are that 1,100,000 people were killed and 100,000 were enslaved.

---

37. Ibid., 7.1-3.
38. Ibid., Preface, 1,12.

It may well be, however, that the statement in verse 21 is deliberately hyperbolic, a stock saying for an indescribably horrendous time. In other words, it may be proverbial, designed to emphasize how truly horrible an event it was. Biblical scholars have long recognized that oracles of judgment are often couched in language that is universal and radical. "Such judgment is often framed in terms of prophetic hyperbole, a common apocalyptic device used by the writers of Scripture."[39] Take a moment and carefully read these texts from the Old Testament and note the verbal parallels with our Lord's statement in Matthew 24:21. I think you will readily see that Jesus is simply employing the terminology widely known in the ancient world for horrific judgment and intense calamity. Neither those who used these terms in the Old Testament nor Jesus himself ever intended for such language to be pressed in such a way that it precluded the possibility for subsequent periods of equal or even more intense judgment to occur. For example (be careful to note the italicized words):

"There shall be a great cry throughout all the land of Egypt, *such as there has never been, nor ever will be again.*" (Exod. 11:6)

"Behold, about this time tomorrow I will cause very heavy hail to fall, *such as never has been in Egypt from the day it was founded until now.*" (Exod. 9:18)

"The locusts came up over all the land of Egypt and settled on the whole country of Egypt, such a dense swarm of locusts *as had never been before, nor ever will be again.*" (Exod. 10:14; cf. Joel 1:1-4)

"a day of darkness and gloom, a day of clouds and thick darkness! Like blackness there is spread upon the mountains a great and powerful people; their like *has never been before, nor will be again after them through the years of all generations.*" (Joel 2:2)

"And because of all your abominations I will do with you *what I have never yet done, and the like of which I will never do again.*" (a reference to the impending Babylonian captivity; Ezek. 5:9; cf. Matt. 24:21)

---

39. Gentry, *The Great Tribulation*, 52.

"He has confirmed his words which he spoke against us and against our rulers who ruled us, by bringing upon us a great calamity. *For under the whole heaven there has not been done anything like what has been done against Jerusalem.*" (Dan. 9:12)

"At that time shall arise Michael, the great prince who has charge of your people. And there shall be a time of trouble, *such as never has been since there was a nation till that time.*" (Dan. 12:1)

Look also at similar terminology in the following two texts:

"He [Hezekiah] trusted in the Lord, the God of Israel; *so that there was none like him among all the kings of Judah after him, nor among those who were before him.*" (2 Kings 18:5)

"*Before him there was no king like him*, who turned to the Lord with all his heart and with all his soul and with all his might, according to all the Law of Moses, *nor did any like him arise after him.*" (2 Kings 23:25)

These texts and this unique phraseology prompt Gary DeMar to make this point:

In 2 Kings 18:5 it is written of Hezekiah that there would be no king after him who would show the same devotion to the Lord as he showed. When we get an assessment of Josiah's reign, which *follows* Hezekiah's reign, we are informed that "there was no king like him who turned to the Lord." How can Hezekiah's reign be the greatest (even considering the reign of a future king like Josiah) and Josiah's reign be the greatest (even considering the reign of a past king like Hezekiah)? Is this a contradiction? There are no contradictions in the Bible. The phraseology is obviously hyperbolic, emphasizing complete devotion to the Lord and His law. [40]

The destruction, however, will not run its full course (v. 22). The days will be shortened, either to allow the elect to survive or per-

---

40. Gary Demar, *Last Days Madness*, 110. Cf. also 1 Kings 3:12 with Matt. 12:42.

haps because the presence of the elect in the world mitigates the divine wrath (i.e., common grace).

But according to verses 23-28 one shouldn't look for the second coming of Christ in the chaotic events surrounding Jerusalem's fall. Such troublesome times would prove to be a golden opportunity for false prophets to lead people astray with false expectations of Christ's appearance. But Jesus says, "Don't be swayed by their miracles or their message" (v. 24). They must be careful "not to entertain the rumors that the Jewish Messiah had returned and was waiting in some secluded desert location for them, or in some inner chamber in the besieged city" (v. 26).[41]

Josephus actually records several instances of impostors who enticed people into the desert and elsewhere with promises of the Messiah's appearance. But, "contrary to the claims of these false prophets, Christ's advent will not be shrouded in secrecy or obscurity. It will be spectacular, patent, and universal. Christ's second coming will not only be obvious, it will be as instantaneous, unexpected, and unannounced as the flash of lightning. Though no one will foresee it, all eyes will see it" (v. 27).[42]

Verse 27, notes France, "is a sort of 'aside' which draws a sharp distinction between the events during the siege and the still future *parousia*. The real *parousia*, when it comes, will not be like the claims of impostors during the siege."[43] In other words, "The time of the siege and capture of the city will be characterized by the claims and counterclaims of those who pretend to a messianic role, but the *parousia* of the Son of Man will need no such claims or proofs: everyone will see and recognize it (as he will go on to spell out in verses 36-44). He is thus setting the *parousia* and the end of the age decisively apart from the coming destruction of the temple."[44]

It should be noted that not everyone interprets verse 27 as a reference to the second advent of Christ. In an earlier work, Gentry

---

41. Kimball, *The Great Tribulation*, 142-43.
42. Ibid., 144.
43. France, *Matthew*, 917.
44. Ibid., 918.

represented the view of a few other partial preterists in arguing that this "coming" is the judgment of Christ that appears like a destructive lightning bolt against Jerusalem. "The direction of this judgment coming of Christ in Matthew 24:27 apparently reflects the Roman armies marching toward Jerusalem from an easterly direction. Josephus's record of the march of the Roman armies through Israel shows they wreak havoc on Jerusalem by approaching it from the east." [45] I should point out, however, that in his more recent treatment of the Olivet Discourse, Gentry has reversed his position and now contends that the reference is indeed to the second coming at the close of history. [46]

The enigmatic saying in verse 28 may be taken in one of three ways, depending on one's interpretation of the "coming" in verse 27. Either the second coming of the Son of Man will be obvious and unmistakable, just as one unmistakably infers the presence of a corpse from the presence of vultures, or "it will be as impossible for humanity not to see the coming of the Son of Man as it is for vultures to miss seeing carrion." [47] Or, finally, if the "coming" (v. 27) is the judgment of Jerusalem in 70, the "vultures" (= "eagles") refer to the Roman "eagle" found on the ensign at the head of every Roman legion. If this be the case, it is the Roman "eagle" (vulture) that gathers over the corpse of Jerusalem to pick it clean.

This, then, was *the great tribulation* foretold by Jesus. It is not a future event, but an accomplished fact of history past.

45. Gentry, *The Great Tribulation,* 54.
46. See his book, *The Olivet Discourse Made Easy,* 101-02.
47. D.A. Carson, *Matthew,* The Expositor's Bible Commentary (Grand Rapids: Zondervan, 1984), 504.

Chapter Eight

The Eschatology of Jesus: Matthew 24 and The Olivet Discourse (2)

I n the previous chapter I argued that Matthew 24 can be divided into two parts, each of which provides an answer to the two questions asked by the disciples. In response to our Lord's ominous prediction of judgment on Jerusalem and the temple (see Matt. 23:29-39; 24:2), they asked him: "Tell us, when will these things be, and what will be the sign of your coming and of the close of the age?" (24:3).

His answer was straightforward and to the point. "These things," by which he means the destruction of city and temple will occur before "this generation" passes away (24:34). Within this time frame, there will be false messiahs, wars, political turmoil, famines, earthquakes, persecution, lawlessness, as well as the successful preaching of the gospel to the Gentile nations (24:4-14). None of these events, however, should be interpreted as indicating that the end is at hand. However, when the Abomination of Desolation appears, know that the time of great tribulation and Jerusalem's demise is indeed at hand (24:15-31). If you are discerning and alert to the signs of the times, you will know when "these things" are about to occur (24:32-35).

As for the second coming of Christ and the close of the age, no such signs will be given. No one knows when "that day and hour" will occur, not even the Son of Man himself. So be alert and watchful, lest you be caught unprepared for Christ's return (24:36–25:30).

259

If this understanding of the structure of Matthew 24 is correct, and I believe it is, by the time we get to verse 35 Jesus has answered his disciples' first question ("when will these things be?"). As for the second question concerning his second coming (or the *parousia*) and the end of history, our Lord's answer begins with verse 36 and extends through the close of chapter 25.

This all seems rather simple and to the point, were it not for verses 29-31. Most Christians today take it for granted that this is an obvious description of the second coming of Christ at the end of human history. How could it possibly be otherwise? It seems so "natural." But I urge you not to pre-judge the issue simply because that's what you've always heard and believed. I urge you to "try to hear Jesus' words as they would have been heard by his Jewish disciples as they listened to this answer to their double question, as yet uninfluenced by a tradition which conditions Christian readers now to assume that 'the stars from falling from heaven' and 'the Son of Man coming on the clouds of heaven' *can only* refer to the end of the world and the *parousia*."[1] What I hope to demonstrate, among other things, is that "the 'cosmic' language of 24:29 is drawn directly from Old Testament prophetic passages where it functions not to predict the physical dissolution of the universe but as a symbolic representation of catastrophic political changes within history."[2] In other words, I'm persuaded that verses 29-31 are in fact part of our Lord's answer to the first question asked by his disciples concerning the impending destruction of Jerusalem and its temple. Here is the passage again:

> Immediately after the tribulation of those days the sun will be darkened, and the moon will not give its light, and the stars will fall from heaven, and the powers of the heavens will be shaken. Then will appear in heaven the sign of the Son of Man, and then all the tribes of the earth will mourn, and they will see the Son of Man coming on the clouds of heaven with power and great glory. And he will send out his

1. France, *Matthew*, 893.
2. Ibid., 891.

angels with a loud trumpet call, and they will gather his elect from the four winds, from one end of heaven to the other" (24:29-31).

The problem we face is that it appears Jesus says his coming will occur "immediately after" the tribulation just described in verses 15-28.[3] Mark renders it, "But in those days, after that tribulation" (13:24). The problem is this: if verses 15-28 refer to the events of 70 (and I don't see how any other conclusion can be drawn), why didn't Jesus return at that time? Several possible answers have been suggested.

Most dispensational scholars simply insist that verses 15-28 do not, in point of fact, refer to the events of 70. They refer to a yet future tribulation period immediately preceding the second coming of Christ. This period is usually identified with the seventieth week of Daniel's prophecy, hence seven years in duration. At the other end of the theological spectrum, liberal scholars have simply concluded that Jesus was mistaken about the time of his return.

Yet another interpretation is that the "tribulation of those days" (v. 29) refers not simply to the events of 70 but also to *this entire present age between the two comings of Christ.* Thus it would hold true that "immediately after the tribulation of those days" (A.D. 70 *and* the present age), Jesus will return in glory. D.A. Carson advocates this view in his excellent commentary on Matthew.

Others, who embrace an extreme version of the *preterist*[4] interpretation, insist that the second coming of Jesus was, in fact, his return in 70. His second coming was a coming in judgment against

---

3. The Greek word translated "immediately" (*eutheos*) occurs thirteen times in Matthew's gospel and in each instance describes something that occurs very soon after a preceding event. There is nothing in the word or the context of Matthew 24 that would lead us to believe that Jesus envisioned a gap of now nearly 2,000 years between the events of verses 15-28 and those of verses 29-31.

4. Extreme, hyper, or full preterism contends that not only did the prophesied *parousia* or second coming of Christ occur in 70, so too did the final resurrection, final judgment, and inauguration of the new heavens and new earth. For a helpful critique of hyper-preterism, see *When Shall These Things Be? A Reformed Response to Hyper-Preterism,* edited by Keith A. Mathison (Phillipsburg: P & R Publishing, 2004); and Keith A. Mathison, "A Brief Critique of Full Preterism," in *Postmillennialism: An Eschatology of Hope* (Phillipsburg: P & R, 1999), 235-48.

Israel in the destruction of city and temple, but not a visible return to the earth. J.S. Russell put it this way:

> We are compelled, therefore, by all these considerations, and chiefly by regard for the authority of Him whose word cannot be broken, to conclude that the Parousia, or second coming of Christ, with its connected and concomitant events, did take place, according to the Saviour's own prediction, at the period when Jerusalem was destroyed, and before the passing away of "that generation."[5]

Another possibility is that verse 29 does not refer to what will occur in conjunction with Christ's second coming at the end of the age. Rather, it is a figurative or symbolic description of *the present age itself*, the last 1,942 years or so following the events of 70. In other words, verse 29 describes the characteristic features and course of events throughout the present church age. Therefore, verses 30-31 *alone* describe the actual second coming of Jesus at the close of history.

Finally, a somewhat more moderate version of the *preterist* view which I will seek to defend is that verses 29-31 are not a literal description of the second coming but a symbolic description of the fall of Jerusalem and the destruction of the temple, in the colorful language of Old Testament prophecy. The "coming" of Jesus is not to the earth at the end of history, but to the Father, in heaven, for vindication and enthronement. Unlike those who embrace a full preterist position, these "partial preterists" believe in a yet future, personal, physical, and visible "coming" of Christ to consummate the redemptive purpose of God.[6] This is the view that I will now seek to explain and defend.

The "A.D. 70" Interpretation of Matthew 24:29-31

Once again, what I will argue is that verses 29-31 do not refer at all to the second coming of Christ at the end of the age but rather to

5. J. Stuart Russell, *The Parousia: A Critical Inquiry into the New Testament Doctrine of Our Lord's Second Coming* (Grand Rapids: Baker, 1983 [1887]), 549.

6. See the commentary on Matthew by R.T. France, as well as the writings of N.T. Wright, Peter Walker, David Chilton, Kenneth Gentry, and Gary DeMar.

events associated with the fall of Jerusalem in 70. We have already noted how Matthew 24:15-25 describes events in conjunction with the Roman siege of Jerusalem that transpired in 66–70. But this leads us to expect more information on the actual fall of the city and the effects of this destruction. Matthew's "immediately after" only heightens that expectation. Dare I say, then, that the most "natural" reading of verses 29-31 is that they do in fact provide us with a description of the city's final demise?

As noted, when one reads Matthew 24:29-31 (in particular v. 29), he/she may at first glance have difficulty seeing in it a reference to the destruction of Jerusalem. This is due, in part, to the fact that Matthew's language is compressed. It is also because his language sounds like what most people believe will occur at the second coming. Phenomenal events involving sun, moon, stars, and the powers of heaven don't sound to the twenty-first century mind like a description of what happened in 70. The reason for that is because we mistakenly seek to interpret and understand prophecy by reading the *New York Times*, the Drudge Report, or *Time* magazine, or by watching the evening news on TV rather than by reading the Bible. Remember, *Jesus was speaking to a people saturated by Old Testament language, concepts, and imagery. From the earliest days of their lives they memorized and were taught the Old Testament. Thus, when Jesus spoke to them of things to come he used the prophetic vocabulary of the Old Testament which they would instantly recognize.* Consequently, if we are to understand the meaning of Matthew 24:29-31 and its parallel in Mark 13:24-27 and Luke 21:25-26, we must read and interpret them through a *biblical* (i.e., Old Testament) lens.

Luke refers to "signs" in sun, moon, and stars. Matthew says "the sun will be darkened, and the moon will not give its light, and the stars will fall from heaven." Are these literal, physical, astronomical events that one might see with the naked eye? I don't think so.

In the Old Testament, *such language was used to portray not what is going on in the heavens but what is happening on the earth.* Natural disasters, political upheaval, and turmoil among the nations are often described figuratively through the terminology of cosmic disturbances. The on-going and unsettled turbulent state of affairs among *earthly* world powers is portrayed symbolically by reference to incredible events in the *heavens*. In other words, astronomical phenomena are used to describe the upheaval of earthly dynasties as well as great moral and spiritual changes. Once we learn to read this language in the light of the Old Testament we discover that great upheavals upon earth are often represented with the imagery of commotions and changes in the heavens. As we shall see, when the sun and moon are darkened or the stars fall from heaven, the reference is to the disasters and distresses befalling nations on the earth.[7]

In Isaiah 13:9-10 we read of the impending judgment of God on Babylon, which he describes in this way: "For the stars of the heavens and their constellations will not give their light; the sun will be dark at its rising, and the moon will not shed its light" (v. 10). Clearly, these statements about celestial bodies no longer providing light is figurative for the convulsive transformation of political affairs in the ancient Near East, on earth. *The destruction of earthly kingdoms is portrayed in terms of a heavenly shaking.*

We find much the same thing in Ezekiel as he describes the impending destruction of Egypt: "When I blot you out, I will cover the heavens and make their stars dark; I will cover the sun with a cloud, and the moon shall not give its light. All the bright lights of heaven will I make dark over you, and put darkness on your land, declares the Lord GOD.... When I make the land of Egypt desolate, and when the land is desolate of all that fills it, when I strike down all who dwell in it, then they will know that I am the LORD" (Ezek. 32:7-8, 15).

The destruction of Idumea (Edom) is described in this way: "All the host of heaven shall rot away, and the skies roll up like a scroll. All their host shall fall, as leaves fall from the vine, like leaves falling from the fig tree. For my sword has drunk its fill in the heavens;

---

7. Some examples of how *cosmic events* are used as symbolic portrayals of earthly realities (whether blessing or cursing) include Isa. 60:20; Amos 8:2-9; Zeph. 1:4,15; Isa. 5:30; Jer. 4:23,28; 13:16; Joel 2:10.

behold, it descends for judgment upon Edom, upon the people I have devoted to destruction" (Isa. 34:4-5).

Thus, as William Kimball points out, "when Israel was judged, or when Babylon was subdued by the Medes, or when Idumea and Egypt were destroyed, it was not the literal sun, moon, and stars that were darkened. The literal stars of heaven did not fall from the skies, and the literal constellations were not dissolved or rolled up as a scroll. These figurative expressions were clearly presented in a purely symbolic manner to characterize the destruction befalling nations and earthly powers." [8]

Language that describes the collapse of cosmic bodies, therefore, was often used by "OT prophets to symbolize God's acts of judgment within history, with the emphasis on catastrophic political reversals." [9] Therefore, France concludes that "if such language was appropriate to describe the end of Babylon or Edom under the judgment of God, why should it not equally describe God's judgment on Jerusalem's temple and the power structure which it symbolized?" [10]

In summary, "it is crass literalism," notes Wright, "in view of the many prophetic passages in which this language denotes socio-political and military catastrophe, to insist that this time the words must refer to the physical collapse of the space-time world. This is simply the way regular Jewish imagery is able to refer to major socio-political events and bring out their full significance." [11] Again, "the dramatic and (to us) bizarre language of much 'apocalyptic' writing is evidence, not of paranoia or a dualistic worldview, as is sometimes anachronistically suggested, but of a creative reuse of Israel's scriptural, and particularly prophetic, heritage." [12] It seems only "natural" to conclude that Matthew 24:29 is stock-in-trade Old Testament prophetic language for *national disaster*. Our Lord, therefore, is not prophesying that bizarre astronomical

---

8. Kimball, *The Great Tribulation,* 166.
9. France, *Matthew,* 922.
10. Ibid., 922.
11. Wright, *Victory,* 361.
12. Ibid., 513.

events will occur; he is predicting that the judgment of God will soon fall decisively on the Jewish nation.

If verse 29 is a symbolic description of God's judgment on Israel and the destruction of the city of Jerusalem, what then of verses 30-31? There we read: "Then will appear in heaven the sign of the Son of Man, and then all the tribes of the earth will mourn, and they will see the Son of Man coming on the clouds of heaven with power and great glory. And he will send out his angels with a loud trumpet call, and they will gather his elect from the four winds, from one end of heaven to the other."

Christians today are so conditioned to assume that the "coming" of the Son of Man "on the clouds of heaven" is his return at the close of history that it is hard to gain a hearing for any alternative position. But we must aim to read the text not in terms of our traditions or preferences but from the perspective of Jesus and in the light of the Old Testament Scriptures from which he draws his language.

We must begin by pointing out that nowhere in this passage does Jesus use the term *parousia* (as he does in vv. 27, 37). The Greek word translated "coming" is *erchomenon*, which could mean either "coming" or "going". Be it noted, however, that even if *parousia* were used, it need not point to the second coming. One cannot simply assume that the later, technical Pauline, use of that term is in view here. Says Wright:

> But why should we think – except for reasons of ecclesiastical and scholarly tradition – that *parousia* means "the second coming", and/ or the downward travel on a cloud of Jesus…? *Parousia* means "presence" as opposed to *apousia*, "absence"; hence it denotes the "arrival" of someone not at the moment present; and it is especially used in relation to the visit "of a royal or official personage." [13]

For the ordinary sense of "arrival," Wright points to 1 Corinthians 16:17; 2 Corinthians 7:6, 7; 10:10; and Philippians 1:26 and 2:12.

---

13. Ibid., 341.

From this, he concludes, "the most natural meaning for the word as applied to Jesus would be something like 'arrival on the scene', in the sense of 'enthronement.'"[14] Here the "coming" of the Son of Man in verse 30 is an allusion to Daniel 7:13-14 which speaks *not of a "coming to earth" from heaven but of a "coming to God" in heaven to receive vindication and authority.* This "coming" refers to an event "whereby the authority of Jesus is vindicated over the Jewish establishment which has rejected him."[15] Read with me this crucial text from Daniel:

> [13]I saw in the night visions, and behold, with the clouds of heaven there came one like a son of man, and he came to the Ancient of Days and was presented before him. [14]And to him was given dominion and glory and a kingdom, that all peoples, nations, and languages should serve him; his dominion is an everlasting dominion, which shall not pass away, and his kingdom one that shall not be destroyed. (Dan. 7:13-14)

Clearly, this is a vision not about a descent from heaven to earth, not about the second coming of the Son of Man at the close of history, but rather *a vision of the Son of Man in heaven coming to the Ancient of Days, God the Father, to receive his kingdom.* A new kingdom, a new and everlasting dominion is being established to replace the failed regimes of previous empires. Again, Matthew 24:30-31 is not about the return of Christ at the end of history but about his enthronement as King of kings and Lord of lords in the very middle of history.[16]

This understanding is confirmed by what Jesus says in Matthew 26:64. Standing in the presence of the high priest and members

---

14. Ibid., 341, n. 95.
15. Ibid., 344.
16. We know from 1 Thess. 4:16, as well as the book of Revelation and elsewhere, that Jesus will in fact "descend from heaven" at the end of human history. But nothing in Matt. 24 (or Mark 13 or Luke 21) speaks of Jesus coming "down". It rather speaks of something that is happening in heaven, as the Son of God, the Son of Man, Jesus, comes "to" God the Father, not "down to" the earth.

of the Sanhedrin, Jesus declares, "But I tell you, from now on you will see the Son of Man seated at the right hand of Power and coming on the clouds of heaven." These to whom Jesus spoke are obviously not now alive. Is it not evident that our Lord is referring to an event in the lifespan of those in the first century to whom he is directly speaking? N.T. Wright explains:

> Jesus is not ... suggesting that Caiaphas will witness the end of the space-time order. Nor will he look out of the window one day and observe a human figure flying downwards on a cloud. It is absurd to imagine either Jesus, or Mark, or anyone in between, supposing the words to mean that. Caiaphas will witness the strange events that follow Jesus' crucifixion: the rise of a group of disciples claiming that he has been raised from the dead, and the events which accelerate towards the final clash with Rome, in which... Jesus will be vindicated as a true prophet. In and through it all, Caiaphas will witness events which show that Jesus was not, after all, mistaken in his claim, hitherto implicit, now at last explicit: he is the Messiah, the anointed one, the true representative of the people of Israel, the one in and through whom the covenant God is acting to set up his kingdom. [17]

We simply cannot escape the fact that the coming of the Son of Man on the clouds of heaven was never understood as an ancient form of space travel, but as a symbol for a massive reversal of national destinies within history. R.T. France agrees:

> Jesus is using Daniel 7:13 as a prediction of that authority which he exercised when in A.D. 70 the Jewish nation and its leaders, who had condemned him, were overthrown, and Jesus was vindicated as the recipient of all power from the Ancient of Days.... Jesus, exalted after his death and resurrection to receive his everlasting dominion, will display it within the generation ... by an act of judgment on the nation and capital of the authorities who presumed to judge him. Then they

---

17. Wright, *Victory*, 525.

will see... for themselves that their time of power is finished, and it is to him that God has given all power in heaven and earth. [18]

Let me bring this to a summary with these words of Wright:

> The days of Jerusalem's destruction would be looked upon as days of cosmic catastrophe. The known world would go into convulsions: power struggles and *coups d'etat* would be the order of the day; the *pax Romana* [peace of Rome], the presupposition of "civilized" life throughout the then Mediterranean world, would collapse into chaos. In the midst of that chaos Jerusalem would fall. The "son of man" would thereby be vindicated. That would be the sign that the followers of this "son of man" would now spread throughout the world: his "angels", that is, messengers, would summon people from north, south, east and west to come and sit down with Abraham, Isaac and Jacob in the kingdom of YHWH. [19]

The Sign of the Son of Man in Heaven

If you are still struggling with this, I suspect that it may be due to a mistranslation of verse 30. Literally, verse 30 reads as follows: "And then will appear the sign of the Son of Man in heaven, and then will mourn all the tribes of the land and they will see the Son of Man coming on the clouds of heaven with power and great glory." In other words, Jesus was not telling his disciples that *he* would appear in the sky. Rather, "He told them that they would see a *sign* that proved He was in heaven, sitting at His Father's right hand (Acts 2:30-36)." [20] Those who would witness the events of 70 would see the sign of Jesus' enthronement when they saw Jerusalem's destruction. Thus *the "sign" of the Son of Man being enthroned and vindicated in "heaven" is the destruction of Jerusalem and its temple on "earth"*. It is the *sign* that appears, not the Son of Man. What does the sign signify? It signifies that the Son of Man is in heaven, exalted, vindicated, and enthroned at God's right hand.

---

18. France, *Jesus and the Old Testament*, 236.
19. Wright, *Victory*, 362-63.
20. DeMar, *Last Days Madness*, 165.

There are several questions that need to be addressed, the first of which is the identity of the "tribes of the land".[21] The word translated "tribes" (*phyle*), when used in the New Testament, typically refers to the Old Testament tribes of Israel (see Matt. 19:28; Luke 2:36; Acts 13:21; Rom. 11:1; Heb. 7:13-14; the only exception is Rev. 5:9; 7:9; 11:9; 13:7; 14:6 where the word is found in a stock phrase). France points out "that the reference in Zechariah 12:10-14 is explicitly to a mourning of the tribes of *Israel*, the tribes of David, Nathan, Levi and Shimei being specified, and a final 'all the families that are left' extending the scope to the whole *nation*."[22] In other words, the mourning of "all the tribes of the land" (i.e., the land of *Israel*) is not so much a global lamentation, but rather the response of Israel when they see the vindication of Jesus whom they have pierced. The people of Jerusalem will then recognize how they have mistreated their Messiah, but their mourning will not be the sort that comes from heartfelt repentance but rather a woeful and wailing lamentation that arises from their having witnessed his ultimate vindication and triumph. Tragically, though, it will be too late to escape the consequences of having rejected him.

The "tribes" are to "see" the vindication and enthronement of the Son of Man in heaven, but *how* or in what sense are they to "see" it, that is, to know that it is true? Not perhaps by a celestial phenomenon, but "by what is happening on earth as the temple is destroyed and the reign of the 'Son-of-Man-in-heaven' begins to take effect in the gathering of his chosen people. In that case the 'sign' is not a preliminary warning of an event still to come, but the visible manifestation of a heavenly reality already established, that the Son of Man is in heaven sitting at the right hand of Power (26:64)."[23]

Therefore, this "coming" is not a visible, physical appearance by which Jesus returns to earth (although that will most assuredly occur at the end of history). Rather, they will "see" him in the sense

---

21. The Greek noun translated "earth" (*ge*) can refer generally to the tangible ground, the earth, or more specifically to a particular land area. Often in the New Testament *ge* refers particularly to the "land" of Israel, i.e., Palestine (see Matt. 2:6,20; 27:45; Mark 15:33; Luke 4:25; 21:23; John 3:22; Acts 7:3).
22. France, *Jesus and the Old Testament,* 237.
23. France, *Matthew,* 926.

that they will "understand" or spiritually *perceive* that he is the vindicated and enthroned King.[24] As Gentry points out, "this actually refers to Jesus' ascension [not his second advent]. In the destruction of the temple, the rejected Christ is vindicated as the ascended Lord and shown to possess great power and glory."[25]

The word "angels" (v. 31) literally means "messengers" and possibly refers to *human preaching of the gospel* throughout the world. In the Greek version of the Old Testament (the Septuagint), the Greek word *angelos* is often translated as "messenger".[26] (However, if we should discover that the word actually refers to "angels" in the more traditional sense of spiritual beings who fulfill God's will, "it would then refer 'to the supernatural power which lies behind such preaching.' Then it would teach that the angels of God attend our faithful proclamation of God's Word."[27] This would not be at all surprising, given the fact that according to Hebrews 1:14 we know that angels are commissioned by God to minister to the elect and to serve them in keeping with God's will. The statement in Matthew 24 doesn't tell us in what specific ways the angels function "behind the scenes," so to speak, when we proclaim the gospel, but we may rest assured that in some way they are present to strengthen, guard, and encourage those who proclaim the gospel and perhaps even to restrain the adverse influence of the demonic who would seek to undermine the reception of the gospel (cf. 2 Cor. 4:4).

The reference to the "trumpet" is perhaps an allusion to the means by which the Old Testament Jubilee was announced: "Then you shall sound the loud trumpet on the tenth day of the seventh month. On the Day of Atonement you shall sound the trumpet throughout all your land" (Lev. 25:9). The point of its use here is to declare that with the destruction of the temple the *ultimate* jubilee

---

24. For "seeing" as a reference to "understanding", see John 12:40 (Isa. 6:10); Acts 26:18; cf. 1 Kings 8:29, 52; 2 Kings 2:16; 6:20; 19:16; Isa. 35:5; 42:7, 16; see also Luke 24:31; also note Mark 1:44; Luke 17:22; John 3:3, 36; Rom. 15:21.
25. Gentry, *The Great Tribulation*, 61.
26. See 2 Chron. 36:15,16; Hag. 1:13; Mal. 2:7; see also Matt. 11:10; Mark 1:2; Luke 7:24,27; 9:52; James 2:25.
27. Gentry, *The Great Tribulation*, 63.

year has arrived. That is to say, "by employing imagery from the typological Year of Jubilee in Leviticus 25, the Lord here speaks about the final stage of redemption, which is finally secured as the temple vanishes from history."[28] Jesus himself announced the fulfillment of the jubilee law in his ministry when he quoted from Isaiah 61 in his synagogue sermon (Luke 4:17-21). The ultimate deliverance of God's people and liberation from all "indebtedness" has come in the person of Christ.

The "gathering together" (v. 31) of God's elect is not a reference to the end-time harvest (far less to the "rapture") but to the global growth of the Church that is on-going throughout this present age. It includes both the gathering of the saints into local assemblies or churches (Heb. 10:25; James 2:2) and the universal assembling of the saints into the body of Christ, the universal Church (see Matt. 22:7-13). Gentry explains:

> Through Christ-commissioned gospel preaching by faithful messengers, God gathers the elect into His kingdom from the four corners of the world (Matt. 28:19; Luke 24:47; Acts 1:8; 13:47; 17:30). The phrase "from one end of the sky to the other" does not indicate that the place of the action is in the sky (or heaven) above. The phraseology often signifies nothing more than "horizon to horizon" (Deut. 30:4; Neh. 1:9; compare Matt. 8:11; Luke 13:28-29). Thus, it speaks about evangelistic activity spreading throughout the earth. In fact, it parallels "from the four winds," that is, the four points of the compass. This, of course, Jesus promises in His ministry, despite the failure of His own people: "And I say to you that many will come from east and west, and sit down with Abraham, Isaac, and Jacob in the kingdom of heaven. But the sons of the kingdom will be cast out into outer darkness" (Matt. 8:11-12; Luke 13:29 speaks about all four points of the compass).[29]

Likewise, Wright points to Deuteronomy 30:2-5, which speaks of God's regathering of his children "from all the peoples where the

---

28. Ibid., 61.
29. Ibid., 64.

Lord your God has scattered you. If your outcasts are in the utter-most parts of heaven, from there the Lord your God will gather you, and from there he will take you" (vv. 3-4). Wright contends that the language of this text, echoed in the Olivet Discourse, "suggests strongly that the... passage refers, not to a 'supernatural' or 'heavenly' event, but to this-worldly [evangelistic] activity." [30]

Thus, according to this view, Jesus does not address the issue of his second coming at the end of history until verse 36. Therefore, "all these things" (v. 34) which must take place before "this generation" (v. 34) passes away refers to everything described in verses 4-31, i.e., events leading up to and including the destruction of Jerusalem in 70. In sum,

> the tribes of the earth, having come to understand the significance of the Messiah's suffering, will see what Daniel "saw," namely, the judgment in favor of the Son of Man and his enthronement. What they will literally *see* will be the destruction of the temple, the rejection of national Israel as God's chosen servant, the steady expansion of the gospel into the pagan world, and the eventual collapse of Roman imperialism – but they will *understand* from these developments that spiritual authority has been taken from the old powers and given to Jesus Christ. (cf. Dan. 7:14) [31]

The Lesson of the Fig Tree

From the fig tree learn its lesson: as soon as its branch becomes tender and puts out its leaves, you know that summer is near. So also, when you see all these things, you know that he is near, at the very gates. Truly, I say to you, this generation will not pass away until all these things take place. Heaven and earth will pass away, but my words will not pass away (Matt. 24:32-35).

Still at the center of attention is the question the disciples had asked Jesus back in verse 3. First, when will "these things" be, i.e., the

30. Wright, *Victory*, 363, n. 163.
31. Andrew Perriman, *The Coming of the Son of Man: New Testament Eschatology for an Emerging Church* (Waynesboro, GA: Paternoster, 2005), 55-56.

destruction of Jerusalem and its temple as prophesied in 23:35-36, 38; 24:2? Second, when will you return and consummate the age? The disciples thought the two events would be simultaneous. Jesus says, "No, the destruction of Jerusalem will be in your lifetime. I'll even give you a sign that will warn you of its nearness. But the day of my second coming will not be preceded by signs. It will come only after a period of delay of undetermined duration. Everyone of this present generation will be aware of when Jerusalem will fall, but not even I know when the second coming will occur." To make this point, Jesus employs a *parable* (v. 32).

The fig tree in Palestine loses its leaves in winter and blossoms late in the spring. As they sat on the Mount of Olives, a place famous for its fig trees (some of which grew to twenty-five feet), Jesus perhaps reached up and plucked a branch from one of the trees. After all, he delivered this sermon just before Passover and the fig tree would have been in precisely the condition described in the parable. He pointed out to them the tenderness of the branch as the sap was moving into it and the sprouting of its leaves. His point was that these are indications that summer is close at hand. The *application* of this to the subject at hand will become evident as we examine each part in turn.

The *"fig tree"* (v. 32) does not refer to the nation Israel, nor does the budding of the tree refer to the rebirth of the nation in 1948. There is nothing in the context to indicate he is equating the fig tree with Israel. This theory is based on the unchallenged assumption that Matthew 24 is future; hence, all the arguments for taking Matthew 24 as referring to events preceding and including 70 weigh equally against identifying the fig tree with Israel. Most believe Jesus is appealing to Isaiah 34:4 as a basis for his use of the fig tree; in other words, he was simply using what was close at hand to illustrate his point. Luke 21:29 makes it clear that *any* tree would have made the point, be it a fig tree, oak tree, sycamore, or whatever was close at hand to serve to illustrate his point. Jesus is simply drawing a lesson from nature. Finally, "this generation" (v. 34) points away from a reference to a future Israel to events in their own lifetime.

The phrase *"all these things"* (v. 33a) refers to events described in verses 4-31. "All these things" encompasses those distinctive events which that generation of Jewish Christians would see in conjunction with the destruction of Jerusalem and the temple. When you see "these things", especially the Abomination of Desolation (vv. 15-22 = Roman armies surrounding Jerusalem), you may safely conclude that Jerusalem's destruction is near.

The phrase "he is near" might lead you to think that the reference is to Jesus and his coming at the close of history. But the Greek word is grammatically ambiguous and could be either masculine ("*he* is near") or neuter ("*it* is near"). If masculine, it likely refers to the vindication of Jesus as seen in his coming in judgment. Or it could be that the coming of Jesus to the Ancient of Days in heaven is near or close at hand (Dan. 7:13-14). If neuter, it refers to the desolation, desecration, and destruction of Jerusalem and the temple. And, as noted before, "this generation" (v. 34a) refers to the contemporaries of Jesus who would live to see the events he describes.

In summary, Jesus says: "I want you to be alerted to the approach of Jerusalem's destruction. Here is how you can know when its fall is impending. It will as surely follow the Abomination of Desolation as summer follows the budding of figs. But, on the other hand, when it comes to the timing and proximity of my return and the end of human history, not even I know when that day will occur."

Matthew 24:35 (Mark 13:31) records Jesus' words: "Heaven and earth will pass away, but my words will not pass away." Most commentators have given scant attention to the significance of this statement in its context, simply assuming that our Lord had in mind the destruction and/or collapse of the space-time cosmos at the close of history. However, Crispin H.T. Fletcher-Louis has put forth an intriguing argument "that 'by heaven and earth' is meant the Jerusalem temple and the Torah constitution at the center of which the former stands…. [Thus the phrase 'heaven and earth shall pass away' refers] to the imminent end to the social, religious and economic structure of Israel's covenant relationship with God with the attendant destruction of the temple."[32]

---

32. "The Destruction of the Temple and the Relativization of the Old Covenant: Mark 13:31 and Matthew 5:18," in *Eschatology in Bible & Theology: Evangeli-*

Although this may sound strange to modern ears, he compiles an impressive amount of biblical and extra-biblical evidence that the temple was thought of "as the point at which the creation had taken place and around which it now revolved – the Navel of the Earth (*Jub.* 8:19; *1 Enoch* 26:1; cf. Ezek. 38:12); the meeting point of heaven and earth – the Gate of Heaven."[33] More important still "was the belief that the temple was regarded as the 'epitome of the world, a concentrated form of its essence, a miniature of the cosmos'. The temple was far more than the point at which heaven and earth met. Rather, it was thought to correspond to, represent, or, in some sense, to be 'heaven and earth' in its totality. The idea is readily grasped if its three-fold structure, the sanctuary (supremely the Holy of Holies), the inner and outer courts, are allowed to correspond to heaven, earth and sea respectively."[34] If Fletcher-Louis is correct, we would find in verse 35 additional support for the view that finds the fulfillment of Jesus' words in Matthew 24 in the destruction of temple and city in 70.

The Second Coming of Christ

Whereas the parable of the fig tree makes it possible to know the nearness of Jerusalem's fall, nothing will help you fix the date or proximity of Christ's final return (Harold Camping's pathetic prophetic forecasts notwithstanding). Here, then, is our Lord's answer to the second half of the disciples' question (v. 3). "That day" (v. 36) refers to the second coming at the end of human history. This, then, is a major transition verse in the Olivet Discourse. It's important that we observe the contrasts.[35]

---

cal *Essays at the Dawn of a New Millennium*, edited by Kent E. Brower & Mark W. Elliott (Downers Grove: IVP, 1997), 146.

33. Ibid., 157.

34. Ibid., 157; see Ps. 78:69; Isa. 65:17-18 where the new heavens and earth are related to the restoration of Jerusalem. For more on this, see N.T. Wright, *Simply Jesus,* 132-35.

35. The most helpful and extensive explanation of the many reasons why verse 36 marks a major transition from a description of the destruction of Jerusalem and its temple to a description of the second coming of Christ is provided by Gentry in *The Olivet Discourse Made Easy,* 128-38.

First of all, the "but", with which verse 36 opens, implies a contrast between verse 36 and what has previously been said. Our Lord is clearly moving from the subject of Jerusalem and its temple to that of his parousia.[36] France explains that in verse 36

> we are introduced, it seems, to a new subject. There is, first, the fact that whereas the preceding verses have described an event shortly to occur, and definitely within a generation, this verse introduces an event of the date of which Jesus explicitly disclaims any knowledge. Further, the phrase *peri de tes hemeras ekeines* ("but of that day") is as clearly as possible setting the day it describes in contrast with what has preceded. The phrase *he hemera ekeine* ("that day") is a new one in this chapter [Mark 13]. The events of 66–70 have been described as *tauta panta* ("all these things"), and as *ekeinai hai hemerai* ("those days") (vv. 17, 19, 24; and Matt. 24:22), but the singular has not yet occurred. The inference is clear that a new and distinct day is being described.[37]

Second, the change in subject is also attested by the issue of *signs*. In the first half of the sermon, Jesus gave specifics concerning events preceding and leading up to the destruction of Jerusalem; he gave instructions on how to escape; he even gave them one sign in particular that would unmistakably indicate the imminence of the city's fall. But now, in response to the second half of their question, he says: "No one knows or can know; not even I."

Thus, one event was close at hand (Jerusalem's fall). It would happen within the time span of that generation and would be immediately preceded by the sign of the Abomination of Desolation. The other event (the parousia) would transpire in the future

---

36. "The event predicted in vv. 4-35 has been described as the "coming of the Son of Man," using the participle *erchomenos*, which echoes the vision of Dan. 7:13-14. The only mention of the *parousia* in that section was to say that it will *not* be like the events of those days (v. 27). But now the term *parousia* (which does not occur in the Greek translation of Dan. 7:13-14) comes into play in vv. 37 and 39. Since this was the term used in the second part of the disciples' question, it is clear that that second issue is now being addressed" (France, *Matthew,* 937).

37. France, *Jesus and the Old Testament,* 232.

at a time unknown even to the Lord. No signs will point to that day. Perhaps Jesus spoke this way to keep us from rashly concluding that every new global crisis, war, catastrophic earthquake, or other sort of national or natural upheaval was the clear sign of his return.

Living in the Last Days

Did Jesus provide any information at all of what the last days would be like? Yes. He does describe some of the features of that time in Matthew 24:37-41. There will not be unprecedented global catastrophes or unparalleled calamities that will point people to the impending return of Jesus. Rather, humanity will be immersed in the routine affairs of life. It will be like it was in the days of Noah. The world will be caught completely off-guard by the coming of Christ. People will be engaged in normal, routine occupations of life: farming, fellowship, marriage, etc. (Cf. Luke 17:28-30; 1 Thess. 5:3.). Jesus will come at a time of widespread indifference, normalcy, materialistic endeavors, when everyone is thoroughly involved in the pursuit of their earthly affairs and ambitions (cf. 2 Pet. 3:3-4, 10). His coming will occur at a time so unexpected, so unannounced, that it will catch people in the middle of their everyday routines (see vv. 40-41). When will Jesus come? *Jesus will come at a time when his coming is the farthest thing from people's minds!*

He then employs two illustrations in verses 42-51 to reinforce his point. The first is found in verses 42-44. Has a thief ever called your home to tell you when he planned on breaking in? Did he say, "Hey, I'm coming to steal everything you've got at about 3:30 a.m. Be sure you leave your back door unlocked!" Of course, Jesus is not comparing himself to the character of a thief but to the *coming* of a thief. Both a thief in the night and Jesus' coming are unannounced and unexpected: so be ready!

The second is found in verses 45-51. Watching does not mean sitting quietly and passively as you gaze into the skies. It means serving, being diligent to help others, obeying God. I should point out, however, that N.T. Wright contends that not even verses 36ff. refer to the second coming but rather are an extended warning to the disciples to be prepared for impending judgment. Although I disagree with Wright on this point, we should listen to his argument. He comments on Luke's version of this warning (17:26-36), which refers both to the days of Noah and Lot, as

> times when devastating judgment fell on those who were failing to heed divine warning. Their times were perfectly ordinary, with no special signs of imminent disaster: they ate, they drank, they married and were given in marriage. But when YHWH acted in judgment there was no time to waste. Only those who got out and fled... were saved.... While they were waiting for the moment to arrive, however, there would be many voices urging that Israel's vindication was to be found in this or that new movement. They would long to see one of the days of the "son of man" [Luke 17:22], but would not see it, and would be an open prey to invitations to look at this or that conspiracy or uprising as the way towards vindication. But when it happened there would be no mistaking it: it would be like lightning flashing from east to west, and on that day... they should not stop to pack and get ready, but simply run. [38]

He contends that "being 'taken' in this context means being taken in *judgment*. There is no hint here of a 'rapture', a sudden 'supernatural' event which would remove individuals from *terra firma*. Such an idea," says Wright, "would look as odd, in these synoptic passages, as a Cadillac in a camel-train. It is a matter, rather, of secret police coming in the night, or of enemies sweeping through a village or city and seizing all they can. If the disciples were to escape, if they were to be 'left', it would be by the skin of their teeth." [39]

Conclusion

In conclusion, my argument that Matthew 24:4-31 refers immediately and primarily to the events leading up to and including the destruction of Jerusalem in 70 does not necessarily exclude the possibility that the end of the age is, at least indirectly, also in view.

---

38. Wright, *Victory*, 365-66.
39. Ibid., 366.

It may well be that future events associated with the second advent of Christ at the end of the age are *prefigured* by the destruction of the temple and the city in 70. James Edwards argues "that events surrounding the destruction of the temple and fall of Jerusalem are a type and foreshadowing of a final sacrilege before the eschaton."[40] Thus, the temple is understood as a microcosm of the cosmos, so that its destruction becomes a prophetic or proleptic paradigm for what will occur in the macrocosm at the close of history.

The mistake that many make, however, is in trying to project the historical details of the year 70 into a comparable and proportionate conflagration in literal, historical Jerusalem at the end of the age. They want to suggest that essentially everything that literally happened in the period 33–70 will literally happen again on the same scale in the same part of the world: Palestine. They fail to realize that the events of 70 are at most a prototype on a microcosmic scale of what will occur on a macrocosmic scale when Jesus returns. In other words, the events of 70 *may* well portray in a localized way what will happen *globally* at or in some way associated with the second advent.

Therefore, my opinion is that the pattern of events that transpired in the period 33–70, leading up to and including the destruction of Jerusalem and its temple, *may* function as a *local, microcosmic foreshadowing* of the *global, macrocosmic* events associated with the parousia and the end of history. The period 33–70 conceivably, then, provides in its *principles* (though not necessarily in all particularities), a template against which we are to interpret the period 70–parousia.

In bringing our discussion of the Olivet Discourse to an end, I want to emphasize once again that the destruction of Jerusalem and the temple and God's judgment on Israel in 70 is all about Jesus! It's about who he is and how he reigns as sovereign Lord. It's about the truth of who he claimed to be, as over against the blasphemous lies and rejection of him by the religious leaders in

---

40. James R. Edwards, *The Gospel According to Mark* (Grand Rapids: Eerdmans, 2002), 384.

Israel, together with the extent and duration of his dominion over all creation. This prophecy, therefore, is designed to tell the disciples then (and us now) that the temple is no longer, and never shall be again, where you go to meet God. The temple is no longer, and never shall be again, the place of God's dwelling. The temple is no longer, and never shall be again, the place where blood sacrifice is offered. The temple is no longer, and never shall be again, the place where forgiveness of sins is found. The temple is no longer, and never shall be again, the place where you go to hear God's voice and to learn about who he is. *All these things now are found in Jesus alone.* He is the true temple of God. He is the person and place of sacrifice where forgiveness is found and God's voice is heard and God's glory and presence are encountered. So, when the temple in Jerusalem was razed, leveled, and flattened such that not one stone was left upon another, the people of that day "saw" that everything the temple symbolized and achieved is now found in King Jesus who rules over all the universe. There has been a regime change. The temple is dethroned. Jesus is enthroned. [41]

---

41. My reason for repeating the phrase "and never shall be again" is to stress as emphatically as I can that God will never approve of nor sanction the rebuilding of the physical structure of a temple in Jerusalem, contrary to the argument of virtually all dispensationalists and Christian Zionists. As noted earlier in this book, whether or not the Jewish people in fact rebuild a temple in Jerusalem is irrelevant and unrelated to anything in biblical prophecy. Notwithstanding the presence on the temple site of the Dome of the Rock, a way may be found for a Jewish temple to be built in its place. But it will never be the locus of God's presence or glory or redemptive grace. Should it be built, it would stand as an affront to the incarnation, life, death, resurrection, ascension, and enthronement of the Son of God, the true and final temple of God.

Chapter Nine

The Book of Acts and the Promise of Israel's Restoration

The title to this short chapter is a bit misleading insofar as I intend only to address two passages in the book of Acts that relate to the question of whether or not there is a distinct prophetic future for national Israel. I have chosen these two texts because they are the ones most frequently mentioned by all dispensationalists and some premillennialists. The first one will require less time and space than the second.

Acts 1:6-8

Many are inclined to find evidence for Israel's future national regathering and restoration in the way our Lord responded to a question posed by the disciples. Or perhaps it would be more accurate to say it is in the way he did *not* respond. The question was asked just prior to our Lord's ascension:

> [6]So when they had come together, they asked him, "Lord will you at this time restore the kingdom to Israel?" [7]He said to them, "It is not for you to know times or seasons that the Father has fixed by his own authority. [8]But you will receive power when the Holy Spirit has come upon you, and you will be my witnesses in Jerusalem and in all Judea and Samaria, and to the end of the earth." (Acts 1:6-8)

As noted above, many believe that Jesus declined to answer their question. More than that, had they been wrong in their belief that the kingdom would be restored to Israel, Jesus would have corrected them. The fact that he did neither strongly indicates that he endorsed their prophetic perspective. Or so some say.

A closer look at the larger context of Acts 1 will indicate, on the other hand, that Jesus did in fact answer their question, but in a way that they did not anticipate. The place to begin isn't with the disciples' question in Acts 1:6 but with the teaching of Jesus concerning the kingdom of God in Acts 1:3-5:

> ³He presented himself alive to them after his suffering by many proofs, appearing to them during forty days and speaking about the kingdom of God. ⁴And while staying with them he ordered them not to depart from Jerusalem, but to wait for the promise of the Father, which, he said, "you heard from me; ⁵for John baptized with water, but you will be baptized with the Holy Spirit not many days from now."

Here we see that in the time following his resurrection and prior to his ascension, Jesus had been speaking to them "about the kingdom of God" (Acts 1:3). It would appear that a crucial dimension to this "kingdom" was the promise of the outpouring of and baptism in the Holy Spirit. Indeed, Luke tells us that he was speaking to them of his Father's "promise", as made known by John the Baptizer, that whereas the latter "baptized with water," the Christian community "will be baptized with [more literally, "in"] the Holy Spirit not many days from now" (Acts 1:5). Although the connection between the two is not as explicit as one might hope, it is hard not to conclude that the coming of the kingdom is in some sense directly related to, if not identified with, the outpouring of the Spirit at Pentecost and the globally expansive evangelistic work to which Jesus commissions them in Acts 1:8.

When the disciples asked their question in verse 6, the "kingdom" about which they were concerned was the very one to which Jesus had just referred in verse 3. "The fact that they spoke of its being 'restored to Israel' indicates that they were thinking of it as a national entity with its center located in Jerusalem and its domain encompassing the land of their fathers."[1] But contrary to what many think, Jesus did not avoid answering their question. The disciples had not merely asked a question about the kingdom; they had asked specifically "when" its restoration would occur. Jesus answered by saying, "It is not for you to know times or seasons that the Father has fixed by his own authority" (Acts 1:7a). Although it may appear from this that Jesus refused to address the issue of timing, that's not entirely accurate, insofar as he told them in Acts 1:5b that the Spirit would come "not many days from now" (1:5b). This may well be at least a partial hint to them regarding their inquiry about "when" the kingdom would be restored.

But given the connection previously established between the "kingdom" and the coming of the Spirit (see Acts 1:3-5), I contend that Jesus did in fact answer their question about the restoration of the kingdom. When he immediately declares, "But you will receive power when the Holy Spirit has come upon you, and you will be my witnesses in Jerusalem and in all Judea and Samaria, and to the end of the earth" (1:8), he is telling them precisely the way in which the much anticipated kingdom of God would appear and make its presence known on the earth. Robertson explains:

> The domain of this kingdom, the realm of the Messiah's rule, would indeed begin at Jerusalem, the focal point of Israel's life for centuries. So, unquestionably, Israel would be a primary participant in the coming of the messianic kingdom. Jesus was not teaching a "replacement" theology in which all connection with the promises given to the fathers is summarily settled, and the Israel of old is replaced by the church of the present day. At the same time, the domain of this kingdom cannot be contained within the Israel of the old covenant. Going even beyond Judea and Samaria, this kingdom would break

---

1. O. Palmer Robertson, *The Israel of God: Yesterday, Today, and Tomorrow* (Phillipsburg: P & R Publishing, 2000), 130. As Robertson points out, "restoration of the kingdom after Israel's exile was a major expectation of the prophets of old" (131). See especially Isa. 1:26; 9:7; Jer. 16:14-15; 23:5-8; 33:14-18; 50:19; Hos. 3:4-5; 11:11; Amos 9:11-12; Zech. 9:9-10.

through the bounds of Jewish political concern and extend to the far-thest corners of the earth.[2]

In other words, as Gary Burge has pointed out, our Lord's response "should not be taken to mean that Jesus acknowledges the old Jewish worldview and that its timing is now hidden from the apos-tles."[3] Rather, he is declaring that he will indeed restore Israel, but by a means and in a way that they cannot begin to imagine. Most people hear our Lord's response and think he has failed to respond to their inquiry. *But might it be that his answer is actually found in verse 8* and the impending impartation of spiritual power that will enable them to carry the gospel of the kingdom to the ends of the earth? In other words, Jesus' answer to the question of how and when God will "restore the kingdom to Israel" is wrapped up in the reality of his resurrection, his ascension to the right hand of the Father, and the much anticipated outpouring of the Holy Spirit that will result in the progressive ingathering of the Chris-tian community through gospel proclamation, together with the spread of the gospel beyond the boundaries of Jerusalem, Judea, and Samaria, to the uttermost parts of the earth![4]

Peter Walker contends, and I am in agreement with him on this point, that Jesus was seeking to turn the disciples' attention away from the socio-political concerns that shaped their understanding of the coming kingdom. He was also indicating

> that their forthcoming mission to the "ends of the earth" would itself be an indication of Israel's restoration and the means whereby the truths of that restoration would be implemented upon the world-stage. Israel was being restored through the resurrection of its Messiah and the forthcom-

2. Robertson, *The Israel of God*, 133.

3. Gary Burge, *Jesus and the Land*, 61.

4. Or, as Alan J. Thompson puts it in his book *The Acts of the Risen Lord Jesus: Luke's Account of God's Unfolding Plan* (Downers Grove: InterVarsity Press, 2011), "the inauguration of God's kingdom, or the fulfillment of God's saving promises for his people, are about to be worked out in the pouring out of the Holy Spirit and the declaration of Jesus' reign in Jerusalem, Israel and beyond!"

ing gift of the Spirit. The way in which Israel would then exert its hege-
mony over the world would not be through its own political indepen-
dence, but rather through the rule and authority of Israel's Messiah. The
chosen method of this Messiah's rule was through the apostles' proclamation of his gospel throughout the world bringing people into the "obedience of faith" (cf. Rom. 1:5). Jesus' concern, now as before, was not for a
political "kingdom of Israel," rather for the "kingdom of God" (Acts 1:3).[5]

There are other indications in our passage that the Old Testament
promise of Israel's restoration is to be identified with the creation
and growth of a Spirit-baptized Church and its expansion through
gospel proclamation. Consider, for example, three phrases in
Acts 1:8, each of which reflects the wording in Isaiah that looks
forward to a future salvation and restoration of Israel.[6] The phrase
"when the Holy Spirit has come upon you" (Acts 1:8a) alludes to
Isaiah 32:15 where the prophet describes how the desolation of
God's people will continue "until the Spirit is poured upon us from
on high" (cf. Isa. 44:3-5). The connection between these texts is
strengthened when we observe that Luke describes the promise of
Pentecost as a time when the disciples will be "clothed with power
from on high" (a clear reference to Isaiah 32:15; emphasis mine).
The phrase "you will be my witnesses" (Acts 1:8b) reflects the wording of Isaiah 43:12 where "the people of God will be transformed
and become witnesses to the salvation of God when the new age

---

5. Peter W.L. Walker, *Jesus and the Holy City* (Grand Rapids: Eerdmans, 1996),
   292. It's important to note, however, as Alan Thompson points out, that "Israel
   is in fact mentioned in Jesus' reply. When Jesus refers to Jerusalem as well as
   to 'all Judea and Samaria,' he is of course referring to Israel. Jerusalem was the
   religious capital of Israel, and the phrase 'all Judea and Samaria' was representative of the southern and northern kingdoms of Israel respectively" (*The Acts
   of the Risen Lord Jesus,* 106).
6. Several have recognized these textual connections. In addition to Thompson
   (*The Acts of the Risen Lord Jesus,* 106-08), see especially G.K. Beale, *A New
   Testament Biblical Theology: The Unfolding of the Old Testament in the New*
   (Grand Rapids: Baker Academic, 2011), 138-40; and David W. Pao, *Acts and
   the Isaianic New Exodus* (Grand Rapids: Baker Academic, 2000), 91-93.

arrives."[7] Finally, the phrase "to the end of the earth" (Acts 1:8c) recalls Isaiah 49:6, "I will make you as a light for the nations, that my salvation may reach to the end of the earth." In view of the "clear parallel in Isaiah 49:6 between 'a light for the Gentiles' and 'salvation to the ends of the earth', and the use of Isaiah 49:6 in Acts 13:47 to refer to ministry among Gentiles (cf. 13:46, 48), the phrase 'to the ends of the earth' in 1:8 refers also to the inclusion of Gentiles in this restoration program. What Jesus does then in his reply to the disciples is affirm that God's promises of restoration are about to be fulfilled."[8]

In a nutshell, "the kingdom of God would be restored to Israel in the rule of the Messiah, which would be realized by the working of the Holy Spirit through the disciples of Christ as they extended their witness to the ends of the earth."[9] The restoration of the kingdom is even now occurring as the Church extends the influence of the gospel through the power of the Holy Spirit. Therefore, Jesus is not endorsing their anticipation of a geo-political restoration of the nation Israel to earthly preeminence (either now or in an alleged future millennium). He is declaring rather that the way in which God will bring his kingdom purposes to prophetic consummation is through the Spirit-empowered growth and expansion of a multi-ethnic spiritual body, the Church, the true Israel of God.[10]

---

7. Thompson, *The Acts of the Risen Lord Jesus*, 107.

8. Ibid.

9. Robertson, *The Israel of God*, 134.

10. Space does not allow me to unpack how this principle is found elsewhere in Acts, but Thompson provides an excellent summary of how the language of Acts 2 (the coming of the Spirit at Pentecost), Acts 8:1-25 (the spread of the gospel into Samaria), Acts 8:26-40 (the inclusion of "outcasts" among God's people), and Acts 13:47 (inclusion of the Gentiles), among others, indicates that God's restoration of "Israel" has been inaugurated with the death, resurrection, and enthronement of Jesus in the present age (see *The Acts of the Risen Lord Jesus*, 109-20). Thompson's summation of the significance of Acts 2 and Peter's response to the question, "what does this mean?" (Acts 2:12), must suffice. What it "means" is "that Jesus is Lord and his enthronement as the Davidic King has ushered in the last days, the new age of the Spirit, in fulfillment of God's ancient promises for his people. Israel is being restored, the

Acts 15:13-18

Our second passage in Acts reaffirms what we've just seen in Acts 1:6-8. In fact, I will suggest that Acts 15:13-18 provides us with perhaps the single most explicit affirmation in the New Testament that the salvation of those who now constitute the Church of Jesus Christ is *the fulfillment of the promised regathering of Israel*. Needless to say, this will have tremendous bearing on our question of who constitutes the true people of God.

Here is the text for our consideration.

> [13]After they finished speaking, James replied, "Brothers, listen to me. [14]Simeon has related how God first visited the Gentiles, to take from them a people for his name. [15]And with this the words of the prophets agree, just as it is written, [16]'After this I will return, and I will rebuild the tent of David that has fallen; I will rebuild its ruins, and I will restore it, [17]that the remnant of mankind may seek the Lord, and all the Gentiles who are called by my name, says the Lord, who makes these things [18]known from of old.'"

The Prophecy of Amos

As a result of certain military victories in the eighth century B.C., Israel had become both inwardly prosperous and secure from outward threat, enabling her to extend the boundaries of the nation (2 Kings 14:25). "Such successes inspired national pride and the feeling that Yahweh favored Israel. The development of international trade made the merchants rich. Wealth brought injustice and greed; the poor were neglected, then persecuted. Religion became formalistic. The rich dominated everything and everyone from prophets and priests to judges and the poor who sought justice."[11] Given this context, God commissioned Amos to take

---

exiles are returning to God and the promised age of the Spirit is here because Jesus is Lord and is reigning even now from the right hand of the Father!" (ibid., 112). All this, of course, sets the stage for the most definitive articulation of this truth in Acts 15:13-18 (see below).

11. William Sanford Lasor, David Allan Hubbard, Frederic Wm. Bush, *Old Testament Survey* (Grand Rapids: Eerdmans, 1982), 321.

his message of impending judgment to the ten northern tribes of Israel. They refused to repent. Thus, in 722 B.C. the capital of the northern kingdom, Samaria, fell to the Assyrians. Amos 9:8-10 describes what happened:

> [8]"Behold, the eyes of the Lord GOD are upon the sinful kingdom, and I will destroy it from the surface of the ground, except that I will not utterly destroy the house of Jacob," declares the LORD. [9]"For behold, I will command, and shake the house of Israel among all the nations as one shakes with a sieve, but no pebble shall fall to the earth. [10]All the sinners of my people shall die by the sword, who say, 'Disaster shall not overtake or meet us'."

Although the judgment of Israel is unavoidable (v. 8a), it is not universal (v. 8b). The house of Israel will be punished but not annihilated. It will not be totally destroyed (v. 8b) but shaken, as if in a sieve (v. 9). Although the shaking of Israel in judgment will be severe, "there is always a divine kernel in the nation, by virtue of its divine election, a holy seed out of which the Lord will form a new and holy people and kingdom of God. Consequently the destruction will not be a total one." [12] This ray of hope shines in verse 11: "In that day I will raise up the booth of David that is fallen and repair its breaches, and raise up its ruins and rebuild it as in the days of old."

David's once great "house", promised to him and his seed in perpetuity in the covenant of 2 Samuel 7, is now but a "booth," a mere "hut." The word Amos uses, translated "booth" (ESV, NASB), referred to a rude and temporary shelter for cattle (Gen. 33:17), for warriors in the field (2 Sam. 11:11), laborers in the vineyard (Isa. 1:8), and for the Israelites during the festival of booths (Lev. 23:42-43; Deut. 16:13, 16). This tottering structure made of intertwined branches was Amos's way of describing the condition of the once great "house" or dynasty of David (2 Sam. 7:5, 11; 1 Kings 11:38; Isa. 7:2,13). Thus, "as the stately

---

12. C.F. Keil and F. Delitzsch, *Commentary on the Old Testament* (Grand Rapids: Eerdmans, 1975), X:328.

palace supplies a figurative representation of the greatness and might of the kingdom, so does the fallen hut, which is full of rents and near to destruction, symbolize the utter ruin of the kingdom. If the family of David no longer dwells in a palace, but in a miserable fallen hut, its regal sway must have come to an end."[13]

Literally, Amos says the "hut/booth" of David *is falling* or possibly *is about to fall*. He speaks both of its current condition of fallenness subsequent to a history of division and decay, as well as its impending fall in consequence of the divine judgment that he has so forcefully predicted. Gerhard Hasel thus interprets verse 11 as "a proclamation which expresses that the 'booth of David' has 'fallen' with the disintegration of Israel into two kingdoms at the time of the death of Solomon and that since that time it is 'falling' through the continual loss of much of its former power and splendor as is dictated by the whole chain of events – political, social, and religious – which followed the divisions of the united monarchy to the time of Amos."[14]

However, this "hut/booth" will one day be rebuilt and restored, described in three phrases. First, God will "repair *its* breaches". Second, he will also "raise up *its* [lit., his] ruins". Third, God will "rebuild *it* as in the days of old."

Note the italicized words: "*its* breaches" refers to the tragic division of the Davidic house (which symbolized the kingdom of God) into two kingdoms, north and south. In the phrase, "*its* ruins," the suffix is masculine and probably refers to David himself, indicating that with a new coming David (which, of course, is Jesus) the dilapidated house would rise again. Finally, the last suffix is feminine, referring to the fallen hut which would be rebuilt. Clearly, then, *Amos envisioned a restored Davidic dynasty*. Note the last phrase in verse 11 – "as in the days of old," a reference to the original Davidic promise in 2 Samuel 7:11-16.

In verse 12 Amos declares that this restoration of the Davidic kingdom is in order that Israel might "possess the remnant of

---

13. Ibid., X:329-30.
14. Gerhard Hasel, *The Remnant: The History and Theology of the Remnant Idea from Genesis to Isaiah* (Berrien Springs: Andrews University Press, 1974), 211.

Edom and all the nations who are called by my name." Why is only "Edom" mentioned and not also the Philistines, Moabites, and Ammonites? Evidently Edom (the descendants of Esau) is singled out as representative of a wider circle of people. Because of her marked hostility toward Israel, the role of Edom "was similar to that of the Amalekites, the earliest nation to represent the kingdom of men (Exod. 17:8ff.; Deut. 25:17-19), which stood violently against the kingdom of God. Moreover, Edom's representative role is further stressed by the epexegetical note in verse 12 – "and/even all the nations/Gentiles who are called by My name." [15]

What does Amos mean in saying that the people of the restored Davidic kingdom will "possess" the remnant of Edom? Some see military subjugation in this word, yet in Acts 15 James changes "possess" to "seek". LaRondelle believes that "while Amos prophesied the physical conquest of the Davidic rulership over the remnant of Edom, James translates this political-military kingship into Christ's higher, spiritual conquest and reign over the hearts of gentile believers. Amos' phrase, 'so that they may possess the remnant of Edom,' becomes in Acts 15:17, 'that the remnant of men may seek the Lord'." [16] Walter Kaiser refuses to see in the word "possess" any notion of military conquest. The reference "is not to be understood in a negative or retaliatory sense – i.e., as a punishment to Edom for one or more of its rivalries with Israel. On the contrary, 'Edom' along with the other nations would be brought under that reign of the Davidic King who is to come – the Messiah. This 'remnant' must also share in the covenant promise to David." [17]

Kaiser's point is that Israel takes "possession" of the believing remnant of Edom because they are "owned" by God who has incorporated them into that restored Davidic kingdom and brought them into spiritual submission to his sovereign rule.

15. Walter Kaiser, "The Davidic Promise and the Inclusion of the Gentiles (Amos 9:9-15 and Acts 15:13-18): A Test Passage for Theological Systems," *JETS* 20 (June 1977): 103.

16. Hans K. LaRondelle, *The Israel of God in Prophecy: Principles of Prophetic Interpretation* (Berrien Springs: Andrews University Press, 1983), 150.

17. Walter Kaiser, "The Davidic Promise and the Inclusion of the Gentiles," 102.

Therefore, "the point is not about David's or Israel's military subjugation of Edom or the Gentiles; rather, it is about their spiritual incorporation into the restored kingdom of David that is in view in Amos 9:12. Indeed, had not the promise of God to Abraham and David included a mediated 'blessing' to all the Gentiles?" [18]

Regardless of how one interprets the original meaning of "possess," in the fulfillment of the prophecy in Acts 15 the "remnant of Edom" consists of those who are saved in the judgments that befall her. Likewise, "all the nations" refers to those from among the rest of the Gentiles who are incorporated into the restored kingdom of David. In other words, the "taking possession of the remnant of Edom" and the "rest of mankind seeking the Lord" alike refer to the "ingrafting" of believing Gentiles into the olive tree of Israel (Rom. 11).

Acts 15 and the Jerusalem Council

The Jerusalem Council was convened to address the question of the status of believing Gentiles (see Acts 15:1-2). The issue they faced was this: Must Gentiles become Jewish proselytes, keep the Mosaic Law, and be circumcised, or should they be admitted to the church on the basis of faith alone?

Paul and Barnabas describe in detail the grace of God in saving Gentiles (15:3) and upon their arrival in Jerusalem repeat the story (15:4). This news did not meet with universal approval (15:5). However, based on the testimony of Peter (15:7-11), as well as Paul and Barnabas (15:12), the council decided that they should not discriminate between believing Jews and believing Gentiles. They based their decision on several factors:

- God specifically set apart Peter some ten years earlier to take the gospel to the Gentiles (Acts 10:1–11:18);
- God bestowed the gift of the Holy Spirit on believing Gentiles in the same way he did on believing Jews (Acts 15:8);

---

18. Ibid., 103.

- God refused to distinguish between Jews and Gentiles, cleansing the latter even as he did the former, through faith (15:9);
- It would be useless to require of Gentiles an obedience to the law that not even Jews were able to maintain (15:10);
- Both Jews and Gentiles are saved by the grace of Christ apart from circumcision or any old covenant law (15:11); and
- God blessed the Gentiles with signs and wonders accompanying salvation no less than he did the Jews (15:12).

James then summarizes the evidence and issues his declaration:

> [13]After they finished speaking, James replied, "Brothers, listen to me. [14]Simeon has related how God first visited the Gentiles, to take from them a people for his name. [15]And with this the words of the prophets agree, just as it is written, [16]'After this I will return, and I will rebuild the tent of David that has fallen; I will rebuild its ruins, and I will restore it, [17]that the remnant of mankind may seek the Lord, and all the Gentiles who are called by my name, says the Lord, who makes these things [18]known from of old'."

In light of this, he recommends a policy that minimizes any offense that believing Gentiles might cause among the Jews (15:19-21), but refuses to impose on them any additional requirements.

The Dispensational Interpretation of Acts 15:13-21

Most classical dispensationalists believe that in verses 14-18 James is outlining God's program for the future.[19] They argue that James responds to the problem of Gentile salvation by saying that God has always intended to bless Gentiles as well as Israel, but in their proper prophetic sequence. God purposed "first" (15:14)

---

19. This understanding of the passage is built on the arguments of John Walvoord, as found in *The Millennial Kingdom* (Grand Rapids: Zondervan, 1971), 203-07.

to visit the Gentiles in this present age to take from among them "a people for his name" (15:14b). Only "after this" or "after these things" (15:16a), i.e., after this present age of Gentile salvation, will he "return" (15:16a) in the person of his Son, Jesus Christ, at the second advent, and rebuild or restore the national, earthly, territorial dynasty of David in fulfillment of 2 Samuel 7. This rebuilding of the Davidic "house/kingdom/dynasty" will occur in the millennium. Israel's regathering and restoration in the millennium will also make possible the salvation of Gentiles (15:17).

The dispensational view can be portrayed as follows:

Dispensational View

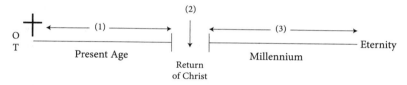

(1) God "first" (15:14) saves Gentiles in this present church age, intervening between the cross and the second coming.

(2) God in Christ will "return" (15:16) at the end of the church age in the second advent or parousia.

(3) God will at that time, i.e., after the things of the present age in which he saves Gentiles, in the millennium, rebuild and restore the national Davidic kingdom or "house" of David.

A Redemptive-Historical Interpretation of Acts 15:13-21

We begin with a critique of the dispensational view. First, the word "first" in James' statement (v. 14) is an echo of Peter's declaration (v. 7) of how "*in the early days* God made a choice among you…" In other words, "first" means "for the first time." It refers to the initial saving work of God among the Gentiles through Peter as recorded in Acts 10 and again through Paul (15:12). Thus "first" cannot mean "first" in the sense of sequence, in contrast to "after this".

Second, James uses the phrase "after these things" (v. 16a; my translation) instead of Amos' "in that day" to emphasize that the "day" in which the tabernacle of David would be rebuilt was "after" the "things" described by Amos in 9:8-10 of his prophecy, namely, the judgment that was to befall Israel as manifested in the progressive deterioration of David's tabernacle. Oswald Allis summarizes:

> The words "After these things I will return and build" do not refer to a time which was still future when James used them. In the Amos passage the words are used simply, "in that day," which is the most general formula used by the prophets to introduce an utterance regarding the coming Messianic age. "After these things I will return and build" is a slightly more emphatic form of statement. Viewed in the light of their context in Amos, they refer to a time subsequent to the complete destruction of the northern kingdom, which had ceased to exist centuries before the New Testament age in which James was living. The words "I will return and build" are simply an emphatic way of saying, "I will build again." There is no warrant for making them refer directly to the second advent. They naturally refer to the first advent and to the whole of the great redemptive work of which it was the beginning and which will culminate in the second advent. The only natural interpretation of this passage is that it refers to the Church age and to the ingathering of the Gentiles during that age, as a signal proof of the world-wide sovereignty of the Son of David.[20]

Third, as Allis briefly noted, the "return" of God mentioned by James in verse 16a, at which time the Davidic tabernacle will be restored, was *future to Amos, not James!* Amos had predicted in 9:8-10 that God would, as it were, "turn away" from Israel in judgment, dispersing her among the nations. But Amos also records the promise that God would "return" in favor to bless his covenant people and build again the dilapidated kingdom of David (cf. Jer. 12:15). Therefore, the "return" in Acts 15:16a is not a technical reference to the return of Christ at the end of the age. Indeed, this Greek word is never used in the New Testament of Christ's second advent.[21]

---

20. Oswald T. Allis, *Prophecy and the Church* (Philadelphia: Presbyterian & Reformed, 1945), 149.
21. See Matt. 17:22; John 2:15; Acts 5:22; 2 Cor. 1:12; Eph. 2:3; 1 Tim. 3:15; Heb. 10:33; 13:18; 1 Pet. 1:17; 2 Pet. 2:18.

The "return" of God to which James refers had *already* occurred in the person and work of Jesus, more specifically, in his glorious exaltation to the right hand of the Father thereby seating David's son on David's throne in fulfillment of David's covenant. *The "rebuilding" of David's tabernacle as a result of this "return" of God was inaugurated by the resurrection and exaltation of Christ and is being progressively realized in the gathering of Gentile believers into the covenant people of God.* J. Barton Payne is certainly correct when he concludes that "the reference [to the rebuilding of David's fallen tent] must be to His [Christ's] first coming; for Acts 15:16 emphasizes that it is this event which enables the Gentiles, from the apostolic period onward, to seek God.... [Then] came the engrafting of the uncircumcised Gentiles into the church, to which Acts 15 applies the OT passage, so it cannot refer to times yet future." [22]

Fourth, the dispensational view makes it impossible for James to say anything relevant to the problem at hand (i.e., the status of believing Gentiles in relation to Jews). At most, they might argue that there is an *analogy* between the future millennial age (outlined by Amos), in which Gentiles will be blessed along with Jews, and the present church age. But this creates a problem, for dispensationalists have always argued that Gentiles in the millennium will have a somewhat inferior status in relation to believing Jews. If James believed this, "then the point to be gained from his quoting of Amos 9:11-12 would be not to grant the Gentiles equal status with the Jews but only a status like that which they would have in the millennium. The result would have been that those who argued that Gentiles must be circumcised to be saved (Acts 15:1) would have been strengthened, and the truth of the gospel (cf. Gal. 2:5) would have been endangered." [23]

---

22. J. Barton Payne, *Encyclopedia of Biblical Prophecy* (Grand Rapids: Baker, 1980), 417.

23. Daniel P. Fuller, *Gospel and Law: Contrast or Continuum? The Hermeneutics of Dispensationalism and Covenant Theology* (Grand Rapids: Eerdmans, 1980), 180.

The key to interpreting this text in Acts is found in the prophetic perspective of Amos. Amos prophesied divine judgment against Israel, to be followed "in that day" by the rebuilding of David's kingdom. Consequently, *the "day" of restoration was future to Amos, not James.* The "things" of which James speaks, "after" which God will return and build David's tabernacle are the judgments against Israel from the time of Amos in the eighth century B.C. to the coming of Christ in the first century A.D. We could portray it this way:

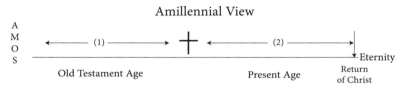

Amillennial View

(1) This is the period of the "things" of which James speaks, namely, the judgments against Israel from Amos to Christ, a time during which David's tabernacle (kingdom) progressively lost its power and prestige.

(2) This is "that day" spoken of by Amos, beginning with the exaltation of David's greater son, the Lord Jesus Christ, and extending to the end of the age, during which time God restores the fallen fortunes of the Davidic kingdom.

The "return" of God to "rebuild" and "restore" the tabernacle of David is preparatory to, indeed, the means by which "the rest of mankind" (15:17a), i.e., the Gentiles, will seek the Lord and be saved. If James finds the fulfillment of Amos' prophecy concerning Gentile salvation in the events associated with the ministries of Peter and Paul (recounted in 15:1-12), then the Davidic kingdom must already in some sense have been restored or at least inaugurated.

The covenant promise in 2 Samuel 7 spoke of a "son" who would ascend the throne of an eternal kingdom (cf. Pss. 89:20-37; 132:11-18). Jesus is that very son of both David and God in and by whom the covenant is fulfilled (see Rom. 1:3; Rev. 3:7; 5:5; 22:16b; see especially Luke 1:31-33). When and in what manner would Jesus, son of David, ascend this throne and fulfill the promise of an ever-lasting kingdom? Has it been postponed until the millennium? Or did Jesus, on the basis of his death and subsequent to his resurrection, ascend to the throne of David in the heavenly Jerusalem from which place of sovereign glory he even now rules as Davidic king? Two texts in Acts answer this question.

At Pisidian Antioch Paul surveys the course of God's redemptive activity from the Exodus to the establishment of the Davidic monarchy. He then declares that it is in Jesus we see the fulfillment of the promise made to David. Look at Acts 13:32-37:

> [32]And we bring you the good news that what God promised to the fathers, [33]this he has fulfilled to us their children by raising Jesus, as also it is written in the second Psalm, "You are my Son, today I have begotten you." [34]And as for the fact that he raised him from the dead, no more to return to corruption, he has spoken in this way, *"I will give you the holy and sure blessings of David."* [35]Therefore he says also in another psalm, "You will not let your Holy One see corruption." [36]For David, after he had served the purpose of God in his own generation, fell asleep and was laid with his fathers and saw corruption, but he whom God raised up did not see corruption.

Consider also the words of Peter in Acts 2:29-36.

> [29]Brothers, I may say to you with confidence about the patriarch David that he both died and was buried, and his tomb is with us to this day. [30]Being therefore a prophet, and knowing that God had sworn with an oath to him that he would set one of his descendants on his throne, [31]he foresaw and spoke about the resurrection of the Christ, that he was not abandoned to Hades, nor did his flesh see corruption. [32]This Jesus God raised up, and of that we all are witnesses. [33]Being therefore exalted at the right hand of God, and having received from the Father the promise of the Holy Spirit, he has poured out this that you yourselves are seeing and hearing. [34]For David did not ascend into the heavens, but he himself says, "The Lord said to my Lord, Sit at my right hand, [35]until I make your enemies your footstool." [36]Let all

the house of Israel therefore know for certain that God has made him both Lord and Christ, this Jesus whom you crucified.

This can't help but suggest, observes F.F. Bruce, that "just as the promise to build a house for David was fully realized not in Solomon but in Christ, so the prediction that David's son would build a house for God was consummated not in Solomon's temple but in the new temple of Christ's body in which His people 'are built ... for a dwelling place of God in the Spirit.'"[24] Thus, as Beale explains, "Jesus is the latter-day cosmic tabernacle in which not only believing Jews but also Gentiles throughout the cosmos may worship."[25] O. Palmer Robertson clearly summarizes what we've seen to this point:

> It is difficult to imagine any way in which Peter could have expressed more pointedly that Jesus Christ's current exaltation fulfilled God's promise to David that his descendant was to reign as the anointed one of Israel. The question cannot be relegated to one of "literal" or "non-literal" interpretation. Jesus Christ "literally" is the descendant of David. He sits "literally" on David's throne, since from both the Old Testament and the New Testament perspectives the "throne of David" is to be identified with the throne of God. As the figures of David's throne and God's throne merged in the theocracy of the old covenant, so God's throne and Jesus' position as heir to David's throne seated at God's right hand merge in the new covenant. Today Jesus reigns "literally" in Jerusalem because the "Jerusalem" of the old covenant represented the place of God's enthronement, just as the "Jerusalem" of the new covenant represents the place of God's throne today.[26]

---

24. F.F. Bruce, *The New Testament Development of Old Testament Themes* (Grand Rapids: Eerdmans, 1973), 79.

25. G.K. Beale, *The Temple and the Church's Mission: A Biblical Theology of the Dwelling Place of God* (Downers Grove: Inter Varsity Press, 2004), 233. Beale provides an especially thorough and persuasive account of James' citation of Amos (232-44).

26. O. Palmer Robertson, *The Christ of the Covenants* (Grand Rapids: Baker Book House, 1980), 221.

And in what way does this bear upon the use in Acts 15 of Amos 9? George Ladd explains:

> James cites the prophecy of Amos 9:11-12 to prove that Peter's experience with Cornelius was a fulfillment of God's purpose to visit the Gentiles and take out of them a people for his name. It therefore follows that the "rebuilding of the dwelling of David" which had resulted in the Gentile mission, must refer to the exaltation and enthronement of Christ upon the (heavenly) throne of David and the establishment of the church as the true people of God, the new Israel. Since God had brought Gentiles to faith without the Law, there was no need to insist that the Gentiles become Jews to be saved.[27]

Conclusion

The resurrection of Jesus from the dead, followed by his exaltation and enthronement at the right hand of the Father, is the inaugural step in the restoration of the fallen booth of David. *The grafting in of Gentile believers is the prophesied regathering of the true Israel.* The restoration of the Davidic kingdom and the fulfillment of the covenant promise in 2 Samuel 7 have been inaugurated in the resurrection and exaltation of David's "greater son," the Son of God, Jesus Christ. It is this, then, that has made possible the rebuilding of the Davidic dynasty which consists in nothing less than the ingathering of believing Gentiles as the true Israel of God (Gal. 6:16). Therefore, to say that believing Gentiles should enter the fellowship of the saints on a different basis from believing Jews is contrary to the prophetic purpose for redemptive history as defined by Amos in the eighth century B.C.[28]

The implications of this for our understanding of God's purpose in redemptive history are significant. We began with the

---

27. George E. Ladd, *A Theology of the New Testament* (Grand Rapids: Eerdmans, 1974), 355.

28. For extended discussion of the exegetical issues involved in James' citation of Amos, see both the article of Kaiser cited above and "James' Use of Amos at the Jerusalem Council: Steps Toward a Possible Solution of the Textual and Theological Problems," by Michael A. Braun, *JETS* 20 (June 1977): 113-21.

foundational principle that the New Testament is God's authorized and inspired interpretation of the Old Testament. When this hermeneutical principle is applied not only to Amos 9 but to the entire corpus of Old Testament prophetic utterances, we see that Israel's destiny is realized first and fundamentally in the life, death, resurrection, and exaltation of Jesus Christ, and by organic extension, in his body, the Church (the true Israel of God).

Chapter Ten

Romans 11 and The "Future" of Israel

Is there a distinctive future for ethnic Israel in which the vast majority of Jewish people will be saved, somehow in connection with the second coming of Christ to earth? Few issues are more hotly disputed than this one, and no text is more frequently cited in the debate than Romans 11.

Many postmillennialists and even some amillennialists agree with premillennialists that Paul in Romans 11 is affirming a future restoration of ethnic Jews to salvific blessing and favor. Of course, neither postmillennialists nor amillennialists who hold to this interpretation envision Israel as a second people of God, separate from the Church (nor, for that matter, do some premillennialists). They insist that the salvation of the nation as a whole will not be for the purpose of restoring Israel to her Old Testament theocratic glory. Rather, believing Jews will be saved into and as a vital part of the body of Christ, the Church, the true Israel of God.

Although advocates of all millennial schemes may feel comfortable in Romans 11, the fact remains that much of the rationale for a post-parousia millennial age is at least indirectly related to a belief that God will save Israel as a nation and fulfill in the earthly millennium his Old Testament promises to her. If it can be shown that Paul does *not* herein affirm a national future for ethnic Israel, the theological underpinnings of premillennialism will be noticeably weakened.

Rather than attempting to comment on each verse, I propose to focus attention on several crucial passages and themes which I believe are determinative of the controversy. The question before us in this passage is whether or not Paul is saying that in the future, in some way related to the second advent of Jesus Christ, the nation of Israel as a whole will be saved? Will there be a future restoration in mass of ethnic Jews? Or is he saying that the salvation of ethnic Jews has occurred and will continue to occur in no other way than that which obtains in the case of ethnic Gentiles, namely, progressively and individually throughout history?

For the sake of brevity, I will call the former view the *Future Restoration* (hereafter FR) interpretation. The latter will be called the *Historical Remnant* (hereafter *HR*) theory. Of course it cannot be disputed, as O. Palmer Robertson reminds us, "that Jews have been saved and will continue to be saved throughout the present dispensation. This kind of 'future' for the descendants of Abraham is granted on all sides. The question instead is whether or not the… [text] under consideration speaks of some distinctive conversion-activity of God among Israel immediately prior to or in conjugation with the return of Christ."[1]

The Problem of the People of God

Key to Paul's argument in Romans 11 is a problem he addressed in Romans 9:1-5, to which I must briefly turn. If Israel is God's covenant people to whom many glorious privileges have been given (9:4-5), how can it be that so few are saved and so many accursed, separated from Christ (9:1-3)? Has God's "word," his covenant promise and eternal purpose, failed? Has the unbelief of the majority of Paul's kinsmen according to the flesh thwarted God's salvific decree, thereby undermining the trustworthiness and fidelity of God's word? Paul's answer to this question is a resounding No! He will labor to demonstrate that God's eternal purpose

---

1. O. Palmer Robertson, "Is There a Distinctive Future for Ethnic Israel in Romans 11?" in *Perspectives on Evangelical Theology: Papers from the Thirtieth Annual Meeting of the Evangelical Theological Society* (Grand Rapids: Baker Book House, 1979), 221 (hereafter cited simply as "Distinctive Future"). This article has been slightly revised and updated in *The Israel of God: Yesterday, Today, and Tomorrow* (Phillipsburg: Presbyterian & Reformed, 2000).

never included the salvation of every ethnic Jew. Their unbelief, therefore, can hardly be cited as evidence against the veracity and immutability of God's word.

Paul makes his point by articulating a principle which will serve him time and again throughout Romans 9–11. It is stated in Romans 9:6b, "For they are not all Israel who are descended from Israel." If God's word of promise and eternal purpose is that all ethnic Israelites (i.e., all those "who are descended from Israel") are to be saved, then clearly his purpose has failed and his word is void. But this is the very thing Paul denies, namely, that God ever intended to save all ethnic Israelites. His purpose has always been to save a remnant within, but not the entirety of, ethnic Israel. Paul is telling us that there is an "Israel" within "Israel," a spiritually elect remnant within the physically ethnic nation. The purpose of this distinction, says John Murray, "is to show that the conventional promise of God did not have respect to Israel after the flesh but to this *true* Israel and that, therefore, the unbelief and rejection of ethnic Israel as a whole in no way interfered with the fulfillment of God's covenant purpose and promise. The word of God, therefore, has not been violated." [2]

Paul proves his thesis in Romans 9:6-13 by appealing to the family of Abraham (vv. 7-9) and to the family of Isaac (vv. 10-13). Although both Isaac and Ishmael are Abraham's physical descendants (i.e., "Israelites"), Isaac alone is a true or spiritual "Israelite." It is likewise with the descendants of Isaac. Whereas both Jacob and Esau are the physical seed of Isaac, indeed they were twins, only Jacob is the sort of "Israelite" whom God purposed to save. Notwithstanding the unbelief of Ishmael and Esau, God remains faithful to his word. Though the physical descendants of Abraham be ever so numerous (Rom. 9:27-29), God will save only a remnant. Neither the presence of Abraham's blood in one's veins nor the mark of circumcision in one's flesh has been or ever shall be a sufficient cause for salvation. Abraham's faith is the only necessary and sufficient condition.

---

2. John Murray, *The Epistle to the Romans* (Grand Rapids: Eerdmans, 1965), 2:10.

The unbelief of Israel as a whole is taken up yet again by Paul at the close of Romans 10. "Surely Israel's unbelief is excusable," comes the charge. "If they did not believe the gospel, it must be because they did not hear the gospel. Right?" Wrong, says Paul, for "their voice has gone out into all the earth, and their words to the end of the world" (10:18). Again the objection echoes, "But if Israel did not believe it must be because they did not understand. Right?" Wrong, says Paul, for "all the day long I [the Lord] have stretched out my hands to a disobedient and obstinate people" (10:21).

Does this mean, then, that God has *rejected* his people whom he foreknew? That is the question Paul addresses in Romans 11. In other words, does widespread unbelief among ethnic Israelites mean that God has withdrawn his covenant promise, reneged on his word, forsaken his beloved, and rejected the people whom he foreknew? God forbid!

But indignant denial is not proof. We feel compelled to ask Paul, "What evidence do you have to prove your point?" "**Me**," says the apostle, "for I too am an Israelite, a descendant of Abraham, of the tribe of Benjamin" (Rom. 11:1b). The suggestion that God has rejected his people is falsified by the salvation of Paul himself. Paul is an example of the remnant within the nation as a whole, an individual who is both an ethnic and elect Israelite. The proof that God has not reneged on his word despite unbelief in the nation as a whole is the same as has been true all through redemptive history, to wit, that God never foreknew or fore-loved in saving grace all the physical descendants of Abraham, Isaac, and Jacob, but only a remnant, of which Paul is a current, living constituent member.

An important consideration here is the identity of the "people" whom God foreknew. Who are they? Who are the "people of God"? Two answers have been given. On the one hand, it would seem that if Paul cites his own salvation as proof that God has not rejected his people then surely the "people" whom he foreknew is the remnant according to the election of grace. This answer, however, has not been accepted by everyone. Both John Murray and C.E.B. Cranfield, for example, insist that the "people" whom God foreknew, the people whom Paul says God has not rejected, is the nation as a whole, ethnic and elect Israel alike. They appeal to Romans 10:21 where ethnic Israel as a national body is in view. They argue that since Romans 11:1 follows immediately upon 10:21 the "people" referred to in the former must be the same as the "people" in the latter. Whereas this view may be correct, it faces two obstacles.

First, we must remember that in Romans 9–11 the title "people of God" may be understood in one of two ways. Certainly ethnic Israel as a whole was God's "people" in that he blessed her with all the theocratic privileges described in Romans 9:4-5. This is undoubtedly the sense in which Israel is God's "people" in 10:21. It is to the nation, the theocratic entity, comprised of Abraham's physical descendants that the divine appeal noted in 10:21 is issued. But if ethnic Israelites are God's "people," why do they not believe? Because, says Paul, there is a "people" within the "people." There is an elect Israel within ethnic Israel (cf. Rom. 9:6). Israelite unbelief in 10:21 must be explained on the same terms as Israelite unbelief in 9:1-5. God never intended to save all ethnic Israelites, i.e., all his theocratic "people," but only elect Israel, the remnant. Therefore, Romans 9:6 could easily have been stated this way: "But it is not as though the word of God has failed. For they are not all my 'people' who are of my 'people'." Similarly, Romans 11:1 could just as easily have been written as follows: "I say then, God has not rejected his people, has he? May it never be! For they are not all Israel who are descended from Israel, i.e., all the ethnic 'people' are not necessarily the elect, remnant 'people'." In other words, *Romans 9:6 and 11:1-2 are making the same point!*

The second reason why the "people" in 11:1-2 may well be the remnant and not ethnic Israel as a whole is because God "foreknew" them. If the "people" in 11:1-2 are all ethnic Israelites, then God's "foreknowledge" of them must be something less than salvific in nature. This is clear, for all concede that not every ethnic Jew has been or shall be saved. But it would appear that in view of Paul's reference to divine "foreknowledge" in Romans 8:29, the burden of proof is on those who argue that "foreknowledge" in 11:2 is *not* salvific. It seems more likely that the "people" whom God foreknew are the elect remnant (cf. 11:5), precisely because they were foreknown, i.e., fore-loved or fore-chosen. Otherwise we are forced to conclude that all the people whom God foreknew in Romans 8:29 are to be called, justified, and glorified, whereas the majority of people whom God foreknew in Romans 11:2 are to be given a spirit of stupor, eyes that see not and ears that hear not! [3]

I should point out that even should it be granted that "people" refers to ethnic Israel as a whole, this in no way substantiates the FR perspective. If by "people" Paul is referring to ethnic Israel as a nation, his point would still be, "No, God has not ceased his saving activity altogether among those whom he elected to theocratic blessing. The proof that God has not totally abandoned ethnic Jews is my own salvation, for I am an ethnic Jew of the tribe of Benjamin." The important thing to note is that on either view the FR finds no support for positing a mass restoration at the end of the age. Paul still maintains that it is the remnant within the nation as a whole, and not the nation itself, that God intends to save. The proof that God still has a saving purpose for ethnic Israel, the proof that God has not rejected his people, is the *present remnant*, not a future restoration.

Paul's appeal to himself in Romans 11:1 for the question of Israel's "future" salvation is crucial. When Paul denies that God has cast off his people whom he foreknew, many immediately and perhaps unconsciously assume something Paul never says. They assume his denial means that God intends to deal uniquely with Israel in the future, at the second advent of Christ. But Paul's question and answer pertain not to some alleged future restoration but to the far more fundamental issue of whether God ever intends to save Israelites at all. And in answer to the question, "has God rejected his people?" the apostle immediately points to himself as living proof that God *is* dealing in a saving way with ethnic Israelites. It is worth noting, says O. Palmer Robertson,

---

3. Murray merely asserts, without proving, that "to foreknow" in 11:2 is generic. The use of the word in 11:2, he says, is "not the particularizing and strictly soteric import found in 8:29" (*Romans*, 2:68). The only reason I can see why Murray takes this position is that otherwise he must adopt the alternative interpretation of "people" in 11:1-2.

That the apostle does not respond to his own question by asserting specifically that God has not cast off his people Israel with respect to some distinctive future reserved for them. This conclusion might be reached by inference; but the apostle specifically points instead to the concrete realities of God's activity among the Jews in the present. He himself is an Israelite, thus indicating that the grace of God is working currently among Judaism.

In the same way then, there has also come to be at the present time a remnant according to God's gracious choice (Rom. 11:5, NASB).

Paul emphasizes specifically the present position of Israel by the phrase "in the present time" (*en to nun kairo*). Dramatically in the current situation a remnant of Israel remains. These two references orient this first paragraph of Romans 11 (vv. 1-10) to the question of God's dealing with Israel in the present hour. Paul's discussion of the OT remnant-concept in these verses as it has been manifested throughout redemptive history intends to alleviate his readers' concern over the present condition of Israel. Not all Jews currently are believing the gospel, to be sure. But never has the salvation of the totality of ethnic Israel been God's determination.[4]

The fact that God intends to include ethnic Jews in his redemptive activity is proven *not* by an appeal to a hypothetical future for the nation as a whole but by the very concrete work of God among Jews in the *present*, of which Paul is one example. Consequently, Paul's answer to his own question "in no way spells out the details of a massive turning of the Jews to Christ at some distant date in the future. His answer deals with the present state of Israel in the gospel era. Indeed the apostle's answer does indicate that ethnic Israel has a 'future.' But this 'future' is integrated explicitly with the current era of gospel-proclamation."[5]

In Romans 11:2-4 Paul illustrates his point by citing the example of Elijah and the doctrine of the remnant. Murray and Cranfield insist that the salvation of a remnant of Jews throughout redemp-

---

4. Robertson, "Distinctive Future," 210-11.
5. Ibid., 214.

tive history, whether in Elijah's day or in Paul's, is a token or pledge that the people as a nation had not been cast off. It is a token or pledge that God would yet save *all* the nation Israel as a nation.

But this simply cannot be true. The appeal to the remnant in Romans 9–11 is to demonstrate or prove that God *never* intended to save the nation as a whole. Paul's point is to show how God is faithful to his word despite extensive unfaithfulness in ethnic Israel. The proof is the remnant. The remnant, of which Paul is a part, is *not* cited to prove that God *will* save the nation, but is cited to explain why he *didn't*! He did not save the entire nation, but only a remnant within it, precisely in order that his sovereign and distinguishing purpose according to the election of grace might be manifest. In saving some, but not all, ethnic Israelites, not based on physical descent or human attitudes or actions, God demonstrates his own glory, power, and unalterable purpose. To suggest that Paul's appeal to the remnant is to prove that God saves a part as a pledge of his intention to save the whole is, I believe, utterly antithetical to the purpose for which Romans 9–11 was written.

Israel's Fulfillment

The FR view finds perhaps its most persuasive data in verses 12-15. Verses 12 and 15 appear to be asserting the same truth: if the transgression, defeat, and consequent rejection of the majority of Israelites have resulted in such glorious salvific blessing for the Gentiles, how much greater must the Gentile blessing be which will result from Israel's "fulfillment" or "acceptance." In other words, if God did great things for the Gentile world when Israel sinned (in rejecting the Messiah), how much more will he do for them when Israel is saved!

The central question here is the meaning of the word "fulfillment" in verse 12 and the word "acceptance" in verse 15. John Murray insists that Israel's "fulfillment/fullness" and "acceptance/receiving" must be the antithesis of her "transgression" and "failure." This means

that Israel is contemplated as characterized by the faith of Christ, by the attainment of righteousness, and by restoration to the blessing of

God's kingdom as conspicuously as Israel then was marked by unbelief, trespass, and loss.... Hence nothing less than a restoration of Israel
as a people to faith, privilege, and blessing can satisfy the terms of this
passage. The *argument* of the apostle is not, however, the restoration of
Israel; it is the blessing accruing to the Gentiles from Israel's "fulness"....
Thus there awaits the Gentiles, in their distinctive identity as such,
gospel blessing far surpassing anything experienced during the period of
Israel's apostasy, and this unprecedented enrichment will be occasioned
by the conversion of Israel on a scale commensurate with that of their
earlier disobedience. We are not informed at this point what this unprecedented blessing will be. But in the view of the thought governing the
context, namely, the conversion of the Gentiles and then that of Israel,
we should expect that the enlarged blessing would be the expansion of
the success attending the gospel and of the kingdom of God.[6]

Clearly, then, Murray believes that verse 15 reiterates the assertion of verse 12. As a result of Israel's transgression and failure
(v. 12) she has been rejected or cast away (v. 15). Israel's fulfillment,
which brings increased riches to the Gentiles (v. 12), is therefore
equivalent to her acceptance which yields a virtual life from the
dead (v. 15). The point Murray is making is this: Since the rejection
(v. 15a) Israel experienced was *national*, their acceptance (v. 15b)
must also be *national*. The restoration must be commensurate in
scale with the rejection. Israel as a whole fell and therefore Israel as
a whole must be saved. Finally, Murray believes that the "life from
the dead" which results from Israel's acceptance into national favor
is salvation for the Gentiles, not bodily resurrection. It is, he says,
"an unprecedented quickening for the whole world in expansion
and success of the gospel."[7] He therefore envisions a worldwide
conversion consequent upon the restoration of the nation of Israel.

The HR view responds to this first by acknowledging that
verses 11-15 describe a sequence in which Jews reject their Messiah, after which Gentiles believe, thereby provoking the Jews to

---

6. Murray, *Romans*, 2:78-79.
7. Ibid., 2:84.

jealousy and faith. This conversion of the Jews in turn leads to an even greater blessing for the world. As we have seen, the FR view, expounded by Murray, contends that Israel's transgression or falling away coincides with the present gospel age, whereas their fulfillment or acceptance refers to a national or *en masse* conversion in the future, at the end of our current Christian era.

The HR interpretation takes a different approach. Note the explanation of O. Palmer Robertson:

> The whole cycle could be considered as having fulfillment in the present era of gospel proclamation. In context, Paul compares the experience of Israel to the experience of the Gentiles. According to verse 30, Gentiles once were disobedient, but now have received mercy. In the same manner, Israel now is found disobedient, that they also now may receive mercy. Both in the case of the Gentiles and the Jews, the full cycle of movement from a state of disobedience to a state of mercy occurs in the present age. From this perspective, the receiving of Israel would refer to the ingrafting of believing Jews throughout the present era, which would reach its consummation at the point in time at which their "fullness" would be realized. The parallel experience of the Gentile world offers no support to the idea that Israel's period of "falling" and "casting away" coincides with the present gospel age, while their "receiving" and "fullness" is reserved for a subsequent era." [8]

It is clear from verse 14 that Paul has in view individual Jewish salvation in the present era, parallel to what the Gentiles now experience, and not some national conversion at the end of the age. There Paul speaks of his hope that by *his* ministry he might move to jealousy his fellow-countrymen and save some of them. This saving of "some," says Robertson,

> ought not to be regarded as the deliverance of some pitiful minutia of Judaism hardly worthy to be compared with the "fullness" to be effected at the end of time. Much to the contrary, this saving of "some" should

---

8. Robertson, "Distinctive Future," 214-15.

be viewed as conjoining integrally with one of the major themes of Romans 11. As Paul says, there remains at the present time a "remnant" according to the election of grace (v. 5). It is not that "some" which the apostle hopes to save is equivalent in number to the "remnant" which he discusses throughout the passage. But the saving of "some" and the maintaining of a "remnant" are interrelated ideas. Paul's hope that "some" would be saved through his current ministry is based on the principle that a "remnant" would remain throughout the ages.[9]

Paul has said in verse 11b that Gentile salvation is designed to provoke Jews to jealousy. Paul is an apostle to the Gentiles, striving to achieve this very effect among his fellow-countrymen in order that they might be saved. This activity by Paul, in *his* day (I emphasize once again) is directly related to the "acceptance" of the Jews in verse 15. As Robertson points out, "the 'for if' (*ei gar*) of verse fifteen connects the 'receiving' [or 'acceptance'] of the Jews with the present ministry of the apostle Paul in the gospel era. By his present ministry among the Gentiles, the apostle hopes to move the Jews to jealousy, and thereby to save some from among Israel. Their 'saving' as described in verse 14 corresponds to their 'reception' in verse 15. In each case Paul describes the hoped-for consequence of his current ministry."[10]

My question for advocates of the FR view, therefore, is this: *How can Paul's ministry in the first century contribute to Israel's "fulfillment" (v. 12) and acceptance" (v. 15) if the latter pertains to only one generation of Jewish people living at the time of Christ's second coming at the close of human history?*

Advocates of the FR view are forced to argue that the "fulfillment/acceptance" of Israel described in verses 12 and 15 pertains to the salvation of but *one generation* of ethnic Jews living at the *end* of the age when Christ returns. But if this is true, how can Paul's ministry to the generation of ethnic Jews in the *first* century sustain any meaningful relationship to it? Or, to put it yet another

---

9. Ibid., 215.
10. Ibid., 211.

way, *if Israel's "fulfillment" refers to her national, en masse conversion at the end of the age, how is it that Paul at the beginning of the age is contributing to it?* Paul very clearly tells us that *his* ministry, in the early stages of this *present* age, is designed to contribute to, or perhaps even hasten, the "fulfillment" and "acceptance" of Israel.

It strikes me as more in keeping with the biblical text that the "fullness" or "fulfillment" of Israel is simply the sum total of all Israel's remnants throughout history, to which Paul contributes by saving some in *his* day. I am forced to conclude that the "fulfillment" of Israel, or her "acceptance," should be viewed from the perspective of what God *has been* doing throughout history and *is doing now* among the Jews, not what many think God will do only at the end of the age. Thus, "the 'receiving' of the 'full number' is being realized. For this reason, it is neither necessary nor appropriate to posit some future date in which the 'remnant' principle will be superceded by a newly-introduced 'fullness' principle. The completed number of the 'remnant' of Israel is identical precisely with the 'fullness' of Israel." [11]

Murray has argued that the salvation or fulfillment or acceptance (vv. 12, 15) of Israel is a mass, national restoration at the end of the age. But in verse 14 Paul perceives himself as contributing to the fullness of Israel by provoking Jews to jealousy, and thereby to salvation, in *his* own day. Again, in verse 31, it is God's saving activity among individual Jews like Paul, *now*, in the present age, by which Israel's fullness is eventually to be attained.

The two views of verses 12-15 that we have been examining thus agree on the *fact* but differ on the *manner* in which the "fullness" of Israel comes in (v. 12), or the manner in which Israel is "accepted" (v. 15). The FR view insists on a one-time, end of the age, en masse restoration of Jews. The HR view, on the other hand, insists that Israel will experience theirs, namely, by individual faith in response to the gospel *throughout the course of the present age.*

There is yet another problem for the FR view that must be addressed. Verses 12-15 assert that the fullness of Israel yields increased blessing for the Gentiles, what Paul in verse 15 refers to

---

11. Ibid., 216.

as a "life" from the dead. Murray takes this to mean that after and as a result of Israel's mass conversion there will occur a spiritual vivification or quickening of the Gentile world. But how can this be if the "fullness" of the Gentiles will *already* have come in, i.e., if the salvation of all elect Gentiles will have *antedated* the coming of Israel's fullness? According to the FR interpretation of verses 25-26, all elect Gentiles will have been saved *before* Israel is restored. For the sake of argument, let us assume that is correct. How then can Israel's restoration yield not only additional but unprecedented Gentile salvation? One answer may be that it is not salvation but some other form of blessing (but what kind? when? how?). Murray will attempt to deal with this by offering a different interpretation of Gentile "fullness" in verse 25. More on this later.

The HR view, however, has a perfectly plausible explanation of the data. During the progressive realization of Israel's fullness in the present age, that is to say, as elect Jews are being saved, there accrues to the Gentile world even greater and more widespread opportunity for salvation than there resulted from Israel's initial unbelief. As Jews are saved, the salvific blessings of the gospel are dispensed throughout and upon the Gentile world with greater and more decisive results than in the first century, when in consequence of Israel's rejection of Messiah the kingdom of God was taken from them and given to a nation bearing the fruit thereof.

In bringing this discussion of Israel's fulfillment to a close, we must briefly note one element in Paul's discussion in verses 16-24. The "first piece of dough" and the "root" (v. 16), in my opinion, refer to Abraham and the patriarchs. Their initial consecration to God is indicative of God's purpose to save ethnic Jews, be they ever so few, throughout history (cf. v. 28). According to Murray, "this fact of consecration derived from the patriarchs is introduced here by the apostle as support for the ultimate recovery of Israel. There cannot be irremediable rejection of Israel; the holiness of theocratic consecration is not abolished and will one day be vindicated in Israel's fullness and restoration." [12]

---

12. Murray, *Romans,* 2:85.

I agree that the consecration of the patriarchs supports the expectation of a restoration of Jews, but why is it simply assumed that this restoration will be national and in mass at the end of the age only? The unproven (and in my opinion false) assumption by Murray and others who espouse the FR view is that the regrafting of Israel, described in verses 17-24, must entail a distinctive future for the nation as a whole. They assume that the figure of the olive tree and regrafting of the natural branches demands or at least implies a corporate inclusion in mass of ethnic Israelites at some definite time in the future.

But Paul clearly draws a parallel between the experience of Israelite believers and Gentile believers. Consider, for example, the statement at the close of his argument in verses 30-31: "For just as you [Gentiles] once were disobedient to God but now have been shown mercy because of their [Israel's] disobedience, so these also now have been disobedient, in order that because of the mercy shown to you they also may now be shown mercy." Through Paul's ministry and that of others, Gentiles are being grafted into the olive tree *when they believe*. As individual Gentiles come to faith (v. 20), says Paul, they receive all the blessings of redemption. Why should we think it is any different for Jews, especially when Paul says in verses 30-31 that it is the same? As Gentiles are saved through Paul's ministry the Jews are provoked to jealousy and saving faith. It is *then*, when they believe, that they are grafted back into the olive tree from which they had been broken off (v. 17).

I am compelled to agree with Robertson that "nothing in the imagery of regrafting suggests a delay in the incorporation of the believing Israelite. As each Jew believes, he becomes a partaker of the blessings of the olive tree. The current ministry of the gospel provides the catalyst for the salvation of the Jews precisely in the same manner as it does for the Gentiles. The major thrust of the apostle's argument about the grafting process is that Israelites experience salvation and incorporation among God's people precisely in the same manner as the Gentiles. Nothing in the figure of ingrafting necessarily communicates the idea of a distinctive and corporate inclusion of ethnic Jews at some future date." [13]

---

13. Robertson, "Distinctive Future," 216.

Life from the Dead

Those who insist on a future restoration of ethnic Jews point to the phrase, "life from the dead," in verse 15b to support their position. There Paul says that if the rejection of the Jews has made possible the "reconciliation" of the Gentile world, then what will Jewish "acceptance" mean but "life from the dead"? This latter phrase must refer to the *final bodily resurrection* at the end of the age. Therefore, the "acceptance" of the Jews that makes it possible must likewise have in view an eschatological, end-of-age restoration.

My response is simply that "life from the dead" does not, in fact, refer to the final bodily resurrection of all believers, and I say this for two reasons. First, we must take note of the relationship between verse 15 and verses 13-14. As noted before, Paul is emphasizing his current, first-century ministry. He has in mind what he (Paul) is doing *then*, not what God will or will not do in the eschaton. The aim of all his efforts, according to verse 14, is to "save some of them," i.e., Jews, his kinsman according to the flesh. Verse 15 is directly related to verse 14 by "for if" (*ei gar*). In other words, verse 15 provides the grounds for verse 14, or perhaps is an expanded explanation of the meaning of verse 14. But the point is that Paul is describing in verse 15 what it means for the Jews to be "saved" (v. 14) through his first-century ministry.

Because of their unbelief, God has rejected them (v. 15a). This resulted in the gospel being extended to the world (i.e., Gentiles). When they (the Jews) believe, God will accept them ("acceptance" in v. 15b). This is tantamount to or consists of "life from the dead". If the relationship of verse 15 to verse 14 is to be maintained, it must be that "life from the dead" (v. 15b) is descriptive of their "salvation" (v. 14b), not bodily resurrection.[14]

Romans 11:15, therefore, is not to be read as parallel to 11:12. In verse 12 there is a clear "much more" argument (typical in Paul).

---

14. It may even be that Paul is alluding in these verses to the parable of the prodigal in Luke 15. When the prodigal returned home, the father declared, "For this my son was dead, and is alive again; he was lost, and is found" (Luke 15:24). The point is that his "faith" is a coming to life again after death.

317

Indeed, "much more" is explicit in the text. But not so in verse 15. In verse 15 Paul is providing an explanation for the "salvation" of individual Jews that he mentioned in verse 14. The point of verse 12 seems to be that if the unbelief of Jews entails riches for the Gentiles, the belief of the Jews will bless Gentiles even more. What that blessing is, is hard to say. Paul never defines it. But this isn't his argument in verse 15. Whereas in verse 15a he does speak of the "reconciliation" that came to Gentiles because of Jewish unbelief, in verse 15b he speaks of the "life" that comes to the Jews because of their belief, a "life" that in verse 14b he referred to as their (Jewish) "salvation."

Also, if "life from the dead" refers to the final bodily resurrection of all people at the end of history, how could Paul possibly say that his first century ministry was contributing to or facilitating that reality? Again, when we see verse 15 in its proper grammatical relation to verses 13-14 ("for if," v. 15a), it is clear that Paul envisions his own efforts, by God's grace, as contributing to the "life from the dead" that comes with God's "acceptance" of the Jews when they believe.

Here I'm repeating what I said earlier, but it's important. Paul is saying, "I labor to bring the gospel to the Jewish people so that they might be saved (v. 14), *because* ('for', *gar*, v. 15a) if I do so and they come to faith they will no longer be 'rejected' by God but 'accepted', and what will this be for them (not for Gentiles, but specifically for the Jews to whom I am ministering) if not 'life from the dead'"?

Second, if "life from the dead" means the final, physical bodily resurrection for all believers, both Jew and Gentile, Paul would be saying that the resurrection is in some sense dependent upon or caused by a corporate or mass restoration of ethnic Jews. Where in all of Scripture do we see anything remotely approaching that? In other words, if the "acceptance" in verse 15 is a reference to an end-of-the-age mass salvation among ethnic Jews, then Paul would be saying that everyone's bodily resurrection is suspended upon it, or can't occur without it, or is in some sense the result of it. Is it really the case that the New Testament teaches us that the final resurrection of believers is causally related to the salvation of national Israel? No.

Advocates of the FR view would be in the awkward position of contending that Paul's point is that we must labor and evangelize the Jews and pray for their mass salvation at the end of history so that we can all be bodily raised from the dead. But nowhere in Scripture is the resurrection said to be the result of, much less caused by, the salvation of the Jewish people. Rather the bodily resurrection of believers is always tied to or grounded in the bodily resurrection of Jesus Christ. It is because of his atoning death and resurrection that I am to be likewise raised in a glorified body. Is this not what Paul said in Romans 8:11 – "If the Spirit of him who raised Jesus from the dead dwells in you, he who raised Christ Jesus from the dead will also give life to your mortal bodies through his Spirit who dwells in you"? Does Paul now (in light of chapter 11) mean to tell us, "Oh, wait a minute. It's true that you will be raised like Jesus was because the Spirit dwells in you, but it's all suspended on and waiting for a mass restoration of Jews at the end of history, and you can't be bodily raised until they come to faith."

Someone might object and say, "No, we're not saying the salvation of Israel is the *cause* of or *reason for* the bodily resurrection of all believers, but only that it is the *occasion when* that will occur." But again, repeatedly in the New Testament we are told that the occasion for the bodily resurrection is the second coming of Christ (see 1 Thess. 4; 1 Cor. 15; and 1 John 3:1-3). We will be bodily raised because of Christ's resurrection (he is the first fruits) and at Christ's return. That's a settled fact repeated in numerous biblical texts. So are we now being asked to believe that Paul is making this grand assertion in Romans 11 that we must be diligent to evangelize the Jews because it's only if and when they come to salvation in mass that we will experience bodily resurrection? If he were making such a huge assertion, especially in light of what he has taught in his other epistles concerning the ground for and time of the bodily resurrection of all believers, would he not have made it more clear and used explicit resurrection language (such as *anastasis*)?

Advocates of the FR perspective must answer the question: "How could, or why would, Paul drop this altogether novel bombshell of an idea at this point in Romans and his ministry to the effect that the great and glorious final bodily resurrection of all believers, both Jew and Gentile, is suspended upon or is the result of a mass corporate ingathering of Jews into the kingdom?" On the other hand, if he's saying nothing more than that the bodily resurrection won't occur until all elect Jews are saved, how utterly trite. Who would ever have thought it could occur before then?

The precise wording Paul employs does not settle the argument. Whereas it is true that "life from the dead" language typically refers to bodily resurrection in the New Testament, we must consider Romans 6:13 where it explicitly refers to regeneration or spiritual life from the dead. We must also take into account that numerous times in the New Testament the new birth and salvation are portrayed as a coming to life out of death (see Eph. 2:1-10 for one clear example).

Thus far, then, I remained unconvinced by the arguments of those who see in Romans 11 a reference to a final, eschatological in-gathering of ethnic Jews. But our study of Romans 11 is far from over. We now turn to the remainder of this remarkable chapter.

Romans 11:25-27

We are now prepared to examine Romans 11:25-27 in which are found the most important statements in this chapter. It is here that the exegetical and theological battle is waged in all its fury. We begin with Paul's declaration in verse 25 that "a partial hardening has happened to Israel." As it turns out, this is one of the few statements on the meaning of which almost all agree. Israel's hardening "in part" does not refer to the degree or time but to the *extent* of the experience in view. Paul is not saying that those hardened are only partially hardened, as if to suggest that their hardening is not as intensive as it could have been. Neither is Paul saying, at least in this phrase, that Israel's hardening is temporary, as if he meant to assert that "*for a while* hardening has happened to Israel." His point is simply that *not all* Israelites in this present age have been hardened. Although a part of Israel is hardened (the precise numerical proportions are not in view here), there have been, are, and always will be some ethnic Israelites who are saved. In summary, Paul is simply repeating in different words what he said in Romans 11:7.

But what does he mean when he says this hardening has happened to Israel "until the fullness of the Gentiles has come in"? Let's begin with the word translated "until" (*achris hou*).

The FR (Future Restoration) view insists that this word "be taken as referring to a point of eventuation that brings the hardening of Israel to an end." [15] The hardening of Israel has a terminus, an event or occurrence at which time the hardening will cease and salvation ensue. "Paul's meaning," says Cranfield, "is not that Israel is in part hardened during the time in which the fullness of the Gentiles is coming in, but that the hardening will last until the fullness of the Gentiles comes in. The entry of the fullness of the Gentiles will be the event which will mark the end of Israel's hardening." [16] The point of this interpretation is that Paul envisions a time after which a change will occur in the spiritual status of Israel: her experience of hardening will terminate with the coming of Gentile fullness. The state of affairs subsequent thereto can only be that of Israel's national salvation.

Advocates of the HR (Historical Remnant) view argue that, on the contrary, "until" need not imply a time after which the hardening of Israel will cease. Robertson appeals to two lines of evidence in support of this response. First, the "hardening" of which Paul speaks is simply the historical or temporal manifestation of God's eternal decree of reprobation, the converse of which is election. If this is true, says Robertson,

> the integral role of "hardening" in the processes of salvation through all the ages should make one pause before asserting too quickly that this "hardening" shall cease. It ought to be noted that Romans 11:25 does not make this assertion. The text does not say "hardening shall cease among Israel." Certainly it is not declared that the overarching

15. Murray, *Romans*, 2:92.

16. C.E.B. Cranfield, *A Critical and Exegetical Commentary on the Epistle to the Romans* (Edinburgh: T.&T. Clark, 1979), 2:575.

principle of God's electing some and hardening of others someday will have no application in Israel. Instead the text affirms a continuation of hardening within Israel throughout the present age. God's decrees of election and reprobation continue to work themselves out in history. As a sovereign distinction was made between the twins Jacob and Esau, so throughout the present age, hardening shall continue. [17]

In other words, the FR view would imply that the principle of reprobation, operative throughout redemptive history (even in Israel; cf. 9:6ff.), will at some future time cease to be. I find this highly unlikely from a theological point of view.

Robertson's second argument is to challenge the traditional interpretation put upon the word "until." He insists that in many cases "the termination envisioned in *achris hou* has a finalizing aspect which makes irrelevant questions concerning the reversal of circumstances which had prevailed prior to reaching this termination point." [18] The force of the word is to carry actions or conditions to their ultimate point, as for example, when Paul declares that he persecuted Christians "until death" (Acts 22:4). Or again, in the days of Noah people were eating and drinking, marrying and giving in marriage, "until" the day that Noah entered the ark (Matt. 24:38). That is, their actions continued up to the time their end came. Robertson also cites Hebrews 4:12; 1 Corinthians 11:26; and 1 Corinthians 15:25. His conclusion is that the "hardening ... until" in Romans 11:25 speaks of eschatological termination. In other words,

> throughout the whole of the present age, until the final return of Christ, hardening will continue among part of Israel. "Hardening... until" too frequently has been understood as marking the beginning of a new state of things with regard to Israel. It hardly has been considered that "hardening... until" more naturally should be interpreted as eschatologically terminating in its significance. The phrase implies not

---

17. Robertson, "Distinctive Future," 218-19.
18. Ibid., 219.

a new beginning after a termination point in time, but instead the continuation of a prevailing circumstance for Israel until the end of time.[19]

Ben Merkle argues in similar fashion, insisting that "what is important is not what will take place *after* the event is completed, but *that* the event is eschatologically fulfilled."[20] He then cites the use of this terminology in 1 Corinthians 11:26 where Paul states that the church is to partake of the Lord's Supper and by doing so proclaims the Lord's death "until" (*achris hou*) he comes. Paul's purpose, notes Merkle, "is not to stress that one day the church will not celebrate the Lord's Supper. Instead his point is that this celebration will continue 'until' the end of time."[21] We find much the same in 1 Corinthians 15:25 where Paul declares that Christ must reign "until" (*achri hou*) he has put all enemies under his feet, the last of which is death itself. "The intended stress is not that a time will come when Christ will no longer reign, but that he must continue to reign until the last enemy is conquered at the final judgment."[22]

I'm not as confident about this point as are Robertson and Merkle. Whereas they are correct in pointing out that "until" *may* have this meaning, it should be openly acknowledged that this is not its most frequent sense. I am not prepared to say with Robertson, for example, that "hardening … until" is *more naturally* interpreted as eschatologically terminating. What I am saying is that it is grammatically *possible* to take the word as Robertson suggests. However, it becomes *probable* only in view of the contextual argument in Romans 11 as a whole. Were it not for other conclusive evidence in Romans 11 favoring the HR interpretation, one would be unwise in arguing for that view based solely on what is an admittedly rare sense of "until" in verse 25.

---

19. Ibid., 220.
20. Ben L. Merkle, "Romans 11 and the Future of Ethnic Israel," *JETS* 43/4 (December 2000): 715.
21. Ibid.
22. Ibid., 716.

Part of that conclusive evidence is found in Paul's statement concerning the "fullness" of the Gentiles. This surely refers to the full number of the elect from among the Gentiles, the salvation of whom is realized progressively throughout the present age, at the end of which the total number thereof will have come in. Almost all interpreters, whether they hold to the FR or HR viewpoint, agree on this meaning. John Murray is the exception, perhaps because he realizes the inconsistency this entails for the FR view (although Cranfield also notes the inconsistency in passing). Let me explain.

Murray interprets verse 12 to mean that *after* the fullness of Israel has come in, i.e., after the final end-of-the-age-mass-salvation of Israel as a nation has occurred, even greater salvific blessing will accrue to the Gentiles. "Thus there awaits the Gentiles," says Murray, "in their distinctive identity as such, gospel blessing far surpassing anything experienced during the period of Israel's apostasy, and this unprecedented enrichment will be occasioned by the conversion of Israel on a scale commensurate with that of their earlier disobedience."[23] It is here that the problem for the FR interpretation becomes acute. For if the fullness of the Gentiles (v. 25) means the total number of elect to be saved, then the salvation of all Israel (which awaits and follows the coming in of Gentile fullness) would terminate any further expansion among the Gentiles of the kind of blessing verse 12 suggests. In other words, if *all* elect Gentiles are to be saved *before* Israel is restored (and according to the FR view, that is what vv. 25-26 assert), how can Israel's restoration yield *subsequent*, additional, indeed unprecedented, Gentile salvation?

The only escape from this difficulty is to interpret the fullness of the Gentiles as something other than the full number of elect Gentiles to be saved. According to their interpretation of verses 12-15, Murray, and the FR view in general, must somehow make room for unprecedented Gentile salvation *after* Israel's final, national restoration. But verses 25-26 will not permit this! Murray obviously recognizes this and proceeds to say that Gen-

---

23. Murray, *Romans*, 2:79.

tile fullness denotes "unprecedented blessing" for them but does not exclude even greater blessing to follow. The "greater blessing" to follow the final restoration of national Israel is, of course, the conversion of the world in accordance with Murray's postmillennial eschatology.

This seems to me to be altogether inadequate. Not only does it strain the sense of the term "fullness," but Paul's statement that at the end of the age this fullness will have "come in" or will have reached its culmination is emptied of significance if in fact beyond that point there is yet more Gentile "fullness" to come. In other words, if, according to Murray, Israel's national salvation must *await* the coming in of Gentile fullness, how can Gentile fullness extend *beyond* the salvation of Israel? Or again, if Gentile fullness does *not* terminate with Israel's salvation, as Murray is forced to say, why must Israel's salvation await it?

Murray rightly insists that the fullness or fulfillment of Israel in verse 12 and the fullness of the Gentiles in verse 25 are similar, if not identical, in significance. Therefore, since Israel's fullness entails a mass national salvation at the end of the age (so says Murray), it is only natural to assume that the coming in of Gentile fullness implies the same for them. Thus, Murray's view entails the following end-of-the-age scenario:

mass salvation of Gentiles → mass salvation of Israel → yet another mass salvation of Gentiles.

Is this really what Paul is saying?

Finally, it is far more likely that the coming in of Gentile fullness is what Paul earlier described in verses 16-24 under the imagery of unnatural branches being grafted into the olive tree as they come to faith in Christ, a process on-going in the church age from Paul's day to the present. If so, then on Murray's FR view the fullness of the Gentiles comes in a manner radically different from the way in which Israel's fullness comes in. Gentile fullness would be a progressive, throughout-history occurrence, whereas Israelite fullness would be an instantaneous, at-the-end-of-history occurrence.

But this would violate the point of verses 16-24 and verses 30-31, namely, that both Gentile and Jew are now (from Paul's perspective) and into the future being saved, and are together and in parallel fashion being grafted into the one olive tree.[24]

"And in this way all Israel will be saved"

This brings us to the crucial phrase, "and in this way (or, thus) all Israel will be saved." There are two important questions to be addressed. First, who or what constitutes "all Israel," and second, what does Paul mean by the words "and in this way"?

As far as our first question is concerned, there appear to be five possible answers. "All Israel" may refer to

(1) all ethnic descendants of Abraham of every age; or,

(2) all ethnic descendants of Abraham living in the future when Christ returns; or,

(3) the mass or majority of the ethnic descendants of Abraham living in the future when Christ returns; or,

(4) both elect Jews and elect Gentiles who together comprise the Church of Jesus Christ, the true "Israel of God"; or,

(5) all elect Israelites within the ethnic community of Israel (cf. Rom. 9:6).

View (1) is a form of ethnic universalism. But since Scripture nowhere endorses the notion of a "second chance" to be saved after death, and since Paul has already denied in Romans 9:6ff. that all ethnic Israelites will be saved, this interpretation must be rejected.

View (2), argues Murray, is contrary to the analogy drawn in Romans 11 between Israel's national apostasy and her national res-

---

24. The more I reflect on Murray's interpretation of Gentile "fullness" the more evident it becomes that he alone, among advocates of the FR view, has realized the contradiction between verse 12 and verses 25-26. If Gentile "fullness" refers to the full number of elect Gentiles, the conflict seems inescapable. Unfortunately, Murray's attempt to provide an alternative interpretation of Gentile "fullness" is, in my opinion, the weakest and least coherent piece of exegetical work in his otherwise excellent commentary on Romans.

toration. "The apostasy of Israel, their trespass, loss, casting away, and hardening were not universal. There was always a remnant, not all branches were broken off, their hardening was in part. Likewise restoration and salvation need not include every Israelite. 'All Israel' can refer to the mass, the people as a whole in accord with the pattern followed in the chapter throughout."[25]

View (3) is widely held today. The belief is that Paul is describing an end-of-the-age salvation of the nation as a whole, though not necessarily including every single member of that nation or every single ethnic Jew.[26] There are numerous objections to this view, most of which will be mentioned later on. Here I direct your attention to only one problem with this view. Robertson puts it best:

> The problem in this viewpoint arises from the contradiction created by the proposal that a mass or majority, *though not all*, of Israel shall be saved when the "hardening" is lifted. For the "hardening" in this context refers to the historical outworking of the principle of reprobation, as indicated earlier.... If a day is coming in which the principle of reprobation is to be inactive among Israel, then it must be assumed that every single Israelite living at that time will be saved. If even one Israelite of that period is to be lost, then the principle of "hardening" or "reprobation" still would be active.[27]

Robertson's point is that if one takes "all Israel" to be ethnic Jews living at the time of Christ's return, view (2) is preferable to view (3). *Every* ethnic Jew must be included.

View (4) suggests that a way to avoid all such problems is to take "all Israel" as a reference to the Church, elect Jews and Gentiles who are together the Israel of God (cf. Galatians 6:16). This is Calvin's interpretation:

---

25. Murray, *Romans*, 2:98. See 1 Sam. 7:5; 25:1; 1 Kings 12:1; 2 Chron. 12:1; Dan. 9:11, for the idea of Israel "as a whole" but not necessarily all.

26. For a defense of this view, see especially Barry E. Horner, *Future Israel: Why Christian Anti-Judaism Must Be Challenged* (Nashville: B & Academic, n.d.).

27. Robertson, "Distinctive Future," 223.

Many understand this of the Jewish people, as of Paul were saying that religion was to be restored to them again as before. But I extend the word *Israel* to include all the people of God, in this sense, "When the Gentiles have come in, the Jews will at the same time return from their defection to the obedience of faith. The salvation of the whole Israel of God, which must be drawn from both, will thus be completed, and yet in such a way that the Jews, as the first born in the family of God, may obtain the first place."... [Thus] in Gal. 6:16, he calls the Church, which was composed equally of Jews and Gentiles, the Israel of God, setting the people, thus collected from their dispersion, in opposition to the carnal children of Abraham who had fallen away from faith.[28]

The problem with Calvin's interpretation is that the term "Israel" appears ten other times in Romans 9–11 and always refers to ethnic Jews (cf. 9:4, 6[2], 27, 31; 10:19, 21; 11:1, 2, 7). Also, what becomes of Paul's statement in verse 25, immediately preceding verse 26, that "Israel" is experiencing partial hardening? If "Israel" in verse 25, a clear reference to ethnic Jews, is not carried over to verse 26 with the same denotation, Paul's argument does not make sense.

Note well, however, that regardless of which view one holds, "Israel" in verse 26 is not the precise equivalent of "Israel" in verse 25. According to the FR view, "Israel" in verse 25 refers to the ethnic nation as a whole during the inter-advent period, whereas "Israel" in verse 26 is restricted to one generation of ethnic Jews living at the time of the parousia. The HR view differs only with regard to the use of "Israel" in verse 26, in which case it refers to all *elect* ethnic Jews in the present age. On the HR view, therefore, the distinction between "Israel" in verse 25 and "Israel" in verse 26 is the same as the one Paul makes in Romans 9:6. Nevertheless, the important point which unites the HR and FR theories is their insistence that "Israel" in verses 25-26 is exclusive of ethnic Gentiles.

---

28. John Calvin, *The Epistle of Paul the Apostle to the Romans*, translated by Ross Mackenzie (Grand Rapids: Eerdmans 1973), 225. This view is also endorsed by Robertson in a later work, *The Israel of God: Yesterday, Today, and Tomorrow* (Phillipsburg: P & R Publishing, 2000), 187-92.

View (5) is that "all Israel" means the total number of elect ethnic Jews, the sum total of all Israel's remnants throughout the present, inter-advent age. "All Israel" thus parallels the fullness of the Gentiles (v. 25). "And if 'All Israel' indicates, as it does, that not a single elect Israelite will be lacking 'when the roll is called up yonder,' then 'the fullness of the Gentiles' similarly shows that when the attendance is checked every elect Gentile will answer, 'Present.'" [29]

Responding to Objections

Several objections have been raised against this interpretation by advocates of the FR view. Most of these have already been answered earlier in this chapter. Let me here respond to two others.

Often one hears that Paul must be referring to a future restoration of Jews in verses 25-26, for he has used the future tense repeatedly in this chapter whenever describing salvation. But surely this is no reason for accepting the FR view, for how else could Paul possibly have spoken? If someone in the first century is writing about the salvation of others that has yet to occur, it is only normal that he should employ the future tense. In other words, if Paul is describing in his day (obviously) the manner in which all elect Israelites will come to faith up to the end of the age, how else *could* he have stated it if not with the future tense? May I also remind the reader of the repeated emphasis Paul makes on the present as well (cf. 11:1-2, 5, 31).

Another objection goes something like this: "If all Paul meant to say is that all elect Israel will be saved, the climactic element in verse 26 is lost. Of course all the elect of Israel will be saved! How utterly prosaic!" [30] But this objection fails to realize what that so-called climactic element in verse 26 really is. Paul is not simply asserting *that* all elect Israel will be saved but is describing the mysterious *manner* in which it will occur. That is, *it is not so much*

---

29. William Hendricksen, *Exposition of Paul's Epistle to the Romans* (Grand Rapids: Baker, 1982), 381.

30. See, for example, the argument of Jason C. Meyer in *The End of the Law: Mosaic Covenant in Pauline Theology* (Nashville: B&H Publishing Group, 2009), 191-92.

*the **fact** as it is the **fashion** in which they will be saved*. It is by means of nothing less than the incredible scenario of Jewish unbelief → Gentile salvation → Jewish jealousy and salvation → Gentile blessing. This is the way in which all elect Israel will eventually and progressively come to saving faith. Furthermore, in a context in which the question has been raised whether *any* Israelites will be saved (cf. 11:1-5), it is even less prosaic, indeed, it is profoundly important!

We must also ask whether it is compatible with what we read in the New Testament to suggest that God will in the future obligate himself to save all (or at least most) of a particular group of people based on an external, which is to say, non-spiritual characteristic. Part of the word of the cross is that by his death Jesus Christ has abolished the distinction between Jews and Gentiles *as far as spiritual privilege is concerned*. Jews are still Jews and Gentiles are still Gentiles, but neither has any advantage over the other *simply because* he is a Jew or Gentile (Gal. 3:28). It is spiritual circumcision of the heart, not physical circumcision of the flesh that avails before God (Rom. 2:25-29; Phil. 3:2-3). It is not Abraham's blood but his faith that gains entrance into the olive tree (Gal. 3:16-29). But if the FR view is correct, a different state of affairs shall obtain when Christ returns, in which one's *ethnicity* alone either guarantees or at least greatly increases the probability of being saved.

We must now deal with the second crucial issue in verse 26, namely, the force of the words, "and thus" (*kai houtōs*). Although not impossible, it is highly unlikely that the words should be translated "and then," with a temporal or sequential force. If that were Paul's intent he would probably have used *kai tote* or *eita* or *epeita*. One simply cannot use the phrase "and thus" to prove that Israel's salvation is temporally subsequent to the coming in of Gentile fullness.[31]

The most common meaning of *kai houtōs* ("and thus") is "in this way" (ESV), "in such a manner," or "in accordance with this

---

31. At best, no more than 4 of the 205 instances in which this phrase appears in the New Testament may reasonably be taken in the sense of "and then," "thereafter," "and consequently," or some such idea (cf. John 4:6; Acts 17:33; 20:11; 28:14).

pattern." In other words, Paul is *not* telling us *when* all Israel shall be saved but *how*. All right, then, how shall all Israel be saved? All Israel shall be saved in the way Paul has described in the first twenty-four verses of Romans 11. Robertson explains:

> First the promises as well as the Messiah were given to Israel. Then, somehow in God's mysterious plan, Israel rejected its Messiah and was cut off from its position of distinctive privilege. As a result, the coming of Israel's Messiah was announced to the Gentiles. The nations then obtained by faith what Israel could not find by seeking in the strength of their own flesh. Frustrated over seeing the blessings of their messianic kingdom heaped on the Gentiles, Israel is moved to jealousy. Consequently they too repent, believe, and share in the promises originally made to them. "And in this manner" (*kai houtos*), by such a fantastic process which shall continue throughout the entire present age "up to" (*achris hou*) the point that the full number of the Gentiles is brought in, all Israel shall be saved. [32]

But what about the Old Testament confirmation of this truth which Paul cites in verses 26-27? In these verses Paul combines Isaiah 59:20, 21, and Jeremiah 31:33-34 (and possibly alludes to Isa. 27:9 and Ps 14:7). Although many have simply assumed this is a reference to the second coming of Christ, it seems more likely that Paul has in view the work of Messiah at his first advent. The future tense in the passage ("the Deliverer *will* come ... *will* banish") is future from the perspective of *the Old Testament prophet* who is speaking and not necessarily from the perspective of Paul in the first century. It was by virtue of Christ's atoning death and resurrection that the new covenant has been inaugurated and the foundation laid for the removal of ungodliness from Jacob (i.e., from elect Israel). The forgiveness of sins is available to both ethnic Gentiles and Jews because of what Jesus did at his *first* coming when he ratified the new covenant in his blood (see especially Matt. 26:28; Heb. 8:6-13; 9:15; 10:11-18). It is therefore by means of this which the Deliverer accomplished at his

---

32. Robertson, "Distinctive Future," 222.

first advent that all elect Gentiles ("the fullness of the Gentiles") and all elect Israelites ("all Israel") will be saved.

Finally, what contribution do verses 28-32 make to our discussion? There Paul writes:

> [28]As regards the gospel, they are enemies of God for your sake. But as regards election, they are beloved for the sake of their forefathers. [29]For the gifts and the calling of God are irrevocable. [30]For just as you were at one time disobedient to God but now have received mercy because of their disobedience, [31]so they too have now been disobedient in order that by the mercy shown to you they also may now receive mercy. [32]For God has consigned all to disobedience, that he may have mercy on all.

Most agree that the enmity of the Jews ("they are *enemies* of God") is not subjective, that is to say, it is not their enmity against God but God's enmity against them because of their unbelief. We know this to be the case from the contrast drawn between being, on the one hand, "enemies" of God and, on the other hand, being "beloved." To be an enemy of God is to be the object of his wrath; to be beloved is to be the object of his love and grace.

But who are "they" in verse 28 of whom these things are said? Surely they are "all Israel" (v. 26), those whom God intends to save by taking away their ungodliness and forgiving their sins (vv. 26-27). Consequently, the "enemies" of God and the "beloved" of God are the same people, the elect of ethnic Israel. Their rejection of the Messiah, as a result of which the gospel comes to the Gentiles, incurs divine wrath and enmity. Hence they are God's enemies. But when they are in turn saved, being provoked to jealousy and faith by Gentile blessing, they enter a new relationship with God, that of being beloved because of election (cf. Rom. 5:6-11). Therefore, I disagree with Murray who says that the "election" or "choice" in verse 28 is theocratic, that is, non-salvific, and is therefore different from the "election" of verses 6-7. The failure to observe the connection between verse 28 and the preceding description of the *salvation* of all Israel in verses 26-27 accounts for his error.

It is because all Israel is elect that in God's redemptive purpose they are transformed from a status of enmity to one of love. In saying they are beloved "for the sake of their forefathers" Paul does not mean their election is a result or reward for any supposed merit or innate goodness in Abraham, Isaac, and Jacob (cf. Rom. 9:6-13). Rather, Paul is referring to the divine promise given to Abraham of an elect remnant from among his physical seed, in fulfillment of which "all (elect) Israel" is being saved. Therefore, they are beloved because God promised a saved remnant to the fathers in the Abrahamic covenant, and to his word God is ever faithful. The "gifts" and "calling" of God, therefore, are not non-saving theocratic privileges given to all ethnic Jews regardless of their relation to Messiah. They refer to the products of God's special, saving, electing grace such as faith, hope, love, and peace, that is to say, those spiritual blessings which accompany the salvation of those whom God has called to himself.

The "for" with which verse 30 begins indicates that what follows confirms and illustrates the assertion of verses 28-29. Why is this significant? Simply because in verses 30-31 Paul explicitly declares that the salvation of elect Israel, their experience of being beloved of God in fulfillment of the divine and irrevocable promise given to the fathers, is being realized *now!* Note well in verses 30-31 the three-fold "now" which emphasizes that the salvation to which Paul has just referred is being realized in the gospel era, the *now* of gospel proclamation. The irrevocable gifts and calling of God (v. 29) which account for the ultimate realization of "all Israel's" salvation as God's beloved are being experienced *now* in the present church age. This salvation, this removal of ungodliness from Jacob, this forgiveness of sins, this restoration of all Israel is not said to be restricted to the end of the age, in some way associated with the second advent of Christ, but is *presently* being realized as a result of Christ's *first* advent.

Conclusion

It would appear, then, that Romans 11 does not provide explicit support for the expectation that the mass of ethnic Jews still alive at the second coming of Christ will be brought savingly into the kingdom of God. Of course, on the other hand, neither does it explicitly preclude the possibility of a large-scale conversion of Jews to Christianity. Romans 11, as I understand the chapter, is simply silent on whether or not such a mass turning of Jews to faith in Christ will occur in conjunction with the return of Christ at the close of history. One may, indeed, one *should* certainly pray for this to happen (as one should also pray for the conversion of all people groups throughout the world). But I do not believe Romans 11 gives us biblical warrant for declaring that it assuredly *will* come to pass.

Chapter Eleven

The Kingdom of God: Now and Not Yet[1]

If one does not embrace dispensational premillennialism and its affirmation of a dual redemptive purpose involving two distinct covenant peoples, how should God's purpose in redemptive history be understood? As noted in an earlier chapter, I was greatly helped in answering this question by reading George E. Ladd's book, *The Presence of the Future: The Eschatology of Biblical Realism* (1974), originally published in 1964 under the title, *Jesus and the Kingdom.*

Ladd, it should be noted, embraced a *non-dispensational* form of premillennialism often called *historic* premillennialism. While denying a distinction between Israel and the Church as well as the doctrine of the pretribulation rapture,[2] Ladd affirmed the existence of a 1,000-year, post-parousia earthly kingdom that precedes the eternal state. Although they reject his view of the millennium, most amillennialists and a number of postmillennialists concur with Ladd on the nature of the kingdom of God and its inauguration at the time of Christ's first advent. Thus, whereas these groups differ over the nature and timing of the millennium, they are in agreement in their rejection of dispensationalism and their affirmation of *one people of God.*

---

1. Some of the material in this chapter has been adapted from my contribution to the book, *The Gospel as Center: Renewing Our Faith and Reforming Our Ministry Practices,* edited by D.A. Carson and Timothy Keller (Wheaton: Crossway, 2012), pp. 253-72.

2. See his book, *The Blessed Hope* (Grand Rapids: Eerdmans, 1956).

With Ladd's help, together with others whose contributions I'll note as this chapter unfolds, it became ever more clear that there is in God's redemptive purpose only one people, the elect. This single body of elect people, however, when viewed within the context of biblical history, is comprised of differing individuals and assumes diverse forms. Beginning with Genesis 12, however, God selected out from among all the peoples of the earth one man, Abraham, and pledged himself to him and his seed to be their God. Thus beginning with Abraham and extending to the first advent of Christ, the elect of God were found almost wholly within the bounds of one ethnic body, Israel, the physical descendants of Abraham, Isaac, and Jacob. It is only appropriate that the people of God in the Old Testament should be called *Israel*, for it was in that stage of biblical history that God's elect assumed the form of a national, socio-political group.

Therefore, from Abraham to Christ, or more specifically, from *Moses* to Christ (since with Moses, the Exodus from Egypt, and the giving of the law the nation of Israel was more conspicuous as a national body), it was God's will that his people be definitively set apart as a national theocracy with specific geographical boundaries hedged in by laws to keep them separate from all heathen peoples. Since the coming of Christ, however (as we shall see), he has seen fit to remove the restricting element of the Law and to organize his people as a *Church* which transcends national and geographical boundaries.

The Inaugural Coming of the Kingdom of God

The "blessed hope" of the Christian, and thus the controlling theme of biblical eschatology, is "the appearing of the glory of our great God and Savior Jesus Christ" (Titus 2:13), at which time he will consummate the kingdom of God. To understand what this consummation entails we must first explore the inauguration of God's sovereign rule in the first coming of Christ.

Christ's first-century proclamation of the kingdom of God must be seen in relation to, indeed, in contrast with, the aspirations of the Jewish people of his day. The expectant attitude and hope of the first-century Israelite were for dominion in the land that God had promised to Abraham and his seed, together with an everlasting throne, international supremacy, and above all else the presence of the King himself in power and glory to rule over God's people. The question reverberating in the heart of the Jewish people at the time of Jesus was: "When will Yahweh send the Messiah to deliver us from our oppressors and fulfill the covenant promises given to our fathers? Where is God's promised fulfillment of the kingdom?"

No one disputes the fact that the focus of Christ's ministry was the announcement of *the coming of the kingdom of God*: "The time is fulfilled, and the kingdom of God is at hand; repent and believe in the gospel" (Mark 1:15; see also Matt. 3:2; 4:17; 4:23; 10:7; Luke 4:43; 10:9). The concept of the kingdom most prevalent in the mind of the Old Testament Jew was that of God's visible conquest of his enemies, the vindication and restoration of his people, Israel, to supremacy in the land, and the fulfillment of the promises of a Davidic throne and rule upon the earth in power and glory. "God's kingdom, to the Jew-in-the-village in the first half of the first century," notes Wright, "meant the coming vindication of Israel, victory over the pagans, the eventual gift of peace, justice and prosperity. It is scarcely surprising that, when a prophet appeared announcing that this kingdom was dawning, and that Israel's God was at last becoming king, he found an eager audience."[3] The crucial issue was: when will Yahweh return to Zion to dwell with his people, to forgive and restore them? Jewish hope, notes Wright,

> was concrete, specific, focused on the people as a whole. If Pilate was still governing Judaea, then the kingdom had not come. If the Temple was not rebuilt, then the kingdom had not come. If the Messiah had not arrived, then the kingdom had not come. If Israel was not observing the Torah properly (however one might define that), then the kingdom had not come. If the pagans were not defeated and/or flocking to Zion for instruction, then the kingdom had not come. These tangible, this-worldly points of reference … are all-important.[4]

---

3. N.T. Wright, *Jesus and the Victory of God* (Minneapolis: Fortress Press, 1996), 204.
4. Ibid., 223.

For the religious leaders of Jesus' day as well as the common man, the coming kingdom of God would be a matter of national liberation and the military defeat of the pagan oppressors. This mindset may well have contributed to John the Baptist's bewilderment concerning Jesus:

> [2]Now when John heard in prison about the deeds of the Christ, he sent word by his disciples [3]and said to him, "Are you the one who is to come, or shall we look for another?" [4]And Jesus answered them, "Go and tell John what you hear and see: [5]the blind receive their sight and the lame walk, lepers are cleansed and the deaf hear, and the dead are raised up, and the poor have good news preached to them. [6]And blessed is the one who is not offended by me." (Matt. 11:2-6)

In his response to John's disciples, Jesus was claiming that the fulfillment of the Old Testament hope with its attendant blessings was in fact *present* in his person and ministry. The fulfillment, however, was not taking place along anticipated lines, hence John's perplexity. The unexpected element was that fulfillment *was* occurring in Jesus, *but without the eschatological consummation.* The Old Testament prophetic hope of the coming messianic kingdom of God as promised to Israel *is being fulfilled* in the person and ministry of Jesus, *but not consummated.* The Jews of our Lord's day, in keeping with what they read in their inspired writings, expected the *consummation* of the kingdom, the complete and final overthrow of Israel's political enemies and the ushering in of the age of blessed peace and prosperity in the land. Our Lord, however, came with the message that *before* the kingdom would come in its eschatological consummation it *has come* in his own person and work in spirit and power. The kingdom, therefore, is *both* the present spiritual *reign* of God *and* the future *realm* over which he will rule in power and glory. Thus, George Ladd rightly concludes that

> *before the eschatological appearing of God's Kingdom at the end of the age, God's Kingdom has become dynamically active among men in Jesus' person and mission.* The Kingdom in this age is not merely the abstract

concept of God's universal rule to which men must submit; it is rather a dynamic power at work among men.... Before the apocalyptic coming of God's Kingdom and the final manifestation of his rule to bring in the new age, God has manifested his rule, his Kingdom, to bring men in advance of the eschatological era the blessings of his redemptive reign.[5]

In his response to John's query, Jesus pointed to the binding of Satan as one example of the manifestation of his kingdom reign. "The meaning of Jesus' exorcism of demons in its relationship to the Kingdom of God is precisely this: that before the eschatological conquest of God's Kingdom over evil and the destruction of Satan, the Kingdom of God has invaded the realm of Satan to deal him a preliminary but decisive defeat."[6] Likewise, the very words of Jesus embodied and gave expression to the presence of the kingdom: "The word which Jesus proclaimed itself brought to pass that which it proclaimed: release for captives, recovery for the blind, freeing of the oppressed.... The message creates the new era..., it makes possible the signs of the messianic fulfillment. The word brings about the Kingdom of God. The gospel is itself the greatest of the messianic signs."[7]

Thus the kingdom of God is the redemptive reign of God, or his sovereign lordship, dynamically active to establish his rule among men. There are two decisive and dramatic moments in the manifestation of this kingdom: first, as it is fulfilled within history in the first advent of the Son, whereby Satan was defeated and men and women are brought into the experience of the blessings of God's reign; and second, as it will be consummated at the close of history in the second advent of the Son, when he will finally and forever destroy his enemies, deliver his people and all of creation from evil, and establish his eternal rule in the new heavens and new earth.

---

5. George Eldon Ladd, *The Presence of The Future* (Grand Rapids: Eerdmans, 1974), 139.
6. Ibid., 151.
7. Ibid., 165.

This unexpected expression of the kingdom in its present form as God's redemptive reign is precisely the *mystery* form of the kingdom as illustrated in the parables of Matthew 13. That God proposed to bring in his kingdom is, of course, no secret or mystery. That the kingdom was to come in power and glory was no secret. The *mystery* is a new disclosure concerning God's purpose for the establishment of that kingdom; to be more specific, that the kingdom which is to come in the future in power and glory has, in point of fact, *already entered into the world in advance in a hidden form* to work secretly within and among men (see Mark 4:26-32). Again, here is Ladd's explanation:

> We may conclude that the "mystery of the kingdom" is the key to the understanding of the unique element in Jesus' teaching about the Kingdom. He announced that the Kingdom of God had come near; in fact, he affirmed that it had actually come upon men (Matt. 12:28). It was present in his word and in his messianic works. It was present in his person; it was present as the messianic salvation. It constituted a fulfillment of the OT expectation. Yet the coming and presence of the Kingdom was not self-explanatory and altogether self-evident. There was something about it which could be understood only by revelation. This meant that while the presence of the Kingdom was a fulfillment of the OT expectation, it was a fulfillment in different terms from those which one might expect from the prophets. Before the end of the age and the coming of the Kingdom in glorious power, it was God's purpose that the powers of that eschatological Kingdom should enter into human history to accomplish a defeat of Satan's kingdom, and to set at work the dynamic power of God's redemptive reign among men. This new manifestation of God's Kingdom was taking place on the level of human history and centered in one man – Jesus Christ.[8]

There is, therefore, a dual manifestation of the kingdom of God corresponding in kind to the two comings of Christ himself. He *first* appeared in obscurity and humility, to suffer and die for the

---

8. Ibid., 227-29.

vindication of God's righteousness and the salvation of his people (Rom. 3:23-26). By this means, said Paul, God "has delivered us from the domain of darkness and transferred us to the kingdom of his beloved Son, in whom we have redemption, the forgiveness of sins" (Col. 1:13-14). He will yet appear a *second* time in visible power and greatness to deliver the earth from the curse of sin, to glorify his people, and to establish his sovereign rule forever in the consummated splendor of the new heavens and new earth. Thus, we must think in terms of *both* "the present realm of righteousness or salvation when men may accept or reject the kingdom, *and* the future realm when the powers of the kingdom shall be manifested in visible glory. The former was inaugurated in insignificant beginnings without outward display, and those who accept it are to live intermingled with those who reject it until the consummation. Then the kingdom will be disclosed in a mighty manifestation of power and glory. God's kingdom will come; and the ultimate state will witness the perfect realization of the will of God everywhere and forever." [9]

Israel and the Church: Contrast or Continuity?

This understanding of the purpose of Christ's first coming has profound implications for how we interpret the relationship between Israel and the Church: whether to emphasize contrast or continuity. It is clear that Jesus came as a Jew to the Jewish people to proclaim to them that God was now acting to fulfill his covenant promises. It was against the background and upon the foundation of the covenant promises to Israel, as the natural "sons of the Kingdom" (Matt. 8:12), that he spoke.

However, the nation of Israel as a whole rejected both Jesus and his message of the kingdom. The gravity of Israel's rejection and the judgment of God which resulted is a theme found repeatedly in the Gospel records. [10] The culmination of this judgment is stated

---

9. George Eldon Ladd, *Crucial Questions about the Kingdom of God* (Grand Rapids: Eerdmans, 1952), 131-32.
10. See especially Matt. 11:16-19, 20-24; 12:34; 23:37-39; Mark 8:11-13; 9:19; 13:1-2; 14:58; 15:29; Luke 13:1-5, 6-19, 34f.; 19:41-44; 21:20-24; 23:27-31.

forcefully in Matthew 21:43 (cf. Mark 12:9). There Jesus declared: "Therefore I tell you, the kingdom of God will be taken away from you and given to a people producing its fruits." This judgment of God against Israel for their unbelief and calloused rejection of the Messiah is described by Paul in Romans 11 as the "breaking off of the natural branches."

On the other hand, *a substantial group of Israelites did respond in faith* and received Jesus as the Messiah with his offer of the kingdom. If Jesus offered the messianic kingdom (i.e., its fulfillment as previously described), then *that* very fulfillment was actually realized in and for those who embraced Christ's claims. Thus, the recipients of this messianic salvation became "the true Israel, representatives of the nation as a whole. While it is true that the word 'Israel' is never applied to Jesus' disciples, the idea is present, if not the term. Jesus' disciples therefore are the recipients of the messianic salvation, the people of the Kingdom, the true Israel." [11] Let us never forget that Jesus' disciples, those who accepted his offer of the kingdom, those who would form the nucleus of the emerging Church, were *Jewish.*

It is against the background of the *believing remnant* that this concept of Jesus' disciples as the true people of God is to be seen. They would become, by reason of their acceptance of the kingdom as over against the nation's rejection, the *nucleus* of the new people of God, the Church.

In the Old Testament, the prophets, while viewing Israel as a whole as disobedient and thus subject to divine judgment, always perceived that there yet remained within the unbelieving nation a *remnant* of believers who were the objects of God's love and care. That is, within the nation of *physical* Israelites there was always a *remnant* of *spiritual* (or believing) Israelites (see again Rom. 9:6). *This believing remnant, wherever it may appear and however large or small it may be, is the true people of God.* This theme reappears in our Lord's reference to the disciples as a "little flock" (Luke 12:32). Israel as a whole, *ideally* God's flock, rejected the Messiah; they

---

11. Ladd, *The Presence of the Future,* 250.

were deaf to the voice of the shepherd; "but those who heard and followed the shepherd constitute his fold, the little flock, the true Israel." [12]

Thus, Jesus saw the realization of Israel's true destiny in the circle of his disciples. They are not to be thought of, however, as a "new" Israel, but as the "*true*" Israel, the "true people of God." With Jesus' offer of the kingdom came the fact that acceptance means the realization and fulfillment of the promise. This offer was accepted by the disciples and thus *was* realized and fulfilled in them. They constituted neither a new Israel nor a separate body of believers: rather, they were *the believing remnant within the unbelieving nation.*

This "Church" (Matt. 16:18-19), therefore, is not a wholly distinct and completely new creation or purpose of God, separated from his people of the Old Testament, Israel, and in some sense "replacing" them. Rather, *the Church of the present age is simply the **continuation and maturation** of the believing remnant of Israel, namely, the disciples and all others who received Jesus as Messiah.* Thus, the fellowship or Church established by Jesus stands *not* in opposition to but in direct continuity with the Old Testament Israel. This body *is* "true" Old Testament Israel: the remnant!

When we speak of "one people of God" we should not conclude that the Old Testament saints belonged to the "Church." The "Church" properly and technically had its birthday on Pentecost. Although Acts 7:38 refers to "the *church* in the wilderness" (an obvious reference to Old Testament Israel), and despite the fact that the word *ekklesia* ("church") is used some eighty-six times in the LXX of the nation Israel, let us not forget that the word had not *as of then* attained its technical sense of *the body of Christ*, a congregation of God's people called out from among *all* nations and united by the baptism in the Holy Spirit. It was at Pentecost, and not before, that God's people (at that time, I might add, a people comprised almost wholly of believing *Israelites*, the remnant) became or took on a new form as the "Church," the body of Christ.

---

12. Ibid., 251. Cf. John 10:16.

Therefore, it is appropriate to speak of *Israel* and the *Church*, the titles for God's people in the Old Testament and the New Testament respectively, all the while recognizing in them God's *one* people through whom he will accomplish his purpose.

The Old Testament Land Promises and the Consummation of the Kingdom

As we noted above, the "kingdom of God" refers primarily to the *reign* or *rule* of God over his people. Thus to believe and receive the kingdom of God is to submit to the yoke of God's sovereignty. [13]

On the other hand, God's *rule* manifests itself and is realized in a specific *historical realm*. God is indeed the King of all the earth, but the Old Testament places great emphasis on the fact that he is in a special way the King of his people Israel, and that this rule or reign is to be realized in *her* history and development on the earth. God's kingdom, therefore, as described in the Old Testament has in view his rule over *Israel in the Promised Land*. The Old Testament prophetic hope was both *nationalistic* (because focused in *Israel*, the physical descendants of Abraham, Isaac, and Jacob) and *earthly* (because realized in Canaan, the land of promise).

The promise of the land and God's rule therein is given to Abraham (Gen. 12:1-3; 13:14-17; 15:1-7; 17:1-16), Isaac (Gen. 26:1-5), Jacob (Gen. 28:13-14; 35:12), and is reaffirmed to Moses (Exod. 6:4, 8; 13:5-11; 32:13; 33:1; Num. 10:29; cf. also Num. 11:12; 14:23; 32:11; Deut. 12:8-11). Furthermore, no fewer than sixty-nine times do we find in Deuteronomy a repetition of the promise that Israel would inherit the land; and lest there be any mistake concerning the reference, in several cases the promise is directly identified as that which was given to Abraham, Isaac, and Jacob (Deut. 1:8; 6:10, 18; 7:8; 34:4).

But was not the land promise *forfeited* by Israel's disobedience? Or, if not forfeited, could it have been exhaustively *fulfilled* during the reigns of David or Solomon? No, for the hope of God's rule over his people *in the land* is confirmed by the prophets who

---

13. Cf. Exod. 15:18; Num. 23:21; Deut. 33:5; Isa. 43:15; 2 Kings 19:15; Isa. 6:5; Jer. 46:18; Pss. 29:10; 47:2; 93; 96:10; 97:1ff.; 99:1-4; 145:11ff.

wrote well *after* David and Solomon as awaiting a yet *future* fulfillment.[14]

Recognizing this, some have argued that these prophesied regatherings of Israel in the land do not refer to any future, eschatological (end-time) event, but to an actual historical fulfillment either in the return from Babylonian captivity under Zerubbabel and Joshua (in 536 B.C.) or in a later return under Ezra (in 458 B.C.). My response to this argument comes in three parts.

First, it isn't possible to understand *all* the prophecies as historically fulfilled, for several are conceived of as being fulfilled only "in the last days," "in the day of the Lord" (see Joel 3:17-21; Micah 4:1-8; Ezek. 36-37; Zeph. 3:14-20; Isa. 11:1-9; 25:6-12). We should take special note of Zechariah 10:9-12; 14:1-9, 16-21, which leads Walter Kaiser to comment:

> Yet even after Israel had been restored to the land after the Babylonian exile, the prospect of a regathered, reunified nation still appeared in Zechariah 10:9-12. The importance of this passage and its late postexilic date should not be lost by those who interpret the promise of the land spiritually or as a temporal blessing which has since been forfeited by a rebellious nation due to her failure to keep her part of the conditional covenant. On the contrary, this hope burned brighter as Israel became more and more hopelessly scattered.[15]

Second, even if we grant that the restoration to the land referred to in the texts cited received historic fulfillment in Israel's return from Babylon, *they were restored to the land,* and more specifically, to the land "that I (God) gave to their fathers (Abraham, Isaac, Jacob)" (Jer. 16:15). From this we can conclude that the land promises therefore were *not* exhaustively fulfilled by any previous historical

---

14. See Isa. 2:1-4; 11:1-16; 14:1-3; 25:6-12; 27:12-13; 35:2, 7, 10; 43:1-7; 49:8-16; Jer. 16:14-15; 23:3-8; 30:10-11; 31:8-11, 31-37; Ezek. 11:17-21; 20:33-38; 34:11-16; 36:22-38; 37:1-28; 39:25-29; Joel 3:17-21; Amos 9:15; Micah 4:1-7; 7:18-20; Zeph. 3:14-20; Zech. 8:4-8; 10:9-12; 14:1-9, 16-21.

15. Walter Kaiser, *Toward an Old Testament Theology,* 255.

possession by Israel, such as that described in Joshua 21 or during Solomon's rule. If they had been exhaustively fulfilled at *that* time, on what basis does God continue to fulfill them at such a late (post-exilic) date in Israel's history? Would this not also demonstrate that the land promises were *unconditional*? Otherwise Israel's disobedience in the centuries preceding (including her disobedience which incurred the captivity) would have precluded *any* regathering, for she would have no inheritance in the land at all (having forfeited it through disobedience).

Finally, it hardly seems possible that such historical (post-exilic) restorations to the land could exhaust the original covenant promise, for the post-exilic possession of Canaan was even *less* extensive than the pre-exilic possessions (e.g., under Solomon). Consequently, if the many pre-exilic possessions of the land, which were *more* extensive, did not exhaust the covenant promise, how could the post-exilic possession do so, being far *less* extensive? It seems best, then, to interpret the historical fulfillments under Zerubbabel and Ezra as but partial, and thus as foreshadowings or the first-fruits (i.e., a token/pledge), as it were, of the ultimate and eternal inheritance which is yet future.

At the close of the old dispensation we are left, therefore, with an as yet unfulfilled prophetic hope of God's *earthly* rule over his people according to the promise given to the fathers. Since we have shown that the promised inheritance was neither forfeited nor fulfilled, what options are left? There seem to be two:

Some insist that the land was *figurative* in purpose. That is to say, it was a *prophetic type* of heavenly or spiritual blessings which are either being fulfilled now by the Church or will be fulfilled in the age to come. The earthly Canaan, therefore, was never designed to be literally possessed as an eternal inheritance, but was to serve as a model of a future blessing, heavenly and spiritual in nature. This has been the perspective of many amillennialists, but is fast giving way to a perspective that takes more seriously the importance of the *earth* in God's redemptive purpose.

Indeed, I would argue that the land promise will yet be fulfilled, *literally* and on the *earth*. But the question is "*When*"? It seems that the first option, which views the Old Testament land promise as figurative of purely spiritual blessings is an impoverishment of the Old Testament covenant promise.[16] I prefer to think that a glorious *earthly* consummation of the kingdom rule of Christ is yet to occur in fulfillment of the Old Testament promises. But *when?* As we've already noted, premillennialists insist that the answer is the 1,000-year period known as the *millennium* which, they argue, intervenes between Christ's second coming and the final judgment. According to the dispensational premillennialist, the millennium will witness a virtual restoration of the Old Testament economy: the temple will be rebuilt, the worship of the old covenant will resume, the priesthood will again function as it did during ancient days, and the Levitical sacrificial system will once again be operative.

Many non-dispensational or historic premillennialists, such as Ladd, have another suggestion. Although the Old Testament prophetic hope was both "nationalistic" and "earthly", in light of New Testament teaching on the Church (believers from *every* tribe, tongue, and nation) as the continuation and maturation of the believing remnant of Israel, it seems the "nationalistic" element has disappeared. The covenant promises in the Old Testament surely were given to Israel alone, but the New Testament indicates that *now* (Eph. 2:11-13) the "seed of Abraham" encompasses all the *faithful and all the believing* (Gal. 3:16, 23-29). Believing Gentiles do not have a separate inheritance distinct from that of believing Israelites. Rather, as Ephesians 2 teaches, we (believing Gentiles) have been admitted to the commonwealth of Israel and have become *co-heirs* of the covenant promise given to Abraham, Isaac, and Jacob!

The promise of God's earthly rule over his people has not changed, nor have believing Israelites been disinherited or displaced by the Church. The only change is that concerning the recipients of the promise: none has been deleted, but many have been *added*, i.e., believing Gentiles! The covenant promise was for the "seed of Abraham", which seed *we*, believing Gentiles, *are*,

---

16. See especially the comments of Ladd, *The Presence of the Future*, 59ff. Also note Matt. 5:5 and Rev. 5:10.

through faith in Christ (Gal. 3:26-29). If there is to be a millennium, therefore, it is not primarily Jewish in nature. It is, rather, the rule of Christ over his *one people*, the olive tree, itself comprised of both natural (believing Jews) and unnatural (believing Gentiles) branches. Thus, according to this non-dispensational version of premillennialism, one purpose of the millennial kingdom would be to serve as the time and place (at least initially) wherein the Old Testament promises of God's earthly rule over his people will be fulfilled. Another purpose of the millennium would be that Christ's kingdom might be disclosed *in history*, as a testimony to his ultimate triumph over the powers of sin and darkness.

The second answer, proposed by amillennialists such as Anthony Hoekema and myself, is that the Old Testament prophetic promise of God's rule over his people in the land will be fulfilled in the *new earth*, which inaugurates the eternal state (see more below). According to this view, the Old Testament promise of a Messianic reign among God's people in the land will be literally fulfilled. It will be fulfilled, however, not on the present, unredeemed earth, but on the *new earth* described in Revelation 21–22 (see especially the discussion of this point in conjunction with Heb. 11).

Vern Poythress agrees and calls himself "an earthy amillennialist" (I like that!). I am *earthy*, he explains, "in the sense of emphasizing the hope for a new earth that is a renewal of this earth. Of course, it is not merely a return to Eden, but an advance, a transfiguration of the old order of things in agreement with the pattern of Christ's resurrection, which transfigured the body of his earthly life. But this transfiguration still includes profound aspects of continuity with the present order, rather than being a totally new beginning."[17] Poythress challenges all premillennialists to recognize that the new heavens and the new earth are the great climax of fulfillment, and therefore that "many of the objections that they have had to amillennialism miss the mark when they have to reckon with the new-earth form of amillennialism."[18]

---

17. Vern Sheridan Poythress, "Currents within Amillennialism," *Presbyterion* 26/1 (2000): 21-25.
18. Ibid.

The Resurrection

An oft neglected element in the eschatological hope of the believer is the resurrection of the body. The popular image of a shapeless Christian floating in some ethereal spiritual fog, moving from one cloud in the heavens to another, is due more to Greek dualist philosophy than to the biblical text. The people of God will spend eternity in a body; albeit a glorified and resurrected body, but not for that reason any less physical or material in nature. The reality of this resurrection is explicitly affirmed by Paul in 1 Corinthians 15:50-57, a passage we examined earlier.

2 Corinthians 5:1-5 is another crucial text in this regard. There Paul likens physical death, the dissolution of the body, to the dismantling of a tent. But death should not lead to despair, for "we have a building from God, a house not made with hands, eternal in the heavens" (v. 1). Amid the many interpretations, the best option is to see here a reference to the *glorified, resurrection body*, that final and consummate embodiment in which we will live for eternity. [19] The major objection to this view is Paul's use of the *present tense*, "we *have* a building from God" (not "we *shall* have"). This seems to imply that immediately upon death the believer receives his/her glorified body. But this would conflict with 1 Corinthians 15:22-28, 15:51-56, 1 Thessalonians 4–5, and perhaps 1 John 3:1-3, all of which indicate that glorification occurs at the second advent of Christ. Furthermore, frequently in Scripture a future reality or possession is so certain and assured in the perspective of the author that it is appropriately spoken of in the present tense, as if it were already ours in experience. Thus Paul's present tense "we have" most likely points to the *fact*

---

19. There are two reasons for this. First, the "building" or "house" in verse 1b stands in a parallel relationship with "home" in verse 1a. Since the latter refers to our earthly, unglorified body, it seems reasonable to conclude that the former refers to our heavenly, glorified body. Secondly, the description in verse 1b ("not made with hands," "eternal," and "in the heavens") is more suitable to the glorified body (see especially 1 Cor. 15:35-49). Paul's point would be that our heavenly embodiment is indestructible, not susceptible to decay or corruption or dissolution.

of having as well as the *permanency* of having, but *not* the *immediacy* of having. It is the language of hope.

It has been argued that perhaps Paul uses the present tense because the passing of time between physical death and the final resurrection is not sensed or consciously experienced by the saints in heaven, and thus the reception of one's resurrection body *appears* to follow immediately upon death. But against this is the clear teaching of Scripture that the intermediate state is consciously experienced by those who have died (see 2 Cor. 5:6-8; Phil. 1:21-24; Rev. 6:9-11). If the deceased believer has "departed" to be "with Christ" (Phil. 1:23) and is therefore "with" Christ when he comes (1 Thess. 4:17), it would seem that some kind of conscious existence obtains between a person's death and the general resurrection (this is why we refer to this time as the *intermediate* state).

Even though Paul appears to envision the possibility (probability?) of his own physical death, he still has hope that he will remain alive until Christ returns. Thus he writes:

> ²For in this tent we groan, longing to put on our heavenly dwelling, ³if indeed by putting it on we may not be found naked. ⁴For while we are still in this tent, we groan, being burdened – not that we would be unclothed, but that we would be further clothed, so that what is mortal may be swallowed up by life. ⁵He who has prepared us for this very thing is God, who has given us the Spirit as a guarantee.

Paul speaks here of his desire to be alive when Christ returns, for then he would not have to die physically and experience the separation of body and spirit, a condition he refers to as being "naked" (v. 3) or "unclothed" (v. 4). He much prefers, understandably, to be immediately joined with the Lord in his resurrected and glorified body.

Here in verse 2 (which is repeated and expanded somewhat in v. 4) Paul mixes his metaphors by speaking of putting on or being "clothed" with a "building". But it is more than simply putting on a garment: it is putting on of a garment *over* another. The heavenly body, like an outer vesture or overcoat, is being put on over the earthly body with which the apostle is, as it were, presently clad. In this way the heavenly, glorified body not only covers but also absorbs and *transforms* the earthly one (see Phil. 3:20-21; 1 Cor. 15:53). If he (or we) remains alive until Christ returns he will be found by the Lord clothed with a body (the present, earthly one), and not in a disembodied state (v. 3). To be without a body is to be "naked". Clearly, Paul envisaged a state of disembodiment between physical death and the general resurrection (cf. "unclothed" in v. 4).

But what assurances do we have from God that he will in fact supply us with a glorified and eternal body that is no longer subject to the deterioration and disease we now experience? The simple answer is: the Holy Spirit! Paul's statement in verse 5 is a reminder "that 'the earnest of the Spirit' is not a mere static deposit, but the active vivifying operation of the Holy Spirit within the believer, assuring him that the same principle of power which effected the resurrection of Christ Jesus from the dead is also present and at work within him, preparing his mortal body for the consummation of his redemption in the glorification of his body." [20]

For the Christian, then, death is not to be feared. For we know that whatever illness or debilitation we experience now, whatever degree of suffering or hardship we must face, there is promised to us by the Spirit a glorified, Christ-like, transformed and utterly eternal abode, a body in which there is no disease, no pain, no deprivation, and no decay. The best case scenario, Paul seems to say, is to be alive when Christ returns. That way the believer would transition instantaneously from this "garment" (our current physical body) into that glorified "vesture" (that is and will forever be our resurrected body). Paul prefers not to get "undressed" but to put the garment of eternity over the garment of time in such a way that the former redeems and transforms the latter.

The Final Judgment

The certainty of final judgment is also affirmed by the apostle in 2 Corinthians 5. Paul insists that "whether we are at home or away,

---

20. Philip Edgcumbe Hughes, *Paul's Second Epistle to the Corinthians* (Grand Rapids: Eerdmans 1973), 174.

351

we make it our aim to please him. For we must all appear before the judgment seat of Christ, so that each one may receive what is due for what he has done in the body, whether good or evil" (2 Cor. 5:9-10).

The broader context in 2 Corinthians 4–5 suggests that believers only are in view in this passage. Murray Harris has pointed out that wherever Paul speaks of the recompense, according to works, of all mankind (such as in Rom. 2:6), "there is found a description of two mutually exclusive categories of people (Rom. 2:7-10), not a delineation of two types of action [such as "whether good or evil" here in verse 10] which may be predicated of all people." [21]

Eternal destiny is not at issue in this judgment; eternal reward is (John 3:18; 5:24; Rom. 5:8-9; 8:1; 1 Thess. 1:10). This judgment is not designed to determine entrance into the kingdom of God but blessing, status, and authority within it. Paul is unclear concerning when this judgment occurs. Is it at the moment of physical death, or perhaps during the intermediate state, or possibly not until the second coming of Christ? The most that we can be sure of is that it happens after death (see Heb. 9:27). Having said that, the evidence suggests that it happens at the second coming of Christ (cf. Matt. 16:27; Rev. 22:12), at the close of human history, most likely in conjunction with that larger assize that will include all unbelievers, known to students of the Bible as the Great White Throne judgment (see Rev. 20:11ff.).

Paul clearly emphasizes the *individuality* ("each one") of the final judgment. As important as it is to stress the corporate and communal nature of our life as the body of Christ, each person will be judged individually (no doubt, at least in part, concerning how faithful each person was to his or her corporate responsibilities!). Paul said it in similar terms in Romans 14:12 – "So then *each of us* will give an account of *himself* to God."

As for the manner of this judgment, we do not merely "show up" but are *laid bare* before him. As Paul said in 1 Corinthians 4:5,

21. Murray Harris, *The Second Epistle to the Corinthians* (Grand Rapids: Eerdmans, 2005), 406.

the Lord "will bring to light the things now hidden in darkness and will disclose the purposes of the heart." Murray Harris is right that "not merely an appearance or self-revelation, but, more significantly, a divine scrutiny and disclosure, is the necessary prelude to the receiving of appropriate recompense." [22] Is it not sobering to think that every random thought, every righteous impulse, every secret prayer, hidden deed, long-forgotten sin or act of compassion will be brought into the open for us to acknowledge and for the Lord to judge? And all this, we are reminded, without any "condemnation for those who are in Christ Jesus" (Rom. 8:1).

Most Christians are by now familiar with the term used here, translated judgment "seat" (*bema*). The use of this word in verse 10 "would have been particularly evocative for Paul and the Corinthians since it was before Gallio's tribunal in Corinth that Paul had stood some four years previously (in A.D. 52) when the proconsul dismissed the charge that Paul had contravened Roman law (Acts 18:12-17). Archaeologists have identified this Corinthian *bema* which stands on the south side of the *agora*." [23]

Christ is himself the Judge, consistent with what we read in John 5:22 where he declared that "the Father judges no one, but has given all judgment to the Son." The *standard* of judgment is "what he has done in the body, whether good or evil." Reference to the "body" indicates that the judgment concerns what we do in this life, not what may or may not be done during the time of the intermediate state itself. We will receive from the Lord "what is due." In other words, and somewhat more literally, we will be judged "in accordance with" or perhaps even "in proportion to" deeds done. The deeds are themselves characterized as either "good" (those which "please" Christ, as in v. 9) or "bad" (those which do not please him).

Finally, the result of the judgment is not explicitly stated but is certainly implied. All will "receive" whatever their deeds deserve. There is a reward or recompense involved. Paul is slightly more

---

22. Ibid., 405.
23. Ibid., 406.

specific in 1 Corinthians 3:14-15. There he writes: "If the work that anyone has built on the foundation survives, he will receive a reward. If anyone's work is burned up, he will suffer loss, though he himself will be saved, but only as through fire." The "reward" is not defined and the likelihood is that the "loss" suffered is the "reward" that he or she would otherwise have received had they obeyed.

Jesus mentions a "great" "reward" in heaven, but doesn't elaborate (Matt. 5:12). In the parable of the talents (Matt. 25; cf. Luke 19:12-27) he alludes to "authority" or dominion of some sort (but over whom or what?). Paul says that "whatever good anyone does, this he will receive back from the Lord" (Eph. 6:8). According to 1 Corinthians 4:5, following the judgment "each one will receive his commendation from God". Both Romans 8:17-18 and 2 Corinthians 4:17 refer to a "glory" that is reserved for the saints in heaven. And of course we should consider the many promises in the seven letters to the churches in Revelation 2–3, although it is difficult to know if they are bestowed now, during the intermediate state, or only subsequent to the second coming, and if they are granted in differing degrees depending on service and obedience or are equally distributed among God's children.[24]

Two closing comments are in order. First, our deeds do not determine our salvation, but demonstrate it. They are not the root of our standing with God but the fruit of it, a standing already attained by faith alone in Christ alone. The visible evidence of an invisible faith is the "good" deeds that will be made known at the judgment seat of Christ. Second, we must not be afraid that, with the exposure and evaluation of our deeds, regret and remorse will spoil the bliss of heaven. If there be tears of grief for opportunities squandered, or tears of shame for sins committed, the Lord will wipe them away (Rev. 21:4a). The ineffable joy of forgiving grace will swallow up all sorrow, and the beauty of Christ will blind us to anything other than the splendor of who he is and what he has, by grace, accomplished on our behalf.

---

24. See Rev. 2:7, 10, 17, 23; 3:5, 12, 21; cf. also Matt. 18:4; 19:29; Luke 14:11; and James 1:12.

Hell and Eternal Punishment

Perhaps the most explicit description of hell and eternal punishment is found in Revelation 14:9ff. There we read:

> [9]And another angel, a third, followed them, saying with a loud voice, "If anyone worships the beast and its image and receives a mark on his forehead or on his hand, [10]he also will drink the wine of God's wrath, poured full strength into the cup of his anger, and he will be tormented with fire and sulfur in the presence of the holy angels and in the presence of the Lamb. [11]And the smoke of their torment goes up forever and ever, and they have no rest, day or night, these worshipers of the beast and its image, and whoever receives the mark of its name."

This issue has become an evangelical battleground. Is the torment of the lost a conscious experience that never ends? Or is the punishment a form of annihilation in which, after a just season of suffering in perfect proportion to sins committed, the soul ceases to exist? Does the ascending smoke of their torment point to the unending conscious *experience* of suffering they endure? Or does it signify a lasting, irreversible *effect* of their punishment in which they are annihilated? Those who argue for the latter view contend that there will be no rest "day or night" from torment *while it continues* or *as long as it lasts*. But whether or not it lasts forever or eternally must be determined on other grounds.[25]

Whereas space does not allow interaction with arguments on both sides of this debate, suffice it to say that there is considerable biblical evidence to support the doctrine of eternal conscious punishment. For example, we must keep in mind that the word group which includes "destroy" and its synonyms is used in a variety of ways, some of which do not require or even imply the cessation of existence. Usage indicates that destruction can occur without extinction of being. And before we conclude that the "fire" of hell consumes and utterly "destroys" its object, leaving nothing, we

---

25. A brief, but exceptionally helpful treatment of this issue is provided by D.A. Carson, *The Gagging of God* (Grand Rapids: Zondervan, 1996), 515-36.

must acknowledge that this is *metaphor*, and thus not press the terms to prove something about hell's duration they were never intended to communicate. Hell in the New Testament is described at one time as "utter darkness" and at another time as "a lake of fire." How do these two coexist if they are strictly literal? Thus we must be cautious in drawing rigid doctrinal conclusions about the supposed "function" of fire in hell. Nevertheless, one cannot help but wonder about Matthew 18:8 which speaks of those who are thrown into the "eternal" fire. As Carson says, "one is surely entitled to ask why the fires should burn forever and the worms not die [cf. Mark 9:47-48] if their purpose comes to an end."[26]

We should also note that there are as many texts where *aion* (often rendered "age") means eternal as there are where it refers to a more limited period of time. This argument is indecisive on both sides of the debate. We must also be careful in making emotional appeals to what we, finite humans, consider just recompense for the enormity of our sins. Carson rightly asks whether the magnitude of our sin is established by our own status "or by the degree of offense against the sovereign, transcendent God?"[27] The essential thing, notes Piper, "is that degrees of blameworthiness come not from how long you offend dignity, but from how high the dignity is that you offend."[28] Our sin is deserving of infinite punishment because of the infinite glory of the One against whom it is perpetrated.

To suggest, as some do, that eternal suffering means that God does not achieve consummate victory over sin and evil fails to realize that only sin that goes *unpunished* would indicate a lapse in justice and a defeat of God's purpose. The on-going existence of hell and its occupants would more readily reflect on the glory of God's holiness and his righteous opposition to evil than it would any supposed cosmological dualism. Perhaps the idea of endless punishing is less offensive when the idea of endless sinning is considered.

---

26. Ibid., 525.
27. Ibid., 534.
28. John Piper, *Let the Nations Be Glad! The Supremacy of God in Missions*. Second Edition, Revised and Expanded (Grand Rapids: Baker Academic, 2003), 122.

If those in hell never cease to sin, why should they ever cease to suffer? [29] If one should argue that people pay fully for their sins in hell and at some point cease to sin, why can't they then be brought into heaven (thereby turning hell into purgatory)? If their sins have *not* been fully paid for in hell, on what grounds does justice permit them to be annihilated?

Finally, one must explain Matthew 25:46 and Revelation 20:10-15. Regardless of what one thinks about the identity of the beast and false prophet, no evangelical denies that Satan is a being who both thinks and experiences feelings and sensations. Thus here is at least one such "person" who clearly suffers eternal conscious torment. "We may not feel as much sympathy for him as for fellow human beings, and we may cheerfully insist that he is more evil than any human being, but even so, it is hard to see how the arguments deployed against the notion of eternal conscious suffering of sinful human beings would be any less cogent against the devil." [30]

Heaven on Earth

As noted earlier in this chapter, and contrary to the caricature of amillennialism that many have entertained, the eschatological hope of the Christian is inescapably *earthly* in nature. God's ultimate aim in the redemption of his people has always included the restoration of the natural creation which I believe will come to pass with the introduction of the new heavens and new earth. Nowhere is this more vividly portrayed than in Revelation 21–22. Space permits only a brief summation of the glories of our eternal destiny in the presence of God.

The relationship between this present earth and the new earth is one of both continuity and discontinuity, even as there is between

---

29. See Revelation 22:10-11. On this latter text Carson comments: "If the holy and those who do right continue to be holy and to do right, *in anticipation of the perfect holiness and rightness to be lived and practiced throughout all eternity*, should we not also conclude that the vile continue in their vileness *in anticipation of the vileness they will live and practice throughout all eternity* (*The Gagging of God*, 533)?"
30. Ibid., 527.

our present, corruptible bodies and our future, incorruptible and glorified bodies. We will be in heaven the *same*, though transformed, people that we are now. Yet, the heaven and earth to come are also said to be "new" (*kainos*), a word which typically indicates newness of quality, not time.

One element of discontinuity is the absence of the "sea" in the new creation, which was typically regarded as symbolic of evil, chaos, and anti-kingdom powers with whom Yahweh must contend.[31] As Ladd has noted, in ancient times the sea "represented the realm of the dark, the mysterious, and the treacherous" (cf. Ps. 107:25-28; Ezek. 28:8; Dan. 7:3ff).[32] This is John's way of saying that in the new creation all such evil, corruption, unbelief, and darkness will be banished.

The fullness of God's presence among his people necessarily demands the banishment of any and all forms of suffering associated with the old creation. Gone forever are the debilitating effects of sin (21:3-4). Gone are the "tears" caused by grief and pain and moral failure (in fulfillment of Isa. 25:8). Gone is "death," because its source, sin, will have been eradicated. Gone are "mourning," "crying," and "pain." All such experiences are linked to the "first things" which have now "passed away."

The New Jerusalem is said to have "the glory of God" (v. 11). Whereas in the Old Testament the physical temple was the place where God's glory resided and was manifest, in the new creation God's presence will abide in and with his people. The absence of "night" (v. 25b) points to the unhindered access to God's radiant presence as well as the fact that there will be no darkness to dim the brilliance of divine splendor. Indeed, as 22:5 indicates, the absence of darkness is due to the continual illumination that God himself provides.

In Revelation 22:1 we find the first of several examples where John links the end of history with its beginning. In the consumma-

---

31. See Isa. 17:12,13; 51:9-10; 27:1; 57:20; Rev. 17:8; 21:1; Jer. 46:7-12; and Job 26:7-13.

32. George Eldon Ladd, *A Commentary on the Revelation of John* (Grand Rapids: Eerdmans, 1972), 276.

tion are features which characterized the beginning of time. It is not as though the end is a *reversal* back to the beginning, "but the circumstances of the beginning are viewed as prophetic of the nature of God's purpose in history. In all respects, however, the last things surpass the first in overwhelming measure, as we see in this paragraph."[33] If Genesis 3 tells the story of "Paradise Lost," Revelation 22 tells of "Paradise Regained." *Heaven (on earth!) is but the glorious consummation of God's original design for the Garden of Eden.*

And what will we do in heaven (22:3-5)? We will "serve" God (v. 3). We will "see" God (v. 4a).[34] We will enjoy the depths of intimacy with him (v. 4b). We will experience the fascination of his presence (v. 5a; cf. Num. 6:24-26). We will "reign forever and ever" (v. 5b).

Conclusion

Let me briefly sum up. The kingdom of God is his dynamic reign or sovereign dominion over both his elect people as well as the entirety of his creative handiwork. The inauguration of this kingdom in the first coming of Jesus was manifest in multiple ways, among which were the defeat of the devil, the release of captives from his tyranny, the healing of the sick, the redemption and forgiveness of sins on behalf of those who by faith embraced Jesus as Lord and Savior, and the creation of the "one new man" (Eph. 2:15), the Church, which is comprised of believing Jews and Gentiles, they together being made co-heirs of all the blessings bound up in "the covenants of promise" (Eph. 2:12).

This kingdom, fulfilled in the first coming of Jesus Christ, will be consummated at the time of his second coming. Then will come to pass the bodily resurrection of both elect and non-elect and the judgment of all at the Great White Throne of God. Then, and not until then, will what has already been accomplished in part come to final and comprehensive expression. Then, and not until then, God "will dwell with" his people and "will be with them as their

33. G.R. Beasley-Murray, *The Book of Revelation* (Greenwood, SC: Attic Press, 1974), 330.
34. See Exod. 33:20; Matt. 5:8; John 17:24; 1 Tim. 6:16; 1 John 3:1-3.

God." It is then that "he will wipe away every tear from their eyes, and death shall be no more, neither shall there be mourning, nor crying, nor pain anymore, for the former things have passed away" (Rev. 21:3-4).

Clearly, then, what Christians have traditionally referred to as "heaven" is, as we have seen, eternal life in the presence of God on the new earth. It is there, as the Confessional Statement of the Gospel Coalition makes clear, that "God will be all in all and his people will be enthralled by the immediacy of his ineffable holiness, and everything will be to the praise of his glorious grace." We can do no better than to conclude this chapter with words of Jonathan Edwards:

> If we can learn anything of the state of heaven from the Scripture, the love and joy that the saints have there, is exceeding great and vigorous; impressing the heart with the strongest and most lively sensation, of inexpressible sweetness, mightily moving, animating, and engaging them, making them like to a flame of fire. And if such love and joy be not affections, then the word "affection" is of no use in language. Will any say, that the saints in heaven, in beholding the face of their Father, and the glory of their Redeemer, and contemplating his wonderful works, and particularly his laying down his life for them, have their hearts nothing moved and affected, by all which they behold or consider? [35]

---

35. Jonathan Edwards, *Religious Affections*, The Works of Jonathan Edwards, Volume 2, edited by John E. Smith (New Haven: Yale University Press, 1969), 114.

Chapter Twelve

The Postmillennial View of the Kingdom of God

The most maligned and misunderstood of all eschatological systems is, without question, postmillennialism. The only explanation I received while in seminary was that postmillennialism was the chosen perspective of humanistic liberalism and unworthy of evangelical consideration. People who believed in postmillennialism, so we were told, didn't believe in the inerrancy of Scripture or the depravity of mankind. What I was not told was that from the time of the Protestant Reformation until the emergence of dispensationalism in the nineteenth century, postmillennialism was the dominant conservative viewpoint. But I'm getting ahead of myself. Let's begin by trying to understand postmillennialism on its own terms, not ours.[1]

A Definition of Postmillennialism

Below are two definitions of postmillennialism, one from Loraine Boettner and the other from a more contemporary advocate, Kenneth Gentry. According to Boettner, postmillennialism is

---

1. I have found three works to be especially helpful in articulating a cogent defense of Postmillennialism. They are John Jefferson Davis, *Christ's Victorious Kingdom: Postmillennialism Reconsidered* (Grand Rapids: Baker, 1986), Keith A. Mathison, *Postmillennialism: An Eschatology of Hope* (Phillipsburg: P&R Publishing, 1999), and the most thorough-going treatment available to date, Kenneth L. Gentry, Jr., *He Shall Have Dominion: A Postmillennial Eschatology,* Third Edition: Revised and Expanded (Draper, VA: Apologetics Group Media, 2009).

that view of the last things which holds that the Kingdom of God is now being extended in the world through the preaching of the Gospel and the saving work of the Holy Spirit in the hearts of individuals, that the world eventually is to be Christianized, and that the return of Christ is to occur at the close of a long period of righteousness and peace commonly called the "Millennium." It should be added that on postmillennial principles the second coming of Christ will be followed immediately by the general resurrection, the general judgment, and the introduction of heaven and hell in their fullness. The Millennium to which the Postmillennialist looks forward is thus a golden age of spiritual prosperity during this present dispensation, that is, during the Church age, and is to be brought about through forces now active in the world. It is an indefinitely long period of time, perhaps much longer than a literal one thousand years. The changed character of individuals will be reflected in an uplifted social, economic, political and cultural life of mankind. The world at large will then enjoy a state of righteousness such as at the present time has been seen only in relatively small and isolated groups, as for example in some family circles, some local church groups and kindred organizations. This does not mean that there ever will be a time on this earth when every person will be a Christian, or that all sin will be abolished. But it does mean that *evil in all its many forms eventually will be reduced to negligible proportions, that Christian principles will be the rule, not the exception, and that Christ will return to a truly Christianized world.* [2]

Kenneth Gentry defines it this way:

Postmillennialism expects the proclaiming of the Spirit-blessed gospel of Jesus Christ to win the vast majority of human beings to salvation in the present age. Increasing gospel success will gradually produce a time in history [which they identify with the "millennium"] prior to Christ's return in which faith, righteousness, peace, and prosperity will prevail in the affairs of people and of nations. After an extensive era of such conditions the Lord will return visibly, bodily, and

---

2. Loraine Boettner, *The Millennium* (Nutley, NJ: Presbyterian & Reformed, 1957), 14 (emphasis mine).

in great glory, ending history with the general resurrection and the great judgment of all humankind. Hence, our system is *post*millennial in that the Lord's glorious return occurs *after* an era of "millennial" conditions.[3]

In yet another place, Gentry writes:

> The postmillennial conception of victory is of a progressive *cultural* victory and expansive influence of Christianity in history.... The personal status of the believer and the corporate standing of the Church in salvation *is* ... one of present victory – in principle.... The distinctive postmillennial view of Christianity's progressive victory, in time and history, into *all of human life and culture*, is postmillennialism's application of the doctrine of Christ's definitively completed salvation.[4]

In summary, "the core, distinctive, defining belief within postmillennialism is that Christ will return to the earth *after* the Spirit-blessed Gospel has had *overwhelming success* in bringing the majority of the world to Christ."[5]

Fundamental Tenets of Postmillennial Eschatology

Given the less than flattering reputation that postmillennialism has among mainstream evangelicals, it will do us well to consider carefully its understanding of a number of issues. We begin with the kingdom of God which, according to postmillennialism, is primarily the rule or reign of God spiritually in and over the hearts of men. Thus the kingdom is truly present in this age and is visibly represented by the Church of Jesus Christ. In other words, the kingdom "arrives" and is "present" wherever and whenever people believe the gospel and commit themselves to the sovereignty of

3. Kenneth Gentry, "Postmillennialism," in *Three Views on the Millennium and Beyond*, edited by Darrell L. Bock (Grand Rapids: Zondervan, 1999), 13-14.
4. Gentry, "Whose Victory in History?" in Gary North, ed., *Theonomy: An Informed Response* (Tyler, TX: Institute for Christian Economics, 1991), 215.
5. Gentry, *He Shall Have Dominion*, 90.

Jesus Christ as Lord. Several important features of the kingdom in postmillennial thought are deserving of comment.

The kingdom, says the postmillennialist, is not to be thought of as arriving instantaneously or wholly by means of some cataclysmic event at the end of the age (an event such as the second coming of Christ). Indeed, the very name **POST**-millennialism indicates that Christ will return only *after* the kingdom has come in its fullness. The "arrival" of the kingdom, therefore, is gradual or by degrees.[6] There may well be extended seasons in the life of the Church where little visible and tangible progress is detected, indeed even times when the Church appears to regress in terms of its global influence. But post-millennialists are quick to remind us that we must take the long view and not succumb to the pessimism that easily grows in the soil of short-term setbacks. Whereas Satan's kingdom may appear at times to experience a growth parallel to, if not greater than, that of Christ, the latter will most assuredly overcome all opposition in every sphere of life until the nations are brought into submission to him.

The means by which the kingdom extends itself is the gospel of Jesus Christ. The continuing spread and influence of the gospel will increasingly, and in direct proportion thereto, introduce the kingdom. This gradual (but constantly growing) success of the gospel will be brought about by the power of the Holy Spirit working through the Church. Eventually the greater part, but not necessarily all, of the world's population will be converted to Christ. As Greg Bahnsen explains, "the *essential distinctive* of postmillennialism is its scripturally derived, sure expectation of gospel prosperity for the church during the *present* age."[7]

No one has expressed this more clearly than has Doug Wilson in his small but extremely helpful book, *Heaven Misplaced*. He refers to the postmillennial view as "historical optimism." What he means by this is that "the gospel will continue to grow and flour-

---

6. Andrew Sandlin (*A Postmillennial Primer* [Vallecito, CA: Chalcedon Foundation, 1997]) refers to "the gradual but relentless progress" (29) of Christ's kingdom that was set in motion by the first coming of Christ.

7. Greg Bahnsen, "The Prima Facie Acceptability of Postmillennialism," in *The Journal of Christian Reconstruction*, III (Winter 1976-77), 66.

ish throughout the world, more and more individuals will be converted, the nations will stream to Christ, and the Great Commission will finally be *successfully* completed. The earth will be as full of the knowledge of the Lord as the waters cover the sea. When that happens, generation after generation will love and serve the Lord faithfully. And then the end will come." [8]

This perspective on the prospects of gospel success in this life is illustrated in the postmillennial interpretation of Revelation 19, a chapter which amillennialists and premillennialists understand to be a description of Christ's coming at the *end* of the age. B.B. Warfield, a postmillennialist, writes as follows:

> The section opens with a vision of the victory of the Word of God, the King of Kings and Lord of Lords over all His enemies. We see Him come forth from heaven girt for war, followed by the armies of heaven.... The thing symbolized is obviously the complete victory of the Son of God over all the hosts of wickedness.... The conquest is wrought by the spoken word—in short, by the preaching of the gospel.... What we have here, in effect, is a picture of the whole period between the first and second advents, seen from the point of view of heaven. It is the period of advancing victory of the Son of God over the world.... As emphatically as Paul, John teaches that the earthly history of the Church is not a history merely of conflict with evil, but of conquest over evil: and even more richly than Paul, John teaches that this conquest will be decisive and complete. The whole meaning of the vision of Revelation 19:11-21 is that Jesus Christ comes forth not to war merely but to victory; and every detail of the picture is laid in with a view precisely to emphasizing the thoroughness of this victory. The Gospel of Christ is, John being witness, completely to conquer the world.... A progressively advancing conquest of the earth by Christ's gospel implies a coming age deserving at least the relative name of "golden". [9]

---

8. Douglas Wilson, *Heaven Misplaced: Christ's Kingdom on Earth* (Moscow, Idaho: Canon Press, 2008), 10.

9. B.B. Warfield, "The Millennium and the Apocalypse," in *Biblical Doctrines* (Grand Rapids: Baker Book House, 1981 [1929]), 646-48, 662-63.

At what point, then, does the "millennium" begin? Postmillennialists differ in their response to this question. Some say the millennium covers the entire inter-advent age (i.e., the whole period of time between Christ's first and second comings), whereas others conceive of the present age as in some sense blending or merging into the millennium. In other words, some postmillennialists see the millennial kingdom as present throughout the *whole* of the current age whereas others reserve the word millennium for the *latter day*, publicly discernible, prosperity of the Christian Church.

This ever-increasing success of the gospel will bring in its wake a reduction (although not a total elimination) of the influence and presence of sin. Righteousness, peace, and prosperity will flourish. Thus, writes Bahnsen, "over the *long range* the world will experience a period of extraordinary righteousness and prosperity as the church triumphs in the preaching of the gospel and discipling the nations through the supernatural agency of the Holy Spirit." [10] Old Testament passages such as Psalms 22 and 64, for example, provide textual support for the eschatological expectation that "the growth of the kingdom will reach a point where the majority of men and nations have willingly submitted to Jesus the Messiah." [11] Postmillennialism "does not teach that every individual who has ever lived on earth will be saved, nor does it teach that there will be a time prior to the Second Coming when every living individual will be converted. But it does believe that there is sufficient scriptural warrant to say that at some point in history there will be worldwide conversion on an unprecedented scale." [12] Andrew Sandlin concurs, and argues that the clear message of these and other Old Testament texts "is that there will come a time on earth when God through his Son and people will rule the earth in justice and holiness, producing a worldwide love for himself and his law and a pervasive international peace and great material abundance." [13]

---

10. Bahnsen, "The Prima Facie Acceptability of Postmillennialism," 63.
11. Mathison, *Postmillennialism,* 193.
12. Ibid., 193–94.
13. Sandlin, *A Postmillennial Primer,* 25.

John Jefferson Davis, who has written an excellent book in defense of postmillennialism, adds this important point:

> It should be understood that the postmillennial perspective provides a forecast for the global and long-term prospects of Christianity, but not for the local, short-term prospects of denominations or churches in the nation.... [Thus] the merits of the argument for the postmillennial perspective are not to be tied to the judgments about the present or near-term prospects of the Christian church in America.[14]

The gospel will also sustain a positive influence in every sphere of society: the economic, political, and cultural life of mankind will be vastly improved. The Church will witness nothing less than "the worldwide dominion of Christ and his elect, the re-establishment of Christian civilization and Christian culture."[15] Therefore, this triumph or victory of the Church in the present age is *not* simply the spiritual or invisible victories in the Christian's heart or the internal blessings privately experienced by the Church. The prosperity will be visibly and publicly acknowledged. Every domain of human activity will be renewed according to Christian principles and thus brought into service for the glory of Jesus Christ. It is this progressive subjugation of Christ's enemies and ever-expansive influence of his sovereign lordship, throughout the course of the present age, that Paul has in view when he says in 1 Corinthians 15:25, "For he must reign until he has put all his enemies under his feet." Thus, as several postmillennialists have been heard to say, *"Christ will return to a truly Christianized world."*

The important point to remember is that all of the aforementioned developments will occur in the present age, *before* Christ returns; hence his return is POST (after) millennial.

At the end of the present age, that is, *after* the kingdom has spread visibly and powerfully throughout the world but just *before* Christ

---

14. John Jefferson Davis, *Christ's Victorious Kingdom: Postmillennialism Reconsidered* (Grand Rapids: Baker Book House, 1986), 15.

15. Sandlin, *A Postmillennial Primer,* 32.

returns, there will be a brief time of increased Satanic activity and apostasy (see Rev. 20:7-10). This final rebellion will be crushed by the glorious return of Jesus Christ to the earth, at which time there will immediately follow the general resurrection, final judgment, and eternal state. "In short, postmillennialism is set apart from the other two schools of thought [premillennialism and amillennialism] by its essential *optimism* for the kingdom in the *present* age." [16]

It should also be mentioned that many postmillennialists believe, as do most premillennialists, that a mass conversion will occur among ethnic Israelites. Of course, *unlike* the dispensational premillennialist the postmillennialist denies that this salvation of physical Israel has for its purpose a restoration of the nation in a future earthly millennium.

The central distinguishing feature of postmillennialism which sets it apart from both amillennialism and premillennialism is its belief in the success of the Great Commission in the present age. Simply put, the nations *will be* baptized and discipled to the glory of God. The best summation of postmillennial eschatology is provided by Greg Bahnsen:

> The optimistic confidence that the world nations will become disciples of Christ, that the church will grow to fill the earth, and that Christianity will become the dominant principle rather than the exception to the rule distinguishes postmillennialism from the other viewpoints. All and *only* postmillennialists believe this, and only the refutation of that confidence can undermine this school of eschatological interpretation. In the final analysis, what is characteristic of postmillennialism is not a uniform answer to any one particular exegetical question…, but rather a commitment to the gospel as the power of God which, in the agency of the Holy Spirit, shall convert the vast majority of the world to Christ and bring widespread obedience to His kingdom rule. This confidence will, from person to person, be biblically supported in various ways…. The postmillennialist is in this day marked out by his belief that the commission and resources are with the kingdom of Christ to accomplish the discipling of the nations to Jesus Christ prior to His second

---

16. Bahnsen, "The Prima Facie Acceptability of Postmillennialism," 66.

advent; whatever historical decline is seen in the missionary enterprise of the church and its task of edifying or sanctifying the nations in the word of truth must be attributed, not to anything inherent in the present course of human history, but to the unfaithfulness of the church.[17]

Biblical Support for Postmillennialism

As an amillennialist, I must admit that the textual support cited in defense of postmillennialism is impressive, if not altogether persuasive. Their appeal is to the many passages, especially in the Old Testament, that speak of a time when "all the nations" of the earth and "all the families" of man and "all the kings" of the earth will come and worship the Lord.[18] Let's take note of several of the more important of these texts, with my emphasis added:

[6]As for me, I have set my King on Zion, my holy hill. [7]I will tell of the decree: The LORD said to me, "You are my Son; today I have begotten you. [8]Ask of me, and *I will make the nations your heritage, and the ends of the earth your possession.* [9]You shall break them with a rod of iron and dash them in pieces like a potter's vessel." (Ps. 2:6-9)

[27]*All the ends of the earth shall remember and turn to the LORD, and all the families of the nations shall worship before you.* [28]For kingship belongs to the LORD, and he rules over the nations. (Ps. 22:27-28)

[8]*May he have dominion from sea to sea, and from the River to the ends of the earth! [9]May desert tribes bow down before him and his enemies lick the dust! [10]May the kings of Tarshish and of the coastlands render*

---

17. Ibid., 68.
18. In support of their eschatology, most Postmillennialists would cite the following biblical texts, with special emphasis on those in bold print: Num. 14:21; **Pss. 2:6-9; 22:27-28**; 47; **72:8-11**; 110:1-2; **138:4-5 (cf. 102:15)**; **Isa. 2:2-4; 9:6-7; 11:6-10**; 45:22-25; 65; 66; Jer. 31:31-34; **Dan. 2:31-35**; Zech. 9:9f.; 13:1; 14:9; **Matt. 13:31-33; 28:18-20**; John 12:31-32; 16:33; Acts 2:32-36, 41; **Rom. 11:25-32; 1 Cor. 15:20-26**, 57-58; Heb. 1:8-9, 13; 2:5-9; 1 John 2:13-14; 3:8; 4:4, 14; 5:4-5; Rev. 2:25-27; 3:7-9; 7:9-10; 11:15; 19:11-21.

him tribute; may the kings of Sheba and Seba bring gifts! [11]*May all kings fall down before him, all nations serve him!* (Ps. 72:8-11)

[9]*All the nations you have made shall come and worship before you, O Lord, and shall glorify your name.* [10]For you are great and do wondrous things; you alone are God. (Ps. 86:9-10)

[15]Nations will fear the name of the LORD, and *all the kings of the earth will fear your glory.* (Ps. 102:15)

[4]*All the kings of the earth shall give you thanks, O LORD,* for they have heard the words of your mouth, [5]and they shall sing of the ways of the LORD, for great is the glory of the LORD. (Ps. 138:4-5)

[1]The word that Isaiah the son of Amoz saw concerning Judah and Jerusalem. [2]*It shall come to pass in the latter days that the mountain of the house of the LORD shall be established as the highest of the mountains, and shall be lifted up above the hills; and all the nations shall flow to it,* [3]and many peoples shall come, and say: "Come, let us go up to the mountain of the LORD, to the house of the God of Jacob, that he may teach us his ways and that we may walk in his paths." For out of Zion shall go the law, and the word of the LORD from Jerusalem. [4]He shall judge between the nations, and shall decide disputes for many peoples; *and they shall beat their swords into plowshares, and their spears into pruning hooks; nation shall not lift up sword against nation, neither shall they learn war anymore.* (Isa. 2:1-4)

[6]For to us a child is born, to us a son is given; and the government shall be upon his shoulder, and his name shall be called Wonderful Counselor, Mighty God, Everlasting Father, Prince of Peace. [7]*Of the increase of his government and of peace there will be no end, on the throne of David and over his kingdom, to establish it and to uphold it with justice and with righteousness from this time forth and forevermore.* The zeal of the LORD of hosts will do this. (Isa. 9:6-7)

[6]The wolf shall dwell with the lamb, and the leopard shall lie down with the young goat, and the calf and the lion and the fattened calf

together; and a little child shall lead them. ⁷The cow and the bear shall graze; their young shall lie down together; and the lion shall eat straw like the ox. ⁸The nursing child shall play over the hole of the cobra, and the weaned child shall put his hand on the adder's den. *⁹They shall not hurt or destroy in all my holy mountain; for the earth shall be full of the knowledge of the Lord as the waters cover the sea. ¹⁰In that day the root of Jesse, who shall stand as a signal for the peoples – of him shall the nations inquire, and his resting place shall be glorious.* (Isa. 11:6-10)

¹⁷"For behold, I create new heavens and a new earth, and the former things shall not be remembered or come into mind. ¹⁸But be glad and rejoice forever in that which I create; for behold, I create Jerusalem to be a joy, and her people to be a gladness. ¹⁹I will rejoice in Jerusalem and be glad in my people; no more shall be heard in it the sound of weeping and the cry of distress. ²⁰No more shall there be in it an infant who lives but a few days, or an old man who does not fill out his days, for the young man shall die a hundred years old, and the sinner a hundred years old shall be accursed. ²¹They shall build houses and inhabit them; they shall plant vineyards and eat their fruit. ²²They shall not build and another inhabit; they shall not plant and another eat; for like the days of a tree shall the days of my people be, and my chosen shall long enjoy the work of their hands. ²³They shall not labor in vain or bear children for calamity, for they shall be the offspring of the blessed of the Lord, and their descendants with them. ²⁴Before they call I will answer; while they are yet speaking I will hear. ²⁵The wolf and the lamb shall graze together; the lion shall eat straw like the ox, and dust shall be the serpent's food. They shall not hurt or destroy in all my holy mountain," says the Lord. (Isa. 65:17-25)

¹⁸"For I know their works and their thoughts, and the time is coming to gather all nations and tongues. And they shall come and shall see my glory, ¹⁹and I will set a sign among them. And from them I will send survivors to the nations, to Tarshish, Pul, and Lud, who draw the bow, to Tubal and Javan, to the coastlands afar off, that have not heard my fame or seen my glory. And they shall declare my glory among the nations. ²⁰And they shall bring all your brothers from all the nations

371

as an offering to the LORD, on horses and in chariots and in litters and on mules and on dromedaries, to my holy mountain Jerusalem, says the LORD, just as the Israelites bring their grain offering in a clean vessel to the house of the LORD. ²¹And some of them also I will take for priests and for Levites," says the LORD. ²²*'For as the new heavens and the new earth that I make shall remain before me, says the LORD, so shall your offspring and your name remain.* ²³*From new moon to new moon, and from Sabbath to Sabbath, all flesh shall come to worship before me, declares the LORD.'* (Isa. 66:18-23)

³¹You saw, O king, and behold, a great image. This image, mighty and of exceeding brightness, stood before you, and its appearance was frightening. ³²The head of this image was of fine gold, its chest and arms of silver, its middle and thighs of bronze, ³³its legs of iron, its feet partly of iron and partly of clay. ³⁴As you looked, a stone was cut out by no human hand, and it struck the image on its feet of iron and clay, and broke them in pieces. ³⁵Then the iron, the clay, the bronze, the silver, and the gold, all together were broken in pieces, and became like the chaff of the summer threshing floors; and the wind carried them away, so that not a trace of them could be found. *But the stone that struck the image became a great mountain and filled the whole earth.* (Dan. 2:31-35)

¹³I saw in the night visions, and behold, with the clouds of heaven there came one like a son of man, and he came to the Ancient of Days and was presented before him. ¹⁴*And to him was given dominion and glory and a kingdom, that all peoples, nations, and languages should serve him; his dominion is an everlasting dominion, which shall not pass away, and his kingdom one that shall not be destroyed.* (Dan. 7:13-14)

⁹Rejoice greatly, O daughter of Zion! Shout aloud, O daughter of Jerusalem! Behold, your king is coming to you; righteous and having salvation is he, humble and mounted on a donkey, on a colt, the foal of a donkey. ¹⁰I will cut off the chariot from Ephraim and the war horse from Jerusalem; and the battle bow shall be cut off, *and he shall speak peace to the nations; his rule shall be from sea to sea, and from the River to the ends of the earth.* (Zech. 9:9-10)

[31]He put another parable before them, saying, "The kingdom of heaven is like a grain of mustard seed that a man took and sowed in his field. [32]It is the smallest of all seeds, but *when it has grown it is larger than all the garden plants and becomes a tree, so that the birds of the air come and make nests in its branches.*" [33]He told them another parable. *"The kingdom of heaven is like leaven that a woman took and hid in three measures of flour, till it was all leavened."* (Matt. 13:31-33) [19]

[20]But in fact Christ has been raised from the dead, the firstfruits of those who have fallen asleep. [21]For as by a man came death, by a man has come also the resurrection of the dead. [22]For as in Adam all die, so also in Christ shall all be made alive. [23]But each in his own order: Christ the firstfruits, then at his coming those who belong to Christ. [24]*Then comes the end, when he delivers the kingdom to God the Father after destroying every rule and every authority and power.* [25]*For he must reign until he has put all his enemies under his feet.* [26]*The last enemy to be destroyed is death.* (1 Cor. 15:20-26)

Premillennialists typically interpret the majority of these texts as describing the state of affairs following the second coming of Christ during his millennial reign on the earth. Amillennialists read them as describing either a great harvest of souls just preceding the second coming of Christ or what will occur in the new heaven and the new earth, which is to say, during the eternal state. The language and imagery employed likely reflects the limited perspective of the Old Testament prophet and is therefore couched in terms that were familiar to the people of his day. In other words, the Old Testament author is describing the very real age to come in terms of its ideal present. What would be most relevant and meaningful to the people of his own day is used as a way of portraying what will obtain in the consummation.

---

19. "The main point of this parable [of the mustard seed] is that despite unimpressive beginnings, the messianic kingdom will grow until it is huge" (Mathison, *Postmillennialism*, 108). The parable of the leaven "illustrates the extensive, pervasive growth and influence of the kingdom" (ibid.).

As noted earlier, most postmillennialists concede that not everyone who is alive when Christ returns will necessarily be converted. In other words, they admit that these statements about "*all* the kings of the earth" coming to worship or "*all* the nations" fearing God are not to be taken as expressing a form of soteriological universalism. Could it then be that these texts are Old Testament equivalent expressions to what we find in Revelation 4–5 which speaks of Christ redeeming men "from every tribe and nation and tongue and people"? In other words, what the Old Testament author may be saying is that there will be *representative* believers that hail from *every* tribe and tongue and nation and people, but not that every single person within these nations and peoples and kings will be saved (or even the majority thereof).

The Difference between Postmillennialism and Amillennialism

Many have asked, "How does postmillennialism differ from amillennialism?" I should first point out that prior to the twentieth century "amillennialism" was not a term even in use among Christians. All amillennialists were called postmillennialists. This isn't difficult to understand, insofar as amillennialists also affirm that the second coming of Christ occurs after ("post") the millennial kingdom. All amillennialists also agree that the term itself is of recent origin, although they are insistent that the doctrine to which it points is as ancient as the Church itself. Jack Van Deventer points out that the *International Standard Bible Encyclopedia* (*ISBE*) had no reference for the word amillennialism in its 1915 and 1929/1930 editions. Some have insisted that the term was coined by Abraham Kuyper (d. 1920). Van Deventer believes the earliest use of the label should be attributed to dispensationalist Charles Feinberg in the title to his book, *Premillennialism or Amillennialism,* published in 1936.[20] In any case, the term amillennialism was likely employed to differentiate its view from that of the more optimistic version of postmillennialism.

---

20. Jack Van Deventer, "Amillennial History," http://www.credenda.org/issues/14-2eschaton.php.

Some have jokingly referred to postmillennialism as "*optimistic* amillennialism" or to amillennialism, conversely, as "*pessimistic* postmillennialism"! There is a measure of truth in this, for the critical question is whether or not one conceives of the church age as a time of ever-increasing gospel prosperity. Will Christianity experience both worldwide growth and influence, such that it gradually becomes the rule rather than the exception among the majority of mankind? Amillennialists say No. Postmillennialists say Yes.[21]

Thus what is really at stake is the question of the future prospects for the kingdom of God that is already established on the earth. As far as postmillennialism is concerned, its essential distinctive, its *sine qua non*, is its expectation of gospel prosperity for the Church during the *present* age. Whatever else may be said about it, postmillennialism requires a consistent and confident, biblically grounded assurance that the gospel will be victorious around the globe before the second coming of Christ and the end of the age. Clearly, then, postmillennialists affirm that the Church of Jesus Christ will prosper, in *this* age, both in terms of numerical size and spiritual vitality. Through the gracious power of the Holy Spirit, the vast majority of the human race will be brought to faith in Christ, resulting in worldwide obedience to his kingdom rule. The postmillennial expectation, therefore, is for a Christian world comprised of explicitly Christian nations and peoples.

The Advocates of Postmillennialism

Postmillennialism, according to its modern advocates, was far more widespread in centuries preceding our own. Among those whom they say were postmillennialists include, in no particular order, the following: John Calvin(?) (1509–1564),[22] Theodore Beza (1519–1605),

---

21. Even were an amillennialist to concede this point to his postmillennial friend, he would not need to embrace the entire system, for they might still differ on the nature of the millennium of Rev. 20:1-6, and perhaps as well its location and duration.

22. I have placed a "?" beside the names of those about whom there is still some debate whether they truly and fully embraced postmillennialism. For evidence that points to Calvin's postmillennial leanings, see Gentry, *He Shall Have Dominion*, 102-04.

Peter Martyr Vermigli (1500–1562), Martin Bucer (1491–1551), Thomas Brightman (1562–1607), John Owen (1616–1683), Thomas Boston (1676–1732), William Perkins (1558–1602), William Gouge (1575–1653), Thomas Manton (1620–1677), John Flavel (1627–1691), Stephen Charnock (1628–1680), Richard Sibbes (1577–1635), Samuel Rutherford (1600–1661), Thomas Brooks (1608–1680), Jonathan Edwards (1703–1758), Isaac Watts (1674–1748), Matthew Henry (1662–1714), John Cotton (1585–1652), George Whitefield (1714–1770), Thomas Goodwin (1600–1679), George Gillespie (1613–1649), William Carey (1761–1834), Archibald Alexander (1772–1851), Charles Hodge (1797–1878), Albert Barnes (1798–1870), Richard Trench (1807–1886), Joseph A. Alexander (1809–1860), A.A. Hodge (1823–1886), Robert L. Dabney (1820–1898), William G.T. Shedd (1820–1894), Augustus H. Strong (1836–1921), H.C.G. Moule (1841–1920), Benjamin B. Warfield (1851–1921), O.T. Allis (1880–1973), J. Gresham Machen (1881–1937), James Henley Thornwell (1812–1862), Patrick Fairbairn (1805–1874), Robert Haldane (1764–1842), David Brown (1803–1897), E.W. Hengstenberg (1802–1869), John Murray (1898–1975), Loraine Boettner (1903–1990), J. Marcellus Kik (1903–1965), Greg Bahnsen (1948–1995), David Chilton (1951–1997), Rousas John Rushdoony (1916–2001), and of course those living authors whose works I have cited in this chapter.[23]

Misconceptions of Postmillennialism

Why has postmillennialism received such bad reviews? Why has it, at least in the twenty-first century, been so casually dismissed by most conservative evangelicals? The answer is found in taking note

---

23. Gentry finds in the writings of several early church fathers what he calls "indicators" of "a genuine hope regarding the gospel's victorious historical progress" (*He Shall Have Dominion,* 91). Among these he includes Origen (c. 185–254), Eusebius (c. 260–340), Athanasius (c. 296–372), and Augustine (354–430). He also points to several medieval thinkers such as the Franciscans Peter John Olivi (d. c. 1297) and Abertino de Casale (fl. 1305); the Dominicans Ghehardinus de Burgo (fl. 1254)and Fra Dolcino (fl. 1330); the Beguine Mechthild of Magdeburg (d. 1280); Roman Catholic scholar Arnaldus of Villanova (fl. 1298); and the forerunner of John Huss, Jan Miliciz of Kremsier (fl. 1367).

of several misconceptions and misrepresentations of this school of biblical eschatology.

First, postmillennialism has been mistakenly linked and often identified with belief in the inherent goodness of man. This has occurred despite the fact that the vast majority of postmillennialists today (and perhaps even in the past) are Calvinists. The result is that postmillennialists have been charged with failing to take seriously the biblical pessimism regarding humanity's efforts apart from the sustaining power of divine grace and, as a result, have been accused of saying that the kingdom of God would be ushered in by human effort alone, independently of the Holy Spirit. But not one evangelical postmillennial scholar has ever suggested that the kingdom of God can be advanced by man's efforts apart from God. This sort of misrepresentation must end. What postmillennialists *do* affirm is what they see as the biblical *optimism* regarding man's efforts *through* God.

Second, and related to the above, is the fact that postmillennialism has been mistakenly identified with the notion of evolutionary optimism and other secular notions of historical progress. But the kingdom of God in evangelical postmillennialism is not the product of natural laws of improvement in an ever-upward evolutionary progression, but rather the fruit of the supernatural energy and operation of the Holy Spirit, primarily through the proclamation of the gospel of Jesus Christ.

Third, postmillennialism has been mistakenly identified with theological liberalism and the so-called "social gospel". Thus the kingdom it espoused came to be perceived as some sort of secular utopia that replaced the return of Jesus as the true hope of the church. Iain Murray explains:

> Instead of dependence on divine grace and upon the powerful operations of the Holy Spirit, the new idea of progress substituted concepts of a universal fatherhood of God and of a human race basically good and therefore capable of unlimited improvement. In the same way emphasis was moved from the promises of God as the only basis for the expectation of success to the philosophy of evolution. It is not

therefore surprising that when the new teaching which thus reduced the gospel to the human and temporal became prevalent, evangelical Christians came to suspect all teaching [i.e., postmillennialism] which viewed future history as hopeful. They assumed that any belief in the world-wide success of the gospel must rest on the same errors upon which liberalism relied, and that, just as this naturalistic optimism destroyed faith in eternal salvation by giving Protestantism the false goal of an earthly Utopia, so any outlook which offers an assurance that the victories of the Church will yet be far more extensive in the world must similarly cease to represent Christ's coming as the glorious hope. But these assumptions rested upon a failure to distinguish between two different and indeed inimical schools of thought.[24]

Hope for this earth that is inspired by belief in the power of the Holy Spirit fulfilling the redemptive purposes of God through his church must never be confused with a hope inspired by belief in the power of human legislation, education and moral reform. Not all Christians, though, have been able to distinguish between the two. As Bahnsen points out, "in their zeal to stand against the liberal tide, large numbers of Christians threw the baby out with the bath. In disdain for the evolutionary social gospel, sincere believers were led to reject Christian social concern for an exclusively internal or *other-worldly* religion, and to substitute for the earlier belief in a progressive triumph of Christ's kingdom in the world, a new, *pessimistic* catastrophism with respect to the course of history."[25]

A fourth reason for the misunderstandings that have plagued postmillennialism is the false charge that its advocates teach salvific universalism. Whereas postmillennialists do indeed look forward to a day in which vast numbers shall turn to faith in Jesus Christ, at no time do they expect that all will be converted or that sin will be entirely eliminated prior to the eternal state. Evangelical postmillennialists believe no less fervently than premillennialists

---

24. Iain H. Murray, *The Puritan Hope: A Study in Revival and the Interpretation of Prophecy* (Carlisle: Banner of Truth Trust, 1975), 210.
25. Bahnsen, "The Prima Facie Acceptability of Postmillennialism," 49.

and amillennialists in the doctrine of hell and the irreversible damnation of those who die without Christ.

Fifth, postmillennialists have been accused of being naïve and unrealistic. Appeal is often made to extra-biblical events and historically catastrophic occurrences such as World War I, World War II, the nuclear arms buildup, and the ever-disintegrating moral fabric of Western society, and in our day, especially, the rise of radical Islam and international terrorism. To the minds of many, such facts discredit postmillennialism and confirm the more pessimistic philosophy of history espoused by premillennialism. A number of postmillennialists have labeled this approach to prophecy (and rightly so) as "newspaper exegesis" in which current events (i.e., the Wall Street Journal, Fox News, and USA Today) rather than the Bible itself are studied to determine the future. Needless to say, the decisive factor is not discernible trends in our world or the condition of mankind in general but rather whether or not the Bible, God's inspired Word, foresees the world-wide triumph of the gospel.

John Jefferson Davis reminds us that the postmillennial perspective "provides a forecast for the global and long-term prospects of Christianity, but not for the local, short-term prospects of denominations or churches in the nation." Says Davis:

> It is quite immaterial, then, to an assessment of the postmillennial outlook whether world conditions improve or decline in the short or intermediate term. Christ's kingdom will continue to expand, because the living, risen Christ now is reigning victoriously at the Father's right hand, subduing his foes (1 Cor. 15:25) and empowering the church in its mission (Matt. 28:20). Whatever the immediate course of history might be, the believer's fundamental outlook remains confident and hopeful, because the crucified One now lives and reigns forevermore, the King of kings and Lord of lords (Rev. 19:16). "Hallelujah! For the Lord our God the Almighty reigns" (Rev. 19:6).[26]

---

26. Davis, *Christ's Victorious Kingdom*, 128.

What Davis and other postmillennialists want us to recognize is that their prophetic outlook is more a matter of Christology than of chronology. Their focus is the majesty and authority of the risen and ascended Christ whose power to bring all enemies into subjection to himself is available to the church in its mission today.

Sixth, and finally, postmillennialists have been mistakenly represented as believing that once the tide turns for good, so to speak, all that remains is a progressive increase of righteousness and peace and the utter absence of evil in the world. But all evangelical postmillennialists believe that there yet remains one final outbreak of evil of undetermined length preceding the second coming of Christ. Satan will be released from the restrictions placed upon him (Rev. 20:1-3) and will foment a global rebellion against Christ and his Church (Rev. 20:7-10). There will likely be a final attempt to persecute and oppress the Church on the part of those who participate in this last-gasp effort of the Enemy, but it will be to no avail. Christ will prevail.

Weaknesses of Postmillennialism

There are a number of areas in which postmillennialism appears to fall short. First, postmillennialism appears to minimize one of the primary experiences that will characterize the Church and all Christians throughout this present age, all the way to its end: *suffering with Christ*. Consider, for example, 2 Corinthians 4:7-12. There Paul writes,

> [7]But we have this treasure in jars of clay, to show that the surpassing power belongs to God and not to us. [8]We are afflicted in every way, but not crushed; perplexed, but not driven to despair; [9]persecuted, but not forsaken; struck down, but not destroyed; [10]always carrying in the body the death of Jesus, so that the life of Jesus may also be manifested in our bodies. [11]For we who live are always being given over to death for Jesus' sake, so that the life of Jesus also may be manifested in our mortal flesh. [12]So death is at work in us, but life in you.

As Richard Gaffin has pointed out, here Paul "effectively distances himself from the (postmil-like) view that the (eschatological) life of (the risen and ascended) Jesus embodies a power/victory principle that progressively ameliorates and reduces the suffering of the church.... Until the resurrection of the body at his return Christ's resurrection-life finds expression in the church's sufferings (and ... nowhere else – so far as the existence and calling of the church are concerned); the locus of Christ's ascension-power is the suffering church." [27]

We must also give weight to Paul's portrayal of the universal experience within the scope of the present age. In Romans 8:17-18, he writes that if we are God's children, then we are "heirs – heirs of God and fellow heirs with Christ, provided we suffer with him in order that we may also be glorified with him. For I consider that the sufferings of this present time are not worth comparing with the glory that is to be revealed to us." How long will this experience of suffering with Christ last? How long will the groaning under the weight of weakness last? According to Romans 8:19, 21, 23, it will last until the day of our redemption, the return of Christ. Says Gaffin:

> Until then, at Christ's return, the suffering/futility/decay principle in creation remains in force, undiminished (but sure to be overcome); it is an enervating factor that cuts across the church's existence, including its mission, in its entirety. The notion that this frustration factor will be demonstrably reduced, and the church's suffering service noticeably alleviated and even compensated, in a future era before Christ's return is not merely foreign to this passage; it trivializes as well as blurs both the present suffering and future hope/glory in view. Until his return, the church remains one step behind its exalted Lord; his exaltation means its (privileged) humiliation, his return (and not before), its exaltation. [28]

Furthermore, "as Paul reminds the church just a few verses after the Romans 8 passage considered above (v. 37), *not* 'beyond' or

---

27. Richard Gaffin, "Theonomy and Eschatology: Reflections on Postmillennialism," in *Theonomy: A Reformed Critique* (Zondervan, 1990), 212.
28. Ibid., 214-15.

'[only] after' but '*in* all these things' ('trouble or hardship or persecution or famine or nakedness or danger or sword,' v. 35), 'we are more than conquerors.' Until Jesus comes again, the church 'wins' by 'losing.'" [29] Gaffin concludes:

> Any outlook that tends to remove or obscure the (constitutive) dimension of suffering for the Gospel from the present *triumph* of the church is an illusion. The misplaced expectation, before Christ's return, of a "golden age" in which, in contrast to the present, opposition to the church will have been reduced to a minimum and suffering will have receded to the periphery for an (at last) "victorious" Christendom – that misconception can only distort the church's understanding of its mission in the world. According to Jesus, the church will not have drained the shared cup of his suffering until he returns. The church cannot afford to evade that point. It does so at the risk of jeopardizing its own identity. [30]

Kenneth Gentry responds to Gaffin by insisting that the "suffering" in view in these texts need not be generalized beyond the experience of the apostles and the first-century Church. He does not argue that suffering connected with indwelling sin and creaturely mortality will be eradicated, but he does insist that, as external opposition to the gospel progressively diminishes, suffering for the faith (i.e., persecution) will be reduced to negligible proportions.

Another problem with postmillennialism is that it appears to undermine the New Testament emphasis on the Church's imminent expectation of Christ's return. That is to say, postmillennial-

---

29. Ibid., 216.
30. Ibid., 217-18. Samuel Waldron likewise faults postmillennialism for failing to recognize that "this age will always be morally evil" (*The End Times Made Simple: How Could Everyone be so Wrong about Biblical Prophecy* [Calvary Press, 2003], 46). Passages such as Luke 16:8, Mark 10:30, Rom. 12:2, 2 Cor. 4:4, Gal. 1:4, and Eph. 2:2 portray this present age as one in which evil persists and persecution intensifies. Therefore "we must not look for a golden age before Christ's return.... But we must not be 'pessimillennialists' either and see nothing but apostasy for the visible church" (52).

ism undermines the element of *watchfulness* that is essential to the New Testament Church.[31]

Related to this point is something Vern Poythress has brought to our attention. "Most postmillennialists," says Poythress, "appear to me not merely to have this gospel optimism, but to claim that the Second Coming of Christ cannot take place just yet, because we have not yet seen a sufficiently broad and deep triumph of Christianity worldwide. But I find no way to quantify what sort of victory there must be before the Second Coming. I therefore call myself a 'nonquantitative postmillennialist.' 'Postmillennialist' indicates my appreciation for optimism about the gospel. 'Nonquantitative' indicates that I do not find grounds for postponing the Second Coming. In fact, the Achilles' heel of postmillennialism lies precisely here. The first century church had a keen expectation for the Second Coming, an expectation encouraged by the Apostles. Postmillennialism, when it becomes quantitative, finds it almost impossible in practice to maintain such fervency, because it shifts its practical focus to the prospect of millennial prosperity rather than the Second Coming."[32]

Amillennialists in particular are also quick to point out that, contrary to postmillennialism, the Old Testament identifies the "golden" age of consummate success and triumph with the new heavens and new earth which come only *after the millennium* of Revelation 20 (Rev. 21-22), and thus cannot be identified with it.

I should also mention that the New Testament seems to anticipate that the number of those saved when Christ returns will not be as great as the postmillennialist suggests, and that conditions will be decidedly bad, not good (see Matt. 7:13-14; Luke 18:8; 2 Thess. 2:3-4; 2 Tim. 3:1-5,12-13; 4:3-4). In the parable of the tares in Matthew 13:36-43 "Jesus taught that evil people will continue to exist alongside of God's redeemed people until the time of harvest.

---

31. See especially 1 Cor. 16:22; Rom. 13:11-12; Phil. 4:5; James 5:8; 1 Pet. 4:7; 1 John 2:18; Rev. 1:3; 22:20

32. Vern Sheridan Poythress, "Currents within Amillennialism," *Presbyterion* 26/1 (2000): 21-25.

The clear implication of this parable is that Satan's kingdom, if we may call it that, will continue to exist and grow as long as God's kingdom grows, until Christ comes again."[33] Matthew 7:13-14 is often cited to prove that the ultimate number of those saved will be comparatively small. Postmillennialists respond by pointing out that Jesus was simply describing the state of affairs as it then existed, in his own day, over the course of his earthly ministry. The passage "does not address the question of how many people will *ultimately* accept or reject Christ."[34] In other words, "nothing in the passage indicates that it is describing a permanent state of affairs."[35]

The postmillennial interpretation of Revelation 19–20 also seems forced and artificial. I refer you to my attempt to make sense of that text in the two chapters that address amillennialism and Revelation 20.

Finally, Scripture (especially the New Testament) nowhere explicitly teaches the progressive and eventual wholesale reconstruction of society (arts, economics, politics, courts, education, etc.) according to Christian principles prior to Christ's return. Of course, there may be relative success in this regard in isolated instances. But whereas this may be a significant shortcoming of that version of postmillennialism known as *Theonomy* or *Christian Reconstruction,* it bears little if any connection to the more classical version which focuses on the increasing spiritual success of the gospel in saving the majority of mankind.

I *want* to believe that postmillennialism is true. The notion of a progressive and ultimate triumph of the gospel within history itself such that when Jesus returns he finds a truly Christianized cosmos is profoundly appealing. But as of the publication of this book, I am not yet convinced. I remain an amillennialist.

---

33. Anthony A. Hoekema, *The Bible and the Future* (Grand Rapids: Eerdmans, 1979), 180.

34. Mathison, *Postmillennialism*, 209.

35. Ibid. Douglas Wilson agrees: "When Jesus said that the way was narrow, and that only few would find it, He was speaking specifically about first century Judaism. From that body of people, only a remnant was saved, and then the Gentiles poured in" (*Heaven Misplaced,* 79).

Addendum: The Global Growth of Christianity

Before we too quickly dismiss the expectations of postmillennialism, we should take note of the "State of the Faith," so to speak, in 2011. In his book, *The Triumph of Christianity,* Rodney Stark explains the remarkable growth of the Christian Church in the first 300 years of its existence. He estimates that by the year 350 there were nearly 32 million Christians, comprising approximately 53% of the entire population of the Roman Empire. In 2011 Christianity is by far and away the largest religion in the world, with more than 2.1 billion adherents (this constitutes approximately 41% of the population). Muslims are a distant second with 1.4 billion (27% of the population). He points out that "Christianity is not only the largest religion in the world, it also is the least regionalized. There are only trivial numbers of Muslims in the Western Hemisphere and in Eastern Asia, but there is no region without significant numbers of Christians – even in the Arab region of North Africa and the Middle East, 4 per cent of the population are Christians."[36]

These numbers, however, do not include China, where calculating the size of the Christian Church is extremely difficult. Estimates range anywhere from the low end of 16 million (these are Christian groups officially registered under the terms of the Three Self Patriotic Movement) to the high end of 200 million (given the fact that there are tens of thousands of Chinese house churches that are not recognized by the government and not registered with TSPM). After conducting careful research, Stark says that "it seems entirely credible to estimate that there are about 70 million Chinese Christians in 2011."[37]

When one steps back to consider the staggering growth evident in the global Christian Church, it should give us pause before we too quickly dismiss the postmillennial vision as one of naïve optimism. Of course, the numbers may decrease and those of other

---

36. Rodney Stark, *The Triumph of Christianity: How the Jesus Movement became the World's Largest Religion* (New York: HarperOne, 2011), 392.
37. Ibid., 407.

religions (or perhaps among secularists) may increase. And yes, one may wish to question the legitimacy of many professions of faith among the 40%, especially since this includes not only Protestants but also both Roman Catholics and those of Orthodox conviction. But given that the Christian faith began with a mere 120+ on the Day of Pentecost, the growth is undeniably staggering.

Chapter Thirteen

The Book of Revelation and Biblical Eschatology:

The Chronology of the Seal, Trumpet, and Bowl Judgments

The book of Revelation is believed by most to be the key to biblical eschatology. My aim here, however, is not to examine the entire book in any measure of detail. That would require a volume (perhaps several!) unto itself. What I propose to do, instead, is focus entirely on the seal, trumpet, and bowl judgments that it describes. The way in which these are understood, and in particular the way in which they relate to each other (whether sequential, parallel, or in some other manner) will go a long way in helping us understand the purpose of God in redemptive history. What I hope to demonstrate is that they do not portray what will occur in a seven-year, so-called period of "Great Tribulation" in the future, but describe the judgments of God against an unbelieving world throughout the course of the entire church age. They are, in a manner of speaking, the *commonplaces of human history*. So let's begin by looking at the actual texts of these three sets of divine judgments.

The Text of the Seven Seals, Trumpets, and Bowls[1]

First Seal – 6:1-2 ¹Then I saw when the Lamb broke one of the seven seals, and I heard one of the four living creatures saying as with a voice of thunder, "Come." ²And I looked, and behold, a white horse, and he who sat on it had a bow; and a crown was given to him; and he went out conquering, and to conquer.

First Trumpet – 8:6-7 ⁶And the seven angels who had the seven trumpets prepared themselves to sound them. ⁷The first sounded, and there came hail and fire, mixed with blood, and they were thrown to the earth; and a third of the earth was burned up, and a third of the trees were burned up, and all the green grass was burned up.

First Bowl – 16:1-2 ¹And I heard a loud voice from the temple, saying to the seven angels, "Go and pour out the seven bowls of the wrath of God into the earth." ²And the first *angel* went and poured out his bowl into the earth; and it became a loathsome and malignant sore upon the men who had the mark of the beast and who worshiped his image.

Second Seal – 6:3-4 ³And when He broke the second seal, I heard the second living creature saying, "Come." ⁴And another, a red horse, went out; and to him who sat on it, it was granted to take peace from the earth, and that *men* should slay one another; and a great sword was given to him.

Second Trumpet – 8:8-9 ⁸And the second angel sounded, and *something* like a great mountain burning with fire was thrown into the sea; and a third of the sea became blood; ⁹and a third of the creatures, which were in the sea and had life, died; and a third of the ships were destroyed.

---

1. The translation used for the seal, trumpet, and bowl judgments is that of the New American Standard Bible.

Second Bowl – 16:3 ³And the second *angel* poured out his bowl into the sea, and it became blood like *that* of a dead man; and every living thing in the sea died.

Third Seal – 6:5-6 ⁵And when He broke the third seal, I heard the third living creature saying, "Come." And I looked, and behold, a black horse; and he who sat on it had a pair of scales in his hand. ⁶And I heard as it were a voice in the center of the four living creatures saying, "A quart of wheat for a denarius, and three quarts of barley for a denarius; and do not harm the oil and the wine."

Third Trumpet – 8:10-11 ¹⁰And the third angel sounded, and a great star fell from heaven, burning like a torch, and it fell on a third of the rivers and on the springs of waters; ¹¹and the name of the star is called Wormwood; and a third of the waters became wormwood; and many men died from the waters, because they were made bitter.

Third Bowl – 16:4-7 ⁴And the third *angel* poured out his bowl into the rivers and the springs of waters; and they became blood. ⁵And I heard the angel of the waters saying, "Righteous art Thou, who art and who wast, O Holy One, because Thou didst judge these things; ⁶for they poured out the blood of saints and prophets, and Thou hast given them blood to drink. They deserve it." ⁷And I heard the altar saying, "Yes, O Lord God, the Almighty, true and righteous are Thy judgments."

Fourth Seal – 6:7-8 ⁷And when He broke the fourth seal, I heard the voice of the fourth living creature saying, "Come." ⁸And I looked, and behold, an ashen horse; and he who sat on it had the name Death; and Hades was following with him. And authority was given to them over a fourth of the earth, to kill with sword and with famine and with pestilence and by the wild beasts of the earth.

Fourth Trumpet – 8:12-13 [12]And the fourth angel sounded, and a third of the sun and a third of the moon and a third of the stars were smitten, so that a third of them might be darkened and the day might not shine for a third of it, and the night in the same way. [13]And I looked, and I heard an eagle flying in midheaven, saying with a loud voice, "Woe, woe, woe, to those who dwell on the earth, because of the remaining blasts of the trumpet of the three angels who are about to sound!"

Fourth Bowl – 16:8-9 [8]And the fourth *angel* poured out his bowl upon the sun; and it was given to it to scorch men with fire. [9]And men were scorched with fierce heat; and they blasphemed the name of God who has the power over these plagues; and they did not repent, so as to give Him glory.

Fifth Seal – 6:9-11 [9]And when He broke the fifth seal, I saw underneath the altar the souls of those who had been slain because of the word of God, and because of the testimony which they had maintained; [10]and they cried out with a loud voice, saying, "How long, O Lord, holy and true, wilt Thou refrain from judging and avenging our blood on those who dwell on the earth?" [11]And there was given to each of them a white robe; and they were told that they should rest for a little while longer, until *the number of* their fellow servants and their brethren who were to be killed even as they had been, should be completed also.

Fifth Trumpet – 9:1-12 [1]And the fifth angel sounded, and I saw a star from heaven which had fallen to the earth; and the key of the bottomless pit was given to him. [2]And he opened the bottomless pit; and smoke went up out of the pit, like the smoke of a great furnace; and the sun and the air were darkened by the smoke of the pit. [3]And out of the smoke came forth locusts upon the earth; and power was given them, as the scorpions of the earth have power. [4]And they were told that they should not hurt the grass of the earth, nor any green ... *(cont. on next page)*

Fifth Trumpet – *cont.*

thing, nor any tree, but only the men who do not have the seal of God on their foreheads. [5]And they were not permitted to kill anyone, but to torment for five months; and their torment was like the torment of a scorpion when it stings a man. [6]And in those days men will seek death and will not find it; and they will long to die and death flees from them. [7]And the appearance of the locusts was like horses prepared for battle; and on their heads, as it were, crowns like gold, and their faces were like the faces of men. [8]And they had hair like the hair of women, and their teeth were like *the teeth* of lions. [9]And they had breastplates like breastplates of iron; and the sound of their wings was like the sound of chariots, of many horses rushing to battle. [10]And they have tails like scorpions, and stings; and in their tails is their power to hurt men for five months. [11]They have as king over them, the angel of the abyss; his name in Hebrew is Abaddon, and in the Greek he has the name Apollyon. [12]The first woe is past; behold, two woes are still coming after these things.

Fifth Bowl – 16:10-11 [10]And the fifth *angel* poured out his bowl upon the throne of the beast; and his kingdom became darkened; and they gnawed their tongues because of pain, [11]and they blasphemed the God of heaven because of their pains and their sores; and they did not repent of their deeds.

Sixth Seal – 6:12-17 [12]And I looked when He broke the sixth seal, and there was a great earthquake; and the sun became black as sackcloth *made* of hair, and the whole moon became like blood; [13]and the stars of the sky fell to the earth, as a fig tree casts its unripe figs when shaken by a great wind. [14]And the sky was split apart like a scroll when it is rolled up; and every mountain and island were moved out of their places. [15]And the kings of the earth and the great men and the commanders and the rich and the strong and every slave and free man, hid themselves in the caves and among the rocks of the ... *(cont. on next page)*

Sixth Seal – *cont.*

mountains; [16]and they said to the mountains and to the rocks, "Fall on us and hide us from the presence of Him who sits on the throne, and from the wrath of the Lamb; [17]for the great day of their wrath has come; and who is able to stand?"

Sixth Trumpet – 9:13-21 [13]And the sixth angel sounded, and I heard a voice from the four horns of the golden altar which is before God, [14]one saying to the sixth angel who had the trumpet, "Release the four angels who are bound at the great river Euphrates." [15]And the four angels, who had been prepared for the hour and day and month and year, were released, so that they might kill a third of mankind. [16]And the number of the armies of the horsemen was two hundred million; I heard the number of them. [17]And this is how I saw in the vision the horses and those who sat on them: *the riders* had breastplates *the color* of fire and of hyacinth and of brimstone; and the heads of the horses are like the heads of lions; and out of their mouths proceed fire and smoke and brimstone. [18]A third of mankind was killed by these three plagues, by the fire and the smoke and the brimstone, which proceeded out of their mouths. [19]For the power of the horses is in their mouths and in their tails; for their tails are like serpents and have heads; and with them they do harm. [20]And the rest of mankind, who were not killed by these plagues, did not repent of the works of their hands, so as not to worship demons, and the idols of gold and of silver and of brass and of stone and of wood, which can neither see nor hear nor walk; [21]and they did not repent of their murders nor of their sorceries nor of their immorality nor of their thefts.

Sixth Bowl – 16:12-16 [12]And the sixth *angel* poured out his bowl upon the great river, the Euphrates; and its water was dried up, that the way might be prepared for the kings from the east. [13]And I saw *coming* out of the mouth of the dragon and out of the mouth of the beast and out of the mouth ... *(cont. on next page)*

Sixth Bowl – *cont.*
of the false prophet, three unclean spirits like frogs; [14]for they are spirits of demons, performing signs, which go out to the kings of the whole world, to gather them together for the war of the great day of God, the Almighty. [15]("Behold, I am coming like a thief. Blessed is the one who stays awake and keeps his garments, lest he walk about naked and men see his shame.") [16]And they gathered them together to the place which in Hebrew is called Har-Magedon.

Seventh Seal – 8:1-5 [1]And when He broke the seventh seal, there was silence in heaven for about half an hour. [2]And I saw the seven angels who stand before God; and seven trumpets were given to them. [3]And another angel came and stood at the altar, holding a golden censer; and much incense was given to him, that he might add it to the prayers of all the saints upon the golden altar which was before the throne. [4]And the smoke of the incense, with the prayers of the saints, went up before God out of the angel's hand. [5]And the angel took the censer; and he filled it with the fire of the altar and threw it to the earth; and there followed peals of thunder and sounds and flashes of lightning and an earthquake.

Seventh Trumpet – 11:14-19 [14]The second woe is past; behold, the third woe is coming quickly. [15]And the seventh angel sounded; and there arose loud voices in heaven, saying, "The kingdom of the world has become *the kingdom* of our Lord, and of His Christ; and He will reign forever and ever." [16]And the twenty-four elders, who sit on their thrones before God, fell on their faces and worshiped God, [17]saying, "We give Thee thanks, O Lord God, the Almighty, who art and who wast, because Thou hast taken Thy great power and hast begun to reign. [18]"And the nations were enraged, and Thy wrath came, and the time *came* for the dead to be judged, and *the time* to give their reward to Thy bond-servants the prophets and to the ... *(cont. on next page)*

> **Seventh Trumpet** – *cont.*
> saints and to those who fear Thy name, the small and the great, and to destroy those who destroy the earth." [19]And the temple of God which is in heaven was opened; and the ark of His covenant appeared in His temple, and there were flashes of lightning and sounds and peals of thunder and an earthquake and a great hailstorm.

> **Seventh Bowl** – 16:17-21 [17]And the seventh *angel* poured out his bowl upon the air; and a loud voice came out of the temple from the throne, saying, "It is done." [18]And there were flashes of lightning and sounds and peals of thunder; and there was a great earthquake, such as there had not been since man came to be upon the earth, so great an earthquake *was it, and* so mighty. [19]And the great city was split into three parts, and the cities of the nations fell. And Babylon the great was remembered before God, to give her the cup of the wine of His fierce wrath. [20]And every island fled away, and the mountains were not found. [21]And huge hailstones, about one hundred pounds each, came down from heaven upon men; and men blasphemed God because of the plague of the hail, because its plague was extremely severe.

The Chronology of the Seals, Trumpets, and Bowls

The various attempts to understand the relation between the seals, trumpets, and bowls have issued in five general schemes, within which are a number of additional variations. These major structural arrangements are as follows.

1. Literary / non-chronological

This scheme denies that there is any strict chronological relationship among the seals, trumpets, and bowls. There is, however, a literary sequence or development used by John. In other words, the seven trumpets are an expansion of and follow the seventh seal; the seven bowls, after some intervening visions, follow the seventh trumpet. Although recognizing such progression, we are not to understand it as setting forth the historical or temporal sequence of their occurrence. John is not saying that first come the seven seals and then the seven trumpets and then the seven bowls, as if they followed one another in strict order (twenty-one separate and distinct events beginning with one and ending with twenty-one). Nor is John suggesting that they are in any sense systematically parallel. He is, rather, writing in what has been called "the exalted idiom of an ecstatic experience." [2] That the latter is true we do not deny, but that the seals, trumpets, and bowls display some kind of developed pattern is equally difficult to deny (see below).

2. Strict Sequentialism

According to this view the seals, trumpets, and bowls follow one another in a strict historical, temporal sequence. In other words, they do not in any sense overlap or parallel each other, thus resulting in twenty-one distinct historical events following in numerical order. This scheme may be illustrated as follows:

Seals <u>1 2 3 4 5 6 7</u>

    Trumpets <u>1 2 3 4 5 6 7</u>

        Bowls <u>1 2 3 4 5 6 7</u>

Or possibly even as follows:

    Seals   Trumpets   Bowls

<u>1 2 3 4 5 6 7 1 2 3 4 5 6 7 1 2 3 4 5 6 7</u>

Most futurists hold this view and argue that the first seal, which inaugurates the sequence of twenty-one judgments, begins immediately following the pretribulational rapture of the church. Thus, according to the futurist, all twenty-one judgments occur within that period immediately prior to the second coming known as the great tribulation (generally believed by most futurists to be seven years in length). The futurist believes that all of the visions from Revelation 4:1 to the end of the book are yet to be fulfilled in the period immediately preceding and following the second coming of Christ.

---

2. Robert Mounce, *The Book of Revelation* (Grand Rapids: Eerdmans, 1977) 184.

3. Strict Parallelism

According to this view, the seals, trumpets, and bowls are numerically and historically parallel. Since all three series come to the same final conclusion (climactic judgment, the second coming, the establishing of the kingdom of God), they ought to be viewed as parallel, giving differing aspects of the same process rather than temporally successive stages of it. Merrill Tenney[3] and William Hendriksen[4] hold to this. However, Tenney places the seals, trumpets, and bowls in the days of the great tribulation whereas Hendriksen sees them as describing what occurs during the entire inter-advent age, i.e., the period from the first coming of Christ to the second. This view (whether that of Tenney or Hendriksen) may be illustrated as follows:

Seals	1 2 3 4 5 6 7
	SECOND
Trumpets	1 2 3 4 5 6 7
	ADVENT
Bowls	1 2 3 4 5 6 7

The strength of this view is that it recognizes the obvious similarities between some of the events in each series. This is especially true of the trumpets and bowls which are amazingly similar. Its weaknesses, however, will be noted below. An accurate understanding of their relationship must give equal weight to their dissimilarities as well.

4. Sequential / Parallel

This view understands the seals, trumpets, and bowls to be essentially sequential but with certain elements of parallelism. There are a number of variations within this structural scheme and each is worthy of consideration. But first, what are the reasons that lead people to believe that the basic relationship is sequential?

---

3. Merrill C. Tenney, *Interpreting Revelation* (Grand Rapids: Eerdmans, 1958), 41.
4. William Hendriksen, *More Than Conquerors: An Interpretation of the Book of Revelation* (Grand Rapids: Baker Book House, 1977), 22-31.

The *prima facie* reading of the text seems to suggest that the series are sequential. We read of seven seals which are then followed by seven trumpets which are again followed by seven bowls, the latter called the "last plagues" in which "the wrath of God is finished" (15:1). There is also an increase in the intensity of the judgments which is easily explained if they are sequential (rather than simultaneous). Each series appears to raise the crescendo of divine judgment to a higher pitch, and some form of sequence would seem to explain this. Finally, it is difficult to explain the dissimilarities between the seals, on the one hand, and the trumpets and bowls, on the other, except under the sequential view. It would appear, however, that a strict sequentialism is unlikely. Thus, several alternatives have been suggested which seek to combine both elements of sequence and parallelism.

a. Here is the first suggested scheme:

Seals 1 2 3 4 5 6 /   7 /

        Trumpets / 1 2 3 4 5 6 / 7   /

                        Bowls 1234567 /

According to this view, the sixth seal brings us to the threshold of the second coming. The contents of the seventh seal **are** the seven trumpets and the contents of the seventh trumpet **are** the seven bowls. The problem here is that this view must assume that the seventh seal has no content of its own other than the seven trumpets. But a close examination of Revelation 8:1-5 indicates that the seventh seal does indeed have content. Also, there is no reason to believe that the contents of the seventh trumpet are the seven bowls, for Revelation 11:15-19 clearly ascribes much content to the seventh trumpet and the bowls do not appear until 16:2. Finally, this scheme fails to recognize the undeniable similarities between the trumpets and bowls.

b. Another scheme which includes both the basic sequence pattern and an element of parallelism is as follows:

Seals 1   2   3   4   5   6   7

Trumpets 1 2 3 4 5 6 7

Bowls 1 2 3 4 5 6 7

This is Robert Gundry's[5] position and is preferable to the preceding scheme in that the sixth seal is shown to bring us to the very threshold of the end with the seventh seal, seventh trumpet, and seventh bowl all at the consummation. But this view also suffers from a failure to deal with the trumpet / bowl similarities.

c. A third alternative in which elements of both sequence and parallelism are found has much to commend itself. The basic sequential element is retained, insofar as the seals are followed by the trumpets and the bowls. The parallelism is found with respect to the latter two series.

According to this view, *the seven seal judgments describe what will transpire throughout the entire course of the present church age.* They are descriptive of the forces and events that have been, now are, and will be operative between the two comings of Christ. They are not restricted to the final few years before Christ's coming, but the seventh seal itself does in fact bring us to the second advent of our Lord. On the other hand, *the seven trumpet and seven bowl judgments are together clustered at the close of human history.* They overlap somewhat with the last two or three seal judgments, but are particularly applicable to the final few years preceding Christ's return. Thus the first five seals describe events which are to be operative during the whole of the present Christian dispensation (although the fifth seal may bring us into the final days of history). The sixth seal brings us to the very threshold of the end, being a general descriptive overview of what will occur immediately prior to the parousia (second advent). Then the seventh seal is broken.

---

5. Robert H. Gundry, *The Church and the Tribulation* (Grand Rapids: Zondervan, 1973), 74-77.

Thus the sixth and seventh seals bring us to the end of the age (sixth seal) and to the second advent itself (seventh seal). With the opening of the seventh seal we also have the opening of the book and the outpouring of its contents, namely, the seven trumpets and the seven bowls, both of which describe judgments that are clustered at the end immediately prior to and possibly somewhat simultaneous with the second advent of Christ.

This view emphasizes the fact that the seals must first be removed or broken before the book/scroll (of Revelation 5) can be opened. The breaking of each of the seals does not point to the progressive opening of part of the book, chapter by chapter, as it were. Rather, all the seals are preliminary to opening the book. This seems right since the seals are on the book to prevent it from being opened and to protect its contents. The book contains the prophecies of the end of the age, "but the end is not a single event but consists of a whole complex of events. It includes the outpouring of God's wrath upon a rebellious civilization, the judgment of the Antichrist and the destruction of his hosts, as well as the resurrection of the dead and the establishment of the Kingdom of God. So we may conclude that the sixth seal brings us to the threshold of the end; and then John stands back, as it were, to tell the story of the end in greater detail. The breaking of the seventh seal opens the book and begins the story of the events of the end time; this is the substance of the remainder of the Revelation."[6] In other words, *the contents of the book are the seven trumpets and seven bowls.*

This particular scheme may thus be portrayed:

1st Coming of Christ				2nd Coming of Christ		

Seals	1	2	3	4	5	6	7
Trumpets		1	2	3	4	5	6	7
Bowls		1	2	3	4	5	6	7

---

6. George E. Ladd, *A Commentary on the Revelation of John* (Grand Rapids: Eerdmans, 1972), 109.

5. *Progressive Parallelism / Recapitulation*

This last view is essentially the same as the immediately preceding one, with one major exception. This view contends that the trumpet and bowl judgments are, like the seals, descriptive of events throughout the course of history between the two advents of Jesus. The question may be asked, "How does this view differ from that of William Hendriksen (option 3) cited above?" The only significant difference is that this view recognizes that the trumpets and bowls bear a similarity with each other much deeper than with the seals. Indeed, in the vision of the trumpets John sees the preliminary, introductory aspect of a judgment, of which the corresponding bowl is the intensified and consummate expression. Thus the trumpets and bowls are essentially two sides of the same coin (of judgment). The trumpet judgment is, relatively speaking, the initial, moderate outpouring of divine wrath, whereas the bowl judgment is the final, full outpouring of wrath. This alone adequately accounts for the rising crescendo of intensity as one moves from the trumpets to the bowls.

A closer look at the trumpet and bowl judgments will reveal their inescapable similarities. The only place where this is less than explicit is with the first in each series. But even then, there is similarity of language.

(1) **With the first trumpet** there is hail and fire mixed with blood thrown to *the earth*; ⅓ of the earth, trees, grass burned (⅓ denoting the initial, partial judgment of the trumpet). **With the first bowl** *the earth* and its inhabitants are afflicted with sores.

(2) **With the second trumpet** ⅓ of *the sea* becomes *blood* and ⅓ of everything in it dies (again, note the partial extent of the judgment). **With the second bowl** *the sea* again becomes *blood*, but now everything dies (indicating the full and final expression of this judgment).

(3) **With the third trumpet** only ⅓ of *the rivers, springs, and waters* become bitter and many *people die* from drinking them. **With the third bowl** there is no limitation placed on how much of *the rivers, springs, and waters* are affected. Once again, many *people die* from drinking.

(4) **With the fourth trumpet** ⅓ of *the sun, moon, and stars* are smitten and there is darkness (again, a partial judgment). **With the fourth bowl** again *the sun* is the focal point, but instead of bringing darkness a worse judgment is inflicted: they are scorched.

(5) **With the fifth trumpet** *unbelievers are tormented* by locusts for five months (again, a specific, limited duration; hence, a partial judgment) and are in such pain that they long to die. **With the fifth bowl** *unbelievers are tormented* and their pain is so bad that they gnaw their tongues and blaspheme God. Note also that in the fifth trumpet the *king* over the locusts is Satan. In the fifth bowl the *throne and kingdom* of the beast are mentioned (described this way because in Rev. 13:2 Satan is said to have given the beast his *throne*).

(6) **With the sixth trumpet** four angels who are bound at *the great river Euphrates* are released and ⅓ of mankind is killed (again, partial judgment). *Three demonic plagues* that are associated with a huge *army prepared for battle* are responsible for killing them. **With the sixth bowl** *the great river Euphrates* is dried up and *three demonic spirits* gather the people for the final *battle*, Armageddon.

(7) **With the seventh trumpet** we have reached the *consummation*. There *are loud voices* in heaven speaking. There is *lightning, sounds, and peals of thunder*. The *temple* of God is mentioned, as is the *throne*. Divine *wrath* comes upon unbelievers. There is an *earthquake* and a *hailstorm* (partial judgments). **With the seventh bowl** we have again reached the *consummation* ("It is done," 16:17). There is a *loud voice* from heaven speaking. There are *lightning, sounds, and peals of thunder*. The *temple* of God is mentioned, as is the *throne*. Divine *wrath* again comes upon unbelievers. There is *an incomparably great earthquake* and a *hailstorm with 100 pound hailstones* (intensified, consummate judgments).

Once again, it would appear that what we see in the relationship of the trumpets to the bowls are two successive stages to the same judgments: one introductory and partial, the other consummative and complete. Perhaps, then, we could portray the seals, trumpets, and bowls in this way:

	1st Coming of Christ					2nd Coming of Christ	
Seals	1	2	3	4	5	6	7
Trumpets	1	2	3	4	5	6	7
Bowls	1	2	3	4	5	6	7

All three series of seven judgments (seals, trumpets, bowls) portray events and phenomena that occur repeatedly throughout the course of history between the first and second comings of Christ. All three series of seven judgments bring us to the consummation at the close of human history where we see the final judgment of unbelievers, the salvation and vindication of God's people, and the full manifestation of the kingdom of Christ.

I'm not suggesting, as have some, that the seven seals, seven trumpets, and seven bowls themselves, or at least the first six in each series, occur sequentially in history, as if the second in each series can't occur until after the first, and the third can't occur until after the second, and so on. According to my understanding of the text in Revelation, all (or at least the first six) of the seal, trumpet, and bowl judgments are released by the sovereign Christ at the beginning of the present inter-advent age. *These judgments and plagues are thus descriptive of the commonplaces of human history, i.e., they can and do occur at any and all times throughout the course of the present age and do not necessarily sustain a temporal relationship to each other.*

It is only with the seventh in each series (and perhaps with the sixth trumpet and bowl) that we are assuredly at the close of history. I previously argued that it would be best to interpret the bowls as indicating that these judgments will progressively increase in their intensity and extent and that divine longsuffering and delay will eventually yield to final and consummative wrath. Upon further reflection, I do *not* think the contrast between the partial trumpet judgments and the complete bowl judgments is to be taken as indicating that the trumpets must *first* be sounded, bringing limited judgment, *then* to be followed by the outpouring of the bowls, which bring universal judgment. For this would be to say that there is a historical or chronological sequence between the trumpets and bowls, something I do not believe.

I now believe that the trumpet and bowl judgments are not only literarily and thematically parallel, but also ***temporally parallel***. The fact that the trumpet judgments are partial and the bowl judgments are complete simply indicates that *what can occur in a limited or partial manner at any point in history between the two advents of Christ, can also occur, at any point in history between the two advents of Christ, in a universal or more thorough-going manner. The effect or impact of these plagues of judgment on the unbelieving world is at one time and in one place restricted, while at another time in another place, widespread.* Thus, here is my interpretive scheme:

1st Coming   2nd Coming
of Christ   of Christ

Seals
Trumpets
Bowls

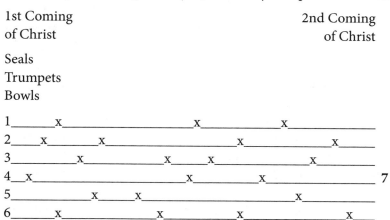

Clearly, this interpretive scheme is based on the belief that Revelation presents us with a description of principles and events that transpire throughout the entire course of church history, between the two advents of Jesus. In other words, contrary to the futurist interpretation, Revelation is not concerned merely with events at the close of history, immediately preceding the second coming of Christ. Rather, there are multiple sections in the book, each of which recapitulates the other, that is to say, each of which begins with the first coming of Christ and concludes with the second coming of Christ and the end of history. Each of these sections provides a series of progressively parallel visions that increase in their scope and intensity as they draw nearer to the consummation. This is what is called the principle of *recapitulation*. Let me make several comments in this regard.

First, an objection often raised by the futurist to the concept of progressive parallelism or recapitulation is the fact that John repeatedly moves from one vision to the next by using a phrase such as "after this," or "after these things," or "and I saw." The futurist contends that this indicates John is writing down the temporal sequence in which the visions occur in history, which is to say, one right after another. But these phrases need only indicate *the sequence in which John **saw** the visions*. In other words, those phrases that serve to connect or link one vision with another are *literary* in nature, not historical. They tell us that John first saw vision "A" *and then* saw vision "B" and *after that* saw vision "C," but not necessarily that the events in vision "A" *occur* before those in vision "B" or that the events of vision "C" *occur* after those of vision "B."

Second, a good example of this is in the relationship between Revelation 6 and 7. In 7:1 John says "After this I saw . . ." He then relates the commandment given to the four angels, "Do not harm the earth or the sea or the trees" (7:3). Yet, chapter 6 describes what is surely a massive harming of the earth. Thus, chapter 7 may follow chapter 6 *in John's visions*, but it does not seem to follow it in the order of actual events.

Third, another example is found by comparing the sixth seal (6:12-13) with the fourth trumpet. Most futurists interpret the book "literally." Thus they believe that in the sixth seal the sun, moon, and stars cease to shine. But in the fourth trumpet they are said to be diminished in their light by only ⅓. It seems, then, that whereas the *vision* of the trumpets follows the *vision* of the seals, they do not sustain a chronological relationship to each other.

Fourth, it was noted above that the trumpets and bowls are clearly parallel to each other. But there are also similarities in structure between the seals and trumpets which may contribute to the possibility that they, too, are parallel. Observe that both the seal and trumpet judgments have a **four + three structure**. The first four seal judgments are clearly a set (the four horsemen) as are the first four trumpets (insofar as the last three trumpets are set apart and called the "three woes" – 8:13; 9:12). There is also a **four + three structure** in the bowl judgments, although not as explicit as in the seals and trumpets. Notice that the first four bowls apply to the same four divisions of creation (earth, sea, fresh waters, heavens) as did the first four trumpets. The last three bowls pertain to judgment of the beast and his kingdom.

Fifth, one should also note that both the seals and trumpets share another structural feature that may be described as **six + parenthesis/ delay + one**. The first six seals bring us to a point at which we expect final and consummate judgment. But the narrative is then interrupted, so to speak, with a parenthetical description of the 144,000 and the innumerable multitude. In other words, there is a noticeable *delay* in judgment as John addresses the experience of God's people in the midst of judgment. So, too, with the trumpets. The first six again bring us to the brink of consummation. There is then, again, a parenthetical insertion (10:1–11:14), that would appear, again, to point to *delay* in judgment. Here, too, the subject of the parenthesis is the experience of God's people. But when we come to the seven bowls there is *no delay*. "This series moves with unimpeded rapidity to the seventh and final judgment."[7] The time for patience and long-suffering is over. Men have shown themselves unwilling to repent. Judgment thus comes swiftly and without mercy. Richard Bauckham sums up:

> In the first intercalation [i.e., parenthesis] (7:1-17), the delay is for the sake of protecting the people of God from judgments, so that they may triumph in heaven, while in the second intercalation (10:1– 11:13) the delay is for the sake of the prophetic witness of the people of God. The relationship between the first two series of judgments and the two intercalations is the structural means by which John is able to relate the story of God's judgment on an unbelieving world to

---

7. Richard Bauckham, *The Climax of Prophecy: Studies on the Book of Revelation* (Edinburgh: T & T Clark, 1993), 14.

the story of God's people in an unbelieving world and their witness to that world.[8]

Sixth, remember that the futurist contends that Revelation is a virtually linear, chronologically sequential description of events within a short span of time at the close of human history. But if that were the case, how does one explain the numerous scenes of consummative judgment and salvation? In other words, there are several passages scattered throughout Revelation that portray the final outpouring of divine wrath and the consummation of God's kingdom. For example, see 6:12-17; 7:9-17; 11:15-19; 14:14-20; 15:2-4; 16:17-21; 17:1–18:24; 19:1-21; and 20:7-15. These can be explained only on the assumption that each is the conclusion of a section that is largely parallel with every other section, all of which describe events beginning with the first coming of Christ and leading up to his second coming and the final judgment.

My view of the book of Revelation is thus something of a mixture of the various schools of interpretation and is best represented in the commentary by G.K. Beale, who explains:

> Accordingly, no specific prophesied historical events are discerned in the book, except for the final coming of Christ to deliver and judge and to establish the final form of the kingdom in a consummated new creation – though there are a few exceptions to this rule. The Apocalypse symbolically portrays events throughout history, which is understood to be under the sovereignty of the Lamb as a result of his death and resurrection.... [Thus] the majority of the symbols in the book are transtemporal in the sense that they are applicable to events throughout the "church age."[9]

A Brief Word about Interpreting Symbolism in the Book of Revelation

In Revelation 1:1 we are told that God "made known" to John the contents of the book through an angel. Whereas the verb *semaino*

8. Ibid., 13.
9. G.K. Beale, *The Book of Revelation: A Commentary on the Greek Text* (Grand Rapids: Eerdmans, 1999), 48.

often simply means "make known, report, communicate," its "more concrete and at least equally common sense is 'show by a sign,' 'give (or make) signs (or signals),' or 'signify.' ... *Semaino* typically has this idea of symbolic communication when it is not used in the general sense of 'make known.' ... The Gospel writers use the cognate noun *semeion* repeatedly to refer to Jesus' miracles as outward 'signs' or 'symbols' of his attributes and mission." [10] It is most likely, then, that John's choice of *semaino* instead of *gnorizo* ("make known") was intentional. His point is that symbolic visions and their interpretation are going to be the primary means of communication in his book. We should also note the use in 1:1 of the verb "to show" (*deiknumi*). God the Father gave Jesus a revelation that he was to "show" his servants. This is a word that refers "to a revelation through the medium of symbolic heavenly visions communicated through an angel." [11] Throughout the book we read how John "saw" these pictorial revelations that were "shown" to him.

Most dispensational commentators contend that we should interpret the images in Revelation literally except where the context dictates otherwise. I contend that just the opposite is the case. The essence of Revelation is symbolic imagery. The language is predominantly figurative and should be interpreted as such except where a literal understanding is required by the context. Thus quite "literal" truth is communicated by means of highly figurative and symbolic visions in Revelation. Kenneth Gentry put it this way:

> We must be careful to distinguish between a "figurative" use of language (a legitimate function of the grammatical-historical method) and a "spiritual" interpretive methodology. Figurative expressions portray *historical events* by means of colorful, dramatic, and overdrawn descriptions. Spiritual interpretation, however, is a system of hermeneutics that evacuates all historical sense from a text in order to replace it with an abstract spiritual reality. [12]

---

10. Ibid., 51.
11. Ibid., 52.
12. Gentry, *The Great Tribulation: Past or Future?* 15.

Robert Mounce makes much the same point. The fact "that the language of prophecy is highly figurative has nothing to do with the reality of the events predicted. Symbolism is not a denial of historicity but a matter of literary genre."[13]

When interpreting Revelation it is important to keep in mind four levels of communication or revelation.[14] There is first *the linguistic level*. This is the text itself as recorded by John, i.e., the configuration of words that we read in the book. Second is *the visionary level*. This is John's actual visionary experience. Through the Spirit and the mediation of an angel, God gave John visions that later formed the basis for what is textually recorded in the book. Third, *the referential level* consists of the particular historical identification of the objects seen in the vision. In other words, the object or image seen usually stands for or symbolizes something or someone that appears in history. Finally, *the symbolic level* has in view the meaning of the historical referents. It is one thing to identify to what, in historical reality, the image points. It is yet another thing to ascertain what the image connotes or means or says about its referent.

Poythress uses the beast in Revelation 13 as an example. On the linguistic level we have the actual text of Revelation 13:1-8 which John wrote and sent to the seven churches in Asia. Before writing that text John had a visionary experience "in the Spirit" (1:10; 4:2) as a result of which he "saw" the beast. But the beast stands for or symbolizes something or someone in history. In all likelihood, its seven heads and ten horns also have historical referents of their own. Lastly, the symbolic imagery in which the beast is, as it were, clothed, means something in terms of the beast's character and activity. This information about the beast, notes Poythress, "is conveyed in symbolic, imagistic form rather than through literal photographic depictions or through unadorned prose description. The description of the beast in 13:1-8 is not intended as a photographic rendering of a literal animal but as a symbolic representation of

---

13. Mounce, *Revelation*, 218.
14. See Vern Sheridan Poythress, "Genre and Hermeneutics in Rev 20:1-6," *JETS*, Vol. 36 (March 1993): 41-54.

a human being or an historical institution. Hence understanding the significance of the imagery involves making a transition from symbols to actual historical significance." [15]

Other examples could be cited, such as the vision of Christ in 5:6-8. There is the actual linguistic material in verses 6-8 (the words themselves). There is the visionary experience of John in "seeing" Christ in the form of a lamb. There is the referential level, in which the lamb points to Christ, enthroned at God's right hand. And there is the symbolic level, where we ask about the meaning of a lamb, its seven horns, its seven eyes, etc.

Beale points to 19:7-8 as yet another, among many, examples. There we have the linguistic elements that can be read or heard. "The images of a bride and fine linen garments are what John saw on the visionary level. On the referential level the picture of the bride and bridegroom's wedding refers to actual believers enjoying some form of communion with Christ, probably after his second coming. Finally, the symbolic level refers to whatever we determine to be the precise meaning of the communion of the bride with the bridegroom and of the wedding imagery in general." [16]

The tendency of some dispensational commentators who take a strictly futurist reading of the book is to "understand the visions as direct reproductions of historical events that are so strange and extraordinary that they could not have occurred in past history up to the present; therefore, they portray literally events to happen in the future, directly before Christ's final coming." [17] In other words, they argue for a straightforward correspondence between the textual description and a historical event. In effect, they ignore the visionary and symbolic levels of communication by collapsing them into the referential, historical – i.e., they move from the first to the third levels of communication (see above) as if what the text records is literally what history reveals. Simply put, we must recog-

---

15. Poythress, "Genre and Hermeneutics," 42.
16. Beale, *Revelation*, 53.
17. Ibid.

nize that the descriptions in Revelation are "*descriptions of symbols, not of the reality conveyed by the symbols.*"[18]

We must also be careful to remember that simply because something is portrayed in figurative or non-literal terms does not mean it is less truthful or less real. In other words, *literal* is not synonymous with *true* nor is *symbolic* synonymous with *false or mythological.* How then might we know if a text is figurative or literal? Here are a few guidelines:

First, would there be a mismatch between subject and predicate if the sentence were taken literally? In other words, when we read that "God's name is a high tower" we are obviously dealing with a linguistic mismatch: God's name is not physically identical to a building of inanimate stone or brick. We see this in Revelation 1:20 where John says, "the seven lampstands are the seven churches." Again, when David declares, "The Lord is my shepherd," he is using the latter word in a metaphorical sense. As Bruce Waltke has pointed out, "the word 'shepherd,' which is at home with words which have reference to animal husbandry, is here transferred and juxtaposed with the Lord, a word pertaining to a transcendent, spiritual being.... When David prayed, 'Cause me to hear joy and gladness,' he juxtaposed objects that refer to an emotional state with a verb that refers to a physical activity."[19]

Second, if taken literally, would the statement be logically absurd or contradictory to what we know from the rest of Scripture or from creation? When we read that "the mountains clapped their hands" it is obvious we are dealing with figurative language. So, too, when John says that he "ate" the book (Rev. 10:10).

Third, context must always be consulted. Often there are clues both in what precedes and what follows that will alert us to the presence of symbolic language. When it comes to the book of Revelation, we need to determine if there is clear and repeated figurative use of the same word elsewhere.

---

18. Bruce M. Metzger, *Breaking the Code: Understanding the Book of Revelation* (Nashville: Abingdon Press, 1993), 14 (emphasis his).

19. Bruce K. Waltke, "Historical Grammatical Problems," unpublished paper, 56.

Fourth, the two most common figures of speech are *simile* and *metaphor*. A simile is an explicit or formal comparison which employs words such as "like" or "as." There are over seventy similes in the book of Revelation alone. Take for example Revelation 1:14 where we read that "the hairs of his head were white, *like* white wool, *like* snow. His eyes were *like* a flame of fire" (emphasis mine). A metaphor is an implicit or unexpressed comparison in which one thing is described in terms of another. Unlike the simile which says "A is like/as B," the metaphor directly asserts that "A is B." Two metaphorical statements are found in Revelation 1:20b where we read: "the seven stars *are* the angels of the seven churches, and the seven lampstands *are* the seven churches" (emphasis mine).

We should also keep in mind that not everything in a symbolic vision is necessarily meant to be interpreted. For example, "when John tells us that the heavenly Jerusalem is a perfect cube, fifteen hundred miles in length, breadth and height, and that it is con- structed of pure gold, transparent like crystal, he obviously does not expect us to visualize [or interpret] it, but is setting out to over- whelm the imagination."[20] Another example would be the vision of the risen Christ in Revelation 1. Whereas there may be theological significance in a few of the items, Caird insists that any attempt to compile a catalogue of meanings for each element is "to unweave the rainbow."[21] In other words,

> John uses his allusions not as a code in which each symbol requires separate and exact translation, but rather for their evocative and emo- tive power. This is not photographic art. His aim is to set the echoes of memory and association ringing. The humbling sense of the sub- lime and the majestic which men experience at the sight of a roar- ing cataract [waterfall] or the midday sun is the nearest equivalent to the awe evoked by a vision of the divine. John has seen the risen

20. G.B. Caird, *The Language and Imagery of the Bible* (Grand Rapids: Eerdmans, 1997 [1980], 149.
21. G.B. Caird, *A Commentary on the Revelation of St. John the Divine* (New York: Harper & Row, 1966), 25.

Christ, clothed in all the attributes of deity, and he wishes to call forth from his readers the same response of overwhelming and annihilating wonder which he experienced in his prophetic trance.[22]

My aim in this all too brief section on symbolism was to provide a few helpful hints when it comes to our exploration and interpretation of Revelation. I'm convinced that much of the sensationalistic and misleading prognostications of prophetic pundits in our day could be avoided if only we paid closer attention to the genre of this remarkable book and the principles by which it should be read.

Addendum – The Appeal of Preterism

This examination of the seal, trumpet, and bowl judgments in Revelation, together with the coming analysis of the beast (Antichrist?) in Revelation 13 and 17, as well as my treatment of the millennial issue in Revelation 20, is largely dependent on the assumption that the Apocalypse was written subsequent to the destruction of Jerusalem and its temple in A.D. 70 The most widely held date for the composition of Revelation is sometime in the early 90s of the first century. However, if a case can be made for an early authorship, sometime prior to the siege on Jerusalem in 66–70, virtually everything that I've said about the book of Revelation would need to be revised. Those who embrace a pre-70 composition for Revelation typically identify the Roman emperor Nero as the beast/Antichrist. The most prolific and persuasive of these scholars is Kenneth L. Gentry, Jr., whose two books on the subject, *Before Jerusalem Fell: Dating the Book of Revelation* (Atlanta: American Vision, 1998), and *The Beast of Revelation* (Tyler, TX: Institute for Christian Economics, 1989) are widely acknowledged to be the best available defenses of this theory.[23]

---

22. Ibid., 25-26.
23. One should also consult Kenneth L. Gentry, Jr., *The Book of Revelation Made Easy* (Powder Springs, GA: American Vision Press, 2008); Gary DeMar, *Last Days Madness: Obsession of the Modern Church* (Atlanta: American Vision, Inc., 1997); Gary DeMar and Francis X. Gumerlock, eds., *The Early Church and the End of the World* (Powder Springs, GA: American Vision, 2006);

Gentry contends that Revelation has two fundamental purposes relative to its original audience. "In the first place, it was designed to steel the first century Church against the gathering storm of persecution, which was reaching an unnerving crescendo of theretofore unknown proportions and intensity. A new and major feature of that persecution was the entrance of imperial Rome onto the scene. The first historical persecution of the Church by imperial Rome was by Nero Caesar from A.D. 64 to A.D. 68. In the second place, it was to brace the Church for a major and fundamental reorientation in the course of redemptive history, a re-orientation necessitating the destruction of Jerusalem (the center not only of Old Covenant Israel, but of Apostolic Christianity [cp. Ac. 1:8; 2:1ff.; 15:2] and the Temple [cp. Matt. 24:1-34 with Rev. 11])."[24]

I must confess that I feel drawn to this position, although I'm not yet persuaded. Perhaps the long-awaited commentary on Revelation that Gentry has promised will convince me. Until then I remain committed to the late date for John's book.

What follows is a brief summary of the primary arguments for a preterist or A.D. pre-70 composition of Revelation.[25] I'm sure advocates of this view would prefer that I make a more thorough presentation of their position, but space constraints simply don't allow it. The books cited in the footnotes should more than compensate for what I omit. Perhaps the best way to proceed is simply to briefly enumerate the arguments one by one.

David Chilton, *Paradise Restored: An Eschatology of Dominion* (Tyler, TX: Reconstruction Press, 1985) and *The Days of Vengeance: An Exposition of the Book of Revelation* (Ft. Worth: Dominion Press, 1987); and Hank Hanegraaff, *The Apocalypse Code* (Nashville: Thomas Nelson, 2007).

24. Gentry, *Before Jerusalem Fell*, 15-16.

25. The word "preterist" comes from the Latin word *praeteritus* which means "gone by" or "past". Proponents of this view thus contend that "the closer we get to the year 2000, the farther we get from the events of Revelation" (Gentry, *Four Views*, 37; who obviously made that comment during the 1990s). The major prophecies of the book, so they argue, were fulfilled either in the fall of Jerusalem in 70 (which would, of course, necessitate the earlier date of composition) or in the fall of Rome in 476.

(1) The argument is made that the temple in Jerusalem is described in Revelation 11:1-12 as still standing when Revelation was written. It is inconceivable to the preterist that John would have portrayed it this way if in fact it had been destroyed some twenty to twenty-five years earlier. Some who argue for a late date for Revelation concede that at least these verses must have been written before 70 and were simply borrowed by John from that earlier source and included in his final composition. But there is no literary evidence in the text itself that 11:1-12 originated in an earlier composition and it runs counter to the fundamental unity of the book.

(2) The preterist also insists that if the city and temple had indeed been utterly destroyed before Revelation was written, surely some reference to this epochal and monumental eschatological event as an accomplished fact of past history would be found in John's book.

(3) In Revelation 17:9 "seven mountains" are mentioned, which most agree is an allusion to Rome and its seven hills. These mountains are said to represent seven kings, five of which have fallen, one which "is", and the other yet to come. The sixth king is the one in power as John writes. Advocates of an early date for the book insist that the first of these kings is Augustus, the first official Roman emperor. The sixth is Galba, who reigned briefly after Nero's death (68–69). Some (such as Gentry) argue that Julius Caesar is the first king, thereby making Nero the sixth and Galba the seventh. In any case, this listing of the seven kings dates the book's composition to the late 60s of the first century. [26]

(4) Using Hebrew transcription, the numerical value of "Nero Caesar" is 666. If the Beast is portrayed in Revelation 13 as active at

---

26. Stephen Smalley (*Thunder and Love: John's Revelation and John's Community* [Milton Keynes, U.K.: Nelson Word, 1994]) makes a case for Vespasian as the sixth king who "is", with Titus being the seventh who "is to come" but who will reign only for a short time (two years, in fact). The eighth, who will eventually be destroyed, is Domitian. Smalley opts for composition sometime during the Jewish war of 66–74, most likely just before the fall of Jerusalem to Titus, Vespasian's son, in 70.

the time of writing, it would point to Nero and thus a pre-70 date for the book's composition.

(5) One of the strongest arguments for a pre-70 date for Revelation is John's repeated declaration that the time of the fulfillment of the book's prophecies is near. "Near" and "shortly", they contend, mean precisely that; not 1,940 years later. For example (emphasis mine throughout):

> Revelation was given "to show to his servants the things which *must soon take place.*" (Rev. 1:1)

> "Blessed is the one who reads aloud the words of this prophecy, and blessed are those who hear, and who keep what is written in it, for *the time is near.*" (Rev. 1:3)

> "And said to me, 'These words are trustworthy and true. And the Lord, the God of the spirits of the prophets, has sent his angel to show his servants what *must soon take place*.'" (Rev. 22:6)

> "And behold, *I am coming soon.*" (Rev. 22:7a)

> "And he said to me, 'Do not seal up the words of the prophecy of this book, for *the time is near*'." (Rev. 22:10)

> "Behold, *I am coming soon*, bringing my recompense with me, to repay everyone for what he has done." (Rev. 22:12)

> "He who testifies to these things says, '*Surely I am coming soon*.' Amen. Come, Lord Jesus!" (Rev. 22:20)

Preterists also point to several similar texts, such as,

> "Therefore repent. If not, *I will come to you soon* and war against them with the sword of my mouth." (Rev. 2:16; most believe, however, that this "coming" of Christ is in spiritual discipline of the unrepentant in the church at Pergamum)

"*I am coming soon.* Hold fast what you have, so that no one may seize your crown." (Rev. 3:11)

"The second woe has passed; behold, the third woe is *soon to come.*" (Rev. 11:14)

(6) Preterists argue that the conditions in the seven churches (Revelation 2–3) best correlate with what we know to have been true of pre-70 Jewish Christianity.

(7) An appeal is also made to the parallel but contrasting commands given to Daniel and to John. In Daniel 12:4a we read, "But you, Daniel, shut up the words and seal the book, until the time of the end." But in Revelation 22:10 John receives this exhortation: "And he said to me, 'Do not seal up the words of the prophecy of this book, for the time is near.'" As Gentry points out, "Daniel's expectations are long term; John's are short term."[27] This would seem to suggest that John was writing Revelation while anticipating that its events were impending or looming in his own day. He did not write about events that were 2,000 years in the future, but spoke pastorally as well as prophetically to first century Christians to encourage them to persevere in the face of persecution already underway and soon to intensify.

(8) The numerous references in Revelation to a time period of some 3½ years (whether "a time, times, and half a time" [12:14] or "forty-two months" [11:2; 13:5] or "1,260 days" [11:3; 12:6]) fits almost perfectly into the time frame of 66–70 during which Rome laid siege to Jerusalem and eventually destroyed both the city and temple.

(9) Although it may initially sound strange, one of the stronger arguments for the early date of Revelation is the weakness of the argument put forth in defense of the late date based on the questionable testimony of Irenaeus, Bishop of Lyon (c. 103–202). Virtually everyone who embraces the traditional late date for the composition of Revelation cites the following from Irenaeus, written sometime between 180 and 190:

---

27. Gentry, *The Book of Revelation Made Easy*, 19.

We will not, however, incur the risk of pronouncing positively as to the name of Antichrist; for if it were necessary that his name should be distinctly revealed in this present time, it would have been announced by him who beheld the apocalyptic vision. For that was seen no very long time since, but almost in our day, towards the end of Domitian's reign.[28]

The argument put forth is that the antecedent of the verb translated "that was seen" is "the apocalyptic vision," a reference to the book of Revelation. Irenaeus asserts, so we are told, that this visionary experience occurred "towards the end of Domitian's reign" (or sometime in the last decade of the first century).

My aim is not to provide an extensive response to this argument, as that has been provided both by Kenneth L. Gentry, Jr., and D. Ragan Ewing.[29] Here I will only summarize two counter-arguments. First, many have argued that the antecedent of "that was seen" is not "the apocalyptic vision" but instead "him" who saw it, namely, John the Apostle. The point being that *John* was observed to have lived into the 90s when Domitian ruled Rome. Second, many question the wisdom of regarding Irenaeus as a trustworthy source in this regard. This isn't to minimize the importance of Irenaeus as an early church father, but only to recognize that he is not infallible, and on other occasions was guilty of historical blunders, not to mention a variety of theological oddities.[30]

---

28. Irenaeus, *Against Heresies*, 5.30.3, *The Ante-Nicene Fathers* (New York: Christian Literature, 1885), 1:559-60; translated by Alexander Roberts and James Donaldson.

29. Kenneth L. Gentry, Jr., *Before Jerusalem Fell: Dating the Book of Revelation*, revised edition (Atlanta: American Vision, 1998), 41-67; and D. Ragan Ewing, "The Identification Of Babylon The Harlot In The Book Of Revelation," a Thesis presented to the Faculty of the Department of New Testament Studies, Dallas Theological Seminary (July 2002). All subsequent citations of this thesis come from the version found at www.bible.org (which lacks pagination).

30. Specifically, he portrayed the Apostle James as the same person as the brother of Jesus (*Against Heresies*, 2.22.5) and believed that Jesus himself lived to be fifty years old (*Against Heresies*, 3.12.14).

But one also hears frequently that there was virtual unanimity among the church fathers in support of a late date for Revelation. This must be tempered with two important facts. First, although the majority of references among the fathers point to a late date, virtually all of them do so based (yet again) on the singular testimony of Irenaeus! That is to say, "the allegedly numerous 'testimonies' to the Domitianic date are in reality merely a chorus of voices echoing *one* testimony [namely, that of Irenaeus]."[31] Thus, if Irenaeus' view is questionable, what becomes of those whose primary (and sometimes sole) appeal is to him? Second, there are a number of exceptions to this "virtual unanimity," documentation for which can be found in both Gentry[32] and Ewing.

(10) Perhaps the most persuasive evidence for an early date for Revelation comes from the aforementioned Th.M. thesis by D. Ragan Ewing, submitted to the faculty, of all places, at Dallas Theological Seminary! Ewing's thesis is that the Harlot/Prostitute of Revelation 17–18 is not Rome, as traditionally argued by all who embrace a late date for Revelation, but rather Jerusalem. I only have room for a brief summation of his primary arguments.

One of the primary reasons people have identified Babylon with Rome is that a number of Jewish sources clearly do so. However, these sources are all from a time after 70. It is understandable that Jews living *after* the destruction of the temple and city would refer to Rome as Babylon. After all, it was Babylon that first destroyed both city and temple in the sixth century B.C., followed again in the first century A.D. by a similar devastation at the hand of the Romans. Therefore, this argument is valid only on the assumption of a late date for Revelation. If the book was composed in the 60s, on the other hand, it carries no weight as a reason why Jerusalem itself could not be described metaphorically as Babylon.

Advocates of the Babylon = Rome view point to the exalted language used to describe Babylon, such as Revelation 17:18. There the woman/harlot "is the great city that has dominion over the

---

31. Ewing, "The Identification of Babylon."
32. See especially, *Before Jerusalem Fell*, 68-109.

kings of the earth." Although at first glance this seems more fitting as a description of Rome, the designation "the great city" is used explicitly of Jerusalem in Revelation 11:8 and perhaps also 16:19 (see "the city" in 14:20, a likely reference to Jerusalem as well).

This city is then portrayed as having "dominion over the kings of the earth," language that again seems more applicable to Rome than Jerusalem. But the language here is probably hyperbolic, as is found in Psalm 48:2 where Jerusalem is said to be "the joy of all the earth" because it is "the city of the great King." Ewing argues that such language is warranted by the fact that "as God's covenantal mediators, it is Israel through whom God exercises His kingly rule." Thus the descriptive language in Revelation 17:18 is theological, not political, and focuses on the mediatorial role Jerusalem was designed to play in the messianic rule of Christ.

Another text of importance is Revelation 17:9 and its reference to "seven mountains on which the woman is seated." Many insist that this is an obvious allusion to Rome, which topographically sat upon seven hills. However, whereas the "seven hills" language was known in the western Mediterranean regions, there is virtually no evidence that Rome was understood or referred to this way in Asia Minor. "A more likely connection," says Ewing, "is the association of mountains with the symbolism of power and kings/kingdoms that is to be found in the Old Testament and other Jewish works." Thus "it may be that the seven mountains are best understood from a Jewish mindset as a symbol of completeness of authority, or fullness of royal power." Ewing also points to *1 Enoch* 24–25 where the writer speaks of Jerusalem as seated among "seven dignified mountains." Given the importance of *1 Enoch* and its striking affinities with Revelation, it is not unlikely that John could use the language of seven mountains in alluding to Jerusalem rather than Rome.

Key to Ewing's argument is Revelation 11:8, where John explicitly calls Jerusalem "the great city." Note also that in this same passage we are given precedent for metaphorical names being applied to Jerusalem, specifically, the names of Israel's ancient enemies. In Revelation 16:19 we read of "the great city" that is juxtaposed with "the cities of the nations." If the latter has in view "the cities of the

Gentiles" (*ton ethnon*), the identification of "the great city" with Jerusalem becomes even more probable. We also read in 16:19 that the "great city" "was split into three parts," a possible allusion to Ezekiel 5:1-5 where God instructs the prophet to divide his hair into three parts as an illustration of the coming judgment upon *Jerusalem.*

Ewing cites a number of other arguments to support his thesis. For example, in Revelation 17:4 and 18:16, the harlot is arrayed "in purple and scarlet, and adorned with gold and jewels and pearls." This is almost identical to the description of *Israel's* high priest, as found in the LXX of Exodus 25:3-7; 28:5-9, 15-20; 35:6; 36:9-12; 36:15-21. Also, the fact that the woman is portrayed as a "harlot" or "prostitute" is significant insofar as in the Old Testament prophets the imagery of a people or city committing adultery is consistently a reference to *covenant* unfaithfulness.[33] His point is that "one cannot commit adultery against God if one is not married to God. It is difficult to conceive of any city other than Jerusalem that would be described as the covenant-breaking harlot in Revelation, especially in light of the dozens of times she has been given this appellation already throughout the Old Testament."[34] Related to this is the fact that the harlot is to be repaid "double for her deeds" (18:6), a phrase used only in the Old Testament against God's covenant people Israel.

Ewing also cites Revelation 17:5 where we read that "on her forehead was written a name of mystery: 'Babylon the great, mother of prostitutes and of earth's abominations.'" This may allude to Jeremiah 3:3 where God indicts Jerusalem as a harlot by declaring, "you have the forehead of a whore" (see also Exod. 28:36-38).

Some have challenged the Babylon = Jerusalem thesis due to the portrayal of sea trade and economic influence attributed to the former in Revelation 18. But Ewing, citing the work of Iain

---

33. To make his point, Ewing cites such texts as Ezek. 16:15, 17, 28, 35, 41; 23:1-21, 44; Isa. 1:21; 57:3; Jer. 2:20; 3:1; 13:27; Hos. 2:2-5; 4:12, 15, 18; 5:4; 9:1; Micah 1:7.
34. Ewing, "The Identification of Babylon."

Provan,[35] argues that John is employing familiar Old Testament prophetic language to express the severity of the fall of a city. It need not be the author's intent that the detailed imagery be a literal description of the situation prevalent in that day. Rather, the language is that of a formal lament largely derived from the one applied to Tyre in Ezekiel 26–28. The point may well be something along the lines of, "You, Babylon, are tragically fallen just as was Tyre and historical Babylon." The specific details that comprise the lament need not find explicit historical correspondence in the circumstances of first-century Jerusalem. They are here used rhetorically to portray the magnitude of judgment that will come on potentially any city or nation that apostatizes.

One must also account for the language of Revelation 18:24 where it is said of Babylon that "in her was found the blood of prophets and of saints, and of all who have been slain on earth." This appears to be a reference to Jesus' words of judgment pronounced against Jerusalem in Matthew 23:34-35 – "Therefore I send you prophets and wise men and scribes, some of whom you will kill and crucify, and some you will flog in your synagogues and persecute from town to town, so that on you may come all the righteous blood shed on earth, from the blood of innocent Abel to the blood of Zechariah the son of Barachiah, whom you murdered between the sanctuary and the altar." Whereas Rome was guilty of killing Christians, she cannot be charged with the death of the Old Testament prophets.

Then there is the fact that the beast, most likely Rome when Revelation was written, not only interacts with the harlot but eventually hates her and destroys her. How can Rome hate and destroy Rome? If, on the other hand, Jerusalem is the harlot attacked by beastly Rome, the imagery in 17:16 ("And the ten horns that you saw, they and the beast will hate the prostitute. They will make her desolate and naked, and devour her flesh and burn her up with

---

35. Iain Provan, "Foul Spirits, Fornication and Finance: Revelation 18 from an Old Testament Perspective," in *JSNT* 64 (1996): 81-100.

fire") makes perfectly good sense, for as we know Rome destroyed Jerusalem in the siege of A.D. 70

Finally, Ewing points to the fascinating literary contrast between the harlot of Revelation 17–18 and the bride of Revelation 21. "Jerusalem's rejection of her Messiah, who had come as her husband, sets the stage for the Messiah to take another bride. And if this new bride is called the 'New' Jerusalem, a likely corollary is that the former, unfaithful woman was the *Old* Jerusalem." [36]

If the preterist, A.D. pre-70 composition of the book of Revelation can be substantiated, all the judgments portrayed through the imagery of seven seals, seven trumpets, and seven bowls must be taken as descriptive of God's wrath against apostate Israel during the siege by the Roman armies, 66–70, which resulted in the utter destruction of both the city of Jerusalem and its temple. If not entirely persuasive at this point, the preterist interpretation of Revelation is surely worthy of deeper and more incisive exploration.

---

36. Ewing, "The Identification of Babylon."

Chapter Fourteen

Amillennialism, Revelation 20, and The Binding of Satan

When I make known my millennial convictions, after getting over their initial shock and incredulity, it's not uncommon for my premillennial friends to say: "But Sam, how can you say you embrace a 'millennial' option when you don't even believe in a millennium?" As you'll soon come to see, *I most assuredly do believe in the reality of a literal millennial kingdom.* The reason for this misunderstanding is the label most commonly used to describe the view I'm prepared to defend: *amillennialism.*

You've no doubt heard someone described as being "apolitical" or perhaps "amoral" and you know what is meant. Similarly, to say that I am "**a**millennial" (where the alpha privative "a" seemingly negates the word "millennial") exposes me and others to the charge that we deny the existence of what is clearly taught in Revelation 20. As you will soon see, the "millennium" that I believe John describes in the Apocalypse is concurrent with the church age in which we live and consists of the co-regency with Christ of those believers who have died and entered into the glory of the intermediate state. More on that shortly.

Many mistakenly identify **pre**millennialism with **pro**-millennialism, as if to say that only premillennialists believe in the millennial kingdom of Christ and are *for* it. If I may be allowed to turn the terminological tables for a moment, just to show how the debate has been skewed in favor of the other side, I would contend that it is the premillennialist who is really an a- or anti-millennialist, for he denies and disbelieves in the heavenly reality of the millennium as it is taught in Revelation 20. Biblical millennialists, in the true sense of that term, are those who affirm that the millennium is one and the same with the experience of those saints who rule with Christ even now in the intermediate state, whereas the real a-millennialists are those who deny it. They deny that concept of the millennium the Bible clearly affirms and are, therefore, a-millennial. Of course, I realize how strange that sounds to most who are reading this book. But it goes to show how thoroughly ingrained premillennialism is in the minds of most Christians today. It also reveals how the deck is psychologically stacked against the amillennialist from the outset of the discussion. I am not so naïve as to believe that anyone will adopt these new labels. But at least when we use them we should do so with an understanding of their inadequacies. I do not propose to coin some new term to replace the standard "amillennialism" (although the term "realized millennialism" has been suggested by some). I am afraid it is here to stay. That said, we must proceed.

A Definition of Amillennialism

As noted, amillennialism has suffered greatly in the past because of its apparent negative character. In other words, definitions of amillennialism have focused more upon what the view *denies* (namely, a chronologically precise 1,000-year, this-earthly reign of Christ between his second coming and the eternal state) than on what it *affirms*. In order best to counter this negativism, the definition of amillennialism presented here will concentrate on its fundamental *affirmations* concerning eschatological truth.

Contrary to what the name (**a**millennialism) implies, amillennialists *do* believe in a millennium. The millennium, however, is *now*: the present age of the Church between the first and second comings of Christ in its entirety *is* the millennium. Therefore, while the amillennialist does *deny* the premillennial belief in a personal, literal reign of Christ upon the earth for 1,000 years *following* his second coming, he *affirms* that there is a millennium and that Christ rules. However, this messianic reign is not precisely

1,000 years in length and it is wholly spiritual (in the sense that it is non-earthly, non-visible, non-physical, but no less literal) in nature. "This millennial reign is not something to be looked for in the future;" writes Hoekema, "it is going on now, and will be until Christ returns. Hence the term *realized millennialism* is an apt description of the view here defended – if it is remembered that the millennium in question is not an earthly but a heavenly reign."[1]

Amillennialists have differed on the precise character of this spiritual rule of Christ. An increasing number, such as myself, contend that the millennium is restricted to the blessings of the *intermediate state*; that is to say, the millennium as described in Revelation 20:4-6 refers to the *present reign of the souls of deceased believers with Christ in heaven*. Others would go a step farther and restrict the experience of the millennial blessings to the "martyrs" now in heaven with Christ (those who were slain while on the earth by reason of their testimony for Christ and the gospel). Other amillennialists interpret the millennium as encompassing all the inward spiritual triumphs experienced by the Church on earth (i.e., Christ ruling in the believer's heart).

As a direct corollary to the above, amillennialists maintain that there will, therefore, be no millennium in the sense of a semi-golden era of earthly prosperity for the kingdom *before* Christ returns. There will be no visible earthly expression of Christ's reign over the world as a whole (other than what may be seen in the expansion and spiritual influence of local churches); the Church will not *Christianize* the nations, nor will it gain a dominant or widespread influence throughout the earth. Thus it is here, and for all practical purposes *only* here, that amillennialism differs from postmillennialism.

According to the amillennialist, there will be a parallel and contemporaneous development of good and evil in the world which will continue until the second coming of Christ. Thus, "despite the fact that Christ has won a decisive victory over sin and evil, the kingdom of evil will continue to exist alongside of the kingdom of God until

---

1. Anthony Hoekema, *The Bible and the Future* (Grand Rapids: Eerdmans, 1979), 235.

the end of the world."[2] The amillennialist, then, agrees with the pre-millennialist that history will witness a progressively worsening situation in which the Church of Jesus Christ will experience an increasingly widespread and oppressive time of suffering and persecution.

At the end of the age there will emerge an intensified form of tribulation and apostasy. Whether or not there will likewise appear a *personal* Antichrist is a point of dispute among amillennialists (a subject I will address in two subsequent chapters). It should be pointed out that the amillennialist does not identify this period of tribulation with Daniel's seventieth week, as does the dispensational premillennialist, nor does he define its purpose as having anything to do with the restoration of national theocratic Israel. Some amillennialists (perhaps even most), however, *do* believe in a mass salvation of ethnic Israel at the end of the age. Christ's return at the close of this period will synchronize with the general resurrection and general judgment of all men, believers and unbelievers alike, to be followed *immediately* by the eternal state (the new heavens and the new earth). In other words, here is the major point of difference between the amillennialist and premillennialist: the former denies whereas the latter affirms an earthly, visible rule of Christ for 1,000 years *between* his second coming and the final resurrection, judgment, and introduction of the eternal state.

Other Distinctives of Amillennialism

Among many amillennialists of the past, most Old Testament prophecies which appeared to teach an earthly kingdom were understood *not* as pointing to future, physical, geo-spatial realities, but were to be interpreted figuratively. In other words, they were viewed as descriptive of *spiritual* blessings now being fulfilled in the Church. Recently, however, and as noted in a previous chapter, Anthony Hoekema has popularized (although he did not invent) a view which takes a more serious, or should I say *more literal and earthly*, perspective concerning these prophecies. Concerning such Old Testament texts, Hoekema writes:

---

2. Ibid., 174.

Dispensationalists commonly say that we amillennialists spiritualize prophecies of this kind by understanding them as being fulfilled either in the church of this present age or in heaven in the age to come. I believe, however, that prophecies of this sort refer neither primarily to the church of this age nor to heaven, but to *the new earth*. The concept of the new earth is therefore of great importance for the proper approach to Old Testament prophecy. All too often, unfortunately, amillennial exegetes fail to keep biblical teaching on the new earth in mind when interpreting Old Testament prophecy. It is an impoverishment of the meaning of these passages to make them apply only to the church or to heaven. But it is also an impoverishment to make them refer to a thousand-year period preceding the final state. They must be understood as inspired descriptions of the glorious new earth God is preparing for his people.[3]

I concur with Hoekema on this point. As noted earlier, the Old Testament promises of God's royal reign over his people in the land he promised to the patriarchs will be fulfilled in geo-spatial terms on the new earth as described in Revelation 21–22.

The Interpretation of the Book of Revelation

Most amillennialists interpret the book of Revelation according to what is called *progressive parallelism*, the view that I defended briefly in the previous chapter. According to this view of the book, "Revelation consists of seven sections which run parallel to each other, each of which depicts the church and the world from the time of Christ's first coming to the time of his second."[4] This has also been called the *Recapitulation* view, meaning that the structure of Revelation does not relate consecutive events but frequently covers the same ground from different perspectives.[5]

Therefore, according to this view Revelation 20:1 is *not* to be thought of as following in chronological order chapter 19 (which

---

3. Ibid., 205–06.
4. Robert, Clouse, ed., *The Meaning of the Millennium: Four Views* (Downers Grove: IVP, 1977), 156–57.
5. The most popular scheme envisions the seven sections as: (1) ch. 1–3; (2) ch. 4–7; (3) ch. 8–11; (4) ch. 12–14; (5) ch. 15–16; (6) ch. 17–19; (7) ch. 20–22.

describes the second coming of Christ). Rather, it takes us back once again to the *beginning* of the New Testament era and *recapitulates* the entire present age (that is to say, it describes the same period in different but complementary terms). By doing this the amillennialist is able to interpret *the binding of Satan* in Revelation 20:1-3 as having occurred during our Lord's earthly ministry, and *the 1,000-year reign* (i.e., the millennium) of Revelation 20:4-6 as describing in symbolic language the entire inter-advent age in which we now live. Therefore, the 1,000-year period is no chronologically literal piece of history; it is a symbolic number coextensive with the history of the Church on earth between the resurrection of Christ and his return. For more on this, we now turn to an exposition of this important passage.

Revelation 20

Unfortunately, the discussion of this text has been muddled by statements such as: "The premillennial interpretation of Revelation 20 is superior because it is *literal*, whereas the amillennial interpretation *spiritualizes*, and therefore dishonors, God's Word." Suffice it to say, in the words of Arthur Lewis, that

> the essential and concrete aspects of the text may not be "spiritualized" out of existence. The martyred and enthroned saints are real, the angel who binds Satan is real, Satan himself is very real, and the wicked nations in revolt against the King are real nations and part of history. The question is not, therefore, which view is the more literal, but which correctly understands the place and purpose of the thousand years.[6]

---

6. Arthur Lewis, *The Dark Side of the Millennium: The Problem of Evil in Rev. 20:1-10* (Grand Rapids: Baker Book House, 1980), 50. An all-too-typical misrepresentation of amillennialism is the statement by Ergun Caner that "Amillennialists approach the book of Revelation allegorically" ("The Patience of Hope: Premillennialism and the Soon-Coming King (1 Thess. 1:1-10)," in *The Return of Christ: A Premillennial Perspective,* edited by David L. Allen & Steve W. Lemke [Nashville: B & H Academic, 2011], 35).

The point is simply that the millennium for which I will argue is just as real and literal as the millennium for which the premillennialist contends. The first interpretive task before us is the account in verses 1-3 of Satan's imprisonment in the abyss [7] (or, "bottomless pit," ESV) for a period of 1,000 years.

Revelation 20:1-3 and the Binding of Satan

Premillennialists believe this vision constitutes one of the strongest confirmations of their prophetic scenario. They point to two significant features.

First, they insist that the relationship between the events of Revelation 19:11-21 and those of 20:1-3 is one of *chronological and historical sequence*. In other words, they argue that the events of 20:1-3 happen immediately after those of 19:11-21. Consequently, the binding of Satan for a millennium is historically subsequent to (i.e., after) the second coming of Christ. Second, they insist that the New Testament evidence concerning the extent of Satan's activity in this present age is incompatible with the description of the restrictions imposed upon him by the angel in Revelation 20:1-3. [8]

---

7. The word translated "abyss" occurs nine times in the New Testament, eight of which refer to the abode of demons (the exception being Romans 10:7 where it refers to the abode of the dead in general). According to Robert Mounce, the abyss was thought of "as a vast subterranean cavern which served as a place of confinement for disobedient spirits awaiting judgment" (*The Book of Revelation* [Grand Rapids: Eerdmans, 1977], 352). In Revelation 9:11 Satan is referred to as "the angel of the bottomless pit (or abyss)," most likely because he is *in* the abyss, the place from which he dispatches his demonic hordes (9:1-3) and commissions the beast (11:7; 17:8). Although this point should not be pressed, it may be that Satan is "in" or "of" the abyss precisely because he was consigned and sealed therein at the inception of this present age, only to be released at its close. In other words, it may be that Satan is described as being "of the abyss" in 9:11 because that is the place of his current incarceration. If so, this would support the identification of the 1,000 years of 20:1-3 with the present age preceding the second coming of Christ. If you are wondering how Satan can be "incarcerated" in the "abyss" and yet still active in the earth, see below.

8. This "angel" is anonymous, as is the case with sixty-five of the sixty-seven occurrences of the word in Revelation. However, Sydney Page suggests that

Since Satan is most certainly not bound now, so they tell us, the events of verses 1-3 must be future.

I will respond to each of these two arguments in turn.

The premillennialist insists that beginning with Revelation 19:11 and extending through 21:1 we have a series of visions that are historically and chronologically sequential. The premillennialist appeals to two arguments. First, much is made of the phrase "and I saw" (*kai eidon*), which occurs in 19:11, 17, 19; 20:1, 4, 11; 21:1. This, they argue, indicates that what John "saw" in chapter 20 follows chronologically and historically upon what he "saw" in chapter 19. Consequently, the binding of Satan and the millennial kingdom are yet future, subsequent to the second coming of Christ.

However, the phrase translated "and I saw" appears countless times in Revelation and need only indicate *the sequence in which John received the visions*. It does not necessarily indicate any historical relation among the many visions themselves. In other words, I'm happy to concede that the words "and I saw" indicate the next vision *seen* by John, but not necessarily the next vision that follows in actual historical sequence. The latter can only be determined by

---

the "angel" of Revelation 20:1 might be Michael. He bases his argument on the possible parallel between the "restrainer" of 2 Thessalonians 2 and the angelic restraint of Satan in Revelation 20:1-3. "It is tempting to speculate," notes Page, "that the restrainer mentioned by Paul might be the angel Michael, since he appears as the one who defends God's people from those who oppose him in Dan. 10:13,21; 12:1, and Paul's teaching in 2 Thessalonians 2 is rooted in the Danielic prophecies. If this identification is accepted it would constitute another link with Revelation 20, for the binding of Satan is pictured as the work of an angel there. Moreover, although the angel who binds Satan is unnamed, there is reason to think that the seer had Michael in view. Revelation 12 describes a heavenly battle between the armies of Michael and Satan that results in Satan and his forces being cast out of heaven. What happens to the devil according to Revelation 12 exhibits enough similarity to what is pictured in Rev. 20:1-3 to prompt the suggestion that a single experience is in view in both" ("Revelation 20 and Pauline Eschatology," in *JETS* 23 [March 1980], 34-35). Whereas Page's identification of the angel in Rev. 20:1-3 with Michael, if correct, would not prove that Satan was bound at the inception of this age, it would certainly lend support to that thesis.

examining the content of what John saw. The phrase "and when" (*kai hotan*) in 20:7, being decidedly temporal in force, simply indicates that the events of 20:7-10 follow historically upon the events of 20:4-6 and 20:1-3, a fact which no one denies.

If we were to take the events of 20:1-3 as historically subsequent to the events of 19:11-21, a serious problem arises in that 20:1-3 would describe an action designed to prevent the Satanic deception of the very nations who had already been *deceived* (16:13-16) and consequently *destroyed* in 19:19-21. In other words, it makes little sense to speak of protecting the nations from deception by Satan in 20:1-3 *after* they have just been both deceived by Satan (16:13-16; cf. 19:19-20) and destroyed by Christ at his return (19:11-21; cf. 16:15a, 19). [9]

Note also the similarity between Revelation 19:17-21 and 20:7-10. It seems that John is providing us with parallel accounts of the same conflict (Armageddon) rather than presenting two entirely different battles separated by 1,000 years of human history (as the premillennialist contends). This deserves some attention.

Amillennialists believe there are three texts in Revelation that describe what has come to be famously known as Armageddon, the final battle when Jesus Christ returns to this earth accompanied by the armies of heaven to defeat and destroy his enemies. They are Revelation 16:12-16; 19:17-21; and 20:7-10. Although each has a different focus, they are complementary portrayals of the second coming of Christ.[10] They differ primarily because chapter 19 is concerned

---

9. For this point, as well as much of what follows, I refer the reader to R. Fowler White's excellent article, "Reexamining the Evidence for Recapitulation in Rev. 20:1-10," *WTJ* 51 (1989):319-44. Dallas Seminary professor, Harold Hoehner, responded to White in "Evidence from Revelation 20," *A Case for Premillennialism: A New Consensus,* edited by Donald K. Campbell and Jeffrey T. Townsend (Chicago: Moody Press, 1992):235-62. White then responded and, I believe, thoroughly put to rest Hoehner's objections in "Making Sense of Rev. 20:1-10? Harold Hoehner Versus Recapitulation," *JETS* 37/4 (December 1994): 539-51.

10. This is yet another example of recapitulation in Revelation, in which the same period of time is described from differing vantage points with different imagery in order to secure a different, but still complementary, emphasis.

with the war as it relates to the participation and fate of the beast, his followers, and the false prophet, whereas chapter 20 is concerned primarily with the role of Satan. Also, it stands to reason that having given a detailed and vivid description of the war in chapters 16 and 19, John would find it unnecessary to repeat such detail in chapter 20.

In Revelation 16 the enemies are "the kings of the whole world" (16:14). In Revelation 19 they are "kings" and "captains" and "mighty men," indeed they are "all men, both free and slave, both small and great" (19:18). In Revelation 20 they are "the nations that are at the four corners of the earth, Gog and Magog" (20:8). They are all specifically gathered together for "the war" (cf. Rev. 19:19; 20:8). The use of the definite article ("the") points to a well-known war, the eschatological war often prophesied in the Old Testament between God and his enemies (cf. Joel 2:11; Zeph. 1:14; Zech. 14:2-14).[11]

The place of this eschatological war is called *Har-Magedon* (16:16). This poses a problem for those who believe a literal battle at the literal site is in view, insofar as there is no such place as the Mountain of Megiddo (which would be the most literal rendering of the word). Megiddo was itself an ancient city and Canaanite stronghold located on a plain in the southwest region of the Valley of Jezreel or Esdraelon. Although situated on a tell (an artificial mound about 70 feet high; others say it was anywhere from 130 to 200 feet), it can hardly be regarded as a mountain! The valley of Megiddo was the strategic site of several (more than 200, according to some estimates) significant battles in history (see Judg. 4:6-16; 5:19; Judg. 7; 1 Sam. 29:1; 31:1-7; 2 Kings 23:29-30; 2 Chron. 35:22-24). It makes sense that the vicinity would become a *lasting symbol for the cosmic eschatological battle between good and evil.* As Robert Mounce accurately notes,

> geography is not the major concern. Wherever it takes place, Armageddon is symbolic of the final overthrow of all the forces of evil by

---

11. This point is confirmed when one observes the absence of the definite article in Rev. 9:7, 9; 11:7; 12:7, 17; and 13:7.

the might and power of God. The great conflict between God and Satan, Christ and Antichrist, good and evil, that lies behind the perplexing course of history will in the end issue in a final struggle in which God will emerge victorious and take with him all who have placed their faith in him. This is Har-Megedon.[12]

To put it simply, *Armageddon is prophetic symbolism for the whole world in its collective defeat and judgment by Christ at his second coming.* The imagery of war, of kings and nations doing battle on an all-too-familiar battlefield (Megiddo), is used as *a metaphor of the consummate, cosmic, and decisive defeat by Christ of all his enemies* (Satan, beast, false prophet, and all who bear the mark of the beast) on that final day. "This suggests that 'Armageddon' is not a specific place that can be located on a map or reached with the help of GPS equipment. Like 'Babylon' and 'Euphrates' in the book of Revelation, 'Armageddon' is a typological symbol of the final battle between God and his enemies."[13]

It's important to note that in 19:17-18 the angel announces the coming destruction of the beast, false prophet, and their followers through the same imagery found in Ezekiel 39:4, 17-20 where the defeat of Gog and Magog is described. The picture of vultures or other birds of prey feasting on the flesh of unburied corpses killed in battle (see also Rev. 19:21b) was a familiar one to people in the Old Testament.[14] Yet we read that it is Gog and Magog who are defeated in the battle of Revelation 20:7-10 (see v. 8). The point is simply that the "war" of Revelation 19 and the "war" of Revelation 20, together with the "war" of Revelation 16, are one and the same, the defeat of the nations of the earth, Gog and Magog, who had aligned with the Beast against our Christ.[15]

---

12. Mounce, 302.

13. Schnabel, *40 Questions*, 233. For more historical and geographical detail on Megiddo, see Eckhard Schnabel, question 28.

14. Cf. Deut. 28:26; 1 Sam. 17:44-46; 1 Kings 14:11; 16:4; 21:24; 2 Kings 9:10; Jer. 7:33; 15:3; 16:4; 19:7; 34:20; Ezek. 29:5.

15. A few dispensationalists continue to defend the utterly indefensible view that Gog, the so-called "prince of Rosh," is the leader of modern day Russia, and

The "kings of the earth" are gathered together for "the war" (19:19; already noted in 16:14, 16; cf. 20:8). The same Greek phrase, "the war" (*ton polemon*), is used in all three texts (16:14; 19:19; 20:8). In fact, in 16:14 and 20:8 the same extended phrase "to gather them unto the war" (*sunagagein autous eis ton polemon*) is used. This confirms yet again that John had one and the same "war" in view. Premillennialists have to disagree, for they see the "war" of chapters 16 and 19 as a reference to "Armageddon" at the time of the second coming of Christ but view the "war" in chapter 20 as a different one that occurs subsequent to the millennium. I remain convinced that "the war" John notes in 16:14, 19:19, and 20:8 is one and the same war, thus supporting the idea that John is providing us, by means of literary recapitulation, differing perspectives on the same events. Thus Gog and Magog in Revelation 20:8 are identical with the kings and nations and all who are here portrayed as resisting the lordship of Christ. Gog and Magog are all the unbelieving inhabitants of the earth who in their rebellion against God and the Lamb follow the Beast and receive his mark. Fowler White correctly concludes that

> if we are expected to interpret the revolts in Revelation 19 and 20 as *different episodes* in history, we would hardly expect John to describe them in language and imagery derived from the *same episode* in Ezekiel's prophecy. On the contrary, John's recapitulated use of Eze-

---

that "Meshech" refers to Moscow. Likewise, "Tubal" is said to be the province of Tobolsk. For a thorough refutation of such nonsense, see Gary DeMar, *Why the End of the World is Not in Your Future: Identifying the Gog-Magog Alliance* (Powder Springs, GA: American Vision Press, 2008); Edwin Yamauchi, *Foes from the Northern Frontier: Invading Hordes from the Russian Steppes* (Grand Rapids: Baker Book House, 1982); as well as Eckhard Schnabel, *40 Questions About the End Times* (Grand Rapids: Kregel, 2011). Furthermore, as Yamauchi later points out, "Rosh" actually means "chief" or "head" and the modern word "Russia" is derived from *Rus*, "a Scandanavian word that was introduced into Ukraine in the Middle Ages. Meshech and Tubal are attested in cuneiform texts as Mushku and Tabal, areas in central and eastern Turkey" ("Updating the Armageddon Calendar," *Christianity Today* [April 29, 1991]: 51).

kiel 38-39 in both 19:17-21 and 20:7-10 establishes a *prima facie* case for us to understand 20:7-10 as a recapitulation of 19:17-21. If 20:7-10 is indeed a recapitulation of 19:17-21, then 20:7-10 narrates the demise of the dragon (Satan) at the second coming, while 19:17-21 narrates the demise of the beast and the false prophet at the second coming. Any other interpretation of how to relate these two judgment scenes, both of which are modeled on Ezekiel 38-39, will have to bear the burden of proof. [16]

So what, then, is Armageddon? I can do no better than to summarize this momentous conflict with the words of premillennialist Eckhard Schnabel:

> The battle of Armageddon brings the final defeat of the evil forces that rebel against God and resist Jesus Christ. It is not an actual military battle in Israel. A literal fulfillment would have been theoretically possible in the first century when armies fought on horses with swords and spears and arrows. However, even then it would have been impossible to picture all the people of the earth assembled at Megiddo in the Jezreel Valley in order to wage war against God's people, not to mention that Old Testament prophecies expected the final battle to take place in Jerusalem and on Mount Zion. The final battle of history is the destruction of the political, cultural, and religious systems of the world (the Beast and the false prophet) that opposed God and the defeat of the ungodly who refuse to follow Jesus (the Lamb). This last battle takes place when Jesus returns for the final judgment. Jesus wins the final victory of human history – not with military might, but with the word of God. [17]

Furthermore, the premillennial view of historical succession between chapters 19 and 20 also runs counter to the declaration of Hebrews 12:26-28. As noted above, according to premillennialism, there will be *two* wars, *two* cosmic dissolutions, one before the millennium (16:17-21; 19:11-21; cf. Matt. 24:29) and one after it

---

16. R. Fowler White, "Reexamining the Evidence for Recapitulation," 327.
17. Schnabel, *40 Questions*, 237.

(20:9-11). But in Hebrews 12 we read: "At that time his voice shook the earth, but now he has promised, 'Yet once more I will shake not only the earth but also the heavens.' This phrase, 'Yet once more,' indicates the removal of things that are shaken – that is, things that have been made – in order that the things that cannot be shaken may remain. Therefore let us be grateful for receiving a kingdom that cannot be shaken, and thus let us offer to God acceptable worship, with reverence and awe" (vv. 26-28). Clearly, the author is describing the cosmic consequences of the appearance of the Divine Judge, first at Sinai, and then finally at the end of the age. He could hardly have been more explicit when he said, "Yet once (*hapax*) more I will shake not only the earth, but also the heavens" (v. 26). But according to premillennialism he should have said, "Yet *twice* more …," that is, once before the millennium and a second time after it. A more viable interpretation is the one which interprets the account of destruction in 20:9-11 as an abbreviated recapitulation of the destruction in 6:12-17, 16:17-21, and 19:11-21.

Another argument employed by the premillennialist is the fact that according to Revelation 20:10 Satan is cast into the lake of fire where the beast and false prophet *already are*. Therefore, the latter two characters must have been cast into the lake of fire *before* the millennium (19:20). This argument is based on a mistranslation of Revelation 20:10. The text literally reads: "and the devil, the one who deceives them, was cast into the lake of fire and brimstone, where also the beast and false prophet, and they shall be tormented day and night forever and ever." The NASB supplies the verb "are" (Gk., *eisi*; the ESV renders it "were"), wrongly so in my opinion. The verb to be supplied should probably be "were cast" (*eblethesan*) from 19:20. Thus the text would read: "and the devil … was cast into the lake of fire and brimstone, where also [*hopou kai;* cf. 11:8 for a similar usage] the beast and false prophet **were cast** (*eblethesan*)."

So, when were the beast and false prophet cast in? The answer would appear to be, at the conclusion of *the* war, when the devil himself was cast in. The three *jointly* instigated the Armageddon/Gog–Magog revolt and are therefore *jointly* cast into the lake of fire to be *jointly* tormented forever and ever. The text does not say that the beast and false prophet were "already" in the lake of fire when Satan was cast in. Even if it did, this need only imply that after the war the beast and false prophet were first judged and cast into the lake of fire, a judgment and fate then immediately applied to Satan.

The suggestion that the judgment of the beast and false prophet precedes by 1,000 years that of the devil ignores the parallel between *the* war of chapter 19 and *the* war of chapter 20. There are not two wars with two judgments, but one war and judgment described from two distinct but complementary vantage points. First, in chapter 19, John relates the destruction of the beast and false prophet, and second, in chapter 20, that of Satan.

All that we may legitimately conclude is that the *vision* given to John of the beast and false prophet being cast into the lake of fire precedes the *vision* given to him of Satan being cast in. In order to prove the historical antecedence of the former to the latter, far more is needed than what the text itself supplies. It is just as likely, if not more so, that what we have here is simply the *literary* antecedence of one vision to another, not the historical sequence of their respective contents.[18]

---

18. One additional factor in determining the literary structure of Revelation, specifically the relation between chapters 19 and 20, is the motif of "angelic ascent and descent." There are four occasions in Revelation where an angel is said either to "ascend" or "descend" (7:2; 10:1; 18:1; and 20:1). In 7:2; 10:1; and 18:1, the angelic ascent/descent initiates a vision that temporarily suspends whatever historical or chronological progress had heretofore obtained, and introduces an interlude that is *recapitulatory* in nature. That is to say, the visional interlude inaugurated by this distinctive angelic activity has its *beginning* at a point in history antecedent to the event(s) depicted in the opening of the preceding vision and its *ending* at a point in history contemporaneous with the concluding event of the preceding vision. If this pattern holds true in 20:1 it would indicate that the relation between chapters 19 and 20 is not one of historical progress (as the premillennialist contends) but of *literary recapitulation*. The angelic descent of 20:1 signals a visionary interlude, the historical beginning of which antedates the inaugural events depicted in 19:11-21. This pattern, of course, cannot of itself prove recapitulation, but it does provide support for that view of the structure of Revelation when taken in conjunction with other factors. For a defense of recapitulation or progressive parallelism in the book of Revelation as a whole, see William

The second of the two arguments from Revelation 20:1-3 employed by premillennialists pertains to the nature and extent of Satan's binding. Premillennialists insist that Satan's imprisonment in 20:1-3 is not compatible with the dimensions of his present activity as portrayed in the New Testament epistles.[19] G.R. Beasley-Murray, for example, argues that the angel in 20:1 "reduces Satan to impotence." The "incarceration of the Devil," says Beasley-Murray, "is trebly circumscribed. He is bound up, locked in, and sealed over. The writer could hardly have expressed more emphatically the inability of Satan to harm the race of man."[20] Wayne Grudem likewise contends that "the imagery of throwing Satan into a pit and shutting it and sealing it over him gives a picture of total removal from influence on the earth."[21]

Hendriksen, *More Than Conquerors: An Interpretation of the Book of Revelation* (Grand Rapids: Baker Book House, 1977), 22-64; Benjamin B. Warfield, "The Millennium and the Apocalypse," *PTR* 2 (Oct 1904): 599-617; Anthony A. Hoekema, *The Bible and the Future* (Grand Rapids: Eerdmans, 1979), 223-27, and the more recent commentaries by G.K. Beale and Dennis Johnson. Although not typically conservative in her conclusions, helpful insights are provided by Adela Y. Collins in her two books, *The Combat Myth in the Book of Revelation* (Missoula: Scholars Press, 1976), 5-13, and *The Apocalypse* (Wilmington, Delaware: Michael Glazier, Inc., 1979), xii-xiv. Meredith Kline, in his unpublished class notes, "A Study in the Structure of the Revelation of John," likewise argues for recapitulation, but offers a slightly different interpretation than Hendriksen. According to Kline, the book contains five synchronous sections or cycles of visions, sandwiched, as it were, between an Introduction/Conclusion and a portrait of the Church in the World / in Glory. Each cycle takes us back to the beginning of the Christian era and concludes with the end of the age, God's judgment, and Christ's return (1:1-8 = Introduction; 1:9–3:22 = The Church Imperfect in the World; 4:1–8:1 = The Seven Seals; 8:2–11:19 = The Seven Trumpets; 12:1–14:20 = The Deeper Conflict; 15:1–16:21 = The Seven Bowls; 17:1–21:8 = The Final Judgments; 21:9–22:5 = The Church Perfect in Glory; and 22:6-21 = Conclusion).

19. For example, in 1 Cor. 5:5; 2 Cor. 4:3-4; Eph. 6:10-20; 1 Thess. 2:18; James 4:7; 1 Pet. 5:8-9; 1 John 4:3; 5:19.

20. G.R. Beasley-Murray, *The Book of Revelation*, NCBC (London: Marshall, Morgan, and Scott, 1974), 285.

21. Wayne Grudem, *Systematic Theology: An Introduction to Biblical Doctrine* (Grand Rapids: Zondervan, 1994), 1118.

However, the question must be asked: "In regard to what is Satan bound? Is the binding of Satan designed to immobilize him from any and all activities?" The premillennialist thinks so. Beasley-Murray tells us that Satan's binding entails his inability "to harm the race of man." But that is not what John says. The premillennial interpretation errs in that it has attempted to universalize what John explicitly restricts.

Two statements in Revelation 20 tell us the purpose of Satan's imprisonment. First, in verse 3, John says that Satan was bound "*so that he should not deceive the nations any longer*." Then secondly, in verse 8, John tells us that upon his release from the abyss Satan will come out "to deceive the nations which are in the four corners of the earth, Gog and Magog, to gather them together for the war." Note well what John does and does not say. He does *not* say that Satan was bound so that he should no longer persecute Christians, or so that he should no longer prowl about "like a roaring lion" (1 Pet. 5:8) devouring believing men and women. He does *not* say that Satan was bound so that he should no longer concoct schemes to disrupt church unity (2 Cor. 2:11), or so that he should no longer disguise himself as an angel of light (2 Cor. 11:14). He does *not* say that Satan was bound so that he should no longer hurl his flaming missiles at Christians (Eph. 6:16), or so that he should be kept from thwarting the plans of the Apostle Paul (1 Thess. 2:18) or other church planters.

Rather, John says that Satan was bound so that he should no longer deceive the *nations* (v. 3), the purpose behind which is to mobilize them in an international rebellion against the city of God (v. 8). And the language John employs in 20:1-3 makes it clear that there is no possible way for Satan to do so during the 1,000 years. The restriction on this particular aspect of his sinister ministry is absolute and invincible. *The intent of the devil is to incite a premature eschatological conflict, to provoke Armageddon before its, that is to say, before God's time. But the exalted Christ, through the agency of an angelic being, has temporarily stripped Satan of his ability to orchestrate the nations of the earth for the final battle* (regardless of the form that battle might assume).

The final offensive against the Lamb and his elect shall come only when the restriction placed on *this* element of Satan's work is lifted. For the duration of the present Christian era Satan's hand is stayed. Upon release from his imprisonment he will dispatch his demonic hordes "which go out to the kings of the whole world, to gather them together for the war of the great day of God, the Almighty" (Rev. 16:14).

Although Satan may and will do much in this present age (as the New Testament epistles clearly indicate), there is one thing of which John assures us: *Satan will never be permitted to incite and organize the unbelieving nations of the world in a final, catastrophic assault against the Church, until such time as God in his providence so determines.* That event, which the Lord will immediately terminate with the fiery breath of his mouth (Rev. 20:9), will come only at the end of this age.

John does not say Satan's activity is altogether eliminated, but that it has been effectively curtailed *in one particular domain.* The binding is absolute and, at least for the duration of a "millennium," unbreakable. That is to say, it is a binding which is intensive, so far as it goes, but is nowhere said to be extensive in relation to all that Satan does. It is designed solely for one purpose, to prohibit and inhibit a Satanic plot to deceive the nations into a war which, in view of the prophetic plan and power of God, is both premature and futile.

Other amillennial interpreters would prefer to expand the limitations placed on Satan by the binding of 20:1-3. Both Anthony Hoekema and William Hendriksen, for example, argue that one form of deception that Satan perpetrated prior to Christ's first advent pertains to the gospel. There is a sense in which prior to Christ's first coming all "nations," with the exception of Israel, were "deceived" by Satan and thus prevented from embracing the truth (with certain notable exceptions, of course). The universal expansion and embrace of the gospel (Matt. 28:19) subsequent to Christ's advent, so they argue, is the direct result of Satan's incarceration. Hoekema and Hendriksen thus identify the binding of Satan in

Revelation 20 with the decisive defeat he suffered at the time of our Lord's first advent.[22]

Especially relevant in this regard is Paul's statement in Acts 26:16-18 concerning the mission given him by the exalted Christ:

> But rise and stand upon your feet, for I have appeared to you for this purpose, to appoint you as a servant and witness to the things in which you have seen me and to those in which I will appear to you, delivering you from your people and from the Gentiles – to whom I am sending you *to open their eyes, so that they may turn from darkness to light and from the power of Satan to God*, that they may receive forgiveness of sins and a place among those who are sanctified by faith in me. (italics added)

The Gentiles ("nations") are portrayed as being in darkness with respect to the gospel, having been blinded ("deceived") while under the dominion of Satan. However, as a result of Christ's first coming, such deception no longer obtains. The nations or Gentiles may now receive the forgiveness of sins and the divine inheritance. Hendriksen draws this conclusion:

> In Rev. 20:1-3 the binding of Satan and the fact that he is hurled into the abyss to remain there for a thousand years indicates that throughout this present Gospel Age, which begins with Christ's first coming and extends nearly to the second coming, the devil's influence on earth is curtailed so that he is unable to prevent the extension of the church among the nations by means of an active missionary program. During this entire period he is prevented from causing the nations – the world in general – to destroy the church as a mighty, missionary institution.... By means of the preaching of the Word as applied by the Holy Spirit, the elect, from all parts of the world, are brought from darkness to light. In that sense the church conquers the nations, and the nations do not conquer the church.[23]

---

22. See Matt. 12:29 where the same word for "binding" (*deo*) occurs; also cf. Luke 10:17-18; John 12:31-32; 16:11; Col. 2:15; Heb. 2:14; 1 John 3:8.

23. William Hendriksen, *More Than Conquerors*, 226-27.

It's entirely possible that these two views may be combined. Perhaps one of the principal means Satan hoped to employ in order to mobilize the nations for war was the pervasive spiritual darkness and unbelief in which they languished. But with the worldwide spread of the gospel, the necessary power base from which Satan would launch his attack has been dismantled. In other words, it is the influence of the Church, as a result of the universal preaching of the gospel, which inhibits the activity of Satan in this particular regard. Though Satan still blinds the minds of the unbelieving (2 Cor. 4:4), he is providentially restricted from hindering the pervasive expansion of the gospel throughout the world. Satan may win an occasional battle, but the war belongs to Christ!

Answering a Premillennial Protest

The premillennialist is often heard to say, in response to my argument, that if the binding of Satan in Revelation 20 refers to what happened at the first coming of Christ, it is inconsistent with what is said of Satan in Revelation 12. That is to say, in Revelation 12 Satan is cast down to the earth at the time of Christ's first coming. But how then can Satan be bound and cast into the abyss, also at the time and as a result of the work of Christ in the first century?

But it seems this would be problematic only if one insists on reading Revelation 20 in a woodenly literal and even physical way, when in fact the language there, as is the case throughout Revelation, is highly symbolic. In other words, the premillennialist seems to be saying that we are to understand Revelation 20 as teaching that a physical, geo-spatial movement is involved to a localized geo-spatial place called the abyss. On this basis they appear to be saying that since the devil moves spatially from heaven to earth in Revelation 12 and spatially from the earth to the abyss in Revelation 20 that they can't be regarded as somehow both connected to Christ's defeat of the devil in the first century.

But if the premillennialist insists on saying that Satan's being cast into the abyss in Revelation 20 must be interpreted in a literal, spatial way, what does he do with the rest of the imagery in that passage? Must we believe that the angel who came down from heaven was physically holding a literal key that literally could lock and unlock a pit? What kind of door was on this pit? What kind of lock held it fast? I suppose then there was only one way of entry into this pit and that it was sealed all around to prevent escape. It must have been something other than a physical pit because Satan is a spiritual being and could not be held by mere material bonds. Must we also believe this angel was holding a literal chain, one with physically material links that could be measured as perhaps 10 feet long or even 100 feet long, a chain that could literally restrain a spiritual being like Satan? And did this angel literally "seize" the devil, i.e., grab him and take hold of him and somehow wrestle him into submission so that he could be incarcerated in the pit?

I suppose the premillennialist must also believe that Satan was a literal, physical serpent, as he is called in verse 2. But of course no premillennialist believes that. They believe that this is symbolic imagery. But must we not assume that the premillennialist is forced to believe that the "pit" or abyss into which Satan was thrown was literally shut and sealed, somehow with a door that could be locked or a wall or stone or something to secure him within it.

My point is that I think most, if not all, premillennialists would readily acknowledge that all of this is symbolic imagery designed to teach a very real and, yes, even literal spiritual and theological truth. The point of talking about an "abyss" and a "chain" and a "key" and "sealing" and "shutting" up within this abyss one who is a serpent is to emphasize that Satan is or will be restrained from some particular activity for the duration of what is called the millennium. But to argue that Satan cannot be cast down to the earth in Revelation 12 and also be incarcerated in the abyss, both as a result of the work of Christ in the first century, is to press this sort of imagery beyond the breaking point and well outside the bounds of what the nature of this sort of language is designed to accomplish.

The singular point of Revelation 20 is simply to portray in graphic terms the spiritual restraint placed on Satan to assure the saints who are suffering that his design for deceiving the nations during the time of the millennium cannot be attained. But to argue that Satan being cast down to earth in Revelation 12 precludes him also being restricted from deceiving the nations during the millennium is to force onto highly symbolic imagery a physical and material sense that is inconsistent with the literary genre of Revelation itself. As I read Revelation 12 and 20 it makes perfectly good sense to me that because of the life, death, resurrection, and exaltation of Christ to the right hand of the Father, Satan has suffered a decisive defeat. That defeat is manifest in several ways. On the one hand, Satan has lost the legal and moral grounds on the basis of which he had formerly accused God's people. Those accusations no longer carry force. This defeat is portrayed in the symbolic language of his being thrown to the earth. But surely the premillennialist wouldn't argue that Satan was never on the earth before that moment? If Satan already had access to the earth before Christ's defeat of him at the cross and resurrection, and surely he did as the experience of Job and Jesus both bear witness, then we cannot press the language of Revelation 12 to mean that he literally and spatially was transferred from heaven to earth. Again, the point of the language in Revelation 12 to the effect that he was thrown down to earth is to communicate to God's people that the devil's work of trying to undermine their status with God is over. Christ has defeated him. His accusations no longer carry force. He has lost any access to the throne of heaven where he might raise such charges against them. And this glorious theological reality, dare I say this glorious and *literal* theological reality, is portrayed in highly symbolic imagery of Satan being thrown down to the earth.

Satan's defeat, therefore, is manifest in several ways. We've seen how Revelation 12 portrays it. Now in Revelation 20 it is manifest in yet another way. Not only has Satan lost his power to successfully accuse Christians, but God has also taken steps to restrict him from preventing the gospel to extend to the nations of the earth. He has also taken steps to prevent him from fomenting a premature rebellion of the nations of the earth in an attempt to destroy the church and to provoke a premature outbreak of Armageddon. And he communicates this gloriously literal and very real theological truth by employing the imagery of Satan being held prisoner in a pit. I see no reason why these two texts cannot stand simultaneously and side by side as vividly symbolic yet incredibly real portrayals of the impact of Christ's death and resurrection and exaltation on Satan.

To insist that Satan cannot be truly in the abyss because he has been thrown down to the earth is, again, to impose a rigidly wooden and artificial structure on symbolism that it simply isn't designed to sustain. Both Revelation 12 and 20, in their own ways, and by means of differing symbolic language, describe the victory of Christ over Satan: in chapter 12 it is Satan's defeat in terms of his efforts to accuse God's people of sin; in chapter 20 it is Satan's defeat in terms of his efforts to hinder the spread of the gospel and to provoke a global assault on the Church of God. Each has its own unique symbolic imagery and each communicates its own glorious and very real truth. They are perfectly compatible with each other.

Eckhard Schnabel's Premillennial Alternative

Eckhard J. Schnabel has a slightly novel interpretation of "the nations that are at the four corners of the earth, Gog and Magog" (Rev. 20:8), who are deceived by Satan and gathered for battle following the millennium. They are the unrepentant of human history who lived *before* the second coming of Christ. According to Schnabel, when Christ returns they are killed and consigned to the abyss where they remain with Satan for the 1,000 years of the earthly millennial kingdom (Rev. 20:1-3). In other words, these are identical with the kings of the earth and the captains and mighty men (Rev. 19:18-19), together with others, "both slave and free, both small and great" (Rev. 19:18b), who opposed Christ at his return and were summarily and swiftly slain (Rev. 19:21). This would also include all the unredeemed of every age who rejected Christ and have been imprisoned in Hades awaiting the final judgment. According to Schnabel, the Abyss and Hades are synonymous and together refer to the realm of the dead. All these unrepentant and unbelieving sinners are "the rest of the dead" who "did not come to life until the thousand years were ended" (Rev. 20:5). Thus, when Satan is released from the abyss after the 1,000 years (Rev. 20:2-3), all these unbelievers who were there with him are "resurrected" and join Satan in one final assault against Christ and his people. According to Schnabel, during this 1,000-year incarceration in the abyss, "Satan's followers saw that following the ancient Serpent, and his claim to godhood, only leads to death. They were able to see his lies: wanting to be like God by knowing good and evil (Gen. 3:5) indeed leads to death, just as God had told Adam and Eve. The Serpent's deception is unmasked: he has nothing to offer but death. John does not provide an explicit answer to the question as to why it is part of God's plan (note the term 'must' in Rev. 20:3) that the 'nations' be deceived a final time. The answer is to be found in the following thought: the fact that the sinners who had been deceived by Satan before are now deceived by him again, after being in his company in the Abyss for a thousand years, proves their total depravity" [24] and demonstrates that they are worthy of eternal punishment. So, according to Schnabel, all the unredeemed who fell for Satan's deception the first time, before the millennium, now "fall for it a second time" after the millennium.

The primary motivation for this interpretation is that it appears to solve a major premillennial problem. As mentioned earlier, the premillennialist must account for where the people come from who comprise the "nations" whom Satan will deceive at the close of the millennium. If all unbelievers are slain at the time of the second coming of Christ, only resurrected and glorified believers will populate the millennial kingdom. As also noted earlier on several occasions, most premillennialists try to evade this problem by insisting that not all unbelievers die at the second coming. Those who survive and enter the millennium in their natural, physical bodies will then bear children, who in turn will bear children, and so on, many of whom at the close of the millennium, having never come to faith in Jesus, will comprise the unbelieving nations who rebel one final time at the behest of Satan. Schnabel finds this unconvincing, so he must account for these unbelieving nations by some other means.

24. Eckhard Schnabel, *40 Questions About the End Times* (Grand Rapids: Kregel, 2011), 274.

There are several problems with this version of premillennialism. First, if all unrepentant and unredeemed humanity are dead in the abyss/Hades, what need is there for Satan to be bound at all? According to Revelation 20:3, the purpose for Satan's incarceration is to prevent him from deceiving the nations. But if the nations no longer exist on the earth, having already been consigned to the abyss (which is precisely what Schnabel proposes), who could possibly constitute those who are the potential objects of his deceptive lies? In other words, if all the saved are reigning with Christ in the millennium on earth and all the lost are imprisoned with Satan in the abyss/Hades, what's the point of his being bound? What need would there be for this? In order to deceive the nations there must be nations to deceive! Yet, according to Schnabel's own reckoning, the only "nations" whom Satan could possibly deceive are present with him in the abyss where neither he nor they can do anyone any harm!

Second, Schnabel, like all premillennialists, argues for chronological sequence between Revelation 19 and Revelation 20. Thus on his view the wicked are deceived by Satan and killed at the beginning of the millennium, raised at the end of the millennium, deceived yet again by Satan, destroyed in the final battle of 20:7-10 ("fire came down from heaven and consumed them"), but are then portrayed in 20:11-15 as "standing before the throne" of God (20:12), very much alive, there to be judged. It appears that Schnabel must have the wicked being raised twice: first at the end of the millennium as they join Satan in this final rebellion, only to be destroyed, and then raised a second time in order that they may appear before the judgment throne of God.

Third, Schnabel must also account for the reference in 20:8 to the nations that are at "the four corners of the earth." How can this be if they are in the abyss or Hades? It would seem that either they are physically alive, scattered abroad on the face of the earth, or they are physically dead, languishing in an immaterial state in Hades. Schnabel's explanation is that "the four corners of the earth" and "Hades" are one and the same. However, in Revelation the number four is the number of the *world*. For example, the earth not only has four corners (7:1; 20:8) but also four winds (7:1). The created world is categorized in four divisions. Whereas all other doxologies in Revelation are either seven-fold (5:12; 7:12) or three-fold (4:9, 11; 19:2), in 5:13 we read of "every creature in *heaven* and on *earth* and *under the earth* and in the *sea*" offering to God a four-fold doxology: "blessing and honor and glory and might". According to Richard Bauckham, "Revelation makes greater use of an alternative fourfold division of creation: earth, sea, (rivers and) springs, heaven (8:7-12; 14:7; 16:2-9). These four parts of creation are respectively the targets of the judgments of the first four trumpets (8:7-12) and the first four bowls (16:2-9)." [25] It is certainly no accident, notes Bauckham, "that the list of cargoes which Babylon (Rome) imports from 'the merchants of the earth' (18:11-13) comprises twenty-eight (4x7) items. They are listed as representative of *all* the products of the whole *world*." [26] We should also note the four references to the seven Spirits (1:4; 3:1; 4:5; 5:6) which undoubtedly represent the fullness of divine power "sent out into all the earth." Related to this are the four references to the seven churches (1:4, 11, 20 [twice]), suggesting that they represent all the churches of the world. Simply put, to reduce "the four corners of the earth" (20:8) to nothing more than a reference to the abyss or Hades is inconsistent with the numeric symbolism found in the book as a whole.

In summary, is this really the end-time scenario that John and other biblical authors envision? Let me walk you through it again. According to Schnabel's view, the unbelieving nations are killed at the second coming of Christ, and then cast into the abyss with Satan where for 1,000 years they suffer in his presence and are witnesses to his lies and obvious and inevitable failure. Satan is there so that, for the duration of the 1,000 years, he may no longer deceive the very unbelievers who are with him in the abyss! At the close of this 1,000 years God releases Satan and raises from the dead all unbelievers. Now, in their resurrection bodies, they all yield once again to Satan's deceptive lies and join him in march-

25. Bauckham, *The Climax of Prophecy*, 31.
26. Ibid.

ing against Christ and his people (Rev. 20:9a). Fire descends from heaven and consumes them (Rev. 20:9b).

What happens next to all the unbelieving people of all human history? Evidently they are then cast yet again (!) into the abyss or Hades, for in Revelation 20:13 we are told that at the time of the final judgment "Death and Hades gave up the dead who were in them, and they were judged each one of them, according to what they had done." So, having been killed and cast into Hades (at the beginning of the millennium) and then raised from the dead and then killed again and then cast yet again into Hades (at the end of the millennium), they are now for the final time (!) raised to stand before the Great White Throne of God to be judged. Once again, may I humbly suggest that these are the sort of exegetical maneuverings and theological oddities that one is forced to embrace when one insists on extending death and deception, together with resurrections and judgments, beyond the time of the second coming of our Lord.

Is it not far more in keeping with the text that these wicked, unbelieving "nations" whom Satan deceives and leads into battle against Christ are the same wicked, unbelieving nations of Revelation 19:17-21 who "make war against him who was sitting on the horse and against his army" (Rev. 19:19; an obvious reference to Jesus and his people)? This, of course, would mean that the "millennium" is coterminous with this current church age, during which Satan is prevented from deceiving the nations into a premature global assault against Christ (i.e., Armageddon). It would mean that the "nations" whom Satan once again seeks to deceive, following his release, are the multitude of unbelievers alive at the time of Christ's second coming at the close of history. Following this final war (i.e., Armageddon), Satan is thrown together with the beast and false prophet into the lake of fire (20:10). Then, as verses 11-15 make clear, the unbelieving dead of every age are one and all at the same time raised to stand before the Great White Throne of God. They are "judged by what was written in the books, according to what they had done" (20:12). Their eternal destiny is "the lake of fire," the "second death" (20:14-15), from which there is no escape.

Amillennialism should not be embraced merely for its simplicity, but one cannot help but admire the straightforward way in which it conceives the end times: The dead in Christ "live" and "reign" with the Lord throughout the course of this present church age (= the millennium), during which time Satan is prevented from hindering the spread of the gospel to the nations and is unable to foment a premature global conflict (Armageddon), at the close of which Satan is granted his freedom to deceive the nations; he gathers them for the war of Armageddon, Christ returns from heaven with his saints and consumes them all, Satan is judged and cast into the lake of fire, the unbelieving dead are all raised to stand judgment, and are in turn cast into the lake of fire to suffer the second death.

Chapter Fifteen

Amillennialism, Revelation 20, and The First Resurrection

We now come to the focal point of the eschatological hostilities which divide premillennialists from amillennialists, namely, the meaning of the "first resurrection" in Revelation 20:4-6. Although for many years a premillennialist, I am now persuaded that Revelation 20:4-6 is concerned exclusively with *the experience of the martyrs in the intermediate state.* Notwithstanding their death physically for disobedience to the beast, they live spiritually through faith in the Lamb. Although a number of amillennialists identify the "coming to life" in 20:4 with regeneration (the new birth), I am inclined to follow the suggestion of others, such as Meredith Kline and Anthony Hoekema, that John is describing entrance into the intermediate state and the blessings of life it brings. My explanation and defense of this interpretation will come later on. But first I must respond to the premillennial view of the passage.

Although there are variations among premillennialists, especially between dispensationalists and non-dispensationalists, most forms of premillennialism hold in common the following points.

The "coming to life" in 20:4b is a physical, bodily resurrection of believers that occurs at the second coming of Christ *before* the millennium. The "coming to life" in 20:5a is also a physical, bodily resurrection, but of unbelievers *after* the millennium. Therefore, the bodily resurrection of all mankind comes in two stages separated by 1,000 years. The elect are raised before and the non-elect after this millennial reign of Christ upon the earth.

Following are the principal arguments used by premillennialists to defend this view of Revelation 20, the first of which has come to be known as *Alford's Dictum*. Henry Alford famously declared:

> If, in a passage where *two resurrections* are mentioned, where certain *psuchai ezesan* at the first, and the rest of the *nekroi ezesan* only at the end of a specified period after that first, – if in such a passage the first resurrection may be understood to mean *spiritual* rising with Christ, while the second means *literal* rising from the grave; – then there is an end of all significance in language, and Scripture is wiped out as a definite testimony to any thing. If the first resurrection is spiritual, then so is the second, which I suppose none will be hardy enough to maintain: but if the second is literal, then so is the first.[1]

Whereas Alford's dictum is a helpful principle of interpretation, I do not believe it applies in this particular passage. Other texts in which it does not apply include John 2:18-22; 11:25-26; Matthew 8:22; Luke 9:24; John 6:49-50; and possibly 1 Peter 3:1; 1 Corinthians 15:22; Romans 9:6; 2 Corinthians 5:21. Amillennialists have almost uniformly appealed to John 5:25-29 as a clear exception to Alford's dictum. Here a "spiritual" and a "physical" resurrection are spoken of in the same context. (See the Addendum below.)

The second argument employed is an appeal to the Greek term (*anastasis*) translated "resurrection". This noun appears forty-two times in the New Testament, thirty-nine of which refer to bodily resurrection from the dead (for an exception, see Luke 2:34). The remaining two occurrences are in Revelation 20:5 and 6, their meaning yet to be determined. The substance of this argument for premillennialism is noted and acknowledged. But is it altogether convincing and compelling? I think not, and here is why.

---

1. Henry Alford, *The Greek Testament* (Chicago: Moody Press, 1968 [1958]), IV:732-33.

Let us assume, for the sake of argument, that John might wish to describe life in the intermediate state in Revelation 20:4-6. How else could he have done so, other than the way he has, and still secure the needed emphasis? That is to say, if John's purpose were to encourage and console believers who were facing martyrdom, and if, in doing so, he wished to throw into sharp relief the contrast between what the beast might do to them *physically* and what the Lamb will do for them *spiritually*, what better, more appropriate, or even more biblical way could he have done so than by assuring them that though they may *die physically* at the hands of the beast they will *live spiritually* in the presence of the Lamb? I can think of no more vivid way of making this point than that of *life* beyond and in spite of *death*.

If John were attempting to describe the blessings of the intermediate state for those facing martyrdom, what terminology could he possibly have used, other than what he does use, and still maintain the desired emphasis? There simply is no other Greek noun besides *anastasis* that would adequately make the point. The only other Greek nouns in the New Testament which mean "resurrection" are *exanastasis,* used only in Philippians 3:11, and *egersis,* used only in Matthew 27:53. Both of these texts refer to physical resurrection also.[2]

In sum, if John wished to describe entrance into the intermediate state in terms of a resurrection (and that would certainly be appropriate given the prospects for martyrdom among those to whom he was writing), with what Greek noun other than *anastasis* could he have done it? There are few who will deny that Scripture uses the terminology and imagery of physical resurrection to describe spiritual life (see Ezek. 37; Eph. 2:1-6; Col. 2:12-13; 3:1; Rom. 6). Why, then, should we object to the use of the terminology and imagery of physical resurrection to describe spiritual life in the intermediate state, especially when such "life" is contrasted

---

2. On this see Murray J. Harris, *Raised Immortal: Resurrection and Immortality in the New Testament* (Grand Rapids: Eerdmans, 1983), especially the Appendix, "The Terminology of Resurrection in the New Testament," 269-72.

with "death"? I am sure John knew that *anastasis* might well evoke the notion of bodily resurrection in the minds of his readers. That is why, I believe, he explicitly identifies those of whom he predicates this resurrection as the "*souls of those beheaded.*" He knew that such a phrase, even more so in view of the parallel in Revelation 6:9-11, would have alerted his readers (prospective martyrs) that the kind of resurrection in view was spiritual life after physical death. When we add to this the fact that only here in all the New Testament is the ordinal "first" appended to the noun "resurrection," and reflect on its significance, the possibility of the amillennial position is strengthened (more on this point below).

Note well: I said the *possibility* of this particular amillennial interpretation. I do not want to be misunderstood at this point. I am *not* saying that John's use of *anastasis* demands the amillennial interpretation. It is entirely possible that *anastasis* means physical, bodily resurrection in Revelation 20. At no time have I suggested that *anastasis* is inappropriate as a description of physical, bodily resurrection. All that I have argued for is that, *assuming* John wished to describe the intermediate state, and given the historical context in which he was writing as well as the immediate prospects for martyrdom among his readers, and in view of the limitations on terminology at his disposal, *anastasis* would not be an inappropriate word to make his point. Whether or not this interpretation of *anastasis* is *probable* must be determined on other grounds. At this point all I wish to establish is that the premillennial argument based on the traditional definition of *anastasis* is something less than compelling.

The premillennialist also appeals to the use of the verb translated "come to life" (*zao*) in the New Testament. This verb is used twice in our passage (vv. 4, 5). The point is that when *zao* is used of resurrection, i.e., of "coming to life" after death, it almost always is physical, bodily resurrection (Matt. 9:18; Rom. 14:9; 2 Cor. 13:4; Rev. 2:8).

However, this verb occurs some 130 times in the New Testament and has well over a *dozen different* connotations. It can refer to ordinary physical existence in the here and now, to the living

God, to living water, to living eternally, to Christ's living now in heaven as exalted Lord, to the way we conduct ourselves ethically, and to spiritual regeneration and conversion, just to mention a few. It is even used of living in the intermediate state in Matthew 22:32 (cf. Luke 20:38; John 11:25-26).

We should not be surprised that John might choose to describe the experience of the martyrs in the intermediate state as "living". The intermediate state is a *spiritual living after physical death*, is it not? Jesus *did* promise his people in Revelation 2:10-11 that because of their faithfulness unto *physical death* he would give them the crown of *life*, did he not? And did he not say that the kind of *living* granted to those who die for their faith is such that secures them against the second *death*, even as John tells us in 20:6 that the second *death* has no power over those who *live* by virtue of the first resurrection? These parallels between Revelation 2:10-11 and 20:4-6 are unmistakable.

On what grounds, then, should anyone object to John's describing the experience of the intermediate state as "living (spiritually) with Christ," especially in view of the intended contrast with the physical death they suffer at the hands of the beast? I do not know of another text descriptive of the intermediate state in which *any* verb is used to describe the quality of life experienced there by the saints. Why, then, should anyone object to the suggestion that John uses such a common, well-known term as *zao* in Revelation 20? I am again led to conclude that *zao*, like *anastasis*, is entirely fitting as a description of the nature and blessedness of the intermediate state. Such could not help but encourage and strengthen those who face the possibility of physical death for their faith, be it then or now.[3]

---

3. Wayne Grudem argues that what the amillennialist means by this verb is "coming into the presence of God" (*Systematic Theology*, 1119) and that "no other examples of that word in the New Testament take the sense, 'come into the presence of God'" (1119). But no amillennialist of whom I am aware ever argues that this is what is intended by the use of *zao*. The word means to "live", which as we've seen is certainly true of the experience of those who are presently with Christ in the intermediate state. On a slightly more technical level, the question of whether the aorist *ezesan* should be translated as ingressive

Finally, the premillennialist insists that the words "one thousand years" (*chilia ete*) must mean literal years, which is to say, arithmetically and chronologically precise years. As anyone who has studied Revelation knows all too well, deciphering numbers in this book is an incredibly difficult task. One need only observe the dispute down through the centuries over the meaning of 666!

In other texts "one thousand" rarely if ever is meant to be taken with arithmetical precision. This is true whether the context is *non-temporal* (Ps. 50:10; Song 4:4; Josh. 23:10; Isa. 60:22; Deut. 1:11; Job 9:3; Eccles. 7:28), in which case the usage is always figurative, indeed hyperbolical, or *temporal* (Deut. 7:9; 1 Chron. 16:15; Pss. 84:10; 90:4; 105:8; 2 Pet. 3:8). What is the significance of the number 1,000 here? According to David Chilton, just "as the number *seven* connotes a fullness of *quality* in Biblical imagery, the number *ten* contains the idea of a fullness of *quantity; in other words, it stands for *manyness.* A thousand multiplies and intensifies this (10 x 10 x 10), in order to express great vastness (cf. 5:11; 7:4-8; 9:16; 11:3,13; 12:6; 14:1,3,20)." [4] For example, we are told in Psalm 50:10 that God owns "the cattle on a thousand hills." Obviously this "does not mean that the cattle on the 1,001st hill belong to someone else. God owns all the cattle on all the hills. But He says 'a thousand' to indicate that there are many hills, and much cattle." [5] Benjamin B. Warfield takes much the same approach:

> The sacred number seven in combination with the equally sacred number three forms the number of holy perfection ten, and when this ten is cubed into a thousand the seer has said all he could say

---

("came to life" or "began to live") or constative ("they lived") is not an especially important one. In support of the ingressive view one may cite Rom. 14:9 and Rev. 2:8. In support of the constative view one might appeal to its correlation with "and they reigned with Christ a thousand years," the latter obviously being constative in force, and the fact that in the majority of cases in the New Testament, when in the aorist, *zao* is constative.

4. David Chilton, *The Days of Vengeance: An Exposition of the Book of Revelation* (Ft. Worth: Dominion Press, 1987), 506-07.

5. Ibid., 507.

to convey to our minds the idea of absolute completeness.... [There-fore] when the saints are said to live and reign with Christ a thousand years the idea intended is that of inconceivable exaltation, security and blessedness as beyond expression by ordinary language.[6]

Summary

I have responded in this chapter and the preceding one to what I perceive to be the strongest arguments favoring the premillennial interpretation of Revelation 20:4-6. My conclusion is that whereas each of these arguments is entirely possible, none of them is com-pelling. In each instance there is a viable alternative. This alternative becomes persuasive when the rest of the New Testament witness is brought to bear on Revelation 20. The task now at hand is to pro-vide a cogent amillennial interpretation which not only does justice to the exegetical and theological data in 20:4-6, but is also compat-ible with what we have seen to be the testimony of the remainder of the New Testament on the subject of the kingdom of God.

The Amillennialist's Millennial Kingdom

It is one thing to offer a critique of a cherished and widely held view of the millennium. It is something else to construct in its place a cogent and persuasive alternative. In the minds of many this has been the principal deficiency in the vast majority of amillennial treatments of eschatology. Whether or not this criticism is justi-fied, I offer this chapter as an attempt to supply what many insist has been conspicuous by its absence: an amillennial explanation of the first resurrection that deals fairly and fully with the textual data. In the light of what has already been said concerning this controversial passage, I wish to make four crucial points.

(1) That John is talking about *the intermediate state* in Revela-tion 20:4-6 seems obvious once the parallel with Revelation 6:9-11 is noted. In my research I have not as yet encountered one premi-llennial author who denies that Revelation 6:9-11 is a vision of the heavenly bliss of those who have suffered martyrdom for Christ.

6. B.B. Warfield, "The Millennium and the Apocalypse," *PTR* 2 (Oct 1904), 608-09.

Yet when they encounter virtually the same terminology in Revelation 20 they can only see a post-parousia millennial kingdom on the earth of embodied believers. A careful examination of these two passages, however, will reveal that they are describing the same experience.

Revelation 6:9	Revelation 20:4
"And … I saw" *(kai eidon)*	"And I saw" *(kai eidon)*
"the souls of those who had been slain" *(tas psuchas ton esphagmenon)*	"the souls of those who had been beheaded" *(tas psuchas ton pepelekismenon)*
"because of the word of God" *(dia ton logon tou theou)*	"because of the word of God" *(dia ton logon tou theou)*
"and because of the testimony which they had maintained" *(dia ten marturian hen eichon)*	"because of the testimony of Jesus" *(dia ten marturian Iesou)*

That John is describing the same scene, namely, that of the blessedness of the intermediate state, seems beyond reasonable doubt. The key is that John, in both instances, is describing the experience of disembodied "souls" *(psuchas)* who had been martyred for their faith in Jesus Christ.

(2) The emphasis in Revelation on the blessedness of Christian death confirms that 20:4-6 is concerned with the bliss of the intermediate state. We read in Revelation 14:13, "Blessed are the dead who die in the Lord from now on! Yes, says the Spirit, that they may rest from their labors, for their deeds follow with them." This sabbath blessing, Meredith Kline explains,

> is very much the same as the millennial blessing of Revelation 20:6. For the biblical concept of sabbath rest includes enthronement after the completion of labors by which royal dominion is manifested or secured (cf., e.g., Isa. 66:1). The sabbath rest of the risen Christ is his kingly session at God's right hand. To live and reign with Christ is to

participate in his royal sabbath rest. In Revelation 20:6 this blessedness is promised to those who have part in "the first resurrection" and in the Revelation 14:13 equivalent it is pronounced on the dead who died in the Lord.[7]

Especially relevant in this regard is the letter to the church at Smyrna in Revelation 2 and its emphasis on the blessedness of Christian death. It also parallels 20:4-6 in several crucial respects. To the believers in Smyrna Jesus speaks these words of encouragement and comfort:

> [10]Do not fear what you are about to suffer. Behold, the devil is about to throw some of you into prison, that you may be tested, and for ten days you will have tribulation. Be faithful unto death, and I will give you the crown of life. [11]He who has an ear, let him hear what the Spirit says to the churches. The one who conquers will not be hurt by the second death (Rev. 2:10-11).

The first thing to note is that, contrary to what premillennialists have typically argued, the activity of Satan here is perfectly compatible with what we read in Revelation 20:1-3 concerning his being bound in the abyss for the duration of the millennial kingdom. As I pointed out in the previous chapter, that binding is designed to prevent Satan from keeping the nations in spiritual darkness and from orchestrating their global assault against the Church of Jesus Christ. But this has no bearing on Satan's on-going efforts to tempt, torment, persecute, and, as is the case here in Smyrna of the first century, cause the deaths of faithful Christian men and women.

There are several other things to note in this passage, each of which draws our attention to the obvious parallel in Revelation 20. First, it speaks of *martyrdom* as the result of steadfast faith ("be faithful unto death"; Rev. 2:10). Second, the faithful are promised "the crown of *life*" (Rev. 2:10). And third, the faithful martyrs are exempt from the *second death* ("he who overcomes shall not be hurt

---

7. Meredith Kline, "The First Resurrection," *WTJ* 37 (1975): 373-74.

by the second death"; Rev. 2:11). Thus Jesus encourages believers in Smyrna to remain faithful unto physical death and he will give them the crown of life. He reminds them of this because he knows that the power to persevere comes from a vibrant faith in the certainty of God's promised reward. Those who do not love "their lives even unto death" (Rev. 12:11) are granted a "life" that infinitely transcends anything this earthly existence could ever afford. Jesus does not call for faithfulness unto death without reminding his people that there awaits them a quality and depth of true and unending life that far outweighs whatever sacrifice is made in the present. These parallels between Revelation 2 and 20 are certainly more than coincidental. Kline makes this clear:

> The equation of the state of Christian death referred to in this letter with "the first resurrection" state of Revelation 20 is of course firmly established by the common contextual mention of "the second death" (not found in any other context), the same assurance of deliverance from this "second death" being given in both cases. But "the crown of life" promise in Revelation 2:10 is also a strong confirmation of this equation. The crown, *stephanos,* though it might be the festive garland, might also be the royal crown. If the latter image is intended here, the "crown of life" promised to the Christian dead is precisely the nominal equivalent of the verbal "they lived and reigned" in the account of the experience that attends the "first resurrection" in Revelation 20:4ff. [8]

When taken in conjunction with the promise to the overcomer in Revelation 3:21 that he will be *enthroned with Christ* (yes, the dead in Christ *do* reign!), the blessings of the intermediate state are encouragements indeed to those whose physical lives are to be taken by the beast. Since John (and Jesus) in Revelation 2–3 conceived of the intermediate state as "souls" living beyond death (hence a *resurrection*), and as an experience characterized by enthronement with Christ (hence *reigning* with him), we should

---

8. Ibid.

not be surprised that in Revelation 20 he likewise describes the intermediate state as *souls living and reigning with Christ!*

(3) John could hardly have been more explicit concerning the location, and therefore the nature, of the millennial rule of the saints when he said that he saw "thrones" *(thronous)*. Where are these thrones upon which the saints sit, which is also to ask, what is the nature of their millennial rule? Let's begin with several observations about the use of the word "throne" *(thronos)* in the book of Revelation.

The word *thronos* appears sixty-two times in the New Testament, forty-seven of which are in the book of Revelation. Twice (2:13; 13:2) it refers to Satan's throne (being synonymous with his authority or power) and once to the throne of the beast (16:10). On four occasions it refers to God's throne on the *new* earth in consequence of its having *come down from heaven* (21:3, 5; 22:1, 3). In every other instance (forty times) *thronos* refers to a throne in *heaven,* either that of God the Father, of Christ, of the twenty-four elders, etc.

Why, then, does the premillennialist argue that *anastasis* ("resurrection") must mean physical resurrection, although it occurs *nowhere* in Revelation outside chapter 20, but ignores *thronos* which never in Revelation refers to anything other than a heavenly throne (and that, in forty texts!)?

Consider the use of *thronos* in the rest of the New Testament. Of the fifteen occurrences of *thronos* outside Revelation, seven are explicitly heavenly. In Luke 1:52 it refers figuratively to the power and authority of earthly rulers. In Colossians 1:16 it refers to angelic (demonic?) beings. In Luke 1:32 the angel Gabriel refers to the "throne" of David on which the coming Messiah will sit in fulfillment of the divine promise, to which Peter makes explicit reference in Acts 2:30. In the verses which follow it is clear that Peter envisioned Christ's resurrection and exaltation to have resulted in his enthronement at the right hand of the Father in fulfillment of Gabriel's declaration.

There are four additional usages of *thronos* (Matt. 19:28 [twice]; 25:31; and Luke 22:30), each of which falls in the same category as Revelation 20:4. In other words, whether the "thrones" in these texts are earthly or heavenly is the very point that stands to be proven. Therefore, one cannot appeal to these passages in support of either view. Otherwise one would be guilty of begging the question. Thus, when we look at all other relevant occurrences of *thronos*, whether inside or outside the book of Revelation, they are without exception heavenly. There is nothing to suggest that they pertain to a millennial earth, either in location or character.

(4) The final point I wish to make concerns the significance of the ordinal "first" (*protos*) in the phrase "first resurrection" (20:5-6), and the theological contrasts that John has established in the text.[9] Before the premillennialist makes much of the meaning of *anastasis* ("resurrection"), he must address the fact that nowhere else in Scripture is this noun (*anastasis*) qualified as being the "first" (*protos*). The importance of this for determining the meaning of "resurrection" must therefore be duly noted.

We begin by noting that in Revelation 21:1-5 the Apostle John contrasts what is "first" with what is "new" (*kainos*). Observe that the consummation of history brings "a *new* heaven and a *new* earth" (v. 1) and a "*new* Jerusalem" (v. 2). Indeed, God will make "all things *new*" (v. 5). Thus we see that the word *first* is used for what is superceded or replaced by the *new*: the *first* heaven and the *first* earth "passed away" (v. 1). Indeed, when God makes all things *new*, all "the *first* things" pass away – tears, death, sorrow, crying, pain (v. 4). Unfortunately, the ESV renders verses 4 with the word "former" things, but it is the same Greek term as found in verses 1-2 where it is rightly rendered by the word "first." Therefore, to be *first* means to belong to the present state of affairs which is passing away. As Meredith Kline explains, "*Protos* ('first') does not merely mark the present world as the first in a series of worlds and certainly not as the first in a series of worlds all of the same kind. On the contrary, it characterizes this world as *different in kind* from the 'new' world [emphasis mine]. It signifies that the present world

9. I'm deeply indebted for this argument to Meredith Kline and his two articles, "The First Resurrection," *WTJ* 37 (1975):366-75, and "The First Resurrection: A Reaffirmation," *WTJ* 39 (Fall 1976): 110-19.

stands in contrast to the new world order of the consummation which will abide forever." [10]

We also see in Revelation 21 that "second" *(deuteros)* is another term for "new". Thus, the death that is identified with the lake of fire and is the eternal counterpart to the death that belongs to the order of *"first* things" (v. 4) is called "the *second* death" (v. 8). Thus *second* as well as *new* serves as the *qualitative opposite* of *first*.

Let me try to put this in easier and more intelligible terms. Whatever is *first* or *old* pertains to the *present* world, that is to say, to the world that is transient, temporary, and incomplete. Conversely, whatever is *second* or *new* pertains to the *future* world, to the world that is permanent, complete, and is associated with the eternal consummation of all things. The term *first* is therefore not an ordinal in a process of counting objects that are identical in kind. Rather, whenever *first* is used in conjunction with *second* or *new* the idea is of a *qualitative contrast* (not a mere numerical sequence). To be *first* is to be associated with this present, temporary, transient world. Whatever is *first* does not participate in the quality of finality and permanence which is distinctive of the age to come.

This idea is present in other passages as well. For example, the Mosaic covenant, being temporary and pre-consummative, is described as the "first" or "old" covenant, in contrast with the Messianic covenant which is the "new" or "second" one (Heb. 8:7, 8, 13; 9:1, 15, 18; 10:9). This contrast between the first and new covenants, Kline concedes, "does not correspond exactly to that between the first and new worlds in Revelation 21, but in both cases the reality described by the term 'first' is one that passes away. In Hebrews as in Revelation 21 *protos* ["first"] is used for the provisional and transient stage in contrast to that which is consummative, final, and enduring." [11] A similar usage of "first" as the qualitative antithesis to what is "second" or "new" is seen in 1 Corinthians 15 as it pertains to the "first" and "second" or "last" Adams.

---

10. Kline, "The First Resurrection," 366-67 (emphasis mine).
11. Ibid., 368.

How does all this affect our understanding of the "*first* resurrection" in Revelation 20? To begin, we should observe that explicit reference to the *first* resurrection and the *second* death strongly implies, if it does not demand, a *second* resurrection and a *first* death. Therefore, we have four events, three of which are easily identified.

(1) There is first of all, the *first death*, which is obviously a reference to physical, bodily death. It is the death to which the martyrs were subjected when the beast beheaded them for refusal to worship his image.

(2) Then we have the *second death*, that is, a non-physical death which consists of eternal punishment.

(3) Thirdly, the *second resurrection*, implied by the existence of a first resurrection, is certainly the physical, bodily resurrection of the unjust (cf. 20:11-15).

It seems reasonable, then, that the first resurrection will sustain to the second resurrection the same relationship which the first death sustains to the second death. So what, then, is that relationship? The first death, as we have seen, is literal and physical, whereas the second death is spiritual and non-physical. The "first" death, because it is "first," relates to this present world with its transient and pre-consummative character, whereas the "second" death, because it is "second," relates to the next world, the consummation, with its permanent and eternal character. Surely, then, since the second resurrection is literal and physical and pertains to the consummate and eternal order, the first resurrection, because it is "first," must be spiritual and non-physical and pertain to the pre-consummative, temporary, and transient order of things.

What all this means is that there are two facts which prevent us from identifying the first resurrection as a physical, bodily resurrection (as the premillennialist insists we must). There is first of all the ordinal *first*. That which is "first" belongs to the order of the present passing world. "The first resurrection" must then be something *this* side of bodily resurrection, some experience that does not bring the subject of it into his consummated condition and final state. Remember: the premillennialist says that if we have a "first" event, in this case a resurrection, we should expect a "second" one of the same kind (Alford's dictum). We now see this is false. The usage of "first" does not suggest a mere numerical sequence of events of like character, but a qualitative contrast between events of a *different* character!

The second factor which excludes the premillennial view is the contrast that John intended to establish between first and second resurrection as well as between first and second death. Observe that when John proceeds to describe the bodily resurrection of the lost in 20:11-15, he avoids using the term "resurrection." Instead, he refers to it, paradoxically, as the second "death" because of the destiny in which it issues (namely, the lake of fire). That which is bodily *resurrection* for the lost is in reality their second *death.*

Similarly, when John proceeds to describe the bodily *death* of the saved in 20:4-6 he avoids using the term "death." Instead he refers to it, paradoxically, as the first "resurrection" because of the destiny in which *it* issues (namely, living and reigning with Christ). That which is bodily *death* for the saved is in reality their first *resurrection.* Observe, then, the beautiful irony in John's language:

- The believer DIES PHYSICALLY but experiences SPIRITUAL RESURRECTION!

- The unbeliever is RESURRECTED PHYSICALLY but experiences SPIRITUAL DEATH!

For the Christian, to die is resurrection. For the non-Christian, to be resurrected is to die. The premillennial interpretation which says that because the second resurrection is literal and bodily, the first resurrection must also be literal and bodily, fails to consider the significance of the ordinal "first" as well as the ironical and paradoxical language which John employs. In Revelation the apparent defeat of the Christian in physical death is, in point of fact, a spiritual victory that leads to life (see 2:10-11; 6:9, 11a; 12:11; 14:13).

Conclusion

Let me briefly sum up what I believe Revelation 20:1-10 is saying. John has a vision of the binding of Satan that is designed to prevent our ancient enemy from leading the unsaved nations into a premature provocation of the final battle, Armageddon. In addition, so long as Satan is restrained in this way the gospel may spread beyond the borders of Israel to bring salvation to the Gentile world. John also sees the martyred saints: those who had refused to worship the beast but instead remained faithful to Jesus Christ. In spite of having lost their physical lives, they are raised to life together with Christ in the intermediate state (as disembodied souls) where they rule and reign with the Lord for the duration of the present church age (cf. 2 Cor. 5:6-10; Phil. 1:19-24; Rev. 6:9-11). These faithful servants are truly blessed and holy, as they will never suffer the second death. Indeed, they reign as priests of God and of Christ (cf. Rev. 3:21). Near the close of the current church age, as the "1,000" years approaches its end, Satan will be released from the abyss and all restraints will be lifted. He will deceive the unbelieving nations into thinking that an assault against Christ and his Church will succeed, only to suffer sudden and decisive defeat when the Lord Jesus returns from heaven with those believers who have until now shared his dominion and rule (Rev. 20:7-10).

Addendum A:
Alternative Amillennial views of the "First Resurrection"

Several amillennial interpreters have conceded the validity of Alford's dictum but have remained amillennial, one of whom is Philip E. Hughes.[12]

Hughes agrees with the premillennialist that the resurrection referred to in both instances of *ezesan* must be physical or bodily. He remains an amillennialist, however, by arguing that the "first resurrection" is not that of Christians immediately prior to a future millennial reign, but is that of *Jesus Christ* in whose resurrection

---

12. Philip E. Hughes, "The First Resurrection: Another Interpretation," *WTJ* 39 (Spring 1977): 315-18.

Christians share. John says in 20:6 that "he who shares in" the first resurrection is blessed. Since one does not "share" (lit., "one who has a part in," *ho echon meros en*) in his *own* resurrection but in that of another, the bodily resurrection of Jesus is in view, a resurrection with which we are identified and of which we partake by virtue of that relation with Christ through faith described by Paul as being "in Christ" (see Rom. 6:4; Col. 2:12ff.; 3:1; Eph. 2:4-5). [13]

Similar to this view is the one espoused by Norman Shepherd. [14] Shepherd contends that the "first resurrection" occurs for the believer in *Christian baptism* (Col. 2:12; Rom. 6:4). It is essentially synonymous with conversion, and therefore Shepherd, like Hughes, also appeals to Colossians 3:1 and Ephesians 2:5-6. Although in Revelation 20:6 no explicit reference is made to a "second resurrection," it is certainly implied. This second resurrection refers to the resurrection of the body (of all the elect) at Christ's second advent. In the light of other texts (Rom. 8:18-23; 2 Pet. 3:13; Rev. 21:1), Shepherd argues that this second resurrection is more than merely a resurrection of the body, but is *cosmic* as well. Thus he concludes that "the distance between the first resurrection and the second resurrection is not a thousand years between the 'literal' resurrection of the just and the 'literal' resurrection of the unjust. It is rather the distance between the resurrection of Jesus Christ in whom and with whom believers are raised by baptism, and the resurrection of all things at the end of the age." [15]

Whereas Hughes and Shepherd concede Alford's dictum but find a reference to *physical* resurrection in both occurrences of *ezesan*, James Hughes [16] and Anthony Hoekema [17] concede Alford's

---

13. Another who takes this view is Samuel E. Waldron in his book, *The End Times Made Simple: How Could Everyone Be So Wrong About Biblical Prophecy?* (Amityville, NY: Calvary Press, 2003).

14. Norman Shepherd, "The Resurrections of Revelation 20," *WTJ* 20 (Fall 1974): 34-43.

15. Ibid., 43.

16. James Hughes, "Revelation 20:4-6 and the Question of the Millennium," *WTJ* 35 (1973): 281-302.

17. Anthony Hoekema, *The Bible and the Future* (Grand Rapids: Eerdmans, 1979), 223-38.

dictum but see a reference to *spiritual* resurrection in both cases
(something Alford refused to believe anyone was "hardy" enough
to maintain). But how can it be said, someone might ask, that the
non-elect are raised *spiritually* after the millennium? The point
James Hughes and Hoekema both make is that this is precisely what
the text does *not* say. Both men deny that the word "until" *(achri)*
demands a change after the point to which it refers is reached. In
saying that the non-elect dead do not "come to life" until the 1,000
years are finished, John is *not* implying that after the 1,000 years are
finished they *will* "come to life." Hoekema explains:

> When he says that the rest of the dead did not live or come to life, he
> means the exact opposite of what he had just said about the believing
> dead. The unbelieving dead, he is saying, did not live or reign with Christ
> during this thousand-year period. Whereas believers after death enjoy
> a new kind of life in heaven with Christ in which they share in Christ's
> reign, unbelievers after death share nothing of either this life or this reign
> .... The Greek word here translated "until," *achri,* means that what is said
> here holds true during the entire length of the thousand-year period.
> The use of the word *until* does not imply that these unbelieving dead will
> live and reign with Christ after this period has ended. If this were the
> case, we would have expected a clear statement to this effect. [18]

It is true, of course, that in certain cases "until" does not demand
a reversal of the circumstances which had prevailed antecedent to
the time to which it refers. However, in the three other instances
in Revelation in which *achri* is used with the aorist subjunctive
(7:3; 15:8; 20:3) the implication is certainly of a reversal of circumstances once the point of termination is reached. Contextually, as
well, the indication is that subsequent to the termination of the
1,000 years significant changes obtain, specifically, the release of
him who, during the 1,000 years, was bound.

Even more decisive is the content of 20:11-15 in which the non-
elect dead, i.e., those who did not live during the 1,000 years, are

---

18. Ibid., 236.

said to stand before the Great White Throne for purposes of judgment. In other words, the non-elect dead *do* live after the 1,000 years in the sense that they are raised physically in order to be cast into the lake of fire. Of course, Hoekema and James Hughes must reject any identification of the "resurrection" in 20:11-15 with that in 20:5, for they have accepted Alford's dictum, to wit, that both occurrences of *ezesan* necessarily refer to resurrections of identical character.

In response, I must agree with the premillennialist here that the strong implication of both grammar and context is that the rest of the dead do indeed "come to life" (whatever that may mean) after the 1,000 years are completed. And since I am not convinced by Philip Hughes or Norman Shepherd that the first resurrection is physical or bodily, I am compelled to reject Alford's dictum. I do in fact believe that the first resurrection is *spiritual* and that the resurrection of the non-elect after the millennium is *physical*.[19]

Addendum B:
A Response to George Ladd on John 5:25-29

Amillennialists have often pointed to John 5:25-29 as a clear counter-example to Alford's dictum. In that passage we find reference to two resurrections, the first of which is spiritual in nature (v. 25) while the second is physical (vv. 28-29):

> [25]Truly, truly, I say to you, an hour is coming, and is now here, when the dead will hear the voice of the Son of God, and those who hear will live. [26]For as the Father has life in himself, so he has granted the Son also to have life in himself. [27]And he has given him authority to

---

19. Jay Adams contends that "the rest of the dead" (20:5) are not the non-elect dead but all other non-martyred Christians. Thus the "living and reigning with Christ for a thousand years" is a special prerogative and blessing given to the martyrs to enjoy in heaven between Christ's two comings. The fullness of this experience will not be received by other, non-martyred Christians, until after the heavenly millennium, i.e., not until the new heavens and new earth. See Adams's book, *The Time is at Hand* (Nutley, NJ: Presbyterian and Reformed, 1974 [1966]).

execute judgment, because he is the Son of Man. [28]Do not marvel at this, for an hour is coming when all who are in the tombs will hear his voice [29]and come out, those who have done good to the resurrection of life, and those who have done evil to the resurrection of judgment.

George Ladd objects to the amillennial appeal to this text as being analogous to Revelation 20. He insists that the two passages are not sufficiently similar, for "in the gospel, the context itself provides the clues for the spiritual interpretation in the one instance and the literal in the other." [20] But in Revelation 20, says Ladd, there is no such contextual clue that the resurrections are of a different order.

On this, however, I beg to differ. In the first place, why must the immediate context *alone* be determinative? Just because the immediate context of John 5 provides its own clues and that of Revelation 20, at least according to Ladd, does not, is hardly sufficient reason to reject the amillennial interpretation of the latter. If John does not supply an extensive elaboration in Revelation 20 as he does in John 5 to the effect that the resurrections are of a different nature, it could very well be because the *broader* context of Scripture has already provided the necessary indications. In the New Testament we read of only *one* general resurrection, we read of *no* intermediate or post-Parousia millennial age, and the second advent of Christ is repeatedly and uniformly portrayed as ushering in the perfection of the eternal state. In view of this I hardly think John thought it necessary to expand greatly upon his comment. Besides, his purpose is to record a vision, not to write a theological commentary on its meaning. In fact, only rarely in Revelation does John interpret his visions for us.

Furthermore, and contrary to Ladd, I am persuaded that John did in fact provide clues in the immediate context that would signal his readers to a difference in the nature of the resurrections. One such clue is the intervening millennium itself. Another is the ordinal "first," used with "resurrection," only here in all the New Testament. The predication of such a resurrection to disem-

---

20. George Eldon Ladd, *A Commentary on the Revelation of John* (Grand Rapids: Eerdmans, 1972), 266.

bodied "souls" of martyrs is yet another clue that the "coming to life" subsequent to their physical death is something other than bodily. The implied qualitative contrasts between the "first death" and the "second death," as well as between the "first resurrection" and "second resurrection," also indicate that John is speaking of two resurrections of contrasting character. Of course, the ultimate rationale for rejecting the application of Alford's dictum to Revelation 20:4-6 must come from the cogency of the amillennial interpretation of the passage itself.

Addendum C:
Who are the Occupants of the Thrones in Revelation 20:4a?

The question of precisely how many groups are mentioned in Revelation 20:4 and who they are is a complicated one, the answer to which requires some knowledge of Greek. Several possibilities exist which I want to explore in this addendum. (If you aren't drawn to such technical discussions, you should probably move on to the next chapter!)

(1) It may be that the anonymous throne-sitters are the heavenly court, comprised of who or what we don't know. In Daniel 7:9 we read that "thrones were placed" and in 7:10 that "the court sat." The function of this heavenly assize in Daniel 7:21-22, 26 is to vindicate or pass judgment in favor of the saints who had suffered the tyranny of the little horn. Similarly, in Revelation 20:4 the heavenly court is convened in order to exact vengeance on the enemies of the faithful dead. On this view the occupants of the thrones in 20:4 are distinct from the martyrs.

There are also two slight variations within this approach that can best be seen by noting how the NASB translates this verse – "And I saw thrones, and they sat upon them, and judgment was given to *them*." One interpretation is that the occupants of the thrones are not the antecedent of the italicized "them". If this be the case, then judgment is exercised by the court *on behalf of* (dative of advantage) "them," the latter being the martyrs. This would harmonize well with Daniel 7 but is grammatically unlikely.

The other approach contends that the occupants of the throne are indeed "those" to whom judgment was given. Thus the authority and power to judge is given to them (dative of indirect object) in order that they might execute vengeance upon those who have persecuted the saints.

(2) If the occupants of the thrones are distinct from the martyrs, but do not comprise the heavenly court, several other possibilities emerge. They could be the Triune God, Father, Son, and Holy Spirit. But how could it be said that "judgment was *given* to them"? Given by whom? Perhaps the occupants of the thrones are the twelve apostles (cf. Matt. 19:28). Or perhaps they are the twenty-four elders of Revelation 4, who are viewed as representatives of the Church and Israel. It is almost certain, however, that the twenty-four elders are non-human, most likely angelic beings (see Rev. 4:4-11; 5:8-10; 7:9-11).

(3) Another view is that the occupants of the thrones are inclusive of but not limited to the martyrs. That is to say, the throne-sitters are the saints of all ages, from among whom John then singles out for special mention the martyrs, i.e., "the souls of those who had been beheaded."

(4) It must also be determined whether those "who had not worshiped the beast or its image and had not received its mark on their foreheads or their hands" constitute yet another group or are simply the martyrs described in more detail. Derwood C. Smith suggests that two groups are in view. His reasons are, first, that if the relative has its antecedent in "souls" it would be *haitines,* and second, the first group is described with the perfect tense and the second with aorists.[21] However, the masculine of the relative pronoun may be a *constructio ad sensum,* not infrequent in Revelation. Also, the shift in tense can hardly be the basis for differentiating between the two unless other exegetical and contextual factors corroborate. Besides, the aorists may justifiably be translated "had not worshiped" and "had not received" (as the ESV suggests). The

---

21. Derwood C. Smith, "The Millennial Reign of Jesus Christ: Some Observations on Rev. 20:1-10," *RQ* 16 (1973): 219-30.

issue, then, turns on how one takes the relative clause "and those" in the phrase "and those who had not worshiped the beast or its image."

The relative *hostis* occurs nine times in Revelation, five of which are nominative, masculine, plural (1:7; 2:24; 9:4; 17:12; and here in 20:4). In 2:24, 9:4, and 17:12 the "who" refers to the preceding group and supplies additional information. Only in 1:7, however, is the relative preceded by *kai* ("and") and there it singles out a special class or group from the more general body in the preceding statement. If this were followed in 20:4 it would mean that *kai hoitines* introduces a special category of beheaded saints, namely, those who were beheaded because they refused to worship the beast. But this would imply that some were martyred for a reason *other* than their resistance to the beast, which makes little sense in the larger context of the book.

It seems, then, that if one chooses to take the relative as introducing a second group it will have to be a group altogether different from the preceding, which is to say, non-martyrs. This is Henry B. Swete's position. He describes them as "confessors," that is to say, those who suffered persecution and reproach but were not martyred for their faith. [22]

(5) On the whole I think it is best to take the relative as introducing a more complete description of its antecedent. The *kai* will therefore be explicative in force, translated "namely," or "that is." There is, therefore, only one group in view: the martyrs. These are the ones who had been beheaded for their witness, which consisted of their faithful obedience to God's word and their refusal to worship the beast or receive his mark.

I also believe that these martyrs are indeed the occupants of the thrones in 20:4a. This may well find confirmation in Revelation 4:2-3. There John sees a throne in heaven and "one seated" on it (who, at least initially, remains anonymous). John immediately proceeds in 4:3 to describe who this throne-sitter is. It is possible

22. Henry B. Swete, *Commentary on Revelation* (Grand Rapids: Kregel Publications, 1977 [1911]), 262.

473

that in 20:4b John likewise intends to describe the throne-sitters of 20:4a when he refers to the martyrs. The principal difference between the two texts is that in 4:3 the one described is specifically identified as "he who sat there," whereas in 20:4b no such reference is made. However, if the martyrs are those who lived and "reigned" with Christ (and few, if any, would deny this), John may be providing us with the clue we need to identify the martyrs of 20:4b with the occupants of thrones in 20:4a. That is to say, reigning with Christ (20:4b) is simply another way of saying, "then I saw thrones, and seated on them . . ." If this is correct, we might then take *kai* as explicative ("namely," or "that is"). Thus 20:4b would function as something of an appositional expansion upon the identity of those in 20:4a. The same sense may be achieved without pressing the *kai* into such service by simply taking 20:4a as something of a summary or opening synopsis of the vision, with the remainder of 20:4 functioning as an elaboration or more detailed analysis of who sat on the thrones, why, and what it means for them.

Chapter Sixteen

The Antichrist in Biblical Eschatology: A Study of Revelation 13 and 17

There is hardly a more fascinating and controversial topic in eschatology than that of the Antichrist. Is the Antichrist the same as the beast of Revelation? Is there more than one Antichrist? Is he a figure of past history or the future? Is the Antichrist a person or a power or a movement, or some combination of all? These and other questions will arise as we try to make sense of this concept.[1]

There is good reason for devoting two chapters to this subject and it has nothing to do with the contemporary fascination with the concept of Antichrist or the number 666 (although I will have something to say about both these issues). The reason is found, first, in the light that a study of this subject sheds on the broader subject of biblical eschatology. Second, a focus on this theme will require that we examine several important biblical texts that bear directly on eschatology in a variety of ways. So let's begin.

---

1. The best treatment of the concept of Antichrist from a historical perspective is by Bernard McGinn in his book, *Antichrist: Two Thousand Years of the Human Fascination with Evil* (San Francisco: Harper, 1994). See also Robert C. Fuller, *Naming the Antichrist: The History of an American Obsession* (Oxford: Oxford University Press, 1995), and Kim Riddlebarger, *The Man of Sin: Uncovering the Truth about the Antichrist* (Grand Rapids: BakerBooks, 2006).

Who or What is the Beast?

A recurring theme both before and during the time of the Protestant Reformation was identification of the Antichrist either with the Roman Catholic Church in general or the papacy in particular. Among the pre-reformers, John Wycliffe (late fourteenth century) believed the papacy itself, as an institution, rather than any one particular Pope, was the Antichrist. John Hus (1372–1415), the Bohemian reformer who was burned at the stake for his opposition to the Roman Catholic Church, embraced Wycliffe's view as well. Virtually all the Protestant Reformers, including Martin Luther and his associate Philip Melancthon, together with the English reformers and most Puritans, identified the Antichrist with the Roman Catholic Church, or more particularly, the office of the papacy. According to John Calvin, "Daniel [Dan 9:27] and Paul [II Thess. 2:4] foretold that Antichrist would sit in the Temple of God. With us, it is the Roman pontiff we make the leader and standard bearer of that wicked and abominable kingdom." [2]

Most evangelicals today, especially those who embrace the futurist perspective on Revelation, refer to the beast as the eschatological or end-time Antichrist, a literal human being who will deceive the world and persecute the Church during the closing few years preceding the second advent of Jesus. Consider this statement by Dave Hunt:

> Somewhere, at this very moment, on planet Earth, the antichrist is almost certainly alive – biding his time, awaiting his cue. Banal sensationalism? Far from it! That likelihood is based upon a sober evaluation of current events in relation to Bible prophecy. Already a mature man, he is probably active in politics, perhaps even an admired world leader whose name is almost daily on everyone's lips. [3]

---

2. John Calvin, *Institutes of the Christian Religion*, edited by John T. McNeill (Philadelphia: The Westminster Press, 1975), Book IV, Chapter two, 12.

3. Dave Hunt, *Global Peace and the Rise of Antichrist* (Eugene, OR: Harvest House, 1990), 5.

Our approach will be to examine Revelation 13 and 17 and their portrayal of the beast, together with the Johannine Epistles and 2 Thessalonians 2.[4] These passages have become the primary source for the idea both of an individual Antichrist at the end of the age and the emergence of a unified, one-world, government under his authority. Both of these concepts, however, are largely dependent on a strictly *futuristic* interpretation of the book of Revelation. If, on the other hand, Revelation 13 and 17 are describing the oppressive reign of the "beast" and "false prophet" (whoever or whatever they may be) *throughout the course of the inter-advent age*, these views will need to be re-examined to determine if they have biblical support.

Revelation 13:1-2

[1]And I saw a beast rising out of the sea, with ten horns and seven heads, with ten diadems on its horns and blasphemous names on its heads. [2]And the beast that I saw was like a leopard; its feet were like a bear's, and its mouth was like a lion's mouth. And to it the dragon gave his power and his throne and great authority.

It would appear that Revelation 13:1-18 is temporally parallel with Revelation 12:6, 13-17 and explains in more detail the precise nature and extent of the dragon's (Satan's) persecution of the people of God. In fact, Revelation 13 describes the earthly governmental, political, economic, as well as individual, powers of the earth through whom Satan works. Though Satan has been defeated (12:7-12), he can still oppress the saints (v. 12). And the primary way in which he exerts this nefarious influence and wages war against the seed of the woman (Rev. 12:17) is through the activities and oppression of the beast. Here John narrates his vision of the dragon standing on the seashore, calling forth his agents through whom he will carry out

---

4. In Chapter Four I argued that the most likely interpretation of Daniel 7, 8, and 11 is that the "little horn" is not a reference to an eschatological Antichrist but refers, instead, to Antiochus Epiphanes IV, the second century B.C. enemy of the Jewish people who desecrated the Temple. However, while not a direct reference to antichrist, it may be that Antiochus was something of a prototype of any and all who align themselves with Satan against the kingdom of Christ.

his persecution of the people of God. The "war" which the dragon is said to wage with the Church (Rev. 12:17) is actually undertaken by his servants as portrayed in chapter 13.

There can be no mistaking the fact that Revelation 13:1-2 is a creative re-working of Daniel 7:1-7. Therefore, several points should be noted. In Daniel 7 we read about four beasts who rise up out of the sea, which in Scripture is often symbolic of evil, chaos, and anti-kingdom powers with whom Yahweh must contend (see Isa. 17:12, 13; 51:9-10; 27:1; 57:20; Rev. 17:8; 21:1; Jer. 46:7ff.; Job 26:7-13). We should also note that the image of an evil sea monster always symbolizes *kingdoms* that oppose and oppress Israel (especially Egypt and Pharaoh; see especially Pss. 74:13-14; 89:10; Isa. 30:7; 51:9; Ezek. 29:3; 32:2-3; Hab. 3:8-15). It may be that John's reference to the "sea" is synonymous with the "abyss", the source or abode of those demonic powers that are opposed to God. Recall that in Revelation 11:7 the beast has already been described as rising up "from the abyss".

The first sea-beast is like a *lion*, the second resembled a *bear*, and the third was like a *leopard*. These three are all now found in the one sea-beast of Revelation 13:2 who is said to be "like a *leopard*; its feet were like a *bear's*, and its mouth was like a *lion's* mouth." Likewise, the fourth sea-beast in Daniel 7 is said to have *ten horns*, as is also the case with the sea-beast in Revelation 13. In other words, whereas the four beasts of Daniel 7 represent four historically successive world empires,[5] the sea-beast of Revelation 13 is John's **creative composite** of them all. *All the evil characteristics of those four kingdoms are now embodied in the one sea-beast who becomes Satan's principal agent in persecuting the people of God.* The point would seem to be that the "beast" of Revelation 13 is primarily *corporate* in nature, rather than personal.

The "dragon" (i.e., Satan) of Revelation 12:3 is said to have "seven heads and ten horns, and on his heads seven diadems." Here in 13:1 the beast who is beckoned from the sea to do the dragon's work likewise has seven heads and ten horns, but he now has ten

5. Possibly Babylon, Media-Persia, Greece, and Rome, but more likely Babylon, Media, Media-Persia, and Greece.

(rather than seven) diadems that appear on his horns (rather than on his heads). Nevertheless, it is explicitly stated that the sea-beast receives "his power and his throne and great authority" from the dragon of Revelation 12. The "crowns" or "diadems" point to the beast's false claim of sovereignty, royalty, and authority, in opposition to the true King, Jesus, who also wears "many diadems" (19:12,16). The "blasphemous names" on his seven heads probably represent the beast's arrogant claims to divinity/deity.

Because of the figurative use of numbers in Revelation, it is unlikely that "seven" and "ten" are to be identified literally and only with a specific series of rulers or kingdoms, whether in the first century or thereafter. More likely is the suggestion that both "seven" and "ten" emphasize "the completeness of oppressive power and its worldwide effect" as well as "the all-encompassing span of time during which these powers hold sway."[6] We should also note that Daniel's four beasts, the tradition on which John draws, have seven heads between them, since the fourth itself has four heads (Dan. 7:6), while none has horns except the fourth, which has ten (7:7).

The Johannine Epistles

Interestingly, the only place in the New Testament where the word "antichrist" appears is in the Johannine Epistles, not in Revelation. *Nowhere in Revelation is the "beast" ever called "antichrist"*. In his first epistle John emphatically states (1 John 2:18) that we may know this is (the) last hour because of the existence and activity of many antichrists. He says: "Children, it is the last hour; and as you have heard that antichrist is coming, so now many antichrists have come. Therefore we know that it is the last hour" (2:18).[7]

Later, in 1 John 2:22, he writes: "Who is the liar but he who denies that Jesus is the Christ? This is the Antichrist, he who denies the Father and the Son." The spirit of the Antichrist, says John, is

---

6. G.K. Beale, *The Book of Revelation: A Commentary on the Greek Text* (Grand Rapids: Eerdmans, 1999), 684, 686.
7. Note well that the entire period between the first and second comings of Jesus = the "last days". See Acts 2:17; 2 Tim. 3:1; Heb. 1:2; 1 Pet. 1:20 (cf. 1 Cor. 10:11).

found in anyone who denies that Jesus is God come in the flesh (1 John 4:3). Again, in 2 John 7, he writes: "For many deceivers have gone out into the world, those who do not confess the coming of Jesus Christ in the flesh. Such a one is the deceiver and the antichrist." Thus, for John, "antichrist" is

- Anyone "who denies that Jesus is the Christ" (1 John 2:22)
- Anyone "who denies the Father and the Son" (1 John 2:22)
- "Every spirit that does not confess Jesus" (1 John 4:3)
- "Those who do not confess the coming of Jesus Christ in the flesh" (2 John 7)

The term "antichrist" is a combination of *anti* (against or instead of) and *christos* (Messiah, Christ). It is ambiguous whether the Antichrist is merely one (or anyone) who opposes Christ as his adversary or enemy, or is also a specific person who seeks to take his place. Most have believed that Antichrist is a lying pretender who portrays himself as Christ; he is a counterfeit or diabolical parody of Christ himself (see 2 Thess. 2:3-12). B.F. Westcott has well said: "It seems to be most consonant to the context to hold that *antichristos* here describes one who, assuming the guise of Christ, opposes Christ."[8] Thus, "the Antichrist assails Christ by proposing to do or to preserve what He did while he denies Him."[9]

Although John's readers have been told that Antichrist's appearance is yet future, "even now" many antichrists have already come. Paul wrote in 2 Thessalonians 2:7 that "the mystery of lawlessness is already at work." In 1 John 4:3 he points out that the spirit of Antichrist is "*now*," "*already*" at work in the world. Most believe that what John means in 1 John 2:18 is that the "many antichrists" (those who in the first century were denying the incarnation of Jesus) are forerunners of the one still to come. Because they pro-

---

8. B.F. Westcott, *The Epistles of St. John, The Greek Text with Notes* (Grand Rapids: Eerdmans, 1950 [1892]), 70.
9. Ibid.

claim the same heresies he/it will proclaim and oppose Christ now as he/it will oppose him then, they are rightly called antichrists (especially in view of their denial of Christ in 1 John 2:22-23).

The antichrists of 1 John 2:18 are the false teachers against whom the epistle is directed. They are the ones whom John wishes to expose by means of the application of his "tests of life". In 1 John 2:19 he indicates that at one time they were "members" of the community which professed faith in Christ. They were actively involved in the ministry of the Church and until the moment of separation were hardly distinguishable from the rest of the Christian society. The essence of *Antichrist*, the height of heresy and the lie "par excellence", is the denial that Jesus is the Christ (1 John 2:22).

The use of the definite article ("*the* liar") points to such a person as the one in whom falsehood finds its most complete expression. To deny that Jesus is the Christ is more clearly explained in 1 John 4:2-3. It is more than simply denying that Jesus is the Messiah prophesied in the Old Testament. If these men were proto-Gnostics they probably argued that "Jesus" was a mere man upon whom the "Christ" (a divine emanation) descended at his baptism and from whom he departed before the cross. Jesus was a man invested for a brief time with divine powers (perhaps "adopted" by the Father). They denied that the man Jesus and the Eternal Son were and are one and the same person.

The consequence of this heresy is that "no one who denies the Son has the Father" (1 John 2:23a). "If the heretics thought that they could 'have' God without believing in Jesus, they were completely mistaken. It is only through the Son that we know that God is Father, and it is only through the Son and his propitiatory death that we can have access to God as Father." [10] To "have" the Father is to know him (2:3-4) and to abide in him (2:6), clearly a reference to salvation. All knowledge of God the Father must come only through the Son (see Matt. 11:27; John 1:18; 14:9-11).

---

10. I.H. Marshall, *The Epistles of John* (Grand Rapids: Eerdmans, 1978), 159; see John 14:6.

Some have argued that John's point is that there is no other "antichrist" than the "one" even then operative in his day or the "one" who takes up and perpetuates this heresy in subsequent history. In other words, *anyone in general* can be "antichrist", if he or she espouses this heresy, but *no one in particular*, whether in the first or the twenty-first centuries, is *the* Antichrist as if there were only one to whom the others look forward. In other words, the "antichrist" who his readers were told was yet to come is "now" with them in the form of *anyone* who espouses the heretical denial of the incarnation of the Son of God. According to Gary DeMar, for example, "it is possible that the early church 'heard' that one man was to come on the scene who was to be *the* Antichrist. John seems to be correcting this mistaken notion."[11] Says B.B. Warfield:

> John is adducing not an item of Christian teaching, but only a current legend – Christian or other – in which he recognizes an element of truth and isolates it for the benefit of his readers. In that case we may understand him less as expounding than as openly correcting it – somewhat as, in the closing page of his Gospel, he corrects another saying of similar bearing which was in circulation among the brethren, to the effect that he himself should not die but should tarry till the Lord comes [John 21:18-23].[12]

The question still remains: Is the *beast* of Revelation the same as the *Antichrist* of 1 and 2 John?

A Time, Times, and Half a Time

The identity of the beast in Revelation 13 is revealed to some degree by the reference to the *duration* of its (his?) reign. According to 13:5-7 (see below), the beast makes war with the saints for a period of *forty-two months*, the same length of time, according to Revelation 11:2, that the "holy city" [i.e., the people of God] is trampled

---

11. Gary DeMar, *Last Days Madness* (Atlanta: American Vision, Inc., 1997), 227.
12. B.B. Warfield, "Antichrist," in *Selected Shorter Writings of Benjamin B. Warfield* (Nutley: Presbyterian and Reformed Publishing Company, 1970), 1:357.

upon. Many believe this is an echo of Daniel's "a time, times, and half a time" (Dan. 7:25: 12:7), during which period the "little horn" (believed by many to be the Antichrist) oppresses the people of God.

Is this a reference to some chronologically precise period of time, or is it a symbolic reference to any period of time, regardless of duration, in which certain characteristic features and events are prominent? One's answer to this question will largely depend on the interpretation given to Daniel 9:24-27 and the prophecy of the seventy weeks.

As we noted in an earlier chapter, dispensational interpreters are uniform in declaring that the seventy weeks are weeks of years, hence 490 years. They believe that sixty-nine of these weeks transpired between the time of Daniel and the crucifixion of Jesus. The sixty-ninth week, or remaining seven years of the original 490, is yet future. This future seven-year period is designated the great tribulation in which the "little horn" or antichrist will hold sway. It is not until the middle of that seven-year period, however, that the "little horn" begins to persecute the people of God. In other words, he persecutes and oppresses them for 3½ years. Thus the dispensationalist says the "time, times, and half a time" of Daniel 7:25 = the last 3½ years of the Great Tribulation period.

Non-dispensationalist interpreters do not believe that the seventieth week or seven-year period of Daniel 9:24-27 is future. I earlier argued that the destruction of Jerusalem and its temple in A.D. 70 is the middle of Daniel's seventieth week and that the present church age is its latter half. On this view, the period "time, times, and half a time" is a reference to the whole of this present era, what we typically refer to as the church age. In other words, if I may be permitted to give you my conclusion up front, "a time, times, and half a time," or "42 months," or "1260 days," or "3½ years," are all *theological*, not chronological, designations. They have in view the *kind* or *quality* of time, not its duration. The important thing is *not how long* events happen but *what kind* of events happen.

Let's go back for a moment to Daniel 7:25 (12:7) where we note that the expression is not in terms of years, days, months, weeks, or any such chronological measure. Rather, we read of a *"time, times, and half a time,"* by which we may take Daniel to mean $1 + 2 + \frac{1}{2} =$

3½. But 3½ *what*? In Revelation there are several texts in which a similar if not identical designation is found:

Rev. 11:2 = forty-two months = the period during which the nations will trample the holy city.

Rev. 11:3 = 1260 days (or forty-two months of thirty days each) = the period during which the two witnesses will prophesy.

Rev. 12:6 = 1260 days = the period during which the "woman" is nourished by God in the wilderness.

Rev. 12:14 = a time, times, and half a time = the period during which the "woman" is nourished in the wilderness.

Rev. 13:5 = forty-two months = the period during which the beast acts with authority and blasphemes.

(Note also Rev. 11:11 and the 3½ *days*, the period during which the two witnesses lie dead in the streets.)

One's understanding of these time references will depend on how one interprets the events prophesied to occur within each respective period. It is not my purpose to explain what the events in Revelation 11–15 are. Suffice it to say that in my view these designations (forty-two months = 1260 days = time, times, and half a time = 3½ years) *all refer to the entire present age intervening between the two comings of Christ.* In other words, they are but literary variations for the same period. I do not believe that either Daniel or John intended us to take these references as chronologically precise periods that may be specified on a calendar.

Observe that there will first be a "time," the precise length of which is not stated. Nothing is said that would lead us to believe it refers to one day or month or year. Following this is the plural "times," which most believe is a doubling of the previous term (although it must be admitted that there is no way to know if the "time" is doubled or quadrupled or even multiplied by ten, etc.). If "time" (one) is in fact doubled to "times" (two), we should likely expect the next in the series to be doubled yet again, resulting in four. Instead, we are told of its shortening to a "half time" (1/2). Thus, instead of an ever-increasing expansion of power or rule the anticipated sequence is broken off. What appeared to be moving toward seven (1+2+4) is halved, reduced to three and one-half (1+2+1/2). The power of the little horn initially grows and intensifies (from a "time" to "times"), but then is just as suddenly cut short (to "half a time").

There is evidence that the number 3½ gradually became a stereotypical or stock designation in apocalyptic literature for a period of persecution and distress, regardless of its chronological duration. As for references to this time frame in biblical literature, we should note the 3½ years of drought during the rule of Ahab and Jezebel in 1 Kings 17–18; Luke 4:25; and James 5:17. One especially thinks of the approximately 3½ years during which Antiochus Epiphanes persecuted the Jewish people and defiled the temple.[13] D.A. Carson believes that event was the primary catalyst for why this particular time span (1,260 days or 3½ years or time, times, and half a time, or forty-two months) "became a symbol in Jewish consciousness of a period of time when one faces great suffering and struggle, but with the assurance that God will triumph in the end."[14] The Church today, says Carson, is "in that time of suffering and struggle. We are living through a compressed time, but there will be persecution and opposition and antagonism from this beast until the consummation takes place."[15]

---

13. The precise length is disputed: some say it was from June 168 to December 165 B.C.; others, from December 168 to the middle of 164 B.C.; and others say it was closer to three years, from Chislev or December 168 to the same month in 165 (see 1 Macc. 1:57; 4:52).
14. D.A. Carson, "This Present Evil Age," in *These Last Days: A Christian View of History,* edited by Richard D. Phillips and Gabriel N.E. Fluhrer (Phillipsburg: P & R Publishing, 2011), 27.
15. Ibid. Some have suggested that the number 3½ came to be symbolic of distress and difficulty in light of the 3½ months that intervened between the winter solstice and the Babylonian festival of Marduk. Thus, Isbon Beckwith writes: "The theory is plausible that he [Daniel] derives the number [3½]

The reference to forty-two months is possibly taken from the forty-two years of Israel's wilderness wandering (the initial two years followed by the forty God inflicted upon her), and the forty-two stations or encampments of Israel while in the wilderness (Num. 33:5ff.). Others suggest that 3½ signifies a broken seven, and thus becomes a symbol for the interruption of the Divine order by the malice of Satan and evil men, a period of unrest and trouble.

The strongest argument for interpreting these references as theological and not chronological is the book of Revelation itself. The events which occur within these periods are, in my view, such that will transpire throughout the present age. Hence the *forty-two months = 1260 days = time, times, and half a time = 3 ½ years = the present inter-advent age.* In the light of this, many commentators suggest that the period is simply an expression for the time of tyranny until the end comes, the period of eschatological crisis, the age of persecution and pilgrimage for the people of God however long it may be. "The figure [thus] becomes a symbol like the red cross or the swastika, a shorthand way of indicating the period during which the 'nations,' the unbelievers, seem to dominate the world, but the 'people,' God's people, maintain their witness in it."[16]

In sum, it would seem that in describing the era of the "little horn" (in Daniel) and the "beast" (in Revelation) as a "time, times, and half a time," the biblical authors are *not* attempting to tell us *how long* he/it will hold sway, as if by 3½, forty-two, or 1260, they were specifying a period that is chronologically precise. It is *not* the *length* but the **kind** of time that is meant. In other words, 3½ and forty-two and 1260 are *not a description of the chronological quantity of the period but rather of its spiritual and theological quality.*

---

from Semitic tradition, that primarily it figured the three months or more during which nature is in the grasp of frost and cold and that it afterwards became a symbol of the fierce period of evil before the last great triumph, a symbol of the time of the power of Antichrist, 'the times of the Gentiles,' Lk. 21:24, or more widely, the symbol of any period of great calamity" (*The Apocalypse of John* [Grand Rapids: Baker, 1979 (1919)], 252).

16. Michael Wilcock, *I Saw Heaven Opened* (Downers Grove: Inter-Varsity Press, 1975), 106.

Therefore, if the period 3½ years = forty-two months = 1260 days = time, times, half a time, all refer to the entirety of the present inter-advent age, the beast cannot be *merely* an individual living at the end of human history. Rather, the beast would be a symbol for the system of Satanically inspired evil, and thus opposition to the kingdom of God, that throughout history has manifested itself in a variety of forms, whether political, economic, military, social, philosophical, or religious. Alan Johnson provides this excellent explanation. The beast, notes Johnson,

> is not to be identified in its description with any one historical form of its expression or with any one institutional aspect of its manifestation. In other words, the beast may appear now as Sodom, Egypt, Rome, or even Jerusalem and may manifest itself as a political power, an economic power, a religious power, or a heresy (1 John 2:18, 22; 4:3).... This interpretation does not exclude the possibility that there will be a final climactic appearance of the beast in history in a person; in a political, religious, or economic system; or in a final totalitarian culture combining all these. The point is that the beast cannot be limited to either the past or the future.[17]

The "blasphemous names" on the beast's heads (Rev. 13:1) indicate that he/it challenges the supremacy and majesty of God by denying and defying the first commandment: "You shall have no other gods before me" (Exod. 20:3). Therefore, says Johnson,

> whatever person or system – whether political, social, economic, or religious – cooperates with Satan by exalting itself against God's sovereignty and by setting itself up to destroy the followers of Jesus, or entices them to become followers of Satan through deception, idolatry, blasphemy, and spiritual adultery, embodies the beast of Revelation 13. The description John gives of the beast from the sea does not describe a mere human political entity such as Rome. Rather, it describes in archetypal language the hideous, Satan-backed system of deception and idolatry that may at

---

17. Alan Johnson, *Revelation*, The Expositor's Bible Commentary (Grand Rapids: Zondervan, 1981), 129.

any time express itself in human systems of various kinds, such as Rome. Yet at the same time John also seems to be saying that this blasphemous, blaspheming, and blasphemy-producing reality will have a final, intense, and, for the saints, utterly devastating manifestation.[18]

The beast, then, is a trans-cultural, trans-temporal symbol for all individual and collective, Satanically-inspired, opposition to Jesus and his people. It is anything and everything (whether a principle, a person, or a power) utilized by the enemy to deceive and destroy the influence and advance of the kingdom of God.

Thus, the beast is, at one time, the Roman Empire; at another, the Arian heresy (fourth century). The beast is, at one time, the Emperor Decius (third-century persecutor of the Church); at another, secular evolutionary Darwinism (in the twenty-first century). The beast is the late medieval Roman Catholic papacy, modern Protestant liberalism, Marxism, the radical feminist movement, the Pelagian heresy of the fifth century, communism, Joseph Stalin, the seventeenth-century Enlightenment, eighteenth-century deism, Roe v. Wade, the state persecution of Christians in China, the publication of the book *The Myth of God Incarnate* in the mid-1970s, radical Islamic fundamentalism, angry twenty-first-century atheism, etc. Each of these is, individually and on its own, the beast. All of these are, collectively and in unity, the beast. Will there also be a *person* at the end of the age who embodies in consummate form all the characteristics of the many previous historical manifestations of the beast? If so, should we call this person the Antichrist? To answer that question we now return to our study of Revelation 13.

Revelation 13:3

[3]One of its heads seemed to have a mortal wound, but its mortal wound was healed, and the whole earth marveled as they followed the beast.

John sees the beast with a wound on one of his heads. The word translated "wound" (*plege*) is used throughout Revelation (eleven

---

18. Ibid.

times) for the "plagues" that God inflicts on an unbelieving world. In other words, the likelihood is that God is the one who strikes this blow in judgment against the beast. In Revelation 13:14 it is said to have been "wounded by the sword," recalling Isaiah 27:1 which says that "in that day the Lord with his hard and great and strong sword will punish Leviathan the fleeing serpent, Leviathan the twisting serpent, and he will slay the dragon that is in the sea."

Although we must not seek to identify or reduce the beast to any one historical event, institution, or person, John does appear to use the historical career of the Roman Emperor *Nero* as a way to illustrate in graphic terms the character and agenda of this archenemy of the kingdom. Although Nero is nowhere explicitly mentioned in Revelation, Richard Bauckham contends that "John would have seen the historical Nero as the figure in whom the imperial power had so far shown most clearly its antichristian tendency: as self-deifying absolutism which sets itself against God and murders his witnesses (cf. 11:7; 13:5-7). The impending confrontation between the beast and the followers of the Lamb would appear to John as an apocalyptic extension and intensification of the Neronian persecution."[19]

According to Bauckham, and I agree, John has made creative use of the historical Nero and the legend surrounding his return to describe the nature and career of the beast. John uses Nero because he was the first and most obvious and hideous example of the antichristian imperial power that threatened the people of God. "For John," notes Bauckham, "Nero ... was the emperor who incarnated and demonstrated most fully the demonic nature of the beast in its opposition to God and his people."[20] The legend of Nero's return thus proved helpful to John because he could adapt it to serve his own portrayal of the conflict between the beast and the Church. Nero's own "death," "resurrection," and "return" (*parousia*) provided a perfect canvas on which John could paint both the character and course of the beast's attempt to rival God. In John's day that

---

19. Richard Bauckham, *The Climax of Prophecy*, 412.
20. Ibid., 442.

beast was Rome. In subsequent centuries it is any and all individual and collective attempts to oppose the kingdom of God and his purposes in Christ.

Those who find the *Nero redivivus* legend in Revelation 13 point to verse 3 as one particular historical manifestation of this death-wound / healing scenario. Whereas Nero committed suicide in 68, some thought he never died. Others believed he died but was raised from the dead. It may have appeared that the beast (i.e., Rome) was slain with Nero's death, since it brought a dramatic decrease in the persecution of Christians. As Bauckham has pointed out,

> Nero's suicide, which was also the end of the Julio-Claudian dynasty, was a death-blow to the imperial power, because it coincided with the beginning of the period of chaos, the so-called "year of the four emperors" [i.e., 69], in which more than one claimant was contesting the imperial rule, in which various provinces hoped to be able to throw off Roman rule, and in which the survival of the empire was put in very serious question. Jews and Christians alike must have hoped that this near-disintegration of the empire was the divine judgment from which Rome would never recover. [21]

However, Vespasian soon solidified the empire once again, so that the Roman beast appeared to have fully recovered. Thus, whereas we read in 13:3 that only one of the beast's heads was wounded, we read in 13:12, 14 that it is the beast itself that recovers from the wound. Thus, Bauckham concludes that "the year 69 threatened the survival of the empire and ruptured the empire's history in a way which made a deep impression on those who lived through it and which fully justifies a description of it as a mortal wound from which the imperial power miraculously recovered." [22]

Of great importance is the way John describes the beast in terms that echo the person and work of Christ. In other words, for John, *the beast is an imitation or Satanic parody of Jesus Christ.*

---

21. Ibid., 442-43.
22. Ibid., 443.

For example, in Revelation 13:3 the phrase "as if it had been slain," echoes Revelation 5:6 where the same phrase is used of the Lamb of God. "It is clearly intended to create a parallel between Christ's death and resurrection, on the one hand, and the beast's mortal wound and its healing, on the other." [23] This also may suggest that the "wound" or "plague" suffered by the beast was inflicted by Jesus through the latter's death and resurrection. It appeared as though the wound was a fatal one. In one sense, it really was. The devil suffered a spiritually fatal blow at Calvary. Despite defeat, however, the devil and his forces, as manifest in and through the "beast," continue to exist. The imagery of a "fatal" blow followed by continued life ("its mortal wound was healed") may well point to what we see in Revelation 12:7-12. There Satan is defeated. He loses his legal grounds for accusing the saints. His moral authority over them is gone. Yet he continues to thrive on earth and to persecute, and often times kill, the people of God. It is this continuing presence of Satan, in and through the beast, in spite of his apparent defeat at Calvary, that amazes the unbelieving world and wins their allegiance and worship.

Some have wondered about John's use of the word translated "as if" (*hos*). Clearly this word in Revelation 5:6 does not imply that Jesus' death wasn't real. Neither should it be taken this way in 13:3. As Bauckham explains, "the use of *hos* ['as if'] is a feature of John's visionary style ... which may here indicate that neither the Lamb nor the beast is actually dead when John sees it in his vision, because it has already come to life again." [24]

There is yet another parallel between the beast and the Lamb in 13:14. There John says the beast "yet lived" and uses a verb (*ezesen*) that is found in Revelation 2:8 with reference to the resurrection of Jesus (cf. 1:18). Note also that the universal worship of the beast (13:4, 8) following its "death and resurrection" parallels the universal worship of the Lamb (5:8-14) following his death and resurrection! In 13:2 we read that the dragon (Satan) gives the beast

23. Ibid., 432.
24. Ibid.

his power, throne, and authority. This parallels the Father's gift to the Lamb of authority and a place on his throne (2:27; 3:21). We should also note that both Jesus and the beast have swords (13:10; 20:4), both have followers who have their names written on their foreheads (see 13:16-14:1), and both have horns (5:6; 13:1, 11).

It would seem, then, that the beast is primarily Satan himself "as he repeatedly works through his chosen agents throughout history [Nero certainly being one]. Therefore, whenever any major opponent of God reaches his demise, it appears as if the beast has been defeated, yet he will arise again in some other form, until the end of history. Such revivals make it appear as if Christ's defeat of the devil was not very decisive. But such revivals are under the ultimate hand of God, who 'gives authority.' " [25] Beale thus concludes:

> The significance of the parallels is that the chief opponent of Christ cannot be limited to one historical person [such as Nero] or epoch. That is, just as Christ's rule spans the whole church age, so the evil activities of his ultimate counterpart, the devil and his servants, span the same time. This analysis leaves open the possibility of an Antichrist who comes at the end of history and incarnates the devil in a greater way than anyone ever before. Whether this consummate expression of evil will be manifested in an individual or an institution is hard to say. Probably, as throughout history, so at the end the individual tyrant is not to be distinguished from the kingdom or institution that he represents.... Consequently, it is better to link the beast's resuscitation to the repeated rise and fall of oppressive states, world systems, or social structures that continue because the devil continues to inspire opposition to God's people, even though he has been decisively defeated by Christ.[26]

---

25. Beale, *Revelation,* 691.

26. Ibid., 691-92. I mention here in passing a standard view among dispensational futurists that the "wounding" and "healing" of one of the beast's heads in 13:3 is to be taken literally. Hal Lindsey, for example, says that he "does not believe it will be an actual resurrection, but it will be a situation in which this person has a mortal wound. Before he has actually lost his life, however, he will be brought back from this critically wounded state. This is something which will

Revelation 13:4

[4]And they worshiped the dragon, for he had given his authority to the beast, and they worshiped the beast, saying, "Who is like the beast, and who can fight against it?"

This passage refers to the devotion of the unbelieving world to anything and anyone other than Jesus. The power and influence of the beast, in whatever form it manifests itself, is grounds for their declaration concerning what they perceive to be the beast's incomparable authority: "Who is like the beast, and who can fight against it?" Indeed, this is the precise terminology found throughout the Old Testament that is applied to YHWH (see Exod. 8:10; 15:11; Deut. 3:24; Isa. 40:18, 25; 44:7; 46:5; Pss. 35:10; 71:19; 86:8; 89:8; 113:5; Micah 7:18). "This is a further attempt at Satanic imitation of God. In all these OT texts Yahweh's incomparability is contrasted polemically with false gods and idols."[27]

Revelation 13:5-10

[5]And the beast was given a mouth uttering haughty and blasphemous words, and it was allowed to exercise authority for forty-two months. [6]It opened its mouth to utter blasphemies against God, blaspheming his name and his dwelling, that is, those who dwell in heaven. [7]Also it was allowed to make war on the saints and to conquer them. And authority was given it over every tribe and people and language and nation, [8]and all who dwell on earth will worship it, everyone whose name has not been written before the foundation of the world in the

cause tremendous amazement throughout the world" (*The Late Great Planet Earth,* 108). According to Robert Van Kampen, "There is little doubt in the author's [i.e., John's] mind as to which of those two [Nero or Hitler] will return [by way of bodily resurrection] as the Antichrist. Without question, Hitler alone fully and unquestionably meets all the requirements, and he certainly was the historical embodiment of Antichrist's supremely evil nature" (*The Sign* [Wheaton: Crossway, 1992], 208). Some who at one time believed Ronald Reagan was the Antichrist speculated that the head wound suffered by press secretary James Brady during the assassination attempt on Reagan's life, from which Brady at least partially recovered, was the fulfillment of 13:3!

27. Beale, *Revelation,* 694.

book of life of the Lamb that was slain. [9]If anyone has an ear, let him hear: [10]If anyone is to be taken captive, to captivity he goes; if anyone is to be slain with the sword, with the sword must he be slain. Here is a call for the endurance and faith of the saints.

These verses simply portray yet again what we see throughout Revelation: the beast's (Satan's) blasphemy of God and persecution of his people throughout the present church age. The statement "to make war" (v. 7) "does not mean to wage a military campaign but refers to hostility to and destruction of the people of God in whatever manner and through whatever means the beast may choose . . . . 'To conquer' [or, 'overcome'] them refers not to the subversion of their faith but to the destruction of their physical lives."[28]

The mistake of dispensational interpreters of Revelation is to project these events into a future "tribulation" period unrelated to the situation, circumstances, and practical needs of all those believers resident in the late first century in the seven churches of Asia Minor. Whatever Revelation 13:1-10 means, it applies to the people of John's day to whom the book was written. Confirmation of this is found in verse 9, where we find the familiar exhortation, "If anyone has an ear, let him hear." The only other place this exhortation appears is at the conclusion of each of the seven letters in Revelation 2–3. Thus, verses 9-10 describe the appropriate response of Christians to the deception and persecution portrayed in verses 1-8.

Revelation 13:10 is a paraphrase that combines Jeremiah 15:2 and 43:11. John's point is that believers are not to offer physical or violent resistance to their persecutors but are to faithfully submit to whatever destiny awaits them as they persevere in their trust in Jesus. As Charles put it, "The day of persecution is at hand: the Christians must suffer captivity, exile or death: in calmly facing and undergoing this final tribulation they are to manifest their endurance and faithfulness."[29]

---

28. Alan Johnson, *Revelation*, 132. The language used here is also reminiscent of Revelation 11:2, 7. Note especially that the description in 13:6 of the saints in heaven as the "tabernacle" is virtually identical with 11:1-2 where the saints on earth are portrayed as the "temple" of God.

29. R.H. Charles, *The Revelation of St. John: A Critical and Exegetical Commentary* (Edinburgh: T.&T. Clark, 1975), 1:355.

Revelation 13:11-12

[11]Then I saw another beast rising out of the earth. It had two horns like a lamb and it spoke like a dragon. [12]It exercises all the authority of the first beast in its presence, and makes the earth and its inhabitants worship the first beast, whose mortal wound was healed.

Now John sees yet another beast, this one arising from the earth (cf. Dan. 7:17). Like the first beast it too is a demonic parody of Jesus, for it has two horns of a "lamb." Perhaps it has "two" horns instead of seven in order to mimic the two witnesses, the two lamp-stands, and the two olive trees of Revelation 11:3-4. There have been numerous suggestions as to the identity of this "earth beast."

- the Jewish religious system of the first century that conspired with the Roman state to suppress and persecute the early church (this is the view of several preterist interpreters),

- the Roman imperial priesthood that sought to enforce worship of Caesar,

- the priesthood of the Roman Catholic Church,

- the Pope (so argued the Protestant Reformers),

- a literal individual living and working in conjunction with the Antichrist at the end of the age,

- the most cogent interpretation is that *this "earth beast" is a figurative portrayal of the presence and influence of false teachers, particularly false prophets, throughout the course of church history* (see especially Matt. 7:15-23).

This beast is later called "the false prophet" (16:13; 19:20; 20:10) and together with the dragon and the sea-beast forms the unholy trinity of the abyss. False prophets and deceivers were prevalent throughout the early Church as evidenced by the consistent apostolic (Peter, Paul, John) warning concerning their influence (see especially 1 John 4:1-6). The aim of false prophets is to mislead the people of God by diverting their devotion from Jesus to idols. They aim to make the claims of the first beast plausible and appealing and, as is especially the case in Revelation 2–3, to encourage ethical compromise with the culture's idolatrous and blasphemous institutions (cf. the Nicolaitans, the false apostles, Jezebel, etc. in Revelation 2–3). Thus the "false prophet" or land-beast stands in immediate opposition to the true prophets of Christ symbolized by the two witnesses in Revelation 11.

It is obvious from the above that I do not believe the "false prophet" is a single eschatological figure who will appear at the close of history to assist the Antichrist. As Johnson notes, "if the thought of a nonpersonal antichrist and false prophet seems to contradict the verse that describes them as being cast alive into the lake of fire (19:20), consider that 'death' and 'Hades' (nonpersons) are also thrown into the lake of fire (20:14)."[30]

Revelation 13:13-15

[13]It performs great signs, even making fire come down from heaven to earth in front of people, [14]and by the signs that it is allowed to work in the presence of the beast it deceives those who dwell on earth, telling them to make an image for the beast that was wounded by the sword and yet lived. [15]And it was allowed to give breath to the image of the beast, so that the image of the beast might even speak and might cause those who would not worship the image of the beast to be slain.

This (these) false prophet (prophets) tries to mimic the ministries of both Moses and Elijah. Even in Exodus (7:11) Pharaoh's court magicians, with their secret arts, performed many of the same "great signs" as did Moses (see also Matt. 7:22; 2 Thess. 2:9). Among the obvious parallels between this "false prophet" and an "apostle" of Jesus, we note: "(1) the beast is a successor of his master in both ministry and authority (Rev. 13:12a; cf. Acts 1:1-11), (2) his attempts to persuade others to worship his master are inextricably linked to his master's resurrection (Rev. 13:12b, 14b; cf. Acts 2:22-47), and (3)

---

30. Alan Johnson, *Revelation*, 134.

he performs miraculous 'signs' as concrete manifestations of his authority (Rev. 13:13; cf. Acts 2:43; 5:12; 15:12)."[31]

These verses describe vividly the idolatrous aims of the false prophet. The picture is clearly drawn from Daniel 3 and the command that all should worship the image of Nebuchadnezzar. Perhaps also the command to engage in idolatrous worship of the beast alludes in part to the pressure placed on the populace and the churches in Asia Minor to give homage to the image of Caesar as god. Beale contends that verse 15 recalls "various pseudo-magical tricks, including ventriloquism, false lightning, and other such phenomena, that were effectively used in temples of John's time and even at the courts of Roman emperors and governors. The 'signs' may also include demonic activity, since demons were thought to be behind idolatry (see on 9:20). 'It was given to him to give breath' is a metaphorical way of affirming that the second beast was persuasive in demonstrating that the image of the first beast (e.g., of Caesar) represented the true deity, who stands behind the image and makes decrees."[32]

With the story of Daniel's three friends still in mind, John portrays Christians of his day as being pressured by this latter-day Babylon (Rome) to worship the image of Caesar, i.e., the state (as inspired and energized by the dragon, from whom the state/beast receives its authority and power). Whereas the immediate idea in John's mind may well be the attempts by the imperial priesthood to seduce the people of God into worshiping the image of a Roman ruler, Johnson reminds us that "the reality described is much larger and far more transhistorical than the mere worship of a bust of Caesar."[33] Using the well-known story of Nebuchadnezzar, "John describes the world-wide system of idolatry represented by the first beast and the false prophet(s) who promotes it. John describes this reality as a blasphemous and idolatrous system that produces a breach of the first two commandments (Exod. 20:3-5)."[34]

---

31. Beale, *Revelation*, 709.
32. Ibid., 711. It is interesting to observe also that the two witnesses of Revelation 11 were given "breath" (*pneuma*) and "came to life". Perhaps the giving of "breath" (*pneuma*) to the image of the beast is yet another parody of the truth.
33. Johnson, *Revelation*, 135.
34. Ibid.

Revelation 13:16-17

[16]Also it causes all, both small and great, both rich and poor, both free and slave, to be marked on the right hand or the forehead, [17]so that no one can buy or sell unless he has the mark, that is, the name of the beast or the number of its name.

Many believe the reference to receiving a "mark" (*charagma*; found in 13:16, 17; 14:9, 11; 16:2; 19:20; 20:4) is an allusion to the ancient practice of branding or tattooing. David Aune[35] has documented several purposes for the latter:

- Barbarian tribes in antiquity practiced tattooing as a means of tribal identification.

- The Greeks used tattoos primarily as a way to punish both slaves and criminals. As such, it was a mark of disgrace and degradation, thus accounting for the methods of removal discussed in ancient medical literature.

- Tattooing could also be a mark of ownership, similar to the branding of cattle.

- In a number of ancient religions, tattooing indicated dedication and loyalty to a pagan deity.

Some have found the background for the "mark" of the beast in the Jewish practice of wearing *tephillim* or phylacteries. These were leather boxes containing Scripture passages (cf. Exod. 13:9,16; Deut. 6:8; 11:18; Matt. 23:5) that were worn either on the *left* arm (facing the heart) or on the forehead. The mark of the beast, however, was to be placed on the *right* hand. Others have pointed out that the word "mark" was used of the emperor's seal on business contracts and the impress of the Roman ruler's head on coins. Perhaps, then, "the mark alludes to the state's political and economic 'stamp of approval,' given only to those who go along with its religious demands."[36]

---

35. David Aune, *Revelation 6-16* (Nashville: Thomas Nelson Publishers, 1998), 2:457-59.
36. Beale, *Revelation*, 715.

It seems quite clear that the "mark" of the beast on his followers is the demonic counterpart and parody of the "seal" that is placed on the foreheads of the people of God (see 7:3-8; 14:1; 22:4). "Just as the seal and the divine name on believers connote God's ownership and spiritual protection of them, so the mark and Satanic name signify those who belong to the devil and will undergo perdition."[37] Since the seal or name on the believer is obviously invisible, being symbolic, it seems probable that *the mark of the beast is likewise a symbolic way of describing the loyalty of his followers and his ownership of them.*

The reason for the mark being placed on either the forehead or the hand is at least two-fold. In the first place, as noted above, this is a demonic parody of the Jewish phylacteries which were worn on either the left arm or the forehead. Secondly, it may be that the forehead points to one's ideological commitment and the hand to the practical outworking or manifestation of that commitment. The reference to socio-economic sanctions points to the hardship under which Christians are often compelled to live due to their commitment to Christ. This is present not only in Revelation (cf. 2:9; 3:8) but also in other New Testament texts (Heb. 10:34; Rom. 15:26).

Revelation 13:18

[18]This calls for wisdom: let the one who has understanding calculate the number of the beast, for it is the number of a man, and his number is 666.

Two issues need to be addressed as a prelude to our study of the mark of the beast. First, we need to be familiar with the legend of Nero's return, which was circulating in more than one form when John wrote his book. Second, we need to examine the meaning of the number 666 and its relation to the beast. That these two matters are closely intertwined will become evident as we proceed.

The Legend of Nero's Return [38]

Nero was the only child of Julia Agrippina, the great granddaughter of Augustus, and Domitius Ahenobarbus. He was born on Decem-

---

37. Ibid., 716.
38. The best treatment of Nero is found in Bauckham, *The Climax of Prophecy*, on which I have relied for the following portrayal.

ber 15, A.D. 37. Following the death of Nero's father, his mother married her paternal uncle who subsequently adopted Nero at the age of twelve. In 53 he married Octavia, daughter of the Emperor Claudius. The latter died on October 13, 54, leading to Nero's accession to the throne.

The first seven to eight years of Nero's reign were remarkably good and productive. Things began to change when in 62 he divorced Octavia (who had failed to bear him a child) and married Poppaea Sabina. In the early hours of June 19, 64, a devastating fire broke out around the Circus Maximus and spread north through the valley between the Palatine and the Esquiline. Unable to silence rumors that he himself had set the fire, Nero found a scapegoat in the emerging Christian community, which he persecuted with intense cruelty. It is generally believed that both Peter and Paul were martyred as a result of Nero's rage against the Church. In addition to the numerous political murders for which he was responsible, Nero killed his own mother, bringing him the unwelcome title "The Matricide" (mother-killer). His dictatorial style of leadership, combined with his self-indulgent personality, provoked the opposition of the Roman senate and aristocracy, although he remained popular with the general population of Rome.

Suspicion was only intensified by Nero's love for the east and its cultural expressions. He toured Greece in 66–67 and was especially popular in Parthia. The Jewish War broke out during Nero's reign and he sent Vespasian to quell it (the latter's son, Titus, was responsible for the final destruction of both city and temple). Nero was declared a public enemy by the Senate in mid A.D. 68 and troops were sent to arrest him. On hearing this, he fled to the villa of his ex-slave Phaon where he committed suicide by thrusting a dagger into his throat.

As noted earlier, whereas the name "Nero" nowhere appears in Revelation, John most likely would have seen in this historical figure the perfect prototypical embodiment of that anti-Christ, anti-Christian spirit which is characteristic of the entire church age. I agree with Bauckham that "the impending confrontation between the beast and the followers of the Lamb would appear to

John as an apocalyptic extension and intensification of the Nero-nian persecution." [39]

It may well be that the mysterious circumstances surrounding Nero's death gave rise to rumors that he was actually still alive and would soon return to seek revenge on his enemies. Several Nero impostors emerged. The first appeared one year after his death in July, 69. This one not only physically resembled Nero but was also, like the emperor, an accomplished musician. "He appeared in Greece, where he mustered some support, set sail for Syria, but was forced by a storm to put in at the island of Cythnos in the Cyclades, where he was captured and killed. His dead body was taken to Rome via Asia (Tacitus, *Hist.* 2.9)." [40] A second impostor by the name of Terentius Maximus, who also resembled Nero, appeared in 80. It is not known how he came to an end. At least one more pretender appeared during the reign of Domitian in 88–89 and must have been fresh in John's mind as he wrote Revelation.

The legend of Nero's return is first found in the Jewish Sibylline Oracles. One of the more important features is how Nero is portrayed as identified with the Parthians whose armies he will lead in an invasion of the Roman west. He is also portrayed as the eschatological adversary of the people of God who will destroy both them and the holy city. Bauckham makes this important point:

> Scholars have frequently referred to the legend of Nero's return as the Nero *redivivus* myth. This term is misleading, since it implies a belief that Nero had died and would return from death. The sources we have examined attest that the belief, up to at least the end of the first century, was that Nero had not died but was still alive, in hiding somewhere in the east, and would return across the Euphrates. [41]

The view that he would rise from the dead, says Bauckham, probably derives from the exegesis of Revelation 13:3, 12, 14 as referring to Nero.

---

39. Bauckham, *The Climax of Prophecy*, 412.
40. Ibid., 413.
41. Ibid., 421.

As I said earlier in this chapter, in conjunction with our study of Revelation 13:3, John has adapted the legend of Nero's return to paint his portrait of the oppressive career of the beast. Nero constituted the most obvious and ready-at-hand embodiment of that antichristian power which opposes and oppresses the people of God. Against the backdrop of Nero's "death, resurrection, and return" John is able to portray the beast's career of persistent persecution of the Church. For the people of God in the first century, that "beast" was the Roman imperial power. In subsequent centuries and in our own day as well it is seen in any and all attempts, whether by individuals, institutions, or movements, to thwart God's kingdom in Christ. Whether or not this "beast" is also to manifest itself at the end of the age in a single individual, popularly known as the Antichrist, is yet to be determined.

That John used the Nero legend to paint his portrait of the beast is also evident from the reference in Revelation 13:16-18 to the "mark" of the beast or the "number" of his name: 666. To that we now turn our attention.

The Mark of the Beast: 666

The meaning of the number 666 has puzzled students of the Scriptures ever since John first wrote Revelation 13:8. There are essentially three schools of thought on the problem.

First is the *Chronological View*. Some have thought that the number refers to the duration of the life of the beast or his kingdom. William Barclay explains:

There are some few who have wished to take the number 666 chronologically. In A.D. 1213 Pope Innocent III called for a new crusade because he held that Muhammadan [Islamic] power was destined to last for six hundred and sixty-six years, and at that time that period was near to an end. Certain others have taken it to refer to the six hundred and sixty-six years between Seleucus in 311 B.C. and the emergence of Julian the Apostate in A.D. 355. Finally, it has been suggested that the reference is to the year A.D. 666, in which year, it is said, Pope Vitalian decreed that all public worship should be in Latin. [42]

---

42. William Barclay, *Evangelical Times*, 70 [1958], 295.

Very few, if any, hold this view today.

Second is the *Historical View*. According to this school of thought, the number is believed to refer to some historical individual, power, or kingdom. This is easily the most popular interpretation and is based on a practice in ancient times called **Gematria** (from the Greek *geomatria*, from which we derive our English word "geometry"). This practice, found in both pagan and Jewish circles, *assigns a numerical value to each letter of the alphabet*. For example, using the English alphabet, the first nine letters would stand for numbers one through nine (A = 1; B = 2; C = 3; etc.), the next nine letters for numbers ten through ninety (J = 10; K = 20; L = 30; etc.) and so on. If one wished to write the number "twenty-three," for example, it would appear as "KC" (K = 20 + C = 3). There is a well-known and oft-cited example from a bit of graffiti found in the city of Pompeii which reads: "I love the girl whose number is 545". Apparently the initials of her name were *ph* = 500; *mu* = 40; *epsilon* = 5.

There is another method, less important to us, called **Isopsephism** that seeks to establish a connection between two different words or names by showing that their numerical values are the same. One such *isopsephism* concerns Nero in a verse taken from the historian Suetonius (*Nero 39*). It reads: *Neopsephon Neron idian metera apekteine* = "a new calculation: Nero killed his own mother." The point is that the numerical value of the name "Nero" is the same as that of the phrase "killed his own mother"!

Third is the *Symbolic View*. Virtually all other numbers in the book of Revelation are figurative or symbolic of some spiritual or theological reality and give no indication that the calculations entailed by *gematria* are in view. Thus, according to this view, the number refers to the beast as *the archetype man* who falls short of perfection in every respect. Triple sixes are merely a contrast with the divine sevens in Revelation and signify incompleteness and imperfection. 777 is the number of deity and 666 falls short in every digit. Again, "three sixes are a parody of the divine trinity of three sevens. That is, though the beast attempts to mimic God, Christ, and the prophetic Spirit of truth, he falls short of succeeding."[43] Thus the number does not identify the beast, but *describes* him. It refers to his *character*.

Furthermore, if a particular historical individual were in view, why didn't John use the Greek *aner / andros* instead of *anthropos / anthropou*? The former means "man" as over against woman, child, etc. The latter, however, is generic, i.e., it speaks of "man" as a class over against, say, animals or angels (see also Rev. 21:17 for the use of the generic "man's measure" / "angel's measure"). Also, if a particular historical person were in view, John could have made that explicit by saying a "certain" (*tinos*) man or "one" (*henos*) man. If this view is correct, we should translate: "for it is *man's* number." This stresses the character or quality of man as apart from Christ forever short of perfection, completely epitomized in the beast.

Revelation 17:7-18

We now turn our attention to the beast with seven heads and ten horns on whom the great harlot is seated. The narrative begins in Revelation 17:7.

> [7]But the angel said to me, "Why do you marvel? I will tell you the mystery of the woman, and of the beast with seven heads and ten horns that carries her. [8]The beast that you saw was, and is not, and is about to rise from the bottomless pit and go to destruction. And the dwellers on earth whose names have not been written in the book of life from the foundation of the world will marvel to see the beast, because it was and is not and is to come. [9]This calls for a mind with wisdom: the seven heads are seven mountains on which the woman is seated; [10]they are also seven kings, five of whom have fallen, one is, the other has not yet come, and when he does come he must remain only a little while. [11]As for the beast that was and is not, it is an eighth but it belongs to the seven, and it goes to destruction. [12]And the ten horns that you saw are ten kings who have not yet received royal power, but they are to receive authority as kings for one hour, together with the beast. [13]These are of one mind, and they hand over their power and authority to the beast.

---

43. Beale, *Revelation*, 722.

[14]They will make war on the Lamb, and the Lamb will conquer them, for he is Lord of lords and King of kings, and those with him are called and chosen and faithful."

[15]And the angel said to me, "The waters that you saw, where the prostitute is seated, are peoples and multitudes and nations and languages. [16]And the ten horns that you saw, they and the beast will hate the prostitute. They will make her desolate and naked, and devour her flesh and burn her up with fire, [17]for God has put it into their hearts to carry out his purpose by being of one mind and handing over their royal power to the beast, until the words of God are fulfilled. [18]And the woman that you saw is the great city that has dominion over the kings of the earth."

As we turn our attention briefly to Revelation 17 we immediately see a striking contrast with Revelation 13. In the latter the *success* of the beast is portrayed. Though struck down by divine judgment, he miraculously recovers, wages war on the saints, and conquers them (13:7). "Of course," as Bauckham notes, "it is only from the perspective of the beast and his worshippers that this is victory. Elsewhere, John refers to the same occurrence – the saints' faithful witness to death at the hands of the beast – as their victory over him (15:2)."[44] In Revelation 17, on the other hand, the inevitable *defeat* of the beast is portrayed. "Unlike his resurrection, his eschatological coming fails to vindicate his divinity. He comes only to go to destruction."[45]

The beast is here described as one who "was, and is not, and is about to rise from the bottomless pit and go to destruction" (v. 8). This is clearly a parody of God who on several occasions has been described as the one "who was and who is and is to come" (4:8; cf. 1:4, 8). Note first of all that the negative middle term "is not" and the third term "is to come" are probably a parody of Christ's death and resurrection. That the beast "is not" points to the continuing effects of his having been decisively defeated at the cross of Christ.

44. Bauckham, *The Climax of Prophecy*, 437.
45. Ibid.

That the beast yet "lives" to persecute the people of God is why the earth-dwellers wonder and follow after him/it. Also observe that whereas the resurrection of our Lord results in his being "alive forevermore" (Rev. 1:18), the beast's "resurrection" serves only to bring about his "destruction".

On the other hand, Bauckham contends that the reference to the beast's "coming up" or "rising" up is a parody not of the resurrection of Christ but of his *parousia* or second coming. We noted earlier that God's "coming" refers to his coming at the end of the age in the person of Christ to judge the world and consummate the kingdom. The description of the beast's "coming" or "rising up" thus is a parody of the eschatological return of Christ. The beast comes up from the "bottomless pit" while Jesus comes down from "heaven" (cf. 19:11).

A Mind with Wisdom

Our primary concern is with the portrayal of the beast in Revelation 17:9-11. There are two primary interpretive approaches to this difficult passage: the historical view (within which are two options) and the symbolic view.

The Historical Interpretation

The first approach believes that the city and empire of Rome are principally in view. The "seven mountains" (v. 9) are a reference to the seven hills on which Rome sat (Palatine, Capitoline, Aventine, Caelian, Esquiline, Viminal, and Quirinal). These seven mountains or hills are further identified with seven kings, five of whom are in the past, one presently rules, and the last has not yet come. The debate concerns which seven of the many Roman emperors are in view. One's decision depends on two factors. First, when was Revelation written? Knowing this will tell us the identity of the king who "is." Second, with which Roman emperor did John begin his count of seven?

Here is the list of Roman emperors, and the duration of their reigns, beginning with Julius Caesar.

Julius Caesar (101–44 B.C.)
Augustus (27 B.C. – A.D. 14)
Tiberius (A.D. 14–37)
Caligula (A.D. 37–41)
Claudius (A.D. 41–54)
Nero (A.D. 54–68)
Galba (A.D. 68)
Otho (A.D. 69)
Vitellius (A.D. 69)
Vespasian (A.D. 69–79)
Titus (A.D. 79–81)
Domitian (A.D. 81–96)
Nerva (A.D. 96–98)

According to **scheme A**, the list begins with Julius Caesar and proceeds through Augustus, Tiberius, Caligula, Claudius, Nero, and finally Galba.

In **scheme B**, the first six are the same as in A. But the seventh is Vespasian (69–79), skipping Galba, Otho, and Vitellius.

In **scheme C**, Julius Caesar is skipped and the series begins with Augustus and runs consecutively through Tiberius, Caligula, Claudius, Nero, Galba, and concludes with Otho.

According to **scheme D**, the series begins with Augustus and runs through Nero. Galba, Otho, and Vitellius are omitted, making Vespasian the sixth and Titus the seventh.

As stated above, one key is the statement in verse 10 that "one is", i.e., the sixth king is ruling at the actual time of John's writing of Revelation. If we adopt scheme "A" and begin the series with Julius Caesar, the sixth king is Nero and the seventh is Galba, who according to verse 10 remains only "a little while" (which would be historically true, for Galba ruled only from October 68 to January 69). But this would require a date of composition for Revelation in Nero's reign, a view that is possible, but not likely.

View "B" arbitrarily omits Galba, Otho, and Vitellius. This is justified by appealing to the brevity of their reigns. However, brief though they were, they were still legitimate Roman emperors. As a matter of historical note, Galba was stabbed to death, decapitated, and his corpse mutilated; Otho committed suicide with a dagger (similar to Nero); and Vitellius was beaten to death. On view "B" Vespasian would be the seventh, but his rule was almost eleven years (is that consistent with "a little while"?).

If one begins counting the seven with Augustus, schemes "C" and "D" are possible. On view "C" John would be writing Revelation during Galba's reign (late 68–early 69), making Otho the seventh (whose time in office in 69 lasted from January 5 to April 16, which would certainly qualify as "a little while"). View "D" chooses to omit Galba, Otho, and Vitellius, making Vespasian the sixth (during whose reign John wrote Revelation) and his son Titus the seventh (whose reign lasted little more than two years).

The simple fact is, no scheme satisfactorily leads to Domitian as the sixth king who "is" reigning when John wrote Revelation (early 90s). Be it also noted that if the seven hills point to Rome one would hardly need special divine wisdom to figure it out (as verse 9 asserts). In other words, "any Roman soldier who knew Greek could figure out that the seven hills referred to Rome. But whenever divine wisdom is called for, the description requires theological and symbolical discernment, not mere geographical or numerical insight." [46]

The second option is to interpret the seven mountains of verse 9 as a reference not to Rome or any of its emperors but to seven *world empires* that oppressed the people of God. [47] Five of these pagan empires belong to past history from John's perspective: Egypt, Assyria, Babylon, Persia, and Greece. A sixth kingdom, Rome, ruled the world when John wrote (hence, Rome is the one who "is"). The seventh, i.e., "the other [who] has not yet come," is the emergence of a world empire at the close of history.

Many futurist interpreters of the book take this view and believe the seventh empire will be a revival of ancient Rome. They appeal to Revelation 13:3 and argue that the "mortal head wound" suffered by the beast was the fall of ancient Rome and the miraculous recovery

---

46. Johnson, *Revelation,* 162.
47. Cf. Dan. 2:45; 7:17; Jer. 51:25; Isa. 2:2; 41:15; Pss. 30:7; 68:15-16; Hab. 3:6.

(or resurrection) that astounds the world is the modern-day revival of Rome in all its power and glory. According to Revelation 17:11, the beast not only *has* seven heads; he also somehow *is* himself an eighth head. The beast is an eighth empire and is somehow related to ("of") the first seven. That is to say, out of revived Rome will emerge yet another pagan power related to the previous seven, but nevertheless distinct in its own right. This, then, would be the final manifestation of pagan opposition to the kingdom of God.

One major problem with this view is that in order to make the five + one + one scheme of empires work it unjustifiably omits the devastating persecution of the people of God by the Seleucids of Syria and the evil Antiochus Epiphanes. Also, if the seventh world empire in this list has yet to appear, what does one do with the many major world empires that have come and gone in the past 1,600 years, especially those that sorely persecuted and oppressed the Church?

The Symbolic Interpretation

I believe there is a better solution, one that is more consistent with John's use of *numerical symbolism*. On this view "seven" is not numerically precise but points figuratively to the idea, as it often does, of fullness or completeness (see Rev. 1:4, 20; 4:5; 5:6). As in Revelation 12:3 and 13:1-2, notes Beale, "fullness of oppressive power is the emphasis here. Therefore, rather than seven particular kings or kingdoms of the first century or any other, the seven mountains and kings represent the oppressive power of world government throughout the ages, which arrogates to itself divine prerogatives and persecutes God's people when they do not submit to the evil state's false claims." [48]

The seven heads of the beast, therefore, signify totality of blasphemy and evil. "It is much like our English idiom 'the seven seas,' i.e., all the seas of the world." [49] In sum, *seven does not point to quantitative measure but to qualitative fullness*. In John's day the particular manifestation of the beast was, of course, Rome. This may

48. Beale, *Revelation*, 869.
49. Johnson, *Revelation*, 163.

well have been what influenced him to use the figurative number "seven" (with reference to its hills), although he would have insisted that the Beast is far more than Rome.

John says that five heads of the age-old beast have fallen or been slain. In this sense the beast "is not" (vv. 8, 11). But though defeated, he lives on (he "is", v. 8) because the sixth head is still very much in power (v. 10). And a seventh is yet to appear. John's point, then, in verse 10,

> is to inform his readers how far they stand from the conclusion of the full sequence of seven oppressive rulers. He tells them that only one more short reign will elapse until the end of the oppressive dominance of Rome, which represents all ungodly oppressive powers. As elsewhere, John tells the churches that the end is not far off and could come quickly: "the other," that is, the seventh, "has *not yet* come." This is to be understood, as elsewhere, as a near expectation. Thus an idea of imminence is expressed, but there is an indeterminate distance between the present and the future end.[50]

In summary, the first six "heads" or kingdoms last a long time, throughout the course of history, in contrast with the seventh, and final earthly incarnation of evil, which will fail to sustain a lengthy tenure. It will remain only a short time. When John says in verse 11 that the beast not merely "has" seven heads but "is" itself an eighth head that is in some way related to the seven, his point is that the manifestation of the dragon/beast through one of their authoritative heads (or earthly kings) at any particular point in history is tantamount to the full presence of the beast.

We must also determine the meaning of the "eighth" head. Beale argues that "the mention of an eighth king is not a literal quantitative referent to an actual eighth king in a historical order of succession from the seven preceding kings. Rather, 'eighth,' like 'seven,' has a figurative meaning. 'Eight' likely had such signifi-

---

50. Beale, *Revelation*, 871.

cance in earliest Christianity,"[51] being a symbolic reference to the day of Christ's resurrection, and even of Christ himself (recall that, using the method called *Gematria*, the sum of the Greek letters in the name "Jesus" = 888). Therefore, calling the beast an "eighth" may be another way of referring to his future attempted mimicry of Jesus who in his resurrection inaugurated the new creation.

Richard Bauckham makes several observations based on his understanding of numerical symbolism in Revelation. One possibility is the fact that 666, the number of the beast, is the double triangle of eight (i.e., 666 is the triangle of thirty-six, which is the triangle of eight). Or again, 666 is the eighth doubly triangular number (in the series 1, 6, 21, 55, 120, 231, 406, 666). Thus the beast is, in a sense, both the "eighth" in that particular series of numbers and also related to the first "seven". Another approach is to observe that the beast is called an "eighth" because "he is one of the seven recurring as a kind of final excess of evil. In him completeness [as symbolized by the first seven] becomes excess."[52]

Bauckham also believes the "seventh, yea eighth" sequence is an example of the Hebrew idiom known as *graded numerical saying* in which two consecutive numbers are used in parallel to indicate something that is illustrative and representative rather than literally exhaustive. For example,

"There are six things that the LORD hates, seven that are an abomination to him." (Prov. 6:16)

"The leech has two daughters; 'Give' and 'Give', they cry. Three things are never satisfied; four never say, 'Enough'." (Prov. 30:15)

"Three things are too wonderful for me; four I do not understand." (Prov. 30:18)

"Under three things the earth trembles; under four it cannot bear up." (Prov. 30:21)

---

51. Ibid., 875.
52. Bauckham, *The Climax of Prophecy,* 405.

"Three things are stately in their tread; four are stately in their stride."
(Prov. 30:29)

"Give a portion to seven, or even to eight, for you know not what
disaster may happen on earth." (Eccles. 11:2)

"And he shall be their peace. When the Assyrian comes into our land
and treads in our palaces, then we will raise against him seven shep-
herds and eight princes of men." (Micah 5:5)

I must confess that, in the final analysis, the meaning of verses 9-11
may well remain in obscurity!

The Ten Horns

The next task is to determine who or what constitutes the "ten horns."
Those who embrace the historical view above usually find here ten
literal rulers of the ten Roman provinces or perhaps ten specific
nations in what they believe will be a revived Roman Empire (hence
the wild speculation and jubilation of some futurists when it was
announced in January, 1981, that the European Common Market
had just admitted its tenth member nation).[53]

But as we have seen, the number "ten," like "seven," is figurative. It
likely symbolizes the variety and "multiplicity of sovereignties in confederacy that enhance the power of the beast."[54] Johnson then goes
on to identify the ten with "the principalities and powers, the rulers

---

53. In 1957 the six original nations were Italy, France, Belgium, Germany, Lux-
    embourg, and the Netherlands. On January 1, 1973, the number of member
    nations increased to nine when the United Kingdom, Denmark, and Ireland
    joined. People began to sense the impending end of the age when Greece
    became the tenth(!) member in 1981. This excitement (or nervousness!) was
    short-lived. Spain and Portugal joined in 1986, and Austria, Finland, and
    Sweden joined in 1995. An additional ten countries joined in 2004 (Cyprus,
    Czech Republic, Estonia, Hungary, Latvia, Lithuania, Malta, Poland, Slovakia
    and Slovenia), and in 2007 Romania and Bulgaria got on board. The EU had
    twenty-seven member nations in 2010. By the time this book is released one
    can only speculate at what the number of member nations might be.
54. Johnson, *Revelation*, 165.

of the darkness of this world, the spiritual forces of evil in the heavenly realms that Paul describes as the true enemies of Jesus' followers (Eph. 6:12). To be sure, they use earthly instruments, but their reality is far greater than any specific historical equivalents. These 'kings' embody the fullness of Satan's attack against the Lamb in the great eschatological showdown. They are the 'kings from the east' (16:12-14, 16), and they are also the 'kings of the earth' who ally themselves with the beast in the final confrontation with the Lamb (19:19-21)." [55]

I'm more inclined to see the ten horns as representing any and all kings, i.e., the totality of the powers of all nations on the earth, which align themselves with the beast in a final attempt to crush the Church. Their unified purpose in giving their power and authority to the beast (v. 13) is the result of God's providential control (v. 17) pursuant to the fulfillment of God's eternal prophetic purpose.

The scenario portrayed in Revelation 17:16-17 is stunning. Evidently at the end of the age the nations of the earth (i.e., the "ten horns = ten kings") will conspire with the beast for the purpose of destroying the harlot. Beale takes this to mean that "the political side of the ungodly world system will turn against the heart of the social-economic-religious side and destroy it." [56] The harlot, i.e., the apostate church together with every false religious institution and/or system, will be destroyed by a coalition of political and/or military powers. The Old Testament language behind the demise of the harlot comes from Ezekiel 23:25-29, 47. Three metaphors are used to describe this event: her "nakedness is exposed like that of a whore, she is devoured like a victim of a fierce beast, and she is burned like a city." [57]

The amazing thing is that *the ten kings are inspired and energized to do this by God* (v. 17)! This incredible internecine conflict between the religious and political spheres of the ungodly world system is so foolish, short-sighted, and ultimately self-destructive that only the hand of God could account for it. This is a theologically fascinating assertion. Clearly, it is against God's *will* for

---

55. Ibid., 166.
56. Beale, *Revelation*, 883.
57. Ibid.

anyone to assist or align with the beast, for the beast's ultimate aim is to wage war with the Lamb. Nevertheless the angel says (literally), "God gave into their [the ten kings] hearts to do his will, and to perform one will, and to give their kingdom to the beast, until the words of God shall be fulfilled" (v. 17). *Therefore God **willed** (in one sense) to influence the hearts of the ten kings so that they would do what is against God's **will** (in another sense).*

Conclusion

We've covered an incredible amount of biblical territory in this chapter, and much could be said by way of summary and conclusion. But I will restrict myself to one final comment.

I want to draw attention one more time to an issue that continues to inflame debate concerning the end times and contributes greatly to the overall hysteria that serves only to discredit the Christian community in the eyes of the world. I have in mind the belief by many that the "mark" of the beast is a literal tattoo, implant, or imprint of sorts, or perhaps some other physiological branding by which his/its followers are visually identified. The popular notion among many Christians (usually of the dispensational, futurist school of interpretation) is that some such designation, whether "the name of the beast" or "the number [666] of its name" (Rev. 13:17) will be forcibly imposed on people living in the final few years prior to the coming of Christ. If one wishes to buy or sell and thus survive in the days ahead, he/she must submit to this means of identification.

Needless to say, this interpretation is entirely based on a futurist reading of Revelation, such that what John describes pertains largely, if not solely, to that last generation of humanity alive on the earth preceding the second coming of Christ. If, on the other hand, as I have argued, the book of Revelation largely portrays events that occur throughout the entire course of church history, this view is seriously undermined. As I argued earlier, we should understand the "mark" of the beast on the right hand or forehead of his/its followers to be a Satanic parody (a religious rip-off, so to speak) of the "seal" that is placed on the foreheads of God's people (Rev. 7:3-8; 14:1; cf. 22:4). G.K. Beale is again surely right: "Just as the seal and the divine name on believers connote God's ownership and spiritual protection of them, so the mark and Satanic name signify those who belong to the devil and will undergo perdition." [58]

Since the seal or name on the believer is obviously invisible, being symbolic, it seems quite certain that the mark of the beast is likewise a symbolic way of describing the loyalty of his followers and his ownership of them. Would that the day might come when Christians forgo the embarrassing and sensational efforts to locate the mark of the Beast in a computer chip to be placed under the skin or some other technological means to differentiate his followers from those of Christ.

Addendum: Analyzing 666

It may be that John is trying to tell us that the numerical value of Nero's name has theological significance. This we see by observing the peculiar mathematical characteristics of the number 666.[59]

(1) A **triangular** number is the sum of successive numbers (1 + 2 + 3 + …). Thus ten is the "triangle" of four; i.e., it is the sum of all the numbers up through four (1 + 2 + 3 +4 = 10). The first four triangular numbers (1, 3, 6, 10) can be represented as equilateral triangles:

```
 X          X          X              X
          X   X      X   X          X   X
                   X   X   X      X   X   X
                                X   X   X   X
```

Each triangle is formed by the series of numbers that are to be added. The side of each triangle is equal to the last number in the series. The actual number of units in each case is the triangular number.

(2) A **square** number is the sum of successive *odd numbers* (1 + 3 + 5 + …). Thus, for example, sixteen is the sum of all the odd numbers up through seven (1 + 3 + 5 + 7 = 16). The first four square numbers (1, 4, 9, 16) can be represented as a square:

---

58. Ibid., 716.
59. In what follows I am heavily dependent on the remarkable research and insights of Richard Bauckham in his book, *The Climax of Prophecy*, 390-407.

```
X          X  X        X  X  X        X  X  X  X
           X  X        X  X  X        X  X  X  X
                       X  X  X        X  X  X  X
                                      X  X  X  X
```

Each number added (after one) forms two sides of the square. So, unlike a triangular number, the side of each square is not the last number in the series. It is, rather, the square root. Sixteen is the sum of the odd numbers up through seven but it is the square of four.

(3) A **rectangular** number is the sum of successive *even numbers* (2 + 4 + 6 + ...). Thus twenty is the sum of all even numbers up through eight (2 + 4 + 6 + 8 = 20). These numbers can be represented as rectangles in which one side is one unit longer than the other, so that the first four rectangular numbers (2, 6, 12, 20) can be represented as follows:

```
X  X        X  X  X        X  X  X  X        X  X  X  X  X
            X  X  X        X  X  X  X        X  X  X  X  X
                          X  X  X  X        X  X  X  X  X
                                           X  X  X  X  X
```

Thus a rectangular number can be thought of as the product of two successive numbers ($2 \times 3 = 6$, $3 \times 4 = 12$, $4 \times 5 = 20$).

It is also possible to envision these three classes of numbers in corresponding numbered series. For example, the fourth triangular number corresponding to the fourth square number and the fourth rectangular number and so on. The first thirty-six numbers in the three series may be seen at the end of this addendum.

Note that every rectangular number is double its corresponding triangle. For example, the twentieth rectangular number is 420 which is double the twentieth triangular number of 210. Also, a square added to the number of its place in the series (which is the same as its square root) equals the corresponding rectangular. For example, forty-nine is the seventh square number. So, if you add forty-nine to seven you get fifty-six, which happens to be its corresponding rectangle.

516

Another interesting fact is that the sum of two consecutive triangular numbers equals the square corresponding to the second of them. For example, if you add fifteen and twenty-one (the fifth and sixth triangular numbers) you get thirty-six (the square number corresponding to twenty-one, the second in the series).

666

What we learn from this is that **666** is a remarkable number. First of all, it is a ***doubly triangular number***. That is to say, it is the "triangle" of thirty-six (1 + 2 + 3 + ... = 666), and thirty-six is also a triangular number, being the "triangle" of eight (1 + 2 + 3 + 4 + 5 + 6 + 7 + 8 = 36). Such doubly triangular numbers are quite rare. The series runs 1, 6, 21, 55, 120, 231, 406, 666, 1035, 1540 .... As Bauckham notes, "it seems rather unlikely that the number of the beast should be one of these numbers purely accidentally."[60] Moreover, 666 is the "triangle" of a number (36) which is not only triangular but also square (6 × 6 = 36). Numbers that are both triangular and square are even rarer than doubly triangular numbers. The first three are 1, 36, 1225! "That 666 is the 'triangle' of such a number makes it a very remarkable number indeed. The next such number is 750925 (the 'triangle' of 1225)!"[61] Bauckham makes this important point:

> The nature of numerological symbolism means that we can attempt to identify the principal significance which John saw in his numbers, but we cannot set a limit to the chain of further significance which the numbers could have generated. John was setting his readers thinking. Given the ancient attitude to the significance of numbers, he would probably not have denied dimensions of significance to this numbers which he himself had not discovered but which his readers might discover.[62]

Let's take note of a few other interesting numerological factors in Revelation related to what we've already seen.

---

60. Ibid., 394.
61. Ibid.
62. Ibid., 397.

- We are told in 13:18 that the number of the beast, 666, "is the number of a man." In 21:17 we are told that the angel who showed John the new Jerusalem measured its wall: "144 cubits according to human measurements, which are also angelic measurements." Thus we see a contrast between 666, the number of the beast, and 144 the number/measure of an angel. Interestingly, just as 666 is the numerical value of the Greek word "beast" (*therion*) written in Hebrew letters, so 144 is the numerical value of the Greek word "angel" (*angelos*) written in Hebrew letters!

- Observe also the arithmetical contrast between the two numbers: 666 is triangular while 144 is square. In fact, 144 is the twelfth square number, that is, it is the square of twelve. Clearly it is the number that most aptly represents the New Jerusalem. Bauckham then points out that "the measurements of the city and its wall – 12,000 stadia (21:16), 144 cubits (21:17) – certainly also relate to the people of God who are reckoned by the symbolic number of 144,000 in 7:4-8 … and 14:1. These are the people who will find their home in the new Jerusalem, with its dimensions of 12,000 stadia and its wall of 144 cubits."[63]

- It would seem, then, that *triangular numbers* represent the beast while *square numbers* represent the people of God. What proves fascinating is that when John turns to describe the period during which these two (the beast and the Church) oppose each other he uses *rectangular numbers*. Recall that the *rectangular* numbers forty-two and 1260 are used by John to designate the period (forty-two months, 1260 days) both of the reign of the beast and the ministry of the Church under God's protective care. It is the period both of the beast's war and the Church's witness.

---

63. Ibid., 399.

- Bauckham finds additional significance in the rectangular numbers forty-two and 1260 by noting their place in the series and their corresponding square numbers.

	6th	35th
Square	36	1225
Rectangular	42	1260

- As a rectangular number forty-two is 6 × 7 and is the sum of the even numbers up through twelve. 1260 is 35 × 36 and the sum of the even numbers up through seventy. Needless to say, both twelve and seventy are highly symbolic and significant numbers in Jewish thought and in the Revelation. But look especially at the square numbers to which these rectangulars correspond. Thirty-six, which is both a square and a triangular number, is the triangular root of 666. It is the first such number after one, the next number in the series being 1225, the square which corresponds to the rectangular 1260. And 1225 is itself the triangle of forty-nine, the "jubilee" number of 7 × 7, which is a very special number in Jewish thought.

- Related to the above is the fact that when John uses forty-two months he is referring to the period of the beast's reign (Rev. 11:2; 13:5), but when he refers to the period of the church's prophesying and protection he uses 1260 days. "This may be because 42 is the sixth rectangular number and corresponds to 36, the triangular root of 666, and so is more closely associated with the beast, whereas both 1260 and its corresponding square 1225 relate to the number of the people of God."[64]

Are we making more of John's numerology than is warranted by the text? Perhaps. But it would also be irresponsible of us to ignore the remarkable mathematical properties of the numbers that play such a major role in his symbolism.

---

64. Ibid., 402.

	1st	2nd	3rd	4th	5th	6th	7th	8th	9th
Triangles	1	3	6	10	15	21	28	36	45
Squares	1	4	9	16	25	36	49	64	81
Rectangulars	2	6	12	20	30	42	56	72	90

	10th	11th	12th	13th	14th	15th	16th	17th	18th
Triangles	55	66	78	91	105	120	136	153	171
Squares	100	121	144	169	196	225	256	289	324
Rectangulars	110	132	156	182	210	240	272	306	342

	19th	20th	21st	22nd	23rd	24th	25th	26th	27th
Triangles	190	210	231	253	276	300	325	351	378
Squares	361	400	441	484	529	576	625	676	729
Rectangulars	380	420	462	506	552	600	650	702	756

	28th	29th	30th	31st	32nd	33rd	34th	35th	36th
Triangles	406	435	465	496	528	561	595	630	666
Squares	784	841	900	961	1024	1089	1156	1225	1296
Rectangulars	812	870	930	992	1056	1122	1190	1260	1332

Chapter Seventeen

The Antichrist in Biblical Eschatology: A Study of 2 Thessalonians 2

To this point I've given no indication of whether or not I believe the multiple and many-faceted manifestations of the "Antichrist" and/or "beast" will assume the form of a single human figure at the close of history. I would be inclined to say No, were it not for 2 Thessalonians 2:1-12. What follows is by no means an exhaustive treatment of the text. For that, other resources are available.[1] My aim is simply to summarize what I believe is Paul's argument and to attempt to identify the figure described here as "the man of lawlessness" (v. 3; a number of Greek manuscripts read "the man of sin").

The difficulty of 2 Thessalonians 2:1-12 is nothing short of legendary. Some commentators simply decline to engage it and confess that they don't know what it means. I am tempted to do the same. I am confident of at least one thing, however, and need to mention it up front. The passage does in fact become incomprehensible when the dispensational concept of a pretribulation rapture is assumed and brought to bear on the interpretation of the text. The return of Christ at the close of history is a singular, unitary event. There is no

---

1. I especially recommend two books by G.K. Beale, *1-2 Thessalonians* (Downers Grove: InterVarsity Press, 2003) and *The Temple and the Church's Mission: A Biblical Theology of the Dwelling Place of God* (Downers Grove: InterVarsity Press, 2004); as well as Kim Riddlebarger, *The Man of Sin: Uncovering the Truth about the Antichrist* (Grand Rapids: BakerBooks, 2006).

such thing as a rapture or translation or catching up into heaven of the Church before the time known as the great tribulation, to be followed, at the tribulation's close, by yet another "return" of Christ to judge and destroy his enemies. Jesus will descend from heaven but once, at which time he will rapture and resurrect his Church to be with him forever. But he will not then return into the clouds of heaven but will continue his descent and destroy his enemies, thereby bringing human history to its close, after which is the creation of the new heavens and new earth (what we typically refer to as the eternal state). My point here is simply to say that to think otherwise of the nature of Christ's second advent is to introduce chaos and confusion into a passage that is already hard enough to crack.

As difficult as 2 Thessalonians 2 is in its own right, it becomes utterly incomprehensible if we do not read it in light of what Paul earlier wrote in 1 Thessalonians 4–5. Most Christians are familiar with his teaching in 1 Thessalonians 4:13-18, but let's briefly rehearse what he said. Evidently some in the Church were worried about those believers, perhaps family members and close friends, who had died physically: Will we see them again? What happens to them when Jesus returns? Have they, by dying, somehow lost out on being included in the glory of that day when Christ comes back? Will they experience the promised resurrection of the body? Whatever the precise nature of their fears, Paul reassures them that when Jesus returns "God will bring with him those who have fallen asleep" (v. 14b). In other words, they are already present spiritually with Christ in the intermediate state, experiencing conscious fellowship with him (see Phil. 1:19-21; 2 Cor. 5:1-10), and Paul wants to reassure the Thessalonians that when Jesus comes back their saved loved ones and friends will be very much in the mix, so to speak. In fact, those who come with Jesus at his return will receive their resurrected and glorified bodies before those do who are living. To use Paul's precise terms, they will "rise first" (v. 16b). Then all believers who are physically alive on earth at the time of Christ's return will be "caught up" or raptured or translated, which is to say, they will then receive their resurrected and glorified bodies and join the Lord, together with their deceased loved ones, and will forever remain with him.

Paul then turns immediately in 1 Thessalonians 5 to remind them that this day of Christ's return, this day when both the living and the dead are raised and glorified and united forever with their Savior, this day which he now calls "the day of the Lord" (1 Thess. 5:2), will come without warning, much like a thief breaks into a house in the middle of the night. This coming will not only entail the rapture and resurrection of believers, as 1 Thessalonians 4 has just declared, but also the "sudden destruction" (1 Thess. 5:3) of non-believers. Later in the chapter Paul explains this to mean that whereas non-believers will experience God's "wrath" (5:9) on that day, believers will "obtain salvation through our Lord Jesus Christ" (5:9). That Paul has in view the second coming of Christ at the end of human history is confirmed by his use of the term "destruction" both in 1 Thessalonians 5:3 and 2 Thessalonians 1:9. No one denies that the latter text describes the *parousia* or coming of our Lord at the end of time. When he does, unbelievers will "suffer the punishment of eternal destruction" (*olethros;* 2 Thess. 1:9), the same fate that will befall those in 1 Thessalonians 5:3 who are in the darkness of unbelief.

All this to say, Christians should be constantly alerted to the possibility of that coming day. Christians are not in spiritual "darkness" (5:4) or ignorance or moral indifference such that the coming of that day will "surprise" (5:4) them. Should they be alive when that day arrives, although they will not have been able to predict the precise time when it occurs, they will, in effect, be able to say: "Of course, we knew it was coming. We've been living sober and circumspect and godly lives in hopeful expectation of its arrival. Praise God that the time has finally come!"

We should also note that in 1 Thessalonians 4:15 Paul refers to this event as the "coming (*parousia*) of the Lord." Although it is true that the word *parousia* can on occasion simply mean "presence" or "arrival" or "appearing," here it refers more specifically and technically to what we know as the second coming of Christ at the close of history. This is important because when we arrive at 2 Thessalonians 2:1 Paul once again addresses the matter of "the coming (*parousia*) of our Lord Jesus Christ." It's difficult, if not impossible, to think that here in his second epistle to the Thessalonian church he had something in mind by the word *parousia* other than what he meant when he used it in his first epistle. The *parousia* in 1 Thessalonians 4:15 is clearly a reference to that time when Jesus appears to rapture and resurrect his Church. One would need convincing evidence otherwise to conclude that he did not have the same thing in mind when the word appears here again in 2 Thessalonians 2:1. This point is reinforced by the second phrase in 2:1. Paul not only writes "concerning the coming (*parousia*) of our Lord Jesus Christ" but also concerning "our being gathered together to him" (2:1b). These are clearly one and the same event. Since the *parousia* in 1 Thessalonians 4 results in our meeting the Lord in the air and "always" being "with the Lord" (1 Thess. 4:17b), it seems only reasonable that Paul has the same event in mind when he speaks of "our being gathered together to him" in 2 Thessalonians 2:1b.

All this reinforces yet another conclusion, this one pertaining to the meaning of "the day of the Lord." As already noted, I see no reason why we should not conclude that the *parousia* of 1 Thessalonians 4 is the first or inaugural event of what Paul refers to in chapter 5 as "the day of the Lord." The day of the Lord is that series of events that begins with the unannounced rapture and resurrection of Christians and continues with the "sudden destruction" (1 Thess. 5:3) of non-Christians. We can also extend this to the teaching of Paul in 2 Thessalonians 1:5-12, where he again mentions the time when Jesus "is revealed from heaven with his mighty angels", the result of which is two-fold: (1) he will be "glorified in his saints" and "marveled at among all who have believed" (2 Thess. 1:10), and (2) he will inflict "vengeance on those who do not know God and on those who do not obey the gospel of our Lord Jesus" (2 Thess. 1:8).

So, "the day of the Lord" is that time (whether it be instantaneous or prolonged), inaugurated by the "coming" (*parousia*) of Jesus when he "will descend from heaven" (1 Thess. 4:16) to rapture and resurrect his people and to bring judgment, vengeance, and destruction on those who have rejected him. Thus, "the day of the Lord" would likely include what we know to be the second coming of Jesus, which entails the rapture and bodily resurrection of believers, together with the bodily resurrection and judgment of non-believers. Since I do not believe there is any evidence in the New Testament for the notion of a "pretribulation" rapture in which the coming of Christ is divided into two phases (one before the so-called tribulation and one after it), I conclude that "the day of the Lord" is a unitary event that primarily encompasses the resurrection and salvation of Christians and the resurrection and judgment of non-Christians.

Unsettling Rumors in Thessalonica

We are now prepared to look more closely at 2 Thessalonians 2 where Paul describes the believers in that city as having bought into the rumor (the "teaching" from some heretical source) that "the day of the Lord has come" (2 Thess. 2:2b). There appear to be two ways of understanding what they had been taught by some false teacher(s). On the one hand, some, such as Greg Beale, argue that "false teachers were claiming that Jesus' future advent had already happened in some spiritual manner: either by his coming in the person of his Spirit (perhaps at Pentecost) or in conjunction with the final (spiritual!) resurrection of the saints."[2] In other words, advocates of an over-realized eschatology had convinced many that the coming of Christ and the gathering of his saints in the final resurrection, described by Paul in 1 Thessalonians 4:14-17, had in some way already occurred. Thus, they could experience what Paul described in 1 Thessalonians 4 while yet remaining in their natural, unredeemed, physical bodies on earth. Whatever it is that Paul had in mind in that chapter, it was entirely a spiritual reality that perhaps elevated believers into some exalted state of religious superiority or triumph.

On the other hand, perhaps they were simply told that they had been "left behind" when the Lord came (*parousia*) and translated or caught up believers to join him in the air. For some reason left

---

2. Beale, *The Temple and the Church's Mission*, 270.

unexplained, they had missed it! Perhaps they had been disqualified on some spiritual or moral grounds. In any case, they were left thinking that the "day" or span of time (don't equate "day" with merely twenty-four hours) during which the saints would be raised and raptured and the non-Christian world would be judged had started, had begun, or was now in some sense here and the process (or event) of salvation and judgment underway. [3]

However, this view itself is not without problems. Think with me for a moment about what this would entail. Evidently the Thessalonians had been duped, either by an alleged prophetic revelation ("spirit"; 2:2a), or a spoken word (perhaps some came declaring: "We heard Paul say that ..."), or perhaps by a letter that purported to have been written by Paul ("a letter seeming to be from us"). The content of this false report was that "the day of the Lord has come." If by the latter Paul is referring to the rapture/resurrection of the saints, this would mean that the Thessalonians not only believed that *they* had been left behind, but that *the Apostle Paul himself* (and his ministry associates; note his reference to "us" in 2:2) also had missed out on this glorious event. After all, the only way Paul could have allegedly declared that "the day of the Lord has come" is if he were alive and present on earth when it happened and then took time to send word to the Thessalonians in effect saying, "I'm sorry to have to tell you this, but we all missed out!" It's one thing for the Thessalonians to think that *they* missed the rapture. But it is something altogether different, if not implausible, in my opinion, for them to think that *Paul*, the man who had written so explicitly of this event in 1 Thessalonians 4, together with his companions and co-workers, had also failed to be "caught up" to meet the Lord in the air.

In any case, Paul's response to this error is to say, "Do you not remember that when I was still with you I told you" (2 Thess. 2:5) that the "day of the Lord" will not start or will not come or begin

---

3. There is no evidence whatsoever that the verb translated "has come" in 2 Thess. 2:2b can mean "is at hand" or "is near," in the sense of it being close but not yet present. It rather means either "is here" or "has begun."

"unless the rebellion comes first, and the man of lawlessness is revealed" (2 Thess. 2:3). If the error taught to them was that the day of the Lord was an altogether spiritual or non-physical event that would transpire while they yet remained on earth, I find it hard to believe that Paul would not directly respond by correcting such an egregious theological heresy. In other words, if all he did was to say, "No, that day can't come until these two events occur," he would leave the Thessalonians (and us) thinking that there was nothing inherently wrong about what the false teachers were saying concerning the *nature* of the *parousia* and resurrection. Their only error concerned its *timing*. One can almost hear how the Thessalonians would have responded: "Oh, o.k., so Paul is on board with the idea that the 'day of the Lord' is entirely spiritual in nature. He hasn't said anything to correct it. He just wants us to remember that it won't occur until these other two events happen first." I'm hard-pressed to believe that Paul would not have immediately and forcefully refuted the "spiritualizing" and "over-realized eschatological" distortion of what the "day of the Lord" entailed.

I don't want to be misunderstood on this point, so let me explain myself yet again in different terms. Beale's thesis is that the Thessalonians had been deceived by some version of an over-realized eschatology, according to which the rapture and resurrection of believers (i.e., the day of the Lord) was entirely spiritual in nature, not physical. One could experience this prophesied event while remaining on earth in one's physical body. Believers may well be spiritually exalted in some strange and unique manner, but they would still be living and breathing on earth. If that is what certain false teachers had been propagating, it makes no sense for Paul to respond by saying: "No, those teachers can't be right, because as I've told you before, there are two events that must occur first." Would he not rather have said: "No, those teachers can't be right, because, as I've told you before, the coming of Christ is personal, public, and visible and our gathering unto him is likewise physical and entails the glorification of our bodies"? With that sort of heresy circulating in Thessalonica, I don't think Paul could have cared less about the issue of timing. Rather he would have been quick to refute the underlying false notions of what constitutes the resurrection of believers. If all he said in response was that two other events must come first, he would leave the Thessalonian Christians saying to themselves: "Well, I guess we at least got right the *nature* of the resurrection even if we were duped into believing something false about its *timing*."

The greater likelihood is that a false teaching had circulated at Thessalonica, under the guise of having come from a prophetic utterance, or even from Paul himself, to the effect that what the apostle had taught them in 1 Thessalonians 4–5 concerning the return of Christ and the resurrection of believers and the judgment of non-believers had already started or had come and somehow passed them by. "No," says Paul. "That can't happen yet. Don't you remember that when I was with you I explained what these two events are that must occur first? They haven't yet occurred, so you know that the 'day of the Lord' is yet future."

Space does not allow me to address this subject in depth, but clearly this passage refutes what many have thought about the concept of *imminence*. Many have taught that no prophesied events must first occur before the rapture/resurrection of the Church. Thus the latter could occur "at any moment," at any time, without any event having first to transpire. But Paul says in no uncertain terms that two events must come first (see below). This does not in any way dampen our zeal or expectation or anticipation of the Lord's return, for it is Jesus that we await, it is Jesus whose face we long to see, and neither the passing of centuries nor the necessity of certain intervening events should diminish our love for his appearing.

Although some have tried to find in the "rebellion" either a reference to the "rapture" of the Church (this was the view of some early dispensationalists) or possibly a political crisis, the use of the word both in the Old Testament (Josh. 22:22; 2 Chron. 29:19; Jer. 2:19; cf. 1 Macc. 2:15) and in the New Testament (Acts 21:21; cf. the verbal form in 1 Tim. 4:1; Heb. 3:12), as well as the contextual references to "false teaching" (2 Thess. 2:1-2, 9-12), point to its normal sense of religious defection or a spiritual and theological "falling away." Those of the preterist school contend that this refers to the civil rebellion by the Jews against Rome, one that precipitated the siege of the city in the period 66–70 and its eventual destruction, along with that of the temple. The majority, however, believe that Paul has in view here a future global apostasy within the professing Christian Church.

Paul reminds the Thessalonians that in conjunction with this religious defection the "man of destruction" will take "his seat in the temple of God, proclaiming himself to be God" (v. 3b).[4] There are four primary ways in which this verse has been interpreted, each a function of the way they understand the "temple of God." Those of the preterist school of interpretation insist that this is the physical temple still standing in Jerusalem when Paul wrote this letter in 50–51, the temple Jesus prophesied would be destroyed in 70. If so, the man of destruction/sin is probably Nero and the events described in this chapter concern the devastation of city and temple in 70. The "coming" of Christ (vv. 1-3, 8), therefore, is not the second advent at the close of history but the "coming" of the Messiah in judgment against Israel in the events of 70.[5] I'll have more to say about the preterist interpretation below.

Like the preterists, dispensationalists also argue that the temple is a literal and physical structure, but not the one that was destroyed in 70. Rather, this is a rebuilt temple that does not yet exist but will some day and in some way be constructed just before or at the inception of the seven-year great tribulation. The man of destruc-

---

4. That taking one's "seat" in the temple or "sitting" therein is figurative for the exercise of authority or the spread of one's influence can be seen from a brief survey of other New Testament uses of this language and imagery (see especially Matt. 23:2; 26:64; Acts 2:30-36; Heb. 1:3; 8:1; 10:12; 12:2; Rev. 3:21), as well as the fifteen occurrences in Revelation where "sitting on a throne" is metaphorical for assuming a position of authority.

5. The best explanation and defense of the preterist view is provided by Kenneth Gentry in his book, *He Shall Have Dominion* (386-94), as well as in his on-line article, "The Man of Lawlessness: A Preteristic Postmillennial Interpretation of 2 Thessalonians 2" (Covenant Media Foundation). See also the extensive study of Gary DeMar in *Last Days Madness* (251-93).

tion/sin, therefore, is the future Antichrist and the "coming" of Christ (vv. 1-3, 8) is his return at the end of history to consummate his purposes on earth.

A third view recognizes elements of truth in both these perspectives but also differs considerably from each. A problem with these first two interpretations is the way they understand the phrase, "the temple of God" (v. 4). The way this language is used elsewhere in the New Testament, especially in the writings of Paul himself, makes it unlikely that it could refer to anything other than the Church, the body of Christ, the only temple in which God is pleased ever again to dwell.

Two points need to be made. First, is it plausible to argue that the temple that was eventually destroyed in 70 or any alleged future, rebuilt temple at the close of history could ever be described as "of God"? As we noted in our examination of the Olivet Discourse, the temple complex was abandoned by Jesus, both physically and spiritually, as he departed and made his way to the Mount of Olives. "Your house," said Jesus, "is left to you desolate" (Matt. 23:38). It has thus ceased to be "God's" house. When Jesus died and "the curtain of the temple was torn in two, from top to bottom" (Matt. 27:51), God forever ceased to bless it with his presence or to acknowledge it as anything other than *ichabod* (the glory has departed).

As I explained in an earlier chapter, just as dramatically as Jesus had entered Jerusalem (Matt. 21:1-17, the so-called "Triumphal Entry") and its temple, he now departs. This once grand and glorious house of God is now consigned exclusively to them ("See, your house is left to you desolate," 23:38). The echoes of God's withdrawal from the temple in Ezekiel's vision reverberate in the words of our Lord (see Ezek. 10:18-19; 11:22-23). The ultimate physical destruction of the temple is but the outward consummation of God's spiritual repudiation of it. Jesus has now left, never to return. Indeed, the action of Jesus in departing the temple and taking his seat on the Mount of Olives (Matt. 24:3) recalls Ezekiel 11:23 where we read that "the glory of the Lord went up from the midst of the city and stood on the mountain that is on the east side of the city."

This applies equally to any supposed future temple that dispensationalists believe will be built in the general vicinity where the Dome of the Rock now stands. It's entirely possible, of course, that people in Israel may one day build a temple structure and resume their religious activities within it. The political and military implications of such, not to mention the religious furor it would provoke, are obvious. Whether or not this will ever occur is hard to say, but if it does it will have no eschatological or theological significance whatsoever, other than to rise up as a stench in the nostrils of God. I say this in light of the consistent New Testament witness concerning the only temple which God would ever again deem to regard as "his". In addition, "Christ's coming as the true temple, priest and sacrifice (so Heb. 7:11–10:22) made the first-century temple obsolete in a redemptive-historical sense." [6]

This brings me to my second point. The phrase translated "temple of God" (*ton naon tou theou*) is found ten times in the New Testament. In Matthew 26:61 the false witnesses at our Lord's trial refer to his statement: "I am able to destroy the temple of God, and to rebuild it in three days." Of course, at the time Jesus uttered these words the structure was still the temple "of God." But it is no less obvious that Jesus had in mind his own body as the unique tabernacle of the Most High which would be raised up from the dead three days following his crucifixion.

In several texts, the phrase "temple of God" clearly refers to the people of God, either the Christian individually or the body of Christ, i.e., the Church, corporately (see 1 Cor. 3:16, 17 [2×]; 2 Cor. 6:16 [2×]). Two texts refer to God's eschatological temple in heaven (Rev. 3:12; 11:19) whereas Revelation 11:1 probably has in view the same thing as 2 Thessalonians 2:4 (and for that reason cannot be cited in defense of either view). The point simply is that every time Paul uses this phrase it is descriptive of the people of God, the Church, the body of Christ. In addition, we should not overlook Paul's statement in Ephesians 2:21-22 that "the whole structure [in reference to the Church, the 'one new man'], being

---

6. Beale, *The Temple and the Church's Mission,* 279.

joined together, grows into a holy temple in the Lord. In him you also are being built together into a dwelling place for God by the Spirit." To these we also add 1 Corinthians 6:19 where Paul describes the body or physical frame of each Christian as "a temple of the Holy Spirit."

Needless to say, it would be somewhat out of place, theologically speaking, for Paul then to revert to an Old Testament perspective on this structure and refer to the physical building which God had abandoned, the building which is no longer the focal point of God's indwelling presence or the place where forgiveness is obtained, as "the temple of God." We must always keep in mind that "Jesus' resurrection was the beginning of the rebuilding of the latter-day 'temple of God'. Israel's former physical temple was but a physical foreshadowing of Christ and his people as the temple." [7] On this view, then, Paul envisions an eschatological, end-of-time Antichrist, a man characterized by sin and destruction who will assume a place of influence and authority within the professing Church from which he will persecute God's people and foment a spiritual apostasy (cf. Matt. 7:21-23; 2 Tim. 1:15; Rev. 3:1; 11:7-13; 20:7-10), all of which must come to pass before the Lord Jesus can return in fullness.

That being said, there are also texts which show that Christians prior to 70 were still gathering at the temple in Jerusalem for worship and evangelism. So perhaps it wouldn't be impossible for Paul to describe the still-standing physical temple as "the temple of God." That is how the people of his day thought of it; certainly the Jews did, and even Christians could have referred to it in this way although they knew that its role in God's redemptive purposes had ended with the death and resurrection of Jesus (see Acts 1:4; 1:8; 19:21; 20:16; 24:11). When we look in the book of Acts we see

---

7. Ibid. This volume from Beale is an extensive defense of that thesis. Beale is also correct to point us to 1 Thess. 4:8 where God is described as the one who "gives his Holy Spirit to" us. This statement is parallel to 1 Cor. 6:19 where Paul asks the church in that city, "do you not know that your body is a temple of the Holy Spirit within you, whom you have from God?"

Christians continuing to maintain close contact with the Jewish community and often appearing both at synagogues and in the temple.[8] My point, then, is that it is not beyond the realm of possibility that Christians such as Paul might refer, by way of concession, to the "temple of God" in accordance with standard usage of that day and time. In doing so, he would not be making a theological statement but simply employing the designation common among the people to whom he was ministering.

Perhaps much of the confusion here can be cleared up by taking note of a fourth option. It may be that Paul is simply alluding to well-known Old Testament texts that describe *the epitome of religious arrogance.* That is to say, he makes use of two passages in which are found claims made by those who promote and pass themselves off as divine. In Daniel 11:36 we read of the self-aggrandizement of Antiochus Epiphanes who was to desecrate the temple and oppress the people of God. He "shall do as he wills," notes Daniel. "He shall exalt himself and magnify himself above every god, and shall speak astonishing things against the God of gods" (Dan. 11:36a). Likewise, in Ezekiel 28:2 we read a description of the egomaniacal prince of Tyre. "Thus says the Lord GOD: 'Because your heart is proud, and you have said, "I am a god, I sit in the seat of the gods, in the heart of the seas," yet you are but a man, and no god, though you make your heart like the heart of a god'" (Ezek. 28:2).

There can be no mistake that Paul's language in 2 Thessalonians 2 is a direct allusion to Daniel 11:36. In both cases this rebellious figure exalts himself above and against every other so-called god, thereby in effect claiming that he himself is God. Likewise, just as in Ezekiel 28:2 where the prince of Tyre declares, "I sit in the seat of the gods," so too in 2 Thessalonians 2:4 the man of lawlessness "takes his seat in the temple of God, proclaiming himself to be God." Paul is not saying that this man of lawlessness literally or physically sits in the actual temple in Jerusalem, whether the

---

8. Acts 2:46; 3:1ff.; 4:1; 5:21ff.; 13:5, 14; 14:1; 15:21; 17:1ff.; 18:4, 7, 19, 26; 19:8; 21:26; 22:19; 24:11-12; 26:21.

temple of the first century or some alleged temple in the twenty-first century. His point is that to claim to be God is to claim that one rightfully belongs in the place from which God reigns. In a word, Paul is employing what appears to be *stock, proverbial language for self-deification.* Therefore, we need not try to identify the "temple" in which this alleged act occurs, for it is not an "act" in any physical or literal sense at all. When one claims to be "god" and exalts oneself above every object of worship one is, in effect, claiming to be seated in the place of deity.

I. Howard Marshall agrees, and suggests that "Paul was using a well-known motif metaphorically and typologically" derived from Daniel and Ezekiel. That is to say, "he has used this language to portray the character of the culminating manifestation of evil as an anti-theistic power which usurps the place of God in the world. No specific temple is in mind, but the motif of sitting in the temple and claiming to be God is used to express the opposition of evil to God." [9] F.F. Bruce appears to take a similar position. He argues that had it been said that "he takes his seat on the throne of God," few "would have thought it necessary to think of a literal throne; it would simply have been regarded as a graphic way of saying that he plans to usurp the authority of God." [10]

The "Restrainer"

Paul doesn't leave it there, however, but proceeds to explain why these two events have not yet happened (or more specifically, why the "man of lawlessness" has not yet appeared). Someone or something is "restraining him now" (2 Thess. 2:6). "His time" (v. 6b), which is to say, the time when in God's purpose the "man of lawlessness" will be revealed has not yet come. This "person" or "thing"

---

9. I. Howard Marshall, *1 and 2 Thessalonians*, New Century Bible Commentary (Eerdmans, 1983), 191-92.

10. F.F. Bruce, *1 & 2 Thessalonians*, Word Biblical Commentary (Waco: Word Books, 1982), 169. Gordon Fee, *The First and Second Letters to the Thessalonians* (Grand Rapids: Eerdmans, 2009), similarly argues that Paul "was simply using well-known 'anti-Christ' events to describe the Rebel's self-deification" (284).

that is now restraining the revelation of the man of lawlessness will "do so until he [the restrainer] is out of the way" (v. 7b). Then the lawless one will be revealed.

But who or what is it that restrained him in Paul's day (v. 6) and will continue to do so "until he is out of the way" (v. 7)? This is a notoriously difficult interpretive question.[11] Whatever view one finally embraces, it seems reasonable to conclude that the ultimate origin of this restraining influence is God. Three factors point me in this direction. First, the restraint is a spiritually positive force in the service of good insofar as it inhibits the revelation and perpetration of evil. Second, the gender of the "restrainer" is neuter in verse 6, but masculine in verse 7. This may suggest that whereas it is ultimately God who exerts the restraining influence, he does so through some secondary means or instrument or historical phenomenon. Third, the purpose of this hindrance to the revelation of the man of destruction is "so that he may be revealed in his time" (v. 6). As Beale rightly notes, "this time is certainly set by God, since the whole segment (2:6-12) is placed within a prophecy-fulfillment framework. God will bring history to a conclusion in his own timing."[12]

In light of this, I'm inclined to see the "restrainer" as perhaps one or a combination of several forces: (1) civil government and its authority and power to resist as well as punish evildoers (cf. Rom. 13:1-4; this would be the case not only in first-century Rome but in other, subsequent, governments up to the present day); (2) the preaching of the gospel and the comprehensive good (spiritually, politically, socially, morally, etc.) that comes in its wake; (3) the ministry of an angel, specifically the same angelic being who "binds" Satan and casts him into a pit for the duration of the present church age (the "1,000 years" of the millennium; Rev. 20:1-10); and (4) the providential power of God expressed in terms of common grace wherein the Spirit restrains the expression of evil both in the

---

11. See the discussions in Beale, *1-2 Thessalonians* (213-221), and Riddlebarger, *The Man of Sin* (130-134).
12. Beale, *1-2 Thessalonians*, 217.

hearts of the unregenerate in general and in the manifestation of the man of destruction in particular.

I will make no attempt (and, in my opinion, no one else should either) to speculate on who this might be, from which country or nationality he will arise, whether or not he is currently living, or any other factors concerning his eventual appearance and activity. The tendency to do otherwise rarely avoids the sort of sensationalism that ultimately brings reproach on the gospel of Christ. The only thing on which any of us can or should speak with certainty, and with celebration, is that this final embodiment or expression of the Antichrist / beast will be destroyed by the Lord Jesus Christ "with the breath of his mouth" and will be brought to nothing "by the appearance of his coming" (2 Thess. 2:8). But we still have a few critically important questions to answer from this passage.

Now!

If I were to open this paragraph by writing, "*And now* let me explain what the next verse means," all of you would understand that my use of the adverb "now" simply means something like, "to move the argument along" or "my next point is" or something similar. In other words, there is a valid use of the adverb "now" that is merely logical and helps explain the relationship between statements in a sentence or paragraph. In other words, it serves to transition from one thought to the next. That is *not* what Paul is doing in verse 6.

Paul is clearly using the word "now" in a temporal sense. It has to do with *time.* "Now" in verse 6 means "in the present day," "at this moment," or something along those lines. But the question must then be asked, Does Paul mean for the word "now" to modify the Thessalonians' knowledge or the activity of the restrainer? I'm quite persuaded that it is the latter of the two. In other words, according to the ESV of verse 6, the restrainer is "now," which is to say, in the first century, during the lifetime of Paul and the Thessalonians, exerting his/its influence to keep the lawless one from being revealed. The KJV is highly misleading in this instance. Its translators connect the word "now" with the *knowledge* of the Thessalonians rather than with the *activity* of the restrainer. The

KJV reads: "and *now ye know* what withholdeth." But clearly Paul isn't saying anything about *when* the Thessalonians stand in possession of this knowledge. Rather he is saying that they know who or what the restraining influence is that currently ("now") exerts his/its power over the lawless one. Gordon Fee is surely correct in saying that what is "at issue is not their already knowing what he is talking about, but the fact that something or someone is 'now' (= currently) holding the Rebel back, so that he will appear at a later time."[13] Of course, the Thessalonians' knowledge is very much at issue here, as the mild rebuke of verse 5 indicates ("do you not remember"). But Paul's point is that what they already know, because he earlier had informed them, is that the restrainer is *now*, currently, holding back the revelation of who the lawless one is as well as what the lawless one will eventually do.

Reinforcing this understanding of the adverb "now" in verse 6 is the use of two similar words in verse 7. There Paul writes: "For the mystery of lawlessness is *already* (Gk., *ede*) at work. Only he who *now* (Gk., *arti*) restrains it will do so until he is out of the way." Thus we see again that the restrainer is currently, in the first century, when Paul and the Thessalonians were very much alive, exerting an influence to inhibit the revelation and activity of the lawless one. Notwithstanding this current work of the restrainer, "the mystery of lawlessness is already at work." In other words, even though the lawless one is not himself active, being restrained, the "mystery" associated with his nefarious work is even now, at present, very much a reality in the world. And again, as if to make his point with even greater clarity, Paul reiterates in verse 7b that the restrainer "now restrains" and will continue to do so until he is out of the way.

Now I suspect (by the way, note that here I've used "now" in a logical, non-temporal sense!) that many of you are wondering why I've labored so long and hard and somewhat repetitively to make the point that Paul makes, namely, that the restrainer is in Paul's day very real, very active, very much at work. So too is the

---

13. Gordon D. Fee, *The First and Second Letters to the Thessalonians*, 287.

mystery of lawless (whatever that means!). Thus the one "who now restrains" (v. 7) in the first century will continue to do so until the time comes for the lawless one to be made known. So, why is this such a big deal? Here's why.

As we've seen, Paul declares that whatever it is that is restraining the revelation of the man of lawlessness is "now" (v. 6) present, already at work to inhibit the manifestation of his evil work. But if the "Antichrist" is an individual human being who was not to be born, far less revealed and released, for at least another 2,000 years, what possible reason would there be for God to impose any restraint on him in the first century? Indeed, it would seem inappropriate even to use the pronoun "him" insofar as this alleged Antichrist was not a living entity (and wouldn't be, from Paul's perspective, for at least 2,000 years!). Someone might respond by saying that Paul didn't know precisely when the Antichrist would be revealed (any more than he knew when the end of the age would occur), whether in the first or twenty-first century. He simply knew that he was coming and that at least two events must occur first. If he was operating on the assumption that he may well have been living in the generation that would witness Christ's return he would necessarily have believed that the restrainer was already in operation.

However, it's one thing to be *open to the possibility* that you are living in the final generation when Christ returns and to *explicitly assert* that such is the case. Paul never does the latter. Yet here in 2 Thessalonians he explicitly asserts that the restrainer is presently ("now") exerting an inhibitive influence to prevent the manifestation of the man of lawlessness. More than that, he had previously told the Thessalonian Christians who or what the restrainer was (v. 5) and not simply that they "may" or "may not" be living in the day when he will be revealed. How could Paul have known and told the Thessalonians who/what the restrainer was if such restraint would not be necessary for at least another 2,000 years? Paul couldn't have been more to the point when he declared in verse 6 that "**you [Thessalonian Christians living in the first century] know** what is restraining him **now [at the same time you are alive]**" and again in verse 7 that he "**now** restrains" him. Paul obviously knew who or what the restrainer was and so too did the Thessalonians. But Paul and the Thessalonians were **wrong** if in fact these events were not to occur for hundreds, even thousands, of years later!

The Preterist Interpretation of 2 Thessalonians 2

As you can see from my discussion of the words "now" and "already" in 2 Thessalonians 2, I have lingering doubts concerning my brief exposition of this passage. They are not sufficiently strong (at least, not yet) that I'm convinced the view I've defended is wrong. But they should be noted. The case for a preterist or A.D. 70 fulfillment of the details in this passage has been made by others and I have no desire to repeat their findings. However, I do want to mention three things in particular that make me less than dogmatic about the position I've taken.

First, a few preterists insist that if the "day of the Lord" and this "coming" of Christ and this "gathering together" to him which the Thessalonians evidently believed had already occurred all refer to events associated with the second coming and our bodily resurrection at the end of history, Paul's way of proving them wrong is admittedly strange (if not to say altogether ineffective). Keith Mathison put it this way:

> Why would Paul have tried to convince a group of believers that the Rapture and the bodily resurrection of all believers had not yet occurred by arguing that the apostasy and revelation of the man of lawlessness must come first? If this chapter is referring to the Second Advent, the Rapture, and the bodily resurrection of the dead, the proof that these things had not yet happened would have been far more simple and obvious. The entire argument of 2 Thessalonians 2 could have been reduced to the single question, "Are you still here?" [14]

Mathison's point is that the obvious proof that these events had not yet occurred is the fact that Paul and the Thessalonians themselves

---

14. Mathison, *Postmillennialism*, 229.

are still alive on the earth in their natural, physical bodies! If Christ had come and all Christians had been resurrected and gathered to him there would be no apostle to tell them so and no church in Thessalonica to hear him say it!

Let me make the point once again, so that there is no mistake about what is being said. If the "coming of our Lord Jesus Christ" and "our being gathered together to him" (2 Thess. 2:1), which Paul refers to as "the day of the Lord" (2 Thess. 2:2), are collectively a reference to the second advent at the close of human history, or even perhaps the rapture (as dispensationalists would have it), Paul's attempt to reassure them that such had not yet occurred, says the preterist, is a strange one indeed. Instead of appealing to events that must come first, i.e., the "rebellion" and the revelation of "the man of lawlessness," why doesn't he simply say: "Folks, pinch yourselves! You're still here. You're still alive. I'm here and alive and writing this to you. What greater proof do you need that these events have not yet occurred?"

In response, I suppose one might argue that this fails to understand precisely what it is that the Thessalonians had been duped into believing regarding the day of the Lord. The false teaching circulating in their church was that the rapture and resurrection had occurred but for some inexplicable reason they had been left behind or left out or for some reason overlooked. Of course they knew they were still alive on the earth. That was the problem and the cause of their distress: "Why have we been left out of those marvelous events that Paul told us about in 1 Thessalonians 4?" One problem with this view is that it implicates, or better still, includes the false teachers themselves. If the Thessalonians had been excluded from the rapture, then so too had the teachers who were spreading this false doctrine. Is it reasonable to think that such men would have devoted themselves to spreading a rumor to the effect that they and the Thessalonian Christians had all been, in a sense, "left behind"?

In any case, the preterist believes a more likely interpretation is that the "coming of our Lord Jesus Christ" and "our being gathered together to him" does not refer to the end-of-the-age second advent but to events associated with the destruction of Jerusalem and its temple in 70. More on this below.

A second reason for the preterist's reluctance to see in this passage a reference to the second coming at the end of history has already been noted at some length. It is found in Paul's assertion that the restraining influence, whoever or whatever it may be, is *already* at work *now* in the first century in preventing the revelation and activities of the man of lawlessness. I won't repeat what I said earlier, other than to ask the question: "Why would Paul affirm that the restrainer was actively at work in the first century and that both he and the Thessalonians already know who/what the restrainer is if the one supposedly being restrained would not be born or make an appearance in history for at least another 2,000 years?"

The third, but less forceful, reason for my lingering doubts concerning any futurist interpretation of this passage is the similarities it bears to our Lord's words in Matthew 24. I'm thoroughly persuaded that the language in Matthew 24:29-31 of the "coming" of the Son of Man and the "gathering" [15] of the elect from one end of heaven to the other refers to events associated with the destruction of Jerusalem and its temple in 70. It seems reasonable, therefore, to conclude that the "coming" and "gathering together" in 2 Thessalonians 2 likewise has to do with the events associated with Jerusalem's destruction and the temple's demise.

Once again, it is essential that the Thessalonians be in a position where they could know that Christ had "come" in the sense in which Daniel 7:13-14 describes it, that is to say, that he had "come" to the Ancient of Days to be vindicated and to receive his kingdom. The clear and obvious way that they were able to "know" if this had occurred was to keep an eye on Jerusalem and its temple. When the prediction of Jesus concerning their destruction was fulfilled, as it was in 70, the Thessalonians would then be assured that he

---

15. The word translated "gathered together" in 2 Thess. 2:1 is *episunagoge*. It is found only one other place in the New Testament (Heb. 10:25). However, the cognate verbal form, *episunago*, is used in Matt. 24:31 (and Mark 13:27) to refer to what occurs in the wake of the events of 70.

had "come" or was "present" and the elect were in process of being "gathered together" to him.

Clearly, the preterist does not believe that "our being gathered together" to Christ has anything to do with a rapture or resurrection. They make much of the fact that the word translated "gathered together" here in 2 Thessalonians 2:1 is *episunagoge*. It is found only one other place in the New Testament, Hebrews 10:25, where it describes an assembly of Christians on earth (i.e., a local church gathering).[16] Thus, "the gathering," says Gary DeMar, "is horizontal and earthly, not vertical and heavenly."[17] Fellow preterist Kenneth Gentry concurs, insisting that "with the coming destruction of Jerusalem and the temple, Christians will henceforth be 'gathered together' in a *separate* and *distinct* 'assembly' (*episunagoge*; the church is called a *sunagoge* in James 2:2). After the temple's destruction God will no longer tolerate going up to the temple to worship (it will be impossible!), as Christians frequently do prior to A.D. 70."[18]

But in what sense can it be said that the gathering together to Christ of the elect must await the revelation of the man of lawlessness? Evidently, it is far more than simply a reference to people getting saved, for that obviously was occurring prior to 70. Paul (and Jesus) must be saying that the worldwide, global, and multi-racial extension of the gospel beyond the bounds of Jewish ethnicity was to a large extent dependent upon the vindication of the Son of Man in heaven. In other words, at least the inaugural stages of the gathering of God's elect "from one end of heaven to the other" awaited the enthronement of the Son of Man and his vindication as visibly manifest in the destruction of Jerusalem and its temple.

The preterist thus contends that all of 2 Thessalonians 2:1-12 pertains to events that transpired prior to and were consummated by the destruction of the city of Jerusalem and its temple by the

---

16. However, the cognate verbal form, *episunago*, is used in Matt. 24:31 (and Mark 13:27) to refer to what occurs in the wake of the events of 70.

17. Gary DeMar, *Last Days Madness*, 258.

18. Kenneth Gentry, *He Shall Have Dominion*, 389.

Romans in 70. Who, then, was the "man of lawlessness"? If this is not a reference to a person who has yet to appear on the scene of history (the so-called "Antichrist"), but actually points to someone in Paul's and the Thessalonians' lifetime, who was he?

The three most common suggestions are that the "man of lawlessness" was either the Roman Emperor Nero, the Jewish high priest Phannias, or a Jewish zealot named John Levi Gischala.[19] The more popular view among these is that Paul is describing Nero. As you will recall from the immediately preceding chapter, Nero was emperor at the time the Jewish War broke out in 66. He dispatched Vespasian to quell the rebellion, but it was the latter's son, Titus, who was ultimately responsible for the final destruction of both the city and temple. Nero fell out of favor with the Roman Senate and was declared a public enemy in 68. Upon hearing that troops were sent to arrest him, he fled to the villa of his ex-slave Phaon and there committed suicide by thrusting a dagger into his throat.

But there are a number of troubling questions that this view struggles to answer (aside from the difficulty it encounters in making sense of v. 1). For example, what constitutes "his time" (v. 6), which is to say the time of his "revelation"? When did he, in a manner of speaking, come out and perpetrate the sort of lawless and sacrilegious activities that Paul describes? It is difficult to identify a particular time during his reign when this occurred. He came to power in 54 and displayed considerable civility and moral restraint for the first seven or eight years. Although things took a turn for the worse in 62 (when he divorced his wife, Octavia), it wasn't until two years later that the great fire of Rome prompted

---

19. Among preterists, Kenneth Gentry opts for Nero, Gary DeMar believes it is Phannias (or another member of the priesthood), while John Bray points to John Levi (see his *The Man of Sin of II Thessalonians 2* [Lakeland, FL: John Bray Ministry, 1997], 26-41. John Levi was a principal figure in the Jewish efforts to overthrow the Roman government and is believed by many to have been the one whose actions provoked Rome's final siege against Jerusalem and its temple. The "restrainer," so it is argued, would have been the Jewish high priest, Ananus, whose death opened the door for the full revelation of Levi and his rebellious ways.

him to lay blame on the Christian community. The persecution that followed was intense and eventually resulted in the martyrdom of both Peter and Paul. This would appear to be the most likely time when "the man of lawlessness" was "revealed" (v. 3).

We know with some measure of confidence that Paul wrote 2 Thessalonians in either 50 or 51, some four years before Nero came to power. Yet Paul clearly indicates that both he and the Thessalonians knew who the man of lawlessness was. This forces the preterist to conclude that by some special revelation God had made known his identity to the apostle, for there was no other way that Paul could have known that a man who, in 50, was still nearly four years from the throne would eventually emerge as the self-aggrandizing, self-deifying threat that Nero ultimately became. This isn't a fatal blow to the preterist view, but it does render it somewhat less likely.

Also, who or what is it that "restrains" the full revelation of Nero's evil deeds? This view must also account for Nero's death. According to verse 8, "the Lord Jesus will kill" him "with the breath of his mouth" and bring him to nothing "by the appearance of his coming." If the latter is not a reference to the second advent but instead points to the "coming" of Christ in judgment against the nation of Israel in 70, the preterist must explain how the latter is responsible for Nero's suicide some two years earlier! This view must also explain in what sense, if at all, Nero's "coming" was "with all power and false signs and wonders" (v. 9). Did he claim to work miracles? If so, do we have any credible evidence to this effect? Finally, if the man of lawlessness was Nero, what was the "rebellion" that together with Nero must first come before the day of the Lord (v. 3)? As noted earlier, the preterist would likely argue that this refers to the civil revolt by the Jews against Rome, one that precipitated the siege of the city in the period 66–70 and its eventual destruction, along with that of the temple. [20]

---

20. Says Gentry, "I believe that it [the apostasy or falling away] speaks primarily of the Jewish apostasy/rebellion against Rome. Josephus certainly calls the Jewish War against Rome an *apostasia* (Josephus, *Life* 4, 9, 10; *J.W.* 2:2:7;

One final problem that, in my opinion, weakens the preterist case concerns verses 1-2. Let's recall that the preterist believes that "the coming of our Lord Jesus Christ and our being gathered together to him" (v. 1) is a description of events associated with the fall and destruction of Jerusalem and its temple in 70. My question is this: Why would the occurrence of that particular event cause the Thessalonian Christians to be "shaken in mind" and "alarmed" (v. 2)? If Paul had taught them often and well about "the day of the Lord" (v. 2b; cf. v. 5 and also 1 Thess. 5:1-11), a day that would have witnessed the judgment of God against their persecutors and those who had been responsible for the cruel crucifixion of their Lord, why would news of its occurrence be the cause of anything but celebration and relief? If this was to be the "day" when the Son of Man was to "come" and be "presented" before the Ancient of Days, that he might be given "dominion and glory and a kingdom, that all peoples, nations, and languages should serve him" (Dan. 7:13-14), would not the Thessalonians have felt renewed confidence in the truth of God's prophetic promise? Would they not have been encouraged in their faith, knowing that in the destruction of Jerusalem there was, on earth, the visible and concrete evidence that, in heaven, their Savior had been vindicated and installed as King of kings and Lord of lords?

Please understand what I'm saying. I believe this is precisely what happened in 70. As we saw in our two chapters on the Olivet Discourse, the judgment against Israel that resulted in the destruction of city and temple was simultaneously the consummate fulfillment of Daniel 7:13-14. My point isn't to deny this truth or to reverse myself on what I argued earlier. My point is simply to suggest that news of this event would not, or at least should not, have provoked alarm or fear or anguish in the Thessalonian church. It seems that only on the assumption that these Christians had been led to believe they had missed out on the resurrection/rapture, which Paul had so meticulously described for them in 1 Thessalo-

2:16:4; 7:4:2; 7:6:1)" (*He Shall Have Dominion*, 391). DeMar appears to favor a religious defection among the Jews as they consistently turned from faith in the one true God (see *Last Days Madness*, 271-86).

nians 4, that we can suitably account for their reaction in 2 Thessalonians 2:2. [21]

I'm not insisting that such questions cannot be answered in a credible way. The preterist certainly believes he has a good and persuasive response to each. At this point, however, I must remain somewhat skeptical of his proposed solution to our problem.

Parousia

I want to briefly address one final point before closing this chapter. Regardless of the view one embraces, an account must be given of Paul's use of the Greek word *parousia*. Most Christians simply assume that this is a technical term used specifically to refer to the second coming of Christ at the close of human history. Undoubtedly it is used in precisely this way in a number of texts, 1 Thessalonians 4:15 being one. Earlier I pointed out that it seems only reasonable to conclude that Paul would employ this term consistently throughout the Thessalonian literature. He uses it in 1 Thessalonians 2:19 to refer to the second coming of Christ, as is also the case in 3:13 and again in 5:23. Although the term itself is not found in 2 Thessalonians 1:5-12, no one denies that this paragraph has in view the *parousia* at the close of history (except, that is, for the hyper-preterists who argue that Christ's "coming" in judgment against Israel in 70 was in fact his second and final "coming" or *parousia*). So when we finally arrive at 2 Thessalonians 2:1, it seems reasonable to conclude that once again Paul's use of *parousia* points to the second advent of our Lord.

All of this makes for a strong case that Paul's use of *parousia* in 2 Thessalonians 2:8 likewise refers to the second coming at the end of human history. If so, then quite obviously Nero cannot be the man of lawlessness and we should continue to look for this arch-

---

21. DeMar tries to account for the reaction among the Thessalonians by saying that they "were concerned about fellow Christians [and perhaps family members] who they believed had gone through a terrible tribulation" (*Last Days Madness,* 267). Although this is certainly possible, I'm not persuaded that it can adequately account for the degree of consternation and emotional agitation that Paul describes.

enemy in the days (years? decades? centuries?) that lie ahead. But the preterist may well respond by asking: What are we to make of verse 9 where the very term *parousia* is used of the "coming" of the lawless one? Could this possibly indicate that Paul does not intend for us to find in this term a unified and technical way of referring to the second coming of Christ? That's certainly a possibility, but not a necessity. We must remember that one of the primary deceptive characteristics of the man of lawlessness is to mimic or counterfeit what is true of Christ. He is in this sense truly "anti"-Christ, i.e., one who attempts to supplant, act in the place of, and imitate the "coming" or *parousia* of the one true Christ. If this be true, then Paul's point in using the term in verse 9 of the "coming" of the man of lawlessness is to point once again to his sinful efforts at making himself out "to be God" (v. 4).

Conclusion

I had hoped to be more definitive in my conclusions concerning the meaning of this passage. I had hoped that by studying the text closely I might contribute something substantive to the never-ending attempt to identify the "man of lawlessness" or at least expand our grasp of what he will do upon his appearance. Alas, I fear I have failed in this regard. As much as I hate to say so, I feel compelled to agree with Augustine and say, "I frankly confess I do not know what [Paul] means" in this text! [22]

---

22. Augustine, *The City of God,* in *A Select Library of the Nicene and Post-Nicene Fathers of the Christian Church,* ed. by Philip Schaff (Grand Rapids: Eerdmans, 1983), Volume 2, Book XX, chapter 19, p. 437.

Conclusion

A Cumulative Case Argument for Amillennialism

My intent in this brief conclusion is certainly not to revisit in detail every argument set forth in the preceding seventeen chapters. After all, I did cover considerable ground on issues beyond that of amillennialism alone. Rather, my aim is to summarize as clearly as possible the *thirty reasons* why I find amillennialism the most cogent biblical account of the purpose of God in redemptive history. Not all of the following arguments are of equal weight. Some point to amillennialism more by implication while the majority, in my opinion, explicitly demand an amillennial reading of the biblical text.

(1) Amillennialism best accounts for the many texts in which Israel's Old Testament prophetic hope is portrayed as being fulfilled in the person and work of Jesus Christ and the believing remnant, his body, the Church. Contrary to all forms of dispensationalism and much of premillennialism, the fulfillment of the Old Testament covenant promises is not to be found in the restoration of national, ethnic Israel, in a literal 1,000-year earthly kingdom, but in the King himself and his new covenant people, the Church, the true Israel of God. The "promises were made to Abraham and to his offspring.... who is Christ.... And if you are Christ's, then you are Abraham's offspring, *heirs according to promise*" (Gal. 3:16, 29).

(2) Amillennialism best accounts for the way in which the Old Testament prophets spoke of the future in terms, images, and con-

549

cepts borrowed from the social and cultural world with which they and their readers were familiar. In other words, they communicated the realistic future glory of God's eschatological purposes in the hyperbolic or exaggerated terms of an ideal present. That realistic future glory will be consummated, not in a semi-golden age intervening between the second coming of Christ and the eternal state, but in the latter alone, on a new earth where righteousness dwells.

(3) Amillennialism best accounts for the presence of typology in Scripture, according to which Old Testament persons and events and institutions find a deeper and intensified expression and consummation in the antitype. This is especially seen in the way Jesus is portrayed as the antitypical fulfillment of the many Old Testament types and shadows.

(4) When the Old Testament speaks of the consummation of God's renewal of creation it knows nothing of a 1,000-year period preceding the eternal state. Rather its focus is on the new heavens and new earth (Isa. 65:17-22; 66:22), consistent with what we read in the New Testament as well (Revelation 21–22). This, of course, is precisely what amillennialism argues for.

(5) Amillennialism provides a superior and more cogent explanation of the seventy-weeks prophecy of Daniel 9, which we saw is designed to evoke a *theological image*, namely, that in the person and work of Jesus God will act to bring about the final jubilee of redemptive history. The ten jubilee framework (i.e., the 490 years or seventy weeks) is thus symbolic of the divine work of redemption, at the conclusion of which the eternal and perfected jubilee will appear: the new heavens and the new earth.

(6) We found amillennialism to be a superior scheme for understanding redemptive history insofar as it alone is consistent with the New Testament testimony concerning the termination of physical death at the time of the second coming of Christ. Premillennialism falls short in that it necessarily entails the perpetuation of death beyond the return of Christ, beyond that point when death is "swallowed up in victory" (Isa. 25:7-9; 1 Cor. 15:52). Paul is quite clear and to the point in telling us that the end of all physi-

cal suffering and human mortality occurs at the time of the return of Christ and the resurrection of the body. At that time, says Paul, Isaiah 25:7-9 will be fulfilled. At the second coming of Christ, says the apostle, "Death will be swallowed up in victory." No physical death can occur after the second coming. If it could, Paul would be wrong in saying that death is swallowed up in victory, in fulfillment of Isaiah 25, at the moment of the second coming.

(7) Yet another affirmation of amillennialism is found in the fulfillment of Isaiah 25:8, where we are told that God will one day "wipe away all tears," a prophecy that according to Revelation 21:1-4 comes to fruition when the new heavens and new earth are created. What makes this an argument for amillennialism is that Paul says Isaiah 25:7-9 will be fulfilled at the time of the second coming (1 Cor. 15:50-55). The point, simply, is that the new heavens and new earth "come" when Christ does, at the end of history, not some 1,000 years later.

(8) A related point is that amillennialism alone is consistent with the New Testament teaching that the natural creation will be delivered from the curse and experience its "redemption," in conjunction with the "redemption" of our bodies, at the time of the second coming of Christ (Rom. 8:18-23). Premillennialism again fails insofar as it requires that the earth continue to be ravaged by war and sin and death. Premillennialists must necessarily believe that the renewal of the natural creation and its being set free from bondage to corruption does not occur, at least in its consummate expression, until 1,000 years subsequent to Christ's return.

(9) Amillennialism is more consistent with the New Testament teaching (2 Pet. 3:8-13) that the new heavens and new earth will be inaugurated at the time of Christ's second coming, not 1,000 years thereafter. Believers in the present age are "waiting for and hastening the coming of the day of God," which is to say they "are waiting for new heavens and a new earth in which righteousness dwells" (2 Pet. 3:12-13). This is the focus of our expectations, not a 1,000-year period within history in which *un*righteousness dwells.

(10) Amillennialism is superior to premillennialism insofar as the latter view requires that one believe that unbelieving men and

women will still have the opportunity to come to saving faith in Christ for at least 1,000 years subsequent to his return. Amillennialism alone affirms the New Testament truth that all hope for salvation terminates with the second coming of Christ. The opportunity for eternal life is now, in the present church age, before Christ comes, not later, in some millennial age, after Christ comes.

(11) Amillennialism alone is consistent with the New Testament teaching that the resurrection of unbelievers will occur at the time of the second coming of Christ, not 1,000 years later following an earthly millennial reign. Thus amillennialism more clearly accounts for John 5:28-29 where Jesus declared that "an hour" is coming when there will be a single and universal bodily resurrection of both believers and non-believers. Premillennialism must posit a gap of 1,000 years between the two.

(12) Related to the previous point is that premillennialism necessarily entails the belief that unbelievers will not be finally judged to suffer eternal punishment until at least 1,000 years subsequent to the return of Christ. Yet 2 Thessalonians 1:5-10 asserts that "those who do not know God" and "who do not obey the gospel of our Lord Jesus ... will suffer the punishment of eternal destruction ... *when he [Christ Jesus] comes on that day* to be glorified in his saints and to be marveled at among all who have believed" (2 Thess. 1:8-10a; emphasis mine; see also Matt. 25:31-46).

(13) Amillennialism alone can account for Paul's declaration that "flesh and blood cannot inherit the kingdom of God" (1 Cor. 15:50-57). Premillennialism again fails because it posits the existence, in a supposed post-parousia earthly millennial reign, of both unbelievers and believers who remain in their natural, "flesh and blood" bodies.

(14) The superiority of amillennialism to premillennialism is also seen in the fact that the former, unlike the latter, does not have to solve the problem of what happens to those believers who experience physical death during the course of this purported earthly millennial reign. Amillennialism does not have to posit the improbable (if not bizarre) scenario in which there are thousands and thousands of individual resurrections occurring subsequent

to Christ's second coming, or, should that be rejected, the notion that those who die in Christ somehow exist in an immaterial state in some undefined proximity to their Savior while he and those believers who are resurrected live and reign on the earth. As I asked in an earlier chapter, is it really the case that the Bible teaches an earthly reign of Christ in which potentially hundreds of thousands (millions?) of physically dead believers hover in his presence, strangely mingling with physically alive unregenerate people, as well as physically alive but unglorified regenerate people, as well as resurrected and glorified people? As noted above, for the premillennialist, the alternative is to assert, without the slightest hint in the Scriptures, that untold multitudes of individual bodily resurrections occur during the millennial age as believers die physically, one after another.

(15) As we noted at great length in Chapter Six, amillennialism is more consistent than any other view with the teaching of the New Testament that the prophesied restoration of Israel is fulfilled in the Church, the true Israel of God.[1] Although many historic premillennialists also affirm this truth, they are then hard-pressed to provide a cogent explanation or rationale for why there would even be a post-parousia millennial kingdom.

(16) A careful reading of Acts 15 also reinforces the truth of amillennialism. In this text we saw that the rebuilding of the tent (or tabernacle) of David refers not to a restoration of ethnic or national Israel in a post-parousia millennial earth, but rather to the resurrection and exaltation of Jesus to the throne of David and the ingathering of souls, in this present church age, from among the Gentiles.

(17) Amillennialism makes the best sense of Hebrews 11. There Abraham, Isaac, and Jacob are said to have persevered in faith, "having acknowledged that they were strangers and exiles on the earth" (Heb. 11:13), all the while they looked forward to "the city that has foundations, whose designer and builder is God" (11:10;

---

1. I have in mind such texts as Matt. 8:10-12; 24:31; Rom. 9:25-26; Rev. 2:17; 3:9; 7:15; and 21:14.

cf. 11:16). That city, of course, is the New Jerusalem. They lived in expectation that the promise would be fulfilled in "a better country, that is, a heavenly one", which must be a reference to the new earth. Clearly, then, even Abraham and his fellow patriarchs understood that the Old Testament promise of a land would not be fulfilled in a this-earthly-territory but in the new earth, the "heavenly" country which God had prepared for them.

(18) Amillennialism also makes more sense of the structure of the book of Revelation. There we find the principle of recapitulation, or progressive parallelism, in which the same period of time (the church age, spanning the two advents of Christ) is described from different but complementary perspectives. If the principle of recapitulation is applicable here, as I believe it is, much of the rationale for reading Revelation in a strictly futurist manner is undermined. Indeed, if this principle is true, Revelation 20:1-10 should be interpreted as a recapitulation of the present church age rather than as following in historical sequence upon the second coming of Christ as described in Revelation 19.

(19) Amillennialism also makes most sense of the literary genre of Revelation and the highly symbolic nature of the language in Revelation 20. The premillennial attempt to read this passage in a woodenly literal way wreaks havoc on an obviously figurative portrayal of the binding of Satan.

(20) Amillennialism is better suited to explain the restriction placed on Satan in Revelation 20:1-3. Contrary to the claims of premillennialism, Satan's binding is not universal, as if during the span of the "1,000 years" he is prevented from doing everything. Rather, he is prevented from perpetuating the spiritual blindness of the nations and keeping them in gospel darkness. He is also prevented from provoking a premature global assault on the Church which we know to be the battle of Armageddon.

(21) Amillennialism alone can account for why Satan must be bound in the first place. According to premillennialism, Satan is allegedly prevented from deceiving the very nations who at the close of Revelation 19 have already been defeated and destroyed at Christ's return. In other words, it makes no sense to speak of

protecting the nations from deception by Satan in 20:1-3 *after* they have been both deceived by Satan (16:13-16; cf. 19:19-20) and destroyed by Christ at his return (19:11-21; cf. 16:15a, 19).

(22) The amillennial reading of Revelation alone makes sense of the obvious parallel between the war of Revelation 16, 19, and 20. This parallel is reinforced when we note that the imagery in Ezekiel 39 related to Gog and Magog is used to describe both the battle in Revelation 19:17-21 and the battle in Revelation 20:7-10. Clearly, these are one and the same battle, known as Armageddon, that consummates the defeat of God's enemies at the time of Christ's second coming. They are just as clearly not two different battles separated by 1,000 years of millennial history. This is all confirmed by reference to "the war" (19:19; already noted in 16:14, 16; cf. 20:8). The same Greek phrase "the war" (*ton polemon*) is used in all three texts (Rev. 16:14; 19:19; 20:8). In fact, in 16:14 and 20:8 the same extended phrase "to gather them unto the war" (*sunagagein autous eis ton polemon*) is used.

(23) Amillennialism best explains Hebrews 12:26-28 where there is only one coming cosmic dissolution (associated with Christ's second coming, the judgment of the nations, and the creation of a new heavens and new earth), not two (as is required by premillennialism; one at the time of the second coming and yet another at the close of a millennial kingdom).

(24) Amillennialism makes more sense of the symbolic nature of the number "1,000" in Revelation 20. In other texts "1,000" rarely if ever is meant to be taken with arithmetical precision. This is true whether the context is *non-temporal* (Ps. 50:10; Song 4:4; Josh. 23:10; Isa. 60:22; Deut. 1:11; Job 9:3; Eccles. 7:28), in which case the usage is always figurative, indeed hyperbolical, or *temporal* (Deut. 7:9; 1 Chron. 16:15; Pss. 84:10; 90:4; 105:8; 2 Pet. 3:8).

(25) Amillennialism recognizes the obvious parallel between Revelation 20:1-6 and Revelation 6:9-11. The latter text unmistakably describes the experience of the martyrs who have been beheaded because of the word of their testimony on behalf of Christ. So, too, Revelation 20 portrays the experience of "souls" beheaded for the sake of their testimony concerning Christ. Simply

put, the cogency of amillennialism is seen in its recognition that in both texts the intermediate state is being clearly portrayed.

(26) Amillennialism alone does justice to the obvious parallel between Revelation 20:1-6 and Revelation 2:10-11. The latter is an encouragement given to prospective martyrs. They are to be faithful unto death and Christ will give them the "crown of life." Likewise, in Revelation 20 those who die for the sake of their witness are granted "life" with their Lord in the intermediate state. Reinforcement of this parallel is found in the fact that only here in chapter 2 and again in chapter 20 is reference made to "the second death," from which the faithful martyrs are promised deliverance.

(27) Related to the above is the fact that in Revelation 3:21 those who persevere under persecution and "conquer" or "overcome" are said to sit and reign with Christ on this throne. This is precisely what is said of the martyrs in Revelation 20. They come to life and reign with Christ for 1,000 years.

(28) Amillennialism alone accounts for the use of the word "thrones" in Revelation 20:4. This word, both inside Revelation and elsewhere in the New Testament, consistently refers to heavenly thrones, not earthly ones. These are the thrones in the intermediate state on which the faithful martyrs sit and rule together with their Lord and Savior, King Jesus.

(29) Amillennialism alone explains the significance of the ordinal "first" as a modifier of "resurrection." Closer study reveals that whatever is *first* or *old* pertains to the *present* world, that is to say, to the world that is transient, temporary, and incomplete. Conversely, whatever is *second* or *new* pertains to the *future* world, to the world that is permanent, complete, and is associated with the eternal consummation of all things. The term *first* is therefore not an ordinal in a process of counting objects that are identical in kind. Rather, whenever *first* is used in conjunction with *second* or *new* the idea is of a *qualitative contrast* (not a mere numerical sequence). To be *first* is to be associated with this present, temporary, transient world. Whatever is *first* does not participate in the quality of finality and permanence which is distinctive of the age to come. Thus the "first resurrection" is

descriptive of life prior to the consummation, which is to say, life in the intermediate state.

(30) Finally, the hermeneutical principle known as the Analogy of Faith is best honored within an amillennial system. When asked for an explicit and unmistakable biblical affirmation of a post-parousia millennial kingdom, premillennialists typically point to Revelation 20, and *only* Revelation 20. But as we have seen, Revelation 20 is neither explicit nor unmistakable in teaching an earthly millennial kingdom. Furthermore, no single passage in an admittedly symbolic and comparatively difficult context should be allowed to overturn (or trump) the witness of a multiplicity of passages in admittedly didactic and comparatively straightforward contexts. To put this same point in the form of a question: Do the statements in other New Testament books concerning end-time chronology *necessarily and logically preclude* the notion of a post-parousia millennial age in Revelation 20? I am convinced that this must be answered affirmatively.

As noted in Chapter Six, my contention is not that the passages in the Pauline, Johannine, and Petrine corpus simply omit reference to a post-Parousia millennial age. If that were the case it is conceivable that we might harmonize Revelation 20 with them, making room, as it were, for the former in the latter. But the texts we examined are not such as may be conflated with the notion of a future millennial kingdom. These passages clearly appear logically to preclude the existence of such a kingdom. My argument throughout this book has been that a premillennial interpretation of Revelation 20 actually contradicts the clear and unequivocal assertions in such texts as John 5, 1 Corinthians 15, Romans 8, 2 Thessalonians 1, Hebrews 11, and 2 Peter 3.

Rather than reading these texts through the grid of Revelation 20, the latter should be read in the clear light of the former. Sound hermeneutical procedure would call on us to interpret the singular and obscure in the light of the plural and explicit. To make the rest of the New Testament (not to mention the Old Testament) bend to the standard of one text in the most controversial, symbolic, and by scholarly consensus most difficult book in the Bible is hardly commendable hermeneutical method. We simply must not allow a singular apocalyptic tail to wag the entire epistolary dog! We must not force the whole of Scripture to dance to the tune of Revelation 20.

That is why I am an amillennialist.

Before closing down this treatment of biblical eschatology, I direct your attention to the visual portrayal of amillennialism in

AMILLENNIALISM

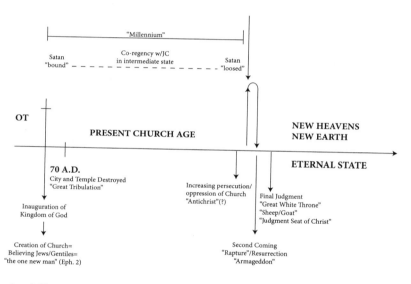

the following chart. I will only briefly highlight the primary points of interest.

As you can see, amillennialism asserts that Satan was "bound" at the first coming of our Lord. This is portrayed by a broken horizontal line, spanning the present church age, to indicate that although the restraint placed on the enemy is total insofar as its stated purpose is concerned, he is still free to operate in a variety of other nefarious ways as outlined in the New Testament. The "millennial" kingdom is represented by a solid horizontal line that extends from the time of the first coming of Christ to his second. This is designed to teach us that those who have died in Christ, particularly those martyred for their faith, share in his reign from within what we typically refer to as the intermediate state. The release of Satan from this restriction occurs at some time immediately preceding the return of Christ, and is in some measure the cause of the increased persecution of the church and the expansive influence of Antichrist (whether conceived as all expressions of resistance to the kingdom of our Lord or in one particular personal manifestation). It at this time that Satan gathers the nations from the four corners of the earth for the great war against God and his Christ.

Now, at the close of the present church age, which is also to say at the close of the millennial reign of the saints in the intermediate state, Jesus Christ will return to earth. All those who have died in faith will be raised first and receive their resurrected and glorified bodies. They will then be joined together with Christ by all living believers who are translated or caught up into heaven or "raptured" into the presence of Christ. At this time they participate with Jesus in his continued descent to earth, constituting, as it were, his royal entourage. Thus the second coming of Christ is a singular event that leads to the resurrection and glorification of all saints of all ages. The global defeat of all Christ's enemies ensues at what we refer to as the battle of Armageddon.

Following Armageddon, all humanity appears at the Great White Throne judgment of God. This judgment is simultaneous, if not entirely synonymous, with the judgment of the sheep and goats (Matt. 25) and the judgment seat of Christ where the saints of God receive their eternal rewards. Those judged are either granted entrance into the new heavens and new earth, i.e., the eternal state, or are cast forever into the lake of fire.

There are many and considerable disagreements among Christians on the subject of biblical eschatology. But none of them is of sufficient urgency or importance that we who trust and treasure Jesus Christ as Lord and Savior cannot unite in our common cry: Even so, come Lord Jesus! Soli Deo Gloria!

Scripture Index

Subject Index

REVELATION
A MENTOR EXPOSITORY COMMENTARY
DOUGLAS F. KELLY

REVELATION

A Mentor Expository Commentary

Douglas F. Kelly

What a great blessing it is for the church to regain clarity about the message of Revelation! Kelly's commentary will prove invaluable in restoring this vital message to the pulpits of our churches and the lives of suffering believers.

Richard D. Phillips,
Senior Minister, Second Presbyterian Church, Greenville, South Carolina

The church, including the Western church and the global South in the global Eastern Church, need to read the book of Revelation now more than ever. Let Douglas Kelly be your guide. I commend the book and I commend the publisher for such a time as this.

Michael Milton,
Chancellor and Chief Executive Officer,
Reformed Theological Seminary, Charlotte, North Carolina

ISBN 978-1-84550-688-9

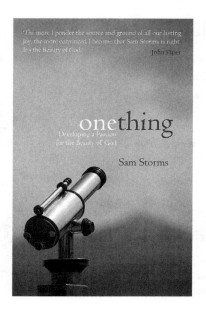

ONE THING

Developing a Passion for the Glory of God

Sam Storms

The more I ponder the source and ground of all our lasting joy, the more convinced I become that Sam Storms is right. It's the Beauty of God. In all His gifts we are to see Him. Especially in the gospel.... Let Sam Storms guide you biblically and waken your heart to the Treasure of Christ who is the image of the Beauty of God.

John Piper,
Senior Pastor, Bethlehem Baptist Church, Minneapolis, Minnesota

ISBN 978-1-85792-952-2

Christian Focus Publications

Our mission statement –

STAYING FAITHFUL
In dependence upon God we seek to impact the world through literature
faithful to His infallible Word, the Bible. Our aim is to ensure that the Lord
Jesus Christ is presented as the only hope to obtain forgiveness of sin, live
a useful life and look forward to heaven with Him.

Our Books are published in four imprints:

CHRISTIAN
FOCUS

Popular works including biographies, commentaries, basic doctrine
and Christian living.

CHRISTIAN
HERITAGE

Books representing some of the
best material from the rich heritage
of the church.

MENTOR

Books written at a level suitable
for Bible College and seminary
students, pastors, and other serious readers. The imprint includes
commentaries, doctrinal studies,
examination of current issues and
church history.

CF4•K

Children's books for quality Bible
teaching and for all age groups: Sunday school curriculum, puzzle and
activity books; personal and family
devotional titles, biographies and in-
spirational stories – Because you are
never too young to know Jesus!

Christian Focus Publications Ltd,
Geanies House, Fearn, Ross-shire,
IV20 1TW, Scotland, United Kingdom.
www.christianfocus.com